HOW I SWEPT MY WAY TO THE TOP

BY DON ASLETT
AMERICA'S #1 CLEANING EXPERT

Some of the stories in Chapters I and 3, and "Control by feel" in Chapter 23, appear in a somewhat different form in *Everything I Needed to Know About Business I Learned in the Barnyard*, copyright 1993 by Don A. Aslett

"Lesson on the homefront" on page 155-157 appeared in the first edition of *Is There Life After Housework?*, copyright 1981 by Don A. Aslett.

Published by

Marsh Creek Press
PO Box 700
Pocatello, Idaho 83204
Phone 208-232-3535
Fax 208-235-5481
www.aslett.com

ISBN 0-937750-34-4

To purchase this book in quantity at a discount, contact the publisher above.

Editor: Carol Cartaino
Production manager: Tobi Alexander
Production assistant: Ryan Roghaar
Cover photo: Jesse Sena
Sculpture on page iii by David Halverson, 1997.

Dedicated to all
who feel they are "stuck"
in a lesser or low-end job.

TABLE OF CONTENTS

ALSO BY DON ASLETT

**Books on decluttering
and personal organization:**

Clutter Free! Finally & Forever

Clutter's Last Stand

Dejunk Live! (Audio CD)

DONE! (How to Have a 48-Hour Day)

For Packrats Only

How to Handle 1,000 Things at Once

The Office Clutter Cure

Weekend Makeover (Lose 200 Lbs. This Weekend)

Other books on home care:

500 Terrific Ideas for Cleaning Everything

Clean Break (with Sandra Phillips)

Do I Dust or Vacuum First?

Don Aslett's Clean in a Minute

Don Aslett's Stainbuster's Bible

HELP! Around the House

How Do I Clean the Moosehead?

Is There Life After Housework?

Let Your Sink So Shine

Make Your House Do the Housework
  (with Laura Simons)

No Time to Clean!

Pet Clean-Up Made Easy

Painting Without Fainting

The Cleaning Encyclopedia

Who Says It's a Woman's Job to Clean?

Business books:
DONE! (How to Have a 48-Hour Day)

From Barnyard to Boardroom

How to Be #1 With Your Boss

Keeping Work Simple (with Carol Cartaino)

Speak Up! A Step-by-Step Guide to Powerful
Public Speeches

The Office Clutter Cure

For professional cleaners:
Cleaning Up for a Living (with Mark Browning)

Construction Cleanup

How to Upgrade & Motivate Your Cleaning Crews

Professional Cleaner's Clip Art

The Brighter Side of the Broom

The Professional Cleaner's Personal Handbook

Writing and publishing:
Get Organized, Get Published! (with Carol Cartaino)

How to Write and Sell Your First Book

You Can, You Should Write Poetry

Other interests:
How Successful People Keep Their Lives
Out of the Toilet (with Sandra Phillips)

If You Can Bake It You Can Make It (with Sandra Phillips)

FOREWORD by Carol Cartaino

*"A resoundingly American success story,
in Don's own words..."*

FORMERLY THE EDITOR-IN-CHIEF OF
WRITER'S DIGEST BOOKS, CAROL
CARTAINO (SHOWN HERE IN OUR
EARLY EDITING DAYS IN CINCINNATI)
HAS EDITED ALL OF MY BOOKS.

Twenty-seven years ago a man with a squeegee tie tack and an outhouse-shaped notebook walked into my editorial office in Cincinnati, and life has never been the same.

At that moment long ago now, an eastern intellectual transplanted to Ohio (me) met a wild man from Idaho—"the cleaning man"—Don A. Aslett, and an unlikely partnership began that continues to this day. I have edited more than 40 books for him, and we have coauthored two together.

You'll learn more about all of that in Chapter 15, so let me just say for now that I've been a book editor all my life. In 40 years in the business, I've met a lot of authors, and they are pretty unusual people for the most part. So it amazes me now more than ever that the *most* unusual author, the most extraordinary and dynamic man I have ever known, the most irrepressible fountain of new ideas and enthusiasm, creator of excitement on the page and in life is... a janitor, a professional cleaner. A man who started a cleaning business to get through college, built it into a highly successful nationwide business, and became a best-selling author and media star. This man of action, charismatic salesman and promoter, big-time business and publishing innovator and entrepreneur, is Don Aslett.

This book is the story of how a farm boy from Idaho managed to do all of this, and why he did it. It is a resoundingly American success story, in Don's own words.

The other 40 books of Don's I edited were mostly a matter of making sense of the outpourings of a vivid imagination, deciphering yellow pages filled with handwriting and often un-translatable spelling, and winnowing out an overabundance of charm (and opinion). Plus pulling "more good stuff" out of Don as necessary, to flesh out his ideas and visions.

The book you hold in your hands, however, was the challenge of my career. Working for big publishers in New York and Cincinnati and elsewhere I did books on and with celebrities, art and photographic books, cookbooks, business books, books of essays and nature study, and how-to and self-help books of all kinds, but nothing quite like this. Had this been any normal book of fact or fiction, I could handle it in a heartbeat. But Don wrote this not as a single start-to-finish manuscript, but in 5,000 different sittings over 60 years, amidst 5 dozen other ongoing projects. In odd moments he recorded every notable experience and emotion: at work, home, or play; on the farm, in sports, at church, in education, entertainment, real estate, and publishing. Then he handed me 16 reams, 57 pounds of manuscript—8,000 typed pages—to edit into a coherent, less than five-pound autobiography.

Sifting through, sorting, narrowing down, and organizing even that many pages would have been no big problem. But in that pile there were two to sixteen versions of many events, accurate in fact, but all written at different times and in different moods, some a paragraph, some a page. This meant a lot of comparing and splicing to get the best. It was hard sometimes, too, to choose from this embarrassment of riches—to use only four Boy Scout stories when there were 34, only 50 work adventures out of 150. (To console ourselves about this, we are making the best of the other funny cleaning stories into a separate book.)

Most parts of the original draft, too, were all written as "stand alone" pieces, often from quite different standpoints and to differing degrees of condensation. Most of the manuscript describing earlier times and events was in "as it happened" narrative; while much of the later copy was overviews written in reflection and contemplation. And some parts of the story were missing and had to be added now. I also read my way through an 18-gallon Rubbermaid tub of press clippings about Don to find quotes from others that give some additional perspective here and there and winnowed through many hundreds (if not thousands) of photographs and other illustrations. I've edited books in days, some in weeks or months, but this is the first in which the process stretched over years.

For the reasons noted above, this book is not a totally seamless narrative, nor does it proceed 100 percent chronologically in all cases. I have tried to make it as smooth a ride as possible, and give you, the reader, a feeling for the full scope and spectrum of this man's life, 70 years of living and 50 years of book and business adventures so far. It was impossible to get even close to everything in here, but I included all of the best, and the message of a man who took a common, low-image business to the heights, made it funny, made it memorable, and became an inspiration to all who wonder if they can ever rise above the mundane and difficult in their lives.

The result? You will be the judge, but I assure you there is nothing quite like this.

Don Aslett's life is a sentence... a paragraph... a page in history that can only be ended with an exclamation point!

INTRODUCTION

If he can do it so can I!

There isn't one of you reading this who hasn't imagined reaching the top of what you take on. We all see ourselves conquering, competing, excelling. We would all like to save a few lives and get a few headlines before we ride off into the sunset. The little business I began half a century ago in an Idaho college town is now one of the tops in the industry, operating in 50 states and Canada and making waves throughout the world. This started with a dream that was different—but not entirely different—from yours.

Let me introduce myself. I am Don A. Aslett, now 72 years old—6 feet tall, 178 pounds, and happily married to a beautiful woman who brought six lovely children into our lives. I'm a toilet cleaner, floor cleaner, window cleaner, a "cleaning man." I got started in this business at age 19 while a freshman at Idaho State University. My business now has thousands of employees and has branched off into several other businesses. I've also written more than three dozen books, sold almost four million copies, and been on *Oprah, LIVE—Regis and Kathie Lee*, the Discovery Channel, and hundreds of other TV and radio shows.

If I could do that starting at the bottom in one of the least prestigious and lowliest occupations around, there is no limit to what *you* can do! There is nothing in these pages that another person couldn't do as well—or better.

Making it all count for something

Rattlesnakes and temperatures of thirty below would be enough reason for many people to shy away from a job, but add glass-slick roads for four months a year, hanging down 30-story buildings on a single rope, fighting mosquitoes, and a 150-mile stretch of employment problems requiring constant checkup and monitoring. This was what one of my associates was up against in the early 1970s. He slaved day and night, risking his neck daily behind the wheel and on scaffolding, and had little time with his wife and family, all in the course of running his area. At the end of the year, he had grossed $750,000 and his expenses were $749,751, a measly $249 profit for the whole year.

As I reviewed his financial statement and reflected on all of that risk and effort for such a tiny reward, I suddenly realized why I love to write. I want to make my and others' mileage count for something and there is no way it can be done better than with a ten-cent pencil or a spare pen and a one-dollar notepad.

All of us go through things similar to those described above. We face the grind and abuse and challenges of life, and all for what? The trip may even be great, but where have we gone and why? If all of those hours, all those aches and tears could just return more than the experience itself. This is exactly why I began to write. Money wasn't my motivation because I learned to paint a house or wash a building and make $500 a day, and writing income is usually a long way from that. Few of us write for money, because it is a tough way to earn a living. We do it because we have something we feel compelled to share, and how can you share better than in a book, poem, or essay? Whether you lose or win in life, all of that mileage, all of that effort, can then live on and change lives and inspire others.

I get up every morning as if it were Christmas morning because through writing, my life is not just my life. My life counts for something because millions of people hear and read about the things that I do. What stimulates us more than an audience of one or 100,000 in the stands, giving us a reason to play the game with everything we have in us?

For decades I struggled to build a business, raise a large family, and keep myself healthy, tough, and trim. I learned seven trades, plus how to design things, perform, speak in public, and write. I've driven over a million miles, and flown almost three million. I've lived and worked in the desert at 120 degrees and in Western winters at 56 below. I've performed marriages and funerals, led Scout troops across the U.S., and driven just about everything with wheels plus tanks and dozers. I've built homes, torn them down, developed property, and worked with and cared for just about every kind of domestic animal. I helped raise eight teenagers (a good place to stop!). All of this got me through life and I had some fun along the way, but now, by writing about it, I'm making it count.

> OUR SCURRY TO SURVIVE OFTEN GOES UNCHARTED, BUT ONCE RECORDED, IT WILL REFUEL, RESTORE, AND REWARD YOU. ALL OF THIS MILEAGE—MAKE IT COUNT FOR SOMETHING!

I hope the stories in these pages inspire you and remind you of the good *you* have done and will do. By the time you reach the end, I hope you will be filled with excitement and energy, not about my life, but about recording at least the most important parts of your own life—first for your own good, and then to share with your family and friends and hopefully the world. Any "wow" you find here is the same wow you have or can have in your own set of circumstances. My life is just an assemblage of a lot of ordinary elements like small town, small school, ordinary job, good friends and community, yet quite unique when pulled together and put into words, annotated, and explained.

Some of this might seem unbelievable, but it's all true! It all happened this way.

The answer to the big question

In my seventies, the question I hear the most is: "Did you ever dream your little part-time college job would end up a world-recognized, multimillion-dollar corporation?"

The answer is yes. I did dream, imagine, and pursue this outcome, and now more than 50 years seems to have passed in a flash, from growing up on a farm to starting a family to finding a niche in cleaning up and making the most of it. Outsiders and onlookers are impressed by what they see as an empire, measuring the size and dollar value of this now nationally recognized business. We who have matured with it find the financial rewards a distant second to the wealth of influence and experience all of this brought—the learning, laughing, loving, travel, books, relationships, and properties gained along the way.

Varsity, the original anchor company I founded as a college student, is now one of the premium facility care providers in the country, siring seven other supporting, related entities, from our own university to retail sales, technology, manufacturing, and other services. It has been and still is quite a trip. I hope you enjoy this—thanks for reading and letting me share it.

Good reading,

Founder, Varsity Contractors, Inc.

A FEW OTHER NOTES
FROM THE AUTHOR

How did this get written?

For more than 50 years, I wrote notes, journal entries, and essays, in moments of delight or ambition, depression or desperation. I tossed them all into a file marked "Biography Some Day." After at least 60 years of following my own recommendations about careful record keeping, I ended up with more than 8,000 typed and handwritten pages (and almost as many pictures).

Then one day I began the process of organizing all of this into a book. It started in November 2003 with a meeting in Pocatello with Carol, my editor, and Tobi, my operations manager. Together we gathered up and crudely organized more than 16 reams of drafts and sent them back to Ohio with Carol. She reviewed, sorted, edited, and spliced her way through 57 jumbled pounds of paper to a first draft of a little over 800 pages, asking me for new bits and pieces as necessary to fill the gaps. The draft manuscript was then read by a half-dozen carefully chosen readers who know me and my life from different vantage points. Then the final editing, splicing, reshuffling, and smoothing process began. The process continued (with at least a year's interruption for another megabook project that cropped up) until November 2007, four years and $150,000 later, not counting printing costs.

THE STARTING POINT—THREE DETERMINED PEOPLE AND MANY PILES OF PAGES, ON THE FLOOR OF OUR OFFICE IN POCATELLO—NOVEMBER, 2003.

P.S. I've never been so analyzed, examined, questioned, or criticized on any other endeavor!

CLOSE ENOUGH—A LITTLE DISCLAIMER FROM DON

This book is primarily composed of a selection from my journal jottings and notes to myself, my impressions and observations, over a 60-year period. Times, dates, casts of characters, and circumstances are presented as they were captured then or now remembered. The miles driven, walked, or flown, and amounts of money cited are pretty close if not perfectly accurate, the height and weight of things might vary a few inches or pounds but not tons. The depth of snow and degree of cold are probably exaggerated a bit as cold gets colder as we age. Traffic is not exaggerated enough. My interpretation of others' feelings and attitudes is my best guess, based on my dealings with people over the past 70 years.

There is a lot of opinion here, and even a little moralizing. I have the experience and credibility to have earned some beliefs and judgments. Have no doubt these are my own personal views—I like the strength of taking a stand.

ACKNOWLEDGMENTS

Considering the span of time this autobiographical record covers, I'd estimate that between family, friends, employees, associates, and fans, more than three million people contributed to its contents (possibly including you). I can't do justice to all of them, so I will only mention a few people directly associated with its actual production.

The collection, filing, and compiling of all of the raw material was handled by my operations managers Tobi Alexander and Nancy Everson. These materials included an early draft of a biography of Don Aslett nicely written by Jamie Warnock, some parts of which have survived into the present volume.

The vision, structure, and four-year editing process were in the capable hands of Carol Cartaino of Seaman, Ohio, who since 1979 has edited my previous 40 books.

The first 800-page rough draft was read and very helpfully annotated by contributors Colonel Gene Kisling (ret.), Shirley (Aslett) Kisling, my sister and a representative of the family, Varsity manager Greg Hoch, Susie Sharp of Hillsboro, Ohio (wife of one of my favorite authors, Dr. Robert T. Sharp), and Annen Vance of Wilmington, Ohio. Freelance editor Kay Burns of Sardinia, Ohio, lent her able assistance to research, copyediting, and miscellaneous editorial chores (including second opinions when needed) in all of the later stages of this project.

The conversion from finished manuscript and narrowed-down illustrations to the handsome finished product you see here was masterfully made (layout and all final details of production) by Tobi Alexander with the help of Ryan Roghaar.

And I can't forget Clark Carlile, who encouraged me to write my first book... and this one.

Chapter 1

GROWING UP IN THE GEM STATE

I was blessed to have not only good parents, but all four grandparents into my thirties...

MOTHER AND DAD IN FRONT OF THEIR '29 CHEVROLET.

Birth of a custodian

I was born July 23, 1935, in Twin Falls, Idaho. My parent's first boy, I came early. The doctor bill was only $6, and relatives and nurses noted in me a certain resemblance to Adolf Hitler. (I was ugly!)

I wonder if the custodian who was cleaning the floor in my hospital room that night had any idea that the brand-new baby watching him would someday be a fellow professional cleaner, responsible for keeping 300 million square feet of floor clean in all 50 states and Canada? A sideways view of the janitor closet across the hall might have been the first sight to strike my infant eyes; the first smell, floor wax or disinfectant cleaner being applied, and right after my mother's heartbeat, the most soothing sound was probably the hum of a buffer out in the hallway.

From then on up, I was a skinny boy in coveralls, with a cowlick and lots of freckles.

What was I like as a kid? According to my mother, I was "always fixing, building, or cleaning something—busy as two bees," and "always eager and willing." From the first I loved neatness and order—before I went to bed I made sure my shoes, tools, and toys were all lined up and organized for the next day.

I had the advantage of good roots. Grandpa Aslett's folks hailed from Bath, England, and Asletts are peppered through Great Britain's records as soldiers, servants, doctors, and pub owners. My grandmother, a Bell, descended from early sawmill owners who crossed the plains by covered wagon in the 1840s and 1850s after migrating to the United States from England. My mother's side, the Ross side, is rooted in Denmark and Scotland, and my ancestors left there to seek religious freedom and agricultural opportunity in America. They pushed a handcart across the continent to settle in the West, surviving the death of children and spouses, drought, Indians, disease, and injury.

All of my ancestors were independent and self-reliant, and reading their well-kept journals inspires me now as much as it did when I was a boy.

> SOMETIMES I THINK CLEANING MUST BE IN MY BLOOD. THERE WERE ASLETTS (HAZLETTS) BACK IN ENGLAND'S CASTLE DAYS AND ONE OF THEM WAS THE EQUIVALENT OF THE DUKE OF THE ROYAL CHAMBER POT.

There were no silver spoons in our family's kitchen, but we had a close family, thanks to my parents and to the fact that for most of my young life we lived on a farm. Together was our way of life, though not necessarily a conscious choice. There were seven of us: my father and mother, Duane and Opal Aslett (formerly Opal Nora Ross), and their five children—one girl and four boys. We lived together, worked together, and played together. My sister Shirley was a year and half older than me, my brother Larry two years younger, and Dee and Rick seven and eight years younger. We were never idle—we always had something going on—something to do, somewhere to be.

Rich in relatives

At the age of eight or nine, I suddenly realized the benefits of relatives—grandfolks, uncles, aunts, and cousins. My father had 14 brothers and sisters; my mother, three sisters, and all of these uncles and aunts were married, with children. This gave us lots of relatives, who came around often. Cousins often stayed a week.

Everything was exciting when the relatives arrived. Young and old, they were among the best advisors—they could and would fill any gaps in parental knowledge or enthusiasm. And they were willing to stop almost anything to play baseball (one of the few entertainments we had then).

WITH MY DAD ON THE HAY RAKE, IN 1937.

Most of my uncles were in road construction or agriculture; one a colonel in the air force. Only one had been to college, and he became an engineer. He invented a way to remove the starch from potatoes, built a factory to do it, and became a millionaire.

I was one of the first to break out of the mold of construction and agriculture, and become a janitor. That might be a disgrace or reverse to some people, but not the Asletts. When I was 34, at the bedside of my dying grandmother (the mother of 15) she said, "Donny, all of my boys went into their own businesses, and employed many people, and I'm proud of that." That was my last conversation with her, and it only reinforced my enthusiasm for the entrepreneurial life. Seeing enterprise all around me as I grew up, I assumed that owning and running my own business was the only way to make a living.

Many people never know their grandparents, and some only get to enjoy them as a child. All four of mine lived until I was in my thirties. What a blessing that was, as all that time they were actively interwoven with our lives. They helped to raise me, and I got to interact with them, listen to them, stay with them, and learn from them. I always appreciated this privilege then and only treasure more now all of the good things I gleaned from it.

I suspect that the confidence I always seemed to have came from an extremely secure set of parents and grandparents. My dad, mother, uncles, and aunts could do, fix, or build just about anything. And even when frost, fire, hail, or disease undid all their hard work, they always managed to overcome the setback and life would roll on as exciting as ever. Life at home, school, and work was filled with purpose—what was planned and dreamed about was done.

My grandmothers were something. My maternal grandmother, Dora Ross, never spoke a bad word about even the worst character in the world. She always

OUR FAMILY IN 1939, ME IN THE MIDDLE.

took care of others first—you never heard anything from her but "May I help you?" or "What can I do?" She was proud of her family and quite a family it was—more like an entire tribe!

My mother, Opal Ross Aslett, topped even these ladies. I have a lot of "mother" stories, and know I could top Abe Lincoln's best about his mother. If ever an eternal optimist lived, someone who could see the positive side of even a sure loser, it was my mother. She made certain our childhood was not only warm and solid and secure, but productive. Mother didn't just cuddle us, she watered and fertilized and pruned and repotted us. She taught us to love good music, art, and gardening, read us books, and took us exciting places. The worst thing she ever called me, when my baseballs broke a fifth window in one year, was "a little pill." Whatever that was!

Mom worked hard in the house and in the fields, was always supportive, and cared for her own and Dad's folks as well as us kids. I never witnessed a bad word or feeling between her and my dad.

When she changed from her farm togs and dressed up to go to town for parts, even when she was in her late thirties, high school seniors and college boys would whistle at her (which really irritated my dad!).

My mother's three sisters were like her, very feminine and full of life and beauty. Never did I hear any profanity, filthy jokes, or sacred things made light of from any of these ladies. The same was true of my sister Shirley, my Aunt Rose, and most of the women in the agricultural community, those I met at school bazaars, ag meetings, and school plays.

This was the main exposure I had to women as a child, and it contributed mightily to my lifetime concept of women. They seemed to radiate quality and goodness, and to have a depth of feeling and nurturing spirit that men often lack. Thus I developed early a reverence, if not awe, for all women. They are the superior beings of our species.

ROSS SISTERS: DONA, OPAL (MOTHER), BETTE, GLENDA C. 1945.

The long road home

Dad was a grade foreman, a boss on road construction for M.K. & Duffy Reed, and had to be where the many new roads were being built, so we moved a lot. The year I was four we moved ten times (yes, in one year!). Another year I attended seven different schools.

In 1941, when I was six, things became a little more permanent. We moved to Twin Falls, Idaho, to a trailer on a vacant lot behind the new house Grandfather Aslett was building. I loved the sound of building and still remember the smell of all that fresh sawdust.

Later my parents bought a house. It seemed like a mansion, though it was only a small house in a nice neighborhood. I lived a lifetime, it seemed, in that little gray-shingled house on Adams Street in Twin Falls, Idaho, but it was really only two years.

I was playing in the dirt one day building imaginary roads with toys when my sister burst out the back door yelling, "The Japanese have bombed Pearl Harbor. We are at war!" I was old enough (had seen enough war movies) to comprehend the terror of this and had nightmares of airplanes filling the sky over Twin Falls. I gathered up the scraps from Grandpa's house-building and carved them into crude airplanes—my own little fleet to defend America. Some of Dad's brothers, one only 17 or 18, enlisted and left. For years names like Corregidor, Bataan, Guadalcanal, Berlin, Sicily, Poland, and Midway were part of our vocabulary. The war was woven through our everyday lives—in newsreels, radio broadcasts, scrap drives, and war songs. We saw a lot of soldiers leave and return and some relatives never come home. Dad was gone most of the time (I hardly knew him then) building roads and airports, but life was still rich, between a wonderful mother, cousins and numerous other close relatives, and a grandfather who would actually sit and play with us.

Like most of the boys of the day, I wanted the genuine Red Ryder BB gun, got beat up by bullies, and enjoyed Ovaltine and secret code rings. I knew every airplane and car name and insignia by the age of seven. Movies were ten cents then and serials from Spy Master to Batman were at the Saturday matinee. Lassie was coming home, and it was tonsil trouble time, and adventure time. I wonder now how I survived some of the rides down into Rock Creek Canyon inside of old tires and barrels.

The war raged on, and when Dad came home every three weeks or so, he seemed like a stranger. Our family of five kids was complete by now. Our nightly treat was listening to Amos and Andy, Jack Armstrong, Sky King, Sergeant Preston of the Yukon, Jack Benny, and others on the radio. Our outdoor life was usually centered on our often muddy backyard, and digging a basement under our house by hand with a bucket (a smart mother's ploy to keep her children occupied).

I remember standing up on a chair in the living room when I was 11 or 12, as Mom fitted my first Scout uniform. Was I ever spiffy and proud! She stitched the last patch on, and as she stepped back to admire her eldest son, she whispered, "Oh Lord, I hope this is the only uniform you'll ever have to wear, Donny!" It was 1946, and our family and friends were still healing from their World War II losses. I never put on a uniform of any kind after that without remembering her quiet entreaty.

The unmatchable pleasures of childhood

Time stretches out for kids—a single season is like a whole generation. Each season had its own excitement. We tingled in anticipation of the first snow. Nothing else in the world seemed to matter when all was blanketed with white, from treetops to icy ponds. And it wasn't wasted, either. Back then we didn't need recreational machines to take advantage of a good snow. The menu for massive adventure included snow forts, snowball fights, snowmen, sledding (on anything from old scoop shovels to Grandpa's oversized overshoes), snow skating, and snow tunnels. Saturday afternoon in the snow with a Flexible Flyer made memories that would last a lifetime. Even snow shoveling was a thrill.

Winter seemed to last forever, but finally—glory upon glory—spring came. All that snow was suddenly gone and the brown, beaten-down, frozen flowers, trees, grasses, and weeds were resurrected into soft new green growth.

A simple thing like lawn was a magic carpet back then. What could be done on a lush open lawn was endless, including games like "Run Sheep Run," "Red Rover," "Kick the Can," "No Bears Out Tonight," "Fox and Geese," and "The Statue of Liberty," and of course walking on it barefoot. And as in the song, "Green, Green Grass of Home" we all had that "old oak tree" to play on.

And then there were the creeks and rivers, and Idaho had plenty of those, fresh from the snow-capped mountains, crystal clear and pure, and too cold to swim in or even to hold your hand in for long. Wading in one of these, keeping your balance in that swift water on slick, water-polished rocks, was an act the circus tightrope walkers never did any better than us.

THERE WERE JUST THREE OF US IN 1941, AT THE START OF WORLD WAR II—MY SISTER SHIRLEY, ME, AND MY BROTHER LARRY. MAN, DID I LOVE THOSE OVERALLS!

And rain! The poets plainly missed the mark when they said, "into every life some rain must fall." Those were sedate adults, a bunch of golfers or picnickers talking to each other—not kids! Rain for us was just a message from heaven to reroute the activities of the day, a fresh new environment in which to mudslide and puddle-splash. Rain never dampened a young spirit, only irrigated it. And as farmers in a desert area, we appreciated it doubly.

What about the sagebrush? Pioneers traveled through it, cowboys sang of it, and I lived in it. Wonderful stuff it was, pungent odor and all. Though you always had to keep an eye out for wood ticks and rattle-snakes, we hiked in it, camped in it, hunted in it, cleared it, played in and under it, and swished each other with it in sagebrush swordfights. When it bloomed, it was beautiful. When it was wet, no perfume could match it, and when snow draped it, it was magical. That shabby-looking shrub growing all over the plains was never plain to us.

Ah yes, childhood! When a bee sting was an important event worth telling everyone about. My childhood had all those Norman Rockwell scenes in real life—the ice cream parlor and the town bully both gave us some extremes of emotion! Playing catch or batting fly balls could make the blood race, as could the sound of a school bell or school bus coming, or an appreciative crowd of your peers all waiting to see one of your homemade puppet shows. Just sitting on a rock by the river could inspire some unforgettable philosophies and dreams.

No ride could equal a ride on one of our hay wagons, or on Grandpa's back. And no king ever felt as grand as I did sitting on a short haystack, being "The King of Bunker Hill." Every bruise or scrape was just another adventure. Mercurochrome and kisses were about the extent of the first aid we had in those days, but I can't remember suffering much pain. Our frustrations were short-lived and pretty elastic, because every one of us knew that we counted. Of rich and poor we were aware, but we never focused on or were impeded by it.

Youth was full of music with no fanfares needed. To hear father break out into a song as we plowed, or to hear Grandpa sing "The Preacher and the Bear," now that was performance!

Childhood was full of fun, magic, and mystery, and most days had so much going on that it was almost sensory overload.

In 1944 Dad got tired of being away from home so often in his job as a traveling construction worker, so he and Mom agreed that with five kids now, they should make some changes. This was no way to raise a family.

I remember well the day he returned after being gone for weeks. He was smiling, happy, and he hugged me. His three-day beard pricked my cheek as he announced that we were moving.

Thus we moved to a rented farm in Jerome, Idaho. It was 160 acres in Sugar Loaf valley on the dry, flat, fertile fields of southern Idaho. Uncle Mel (my favorite uncle, who looked like Spencer Tracy) was going to be Dad's partner in ranching.

We moved into the old house there made of lava rock, and Uncle Mel and his family moved to a house across the road. His children were all girls. He loved kids and this really added to the fun, warmth, and education of life here. I learned cheerfulness from him—he was Mr. Fun, Mr. Positive. He could find the humor in any situation, no matter how grim it might seem at the time.

IN 1944, WE MOVED FROM THE CITY TO THIS SOLID OLD HOUSE BUILT OF LAVA ROCK, ON A RENTED FARM IN JEROME, IDAHO. ALL OF THE BATHROOMS WERE OUTSIDE, AND I BROKE A RECORD 12 WINDOWS HERE.

For the next ten years, from the age of eight to eighteen, I had a first-class relationship with my father. When I wasn't in school, I was with him at least 12 hours a day—at work, play, and meals, and on trips to the neighbors, or the hardware or feed store. He was the hardest worker, best manager, and most positive and moral person I have ever known.

An oasis in the desert

The farm was desert but beautiful. There were hot, dry summers and deep-snow winters. Anything not watered regularly would turn brown and die. We irrigated the fields from man-made canals and ditches, and grew big gardens.

We had an outside bathroom, and no indoor plumbing, so we had to carry in water from the well house several times a day. We washed our clothes in a washhouse, and bathed once a week on Saturday night in big, round tin tubs (with several kids using the same water in turn, according to age).

We had no regular hired help so running the farm was very much a family operation. We all had chores—important, precious chores to do. Coal to fetch, animals to herd and feed and water, cows to milk, potatoes to pick, and beans to weed (fields and fields of them, which we attacked enthusiastically as a family). It was a real adventure to tromp the hay in the stack or the grain in the bins, and no TV special was ever as spectacular as watching the Basques (Spanish shepherds) bring their flocks of sheep past the ranch in spring, heading for the mountain pastures. I got to help Uncle Mel overhaul tractors, and was introduced to the rewards of harvest as well as occasional setbacks and losses.

> From earliest childhood I cannot recall a single day of my life that I didn't know the night before exactly how the following day would be spent and what outcome was expected. At the end of every day, my father or mother would "schedule" tomorrow. We always knew, the minute we woke up, what was going to happen, where, when, why, and how.

By the age of 12 I had graduated to a grown man's work and responsibility with stock and machinery. We worked long hours but had enough fly fishing afternoons, occasional Roy Roger movies, and camping trips to the mountains to savor life at its finest. Relatives would come and stay all night—we relished that. One of the best times was when the "city dude" cousins came to visit on the farm. Once out of their safe, soft city environment, they were at our mercy. Every day was show time, from the table to the stable.

Life here helped to make me aware that anything was possible with enough planning and persistence. One time there was a big red granary (the size of a small house) that needed to be moved to a better location, about 150 feet away. We put some skids under it and hooked it up to the old F-12 Farmall tractor with a heavy chain. The tractor spun its wheels but didn't even shake the granary. Then we hooked our team of horses to the front of the tractor. After much lunging and yelling the granary moved only an inch, so we hooked Uncle Mel's '41 Dodge and our '41 Chevy in front of the horses. Then every member of our two families not driving one of the vehicles got behind the granary and pushed. With much spinning of tires and dust from hooves (and many grunts), it moved. Victory—what a memory!

A life of true riches

We might have been poor in the eyes of the world, but we were rich. We had everything, especially full-time, 100 percent parents.

The ranch was a complete world of its own, full of freedom and passion. We had everything most people only read or hear about now—gardens with fresh fruit and vegetables (even cantaloupe and watermelon), horses, sheep, pigs, and cows. We had dogs to run with, trees to climb, fields to run in, hills for sledding and skiing, and caves to explore. Adventure was as near as a big gravel pile to roll down, the old swimming hole, and the tree swings. The farm was a place of action all year round, and there were few worldly distractions in those days before general stores evolved to malls.

Best of all, we had a nice flat green pasture to play ball in, with dried cow pies for bases. My dream at this point was to be a professional baseball player. I practiced for hours every day, without missing a day, and was always one of the leaders whenever we kids managed to put together a team.

Our time in Jerome seemed like an entire lifetime, though it was just five years.

A new world opens

When I was 12, another new world opened up for me; it was the year I found Scouting. Out of nowhere came Jess Osier, a small-framed, handsome man in his thirties. Why he took it upon himself to organize a troop of Boy Scouts, I'll never know, but that's what he did. There was no church, PTA, no Lions or Elks Club or Chamber of Commerce in that small farming community to sponsor a troop, so on his own time and at his own expense he gathered up 17 boys he didn't even know and created Troop 99, of Jerome, Idaho.

Over the next few years, this handful of boys enjoyed hikes, trips, ball games, camporees, parades, and thrilling Scout meetings. And always with us was Jess Osier—quiet, smiling, and caring. His annual two-week vacation from the implement company where he worked was spent not on himself but on us—Mr. Osier always provided his car, and the money any poor kids needed to go. He shared with us some of the rarest of riches—he cared and he gave.

There wasn't much else going on in our quiet, isolated farm community in 1946, so Scouting received my full attention. Going to Scout camp for the first time, where there were organized activities like skits, courses, competitions, and raft races, seemed like the first phase of going to heaven. There has never been air cleaner, pines taller, silence more profound, or food so delicious. I loved the smells of cooking outside, the feel of slipping into a brand-new sleeping bag, ignoring the hard, rocky ground underneath, and learning about, being able to name, and even eating some of the wild things we'd trod over for years.

Camp meant the smell of wood smoke, the splash of canoe paddles, the sound of the creek and the crackling of the wood fire, the enthusiastic, then fading chatter from the proud tented groups, silly jokes, and excitement for the coming morning. Then lying in a sleeping bag gazing into the heavens, or being hypnotized for hours by the coals of the campfire. All of this was excitement par excellence!

There was one experience that might have contributed to my future choice of a profession. At our third Scout meeting, Mr. Osier announced that we would be going on a hike. I had never been on an official hike in my life, and after reading the Scout manual and looking at the pictures of lines of uniformed boys going on the trail, I couldn't wait for the day. We were given a list of things that we would need to "be prepared" for the hike. This included a canteen to supply the necessary drinking water, especially since we would be hiking in the desert. The official Scout canteen I saw in the book was not within my budget of 60 cents, so I followed my father's example of making whatever he needed, but didn't have or couldn't afford. I decided to make a canteen.

Searching through Mom's cupboards I came upon the perfect container, a flat, quart-sized metal can of Aero Wax. Shaking it, I found only a dribble of wax in the bottom and so was granted permission to have it. I rinsed it out until the water was clean and clear. (Of course I didn't know that cold water wouldn't dissolve the wax that still coated the inside of the can.) I then made an insulating padded cover for it from a piece of old Army blanket, stitching it up nicely with some thick black thread. It was a beaut! After I added a belt loop and carrying strap to it, I was prepared!

The morning of the hike I didn't drink anything before I left home because I wanted to be sure to get as much use out of the canteen as I could. Out into the desert we went, a brisk-stepping line of Scouts. My gurgling canteen at my side gave me great pride and confidence. By ten o'clock it was hot and my mouth was like cotton when we stopped to rest. My first big draft of cool, clear water was not as thrilling as I expected. The heat and slogging had loosened all of the old wax I had failed to clean out of the canteen, and thus what I drank was... diluted wax. It was terrible, and now my mouth tasted like waxed cotton. I wanted desperately to ask a fellow Scout for a drink of water, but I had bragged so much about my homemade canteen being better than their boughten ones that I didn't have the nerve. On we went, my reservoir of waxwater sloshing at my side and me belching wax. For lunch, I'd brought one of Dad's famous cheese and egg sandwiches and two of Mom's peanut butter ones for energy—two of the driest sandwiches you could eat. Trying to wash them down with waxwater was almost impossible.

By three o'clock that afternoon, we were in one of the highest, driest spots on earth. I could spit dust, and had only my can of wax-water to drink. As the desert heat waves danced across the horizon, I could only stagger along, feeling like I'd just licked a few thousand square feet of kitchen linoleum. In a desperate attempt to rid myself of the wax so that I could graciously accept a drink from someone else, I "accidentally" knocked over my canteen. But before two drops of the liquid managed to flow out, an alert nearby Scout leaped up and saved my "water" (which he bragged about all the rest of the day).

That evening coming home, when we walked past a canal of muddy water, my whole soul said, "Dive in and drink." The canal ran through a corral of several thousand cows, but that wasn't why I didn't do it. It was saving face.

By the end of the day, floor wax was in my system and has been ever since.

Good food sense was one of many sound instincts my parents had. My mother was a natural nutritionist, and studied up on it. We ate three meals a day, no in-between snacks, and few sweets. We had gardens and fields full of everything good, and coops and corrals full of fine stock—which meant homegrown eggs and chicken dinners, and the best beef, lamb, and pork, plus wild game like deer, elk, and pheasant. We always had fresh milk and real whipped cream, and you've never tasted butter or cottage cheese until you've made your own, as we did. The fruits and vegetables were fresh to the hour, and raised without pesticides or chemical fertilizers. My mother and grandmothers could make bread, cookies, cakes, and rolls that would shame any bakery. We cellared apples, carrots, and of course, our own homegrown Idaho potatoes, so we had fresh vegetables year round. We canned peaches, cherries, pears, apricots, and applesauce (with a slice of homemade bread this was heaven).

We ate like kings, our freezer was always full, and there was no danger of running out, even in our poorest moments.

We grew sugar beets and they had to be thinned, which was backbreaking work. It was almost impossible to stand up after a day of hoeing beet seedlings. Mexican transient workers passed through from farm to farm, and when we could hire them to help, we did. Boy, were they hard workers—they won praise and positive comments from my dad, and great respect from all of us.

Other family jobs on the farm were picking rocks and weeding beans. Both kept us in the field all day, but our parents worked alongside of us and we could talk, visit, and compete. It was here I learned that a little hustle would get the job done faster, and get praise as well as results.

I always looked thinner than I actually was. I was lean but sturdy, from lifting sacks of grain and thousands of bales of hay, wielding a shovel, and milking cows.

I had plenty of energy and idealism. I planned and envisioned my future life while riding tractors or milking cows. I had plenty of time then to think, reach conclusions, and resolve.

> WHAT SHAPED MY LIFE THE MOST?
> PLENTY OF HARD WORK AND
> ACTIVITY, AND PARENTS WHO
> EXPECTED A LOT OUT OF ME AND
> GAVE ME THEIR TIME AND EXAMPLE
> INSTEAD OF ORDERS.

Facing the chores

Our folks always taught us that a "bad day" had nothing to do with the events of the day; it was determined solely by your attitude.

What was our attitude? I'd wake up before dawn hearing my Dad or Grandpa singing or whistling, or shouting encouragement to the cows as they served them the bales. Some mornings Dad would come out of the house, walk out into the barnyard, look all around him, then take a deep breath and say, "Man, isn't it great to be alive?"

This was the approach to work I learned, so it was a real shock when I left home and saw what so many people elsewhere did: Drag themselves out of bed, down a couple of cups of coffee to get their eyes open, and then grump, groan, and pout their way out to the "barn." That's like deciding right then that the day is going to be miserable. We, not the chores or challenges ahead, solely determine whether we will delight in a day or dread it.

Fortunately, when I was young, horses were still used on the farm. We had two blacks, Doll and Star, and I spent hundreds, maybe thousands of hours behind their rumps haying, harrowing, and harvesting beans. I loved and respected them, and learned precise accuracy with the reins—I could guide them through a gate at a trot with one-inch clearance between the implement tires and the posts.

It was always a pleasure at the end of the day to unhitch the horses, feed them, and watch them trot off to the freedom of the fields. The tractors that came later were faster, but never offered the companionship of the teams.

There were few snowplows in those days, especially in remote areas like ours, and we lived a quarter mile from a highway where motorists often slid off the road or got stuck. When they hiked to our farm in search of help, Dad would cheerfully offer "the boys" (me and my brother Larry, who was eight), to pull them out—not with a tractor. They were as helpless as a car in 24 inches of snow. We did it with the horses. We were small and those horses seemed 30 feet high. They hated to be harnessed as much as we disliked heaving and strapping on those cold, stiff leather rigs. We had to take off our gloves to fasten the snaps and buckles, and I learned to be fast and accurate in the biting cold. I'd attach a chain to the huge doubletree, and then to the bumper of the distressed Dodge. No victory was sweeter than when the wonderful, now willing team—straining, slipping for footing, breathing out their hot, steaming breath—would ease the vehicle to freedom. It felt good to see people's thankful faces. We might have gotten an occasional dime for this, but Dad would always say, "The boys are glad to do it." And we were.

Fences provided many lessons in my life. When I was just nine—an age at which many kids aren't even asked to clean their room—I was assigned several miles of electric fence to walk and later ride along, making sure any weeds beneath it were cleared away. If weeds grew up and touched the wire, they would short it out, and the cows could get into the crops and ruin them, or might eat too much and then bloat and die. In those days, one good cow could be worth about what a car cost, so riding fence was a "do it right or get your butt kicked" responsibility.

Two years later I was building electric and barbed wire fences, miles of them. The next year fences with wooden posts. After the posts were in, we attached and stretched the wire tight enough to sing. I remember once stretching barbed wire with the tractor so tight that it broke in two, and in seconds sawed halfway through one of the big corner posts. It was frightening, and reminded you to always keep your hands and eyes well away. I got plenty of punctures, slashes, and jabs, but fortunately, no serious gashes in more than 50 years of dealing with that deadly wire.

Trying didn't count

We learned on the ranch that tiredness, pain, rain, cold, or discouragement didn't matter—only results did. Trying didn't get the cows milked, hay up, or cattle fed. Tiredness wasn't of any consequence if the sun set and the animals weren't cared for and the water put on the crops. This was good training for success, tough at times, but it always got the job done, which built confidence and ability.

At the age of 13 I was promoted to hay stacker, which meant I got to do a grown man's job up on the stack. As a load (about 700 pounds of hay) was lifted up from the ground and dumped on top of the stack, I would pitch it around to the edges and level it to shape the stack straight and tall. It was the hottest, ugliest job imaginable—hay is heavy and with the hay often came rocks, snakes, wire, and sharp, prickly weeds. It was no picnic, but knowing I was the key member of the crew kept me going. I *had* to keep stacking or everything stopped.

One day I had just leveled a load on our now 15-foot high stack, and I decided to catch my breath. I wanted to lean on the pitchfork, so I jabbed it down hard in the hay, forgetting that my foot was down there too. One of the fork's sharp, pencil-sized tines went right through my shoe and into my foot. Alarmed, I yelled down, "Dad, I've stuck the fork through my foot!" Dad yelled back up, "Well pull it out—there's another load coming!"

I did, and quickly, because a hurt foot wasn't nearly as bad as being buried by a giant load of hay. I didn't get to go limping to the house until the hay was all stacked. These days Dad would probably be run in for child abuse, but the attitude I learned here toward responsibility has blessed my life.

Occasionally when the Basque sheepherders brought their flocks through the desert to the high range, "bum lambs" (abandoned or neglected by their mothers) would be left behind to die or serve as dinner for the trailing coyotes. We would find these little orphans, bring them home, put a nipple on a pop bottle, and nurse them with warm cow's milk. They were as cute as any new baby and the most enthusiastic, appreciative eaters in the world. Mom would warn us not to get "too close" to the lambs, because big, healthy lambs had only one purpose later—lamb chops.

We always sold our pet lambs when they were grown, but in our minds they always lived. To this day I don't eat lamb... just in case.

The coyotes were everywhere with their yapping and wailing, which to our delight scared the willies out of our city slicker cousins when they came to visit. The coyotes looked and sounded bad, but were mainly scavengers, and smart, too. They would hang around the outskirts of the sheep camps, watching for strays. For entertainment, my brother and I would creep close to a flock when it grazed at night and perfectly imitate the howl of coyotes, just to see the Basque shepherd come cussing out of the canvas sheep-camp wagon and fire his rifle in the air.

We did manage to squeeze in other mischief. Our favorite trick was to lay up a supply of hard-packed snowballs and wait for the local train to appear at the beet loading area about half a mile from our house. We'd hide in the rocks or behind bushes, and wait until the train was stopped and the engineers were relaxed, smoking, and leaning out of the cab. Then at the signal, "Charge!" on foot or on horses, we'd rush the train, pelting the crew with snowballs. This was war (even better than robbing a train), and we did it many times, unbeknownst to our parents.

FEW THINGS IN A YOUNG LIFE CAN EQUAL THE BLESSING OF COUSINS. THIS WAS TAKEN DURING HAYING TIME. MY FATHER'S MANY SIBLINGS AND MOTHER'S THREE SISTERS GAVE ME MORE THAN FIFTY FIRST COUSINS, MOST OF WHOM WE PLAYED WITH AND STAYED WITH OFTEN, AT THEIR HOMES OR OURS. THAT'S ME AND LARRY ON THE LEFT.

One day we were right up against that huge, steaming iron monster, when I guess the engineer had enough and pulled the steam release valve. A burst of loud, hissing steam issued out of the side of the train with tremendous force, harmless at that distance, but it scared our horse and us half to death. We ran shrieking for home, as the train crew bellowed with laughter.

One stormy winter evening the highway closed and we took in a stranded couple and we kids sat at their feet while they talked with Mom and Dad. Dad asked the man what he did for a living.

"I'm an engineer on the train through here, and you know there is a renegade raiding party that often attacks the train." We quickly exited to bed, but I caught the look in Mom's eye that she knew exactly whom the stranger was talking about.

Growing up, we all wonder if we measure up to the expectations of our parents and our peers. Back on the ranch, once in a while when our performance was less than expected we'd hear things like "worthless little pups" from Dad, and in a corner of our minds we worried.

But there were many little family events that reinforced security and built self-worth. The one I remember best happened when I was about 13. We were only renting the ranch we lived on, and it was clear by now that my father's dream was to have his own "spread"—I'd hear him discuss it with Mom, his brothers, and the grandfolks. An ideal ranch bordered our property, the "Newman place." For five years, my father eyed and admired it, commented on it, and had even surveyed it for the owner. It had plenty of rich bottomland, generous water rights, and good, sturdy buildings. It was probably out of financial range for Dad, but nevertheless, his dream land indeed.

One July afternoon, Dad, my brother Larry, and I were cleaning out a canal ditch along the Newman fence line. Larry and I had forgotten to feed the chickens again, to close the gate, and a couple of other little oversights, so we were on the border of "worthless little snot"-hood. Along came Mr. Newman, who had been irrigating the adjoining field. He leaned on the fence and greeted my dad, and they exchanged a little horse, cow, crop, and weather information.

Then Newman, gesturing to Larry and me working feverishly to re-cover some dignity with our dad, said, "Those are good boys, Duane. I never had any boys. Tell you what I'll do, I'll trade this whole ranch of mine straight across for those two."

My entire nervous system closed down—we were goners for sure! The deal of a lifetime. Dump two deadbeat boys and get a lifetime dream in one handshake.

Dad, chin on his shovel handle, chuckled, "No, they are keepers." That endorsement of self-worth never left my mind.

Adventure in the rocks and sage

Though nowadays I find killing even cockroaches distasteful, I really gloried in the chance to hunt with my father as a boy. In win-ter the crops were in, the cattle corralled, rows of canned fruit sitting neatly on the cellar shelves, machinery parked for the winter, and the irrigating water (which during the growing season we looked after from 5 A.M. till midnight) shut off. It was a grand time because we had real freedom at last.

After the first snow, Dad would set out his heavily insulated hunting boots, boxes of shiny bullets, and either the .22 or the Winchester .30-30 carbine. Only a half-mile from the house were thousands of acres of tall sage, jutting lava rock, and deep gorges housing rabbits, bobcats, lynx, coyotes, and more. I got to walk behind Dad and savor the smell of sagebrush and gunpowder and the breeze. Our stops to rest on a big ledge of lava rock as the sun began to warm it after an icy night were nothing short of magnificent. I learned much about nature, logic, and ethics on those hunts. Even though at first I was just a two-legged bird dog for Dad, fetching downed pheasants, it was fine with me because I got to go along.

The coyotes were much smarter than us—they could hear and smell us over a mile away. Needless to say, we bagged very few of them, though their pelts were worth $7 or $8 each. Later I used a gun myself, at first to kill rockchucks and rabbits attacking our crops and haystacks.

We lived in the midst of some of the best pheasant hunting country in the U.S.—Jerome County, Idaho. When uncles and cousins came to hunt in pheasant season, it was life at its finest. They brought news from outside, and always a new and more worthless hunting dog that would run ahead and scare most of the pheasants out of the countryside.

Then came Mother and Dad's trip of the year, deer hunting with a group of close relatives who relished the annual trip to kindle friendship, not to kill game. It was a chance to get off the desert and into the mountains, and as a bonus, we had delicious deer and elk meat to eat through the winter.

My father believed in obeying the law. There was no moderation in this—it meant the law to the letter.

When I was 13 my brother Larry and I were still glad to follow behind Dad on hunting expeditions through willow brush and wheat stubble. It was late summer, sage hen season, and we were homeward bound after a long hunt. Suddenly Dad handed me the shotgun and said, "I've got to move some irrigation dams, so you boys can hunt hens on the way home." That 16-gauge in my hands meant more than the keys to a new convertible.

Larry was awed that his big brother was now officially ordained a hunter. The sage hens had been scarce that day and with Dad out of sight, we wanted blood! Slightly out of the way of our homeward course lay a 4-acre pond generally blessed with a wild duck or two. We stalked up to the pond and I shoved the barrel of the shotgun through the cattails. Sure enough, three ducks were bobbing there in a peaceful afternoon breeze. BOOOM! The gun kicked like a horse, and all three ducks were flopping in the water. I sent Larry bird-dogging, he beached my three dead ducks, and we high-tailed it home with our prize.

When I saw the look on Dad's face, it occurred to me that duck hunting season didn't open for three more months, and perhaps I should have searched harder for a sage hen. "Why you pitiful little poachers," he yelled. "You killed those ducks out of season!" As Dad dialed the sheriff, Mom sprang up to plead for a pardon. So they passed sentence themselves: "Go pluck those ducks and bring them to Mom. You shot them, you eat them—no other food until all three are gone." I tell you now that fried duck is like reinforced leather—unchewable and unswallowable. I've never killed a duck since, in or out of season, and I shudder when I see duck on a menu.

My parents' swift judgment saved me, I'm sure, from many bad judgments of my own later in life.

Dad was an iron man, and he decided that smoking, which he enjoyed and most construction men did back in those days, was a poor example to show his kids. My dad could do anything, but I remember how hard it was for him to quit, as he ate raisins and nuts "for his nerves." He did finally manage to quit entirely.

Early the next fall on a frosty morning, Dad and I and a husky, handsome cowboy neighbor had just fixed a sickle bar on the combine. It was a beautiful day, with the smell of wheat in the air. The neighbor lit up a cigarette, and Dad said passionately, "Lord, that smells good." The guy pulled out the pack and offered it to Dad, "Here, Duane, have one." "No," he smiled, "I promised my boys I wouldn't smoke." His commitment to his children really impressed me. The days and weeks were filled with lessons like these from a good father.

Well-timed lessons

My mother was also a master of timing. She knew precisely when to seize a moment to teach a principle so that it would stick with you forever.

One hot July day when I was 13, I'd been lollygagging, griping, and groaning out in the garden, making my mother force me to pull every weed. She waited till I'd reached a complete standstill, and then sat down and told me about a soldier she'd met while in the hospital once. He'd lost his arms and legs in a land mine explosion. This grown man sat there in his bed one day and wept for the opportunity to work in a garden, among the plants and flowers again. I felt so sad for that soldier, and so lucky I could work, I vowed from that moment I would never be lazy again for the rest of my life, regardless of how I felt. The rest of those rows were cleared of weeds mighty quick.

Likewise, my mother could have just given the old "don't drink or smoke" lecture to her kids anytime, but she was smarter than that. I had a bad stomach virus once and was sick—vomiting, dizzy, nauseous to my very toe tips, looking forward to death as a release. As I was leaning over a bucket in agony I remember Mom putting her hand on my forehead and saying, "Donald, remember this is exactly how you feel after you drink alcohol." My brain cells quickly organized a "no way will I ever drink, then" commitment, which has held to this day.

There was plenty of "vivid" (more like livid) vocabulary in the barnyard when I was growing up. Hired men, truckers trying to load stubborn calves, and even a few of my uncles reeled out some of the most creative cuss words imaginable. We kids weren't allowed to repeat any of these words; they were for adults only. We couldn't help hearing them, though, because they generally carried all the way to the house.

Mother had her own way of neutralizing this indecent exposure. She told us to observe carefully, to see if the cussing ever corrected or improved anything, or impressed anyone. We did, and it didn't. The cattle never loaded any differently, no matter how numerous or well constructed the filthy phrases were. No tool or machine that broke ever jumped up and healed itself, no matter how thoroughly it was cursed for breaking. No motor ever started easier or ran more smoothly because it was damned, and smashed fingers and stubbed toes didn't quit throbbing. And we never did see anyone applaud or say, "Wow, that was a great string of words!" So from Mother's masterful appraisal I learned that swearing was a total waste of good emotion and personal prestige, not to mention risky. (If a kid got caught swearing it was the old soap in the mouth sentence.) Thanks to Mom, I don't have to worry about inappropriate vocabulary.

I DID, OVER THE YEARS, DEVISE MY OWN VOCABULARY OF EXCLAMATION, SO IF YOU RUN ACROSS AN UNFAMILIAR INTERJECTION IN THESE PAGES, CHECK OUT P. 379.

Rx for reverses

When questioned on my quick recovery from even "kick in the face" events, I have to again credit my parents.

Even as a boy, I was mature and involved enough to appreciate the importance of crops on the farm. They were not just alive—they were our lifeblood. As soon as winter was over, we prepared the ground. Dad and the whole family spent long days (and some nights) plowing, disking, harrowing, removing rocks, and irrigating before planting. Then expensive certified seed was planted in rows straight as arrows, and a couple of weeks of anticipation followed as all was in nature's hands. Soon, if all went well, we beheld the beauty of vast rows and fields of bean, beet, pea, or potato sprouts emerging from the soil, then popping open into gorgeous, tender leaves.

It was the Fourth of July, our one exciting summer day off from farming, and we woke up to an unexpected late frost. Walking out to the bean field, we beheld devastation. Every one of those perfect plants was blackened and wilted to the ground. All that work, all that investment, all that expectation—all undone. Our beautiful bean crop, our major source of income, gone.

How sorry I felt for Dad, who had the burden of supporting all of us. I saw no tear or slumped shoulder, and heard no snarl, not even a choice curse or two. He just sadly surveyed the loss and said, "Well, we better hustle—plow this under and replant. We still might get some kind of crop." And we did.

A few years later, just a week before we planned to sell our Hereford steers, we found two of them bloated, dead in the feed yard. This loss was a good part of our entire yearly income in those days.

I think I did see a tear in Dad's eye this time, but Mom put her arm around him and said, "Duane, let's be thankful that death stayed in the corral." That moment clarified many values, and remembering it in later years made it easier to look beyond the moment when reverses came.

How often we saw things like our beautiful crop of beans frozen to the ground on the Fourth of July. Failure? Nope! Dad and my uncles wrung their hands for about 30 seconds, then jumped on the machinery, plowed those blackened beans under, and replanted. With an attitude like this you could always win, no matter what blow was dealt.

Chapter 2

GRADE SCHOOL GLORIES

*These were the days of small schools,
but a big world...*

HOW WE SAVORED RECESSES IN GRADE SCHOOL, DURING WHICH BASEBALL WAS OFTEN OUR MAIN ENTERTAINMENT. HERE I AM (SECOND FROM LEFT IN FRONT ROW) WITH A GROUP OF MY CLASSMATES AT THE SUGAR LOAF SCHOOL IN JEROME, IDAHO.

The word "school" was always a pulse-racing positive for me, from the first grade right on up. As a second-grader, I attended a small rural school that had all eight grades in one room.

Miss Wheeler, my third-grade teacher at the much larger Lincoln School in Twin Falls, was a knock-out. She let me lead many class projects because I would volunteer, and I could hammer. I adored her. So much so that I would go to the school on Saturday and walk around that old rock fence in the yard, fantasizing about rescuing her from airplane crashes, charg-

ing crocodiles, falling trees, burning buildings, and numerous other life-threatening situations. She wrote a note to my mother once saying, "Donald is the most handy boy in the class." I was ecstatic. I was eight, and she was my first love, but forgotten quickly when we moved to the next town.

When we moved to Jerome, Idaho, I attended a country school called Sugar Loaf, a two-room building of lava rock. The horse barn was larger than the school. There was a big room, grades five through eight, and a little room, grades one through four, and one teacher for each room. I was in the fourth grade when I arrived here, king of the little room.

In the eighth grade, I met one of the most influential women in my life, a woman named Estelle Ricketts. She looked like Ma Kettle or Katherine Hepburn in *Rooster Cogburn*, and was undoubtedly one of the finest teachers ever to stand in front of a classroom. Her reputation from previous schools was one of ferocious sternness.

Her first day at Sugar Loaf, a big eighth-grade bully sassed her as we were coming in from recess. She grabbed the ball bat out of his hands and smacked it against the side of the rock schoolhouse, shattering it into pieces. Picking up the handiest size piece for whipping, she jerked that hunk of muscle out of his shoes and held him up off the ground all the way into the building, then whacked his hind end unmercifully. Boy, did that help us understand the word *obedience*.

A week later, I was showing off on our outdoor basketball court and she leaped from the sidelines, stole the ball from me, faked and dribbled around me, and made a professional hook shot. This shocked me so bad I almost quit playing basketball. She was something!

The next week, hunting season, two trespassing hunters ignored the No Hunting sign on her ranch. She pulled her old Winchester .30-30 off the wall and fired on them. A good shot, she missed them safely by a couple of feet, and kept them pinned down in the ditch where they took cover until sundown, when they snuck off. This lady meant business, in the classroom and in life.

I was born or developed somehow into a fierce competitor—*first* and *win* were the only two words I cared about. I occasionally duked it out with a challenger from the other end of the valley, Stanley Bird. We'd had numerous disagreements, accomplishing nothing except fat lips and black eyes. One afternoon he snatched a shoe from one of the cutest girls in the class, and she was crying—Don Aslett to the rescue! As he ran full speed across a gravel road, I tripped him and he took a terrible skidding dive. I grabbed the shoe and presented it back to the young lady with a flourish. My glory was short-lived, for Stanley was back on his feet now—fists clenched, teeth bared, bleeding, and coming straight at me.

We fought our way around the school a couple times before Mrs. Ricketts got wind of it, and out she came. By the time she got there, my shirt was ripped off, so she grabbed Stanley by what shirt he had left, and me by the neck. Then calling for the whole school to come, she led us to the flagpole platform in front of the building. She quieted the crowd, then said, "Okay, you two roosters, put your arms around each other and kiss." She had to be kidding! Burn me at the stake or put bamboo splints under my fingernails, but kiss another boy in front of the entire crowd? NO WAY! Flunk us, keep us after school for the rest of the year, but not this, Mrs. Ricketts, please.

"Kiss or I'll knock your blocks off!" She could probably rip the flag-pole out, so we kissed. The most humiliating experience a red-blooded boy could undergo. That cooled every ounce of aggression we had for each other, and we were friends from then on, forever.

Mrs. Ricketts challenged us continually, and would not accept loafing or excuses for lateness. When we met her expectations, she subtly extended recess, or noon hour if the bases were loaded and the game was in full swing. She encouraged me to write and perform, made me feel that I could do anything.

I had the lead in the Christmas play in eighth grade (this wasn't hard to manage, since there were only four of us in the whole class). Afterward Mrs. Ricketts pulled me into the back and said, "You have a face that can do many expressions—you are a natural actor." I believed I was after that, and eagerly volunteered for any available performance.

Her teaching of every subject was masterful. That spring, for the school Easter egg hunt, she put John Green, the kid she'd paddled at the beginning of the year, in charge of hiding eggs for the little kids. While the rest of us hid eggs in the usual kinds of places, John did some creative hiding. To conceal one egg he built a little basket out of the spiny seeds of cocklebur and burdock and hung it in the willows, in plain sight. (No one found it.)

When the hunt and fun were over, Mrs. Ricketts brought him up in front of the class, and showed everyone his little creation. Then she explained the importance of not being afraid to think of the new and different. This built John's confidence, and made us all resolve to be "creative" thereafter.

Another of the most valuable counsels of my life also came from Mrs. Ricketts. When I was growing up, sex wasn't a hush-hush thing, but it wasn't flaunted, either. Growing up on a farm the old "birds and bees" talk wasn't necessary—we saw and understood the reproductive process. One afternoon after lunch, Mrs. Ricketts sat at her desk near us eighth graders and very calmly taught us the power and value of being virtuous. She did it without saying any "sex" words, and didn't bring in the church or state. She simply made us understand the rewards of being morally clean in our conduct toward the opposite sex.

She got the idea across that sexual relations were a sacred, very personal and intimate thing of goodness and value and love, and never at any cost should we humans ever act like barnyard bulls. I don't remember the exact words she used, but I understood it perfectly, and I realized that she had just taught me one of the most important principles of my life. She was not an overly religious person, or a feminist either, just one of the wisest women I've ever known.

I resolved at that moment that I would live a clean life. Sixty years later now, I still remember that simple 15-minute talk.

I'm grateful for the time I spent with Mrs. Ricketts, a handsome, compassionate, powerful woman—a real teacher.

THE OLD LAVA ROCK SUGAR LOAF COUNTRY SCHOOL, WHERE ALL EIGHT GRADES WERE FIT INTO TWO ROOMS. IT HAD A BASEMENT WITH A STAGE FOR CHRISTMAS PLAYS AND MOVIES, AND THE FIRST CRANK TELEPHONE IN THE WHOLE COMMUNITY.

As a child, I always seemed to have the urge to take over and lead whatever was going on. This attitude earned me some black eyes and bloody noses, but never dampened my spirit. I was always the presumptuous organizer of little games and gangs at school and on the farm among the cousins. Later I either put myself in charge or was put in charge of running the grade school sports teams, the recess activities, and after-school play. I lined the kids up, collected the votes for leaders, appointed captains and who was "it," and called out the winners of races. People seemed to like someone to tell them what to do and when, so I did it when needed to get the show on the road.

When you immediately volunteer for things, you usually get first pick, so whenever I heard "Who will...?" at home or school, up went my hand. And it worked. When the traveling nurse lined us up for vaccinations at our country school, I'd always be the first in line, so I could get it over with. Cleaning up, errands, answers, whatever, I didn't want to be last, so I volunteered.

> ONE OF OUR FAVORITE RECESS ACTIVITIES AT THIS RURAL SCHOOL WAS BROAD OR HIGH JUMPING INTO PITS OF DRIED HORSE MANURE. IT WORKED GREAT— BETTER THAN SAWDUST. EVEN THE GIRLS ENJOYED BOUNCING IN THAT TOTALLY ODORLESS FLUFF. AND NOT ONE OF US WHINNIED WHEN WE GREW UP.

Diamond dreams

Recesses in grade school went from "ring around the rosy" to run around the bases. How we savored those recesses and noon hours— there were no TVs or video games then, and few movies. Baseball was about it, our main entertainment. I fell in love with baseball, and lived baseball from the fifth through the eighth grade. I devoured every morsel of baseball information in the school's ancient encyclopedia, and followed the Cleveland Indians in our Sunday paper. (I hated those New York Yankees because they won all the time.)

A rural elementary school in the 1940s not only didn't have gyms, locker rooms, or ball fields (the ball field was a cow pasture nearby), there was about one ball per year, and it had almost disintegrated by fall. After that, it was bring one from home or don't play. Every bat had been repaired with black tape somewhere.

I decided, in preparation for our seventh-grade season, to make sure we had a real baseball—the official 5-ounce, 360-stitch ball with cushioned cork center that Joe DiMaggio and Ted Williams were swinging at. In those days of twenty-cent hamburgers, a good baseball was an expensive $2.75.

So we baseball enthusiasts collected nickels, pennies, and dimes (even got one quarter) and by spring, had enough. I gave the money to my father, who was going to town, and back came our real baseball. No crown jewel was more beautiful or packaged more elegantly. Inside a little square box, wrapped in white tissue paper, was a bright white sphere. It brought oohs and aahs from the whole team, as we passed it around and everyone fondled it, held it up to their cheek, then smelled it—gads, a new baseball smells good. Then we lined up against the window looking wistfully at the snow that we wished would melt. Who would be the first to hit that unblemished, first ever official baseball in our lives at this school?

After all the anticipation, everything that followed was a letdown. In the spring, we played the big game much more gloriously in our minds than on that soggy field. The first hit was a screaming grounder. Besides bouncing and hitting me in the neck, the ball got wet and muddy. We lost it twice in the brush the first day, and we never had to fight over who got to take it home at the end of the school year. After a long drive one day into the wilderness of weeds, rock, and rough terrain, our cherished investment was lost forever.

My eighth-grade experience with baseball was a high. Mrs. Ricketts made me the manager of the team. I tried to pattern my style after Lou Boudreau and Connie Mack, who were some of the best major league managers of the time, and I demanded big-league results from a ragtag bunch of farm kids. Every spare minute, when not herding cows, weeding beans, haying, or doing other chores, we would grab our gear and go to the lower pasture and "bat flies."

The last day of school, at the traditional picnic, Mrs. Ricketts gathered the kids and parents together to reward me for my management efforts. Money and sports equipment weren't too plentiful in that little rural school, and when she presented me with an official catcher's chest protector, my whole being filled with gratitude. I still have that thank-you present 60 years later, a reminder of what can be earned through work and your best efforts.

Years later, one afternoon at my mother's house, I was paging through a scrapbook and came upon several of my old report cards. Quickly noticing the C's (as well as a few A's), I suddenly realized that I was not as smart as I remembered. What really struck me, though, was the teachers' comments, recording behavior rather than intellect. I noticed a few things that ultimately predicted my future more than the grades.

1. I missed very few days of school, had almost perfect attendance. Sick, tired, or whatever, I was there.

2. I always got the assigned work done. Maybe not the best, but I was always prepared.

3. Two of my favorites from the comments: "Don has an interesting way of telling things." "Don intensely takes over and never runs out of energy."

Thanks to strong parents and grandparents and a few key teachers, I grew up with a lot of self-confidence. But in the battle for positions, scores, grades, and distinctions, I saw many natural abilities in my peers that I just didn't have. I met some marvelously gifted students, athletes, musicians, actors, and artists in my life, and watched them "get" the dance step, the athletic play, the trumpet notes, the algebra formula, the puzzle solution in seconds. I had to study, pore over, and practice hours, days, even weeks to achieve similar results. I was always able to hold my own or even rise to some leadership on the ball field, or in the band, classroom, or Scout troop, but it wasn't from talent. It was from grinding effort, tons of extra practice, sheer will, and discipline. Nothing ever came naturally except my vision of things.

Lunch lessons

In those pre-fast-food days, we usually took lunches to school in buckets, brown bags, or whatever container you or your mom could find before the bus came. Then at lunchtime, we all sat in groups, setting our lunches on the table in front of us, and there was a slight delay before diving in, as we all wondered what was in the other people's pails. There were Lexus pails, Fords and Chevys, Roy Rogers tins, the poor kids' sacks, and often the urchins of the school had some unidentifiable morsel tucked in their coat pocket.

The opening of the lunches was generally stressful, and as we quickly scanned the other lunches, I was always shocked to be covetous of those who had neat stuff, especially the kids from families with only one or two kids. Multi-child families usually had "throw it in" food; the others had wax paper-wrapped sandwiches made with store-bought Wonder bread and expensive bologna (lunch meat no less!). The meat sandwiches were stacked on one side and the deluxe dessert sandwiches (like peanut butter and jam) were professionally wrapped and stacked on the other, and three cookies leaned tenderly against the sandwiches, plus often, almost beyond belief, an orange!

We, the commoners of the school, got one orange a year from Santa in the toe of our Christmas stocking, but these kids got one almost every day. I never sniffed a girl's perfume until the junior prom, and it wasn't nearly as stimulating as the smell of an orange being peeled by the luscious lunch kids. There were times when we even begged for the peels and ate them!

It always amazed me how their sandwiches held together, as if they were glued—they could eat them with one hand. For ours, constructed of homemade bread, you needed two hands or it was crumb city. And then the final touch—almost psychologically crippling for us—their sandwiches were cut diagonally! Yes, in creative triangles, something our ordinary mothers and grandmothers never learned. Then to heighten the suspense came the wait to see what was in their brightly colored thermoses. Probably ice-cold milk. When they stopped drinking to get their breath, and before they could lick their lips, one could generally identify the contents. It seemed that milk, Kool-Aid, cocoa, or anything would beat the small Mason jar of prune or apricot juice we had in our lunch.

After all of the upscale-lunch kids got their pretty meal on the way, we, the blue Levi group, quickly so it wouldn't be noticed, reached discreetly into our sack or bucket hoping that the twice as thick, homemade whole wheat bread hadn't crumbled, and that the slices of last night's roast with mustard hadn't slipped out of the sandwich. You couldn't peel the boiled egg unseen in the sack, and doing this in public was always degrading. An old lunch spoon always came with a little jar of fruit. ("You kids will lose the good spoons.") Then instead of a cookie, we had a carrot.

Much later I realized that although our lunches were uglier, they were probably far healthier than theirs, giving us more years of living. Another plus was that there was never quite enough in our lunches—we ate it all and still felt hungry. Those white-bread kids (many of whom are now fat) seldom ate all of their lunch—they would often leave half of one of those precision-cut sandwiches in the pail to take home and feed some spoiled cat or dog. During the rest of the afternoon I would eye the pail sitting on the shelf above the coats and baseball stuff, knowing it contained one quarter of an orange and two halves of whatever. In my entire life, I've had no impulse to steal, except then. If I had ever been locked in there alone during recess, their dogs and cats would have gone without that night.

When hot lunches came to the schools, this torturous social ordeal came to an end. We low-life lunchers loved hot lunch and ate any and all of it gratefully. The spoiled wax paper-wrappees were seldom happy with the scheduled offering; they gladly gave us what they wouldn't eat. I dug out an old lunch pail the other day and contrasted it to the corporate "let's go to lunch" ritual and some good memories came back.

ELEMENTARY-SCHOOL ENTREPRENEUR

I was raised with the idea that the only way to get money was to earn it—winning it, inheriting it, finding it, stealing it, or marrying into it were never even options. I figured out early that if I wanted a ball mitt or watch, it was going to take money—mine—my parents wouldn't just fork it over. Even though we worked every day on the ranch, that was to help support the family and pay for our room and board and clothes. Grandpa and Mom were good for an occasional dime for a double feature movie, maybe a quarter on birthdays, but if you wanted the big bucks, you found a way to earn them.

> MONEY IN MY FAMILY NEVER CAME IN A PAYCHECK, SO I ASSOCIATED IT NOT WITH PURCHASE POWER BUT WITH INDEPENDENCE. I HATED TO ASK OR BEG FOR THE CAR FOR A DATE, OR MONEY FOR A BASEBALL MITT WHEN I WAS GROWING UP, SO WORK WAS NEVER JUST A "JOB" FOR CASH, IT WAS A TICKET TO FREEDOM AND SELF-RELIANCE.

My adventures as an entrepreneur started early. When we lived at Sugar Loaf, we had a chicken coop and 18 chickens, which were my chore. I was allowed to keep and sell any eggs the family didn't eat. I learned perfect care of chickens quick. If I fed them right, on time, and kept the coop clean, I'd get 18 eggs out of 18 chickens every day. If I'd miss a feeding or the water ran out, the egg count would go down.

I dropped the big silver dollars from my egg sales into a cigar box, my first savings. In those days (the '40s), a dollar was a significant hunk of change. Shining and heavy, it just fit in the clutch of a little hand. I remember the sense of power and security my cigar box full of dollars gave me.

Once I had mastered chicken husbandry, I moved on to sales.

When I was seven, the offer on the back of the Red Ryder comic sounded like pure capital gain. Just send my name in on the coupon, and they would send me one hundred envelopes of pretty Christmas seals (the kind you lick and stick on packages). I would sell these for twenty-five cents per envelope, and send them the $25. Then I could choose any of the prizes from the full-color spread. It was 1942, World War II was in full blaze, and there among the prizes was an official-looking Army .45 pistol and holster. Gadfrey! The picture alone made my stomach muscles tighten, so I got my big sister to sign the guardian signature.

Soon the seals were in my hand, and I loaded them all up in my Royal Flyer wagon and hit the streets of Twin Falls. The image of that .45 burning in my mind removed all fear of knocking on doors or facing down dogs. I was hot!

MY FIRST SAVINGS (FROM EGG SALES AND OTHER LITTLE ENTREPRENEURIAL VENTURES) WERE STASHED SECURELY IN AN OLD CIGAR BOX.

At dark that first day, I returned with all hundred envelopes. That was just a warm up, I told myself. Every night that week, I walked down block after block. My first twenty-five cent sale came in three days; it took me about two months to peddle most of the rest. By that time, the remaining sets of seals were worn from being packed and unpacked. On day 40, the front axle of my wagon gave out, so I found a nice rope in my dad's stuff in the garage and tied it to the front of the now slanting vehicle. I discovered thus the principle of friction, as within two days the cement of the sidewalks wore the rope in two. (It turned out to be an expensive lariat, Dad's most cherished possession from his teen days on a ranch.)

I sold in the rain, snow, forever. I went out on days not even the mail carrier or the Jehovah's Witnesses would consider. Just enough people took pity on me and bought to keep me going. Mother then bailed me out by buying the tattered remains of my inventory.

It was a glorious day when I proudly sent the money back, with a big checkmark next to that .45. When the package came, I was trembling so badly I could barely unwrap it. The package felt pretty light for a gun, and when a molded rubber toy in a cheap black holster plopped out, I was horrified. Those dirty crooks! All that work for a fake rubber gun! Not even a pretend soldier would use a rubber gun.

My mother sweet-talked me into finding good in my apparent swindle, so I put the gun in the authentic-looking holster it came in and got down to an imaginary war game. Rounding a corner too fast, I slipped and fell on the holster, and it bent right in half. It was ...*cardboard*!

This was too much! I grabbed the set and rushed up to the trash burner (our kitchen stove, which burned wood and coal). I lifted the lid and held that hard-earned and long-awaited prize over the flames. "I'm going to burn this up!" I said with tear-streaming commitment. Mother didn't rush across the room and grab it out of my hand; she just glanced over. So I lowered it closer to the coals and screamed, "I'm going to burn this up!" She calmly continued to peel potatoes. To show her I meant business, into the fire went the gun set. I slammed the lid down. Surely now Mother would race to the rescue! She didn't. So in seconds it was gone, all those months of work, freezing my little butt off, all my dreams dashed. All that labor, all that emotion, and now Dad's lariat to pay for—it was a loser deal all the way.

It was not entirely without benefit, however. I learned two of the most valuable lessons of my life: Don't totally trust advertising and never lose your temper!

Not to have my entrepreneurial instincts quenched by a single failure, two years later I saw in Mother's Henry Field's garden seed catalog a much better deal. We were on the Jerome farm by now, and how could anything agricultural be untrustworthy? "Send no money" (still hadn't learned about this one yet) and Henry would send me 50 attractive cartons of seeds to be sold for fifty cents each. No one with a garden could refuse, because each carton contained ten packets of guaranteed lettuce, beet, carrot, radish, chard, etc., seed. Once I completed the sales and gathered the $25, I got to keep $5 of *their* money. And as a bonus, they would send me a Bible the size of a postage stamp. To this day, I'm not sure why I wanted a postage-stamp size Bible. But I wanted it bad!

I sent in the little card, the seeds came, and I hit the road—the country road, that is. Neighbors were one, two, three, and four miles away, and I walked. I hoped those seeds germinated faster than they sold—the only things getting planted around there were my feet, one behind the other. I remember walking three miles to the farthest ranch (a wealthy one), a dusty, thirsty, tired, discouraged nine-year-old. I gave the lady of the house my best fifty-cent sales pitch, but she squinted, said "No thanks," and walked back into the house. I trudged the three miles home.

After a month of my wagon wandering, when about two-thirds of my inventory was gone, my folks and relatives figured that buying the seeds from me was cheaper than replacing my shoes, so I finally had $20—Henry's share. (I never did sell the last ten cartons—just donated them to family.) I had fulfilled my oath and covenant with Henry Field, and true to his word, the little Bible came. It *was* just postage stamp size, although it only contained the New Testament. It fit right in my shirt pocket, where I left it that Sunday night. Monday was washday on the farm, and Mom never saw that tiny book in my pocket. It looked like a miniature Manhattan telephone directory when it was sadly dropped by my plate at supper—business number two racked up to experience.

Chapter 3

LAND OF OUR OWN AT LAST

*Happy days home on the range and ballfield,
in the mountains, and classroom, too!*

OUR RANCH HOUSE IN DIETRICH DURING THE WINTER OF
1955. THIS WAS HOME FOR MOST OF MY HIGH SCHOOL DAYS.

By 1949, my folks had carefully saved their money and Dad was shopping for our own farm. I was a freshman at Jerome High School, and my three younger brothers were still in the two-room country school. One evening Dad came home with a glowing report—he'd bought a 400-acre farm north of us in the tiny farm community of Dietrich, Idaho. Dietrich had a population of 160, with 42 kids in the entire high school. It was way out, the last place before the desert. Our nearest neighbors in any direction would be miles away. The farm had a small house, a couple of barns and granaries and other old outbuildings, many acres of rich bottomland, and a healthy share of irrigating or water rights. It even had an 8-by-10-foot bunkhouse, my bedroom for the remaining years I was home. Dad paid just $10,500 for all this!

Since it was spring already, my parents let my sister and me stay in the school we were already attending for the remainder of the year. Shirley stayed with Grandma and Grandpa Ross, and a neighboring family gladly took me in. I gave them free babysitting in exchange and helped with the spring plowing and other chores.

The new farm was only 30 miles away if you went straight across the desert. The day after school ended, my brother Larry and I harnessed the team of horses up to our nice rubber-tired Oliver manure spreader full of tools and equipment, added a lunch, water, and five bales of hay for the horses, and hooked a dump rake on behind the spreader. Then at first light we headed north toward our new home. It was a real "pioneer" trip; my heart swelled with anticipation and a sense of power, to have my own wagon train. We drove through miles and miles of nothing, not even a road, just a trail.

At the end of the day, we pulled into the lonely, empty yard of our new place. But before long, the rest of our stuff arrived via cars and trailers, and Mom had brightened the house with curtains and fresh coats of paint. By the time the big yellow rose and lilac bushes began to bloom, a new litter of pigs had arrived, and the quilts were on the beds, it was home.

Remote and flat and wonderful, the farm was heaven. Sunrises and sunsets here would delight an artist or photographer. We grew hay, wheat, beans, and potatoes, tended feedlot cattle, and rented an additional 3,000 acres of grazing land from the Miller and Nelson farms next door.

It was a good life, but my folks had paid cash, all they had, for the place, so we lived pretty frugally. Our main source of sustenance was two brown Guernsey cows that gave lots of rich milk and also provided all the cream, butter, cottage cheese, and whip cream we could possibly use, plus lots of skim milk left over to feed the pigs. Every week we'd accumulate a tall, narrow four-gallon can full of cream, take it to town, sell it for $9, and get $9 worth of groceries. I remember one day jumping into the back seat of our old '41 Chevy with the cream, headed for town. When we took the first corner the can tipped over and spilled. Our grocery money gone, we turned around and went back home.

The spring that first year was beautiful—the crops were in, and Dad had figured out an efficient irrigating system. All looked bright and then one of us left the granary door open and our two cows found it. A pig will eat until it's full and quit, but not a cow—they will eat and eat and eat, and if what they are eating is green hay or grain, they will bloat, and they did. They both lay out in the yard, tears running down their big brown eyes, and died. What a blow that was—we lost our milk as well as our cash income, and in those days cows were a premium price. Dad found an old broken-down Brown Swiss that gave us just enough milk for the house. Things were so tight after that that we had to hand-pull wild hay for the pigs, but we did have work, which cures or subdues most discouragement.

As we moved into summer, we built new corrals and filled the barnyards with haystacks. The hayfields seemed more fun now because it was our hay, all of it, no rental share to pay. The garden and orchard gave fruit and vegetables that would delight a connoisseur. Dogs and cats appeared, new calves, more pigs, lambs, and I was excited about starting in a new school.

"Growing up on a 3,000 acre cattle and pig farm in Dietrich, Idaho, Aslett said he never made his bed but learned two deep ethics from his parents. Opal Aslett told her son, 'If you act like a pig, you can go out and live with them.' Duane Aslett told his son, 'You can always tell a man by how clean his milk is.'

"Don Aslett made sure there was no hair or hay in his milk buckets."

—Bart Ripp, Tacoma *Morning News Tribune*

WHEATFIELD IN DIETRICH, IDAHO.
PHOTO BY STEVE RITTER.

The bunkhouse on the ranch was a little wooden building away from the main house where my brother and I slept. It had a desk and one pull light in the center, but no heat, water, or bath. The bathroom was 50 feet away, an old two-holer outhouse. On crisp spring, fall, and winter nights when temperatures dropped, we just stacked on the covers. We would leave a flannel bag of wheat on the oil heater in the living room, where the kernels would absorb heat. Then we'd grab it at bedtime, run from the house to the bunkhouse, toss it into the bottom of the bed, crawl in, and put our feet on it—Aah! It cooled off pretty quick, but it was the psychological equivalent of a fancy furnace. As we lay in bed, we could hear the wind in the trees and animal and bird sounds all around. The alarm clock was the sound of the screen door of the house opening and the clumping of Dad's boots as he went out to milk the cows at five-thirty in the morning. If you heard the screen door slam a second time when he finished, your goose was cooked! Oversleeping was a low-down, unmanly thing to do on the farm.

Our average neighbor had 20 or 30 acres of hay; we had 130 acres, at least 500 tons of alfalfa, which had to be cut, raked, baled, hauled, and stacked three times a year. How well and fast you could get the hay up was not only a matter

LARRY AND I STACKING OUR HAY CROP.

of profit but a kind of competition in the rural community. We would go for records mowing, raking, hauling, and stacking. Doing any of it well was skill worthy of recognition.

The year I was 16, Dad was doing so much irrigating it occupied most of his time. My younger brother Larry and I handled the entire hay crop. Dad just expected it and turned us loose.

Haying developed great back muscles, which was a lifelong blessing. In 70 years, I have never had a back problem and could always lift anything. The smell of drying alfalfa was pure ambrosia to a farmer, and seeing a haystack go up was like building pyramids. Feeding hay to enthusiastic cattle was a thrill even in 30 below zero weather.

Though my brothers and I worked for my father, I still felt the urge to pursue some profit-making enterprises of my own. But since we now lived on a ranch surrounded by 80 miles of desert, opportunities for extra income seemed as remote as where we lived. Then one day I heard on the radio that the Kasper Keck Hide and Tallow Yard was paying $5 a ton for prairie bones. Gads! I had fenced and herded on the range for years and seen the bleached bones of expired livestock all over the place. I'd also driven horses and milked cows, had them tromp on my toes, and so knew, as Dad said, "Some of them weigh near a ton." Just think of all the profits lying out there on the prairie waiting to be plucked!

So on foot, with burlap "gunny sack," I scoured the face of many acres in my time off. All those big old bones rubbed blisters on my back as my brother Larry and I carried sack after sack home and stored them in a pile against the granary—just like stacking gold in reserve! Finally, I could subdue the urge to cash in no longer. We hauled them all to old Kasper to be converted to calcium for fertilizer. Dad brought a meager check home—$3.38 (for 1,352 pounds)! Samson slew a thousand Philistines with the jawbone of an ass, which is what I felt like after picking up what seemed like a thousand jawbones for a payoff like that!

Investing in the stock market

I was a freshman in high school when my business world really opened up. I enrolled in a Future Farmers of America (FFA) class, which required that you choose a project for the school year, keep all the books on it, sell it at the end of the year, and show your profit or loss. Everything one needs to know about business would be learned here— choosing, investing, working, accounting, …and full responsibility.

At first, I pictured a majestic 1,500-pound Hereford, a dark green field of potatoes, or possibly an award-winning Holstein cow. But after consulting with my father, I was convinced that I should start in the humblest and most economical way possible, with a brood sow. My father promised he would look for the perfect pig (a bred sow) at the stock sales he attended. Weeks went by, months it seemed, and everyone else in the class had their project going (crops, pigs, sheep, or cows). My classmates who had selected pigs had all purchased their sows, registered breeds with names like Miss Golden Ham and Top Snort IV. Our ag teacher was looking at me nervously. Daily I was asked, "Got your pig yet, Don?"

Then one day as the school bus roared to a stop, I saw our blue stock trailer backed up to the unloading chute by the pigpen. That meant only one thing—I was in business! I jumped up on the rail of the pen, and there, evaluating her new owner, stood the ugliest animal I had ever set eyes on. Her color and breed were unidentifiable, and most of her ears and tail had been frozen off. She had a big dent in her back, and her belly was dragging the ground.

Dad only said, "She has a good look in her eye," and that she was worth the $35 she cost. Man, how I hated to report the arrival of my project to the teacher and record it in the "stock" entry of my P & L. There was a space to enter the animal's name, and mine didn't have one, just an invoice from the sale. I entered her in my record book as Lady Railroad Tie the First and the project began.

For the next four weeks I listened to news of the arrivals of my class-mates' sows' litters, mostly with four or five baby pigs. One sow came through with an amazing eight. Of course, these high-society sows were all young and inexperienced as mothers, resulting in heavy losses. After a week or so, the litters were all reduced, and the sow with eight ended up with only four survivors.

My own sow hadn't farrowed yet, though Dad kept assuring me she would. He was right as usual. My old sow waited until the nicest, sunniest day of spring, skillfully prepared a place for the occasion, and delivered 12 healthy, squeaking little beauties. And she knew enough not to lie on them! I only lost two of the litter, and within a week the pen was active with the remaining ten piglets, five of which were sows. That ugly old critter with a good look in her eye had outproduced all seven of the highbrow sows. I loved it.

Dad pretty much left my hog venture up to me, but one day he eased over to the pen, looked at the pigs for a while, and said, "The feed you owe me will be covered if I take the five males and sell them. You'll have your old sow and the other five little ones and will show a good profit. However, if I were you I wouldn't get too anxious to sell them right now. I'd get all five of them bred, and in a year or so you'll have many times the profits." My pig herd eventually grew to 120, and all of the lessons learned from this would take another book. But one good lesson was enough to start—don't be taken in by looks or degrees; it's results in business that count!

The yearly harvest of those famous Idaho potatoes offered a season of opportunity I capitalized on. In potato season, they let school out for two weeks so that the kids could pick up the potatoes unearthed by big digging machines. Once I'd done the work Dad gave me, I could pick spuds for the neighbors. In four years of picking, my partner and I seldom came in second to anyone. I picked with my sister Shirley—she was, and still is, a hard worker. When we reached the fields and I'd yell out, "We can outpick anyone!" My sister would tell me to shut my big mouth, and then we would work like demons to live up to my boast.

We left the wimps in the dust, but there were always some older kids and grownups who kept up with us, even a little ahead of us. At about three or four o'clock in the afternoon, which was often the hottest part of the day, they would buckle or need a break and we would surge ahead.

Picking 350 sacks (most others did around 200) at seven cents a sack meant at least $12.25 earned a day for each of us, and that was big money. An awesome 400-sack day was a staggering $14 each. At the end of spud season we often had more than a hundred dollars tucked away, which took care of Christmas, school expenses, a piece or two of athletic gear, and even a few ice cream sundaes. I loved picking spuds, loved competing.

We had a great reputation with all the farmers and always had plenty of job offers. Thanks to my dad, we were first in the field in the morning and last to leave at night. There was something about the combination of winning and earning that kept one from ever getting tired!

I learned two big principles of success here—that working long hours and working fast gave you more than normal returns.

The great fence test

Fencing, as noted earlier, was a real training in management. You built it right, and maintained and mended it right, or all the wrong things would happen. Here we had 400 acres of irrigated crops to fence, plus 3,000 acres of leased desert grazing land to ride. I could use a staple puller like Clint Eastwood could a .45.

We tore down miles of old fence and put up miles of new fence. I dug hundreds of deep postholes, up hill and down, often in soil full of gravel, rock, and tree roots, through frost (three feet deep, mind you), and rattlesnake dens.

You had to tamp a post right or it would jiggle. Many times my brother and I, after sweating away for hours, would have five or ten posts in a beautiful straight line and my dad, inspecting the job, would take a running leap and karate-kick the top of each post. If the post bent or moved even a little, out it came and we had to do it over. Finally, between the coaching of a grandfather born in 1888 and watching Dad, we learned how to put in a post so well you'd think it was set in concrete. I remember the day of victory. We had about a dozen posts of a corral in, and Dad did his usual sprint and leap. He kicked the top of one of the posts with all his weight and it was so taut it bounced him onto the ground on his back. He didn't say a word, just brushed himself off and walked away (though I saw a flicker of a smile as he turned toward the house).

No fair weather farmers

We played and worked in cold weather so much it was just part of life, but there were times we were cold to the bone. That was during fall or spring plowing or other tractor work. You couldn't put on enough clothes to keep you warm or keep your butt from freezing into the shape of the tractor seat. Every so often you'd have to dismount and do calisthenics to get blood to your toes, cheeks, and fingers. If you didn't sing as you rode along, your mouth would freeze into an unthawable grimace.

In the winter of 1951, it snowed forever. When they plowed the road it left 6- to 8-foot banks on the sides, and then the wind blew all that snow right back on the road. On Christmas Day another year, we were scheduled for dinner at Grandpa Ross'

OUR FAMILY IN 1950. FRONT: DEE (DEVON), MOM, DAD, RICK (RICHARD). BACK: SHIRLEY, ME, AND LARRY.

house, three miles down the drifted-shut road. It took our team of horses again to accomplish this—we all loaded ourselves onto a wagon with food, presents, and some hay for the team and off to Grandpa's house we did go! We missed one month of school that year and they dropped the mail by plane. The road took weeks to plow out with D-8 Cats. I remember the banks were so high after that we could only hear the school bus coming; we couldn't see it until it turned down our lane.

We learned on the farm that when it's time to work, temperature is irrelevant. Ten below zero only meant that you dressed warmer and started earlier.

One Saturday morning when it was 22 below zero. Dad jumped up enthusiastically after breakfast, rubbed his hands together, and said, "No sense sitting around the house. Let's go pick the manure down so the calves can reach the manger." As we worked to lower the built-up manure where the feeder calves usually stood in front of the manger, little chunks of flint-hard frozen manure flew in all directions. It was downright motivating to know that our hands and feet would freeze up if we stopped moving. It was a clear, bright day and it was refreshing and good to be doing something.

Our production level on the ranch wasn't determined by the weather, but what needed to be done. Days when it was so hot out on those desert fields you could hardly breathe, Dad, Mom, we kids, and even Granddad hit the chores the same as if it were 70 degrees. Sometimes the wind was strong all day, blowing bits of straw, manure, and sand into your face so hard that it stung—you just adjusted by squinting and kept going. One year we had a grasshopper plague, and we were haying in 100-degree weather. As you rode the tractor (no closed cabs in those days) through the field, thousands of hoppers would leap up and many would strike you in the face like miniature missiles—man, they hurt. We'd whine and Dad would say, "Well, you dummies, hold your hand in front of your face and get on with it."

I learned here that there are fair, cloudy, hot, rainy, and chilly as well as cold days, but the same things still need doing. Never worry about the weather, use it as an excuse, or tie your production to it. Just put on a thicker sweater or thinner t-shirt and do what you have to do. Real winners keep moving no matter what the weather.

One winter morning when I was 15 or 16, we loaded some stock into the truck to take to market, as we often did. Going to the stockyard with Dad was always a treat. But this time he tossed me the keys and said, "You take them to the sale—I'll be staying home," and walked away. My first solo trip!

The full weight of responsibility descended after I was alone with our "assets." The roads were full of black ice and every time the cattle shifted, the truck would slide around on the road and I would nearly lose control. I finally arrived and began the process of lining up, signing up, weighing, and bidding, and then picking up the money. I remember the mounting thrill as I got closer and closer to success, the relief when all was done, and the confidence that came with it. Likewise, when Dad jumped off a truck or tractor and said, "It's yours—get it done," fear was always soon converted to confidence. I left the farm believing that there was nothing I couldn't do and that you would never be without a job if you wanted to work.

Duty before dinner

A farmer's livestock is his lifeline, and when a birth occurs in the barnyard, everything is rescheduled around the care of the new arrival.

Meals are interrupted, fishing trips cancelled, dates delayed, bedtime ignored, all personal needs and problems put on hold until the animal is on its feet and feeling fine. Many wet, shivering new calves were carried into the house, dried and cleaned off by the stove, and then carefully placed back in the cozy barn on clean straw. Likewise, when you worked with a team of horses and noon or night came, you fed and watered them before you ate or drank anything yourself—that was the rule of the ranch, no exceptions.

I remember a moment in my young life when I'd scored the crucial points at a ballgame, and my parents and I were applauded by many a friend and neighbor. The next night ball practice ran late, and though I usually hitched a ride for part of the six miles home, that night I walked and ran it all so instead of arriving home at five-thirty, I came dragging in at seven o'clock. On the table Mom had left roast, mashed potatoes, fresh homemade bread, and raspberry jam. I was famished and it was too much to pass up, so I pulled up a chair to dig in. Suddenly Dad appeared at the door: "Have you fed your animals?" (Remember now, I'm a senior in high school, star athlete, his offspring, and on the brink of starvation.) "No, in a minute, Dad." "No real man eats before his cows," he said, yanking my chair from under me and gesturing with his foot toward my fanny as I darted toward the back door. That lesson has been one of the most valuable from Barnyard 101: Your customers and employees come first.

During my teen years I became aware of the complications and challenges of "making a living," watching and listening to Dad, uncles, and grandparents discuss and handle the crops and the cattle and then at harvest time account for their efforts. It was a thrill to see the last row threshed, the last bales of hay for the winter fit securely on top of the stack. Here, too, was the excitement of earning—seeing direct fruit of your labor in measurable amounts.

"Sneak feed" snafu

Dad often liked to pasture our pigs on some rolling grass hills on the Dietrich ranch; to feed them out there, we had to outsmart them. So I learned how to "sneak feed," or steal up to the trough and pour the food in quietly before being detected and engulfed in a mass of milling hogs. I was good at this, but there was one Black Friday that ended my hog-raising desires and nudged me in the direction of a safer occupation.

At this point, we had about seventy 180-pound pigs almost ready for market. They were in a big pasture with a "loafing shed" in the corner. The two large feed troughs were out in the pasture, about a hundred feet from the shed. We had 12 or 15 gallons of swill (sour milk) to feed them daily. This took absolutely perfect maneuvering. If you got to the trough and dumped the milk quickly, by the time the pigs heard or saw anything, you could be out of the way and the hogs would rumble past you to attack the milk. This particular hot August afternoon all 70 of the pigs were sleeping in the straw in the shed. There wasn't a sound or movement, except for an occasional weak snort or twitch and a fly or two droning around. It was an ideal setup—I was in a hurry and knew that if they saw me first, I'd never get them fed before my date that evening. I had my rubber irrigating boots on, so quiet was the word. The large slop pails held 6 or 7 gallons each, and I set them down carefully on the other side of the wooden gate, then eased over. I made one small error, however. When I set down the second bucket, I left the bail up, and just as I got over the fence, the bail fell over with a *clink*.

ME (WITH GUITAR) AND MY BROTHERS IN 1954.

Out of the whole mass of sleeping hogs, only one lone pig seemed to hear it. He reared up with a tuft of straw across his snoot and said, "Oink" (in pig talk, "soup's on!"). I knew I had only one choice now—beat the pigs to the trough. I grabbed those two big buckets and began the 30-yard dash to the feeding spot. But the instant that sentry pig gave the signal, the whole floor of the loafing shed raised up and rumbled toward me. Those pigs were so close together it was like one giant 30-by-60-foot pig heading my way.

I was about to dump the two big pails of milk into the trough when I was hit by a gigantic piggy wedge traveling at what seemed like 30 miles an hour. The pails and I were knocked into the air and fell on the backs of the milling hogs, and they went wild, leaping, squealing, and rooting for the food. When I finally found the ground, I began to flail the hogs with the empty buckets. This only aroused them more. When I was finally out of the pen and in a safe place, I knew I'd smell like a hog for my date. So I decided to make Black Friday complete and miss the date.

HIGH ON HIGH SCHOOL

In those days, what our small schools lacked in extensive programs and curricula, they more than made up for with the personal, one-on-one attention of teachers and coaches. We didn't need courses in Creative Problem Solving or Conflict Management—we had the experts, our parents, who taught us better than any professionally trained person ever could. For the basics of math, history, literature, economics, and social studies, we were well provided, even if there were only eight or ten in a class.

And we knew everyone, yes, every single person in the school and community.

I never had a dull moment in high school—could hardly wait for the day to start. It was a thrill to get the bad classes over with and to get to the good ones. I was part of everything and everything was part of me; all of the girls were beautiful, and all the guys were my friends.

When I went out as a sophomore for basketball after we moved to Dietrich, I didn't make varsity but was top in junior varsity. The first junior varsity game started at 6:30. Milking took longer that day and by the time I got to the gym, warmup was in progress and there was no uniform left for me. So I ran out onto the floor in ugly practice clothes. The coach gave me an old numbered jersey so I could be identified and the game started. In the first minute I scored seven points—the crowd

FRESHMAN

was on their feet, and the coach yanked me out and said, "We're saving you for varsity." Now that was some promotion—one minute in the minors and then on to the big league!

I'll never forget suiting up for the first game in that blue and white varsity uniform. I managed to stay in the varsity and as starting center had three years of fast-paced experience. I had days of losing games by ineptness and of scoring right before the final buzzer to win the game. Winning or losing became almost irrelevant—it was the game I loved.

With enough oily "Brilliantine" on it, my hair was a pretty handsome sight in those days, or so I thought. In fact, I was vain enough to want a wave in my cowlick. During my first practice as a varsity player, I missed a lay-up shot a midget should have been able to make. Convinced my front locks were blocking the shooting eye of their star center, two big coaches sprang out on the floor and carried me struggling into the training room. One held me while the other, with a blunt pair of bandage scissors, sheared off my fine mane right down to the scalp. I was so embarrassed I had Dad butch the whole thing after that.

Dropping that hair was like dropping a bad habit. I was free forever of tending, combing and re-combing, oiling, moussing, conditioning, and blow-drying. More than 50 years later now, I still go "semi-Marine." (It goes well now with my growing forehead, too!)

I played baseball three years in high school, as a catcher my first year, and a pitcher after that. I retained my hope and dream of becoming a big-leaguer someday.

On the very first day of my sophomore year, the big senior athletes were hitting fly balls on the football field to a scrambling mass of underlings trying to catch them, which I humbly joined with my mitt. Pretty soon, the batter smashed a towering hit that sailed over our heads. Instead of backing up fast, like the others trying to get it, I turned around, sprinted with my back to the ball, and made a spectacular over-the-shoulder catch. Then I turned and threw the ball from goal post to goal post, more than 300 feet, so they would know that I was serious about baseball. That brought instant acceptance and some first-day friends.

With the basketball on the court, I never felt like I had control, just played. On the mound pitching, I felt in total control of everyone on the field—I owned the hitters. I pitched a game once against an A league (big city) school, faced 15 batters and struck out all 15.

In my senior year, my fastball was never better, and I went to a New York Yankees baseball scout day, and was picked to pitch a short preliminary game in the *el grande* professional baseball park in front of many fans (there to see the big game later).

I thought I was hot stuff, but was smart enough to know the difference between athletes. Some are naturally gifted, and some methodical, determined workers. I was the latter—I had a small frame and small hands, and weighed only 145 to 150 pounds in high school. But what I lacked in size and dexterity, I had to make up for with determination. Much wisdom I used later in the corporate world I learned here, including the fact that talent, gifts, and natural ability are useless without hard work and the right attitude.

> WALKING THE FIVE MILES HOME AFTER BALL PRACTICE WAS THE MOST GLORIOUS TIME OF MY LIFE. AS I LOPED ALONG, I COULD DREAM AND PLAN AND OUTLINE LIFE, WORK, AND ROMANCE, AND WHEN SOMEONE STOPPED TO OFFER ME A RIDE, IT ONLY INTERRUPTED MY MUSINGS.

The peanut principle

"Making the team" in high school was a great accomplishment—often the first time you were really singled out. You got your name in the paper and all the girls cheered for you. Ethics learned on the farm and from my family made me take all the training rules seriously. While some would cut corners when the coach wasn't looking, I paid full attention to the law of the lap, and all the other rules—be in bed by ten o'clock every weekday, midnight on Saturday, no pop, candy, smoking, or drinking. The coach added one more rule in a training talk—between-meal snacks would cut your wind, so they were out.

I lived those rules without one single violation for all three years of my high school athletics, and missed some dances and the like because of them. Girls were secondary to training rules (you can imagine what a convincing coach we must have had). One day, while I was on my way from one class to another, some kid in the hall had a sack of peanuts. It had been four hours since lunch, and you know how good salted peanuts taste. He handed me a single peanut, which I popped into my mouth and savored immensely. As I swung around the corner, I ran right into the coach, and as I said a quick, "I'm sorry," for bumping him, he grabbed me by the arm and said, "Is that peanut breath?" I was devastated—my perfect record broken and the coach disappointed. "Can't believe you'd do that, Aslett. To work that peanut breath off, that will be seventy extra laps around the gym tonight."

I'm sure that peanut had little effect on conditioning, but the principle of "obedience to the rules" that it stood for made a big impression on me. The degree of disobedience to something isn't the issue; it's the violation of self-discipline and our expectations of ourselves.

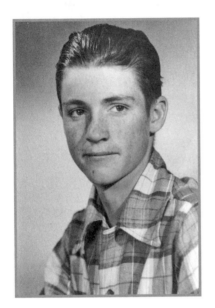

SOPHOMORE

My basketball coach was standing near me in practice one afternoon. I was shooting hot and said as I poised for a 30-footer, "Milkshake says I make it." He bet, and I missed. I hate to lose so I egged, "Double or nothing, coach?" He bet again and I missed again. "You owe me two, Aslett," he said and walked away.

I'd forgotten my gambling debt a week later. Returning from a road game, we stopped in the railroad town of Shoshone, Idaho, to eat at a café that had the best hamburgers in the world and milkshakes so thick in those tall metal mixing cups that they wouldn't even pour. I was famished and had exactly enough money for a hamburger and a shake. I was drooling by the time the waitress set them down in front of me. Before I could touch them, two long, hairy arms reached around me and snatched them both. "You owe me these, right?" "Right." As I sat there starving, the meaning of *owe* really came home to me. I hated that loss, a debt from a flippant bet.

A week later Dad and I attended a tournament in Jerome's new gym. Some pretty serious sports enthusiasts were in the audience. After the game one of my buddies informed me that one of his dad's friends had won $3,000 betting on the game. That was astonishing, and I hurried over to my father. "Dad, Dad, someone won $3,000 on this game!" He turned and said, "That means someone lost $3,000, doesn't it?" That hit me like a heavy barn door. It took us two years of raising herds of cattle in 100-degree fields and 30 below zero feedlots and working hard to feed and care for them, to make $3,000. The thought of losing all that for a bet was sickening—so awful and stupid that I lost all interest in gambling on anything forever.

I had my share of praise and recognition on the ball field and courts, but soon discovered that what you write gets more than a few immediate cheers and onetime sports-page attention. Through grade school and high school whenever I wrote a clever little piece or poem in a Valentine or yearbook, it would delight many. So as a writer on our school paper, I would do little slapstick poems and pieces, then watch fellow students devour them—laugh and take them home to share with others. My humor hopefully made up for the overly creative spelling and made-up words. I also assumed the role of columnist in the school paper, dealing out more than my share of immature judgments and opinions. The power of the pen was not lost on me, even in those early days.

The combination of always volunteering first and always being willing opened up a lot of leadership opportunities for me. In my senior year of high school I was elected student body president, which qualified me to be chosen to represent our high school at Boys' State—which was a week in our capital city of Boise getting to observe real legislators in action and then operating a mock government ourselves. For a small-town farm boy this was awesome—a week away from home and my first train ride. I was fascinated by the surroundings and the dynamic political instruction I received here; it cemented my loyalty to the American system. It also gave me some administrative responsibility and experience in representing others.

> TEEN YEARS WERE FULL OF EXUBERANCE AND PROMISE. EVERYTHING WAS AHEAD OF YOU AND THERE WERE FEW LIMITATIONS. IDEALISM WAS ALLOWED, AS LONG AS YOU DID YOUR CHORES!

Love and basketball

Valentine's Day vibrations started in grade school, as you anguished over the destination of that one card that had the word *love* in it, but as a teen, romance was real. The meaning of love came into focus now as we discovered that there was more (a lot, lot more) to it, that your whole pattern of behavior could be altered by a little unknown called infatuation.

Crushes were well named. When my third-grade teacher got married, I was crushed for weeks. I had plans for her and me when I grew up! In high school often the ones you liked didn't know you existed, and when they did you found yourself speech-less during the first handhold. One movie with your sweetheart lasted a month or two and was replayed in your mind over and over.

When we moved to Jerome, I was out of a little country school into a big town and a massive high school with 500 students. Here I saw my first live cheer-leaders at the first football game—those sweaters and so much bare leg! I was smitten with all three of them. Then we moved to the Dietrich ranch and I was in a small high school again. As a budding athlete, I took sports more seriously than girls, and as noted earlier, took the train-ing rules as seriously as a vow of celibacy. That gives you a hint of my nightlife at that point.

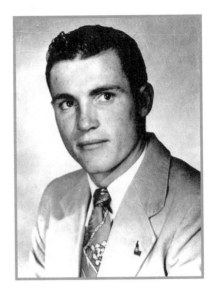

JUNIOR

In a small school, when prom time comes, everyone goes to the dance. I refused, and stood firm, ignoring the hints from my upper classmate's sister that Frieda and several other girls didn't have dates. When pressure from a mother and my best friend were added, I folded and joined the promenade line like everyone else. After the prom, we took the girls home and parked the car in front of Frieda's house, and my friend in the front and his girl began to kiss passionately. Was I em-barrassed—not only had I never kissed a girl, I didn't know how or have the nerve to try. Then my date said, "Beautiful moon tonight, isn't it?" I quickly replied, "Yes, light enough to play basketball!" Of course, that remark was the laugh of the school the next day.

I dated in high school, but never seriously. I liked girls and got along with them well, but they were second to sports, school, and the fun of farm life.

In my junior year Gayle Meservey, who sat across the table from me in study hall, gave me some eye contact and a shy little smile. I mooned around her for a month or two and then finally asked her to the prom later that spring. I had Dad's car (one of those sleek '51 Chevys), and she wore a strapless formal, a corsage, some terrific per-fume—the works. I stopped in front of her house when I took her home and kissed her goodnight, my first! I remembered how soft her lips were all summer, because that was the last date for three months. We had huge hayfields to tend and irrigation schedules to follow, and we worked and worked. I was in love all three months, dreaming of her day and night and looking forward to "next time."

There wasn't any next time, because when I finally came in off the range and went to a dance in late summer, Gayle was engaged to my friend Frank, the catcher on our ball team. This ended that romance, but not my lifetime friendship with both of them. I still visit them often and rib him about stealing my girl—she was a jewel and still is.

No relation to Fred Astaire!

Dancing was a legal and accepted way to get to hug a girl, but even that wasn't worth the agony of having to dance. I had about as much rhythm as a pig. I was a fairly quick-footed athlete, but on the dance floor, I could have been the evening humor act during intermission. My creativity was born here, making excuses to not go to dances. Sick grandmothers and knee injuries were nothing to the reasons I could conjure up to miss a dance. I couldn't even do-si-do in rhythm. So who do I end up dating? Emma Meservey, Gayle's sister—a real live wire, and the most dance-crazy woman ever born. She'd drag me to dances and I'd look anxiously around for someone to cut in (maybe that's why so many of the guys in the school liked me). Leaving high school was a great relief because dances were left behind, along with parental expectations that Don should ask all the need-a-date girls.

Forget the crowd

Most of us have had, at some critical point in our lives, someone who reaches out with a kind hand or insightful word to give us a boost. Even a small nod or note can sometimes have a lifelong impact.

I remember sitting on the training table in the coaches' room (which always smelled like Bengay). It was a big end-of-season game, and the coach, Bob Jones, who was one of those rare combinations of good coach and great man, was taping my ankle. It was spring of my senior year, only a couple of months until I would be out on my own. As Coach Jones snugged that three-inch-wide tape around my swollen ankle, he asked, "Well, Don, what are you going to do after school?" I began to answer in a very general kind of way, "Well, go to college, get a job, maybe get married...." He stopped taping, interrupted my list of mights and maybes, looked me in the eye, and said, "Aslett, you aren't like those other guys, remember that." That's all he said, and all I needed to be channeled into believing my future would not be one of following the crowd.

No glory in glitz

I was definitely not a conformist, never worried about peer pressure on haircuts, clothes, or cars, had a real pragmatic approach. Unless the thing in question was something I really wanted, I just wasn't going to do or own it.

It helped that neither of my parents were fooled by the "pizzazz" of the world. When I was young and impressionable, the colorful, loud, flashy things of fairs, showrooms, and movies sometimes took my breath away. Some of my uncles and others seemed to be having so much fun buying big playthings like the sharpest new cars, and the first and newest of all the trinkets. Neither of my parents ever gloried in glitz, and they always avoided the debts and bad deals that other relatives and neighbors ended up complaining about later. They would let me ooh and aah over the many prizes in life that seemed worthwhile, but always carefully point out the consequences of going after "unworthy" time- and money-consumers. They always bought quality things and took care of them. Waste just didn't happen at our home—waste of time, money, food, animals, land, words, or anything. We were always encouraged to do what counted, not what everyone else did, and to remember that because something was offered, didn't mean we were obligated to take it.

Dad and Mom let us decide how to spend our money, but always suggested alternatives, and reminded us that ordering something was a lot easier than paying for it.

I remember well when the sporting goods salesmen came by with the leather-sleeved letterman jackets, in our school colors. Gadfrey, they were beautiful to see, smell, feel, and picture my new athletic letter *D* (for the Dietrich Devils) sewn on there. They were $30—lots of money in the early fifties. Dad said, "You can probably get that same jacket from Roper's" (a small town clothing store near our hometown). I was crushed to not get the jacket like the others, but I did trust my dad. On our next trip to Roper's, they not only had them, but these were the deluxe model where the leather didn't stop at the shoulder but went clear to the neck in a raglan style—beautiful, and they were $12.95.

Many times, back on the ranch when we were working in the barnyard (spring and fall seemed to be the most susceptible seasons) a neighbor would drive in with a new truck. The doors slammed good and tight, there was no manure dripping out the back or post dents in the bed. The windows had no cracks, the upholstery was unblemished, and there wasn't speck of rust, just shining metal everywhere.

We kids would run up to the spanking new black-tired truck and pet it and walk all around it. Dad never caved in, though I was given to jealousy, and my brother even brought it up. "Why can't we have new?" Dad's answer was that unnecessary debt is real dumb, and that our stuff (every single piece of which was bought used, usually from a "new paint fever" farmer selling out) worked fine. Good equipment and tools can last and function well for decades. The old tractor may be ugly and have a few nicks and weld knots on its skin, but it runs just as well and plows as deep as the new one, which is generally about the same as the old only with new paint and a pretty emblem.

New paint fever—wanting and getting what you don't need and can't afford—has not only put many businesses under, but broken marriages and caused depression and even suicides. Learning to live well with what you have is one of the great, great disciplines of life and business. (It helps to remember that there'll be dents, scrapes, and manure running out the tailgate before long on anything new.)

SENIOR

I had saved around $900 from my FFA and spud-picking projects, and that was a lot of money in the early '50s. Dad suggested that I buy three or four heifers (young cows) with the money. I had all that money safe in the bank and was reluctant to put it in live "stock." "But what if they die?" I asked my father. "What if they don't?" he asked me back.

So I did, and they didn't—I bought, and they thrived. I soon had much more banked and learned risks have rewards—perhaps the greatest lesson of my entrepreneurial career.

Now I went to the next step on the livestock ladder and invested $500 in a bull. Dad said he was going to get some registered Hereford bulls and wondered if I wanted to invest with him. "Two years down the road, a good mature bull can be worth $1,800 to $150,000," he said. "Do you want to invest in one?" Being bullish, even then, I said I did. And so when a herd of registered, "Larry Domino/Republic" baby bull calves was unloaded, Dad said, "Go pick one you want." I sat on the corral a long time to look them over. One cute little curly-faced one finally caught my eye. (My after-the-fact advice now is never pick a bull that looks like Richard Simmons.) Two years later, when the other bulls were making hay with the heifers, mine was in the corral eating hay. He brought $400 as hamburger. Good thing I had some other ventures going.

When I was a junior in high school, Dad had turned 80 acres of the rented Miller place over to my brother and me, and I went into the hay, wheat, and bean business. My brothers and I traded labor and hay for use of our dad's farm equipment. After two summers' harvest, I had my college money in a checking account.

Chapter 4

OFF TO ISU: DAD'S DREAM

*College was the next installment
of a good education...*

IN MY EARLY COLLEGE DAYS.

Growing up, I thought of ivy as just another weed, and the only reason the word *Harvard* was in my vocabulary was that it was the name of a neighbor's dog. Living as I did among entrepreneurs of all kinds (Dad and his eleven brothers were all self-employed, as were my grandfolks), I didn't see getting a degree as essential to making your way in the world. And I'd never met any college-educated people who showed half the smarts of my mother and father, who never went to college.

Nevertheless, I planned to go to college, and for only one reason. My father was a happy, good-natured man who seldom asked for things for himself. But several times I heard him say, "I would love to see one of my kids go to college." I went to college solely because of my love and respect for him, and desire to do something significant for him.

Ivy League... look out!

What a great moment of freedom and assertiveness it was as my friends Marvin Pitman, Walt Jensen, and I shot across southern Idaho's only highway in Walt's shiny 1950 Hudson. We were college bound, and the world was ours.

Money was earned and saved, entrance exams passed, and all the girls back home would surely wait forever for our return. Indeed, life had really begun. Pocatello, Idaho, population 35,000, was an enormous place compared to our hometown of 160. Idaho State was a nice college with an enrollment of 3,000 students that fall of 1953.

At first, it seemed a little more like a sideshow than a learning show. "Hicks" like myself were thrown in with some young people who seemed to have façade and facts mixed up—the pretensions of the fraternity and sorority set and all those trying hard to be intellectual or ivy league was comical, even to us dumb farmers. Back home, we were mature at 16, so frolicking around or worrying about what you wore or silly freshman initiation rites were of little interest to me.

Near the end of my senior year in high school, those of us who had made it clear we were college bound had to declare a major. I hadn't a clue what I wanted to do after college—engineering was one of the more recognizable fields on the career list in the brochure we were given. But the courses required to register for that major, such as calculus and chemistry, were of no interest to me, as my interests beyond agriculture, as far as I was aware of any, were to play pro baseball or be a writer. One major, called graphic arts, caught my eye. The classwork included things like putting out the college newspaper, writing, photography, and printing. So I enrolled as a graphic arts major for my first year of college.

All went well for a while in my new university existence until I began to realize that the many free privileges I enjoyed at home like plenty of food, a car, room, and washing and ironing services, did not exist at school. It was cash on the line. I never imagined how fast my wheat money would scatter in the wind of expenses. I could see that it wouldn't be long until my hog, bull, and hay savings would be gone, too. I didn't expect anyone to pay my way, so for the first time in my life (and the last, by the way), I went looking for a job.

Previously my brothers and I had people ask us to work for them. Here, no one knew me and I was just another college boy looking for a part-time job. I concentrated on the commercial and industrial section of town, and Pitman and I finally landed a job at a soda pop-bottling factory, starting wage seventy-five cents an hour.

The machinery was old and it constantly broke bottles, the mixer leaked oil into the syrup, and the calibration for dispensing the syrup was always out of adjustment, which resulted in inconsistent batches. Kicking the machinery was part of policy and procedure to keep it running. Within a week, we could run the entire operation (washing the bottles, filling and capping them, and loading them on a truck). Good thing, too, because the owner would turn the place over to us and disappear goose hunting for days. Every day was an adventure here, and I was cured of ever being a pop drinker after finding dead mice, bugs, twigs, and other things in the pop under the inspection light.

Payday came at the end of the month, and my 90 hours at seventy-five cents an hour should equal $67.50. The owner handed me a check for a little over forty dollars. Sure I had been cheated, I threw it down on his beverage-stained old wood desk and said, "What are these FICA, Federal, State, and Local 64 deductions? I want my money!" "Those are things we have to take out," he said. "Not out of my check, you don't!" I gave him back the keys to the door, grabbed my sadly reduced check, and walked out the door, determined to eventually work for myself.

It all begins! I began doing what I do now!

This time I went to the college career office and talked to the director of the department, who after listening to the story of my poor pop-bottling payoff said, "Well then, you need to start your own business. People call all the time for help on yards and cleaning." I instantly recognized the opportunity and envisioned the market. When I came home that night I sat down with my roommate Marvin and proposed that we go into business together. We agreed to do it and included another roommate, Johnny Palleria, calling ourselves "The

Announcing Services of
COLLEGE
cleanup and repair
TEAM

We will do odd jobs and household repair such as:

Painting
Grass Cutting
Garden Work
Cleaning Yards
Building Fences
Carpentry Work
Washing Windows
And What Have You?

REFERENCES

Available weekdays 3:15 p.m. on and all day Saturdays. Will work at night if desired. For information and appointments call 1868-R or see us at 553 South 8th Avenue.

John Palleria   **Marvin Pitman**   **Don Aslett**

MY FIRST OFFICIAL PIECE OF BUSINESS LITERATURE.

College Cleanup and Repair Team." This was a bold move for three young bachelors—up to that point, I had never even made a bed. I headed for the graphic arts department, where I designed and printed up our first brochure (page 68), then dropped several hundred off on doorsteps in the neighborhood.

The work turned out to be more fun and educational than school.

Mrs. Milt Smith, our landlady, agreed for a percentage of the profits to take any calls, and we were in business. We passed our cards out all over town and went home to discuss what we were going to do with all of our money. I trembled all day in school anticipating the beginning of our very own operation and rushed home after my last lab. I'd envisioned a page full of calls from people begging us to rescue them from all sorts of dirty situations, but there was only one …"to clean around a furnace." Disappointed, I put on my new coveralls and scampered up the street to do the job.

When I arrived at the address, my vision of greatness was restored. The house was a mansion, one of the finest in town. An attractive woman answered the door and then led me downstairs to the furnace room. She pointed to a narrow space between the coal bin and the furnace hopper. "The coal has fallen in that crack for years and is a fire hazard. Can you get it out of such a tight spot?" I assured her it would be no problem. "How much do you charge?" she asked. It took all of my nerve to blurt out the staggering fee of $1.25 an hour we had decided on. She eyed me over suspiciously and finally said, "Well… okay."

After she left, I tore into the job, quickly devising a way to get the accumulated coal out of its unwelcome resting place. I then dusted and cleaned the whole area in record time and called for her to come down and inspect my job. "Oh my," she said, "that's beautiful work!" Glancing at her watch, she then said, "Let's see, you've been here for 56 minutes… at $1.25 an hour." She pulled out a pad and did logarithms and long division for a few minutes and then said, "That comes to exactly $1.18." She counted it out to the penny with a smile. "You're a good worker and I'll call you again."

I'd expected a little more than the hourly rate for doing that three-hour job in less than an hour. As I turned in the takings of our first day in business and recounted the story, we concluded that business was tougher than we had imagined.

Others in the city began to call; however, by now I had learned a few marketing maneuvers. I took one of our cards over to the college switchboard and told the young woman there to give this number to anyone calling for cleaning or yard work. She did, and the work really began to roll in. One spring month my net income while going to school was an unbelievable $250. In those days, many people working full time weren't making that much. Even though I had some idea of the possibilities in the guidance counselor's office that day, now I could really see the potential. It was hard work and not very glamorous, but you met a lot of interesting people and learned a lot. In fact, it was hard to beat!

We did the work in the morning before school, during the noon hour, after school, and on Saturdays. As jobs picked up we began hiring other college students, and buying a few more tools and ladders as we needed them for jobs.

Out of the more than 75 different teachers I had in high school and college, six were masters, twelve were okay, and the rest were chloroform on the hoof. One of those six masters was Clark Carlile, a speech teacher and author of a well-known speech textbook. He quickly moved me out of freshman (beginner's) speech class into advanced logic and debate classes, and encouraged me to enter the annual speech contests at college. He kept in touch with me and my business after I graduated, and called me up ten or twelve years after I left ISU to encourage me to write a book about my life. I had a real story to tell, he said. How key in my life were people like Clark, who kept his classroom going all throughout his students' lives. In 2007 I shared his ninety-fifth birthday, and he was still offering to proof and contribute to this book!

Finding purpose in life

Going into my own business was practically inborn in me from the independence of a rural upbringing. Another inborn trait that came to the fore at this time was my spiritual side.

I seem to have always had a "Creator consciousness." I don't remember being taught this, it was just there—a clear and strong belief in the existence of a creator, a purpose for life, and a destiny for myself. I knew nothing then of our family legacy of sacrifice and suffering as my pioneer ancestors migrated to this country and crossed the plains for religious freedom.

Although our family did have some Mormon heritage, and I was baptized at the age of eight, I was not exactly steeped in religion in my childhood years. We visited a few churches during Scout week ("a Scout is reverent"), and a traveling preacher came by the school once and insisted that we would all perish unless we were "saved." Mother finally settled on the fact that we needed church, and Dad gave us the choice of going to church or staying home and working in the fields. So we attended a Presbyterian Congregational church in Jerome, Idaho, and a similar little community church later in Dietrich.

I had a good, clean upbringing, but I wasn't necessarily a committed churchgoer. One of my best friends and now roommate Marvin Pitman was an active member of the Church of Jesus Christ of Latter-day Saints (a Mormon). He invited me to go to church with him one Sunday, but I'd heard so many rumors about the Mormons that I wasn't inclined to accept; however, two things finally made me do it.

The first was curiosity. It was clear from my first week in college that the most outstanding students on campus seemed to be Mormon. They were cheerful, clean-cut, and clean spoken, and always seemed to have a sense of purpose. The men were leaders and the girls had a distinguishing glow and high standards.

Second, when I went to the college cafeteria for breakfast on Sunday morning, there were only 70 or so young men there, all in suits and ties. So where were the rest of the students and why were all of these guys dressed like this? Pitman informed me that the rest of the kids were probably still sleeping after a big Saturday night, and these fellows were all going to church early, and then to a priesthood meeting. I liked the dedication and example I saw here so I decided to go with Pitman and check it out.

I soon discovered that these were serious and well-organized church members who loved and used the Scriptures (which I had always read on my own at night in the ranch bunkhouse). I had seen religion talked about, but for the first time now I saw it lived—what the Savior taught in action. I launched into a careful study of the doctrine of the Latter-day Saints and it all fit perfectly with what I had read in the Bible and felt in prayer. It fit too, with the ethics of honest work, good purpose, kindness, thrift, and charity I had learned at home. By the end of the year, I had become an intense and practicing member of the Church.

You're in the Army now!

While I was a freshman, I heard that joining the National Guard was a good way to make some extra cash and maybe have a little immunity from being yanked out of school to go to Korea. So I joined the Army Reserves and loved it! I'm not the kind of person who wants someone else to tell me when to change my underwear, but the order and discipline, the adventure and classes were wonderful. Marching and rifle team precision, driving a big tank, and shooting a 4-foot 75mm cannon were sure fun for a farm boy. I think the officers were a little shocked at my attitude of volunteering for everything—for demonstrations, guard duty in the motor pool, and yes, even doing the dishes in the mess hall, a massive cleaning experience in the camp barracks building.

On my first day in the kitchen, where greasy dishes were sliding in from all sides, we had some Army (probably 1880) issue kitchen soap that just groomed the grease a little. No matter how much of it we used, or how long we soaked or scrubbed, it scarcely affected the slimy dishes and silverware or the stainless steel trays. It took six of us hours to get the dishes done. I took that for two meals, breakfast and dinner. Then I walked down to the PX store, where you could buy normal dish detergent, and bought a jug of it. One squirt of this would put grease on the run. When those greasy cups and plates and trays came pouring in after supper, they hit that hot detergent solution and in a few seconds came out totally clean. We had all the dishes done in 45 minutes, and not just done but spotless, sparkling.

Word of Aslett's kitchen platoon leaked out via a brag by the supervisor of the mess hall, and soon the colonel came in to investigate and congratulate. He looked at the dishes and the clock and he was amazed. How had we managed to outflank the forks and all? I proudly snatched up the bottle of detergent, showed it to him, and said, "Here, Sir, we changed soap—that Army stuff is crap." Calling Army stuff crap (even if it is) is not a good approach to a "go by the rules" colonel. Appalled, he snatched the bottle from me and commanded us to use Army standard issue. So we were reduced back to bathing the dishes in that worthless stuff and watching the grease float on top of the water instead of dissolve.

EVEN MY MILITARY TRAINING SEEMED TO INTERPRET HIDDEN TALENT AND SKILL. WHEN ORDERS WERE CUT ON BIVOUACS OR BARRACKS, I RECEIVED KP AND LATRINE CLEANING ASSIGNMENTS CONTINUALLY. ALTHOUGH I NEVER BECAME A DECORATED HERO ON THE BATTLEFIELD, I WAS THE UNDISPUTED COLONEL OF THE URINAL.

Freshman love

I met a terrific girl my freshman year at ISU, Marilyn Clayton. She was a senior and about the most popular girl and best student in school (the valedictorian that year). She worked in the cafeteria and all the men flirted with her—the jocks, the cool frat cats, and the big California studs. I played humble farm boy and finally my two business partners and I asked her to go with us to a ballgame—a "triple date," you might say. On the way home, when the old Studebaker we paid $25 for quit, my roommates, who had gotten to sit right next to her at the game, drew the duty of getting the car towed or pushed, and I got to walk Marilyn home. We fell in love, and she was something else! She was smart and pretty, and so clean and pure and capable that she could do just about anything.

I had no car, so for dates we walked the cemetery at night and studied together at college. Frisking around like a young colt with a woman a little out of my league (and three years older than me), I did all I could to impress her. I made a big point of being "an outdoor man," which she had said she loved. The last week of college, Dad let me take the car to school to haul things home for the summer, and so I had a week to sweep this woman off her feet. We decided to go on a picnic one afternoon after classes. I packed a lunch and the pistol I'd carried hunting on the ranch and was pretty proficient with. I planned to give her the old "how to shoot a gun" routine after lunch (and reach around and embrace her in the process). I set up some cans a respectable distance away, took my official pistol stance (a week ago I had just qualified as an "expert" marksman in the National Guard), and proceeded to hit the cans a couple of times. "Now you try it, Marilyn, and be careful." I gave her a little coaching and pep talk not to be disappointed if she couldn't hit anything, because handguns weren't easy to aim.

She got in position and ripped off shots so fast I couldn't even count them, and not only hit a can every time, but hit them again while they were rolling. I was stunned. She handed me the gun back with a smile on her face. "Aw, I should have told you, Don. I was the only girl in my family and my dad was a real outdoorsman. All my life he taught me how to hunt and fish and use guns." End of that maneuver!

I liked Marilyn a lot but our days together were numbered. I would soon be going back to a busy farm schedule and to Guard camp, and she had a teaching job in some faraway place. We had only a few classes in these last five days of school and had a car. She usually had to be back in her dorm early, but as we were strolling across campus one afternoon arm in arm, she said she had an all-night pass. We could go to dinner and stay all night at the movies, or better yet go up in the hills and camp out.

This was the '50s, not the '90s. Girlfriends and boyfriends, at least the ones I knew, would park and smooch, kiss and hug, but that was it. Sex was out of the question, but walking together in the pine trees was a little sneaky, yet still in line, so we gathered up some picnic supplies and a couple of blankets and drove up Scout Mountain a few miles south of Pocatello. We walked the mountains and creeks, talked about life, marriage, family, and the future—it was wonderful. We built a fire and sat up all night talking, and when it turned daylight, we loaded up the car and drove back to school.

As luck would have it, on the way out of the hills, blankets piled in the back seat, our hair mussed up, and me unshaven, who would be standing by the side of the road at the Mink Creek stop sign but my Uncle Eddie (Dad's sister's husband, who lived nearby). There was only one Don Aslett and one two-toned Chevy with a 4/L license plate. I spent the rest of the summer worrying if he ever told my parents. It brought to mind at least a million times the old sermon "to avoid the very appearance of evil."

That was the last time I saw Marilyn. She wrote, suggesting marriage. But she was 23, I was 19, and I just wasn't ready, and she was smart enough to understand that. But I never lost the memory of what a quality person she was.

After my first year of college, I went to National Guard summer camp and helped Dad out on the farm, still caught up in my dream of playing professional baseball. By that fall, school seemed secondary to other ambitions. I was packing to go to a New York Yankee baseball training camp in Florida, when my mother came to the bunkhouse and pleaded with me to go to Sun Valley or somewhere and work through the winter and then decide about baseball next spring. I honored her wisdom and wishes and drove up to the famous Sun Valley resort.

A mailman in Shangri-la

Sun Valley was one of the biggest recreation hotspots in the U.S.—a real Shangri-la, and it was only 50 miles from our ranch. I arrived on the right day because the personnel manager needed a replacement for the "deadhead" job, which was carrying inter-company and U.S. mail for the resort.

I was trained for a day and then turned loose. I loved it! I would pick up the mail at the post office in the morning and deliver it throughout

the entire complex, picking up and distributing inter-company correspondence on the way. It was eight solid hours of walking, easy and fun,
so I doubled the frequency of deliveries, which delighted the management. It was more educational than the previous year of college, as I
learned about all the departments of the operation (purchasing, accounting, publicity, hotels, retail sales, food and beverages, etc.).

Everything at Sun Valley had an Alpine theme, and the waitresses at
the Inn in those little Swiss outfits could break any man's heart. I knew
them all and enjoyed flirting with them as I traveled through with my
mail bag.

All the things my parents and grandparents had taught me about
"the work ethic"—going the extra mile, keeping a positive attitude,
finding more to do instead of less—really won over the management. I
got a raise! Wages were very low at the resort; however, room and board
were included. I think I was the only nonmanagement employee who
didn't cash my check on payday, just sent it to the bank. After all, there
wasn't much to spend it on if you weren't a playboy. One of my delivery
stations was the Opera House (Sun Valley movie theater) and since I
had evenings clear, the manager offered me an evening usher job. I had
two jobs now and loved this one, too. Between these jobs, I met many
stars and celebrities (including Gary Cooper, Ann Southern, and the
Shah of Iran), and organized a Sun Valley "outlaw" basketball team.

This was a busy but super good time of my life. I also began to figure
out that wages and pay by the hour offered security and less risk, but
didn't reward ingenuity and hustle much. This further attracted me to
the entrepreneurial path of life.

A life-changing decision

I was so enthused by the change in my life's spiritual footing and
had been so impressed by how outstanding all of the returned missionaries at school seemed to be, I decided to inquire about going on a
church mission myself. This meant serving for two years while supporting yourself. No one had asked me to go, and my parents of course discouraged it because it meant leaving school for a while and they longed
to see me graduate from college. By then, I was what is called in the
church an Elder, 20 years old and afraid of nothing. I still had enough
money left in the bank to pay my way. I was interviewed, and weeks
later received a letter signed personally by the president of the Church.
"You have been found worthy to serve a Mission for the Church of Jesus
Christ of Latter-day Saints and are hereby called to serve in the Hawaiian mission." I would leave in three months.

Date with destiny

About now my lack of a full commitment to any of the charming young women I dated in my teen years finally ended. To help with a community fundraiser, I'd put together a little western band featuring my enthusiastic if inexpert guitar playing and Pitman's accordion, and we played at a few churches and county fairs. We were performing one day in the little town of Richfield, Idaho. Right before us on the program was a reading of the poem "Bobby Shaftoe" by Barbara Morris of Shoshone, Idaho. A shy girl with a heavenly face walked out on the stage and began reading about a roaming sailor. She had a kind, expressive face, beautiful eyes, and her countenance literally glowed. She soon had the audience (including me) under a spell. I'd heard scores of "that's the girl I'm going to marry" stories, and did indeed suddenly have that feeling about her. It was an impression that never left me. I'd met blondes and redheads that could shift my gears, but none that touched my spirit like this.

LOVE AT FIRST SIGHT:
YOUNG BARBARA MORRIS
OF SHOSHONE, IDAHO.

Two weeks later, I heard there was going to be an old-fashioned box lunch auction at a church in Shoshone, where that fascinating, big-eyed girl lived. I went armed with plenty of money and bribed a couple of the local kids to tell me which box was hers. I bid high but somehow bought the wrong box, so I ate with some flattered little 14-year-old while some other guy was sharing Barbara's roast chicken. As I watched them eat she shot back a "come and get me" glance.

Once the meal was over, the field was clear, so we sat and visited a while. She was warm and intelligent, someone you know you'll never tire of. Three days later, I called her and we went to a movie. The show was out at nine o'clock and it wasn't even dark yet, but she was so classy I just drove her home like a gentleman. We pulled up in front of her house and before I turned off the car she said, "Well, I better go in." She gave me a quick hug, and I walked her to the door and shook her hand goodnight. It felt so right—no way was I going to lose this lady.

When I drove into our yard at nine-thirty, Mother came running out. "What happened? Didn't you go on a date?" "Yes, Mother, and I've taken her home," I replied. Barbara's mother was probably equally shocked that Don Aslett could be so disciplined.

Of all the women and girls I ever met (including my first love, Miss Wheeler), I felt best about Barbara. She was pure quality—gentle, affectionate, and always comfortable to be around. I decided to wait until at least the third date before even hinting at a kiss. There was a double feature at the drive-in in Jerome, 20 miles away, so I invited Barbara and picked her up at seven-thirty. I had found a book of baby pictures with clever captions and we had a blast reading and laughing until it got dark and the movie started. The last show ended at 2 A.M., and by the time we got home an hour later, it was a real contrast to our last date. Another quick hug and I just made it home myself in time to do the sunup chores.

I didn't explain this one, either, but I did get a call from Barbara later telling me her mother had invited me to supper, where I got the inevitable question, "Gee, what time did you two get in last night?" I quickly explained how late the last show got out, "and boy, are you a great cook!" We soon became good friends.

After we'd known each other about three months, I had no doubt that Barbara would be the perfect person to spend my life with. We both agreed that if we felt the same when I returned from my mission, marriage was a strong possibility. I left for Hawaii now, and for those two years all women were off the agenda for me. Meanwhile back home Barbara attended college and dated others and wrote to me.

BARBARA GROWING UP.

FROM THE AGE OF 20 TO 22,
I LEFT FOR TWO YEARS,
ENTIRELY ON MY OWN DECISION
AND FUNDS, AND SERVED
A CHURCH MISSION IN HAWAII.

Aloha, Don!

We missionaries had no pick or choice of where we would go, and Hawaii had been a surprise. I had no idea where Honolulu was—I thought it was in China! I bought two suits, twelve white shirts, and a hat and was soon aboard the *SS Lurline,* a luxury ocean liner. In five days, I had moved from the high, dry plains of southern Idaho at 5,000 feet in elevation, to the sea level, humid tropical jungle. Culturally and environmentally, I was in a totally different world, too, from desert to the jungle and ocean, from western U.S. farmers and pioneers to people of all kinds from all over the world.

For two years, from early morning until late in the evening, I taught the people of the islands the Christian message. Missionaries didn't use cars on the islands then, and we (myself and a fellow missionary) walked everywhere in suit, tie, and hat. I got up every morning at five

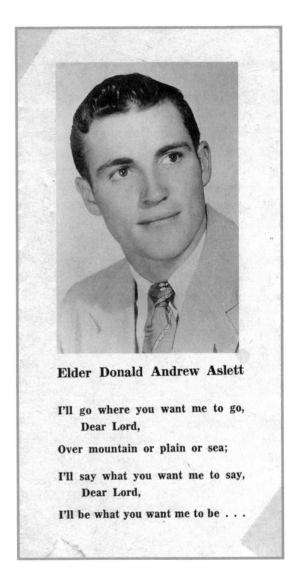

Elder Donald Andrew Aslett

I'll go where you want me to go,
    Dear Lord,

Over mountain or plain or sea;

I'll say what you want me to say,
    Dear Lord,

I'll be what you want me to be . . .

THE MISSION CARD GIVEN OUT
AT MY CHURCH FAREWELL IN 1955.

o'clock, studied the Hawaiian language for an hour, studied the Scriptures for another hour, and then headed out the door.

It was an incredible experience—a hardworking, push-to-the-top-of-myself time, where I focused on others and the spiritual for two intense years. Daily we would visit with people of amazingly varied ethnic backgrounds—Chinese, Japanese, Portuguese, Indians, Filipinos, and of course native Hawaiians. We learned about every religion from Buddhism to Baha'i. It was "arm's length away" for missionaries as far as women were concerned, and we didn't call home the whole time. But every day was exciting, and I saw many people change their lives for the better. I was on the main island of Oahu for eight months, the garden isle of Kauai for eight months, and the small island of Lanai for the last eight months, where I served as the branch president (similar to a priest or pastor of a church).

There was an entire lifetime of experience and growth crowded into these two years. I learned a lot about myself and about my expectations of others. I learned to love all races of people and the Hawaiian culture became a part of me. This was a tremendous educational and spiritual experience, and it started a love affair with Hawaii that continues 50 years later.

ME IN MY MISSIONARY DAYS IN HAWAII, WHEN WE WENT EVERYWHERE IN SUITS AND TIES.

Chapter 5

VARSITY IS BORN!

*Back into that great combination
of earning while learning about life*

On October 5, 1957, I flew home after honorably fulfill-
ing my mission. Two days later, I was back at Idaho State,
enrolled as an education major. Within a week I was back
in the cleaning business. I'd paid for the mission with all
the rest of my savings and so needed to get back to work.

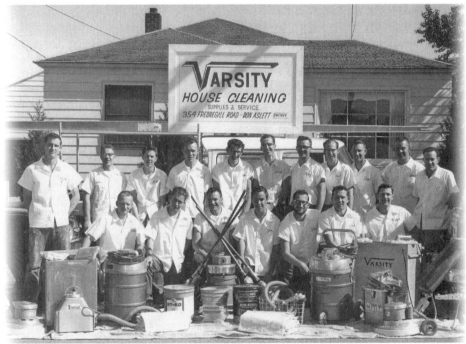

THE EARLY DAYS OF VARSITY, OUR CREW IN 1960.

I also needed a place to stay. One of the professors, Dr.
Ray J. Davis, had recently lost his wife, and he had a nice
brick home right off campus with an upstairs room avail-

able for a single college boy. Dr. Davis was an internationally known author and botanist who turned out to be a wise advisor for me.

I moved my suitcase into the room and then walked over to see my old landlady Mrs. Smith, to see if she knew what had become of the "College Cleanup Team" of three years ago. We were glad to see each other again, and I was informed that in a sense the college team was still operating. She was "kind of" running it from her basement for the boys who wanted to work once in a while. Although the name College Cleanup and Repair Team was legally mine, as Mrs. Smith pointed out, they had used it for the past three years, thus felt entitled to it. My time overseas had made me much more independent and I wanted to make an entirely fresh start, so I assured her that as I reentered the business I would not use this name.

While sitting in my room in Dr. Davis' quiet house searching for a new name for my future business, I envisioned the entire scope of the operation I intended to organize. I saw clearly what I could do and how I was going to do it. This was one of the greatest moments in my life. The picture of what was waiting for me out there was all I needed to totally commit myself to the effort to bring it about.

It took decades of learning and experience before I finally pulled it all off. But that evening as I was planning and dreaming the college-related name "Varsity" came to me. As a varsity athlete myself, I knew the credibility the word "varsity" had—it immediately summoned up "top team," cheers, and cheerleaders. Plus I could spell it without even thinking!

Soon I had an ad in the paper:

By Owner 517-6214

Don Aslett—Professional
Cleaner
Yard Work, what have you
Call CE-2-1256.

On October 18, Varsity Housecleaners received its first job. (I was the sole employee and still working for $1.25 an hour.) The call came from an area of new housing across town, where a woman wanted the outside of all her windows washed.

I had no tools or transportation. I did, however, have $16 left after registration and that was enough to get started. I walked down to the Sherwin-Williams paint store after my last class and walked out with a 5-foot ladder, a bucket, a sponge, and a cake of good old Bon Ami soap. I rustled some worn-out sheets from Dr. Davis, threw the Bon Ami in the bucket and the ladder over my back, and walked the three miles to the job. After two years in Hawaii, the cold Idaho wind was numbing. When I arrived at the house, it was late afternoon and I really had to hustle to get the job done. The water was freezing on the windows by the time I finished the last one. My fingers were numb, and I still remember how good the steak they were eating inside that house looked.

I knocked on the door and told the woman I was done—it had taken two hours altogether. She was happy with the job and wrote me a check for $2.50. I picked up my new equipment and headed back to my room. That was Varsity's first income, the start of my dream.

> DON WORKED SO FAST AND DID SUCH A GOOD JOB ON HIS FIRST WINDOW-WASHING JOB THAT THE WOMAN WHO HIRED HIM URGED A FRIEND OF HERS TO HAVE HIM WASH HER WINDOWS. AGAIN, THE RAPID, EXCELLENT WORK WAS NOTICED (BY A NEIGHBOR) AND DON WAS HIRED TO WORK FOR HER THE NEXT SATURDAY.   —DR. RAY DAVIS

Before I knew it, I was cleaning more windows and then floors. Wall and cupboard cleaning, carpet and upholstery care soon followed. Word got out that there was a willing and inexpensive housecleaner loose in the neighborhood, and soon I had more work than I could handle.

One afternoon a woman called from an elite neighborhood and said she wanted her carpet shampooed. I had never seen a carpet—on the farm we had old linoleum floors.

I ran downtown and rented a rug machine, read the little manual that came with it, and showed up at the woman's house with all of my equipment. She was impressed. The one thing I remembered Mother used to do when she was cleaning was use really hot water. This woman had a big, thick wool carpet. I used 40 gallons of hot water on it, and guess what hot water does to wool? Right—shrinks it! Within two hours, she thought she had a throw rug—the carpet pulled 2 to 3 inches away from the wall in places, and even moved the grand piano! I had to hire a carpet stretcher who labored long to get it to cover the floor again.

A few days later, I was using straight ammonia and lacquer thinner in a small sewing room, and the fumes did in the customer's pet parakeet. Another time I was washing a ceiling with ammonia solution, and some dripped down and left a big white spot on top of a grand piano.

Gradually my reputation spread through Pocatello, and I got better (at cleaning, not ruining). On every job, the homeowner would coach and teach me as I scrubbed, shoveled, and polished. I learned a lot from them and soon could do the work much faster and better.

ONE OF OUR FIRST YELLOW PAGES ADS, AT A WHOPPING $4.20 PER MONTH COST!

A couple of days after I arrived back at school, I saw the beautiful Barbara Morris walking across the campus. After two years of missionary life, hugging a woman sure felt good. A few months of being back together simply confirmed all of the feelings we'd had earlier. We were both in college now, and I wanted to play baseball professionally for a while, and all of our family and friends said, "career first!" But one of the wisest friends we had gave the best counsel, "If you are in love, get married. You'll accomplish twice together what you would individually." That was Thanksgiving Day in 1957. On December 27, 1957 we were married "for time and eternity" in the Idaho Falls Temple. Fifty years later, our union is still strong and flourishing.

When we married, I left the room I rented from Dr. Davis, and rented a one-room apartment at the Sunset Motel, right across the road from the college. Barbara was wonderfully creative in finding places to stash all the cleaning gear we were accumulating, as we had no shop, office, or vehicle, thus no place to store our supplies. Have you ever tried to decorate a small room with a ladder, wall-cleaning machine, and mops and buckets? We had a few lumps under the curtains, boxes covered with tablecloths, tools jammed under the bed, and an end table of stainless steel with casters (the wall-cleaning machine), but it was quite cozy.

OUR FORMAL
WEDDING PICTURE.

"Ignorance is bliss" applied well to the first week of our marriage, as far as food was concerned. Our first home-cooked supper was wieners, and breakfast the next day was wieners with scrambled eggs. Next, we had wieners with baked beans and several times more during the week, it was wieners. What a woman! What a honeymoon!

I was delighted because in my early life wieners were a rarity, a special treat we got if we were good. On the farm, we raised everything and our freezer and cellar were always loaded with prime beef, pork, lamb, venison, elk, and chicken—a gourmet selection. So I thought of steaks and chops as plain old farm food. But wieners came from the store, and meant ball games, camping, and picnics—we couldn't wait for Mom to bring some home.

As we moved into the second week of wiener-hood, I complimented my bride for such thoughtful menu planning. "I'm sorry, Don, but we can't afford steaks or roasts." She had been raised by a widowed mother with three other children and a tight budget, and steak was 89 cents a pound while wieners were only 29. My illusions about my esteemed entree were damaged, and later totally dashed when I got a contract to clean a slaughterhouse, and watched wieners being made out of scraps and dross rather than real meat. My childhood conditioning was dissolved, and steak and roasts have tasted great ever since!

There seems to be a universal belief that when we get more time and money "someday," our relationships will be better. The opposite is true—struggle and survival have unified more people than opulence.

For example, it's better to live poor when first married. Everyone who does it says these were some of their best married days. When they are first married with only each other, this is truly the richest a couple ever gets. Too much comfort, convenience, debt, and distraction after the honeymoon becomes a burden, not a blessing, to a couple. Struggling newlyweds bond twice as firm as highly privileged ones. Scarcity of "stuff" in the beginning seems to create a foundation of co-respect and dependence on each other, and forces a man and woman to team up with and find each other.

When we got married, instead of taking an expensive trip for our honeymoon, we decided that because we had no car, no money, and several term papers due in mid-January, as well as Varsity business to tend to, we would just go back to our new little apartment (it was Christmas vacation) and have a quiet and private week and a half together. That quiet week and a half is still on hold today.

The day after our reception we went back to work in school and business, plus we were busy with plenty of church activity.

Marriage, at least for me, was a smooth transition. Barbara was the kindest and most thoughtful person alive, which offset my "conquer-the-world" rush to get on with things.

Neither Barbara nor I ever liked fighting, and like her mother, she was an unequalled peacemaker. So we never stomped away from one another mad. If we did have a disagreement, she never let me get away with the silent treatment for more than two days. I'd write a sarcastic poem about the incident, and she'd drag my underwear through the stickers and thistles on the way back from the clothesline. We learned to anticipate and defuse each other's potential argument points, and move on to more important things. Barbara was used to going without so there was never any whining and complaining—she amazed all the workers from our cleaning company that she fed or

A SCENE FROM OUR WEDDING RECEPTION IN SHOSHONE, IDAHO.

helped make uniforms for. Because my mother and grandmother were just like her, I figured all women were the same, strong but tender. It didn't take long to find out, after talking to our many newly married employees, that they didn't all enjoy the benefits of a hardworking and supportive wife.

> I NOTICED THREE TOP VIRTUES IN MY WIFE RIGHT AWAY THAT PROBABLY HAD A LOT TO DO WITH WHY WE GOT ALONG. SHE WAS SENSITIVE, INTELLIGENT, AND TOLERANT! BEING MARRIED TO A GENTLE WOMAN WHO NEVER NAGGED, RAISED HER VOICE, LOST HER TEMPER, OR USED PROFANITY WAS A REAL PLEASURE, AND A SUPER MOTIVATION TO PUT FORTH MY BEST EFFORTS.

Along came Luke

That one-room motel apartment is many years in the past now, but some of the happenings there are hard to forget.

The afternoon we moved in, I was about to kiss my wife on the back of the neck when a disturbance at the rear of the apartment caused me to restrain myself temporarily. As I glanced out the window, I saw a smiling, crew-cut young man with squeegee in hand, washing the motel window. This was Arlo Luke, unquestionably one of the most influential people in the success story of Varsity Contractors. Arlo was from Twin Falls, Idaho, a dentist's son, and a freshman in pharmacy at the college. He had a part-time job at the motel as... you guessed it... a janitor. He was newly married also and lived two doors down from us with his bride Jackie. Arlo was a clean-cut blond, 150 pounds of dynamite. He was not one to take second place to anyone or anything. He'd been an all-state defensive tackle in high school, and he and his violin were enthusiastic members of the Idaho State Civic Symphony. We talked to Arlo at the window, met his wife, and it was a foursome visit the entire evening.

Early the next morning Varsity got a call through the motel, a good-sized job, too. I left and scrubbed and cleaned for 12 hours and brought home the first check of 1958, for $21. Shortly after I got home there was a knock at the door and a big voice saying, *"Taw!"* (Maori word of greeting). It was Marvin Pitman, my first college clean-up business partner, just arrived back from a mission in New Zealand. We were glad to see him. We sat up all night talking about Varsity and a new partnership—Aslett and Pitman were in business again.

Marvin said he would buy us a truck, since I already had some equipment. The next day a $250, 1947 Chevy pickup became the first

Varsity vehicle. Varsity's amateur carpentry skills were soon apparent, for nine hours later we had constructed a superb (to us) cleaning camper, and here in all of its splendor it is. We even repainted the truck that day—with brushes!

My wife, dying for a little attention, decided that a surge of domesticity would do the trick. So she put a big pot of pinto beans (my favorite) on the stove and a big batch of biscuits in the oven. I say she put them on, because that's all she did—when she finally remembered them, those pintos looked more like black stallions. The only bright spot in

OUR FIRST CUSTOM-MADE "CLEANING CAMPER."

the smoky room was that it was considered a case of fire damage, and referred to an insurance adjuster, and guess who got the job of cleaning it up? So our company—Barbara and I, with Marvin's help, spent the rest of our honeymoon cleaning burnt bean smoke and odor off the walls and ceiling.

College classes, starting a family, building the business, and church work became our lives for the next seven years. It amazes me now how most of us Varsity men managed to crowd four years of education into everything else that was going on at that time.

We made some important financial discoveries in that month of January—that bidding jobs, for example, sure beat the per-hour bit. I'll never forget the night we came home after our first bid job. When we figured out what we had earned, it was an unbelievable $1.50 an hour, as opposed to the $1.25 we usually charged.

It didn't take long for our name and enthusiasm (and possibly word of our low cost) to get around. Calls began to pour in. The motel was flooded with phone calls, and this "answering service" was free, a great advantage for our overhead. The company was growing, so Marvin and I hired Arlo as our first supervisor, and soon Varsity had four employees. Everything was on the way including our first daughter, Arlo's first daughter, and finals in our college classes.

> OTHER STUDENTS SOON JOINED US, AND MANY OF THEM STAYED WITH US AND BECAME MANAGERS AND MORE.

Our first loser

Business boomed and bigger jobs rolled our way. Just as the snow was melting in March of 1958, the Grims School of Business, a college on the second floor of a big building downtown, called us to bid the cleaning of all 12 of their classrooms and a large hall. We bid $175 for the whole job. The president of the school, after looking over the bid, told us to "go to it!" We were elated, so much so that Barbara and I felt we could now afford our first car and bought a 1951 Chevy for $250. We drove home that weekend to crow a little to our parents about the gold mine we'd found.

When the job started, we knew we'd found a mine all right—a coalmine. We soon realized that we had grossly underbid the job. The 12-foot-high ceilings were covered with ancient water-based paint, almost unwashable, and the rooms seemed to have doubled in size since we bid them. The walls, which looked green, when cleaned, were really light pink—they were unbelievably dirty. We didn't have much experience with cleaning problems or cleaning chemicals then, and we labored days in each room. We built scaffolding, tried putting the cleaning solution in weed sprayers, and everything else we could think of to speed the job up. In contractor's terms, we lost our shirts—the four of us worked evenings and three Saturdays, sunup to sundown, for nothing. A lesson that losses can happen in pursuit of gains, and that this bid business had to be worked out carefully!

It was this spring, while washing walls in the small chamber of commerce office in downtown Pocatello, that I met the chamber president, a salesman supreme. I started telling him our "success story"—six people going to school and learning the scientific approach to scrubbing toilets. His eyes got bigger than my exaggerations and finally he could contain himself no longer and rushed out the door. Minutes later he came back dragging Mr. Stoker, the general manager of the famous Hotel Bannock, where Judy Garland was born in a trunk—a swanky, high-end place for the railroad town of Pocatello. Mr. Chamber of Commerce introduced me as a superman who could clean anything.

Mr. Stoker was impressed, and soon we had our first janitorial contract, cleaning the hotel public areas for a staggering $525 a month. This meant a steady income that we could depend on and so we hired a few more men. There was one small hitch, however—cleaning couldn't start until eleven o'clock each evening and in the bar area not till one in the morning. We could finish cleaning before two in the morning, if we worked really hard.

Our schedules were intense. We left for school at seven-thirty and were usually out by one. Then our work—bidding, painting, and cleaning—kept us busy until nine at night, six days a week. We ate and studied after that as best we could. At eleven-thirty P.M., we went down to the hotel and worked until two A.M., and then home to bed and back up at six to study an hour before starting this routine all over again. Every few days we traded shifts to catch up on sleep, studies, and home life.

The hotel job was an educational one for us. I was innocent of the other side of life—I hadn't heard many women use profanity and judged all womankind by my lovely mother, grandmother, and wife. I trusted everyone, and took people at face value. I'd never been around drinkers and the night hotel and bar crowds were an education in reality. Weirdos of all kinds, ladies of the night, alcoholics, politicians and police on the take, salesmen and promoters living it up with their female partners, married people sneaking around with others, and many other things could be seen here or passing through.

My brother Larry worked for us for a while. He was an ingenious fellow, often pushing his cleaning equipment into the bar at 1:05 A.M. to clean, squealing with delight as he snatched a $5 or $10 bill from the formerly dark floor. This really stimulated the bar cleaners; I wonder now if ol' Larry planted the money just to motivate the late cleaning crew.

Our company gradually moved out of the hotel bar cleaning business, because none of us liked the ambiance or the hours. I do, however, remember one of the last moments of the hotel job. The kitchen was around the corner from the bar and one night as I was mopping up the kitchen, a very inebriated fellow who apparently had missed the men's restroom arrived at the kitchen door. There was a big cauldron of peeled potatoes sitting against the wall. Convinced that the kitchen, with its bright lights and prominent plumbing, was the restroom, the drunk thought this pot was the urinal and proceeded to use it as such. After he finished and returned to the bar, I reported it, but the night cook, also drunk, muttered something like "Good, now I won't have to salt the spuds for the morning hash browns." I didn't order potatoes there for a few years, just to make sure!

The summer of 1958

At first, I thought that summer would bring an easier schedule, but by midsummer, I was looking forward to school starting again so I could get some rest in classes. Full-time work meant bigger and more difficult jobs, and this meant more equipment, more time on the job, and new things to be learned. There were few books and manuals written on housecleaning and building maintenance at that time, and little was known about carpet cleaning. Paint, wall coverings, and floors were also coming out now in many different new styles and types. No one wanted to take a chance of ruining their new home and so would contact us to clean these unfamiliar materials.

We were becoming fairly well known because of our "we really appreciate the work" attitude. Every job would result in several more from neighbors calling us to work. Our housecleaning jobs began to lap over into cleaning business buildings, because many of our customers owned stores or managed businesses. I worked out a system of bidding and would respond to a call by traveling to the house or business to look the job over. Then I would tell the people exactly what the charge would be to complete the job to their satisfaction. I devised a small job sheet card to outline the services agreed upon, as a record for the job and for future reference.

We soon discovered that no matter how cheaply we worked, many people resented us making money. We would always bid jobs, or state a price for them up front. They would ask for an estimate but we gave them a firm price, always. They liked that. If they could see that we lost on the deal, or made a meager amount, they were delighted. But if it looked like we might have made a little extra, they always paid with a hangdog attitude.

I bid the cleaning of a large living room in a nice home once, for instance, for $15. The woman was pleased with my bid and even asked me if I was sure that was enough to do a good job. (It took two days for her to do it herself last year, she said.) By then, I had an automatic wall washer, towels on the end of a hose attached to a pressurized container of cleaning solution. This was sort of a weed-sprayer technology that allowed for fast, no-drip cleaning. That big enamel-painted room was a snap to clean—in 30 minutes I had it gleaming. The woman was devastated. "You did that in half an hour—that means you are making thirty dollars an hour. My husband is a lawyer and only makes ten dollars an hour!" She was bent out of shape and belittled, not by my cheap price or the job result (the best!), but the fact that a student/janitor could make as much as a lawyer.

Likewise, people would chip and chisel away trying to remove old wallpaper, spend a week on one room, and then call us. We had developed a simple "keep wet" system that really worked—"fast patience," we called it. No matter what we bid they smiled with a greedy, satisfied expression and gladly gave us the job. They expected us to be there for days and when they returned home in a few hours or at the end of that same day to find three layers of old wallpaper gone and a clean, glueless, unchipped wall, they were always amazed (and slow in getting out the old purse to pay). When I began to make double what many other people made, I was also working double their hours, taking enormous risks, driving old cars, wearing old clothes, working at top speed, and enjoying it.

Expansion is easy on paper!

September found me registering for my next year of school. Our first daughter, Laura, was born September 30. Marvin had fallen in love with a sweet young woman, and to allow him more time for school and his coming marriage, he decided to leave the partnership and refinish furniture for a living. I bought his share of the operation and now was full owner of Varsity Housecleaning. The business continued to grow and my vision of growth got a little ahead of itself. If I can do so well and do so much, why can't I get two operations go-

BARBARA WITH OUR FIRST BABY, LAURA.

ing, I mused to myself one day. The more I thought about it the better an idea it seemed. A sharp young man who had been working for me was transferring to Utah with his wife to go to school there. He said he would sure like to keep working for me. Expansion was inevitable, and an opportunity for it was knocking on my door!

I offered to set him up in Utah for a percentage of the business. He was all for it as he had no job lined up there and I would be footing the entire bill and taking all the chances. Thus, I made my first major mistake as a businessperson. He was a sharp young man, but he didn't share my philosophy of guts, grind, and sacrifice. The morning he and his wife left for Utah, I loaded up my newest truck with some of the best equipment I had, outlined our agreement, and waved goodbye. The next day we met in Salt Lake City with a friend of mine who was an accounting student. We set him up as our business agent, and then I returned home to let the money come rolling in. Money rolled, but not in. I sent money down a couple of times and seemed to be paying for promises only.

To make a long and sad story short, this expansion was a failure. My Utah manager took care of himself first and didn't worry about our agreement. He did get some contracts on his own, but one day he drove the truck back to me with many additional miles on it, many of them personal. The truck was worn, and there was no equipment in it. He wanted to buy some of our equipment to take care of the contracts he was going to keep—contracts that I paid to get. It took years more to learn that expanding profitably is always easier to do on paper than on the job.

Mistakes in life aren't just erased—they have to be paid for. I was making a living, but going to school and raising a family left me no extra money. After the expansion incident and buying a partner out, funds were short, and the going was tough. Throughout the long, cold winter, pickings remained slim. Classes were tougher this year, plus I was serving in several school and church positions as well. This was the year my financial struggles began. I learned a new and important word: "receivables." As most of you know, these are monies due a company for services already performed. At first, these amounted to a few dollars, then hundreds, then thousands. I was where many businesspeople are today. We were doing plenty of work and I was gaining net worth, but I could barely scrape up enough cash for oatmeal and diapers for the baby. Of course, we couldn't make the men go without a payday, so Barbara and I took the brunt of it. When any appreciable amount of money did arrive, it was only wise to invest it in more equipment. Money for the house was needed, but in the long run, investing it in our education or a new cleaning machine would pay bigger dividends.

After four months at the motel, we had moved to a little apartment in the basement of a nearby house. But this was soon too small for the accumulating equipment, supplies, and the scores of fellow student-employees who were in and out daily. Parking was the biggest problem. Sometimes there were five or six cars parked around our place. This wasn't too popular with the neighbors, who deserved their share of the curb. A second child on the way also prompted us to seek a bigger place to live. At this time, we were also renting the back section of a tombstone shop for our business. We needed a place that was closer and had more room to expand.

We found an ideal small home in a good location. It had a 35-by-60-foot shop at the back of the property, which the present owner used for a carpet cleaning business. We agreed to the price, but needed some money for the down payment. Even though the business was growing, much of a businessperson's worth is generally on paper: equipment, inventory, vehicles, and money on the books but not yet received. With school expenses and the costs of expanding the business, finding the down payment was no easy task.

I could borrow little or nothing because as the bankers put it, "I was self-employed" (which is a risk), and was a janitor, a profession that doesn't suggest security. Yet when any of my employees would buy anything on credit I had to vouch for them. One young fellow bought a new $4,000 sports car with all the trimmings. The bank called me to affirm that he did indeed have a job. "Thank you, we just wanted to make sure he had secure employment," they said, then loaned him the money for the car. But I couldn't borrow because they doubted my employment. I had been taught that character was better collateral than a car, but bankers didn't share my view.

Barbara and I wanted and needed the house and decided that nothing would prevent us from getting it. I gave the real estate people $150 earnest money and told them we would have the down payment in three days.

Barbara went in one direction and I went in another. We were going to try to collect some old bills. Who could be more effective as a bill collector than a woman seven months pregnant with an eleven-month-old baby in her arms? She really brought home the bacon—no one could resist this approach. I was successful too, and between us, we collected $3 more than we needed for the down payment and closing costs. The house was ours and the shop soon sported a 3-by-5-foot sign: VARSITY HOUSECLEANERS.

Our second year of college ended, and the summer found us toiling diligently to sustain ourselves and keep the company growing. Our operation got bigger and supervisors handled many jobs by themselves now. Arlo would run crews as my assistant manager and so would other new men as the jobs multiplied. To organize us better I constructed a large schedule board on which all the jobs were placed under the date they were due to be done. When the men arrived they simply picked up a card describing the job they were assigned to, and noting which of our now three vehicles they were to take, they would pack up and go. This enabled us to run four and five jobs at the same time on the same afternoon. Some confusion occasionally occurred, of course.

Once, for instance, when I added some antifreeze to the truck, the container was leaking so I poured what was left into the only available container at the moment, an empty rug shampoo bottle. I then set it up and away so that no one would find it. Someone did, however, and took it on the job. They were gone for hours and I questioned their late return. It was a carpet-cleaning job, and both men were worn out. One said, "Man, that was tough. We finally got the rug clean, but boy did we have trouble getting that shampoo to foam!" We still boast of having the only recorded antifreeze-cleaned carpet in the world.

At home, I had now remodeled the basement of the house into a big office from which Varsity was run. At this point in the business we began to design forms and systems, many of which we are still using today.

When I reentered college in 1957, I was 22, strong, and in my prime. I still had a baseball dream but I was a married man now and had a business to run. I went out for college baseball and was starting pitcher and lettered three years. My old coach, still looking out for me, set me up to work out with the

SUITED UP AS STARTING PITCHER FOR THE ISU BASEBALL TEAM.

St. Louis Cardinals' minor league in Pocatello. I did it and it gave me a shot of reality. The only things these men talked about were booze and women. My big-league dream had been a wonderful propellant, but I wasn't quite big enough or talented enough to compete with the big Florida and California boys who played year-round. I settled for college ball and church softball and coaching Little League, even those activities dwindling as my family and business grew while I still carried a full-time load of classes.

By this time, I had a number of people working for me. We guaranteed our work, as many businesses do, and were protected by adequate liability insurance. However, workmanship itself cannot be insured. We botched a few jobs in those days; there was no way to avoid it. Due to the lack of information on cleaning techniques, we learned from experience and from the suggestions of the women whose homes we cleaned. We kept good records and gradually became proficient in about everything we did. The jobs that were "disasters" only inspired us to improve our operation.

"Mommy, it's raining downstairs!"

An example of these was one of our early carpet-shampooing jobs. We finally had our own carpet-cleaning machine and were doing more carpet cleaning every week. Carpeting was getting popular, and many old hardwood floors were being covered with carpet. On one job, a woman asked me to put some dye in with my shampoo. She said that it would perk up and brighten her rather dull carpet. I was hesitant, but it was her carpet and she said to do it and assured me everything would be fine. So I added the dye and cleaned the rug. The result was beautiful—the dye had done just what she said it would. The carpet was not only clean but a fresh new green, and the dye hid some of the stains and wear. We added this bit of wisdom to our records and for the next month or so many homeowners were impressed as we shared our secret. (It was easy to do because the carpet cleaner Barbara and I had bought our first house from had left a big shelf of dye behind.) Our new "carpet rejuvenation" program came to a rather expensive end one dark day.

We answered a call to clean a carpet, and the lady of the house was one that even the most dashing entrepreneur would want to impress. "For two extra dollars, Ma'am, we will use super-snort dye additive to give this old carpet a lift." "No," she said. To a hungry young businessman, that means, "I don't understand—tell me again." So I asked again, and she said no a couple more times. Determined to show her I was right, I said, "Okay, I'll add it free!" "If you insist," she said, and I did.

I plugged the machine in, poured in the dye, and got busy on her carpet. I'd done scores of such jobs by now, but this one, when finished, just didn't look right. "Oh," she said, "look at my carpet!" It looked like a dead leopard. I was cool, having learned by now to sweat undetected, on the back of my neck instead of my forehead. "Don't worry, Ma'am, the hydro suds just barely penetrated the fiber flexers" (making it up as I went along). I refilled the shampoo tank and went over it again, but it was no better. I knew I was in trouble, plus she kept saying her truck driver husband would be home any minute. Glancing at his TV chair, I saw a 4-foot span between the seat cushion and where his greasy head hit the back of the chair—he must be 7 feet tall. So I went for broke and went over the carpet a third time with the shampoo release valve fully open. This transformed it from a dead leopard to a dead pinto horse. About then, up the stairs from the basement came her daughter, panicked—"Mommy, it's raining downstairs!" The river running out of my shampoo tank onto that oversoaked carpet was flowing down the heat vents and dripping off the ceiling in the basement. Needless to say I got out of there quick and the family got a new rug at my expense!

The people who replaced the carpet later informed us that her rug was a fiber blend; the cotton had absorbed the dye while the rayon and nylon didn't. That was not the first or last carpet to give up its life in the course of my efforts to become a premier carpet cleaner.

In the old days, we pro carpet cleaners could not get all of the water out of carpets we were cleaning. When we were up against a really grungy one, we had to soak it down, so the carpet stayed wet for days afterward and problems always followed. In one house, we forgot to block the legs of a piano and the steel casters rusted and stuck to the rug (and warped the piano out of tune). In another house, the woman closed up all of the windows after one of these "wet" carpet jobs, trapping in the moisture. When I arrived the next morning after a raving phone call from her, there were long sheets of wallpaper draped all over the rug. I couldn't imagine who would sling wallpaper onto a wet rug, until I found out from the sobbing woman that the wallpaper came off the walls—all that moisture had loosened the glue!

Another of our customers owned a rental house and wanted the carpet cleaned before the next tenants moved in. By now I was perhaps not the best at cleaning carpet, but I was getting pretty good at sniffing out potential problems. The empty living room was large, and on the floor was a thick wool carpet. The former tenants had pets that peed all over it, so we knew a deep, wet suds cleaning would be required and shrinkage might result, unless, my mechanical mind told me, the carpet was anchored to the floor with more than a wimpy tack strip. I had my utility truck with me and the smallest nails in it were 16 penny (more than 3 inches long). I used them to quickly nail the edges of the carpet to the wooden floor beneath. The heads of the giant nails were well hidden by the heavy nap. Then we really put the liquid to it and extracted as much as we could back out with a wet/dry vacuum. The carpet looked fine afterward.

Five hours later, we came back for a final check and blinked about 14 times, unable to believe what we saw. The strength of a shrinking wool carpet is incredible! It had pulled pieces of tongue and groove wood right out of the floor along the walls. There lay our clean carpet, 5 inches away from the wall, trimmed with 20-foot long boards with rows of 16-penny nails sticking out of them. I don't even want to remember how we remedied that one!

Embarrassment, not from work, but as a result of it, was frequent as my business grew. I was elected vice president of the Student National Education Association (SNEA) for the State of Idaho in my sophomore year, and was president-elect the following year. As a sophomore, too, I was chosen Education Student of the Year. A representative of Gamma Phi Beta sorority called the university to arrange a speaker for the next big pow-wow on education. My assumed prominence in the field was noted, and I was assigned to represent the university. On the day of the lecture, I had dyed some upholstery for a customer. The witch's brew she asked me to use was an acid green solution that smelled terrible. While getting ready for my presentation I found that the green stain wouldn't come off my hands, so I decided to keep my hands behind me or in my pockets.

I was minoring in speech, however, and the use of gestures was natural to me. So right in the middle of a point, I threw both hands up in the air. The first few rows of the audience gasped in horror at my apparent affliction, and they looked ill for the rest of my talk.

Most of us Varsity cleaners could be recognized at school by the stains of our trade. A janitor's shoe soles rotted off at the instep from frequent wading in hot chemical strippers, and the right side of a janitor's pants always sagged from carrying 20 pounds of keys around.

Some days we would be on a paint job and leave at twelve-thirty to make a one o'clock class, changing clothes in the car before we rushed in. In sociology class, the girl sitting next to me seemed to be giving me frequent glances. My personal charm aside, I couldn't understand the attraction. Finally, one day she couldn't contain herself any longer. "Excuse me, sir, what are all those different colored spots on your ear?" (These were roller flecks and paint drops I hadn't noticed or washed off in my haste to make class.) I whispered back, "I have leprosy!" The space between our chairs increased.

When I reentered college I joined Army Reserve Officer Training (ROTC). We had a drill every Thursday, in which both we and our gear were supposed to be spotless and spit-polished, top to bottom. My shoes would get specks and drips of paint on them from our painting jobs, so I would give them a coat of gloss black enamel paint on Wednesday night. When the last drill of the year came around, the shoes were pretty heavy from those 36 coats of paint. They looked like something Ronald McDonald would wear. This particular drill was the grand finale of the year, and a real Army general would be there. All of our training would be displayed in this final inspection and drill out on the quadrangle area of the campus.

All week I had reminded myself to give those rainbow brogans their last coating of black enamel, but not until after I had dressed and hustled to the quad did I glance down at my feet. With a horrible sick feeling, I realized I had forgotten to paint-shine my shoes. The company captain and two lieutenants had a conference as to what they would do to get me out of sight. Roadblock guard and supply-room guard were considered, but abandoned because I would be alone and noticed for sure. They decided to leave me in the platoon (one of nine) because they knew the "old man" would inspect only two or three platoons at most. The odds were good that I would be missed.

The band struck up a marching tune and performed a marching spectacular with a snappy "eyes right" to the overweight dignitary. We then formed at rigid attention as the general began to strut up and down the lines of men, eyeing his troops. He passed one... two... three... four platoons, came to ours, stopped, made a left face, and there was no doubt—we were lost! I was in the third column and as the snap of the bolts drew closer, the general finally faced me. His eye went from my paint-sprayed ears to my ammonia-whitened hands and then down to my decorated footwear. Our officers were frozen in their tracks. The general looked back up at me, down at my shoes again. "My God," he said, easing away with a backward glance. The company commander who followed behind him gave me an "I'll kill you" look. All year he had spelled my name with two s's (Asslett) and at that moment, I lived up to it!

I also had a chance to try my hand in the political arena during these years. One afternoon another of my favorite speech/drama/debate professors, Chick Bilyeu, announced to our class that he was going to run for the state senate. I must have clapped the loudest, because after class he asked me (the now well-known college janitor) to be his campaign manager. I was so flattered by the offer I said yes. We took on an old senate incumbent and got beat in the end by 32 votes. I was devastated that a perfect potential senator like Mr. Bilyeu could be beaten by a much less qualified opponent. (Welcome to politics!) On the next term, Bilyeu was elected and served admirably for decades. All of this only added to my college experience.

ARLO AND I AS YOUNG BUSINESSMEN.

Chapter 6

DESTINY RINGS!

"This is Western Electric Bell System calling... can you clean our building?"

In 1958, Varsity began a long, intense, and mutually profitable working partnership with telephone companies.

Then it came, the first contact from a company we later would do millions of dollars worth of work for—the Bell System, said to be the biggest company in the world at the time. I arrived home from an afternoon class in 1958 to find that a call had come in from Western Electric, a Bell System mother company to our local Mountain States Telephone Company. They wanted a bid on some cleaning. I knew the telephone company had built a new building in Pocatello and in a year was going to change from operator-assisted calling to dial service here.

When I went down there that afternoon and walked onto the battleship-gray linoleum floor, I could smell the unique scent of phone cable and other telephone equipment that I would never forget. Western Electric was wiring the building before turning it over to Mountain States. The manager said they needed someone to sweep up wire clippings each night and clean the restrooms and break room, etc. They showed me their special chemically treated Masslinn cloth to dust with and other unique cleaning methods they required.

I bid this at $75 a week for the whole building. When we got the job, I hired a young man to do it, paid him the going wage, and made $45 profit per month. I had never made money before without being personally on the job.

The building manager was pleased with the price and with the work, and as time went on, he gave us more work and more money. We did a good job but best of all began learning the Bell System procedures and practices. By the time Western Electric finished and moved out, we had that new building polished up—the floors looked like sheets of glass and the restrooms sparkled.

The big switchover

Now it was time to transfer from the old "number please" manual office next door to this new dial office. This was called a "cut-over" and it was a grand event, attended by the mayor and many other politicians as well as a platoon of Bell executives. Dignitaries even flew in from the East and exactly at midnight, they pulled the "blocks" and instantly the whole city had dial phone service. We played a bigger role in the switchover than expected.

That night my crew was in the building doing some last touchups while the big bosses were assembling themselves for the speeches and other formalities of the occasion. At 10 P.M., two hours before the big moment, one of our cleaners was sweeping in the frame room. At one end, thousands of wires fastened to the "block" dangled from the ceiling to the floor. As he swept through the wires, they tangled in his awkward Bell sweeping tool, so he yanked the wires and pulled out a large section of the blocks, instantly putting about half the city on dial tone. Alarms went off and a volley of horrified executives barged through the door to see what had happened—the head honcho was so upset that blood vessels bulged out on his neck. "We waited for this event for two years!" he sputtered, "and a stupid janitor has switched over the system!" Pretty funny now, but we didn't laugh then.

Well, they couldn't put the blocks back. So we went home in dishonor yet with a unique honor. That was the first Bell System building in the world to go to contract cleaning, and nearly 50 years later we are still cleaning it (and 3,000 other phone buildings).

With phone service now switched from the old building to the new, all of the Bell personnel were transferred over too, including the custodians—our contract was over. However, our good service had bought us some job insurance. Their three custodians did not have the expertise or energy to keep this big new building to the standard we had established. Within a few weeks, the immaculate new building was a mess. When I came home after class, Barbara gave me a message: "A Mr. Hodge from the telephone building wants to see you." I was there in ten minutes.

The Bell System's nationwide policy then was an "in-house" operation, meaning they did their own cleaning—Western Electric had outsourced a job to us, something completely foreign to Bell's way of doing

THE MAIN TELEPHONE OFFICE IN POCATELLO, OUR FIRST TELEPHONE COMPANY CONTRACT, AND ONE OF THE FIRST BELL BUILDINGS IN THE ENTIRE U.S. TO BE CLEANED BY CONTRACT CLEANERS RATHER THAN IN-HOUSE STAFF.

business. The boss over the new building was a tried and true Bell System manager. He had full respect for Bell's carefully conceived policies, but was also open to new approaches that could save his company money and get a job done better. In short, the man had guts. His name was Les Hodge and he went on with us to save the Bell System hundreds of millions of maintenance dollars!

"I'd like a bid to clean this building," he said, and believe this or not, he didn't hand me a single sheet of specs. I knew the building and gave him a price of $693 a month. With benefits, they were paying the three custodians $3,000 a month for the same job, so the decision was made.

"You've got the job."

That was one of the first of more than 30,000 Bell buildings in the U.S. to eventually go to "contract cleaning," and we, a tiny group of Idaho college kids, started it all.

The manager of Western Electric had been very satisfied with our work and gave us an opportunity to bid a building in Logan, Utah. Soon we had our first out-of-state contract and a month later another Bell contract in Blackfoot, Idaho.

In the late 1950s, I signed a contract with the Mountain States Telephone Company to maintain "call stations" (the official name for phone booths). We set up regular monthly routes and serviced the booths, cleaning them, replacing broken glass, reporting damage, changing burned-out lights, replacing missing directories, and testing the phone to see that it was in working order. We charged around one dollar per visit so we really had to move to make a profit.

The heat, the cold, and the abuse the booths received kept this job from ever being dull. After cleaning a city full, you could lie down at night and count booths instead of sheep. We'd take on any booths anywhere. I did the Sun Valley to Salmon River route just for the beauty of the drive.

An innovation in upkeep

The marvelous phone system whereby we touch a few buttons and communicate anywhere in the world and even in space, at any time of day or night, is nowhere near magic. Bell had all sorts of equipment buildings and relay towers across the continent to accomplish this, on the highest mountains and in the tiniest towns, all of which required upkeep. There were a few large manned equipment buildings with relay towers on top. However, most were smaller (maybe 20 by 20 feet) and called community

ONE OF BELL'S SMALL LOCAL PHONE BUILDINGS, CALLED CDOs (COMMUNITY DIAL OFFICES).

dial offices (CDOs). If they were inside a big downtown building or in a complex like a university, they were called public building exchanges (PBXs); small mountaintop sites were TDY huts, but I never did figure out that acronym. For years, the telephone company just had the visiting phone repairman do a catch-as-catch-can cleaning and maintenance job on these buildings. When the door needed painting or anything else cropped up beyond the repairperson's capacity or job description they would send out a contractor. Since these buildings were often remote, this was expensive.

We had been called in to travel to some of these for an annual floor care session. We would do other work, too, and sometimes our billing for one trip to a CDO to paint a door was $180, counting labor, travel time, and supplies. Although profitable, doing jobs like these all over was running us ragged. One afternoon as I was out in the boonies somewhere waiting for some paint to dry so that I could do a second coat, it occurred to me: Why not set up a route and do cleaning and maintenance on all of these buildings on a regular basis? If we did them once a month, we could do upkeep instead of restoration and repair. This would be much more effective and cheaper than once-a-year overhaul.

I typed up a list of what we had been doing versus what could be done and proposed it to the powers that be, offering a $20 once-a-month maintenance visit. This would cut their upkeep costs in half and keep the buildings in continual top condition, no more "up and down" maintenance. They ate it up, and we ended up with routes of ten to twenty buildings within a given area that could be done in one day. Slowly, we both spotted new needs and added them to our visit list. Our truck had everything on it, and we would pull up in front of a CDO, jump out, clean the floors and the restroom (if there was one there), touch up any nicks in the doors, dust the electronic equipment, change filters, clean and service the booth, police the yard, and vacuum. If there was snow, we shoveled it, and so on. The first thing we did, which they hadn't done in the past 20 years, was put door mats at all building entrances, which cut tracked-in dirt by 80 percent or more.

All these jobs, on an individual, on-demand basis took hours, even days. Now most of our stops per building were 30 minutes and the building was perfect. The union installers, once our opposition, now loved us for doing the cleaning grunt work they once had to do. Soon we had routes all over Idaho, Wyoming, and Utah (my favorite being in the parks of southern Utah). Looking back, it not only benefited the phone company and us, but it was a supreme environmental initiative, saving thousands of gallons of gas! This system was eventually copied by all telephone companies and by our competitors.

Pioneering and new inventions

Our Bell Telephone account was now our main income producer, and they had such a strong network that word of a good job we did for one district would spread and we would get a call from another. Eventually this was the way we made our footprint across the West, and the entire country.

Les Hodge continued to be the most progressive manager I had ever met, next to my father. He was a risk-taking renegade in what was usually a conservative position. When and if anything could be improved upon, Les was the first to put his name and job on the line to do it. Les (who looked like William Holden) had come up through the ranks and he was tough on us, and on everyone. Although a taskmaster, he was also fair and progressive. He had no agenda except to get the best for the Bell System.

I loved working for him—life was always exciting, and we eventually patterned many of Varsity's systems after things we learned from him and others in Bell. Once Les knew us better, the strength of his position, and Varsity's willingness to go anywhere and do anything, enabled us to innovate and develop programs that aided the whole Bell System (and helped lower phone bills). By the time we had completed

four years worth of varied Bell contracts for him, he had us doing jobs we'd never dreamed of doing. We bid anything, tried anything. Before long, besides the cleaning and upkeep we were already doing inside and outside phone buildings, we were killing weeds, doing landscaping, painting towers, washing vehicles, and sealing concrete. Since we already had security clearance and keys, and were often in the

CLEANING BUILDINGS FULL OF HIGH-TECH EQUIPMENT THAT NEEDED TO BE KEPT DUST-FREE WAS AN EXACTING PROCESS, CALLING FOR SPECIAL EQUIPMENT AND PROCEDURES.

buildings cleaning, we were able to do other maintenance work much cheaper than outside competitors.

The Bell System had an awesome accounting and analysis procedure called an "index" whereby costs for a given operation could be compared and evaluated. Les Hodge's index numbers (right here in Pocatello, Idaho) led the entire U.S. on building and vehicle maintenance and other items. He had visitors and calls from all over the country asking how he did it.

The unions hated Les and of course, us right along with him. When news of his contracting finally got back to New York, all the union and other "old system" advocates descended on him. A delegation was sent to straighten him out and get things back to "in-house." Les wouldn't yield, so they threatened him with his job. (It was a super job with lots of great AT&T stock as well.) Les still wouldn't buckle under and these were his last words to the delegation: "The last building evaluation group from your office [New York] just rated my building the cleanest in the entire U.S. I'm saving $2,400 a month, with no accidents, no insurance payments, and no security violations. Now if the company can't buy into these kinds of results [a magic Bell word], then I'm working for the wrong company." They went home and nothing was ever said about the matter again.

> LES HODGE STOOD UP TO
> THE ENTIRE TELEPHONE
> COMMUNICATIONS UNION AND PUT
> HIS CAREER ON THE LINE FOR US,
> RESULTING IN OUR NATIONWIDE
> BELL SYSTEM CONTRACT AND
> SAVING THEM TENS OF MILLIONS OF
> DOLLARS IN THE END.

Together we—Les and Varsity—had broken down the gate. Before long more telephone building maintenance work all over Idaho, Utah, and later Wyoming and Colorado flooded in.

Another first... yanking phones

Another of Les's innovations was in telephone removal. Whenever a customer moved, Bell, who owned all of the phones, needed to retrieve them. The index cost for this nationwide was around $5 per phone, as it was usually done by expensive phone repairers or installers. Since we were all over the place and did many cleaning jobs in conjunction with people moving in and moving out, Les taught us (and some taxi drivers, who also traveled around a lot) to disconnect and remove the phones. For this we were paid fifty cents a phone, which often amounted to a couple of extra bucks a building. We would toss the phones in a black garbage bag and leave them each night in the telephone storeroom in one of the buildings we cleaned. The next morning the Bell supervisors would find a sack of freshly removed phones with not a clue of where they came from. This drove the unions bananas, and as for the index auditors, they couldn't believe it, but results were results. All of Les's phones were out in record time, and his index cost for it was less than a dollar. They never did figure out how he did it.

An excerpt from the Varsity newsletter,

Scrubber's Scribe

Don Aslett and Arlo Luke lived by the Bell System rule that nothing extraneous should remain in the janitor closet. They proved this by throwing out seven boxes of long distance system (billing) cards, which someone had stored in the closet by mistake. They were tossed late in the evening and hauled away by an efficient trash collector to the landfill early the next morning. By late afternoon that same day (after the bills were buried under 20 feet of fill), the accounting department came to get their billing information for the month. But no cards were to be found. We were told that this dumpster dilemma ended up giving some AT&T customers the greatest long distance rate in history—the whole city got a month of free calls!

The business, in between schoolwork, church work and family life, gradually grew. During the school year, we now employed 24 men and one secretary. We had learned by now that our future depended on having good people, not just people who needed a job. We tried to choose students of good character who were hardworking.

One interview I never forgot was the one in which an applicant said to me, "Mr. Aslett, you have too many saints in your company—it's getting to be too goody-goody. You need to hire a good sinner or two like me." I'll admit that was a clever approach that caught me without a reply. I hired him, but never did notice any creative sinning.

I had been taught by my parents and grandparents that charging too much for your services was a sin, just about the same as stealing, so we always bid jobs at a bare, fair minimum. Thus, the only option we had for increasing our income was to learn efficiency: work harder, faster, and longer hours. I found that other people's attitudes were not as conservative as mine; most saw more pay for less work as the ideal. I remember hiring a college student once who needed a job. After two weeks, he came to me and said he wasn't happy with his new job. His answer to my "Why?" was a classic: "Because work takes up all of my time on the job," he said. "What!" I said—I didn't understand. "Well, work takes up all my time on the job. My friend has a good job. He has to read a gauge for five minutes every hour, and the rest of the time he can rest and study and get paid for all of the time he is there." The student left our employment later that day, still hoping to find a no-work job.

"Suited" for the job

Being in the cleaning business, it was only fitting we maintain a clean-looking crew—clean-shaven men with trim haircuts, in clean clothes. To make us even more professional looking, I decided to round up some old navy "whites" (pants and shirts). Barbara sewed the red "flying V" logo I'd come up with on the shirts. Then we showed up at the next job wearing our new matching uniforms. What a difference a $2 pair of used pants and a white shirt made! The owner of the house, who generally watched us like a hawk, left us alone when we worked, and told us where the root beer was in the fridge— we could help ourselves.

The introduction of a uniform was a big step psychologically, and had a rather reluctant buy-in from some of the college freethinkers and nonconformist night workers. The rule now was "wear your uniform at all times when on the job," and because someone like me rules more by suggestion and persuasion than order, a cat-and-mouse game of trying to catch workers out of uniform ensued. This included those who showed up on a job with only half of a uniform because the shirt (or pants) was in the wash. I hinted, pleaded, begged, threatened, fined, and even crept around in the bushes beside buildings we cleaned to catch uniform violators. It got to be a real circus, testing my authority.

One afternoon (after two mean tests at school—a bad day) my crew met me at one o'clock to go on a job. Several of them were uniformless or had only part uniforms, and I decided to get tough. I walked into the shop where men were loading our trucks and said, "We are leaving for the job in 15 minutes. Anyone not in full uniform need not report to work then or hereafter." Men ran to their cars and home and were all back in full uniform in time… and thereafter.

Don meets the unions

Thus far in life, I'd never even heard of regulating work—the only work ethic I knew was to work as hard as you could for as long as you could. You only rested when you were dead tired and if the work wasn't finished, rest wasn't even a consideration. As for a "break," I couldn't conceive of ruining a good working day with interruptions—you ate three times a day, drank on the run, and went to the bathroom in the morning before you left home.

This rural attitude was of course carried into my college cleaning business. We'd do anything, anywhere, anytime, for as low a price as possible. This not only created a problem for Les Hodge, as noted earlier, it irritated the local carpenters', plumbers', and painters' unions.

Having only a limited understanding of unions, I somehow imagined they were actually part of the government, so when a call came requesting me to attend a big union meeting, I complied. The purpose of this meeting, I soon discovered, wasn't to approach me to join the union, but to give me a scare to make me roll over and play dead with Varsity. In other words, it was a meeting to intimidate all of the scabs who had been invading union territory. I was given a chair when I arrived at the hall, along with a few fellow violators. One guy in particular was really sweating it, because he had hired some men for work on the side and not paid them union wages. They had him in a room for 15 minutes and when he came out, he was bowing and cringing and looked like the personification of despair. "Aslett," said a big gruff voice, and now I was escorted into the room and given a seat in the middle of ten men.

The man in charge decided on the soft sell and said, "Aslett, we all admire you and know what you are doing, and it was okay for a while, you were just gravel under our feet, not affecting any of us much. But now with your growth and size, you are taking good money that our men need to support their families. Do you understand that?"

"Yes, I understand, and that money is supporting my family and putting me and twenty others through school."

"That's not the point," he said, raising his voice. "You don't depend on the money for a living. It's our only livelihood. You are working at all hours for a low price when we have to pay overtime and it isn't fair."

"It's fair to me," I said sharply back, and then everyone joined in the discussion.

"You college kids don't need it—you just use the money for beer," said one.

"No one in our company drinks beer," I retorted.

The meeting evolved into a very unfriendly one. I got a little sarcastic and they grew more determined to scare me. Finally, one of them made the ultimate muscle threat: "You have a family and property and we know how to deal with you if you want to play rough."

I just laughed at the overweight fellow who said this. "You guys tell me all this but you can't hurt me because you are not really organized. You have more scabs [nonunion workers] on this committee than I have in town." A silence followed and I continued. "Four out of the ten men sitting here have hired me to do their cleaning because I can do it much more cheaply than they can. I've made them all a good profit." Adam's apples bobbed and feet shuffled. Even the six who had never been involved with me were probably working with someone else on the side, so they didn't know for sure to whom I was referring. The guilty ones stood to lose a lot of their union standing and would be fined if they were found to be using nonunion help.

The chairman stood and said, "Perhaps it would be better if we just forgot the whole thing." All agreed, and I walked forth a free man.

But as Varsity continued to grow, unions continued to badger me. When we were cleaning a truck stop kitchen, a $25 job, two goons showed up and told the owner that if he didn't dismiss us in five minutes they would shut off union gas and food deliveries to his place and close up his business. So the apologetic owner asked us to fold our towels and ladders and leave.

A few months later two of our men were cleaning bird droppings off the sign of a five and ten cent store. It was a small job, but work was stopped and our men thrown off the job because of union pressure on the owner and manager.

Not everyone kowtowed to the demands of the unions. There was a physician in town, a man who looked a lot like Richard Boone, the star of a highly successful western series of the time called *Paladin*. We nicknamed this doctor "Doc Paladin." He had a good practice of his own and was also a physician for the Union Pacific Railroad. We had worked for him at his new home and after it was finished, he gave us the job of cleaning his office. It was Saturday and no one was at the office except the doctor and five Varsity men. In the middle of the job, the phone rang. It was the union calling, and they told "Doc" to get us out of town before sundown. As Paladin the gunfighter would have handled it, Doc responded, "You can go to hell," and hung up. This aroused the union troops and soon two tough-looking guys were there in person. Now Doc was even more direct than in the earlier showdown. "The day I can't hire who I want to clean the toilets and scrub the floors in my own office, a place that I own and run, will be a dark day indeed."

"Yes, but all of the railroad trade will be taken away if you get smart with us."

Doc pointed his finger like a revolver at the union man's chest and said, "Fella, you can take your train, load it up with all of your employees, and drive it _____ (he then specified a popular anatomical location)." We finished the job, and the doctor never lost a patient.

The unions' original purpose of protecting the laborer was a worthy one, but the union workers I too often dealt with were lazy and surly. The bigger the city or convention hall, the worse their manners and productivity. I was picked on, threatened, and had my car windows broken with chains—but none of this interrupted my growth or direction.

I have worked for unions and with them since, as necessary, but never compromised my work ethic and philosophy (only to the extent required by the government, where I comply fully).

Around the clock effort

Although I loved school and was committed to getting a degree, it took constant discipline to keep school and business in proper perspective. I had no choice but to be totally efficient in completing term papers and other assignments. In the evening, I would type up my notes, make an outline of them, and bind them. By doing this, I learned more and had an outline to brief me and keep for future reference.

Working nights made it hard to stay awake in some classes, but somehow all of the Varsity men managed to do it. They had to, to survive. We began to do many supermarket floors—Safeway, Albertsons, Food King, IGA, etc.—and they had to be done in the wee hours. Plowing through our many responsibilities in those days took a share of sacrifice and extraordinary efforts at times.

Our day started at six in the morning (unless we had a supermarket to clean earlier), and most of our classes were in the morning, leaving our afternoons free, except for a couple of labs here and there. At eleven-thirty, when everyone got home from class they would call in and check the schedule. The schedule board would be filled with jobs to be done for the day. We were working more than two dozen men pretty regularly by now, so while making dinner Barbara would tend two toddlers and answer the phone. From noon to one o'clock we ate. The men arrived as they were scheduled, and Barbara would find a replacement for anyone who didn't show. I would estimate the jobs from the morning calls on my way home from school. By one a dozen cars were parked around our house (the mail carrier hated us) and the crews headed out in all directions. Then the afternoon phone calls started. Laura and Karla, our two babies, turned into baby fire horses, for when the phone would ring their mother would jump, and they soon became conditioned to respond the same way.

No one sacrificed more in those days than Barbara. She not only cared for our home and children, but also kept the books for the business, was our bill collector, dispatcher, receptionist, and received the complaints. She also stabilized the wives who were wondering if it was all worth it. When I did off-hour jobs I would bring three or four men home to eat with us, and she cheerfully fed everyone.

Where there's smoke there's . . . a hire

All businesses have pivot points that may lead to growth, open up a new market or new uses for old skills and systems. One of the most significant of these for us was insurance jobs. Most home-owners carry a policy covering damage to a house from fire, wind, or vandals. Since Pocatello was a coal-burning city with cold winters, it was not uncom-mon for a furnace to malfunction and blow smoke and soot throughout a house. Cooking also got out of control (resulting in a grease fire), smokers fell asleep on sofas, and TVs exploded. Jobs like these were called "fire damage," and the homeowner was either paid to re-store the home to its original condition, or to hire professionals to come in and do it. In one to three days, we would often clean the entire inte-rior of a house, fixtures, furnishings, and all! Before long, we were not just cleaning but painting, and then repairing things like burned doors, walls, and floors. This is how I began to learn to build houses. Our flex-ibility and dependability were such that several insurance adjusters started using us regularly. Our service was quick and trouble-free for homeowners and inexpensive for the insurance companies. When we answered the phone and heard, "We've got a smoker for you, Don," it meant good income and often a new account, too.

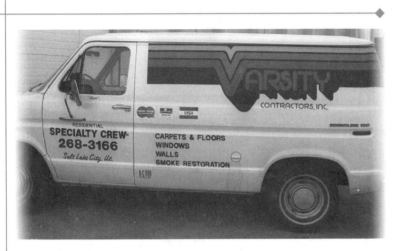

WE SOON FOUND OURSELVES DOING MANY JOBS FOR INSURANCE COMPANIES, CLEANING UP AFTER FIRES, FLOODS, AND OTHER SMALL DISASTERS.

I would look the job over, make up a bid, and call the adjuster. As soon as the bid was accepted, I would pick up the drapes (generally smelling of smoke) and leave them at a dry cleaner who gave us a 20 percent commission. Then I called in the crew and five or six of us hit the house in a well-organized system—went over the walls and ceilings with a rubber pad called a "dry sponge," then washed them, cleaned the windows, cabinets and woodwork, and last shampooed couches, chairs, and carpets. The clean drapes would then be delivered and often hung by the cleaners. We would also work with subcontractors who did major rebuilding and repairs before or after we cleaned up the mess.

My record was getting seven insurance jobs in one day, followed by some real hustling to start and finish them all so adjusters and homeowners would be pleased and competitors wouldn't sneak in.

This type of job was an innocent farm boy's first glimpse of the public "cheating the system." I got a call one day to estimate the cost of a fire loss job at the mayor's house in a nearby city. It was just a little smoke damage from a burning pan, and I planned to bid it at $200. I was just finishing up my calculations when the mayor came in. He knew me, and I knew the company he headed in town. He glanced at my estimate, put his arm on my shoulder, and said, "Two hundred dollars isn't much for all that work, is it?" I told him it was plenty. "How would you like to have a hundred dollars more on top of that?" he asked. "What for?" I said. "Well, I sign the proof of loss and no one will question it. Just change your estimate to four hundred dollars and we'll split the extra." My jaw dropped; I thought he was kidding.

He was an imposing and persuasive man, but if I ever did something that dishonest my father would have run me through our hay chopper. "No, two hundred is really more than enough." I felt foolish arguing with him. "Insurance companies are rich and I've paid thousands into them; there's nothing wrong with it," he said. "Besides, I can say the fire untuned my piano and I had to have it retuned." The more I refused, the guiltier he felt for having made the offer. I didn't yield and from that day on, we always felt a little awkward around each other. I was so disappointed in the man I never even told my wife.

The dishonest mayor wasn't alone, it turned out. It was amazing how on many fire loss jobs where a couple of rooms got a little smoke from a furnace backfire or burning TV set, suddenly the whole house needed to be cleaned, repainted, and recarpeted, just because it was insured. Some people even brought relatives' stuff over to be cleaned. One woman went into her sealed trunks and got out all the clothes, including a wedding dress, and sent them out to be cleaned at the insurance company's expense. What makes us think we should be rewarded instead of just restored when an insurance company is paying?

The speed and efficiency of our work made us attractive to the insurance companies because the quicker the settlement was made and job over, the less time there was for the neighbor who had nicked insurance companies on his past claims to drop in and poison our customers, showing them 20 more ways to rip off insurance people.

Our service soon spread to towns up to 150 miles away. The only drawback of these jobs was the time it took to be paid. By the time renters, owners, adjusters, agents, and the people in the home office drew up, signed, and processed all of the paperwork it was 60 to 90 days, or even six months in some cases, before we got our money.

Just when you figured you'd seen about everything on a cleaning job, something new would surface. One morning we got a call for a fire loss job in a three-bedroom home, so we went to bid on it. A fire in the basement had burned the floor joists badly—the rest of the house was okay, but heavily smoked. There was sticky smoke residue on and in everything.

The owners were real collectors. In the ordinary house fire damage job, for instance, we'd clean about 25 blankets, quilts, rugs, and the like. They had 153. A normal household population of knickknacks and figurines might be 50 to 100; they had over 7,000. The job went on forever—I'd have sworn they were shipping stuff in. But the woman of the house knew every piece and had a story to go with it.

Soap, water, and elbow grease (plus a few brains) would seem to be the main ingredients of cleaning, but we soon realized that a more scientific approach meant more profit and a better job of cleaning. The most common of all cleaning tools (after soap and water) was the cloth or "rag." We learned fast to appear professional in our talk as well as our actions. Calling what we cleaned with a rag was crude, and sounded as if we might be using some stinky old t-shirt on the wall. Likewise, calling paint thinner "thinner" would often cause customers to flinch at the thought that we might be thinning paint before applying it. To enhance our image and build confidence, we would refer to our cleaning cloths as towels, and to thinner as petroleum distillate or enamel reducer. Vocabulary like this would bring smiles from the homeowners.

The towels were literally that—the thickest bath towels we could find cleaned much better than pieces of old sheet or bedspread. Our first towel supply came from the Varsity men scrounging up all of the spare towels around their homes. When that source was depleted, friends, neighbors, and relatives were tapped, and then we had to resort to buying towels. This was hard on the wives. We were all struggling to get through school, making do with repaired and patched things, yet we'd go down to Penney's and buy the thickest, lushest, most deluxe bath towels. We would then come home and cut them in half, fold them once, and sew them into an 11-by-14-inch tube that could be turned inside out when the outside got dirty. "Oh, let us use them just once before you cut them up to clean grease or wipe down toilets!" our wives would beg. But seldom did this occur. Ninety percent of those new towels were cut up and sewed by Barbara, then they quickly went into service in washing walls or other cleaning.

LOADING UP LADDERS AND
SCAFFOLDING FOR A JOB;
ARLO STRAPPING ON THE LOAD.

When the towels got dirt saturated, we'd take them home or to a laundromat, wash and dry them until they were clean and fluffy again, and then start over.

Few laundromats (or for that matter wives) appreciated grungy towels swishing back and forth in their laundry facilities, but laundromats were open to the public after all. We were finally blackballed, however, after a catastrophe. We had used our towels to wipe up five gallons of spilled lacquer thinner on a job, then took the towels down and quickly washed them, not adding any soap because the towels usually contained soap from cleaning operations. Thus little of the volatile thinner was washed away. After washing, we threw the towels in a large gas dryer. Five minutes later, there was a tremendous explosion starring the dryer containing our towels. The lacquer fumes ignited and blew up the dryer and its surroundings, and we, our towels, and our reputation were thrown out—permanently.

YOU WOULDN'T BELIEVE THE THINGS THAT COULD GO WRONG WITH A CREW OF GREEN COLLEGE BOYS AND A FARM BOY MANAGING THEM AND TEACHING THEM HOW TO CLEAN. SOME OF EVEN THE WORST MISHAPS HAD THEIR FUNNY SIDE.

College boys turned loose in a nice home with a picky owner often created "a situation." In one home Ralph Fry, a super polite and cultured Varsity veteran, was running the job. The owner of the home, an elderly woman, stayed right with the crew through just about every square foot of cleaning, checking their work with a magnifying glass. One of the crew left to get some more towels and when he came back through the door, the owner was nowhere to be seen. (She was now sitting in a high-backed overstuffed chair facing the other way.) The young man blurted out, "Is that old bag finally gone?" We all froze. Ralph very calmly, gesturing to the woman he was facing, said, "No, Mr. Brower, the lady of the house dwells at home." The "old bag" didn't even flinch, and eagled-eyed the job to the end.

As Varsity grew we diversified. We boasted in our ads "We clean anything," "Call us, we're ready!" On my first brochure, I listed all sorts of jobs that we were willing to do and added the line, "and what have you." And believe me, people would give us jobs that no one else would touch.

Not exactly our favorite was the "suicide job." This was exactly what the name implied—cleaning up after a suicide. It was an unpleasant chore that usually started with a phone call from the coroner.

"Good morning, Varsity, can we help you?"

"Don, this is Burt. Got a job for you."

"Ah… what kind, Burt?"

"Shotgun. What time will you be here?"

"Ten minutes."

"Check."

On this particular job Arlo was in the office, it was 14 below zero, and things were slow, so I handed him the call card, no need to tell him the nature of it. He took off and when he phoned in later, his voice was strained as he described the job. "Don't send Noel," Arlo said, "he threw up all over on the last one." "Okay, I'll come." I loaded up the van with extras and was soon at the house. The victim had, for the usual unexplainable reason, gone to the family room in the basement and shot himself in the head with a 12-gauge shotgun. The ambulance attendant had to take the body out through the lower patio window. This left a trail of blood from the room all the way around the house to the road. The coroner said that the family wanted things cleaned up and to go ahead before the rest of the family arrived.

Before we could wash the walls and ceiling, fill buckshot holes and paint, we had to scrape off pieces of flesh and other remains. Once we finished, the paint crew started. Our next problem was to figure a way to remove the trail of blood from the icy sidewalk. Because of the extreme cold, the blood was frozen solid. I unloaded our big wet-dry vacuum and Arlo filled several buckets with boiling water with a little bit of ammonia. We applied the hot water and started to scrub. The low temperature and airflow caused the residue we picked up from the sidewalk to freeze quickly inside the hose and wand. Every 20 feet or so, we had to take the hose into the house to flush the bloody slush into the bathtub. The gruesome job was completed three hours after we arrived.

We didn't relish jobs like this. They were an open checkbook for us financially, but by the time we finished, our compassion for the people involved was such that we felt it wrong to bill them at our regular rate. If I recall we billed $29 for the whole job just described—just enough to cover costs, supplies, and paints.

Another not-so-lovely experience was the grill hood vents at the restaurants and cafes that the department of health said had to be "cleaned up or closed up." The owners were generally mad at the health officials and took it out on us as we skated and slid around in those grease-laden caverns, with ammonia and "grease release" strippers running down our arms and necks. Most of the owners were merciful enough to close down the kitchen a day for the purpose, but some didn't, and scraping and scrubbing grease over the top of a hot stove and a 295-pound thoroughly tattooed chef was a stimulating experience indeed.

As a young businessman working mostly for women, I did occasionally get some flirtation and admiration from some of them, which of course always does a little something for your ego. One evening, trying to impress my wife as to what a rare find she had in me for a husband, I commented that a woman we worked for had hinted that we might take a roll on the carpet before I shampooed it. My wife quickly said, "If you were any man at all you would never let yourself get in a position to be asked." A great chop of truth and well-deserved observation!

In fact, jokes and speculations about the additional services sometimes provided by the milkman, handyman, appliance repairman or anyone working in homes while husbands are away have always been greatly exaggerated. We worked hard to maintain a clean reputation in a "dirty" business. I enforced clean-cut conduct in our company at all times, and I'm sure it is one of the things that contributed to our reputation and success.

One of the worst things I ever experienced as a maintenance man occurred during a house-painting job for a Mrs. Willis. We had worked for this woman before—she was a good customer and had boundless confidence in us. She wanted several rooms of her house painted this time. Arlo and two other of our best men and I took on the job.

When we arrived, we found that almost everything in the house had been moved out to the garage. The house was bare except for three things: an enormous china closet with an oval glass door, a huge mirror, and a small pet monkey in a cage. (Yes, a real, live, shrieking monkey!) The china closet, she explained, was so heavy that she just wanted us to move it away from the wall and paint around it. She pointed out that it contained valuable antiques, including precious dishware, stunning goblets and pitchers, magnificent platters, plates with coats of arms and gold trim, silver salt and pepper shakers, etc.—a spectacular collection.

Arlo and I carefully took down the big mirror and set it out in the garage, mixed the paint, and the job began. We were painting the living room and soon reached the wall that the china cabinet blocked, so we prepared to move the 7-foot-high treasure. It was heavy so we moved it very slowly about 6 feet away from the wall, and then went back to work. A minute later, I heard a squeaking, creaking noise and turned to see the large, heavy door of the cabinet swing open. Unbeknownst to us, years before, the front leg of the three-legged cabinet had been broken and after it was repaired that leg was a little shorter than the other two. So when the door swung open, the unit was top heavy and it pitched forward and poured everything out onto the hardwood floor. By the time Arlo and I got to the closet, it was empty and almost everything formerly in it was broken. It took four big boxes to gather up all of the remains of the once priceless collection. We were tempted for a moment to turn the monkey loose and blame him.

Then I had to call Mrs. Willis. She was at her daughter's house next door, and was soon in deep despair over what happened, blaming herself for not telling us about the bad leg on this heirloom. We carried liability insurance, but as she said, there was no way insurance could replace the shattered heirlooms. It was a day of gloom and we did several hundred dollars worth of extra things to try and compensate for what we couldn't help but feel was at least partly our fault.

At ten that evening the paint was dry and we moved everything back into the house. When we went to the garage to get the precious mirror off the couch on which we had so carefully placed it, it had slipped down (with the help of some little neighbor boys playing cowboy in there) against some nearby chair legs. I was afraid to turn the mirror over, and my fears were justified—it was broken.

That was more than I could take. This, too, wasn't our fault, but like the closet, we were there and handled it, and should have kept an eye on it. I went out to a phone booth and called the owner of the glass store in town. "Hi, John—have you got an 84-by-48-inch mirror?" "I do have one exactly that size, an expensive lifetime Fuller mirror." "I want it!" "I'm sorry, Don, but I ordered that for Mrs. Van Snoot and she's waited two months for it."

Taking a big breath, I said, "Tell Mrs. Van Snoot two janitors' lives are at stake—it's a moral emergency!" He still refused, until I finally threatened to not buy any more paint from him. I raced to the store and got the mirror and he ordered another for Lady Van Snoot. The new mirror was exactly the same size as the old one and so we thought that after the day's turmoil we wouldn't say anything right now, just hang it up.

"Oh my," Mrs. Willis said smiling, "That is the most beautiful I've ever seen my mirror look—how did you do it?" So we confessed the second incident. "Oh, you didn't have to do that, boys—it wasn't your fault!" Mrs. Willis never filed an insurance claim and was a continuing customer, but I've never been able to blot from my memory the horrible sound of that beautiful collection breaking. We left that job with a lesson in graciousness unmatched—how could anyone be so kind after a visit from the three stooges plus an extra?

So went the agony and ecstasy of our lives. To the outsider, I was a successful college student businessman; most of the local business-people knew and respected me, and relatives were proud of me and my reputation of being the All-American success story. Several newspapers carried stories about our business, and to the public and even some of our employees I had an enviable station in life.

But between the lines, things weren't quite what they seemed. Getting ahead in the janitorial business back in the late 1950s and early '60s was not easy to do. In-house operations were not sold on contracting out their cleaning. When hard times hit my employees, I played the role of "big daddy." When an employee's car needed repair, I'd loan him a company car and many times even pay for the gas to help him out. When there was no work available, I would often let one of my workers do an unscheduled job around the shop so that he could make some money to feed the kids. As a result, we weren't making much of a profit, just sustaining our families and ourselves as we worked our way through school. This in itself was quite an accomplishment but not the real purpose of a business venture.

No matter how tough things were, however, I had learned that they could be tougher, and they often were. On Christmas Eve that year, the sheriff knocked on the door and served me with a summons for a lawsuit. The woman suing us for $53,000 had fallen while two of my men were cleaning floors early one morning. This was the first, but just one of many suits to follow.

Our big overhead meant more time "tending the store" and less time for school. But I had to keep up with school and so was limited in operating the monster I had created. I wasn't always comfortable with delegation because few others seemed to have the drive and grasp of the business I had.

Barbara and I were determined to finish school, but could see that because of the demands of the business, I would have to continue to take a limited class load. This would mean a long time before getting the old sheepskin. I finally decided not to let the tail wag the dog and cut back the Varsity work and bent my back in schoolwork. Some of my supervisors had only a year more of college to finish so I leased a truck and some of the equipment to them and let them carry out the majority of the daily jobs. I then registered for 19 credit hours (16 was the recommended maximum load). Somehow, I managed to play ball, too, that spring. I was older (26) than most of the players and was strong and settled, and thus was called to pitch in almost every game. I was on the debate team as well. While all of this was tremendously enjoyable, it took a lot of energy. Serving several masters takes its toll, and there was no exception to this rule for me.

Amid this flurry of activity, several financial setbacks occurred. I had been carrying many thousands of dollars on the books in receivables and was careless in managing them, being overly trusting. One morning I woke up and found that we had financial problems. Three big receivables had become impossible to collect. They were insurance jobs, and the checks for the work were made payable to the insured. I failed to get my money from them when it came in and the money was spent. Two of the accounts were close to a thousand dollars, the other $781. That was a lot of money to lose suddenly, especially when the milk bill was past due and equipment payments were due. To make things worse I bought $2,000 worth of chemicals (wax, disinfectant, and the like) and had it delivered to our poorly heated shop. An early frost one night, and my failure to check the heater, cost me the entire $2,000 inventory, and I still had to pay for it.

April 15th rolled around, and I owed several thousand dollars in taxes. We could see no way out—none of the men had any money to help out, and the bank wouldn't loan a janitor/student any money, since we had nothing but used vacuums and old vehicles for collateral. Determined and committed, I came home, washed and polished up our big, beautiful red Pontiac station wagon (easily worth $2,800), drove it down to a lot, and sold it for $1,800, wholesale price. With that and some money I had managed to collect I paid my debts and taxes and had $67 left. I walked to a Western Auto store and bought a three-speed bicycle.

I had no trucks, for they were with my supervisors, so the bike was it, my only mode of transportation. We went without a car for several months. Once in a while, I could grab one of the old cleaning vans in between jobs to get groceries.

Barbara and I were discouraged by the situation we suddenly found ourselves in, but not for long. When we got a few dollars ahead, we went back down to Western Auto and bought Barbara a bike too.

What a fun, close summer we had! We were short on cash but for the first time in years, we had time to use the facilities of the university after our last class. At three o'clock we would load the babies on the back of the bikes and pedal the three miles to the gym and swim for two hours, come home, play with the kids, and study. I still worked the telephone account and other jobs, and this paid the bills.

We even took the first vacation in our lives. We had little money, but we did have two weeks between summer school and the next semester. Barbara's parents wanted to take the kids for a while, so Barbara and I, with $13 cash, started out for the Idaho Primitive Area, the Sawtooth Mountains, and the River of No Return, on our bikes. We packed light, with tennis shoes for wading and walking, sleeping bags, and fishing rods.

We rode 78 miles the first day and about did ourselves in. We carried no food except margarine for frying, one can of stew, and some potatoes. We stopped on the Wood River the first day, where it took us 30 minutes to learn to walk again. Our plans were to live on fish caught out of the streams, and Wood River was one of the prettiest fly-fishing streams around. Soon seven nice fresh rainbows were sizzling in the aluminum foil (our only

A PICTURE I TOOK OF BARBARA DURING OUR BICYCLING ADVENTURE TO THE SALMON RIVER COUNTRY, THE SAWTOOTH MOUNTAINS, AND THE IDAHO PRIMITIVE AREA.

cooking utensil). The beauty of the whole adventure was we didn't have to stay in a crowded, littered, trodden-down campground. We'd just carry our bikes out to an island in the stream and camp, alone and totally undisturbed. It beat any motel by far.

During the next few days, we fished the Salmon River, panned for gold, and rode mile after mile along the Salmon River, several hundred miles in all. The day we turned to head home, we were at the site of the old Sunbeam Dam in Yankee Fork country, and it was 98 degrees, to our amazement, in that mountain area.

We decided to travel back at night, via a shortcut called the Spar Canyon cutoff, because we wanted to cover as many miles as possible before that desert sun rose the next day. Thus we pedaled through a ghostly valley surrounded by steep cliffs, full of bats and eerie growths of bushes and trees. We'd also heard from an old-timer that it was cougar country. When we woke up the next morning we were sure someone had transported us to Death Valley during the night. Compared to the lush green forest, mountains, and streams of the day before, this looked like the Sahara.

After many hot, dry, thirsty miles over sharp rocks, ruts, gullies, and the remains of an old pioneer road, we finally reached the north face of Hill Creek Summit and had to get to the south side to be on the way home, still about a hundred miles away. The three-mile push up to the summit was sheer torture, especially since we were out of water and there were big soda pop trucks roaring by on the highway. We tried to flag them down but they smiled, waved back, and disappeared down the road. So far we had pushed, walked, and ridden over 60 miles of the roughest Idaho mountains and roads imaginable. I promised Barbara we'd make it to Sun Valley that night. Sun Valley was still 30 miles away and we were at a 9,000-foot elevation. It was getting dark and we had to descend Trail Creek Summit, which was about ten miles above Sun Valley. We arrived at the top of the mountain at ten o'clock and it was pitch black. We could hear Trail Creek over the cliff thousands of feet below.

"We aren't going to go down this, are we, Don?"

"Sure, easy as pie."

"No!"

"Oh come on, Honey, we'll have a big steak and a salad."

"NO!"

I thought about telling a cougar story or two to motivate her, but she finally yielded and down we went. We were crazy with heat and hunger and our faces were baked with sunburn (we didn't smell too good, either). At eleven o'clock we pulled into the old mining town of Ketchum, Idaho, and had our steak. My lips were so blistered I couldn't eat the salad. It was an easy 60 miles home the next morning; peddling against a hard headwind was easy, compared to the previous day's experience. What a vacation!

A senior at last!

Being a 27-year-old, well-known entrepreneur senior student had its advantages. Word had circulated through the entire teaching staff (greatly exaggerated, I'm sure) that there was an up-and-coming businessman aboard, and any class I landed in I was treated well. Some teachers would apologize for giving me a B- when I deserved a C-. They were impressed that many of their other students worked for Don Aslett.

When I reentered college as a sophomore after my mission I had left the graphic arts program because this course of study unfortunately seemed to be more about printing than writing. I decided then to concentrate on taking courses that interested and educated me rather than ones that prepared me to make a living. Most people assumed my major now was business or speech. But it was in the area that seemed to give the best opportunity for influencing lives directly—athletic coaching. When I graduated, I qualified for a degree in athletic coaching, and teaching in secondary school.

I was required to take a wrestling class as part of this course of study, and the contestants were paired by weight. I was 170 pounds and matched against another 170-pounder, a 22-year-old who had an Arnold Schwarzenegger physique—bulging muscles and almost no neck. He looked undefeatable to me, and I'm sure I looked spindly. But after milking cows for most of my young life, I had a vice grip. Once I clamped onto his wrists and ankles, the bout was over in seconds. He was amazed, and I never mentioned that the cows deserved the credit.

My last baseball game in my senior year was against Montana State at Bozeman, a double header. I was glad the season was coming to an end. I had four children now, numerous employees, and was working twelve or fourteen-hour days. For practice I ran stairs in the field house (leg strength is key to pitching). Coach Hayes tossed the ball to me before game time and said, "It's your final day on the mound—make it a good one!" The day was perfect, and if you have been to Montana you know why it is called the "Big Sky" state. The sky was crystal blue and went on forever, the grass was the intense green of spring, and the baselines were like gleaming white ribbons. And yes, I put the new baseball up to my face to smell it just like I did back in the sixth grade and felt my stomach tighten—15 years later, it was still just as exciting.

I stepped onto the mound, and the ball felt like it shot out of my hand. I struck out the first six batters, and in the third inning, the first man up tried to bunt to get on base. He popped the ball up in my direction and I dived and caught it, but hit the ground so hard it jarred me enough to walk two batters in a row. One more reached base on an error. So the bases were loaded and a big kid named Knislow came to bat. Sometimes a pitcher just knows a good hitter by his stance, and he stood like Ted Williams. I threw three straight balls, then looking at those loaded bases and not wanting to risk walking a run, I threw the next ball right down the heart of the strike zone. Apparently no one had ever clued this fellow in that "Nobody ever swings at a 3-and-0 pitch." He swung, and when I looked up the ball looked like a BB, a mile high. It cleared the centerfield fence at 420 feet, landing a good 50 feet beyond it. That was spectacular, and he came around third I ran over and shook his hand. Even though the coach told me later, "We don't do that in baseball," I was glad I did. That was the last pitch I ever threw as a uniformed athlete, and my last game was worth every minute.

Education has to end

After two heavy semesters and a full summer school load, there was only a last light semester between my diploma and me. I had completed 47 semester hours that year, including some graduate credits, and needed only to complete practice teaching to have my Bachelor of Arts degree sewed up. So I thought.

An audit of my transcripts found that a required freshman course, Government 101, was missing. It was taught at the exact time I was practice teaching, and I groaned at the thought of yet another semester just for one three-credit-hour course. Thankfully, the teacher was kind enough to allow my wife to attend the course for me until I finished practice teaching. It worked out beautifully, and the only unsettling thing was a sweet feminine voice answering the roll for Don Aslett.

My minor was in speech, and since I was still in school anyway that fall, I took some more graduate courses in it, because I found the field interesting. I conducted lab work, audiological testing, and speech screening. The university had received a grant in speech and hearing and Dr. Vaughn, director of the clinic, offered me an opportunity for a scholarship to get my doctorate, saying they needed progressive ideas and a businessperson's strength in the field if it was ever to gain the recognition it deserved. I was flattered and tempted, but the vision of what I wanted and my thirst for the independence of self-employment induced me to refuse the offer, something for which I was never sorry.

I was also on ISU's championship debate team that semester. This was my final year of debate and oratory and I enjoyed it greatly.

Barbara and I had been without an automobile for several months when I finally talked the bankers into helping me buy a 1959 Chevy panel wagon for $800. They hemmed and hawed and looked down their glasses, but finally loaned me the money. We were an average American family again! We owned a car.

Chapter 7

FINDING PARADISE

Yes, you can take the boy out of the farm,
but never the farm out of the boy!

OUR RANCH IN MCCAMMON, IDAHO, OVERLOOKING A BEAUTIFUL
GREEN VALLEY NESTLED BETWEEN TWO 8,000-FOOT MOUNTAINS.

While work, school, church activities, and family life had been running their rapid course, my childhood and teen memories never left me, and I felt the urge to return to some of the pure and good things I'd had as a boy. Barbara and I sat up a few evenings and made a checklist of the qualities a place should have to be the perfect location to live, raise our kids, and build a new home.

We wanted to stay in Idaho, live in a healthy environment, have full access to church activities, animals, and sports activities for the kids, and to have schools and universities, and our aging parents, all within a reasonable distance. We fed all this information into our

locations checklist. When we compared our list to the map, two towns came up, Hailey and McCammon, Idaho. McCammon was a small one-gas-station, one-store village 25 miles south of Pocatello. After many hours of my spare time combing the area, I found a place we liked at Robber's Roost (from Zane Grey's stories) right on the old Wells Fargo Line road. But the owners wouldn't sell at any price. So we put an ad in the paper, "Home and shop in Pocatello to trade for acreage at McCammon, Idaho." Result: We found a 60-acre paradise.

The property was in an agricultural area only ten miles from Lava Hot Springs, where my father had been raised. The land overlooked a beautiful green valley with a wandering stream, set between two enormous 8,000-foot mountains. The cedar and juniper trees and jagged rock set off a big, beautiful sky full of clean air. There were fresh springs full of watercress and a garden spot with deep, dark, rich soil.

There was no house on the property, only an old log cabin said to have been built by outlaws in the 1880s, a well house, and some dilapidated barns. We traded our college home straight across with a couple who wanted to move to the city for health reasons, and on New Year's Day 1963, we owned the property.

Most of my young life was spent out on the plains of southern Idaho, level land full of lava rocks and sagebrush. It was fertile, but you had to irrigate if you wanted anything green, or crops to grow. We could see the mountains some 50 miles to the north, and when we traveled there to fish or camp the contrast had a big impact on me. How I loved the mountains—majestic, rugged, jagged, and pine-covered, with ice-cold creeks running out of them. When I went out with my fly rod on the rivers or creeks, alone, no one around for miles, I felt like I was the only one in the world and owned it all. I could comprehend eternity here, and hear the sounds of the pines and birds and water. I stored this up and fed on it all my life. The mountains were one thing that never lost savor for me, no matter how old or busy I was.

In January 1963, I finally got my degree. Going to college while being married, running a large business, and having a family—sticking to it in the midst of all this—taught me even more than I learned in my classes. My father (Mother came to my graduation too, of course) got to see one of his children graduate from college. It was worth it!

"DON ASLETT SPENT A RECORD SIX YEARS AS AN UNDERGRADUATE AT THE UNIVERSITY. NOT BECAUSE HE WAS A SLOW LEARNER, BUT BECAUSE HE WAS FOUNDING A SERVICE INDUSTRY 'EMPIRE' AT THE SAME TIME."
—IDAHO STATE JOURNAL

When I graduated we had little money, but had paid our "tuition" in the business world and acquired four things more important to success than even our education or degree. We had:

1. Experience, seasoning, and skills;
2. A good reputation;
3. Established customers, especially the Bell System;
4. Family.

We already had a good start in life.

As soon as I graduated, although we had a big new house in mind for our new property, we decided to move into the small well house there now. That January was record cold. On January 15 I traveled to Denver for one last university debate. It was 40 below zero in Laramie, Wyoming, when we went through. I called Barbara and she had sent the kids to their grandmother's while she prepared for the move.

The next week all six of us moved into the 12-by-16-foot well house. Setting up housekeeping here was hard after the nice home we had in Pocatello. We had to stack up the kids in bunk beds and use a couch for our bed. As Arlo put it, our new dwelling was "the only home in the world where you

WE MOVED OUR WHOLE FAMILY AND OUR KEY POSSESSIONS INTO A WELL HOUSE ON OUR NEW PROPERTY IN MCCAMMON.

can answer the door and cook breakfast while sitting on the toilet." He wasn't exaggerating, either. But we were HOME!

Barbara was pregnant with our fifth child now and living in the well house (which we did for six months) was indeed an experience to forget. When the irrigation pump engaged it rattled the spoons on the table and would wake us all up during the night. The beautiful spring made up for the challenges of living there.

Barbara's turn

Barbara would return to her own studies at the university in the summer. She was still a junior, having cut back on her school schedule due to her involvement in the business and raising our large family. I've never believed that a wife is obligated to work to put her husband through school. A woman is more entitled to a degree and an education than a man. Mak-

BARBARA FINISHED EARNING HER DEGREE IN 1965.

ing a living is easy. If a man has any gumption, if he hustles at all, he can make a living. A degree isn't necessary for that. But a mother has children to raise and that takes all the intelligence and learning you can muster.

Barbara attended school for the next couple of years between mixing cement for me and keeping house. She received her Bachelor of Arts degree as an honor roll student in education in 1965, with the six children we had by then beside her.

Arlo and I still had several telephone buildings and a few other contracts going, so we had some income from the business we had built getting through college. Although developing the McCammon property and running our telephone accounts took some work, for me it was like a day off. I kept the books and tightened things up in order to give good service and spent most of two months at home. I tore down several old barns, saving the wood (ten years later I used it to panel our kitchen in barnwood). I removed about 70 old railroad ties as well and built a 100-foot long barn, entirely out of the lumber I salvaged out of old buildings. I loved the place: all the geese and cranes and wild animals (one day even a moose dropped by).

We had designed a large house for the ranch, and one of my student janitors, an architecture major, drew up the plans and we were ready to build it ourselves. I had helped build a new church during the previous year and was confident that Barbara and I could do it. Two local builders short of work dropped by, looked at the plans, and said that for $8,700 they would construct the center section, enough to live in while we finished the rest. The same day I got a call from the local school district, saying they needed a special education teacher for the next four months. The principal said it would count as one year toward teaching tenure, and since I had taken some graduate courses in audiology and speech therapy, I was qualified.

It seemed to make sense financially and otherwise to put my degree in use while two carpenters started the new house. I did help with the work on the house in my time off, with the goal of moving into a completed center section before we brought our fifth child home from the hospital.

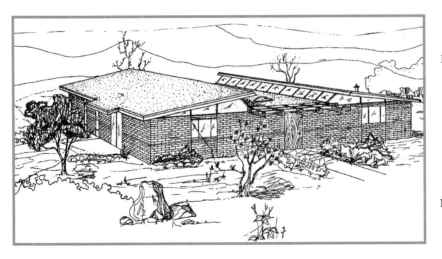

MY ORIGINAL DESIGN FOR OUR McCAMMON HOME WAS DRAWN UP BY ONE OF MY JANITORS, A STUDENT OF ARCHITECTURE NAMED MANUEL MUNOZ.

You might say it was a tie. I was about to install the last side door, closing the house in securely from the elements at last, when I received a call that it was time to go pick up Mother and our new daughter Cindy from the hospital. I dropped my tools and whipped into town. During my absence, our giant Holstein cow entered the opening for the still-unhung door, walked to the middle of the front room, and dropped a huge cow pie, which splashed all over. Powerful stuff! I cleaned it off the floor (which fortunately was tiled) and the walls, but it stained the walls. Even after all of the new coats of paint that have followed, I swear I can still see those spots.

When we bought the farm only two things had come with it—this Holstein cow about to calve, and an old John Deere tractor parked up on the hill. Being a farm boy and FFA cow judge, I knew the cow was as good as its departing owners claimed (people have been known to stretch the truth about cow power). The cow lived up to and beyond all expectations. Her calf weighed 125 pounds at birth rather than the usual 85 or so. Every time I milked the cow it took an hour and she filled two buckets—twice the milk any of our Guernseys ever gave. That was pure labor, and what does a family do with six gallons of milk twice a day? Once you have a cow you must be home every morning and evening—cow care took two hours a day. I could earn $15 an hour cleaning, so this meant that milk for our little family was costing us $30 a day, plus hay.

I finally traded the cow for a huge 5-by-8-foot plate glass window for our new house.

After the carpenters finished the center section, Barbara and I built the rest of the house, constructed largely of masonry and strong wood

A VIEW OF OUR RANCH HOME FROM THE POND IN THE BACKYARD.

WINTER FROM THE SAME VIEW AT "ASLETT ACRES."

beams. Sometimes we'd work until two in the morning together, never getting tired (or at least never realizing it till later). The house when finished was large—over 4,500 square feet—but not luxurious. Later we added a "penthouse" guest room at the top, and an office. The house at that point was over 6,000 square feet, with seven bedrooms.

We didn't think a home should be a shrine for show or treasure storage, a place too fancy to live in. A house is nothing in itself; it is only a structure within which to develop love, raise children, and build a great relationship with your husband or wife, the others you care about, and the community.

We designed and built our home to provide the things a home is supposed to give a family—a place to be together and be comfortable, and have fun. We didn't design our yard and landscaping just to look good; instead, we figured out the best ways to create places for hide and seek and other exciting pastimes for our children, their friends, and our eventual grandchildren. We built ponds for rafting, sloped hills for running and climbing and sledding. We didn't put a basketball hoop in the parking area for our cars; we laid out the basketball court and then found a way to park our cars in it. We built a playhouse in the yard and ball fields, and had a merry-go-round set up most of the time, or a dunking machine. We planted the kinds of trees best for swings, tree houses, and climbing instead of shade and decoration. None of this was by accident. We planned it that way and then worked to bring it to reality.

OUR IDEA OF DECORATION, FOR BOTH HOME AND OFFICE, IS MEANINGFUL FAMILY AND OTHER PERSONAL PHOTOS AND MEMENTOS OF IMPORTANT EVENTS IN OUR LIVES.

Inside, we didn't decorate with paintings or statues, but with pictures of the family and mementoes and awards from our family's notable moments and achievements. Our homes were never finished; our McCammon house was built and improved over a period of 20 years, as we could afford it, and there was always a room or project being built or remodeled somewhere (and we're still at it). Because of this, all our children learned how to be adaptable, flexible, and unimpressed by plushness. The biggest asset was that both of the boys and some of our daughters left home knowing how to build, paint, wire, plumb, and decorate. Our two sons, by the time they were 18, could build a room or home by themselves.

We didn't let convention dictate how we should live—we designed our house to fit our living. We put big windows in the kitchen and small windows in the living room, because we would be in the living room only in the evening when you can't see out anyway. We knew we would be in the kitchen far more in the daytime and so built accordingly. We made sure the house was well suited for gatherings of friends, colleagues, and young people.

The first winter we didn't have a furnace in yet (though we did have a woodstove), so a bit of the 25 below zero weather would seep in, but we didn't have any sick kids. (Maybe the germs froze.) One evening, after someone who nearly got frostbite visiting us reported to our church that we were "destitute," the local clergy visited and offered us welfare, counseling us to not be "too proud" to take it. They didn't stay long (we froze 'em out) and we survived to savor our new furnace the next year.

Creative mailboxes always caught my eye. I liked someone who had more than a post in the ground, like the farmers who adapted wagon wheels, plows, or milk cans for the purpose. I saw a crankshaft on one box and knew here lived a mechanic. I was never slow in claiming or displaying my profession, so when the motor went out on a 19-inch buffer I had a primo mailbox mount. And when the snowplow hit it, it just spun around—eat your hearts out, neighbors!

The hardest work I've ever done

In the classes I taught that spring of 1963, I had "challenged" kids from eight to sixteen. I was creative and animated enough to succeed in teaching them, but the routine of it, especially having to stay at school after classes ended, from three to five o'clock (to impress the public—our principal's rule) convinced me that this would be my first and last teaching job.

I was 28, and had ten years of farm energy stored up. It was the first and only time in my life that I watched the clock instead of racing it. I had been on such a schedule of productivity for the past six years in college and business, and had so many exciting things to do on our new ranch, that those two hours of waiting for the release bell at the end of the day nearly unhinged me.

After the school year ended I launched into a wonderful summer of cleaning phone buildings all over, painting jobs, and doing some finish work on our new home. At the end of August, the phone brought me down from a roof project, and it was the principal of the local high school, asking if I would consider a teaching position there. I told him I couldn't hack the hanging around until five, and he said, "You can leave at three o'clock, beat the students out of the driveway if you want." The subject was speech, my favorite subject of all, and it sounded like an easy six-hour day with good income and tenure, so I said "yes." Within days, I found myself teaching three freshman speech classes and (surprise!) three English classes—one junior class in English literature, and two senior English classes. All my life I had trouble with English—I wouldn't even attempt to diagram a sentence, and didn't know a dangling participle from an unclear antecedent. I barely squeaked through high school and college English, and now I was an English teacher! To make it worse, most of the students had had an English teacher the year before who easily qualified for "English teacher of the world."

Those were days of anxiety. As each lesson came up, I would read ahead, study at home with an intensity I never knew I had in me, and then show up with several creative, off-the-wall approaches to teaching, making clear to my students things never made clear to me. The classes were fun (I could entertain people even with an English book), but I never felt secure.

The many telephone facilities Arlo and I were servicing nights and Saturdays were a pleasant change from and complement to my teaching duties. Not all of our experiences here were equally nice, however.

We had contracted an important Bell building in Jackson Hole, Wyoming, about 150 miles from Pocatello. It was a small building but in our growing relationship with the phone company, it was an important one—our first in Wyoming. Finding help in Jackson was next to impossible. There were jobs galore with good wages and much more prestige than being a janitor. We would hire and train people, and within a few weeks (or days), they would quit. We would repeat the process, and the person would work until a better job popped up in town, and then quit.

Arlo stayed in Jackson three days, cleaned the building himself, and tried to hire someone—nothing! The gross take on the building was $145 per month, so you can imagine the money we were losing, but we couldn't chance giving up the building. Since I was still teaching and Arlo had graduated and was now working full-time as a pharmacist, we both had to be in Pocatello daily, so that meant traveling 300 miles every night for 45 minutes of work. It was mid-January, and the roads were icy and treacherous—mile after mile of twisting roads along cliffs with the South Fork of the Snake River far below. We would leave at nine in the evening and drive for hours, skidding and slipping over icy passes, arrive at the building, clean it as quickly as we could, and head back. We would arrive home at five or six o'clock in the morning in time to go to work again. We discussed busi-

ARLO, NOT LONG AFTER THE INK ON HIS DIPLOMA IN PHARMACY WAS DRY.

ness on these trips and whoever wasn't driving even got a few winks of sleep. We did this for two full weeks, every night except Sunday, until we finally were able to hire someone. It was a nightmare but necessary to honor our contract and commitment to the telephone company. It had to be done at any cost and we did it. We had many situations similar to this over the course of our "Bell" days.

Our Wyoming presence was far less than what we wanted—it would be nine years before we had a meaningful presence there.

In the mid-1960s, when appearing on the media was really something, we got news that our newly hired secretary, Kathy, was one of the finalists for Miss Idaho and was going to be interviewed on the radio. Although she'd only been working for us for a couple of weeks, we were proud and the entire crew assembled at the office to listen. We envisioned a good plug of solid publicity for our enthusiastic little cleaning operation. There must have been a breakdown in our company training program, however. Here's how it went:

"Well, Kathy, it's good to have you on the show today. It must be exciting to be one of the finalists for Miss Idaho. Do you have a job?" asked the host.

"Yes."

"Who do you work for?"

"For Varsity Contractors."

"Great, and just what does Varsity Contractors do?"

"Uh, ah… I don't know what they do."

All of us listening moaned, and a few rolled on the floor.

Another time a bright-eyed, eager young woman joined our busy (and very informal) office as a secretary. It all had to be a little overwhelming, a consideration I always paid too little attention to—telling someone to just "do" things was more my style. When I couldn't remember a first or last name on the draft of a letter, I would address the intended recipient "Dear Horsebreath," figuring that like my wife or the experienced secretaries she could find the real name in the file.

Two days later, reviewing copies of recent letters, I found a perfectly typed one addressed to (gasp!) "Horsebreath Williams." Surely she wouldn't, she didn't… I ran to her desk, "You didn't mail this, did you?" "Oh yes, Mr. Aslett," she said in an innocent and obedient voice, "I typed it up carefully just like you wrote it." It was done, so why get upset. It ended up a cherished memory and a real bond between us, and no, Mr. Williams never said anything.

The logger boot caper

As I designed and planned for the expansion of Varsity, I was determined to cut costs and nonproductive time. One sudden stroke of brilliance here almost cost me my life.

Cedar shingle roofs were popular in our part of the country, but they needed to be maintained. This was usually done by applying a mixture of linseed oil and graphite. A bag of black graphite dust was mixed with linseed oil and left overnight. The next morning, after the dew was gone from the roof, a couple of us would climb up with buckets and brushes and dip into the mixture and work it into the roof. It didn't take long to apply the material but getting the ladder, roof jacks, and other equipment in place on the roof was time consuming. We would generally hook an extension ladder over the peak of the roof to hang on to and use as a stairway as we applied the coating, moving the ladder as we worked our way across the roof.

We always wore tennis shoes for good traction, because graphite is one of the slickest substances known to man, and combined with oil, it made for treacherous treading. Once some of the mixture got on your shoes, the honeymoon was over and you began worrying about your life—the steeper the roof, the bigger the risk.

A new invention came out about this time called the "airless" spray gun. This could spray a strong stream of material over a 3-foot span, and cover an unbelievable amount of area quickly. If a way to maneuver around on a roof faster could be found, this would be a big boost to the profit column. For weeks I thought about it, conjuring up everything from helicopters to 60-foot poles, but nothing seemed really practical until… sure, why not? Some spike-soled logging boots! If lumberjacks could leap around on bobbing logs in the water with them, I should be able to perform like Fred Astaire on a pitched roof, and finish one in an hour instead of the seven or eight it ordinarily took.

When I rushed to town to pick up a pair, I discovered that not every store carried such things. In fact, none of them did. In Montgomery Ward one day I asked the shoe salesman if by any chance he knew where I could secure a pair of logging boots. "Why, yes, Sir, I do, in fact I have a pair right here." He left and came back with a big box. "We never carry these but someone ordered them and then never returned for them." Out they came, and they were beauts—genuine calf-rump leather 14 inches high with a sole armed with neat rows of long, sharp spikes. They were priced at $150 but he would sell them to me for $60 (even though the boots were size 11 and I wore a 9). I walked out of the store whistling, "Bring on the roof!"

In less than a week, my song was answered when a large church in Downey, Idaho, asked us to graphite and oil their roof. Like an athlete dressing for the game of his career, I carefully (with four pair of socks) slipped on my prize boots. They gave me a feeling of power as I crunched across the lawn and started up the ladder. First one step on the roof, and then another, and another, and such a steep roof! I was ecstatic; my brilliant invention was working! I grabbed the airless gun, tromped across the shingles like a Swiss mountaineer, and began to spray, calculating that I'd have the whole $250 job done in two hours.

I was at the height of my glory for at least ten minutes with my trusty spikes gripped into the shingles, and the crew on the ground was cheering. There was, however, a flaw in the engineering of the situation. The soles had to be flat on the roof for the spikes to make contact, so I had to bend at my ankles to the pitch of the roof. This was difficult as the boots were high and stiff, and as my ankles weakened, the spikes lost contact, and the steel-hard leather of the sole edges made contact with the graphite instead. As gravity took over, the sides of the boots hitting and my fingernails trying to dig into the evenly spaced shingles made a nice *clickety-clack* in perfect rhythm, and stopped only when I sailed off the two-story roof. I would have died with my boots on, but providence was kind. After a fall of only seven feet, I landed on the flat roof of the entry, unharmed. (Slipping off anywhere else would have meant a two-story drop.)

I unlaced my marvelous discoveries and donated them to the next garage sale.

A convicted criminal: The State of Idaho vs. Don A. Aslett

Keith Hall and David Johnson were both fine young men, and full of energy and fun. Through the summer of 1965 we laughed, played, and worked hard together, and a great friendship developed between us. Both boys were leaders in school and the community. The two of them had driven to a small farm town with me on Labor Day to finish a painting job prior to the start of school. Heading home, we passed a lot where the state highway department had left several pieces of heavy equipment parked. As we drove by, David quipped, "Boy, Mr. Aslett, that's just what you need to level the road on your new ranch!" (He was referring to a big yellow road grader sitting on the lot). "It sure is," joined in Keith. I answered that there was no chance in the world of hiring a state road grader for a private road, and forgot about the whole thing.

Six hours later, as I was working in our yard, I spotted a big yellow grader coming across the valley. I knew it couldn't be, but…. When the grader slowed up at my gate and turned in, I knew it was! I ran to the gate waving my arms in alarm and sure enough, there sat the two faithful Varsity men, in their white uniforms with a big Varsity emblem on the front. "Are you guys crazy?" I yelled. "Get that thing out of here!" "Oh, don't worry, Mr. Aslett, it's in good hands," and they lowered the blade with great glee and began to grade the lane leading from the road to my house. I learned later that they had fixed a flat tire on the machine, hot-wired it, and drove it over the interstate more than two miles to my house. I pleaded with the two pranksters to return the dirt-moving demon and they, at the height of their glory, assured me that they would take all responsibility for it and take it back when they were done.

After a few passes up and down the road (which they left in far worse shape than it had been), they pulled around the front of the house to make a pass over the front yard. There was a big hole there and they hit it. The front wheel dropped into the pit up to the axle, but unaware of this, they shifted the machine into reverse and backed up. A road grader has tremendous power and traction. The front wheel shifted sideways and the steering bolt snapped and the two front wheels collapsed. There sat the grader on the highest knoll in the area, unmovable.

It was a holiday so no heavy equipment places were open. Needless to say the two boys panicked, realizing there was now no way to return the "borrowed" piece of road equipment. A neighbor who hated to miss out on any kind of action drove down to see if he could help. He provided a large railroad bolt that was lying around his place, and in a few hours, the wheels were restored to a less than perfect alignment. Keith and David couldn't get the grader out of the yard quick enough now, and soon it was limping down the road, with the two front wheels tilting awkwardly inward and leaving a trail of black rubber on the road from my gate back to the state parking lot.

Two days later, up the lane came the county sheriff. He got out of his car and shuffled over to the front yard on which there were large cleat tracks and pieces of yellow, broken parts scattered here and there. "Don, the State of Idaho has reported a road grader stolen and damaged. I heard reports it was out here." I told him the story and he said, "Well, no problem." He talked to the boys, who were then charged with stealing the grader and were to appear in court. I was to attend also, not on charges but to plead for leniency for the boys. When the day came, there sat their mothers, weeping; their innocent boys (neither of whom had ever been in trouble before in their lives) standing before the judge. They were sentenced to make a donation to a boys' ranch and some other things in lieu of a heavy fine, as the judge didn't consider this a malicious premeditated act.

I drove back to my teaching job, relieved that it was all over. Little did I know that my road grader problems had just begun. Two weeks later, I received a call on the intercom during fourth period English class. "Don," a voice on the other end said, "This is Jack [the sheriff]. I've just been handed a warrant for your arrest from the State of Idaho. Shall I come down and get you or do you want to stop by?" Not anxious to expose my students to any hint of criminal activities, I agreed to meet him and we went to the local judge, who read me the charges. "Don Aslett did go onto said property and remove said machine on said day, in violation of Idaho State code 125-00045982." I pleaded not guilty. The judge said a hearing would be set up and I would be contacted.

I walked out again relieved. The two district judges knew me as an honest, industrious toilet cleaner and high school teacher, and surely if I just explained the circumstances, all would be forgiven. I decided it was silly to even think of getting an attorney. I would just take Keith and David with me, and a few words from them would clear everything up. My neighbor Ernie was the manager of a savings and loan company and warned me to get an attorney, saying that anyone who represents himself has a horse's rump for a client.

I received notice that the hearing would be in my hometown of McCammon at the local judge's house, not in the Pocatello district court as I had assumed. I felt a little impulse at last to call an attorney, but dismissed the thought. The two boys and I showed up at two o'clock. The hearing was held in the living room of the judge's small, cluttered home. A soap opera was blaring away on the TV, the judge was unshaven, and his boots were untied. There were a few others there; a state policeman and a representative from the State of Idaho. The state man stood and read the charges and listed the cost of the damage.

The name Aslett was well known in the construction and road building business. My grandfather had 15 children, 11 of them boys, most of whom became associated with Grandpa Aslett in the construction field. An Aslett could run any heavy equipment made—except for me, that is. I was a farmer, teacher, and janitor. I stood and explained my side of the story carefully and ended with, "So you see, your Honor, I had nothing at all to do with it, and the boys have been tried, convicted, and punished for the crime." While I was talking and pleading, I was standing by the judge's desk, and I watched him write out: Damages $270, Fine $500, 30 days in jail.

When I sat down, the judge, without hearing from the boys or any further discussion, creaked to his feet and said, "Huh, it's easy to see that you put them up to it, and likewise you are an accessory. How could they know how to run the thing?" Being a former debate student, I tied him in a knot in a minute with questions like, "You mean to tell me Sears is guilty of that murder in Pocatello last week because they sold the gun used? If it hadn't been for Sears the guy wouldn't have shot the other guy?"

This proved to be a mistake and enraged the old gentleman. He leaped to his feet and said, "I find you guilty as charged, fine you… sentence you… etc. " I couldn't believe what I was hearing. "This is a hearing and under Idaho law a hearing can't be used to determine final guilt," I said. He roared back, "I have the jurisdiction to change this hearing to a trial and I hereby do so!" (Something like that.)

One of the boys jumped up to the rescue. The judge told him to shut up and sit down. I refused to pay and told the judge he was a ridiculous spectacle. The officer there prepared to haul me off to jail. The state policeman who was there waiting for someone else was much more versed on the law than the others, and informed them that they couldn't jail me if I posted bail. This quieted everyone down. I posted a big bail and was a free man for the day.

I left the house convicted of a felony and sentenced in the official records of the court. I contacted one of the best criminal attorneys in the area, Herman McDevitt, who had often been a guest lecturer and evaluator for my college debate team. He shook his head in disbelief and said sarcastically, "Don, with your reputation and fame, if you'd committed a nice clean rape or murder I could get you off, but this... we have a hassle coming." (Ironically Herman was then on a committee to stamp out the injustices of the small-town judges.) The case continued for a few months until the judge died of a heart attack, and not long afterward I received a letter dismissing all charges.

Keith and David paid the lawyer's fees out of their next summer's wages and it was over at last. Life just out of college and mingling with 500 high school kids was full of such adventures.

The second year of high school teaching was better. I had the lesson plans done already, so I could relax a bit. I had some top students who pushed me into studies of poems, essays, and great writers. My senior English literature classes were the best. There was never a dull one, and I was confident enough now to match wits with the kids without lording my position over them.

Teaching was a high every minute—full of challenge, humor, and a chance to learn about people. I was used to long days spent pouring cement, plowing, working on a scaffold, or cleaning floors or walls. But nothing was as exhausting as teaching. I would get home at four o'clock to my lists of exciting farm and family projects just begging to be done. But I'd fall on the couch, unable to move for hours. My wife was sure I had some debilitating disease like mono but it was sheer mental exhaustion. Teaching was

A BUSINESS PHOTO TAKEN WHEN I WAS IN MY LATE TWENTIES.

the hardest work I'd ever done—how do teachers do it year in and year out? I admire teachers—it must be the world's noblest profession.

I loved to teach and put my full effort into any opportunity to do it. When fellow Scouts needed to learn how to do something, I was the first to volunteer. My two years as a missionary in Hawaii were a time of almost total teaching, everyone from Philippine migrant workers to heads of sugar cane and pineapple operations. On the job, I was constantly teaching cleaning and management skills to my new workers. I also taught at many church youth gatherings and workshops, always delighting in finding a better and more creative way to get the message across.

I carried my independence with me to school. I never set foot in the teachers' lounge. In my off hours (before school started, lunch, and my "prep" hour), I stayed in my classroom and visited with students.

One day my turn came on one of the "extra" jobs teachers had to do, monitoring the lunch line to prevent pushing and crowding. It was a trying job, as I didn't know all the students' names and half the community were Harrises, Halls, Bullocks, or Marleys. Plus the students were not slow in the old slight-of-foot game of inching to the front. I hated that job.

When it came time for me to eat, I stood at the end of the line. Students and then faculty members quickly informed me that teachers got to go to the front of the line (cut in). I didn't agree with this, the idea of guarding the students to prevent cutting in, and then being allowed to do that very thing myself, just because I was an adult. I stayed at the end of the line, and several faculty members came back to explain to me that I was supposed to go to the front. I told them age or position doesn't have a monopoly on hunger (plus my captain in the National Guard always let his soldiers eat first), so no thank you.

When some of the rebel students heard of this, I became their hero. Then they put the heat on the rest of the faculty to follow suit. Finally, the principal came to me and said, "You *will* go to the front of the line—you are causing an uprising." That was my last day in the lunchroom. I brought a sack lunch for the rest of my school days.

I loved teaching—many of my students became friends for life. Many later worked for me, some became my bankers, insurance agents, mechanics, grocers, etc. Some who went on to West Point and other major universities returned with a thank-you for my classroom efforts.

Later that year I was asked to coach the junior varsity basketball team. I had a coaching certification, and it was a chance to help kids develop good values and a "can do" attitude. In one pre-tournament game, my starting five were slacking off, so I benched them all and played the second string (five substitutes) the rest of the game. We lost miserably. Lesson learned? Well, not quite. That night as we all got out of the athletic bus, the top five hot dogs got together and all handed me their uniforms (figuring they would teach me a lesson). I told them a quitter is out, so think about it. They stuck to their planned protest, so they were out. They showed up to practice and I said, "Season's over, boys. You made your choice, so go on now to study hall."

After they spent three days in study hall, the head coach came to me and said, "You can't do this. These are my future varsity, and they need to be playing to get experience and develop themselves." "I'm their coach," I told him, "and they are getting experience in decision making and character development."

So they stayed off the team in study hall a while longer and suffered. Now the principal came to see me (he was getting tired of me, I'm sure) and asked why I insisted on being so strict. I asked him just one question, "Do you want to build good men and citizens or good ballplayers? What is the school's goal?" He supported me after that, and they stayed in study hall. (Interesting, but in the next 20 years all five of those boys either worked for me or became good friends.)

Spring of '65—time to decide

Just a few weeks after this I heard from Mountain Bell and Continental Telephone almost simultaneously, offering us contracts on more buildings in Utah and Idaho—something I had envisioned, and worked and planned for. It was a choice now of continuing in the teaching I was enjoying or making a bigger dream happen. It was decision-making time—the Varsity work was now too much to do part-time, so something had to go. I went for my vision and resigned my teaching job in mid-year. The school superintendent held firm to the rules of contract breaking and docked my remaining teaching paycheck soundly, then kindly said, "Well, now that you're out on your own you'll need some work." And he gave me a nice big school painting job.

I NEVER REALLY GAVE UP MY COLLEGE "CAREER" OF TEACHING, I JUST MOVED IT FROM A CLASSROOM SETTING TO THE WORLD OF COMMERCE AND THE WORLD AT LARGE.

Chapter 8

A FULL-TIME COMPANY AT LAST!

What is an entrepreneur?
...someone who thinks he's right!

WE USUALLY MANAGED TO HAVE FUN ON EVEN THE MOST TRYING OF JOBS: MARK BROWNING AND I ON JUST SUCH A JOB (SEE P. 161).

I hit life in my thirtieth year head on—started a sign painting business, a janitorial supply business, Micro-Clean Supply (see p. 447), and began to expand Varsity for the first time into a full-time operation. 1965 was really the first time that Varsity Contractors operated as a full-time company.

I began adding full-time staff, transferring my home office to an office in the city of Pocatello. I finally convinced Arlo to drop his pharmaceutical profession and come with Varsity. He shared my vision and readily joined the ranks of full-time Varsity men and as a result, business really began to take off. Some of the other people who joined me at this time would later be a great influence on my life and the company. One of these was a handsome 19-year-old ISU student from Rigby, Idaho, a plumber's son, Mark Browning. He was sharp, skilled in many things, and learned faster than others. Within months, he was one of my leading men, and a great mentor. (Forty years later, he is president of Varsity.)

Opportunity was everywhere. We weren't lacking initiative or creativity and not only answered our customers' demands but developed many new avenues in the industry. We took on and expanded every niche the telephone or insurance companies gave us. We worked hard— I mean hard—not just 8-hour days but 12, 16, and sometimes even 18 hours or all night too. We always worked fast and the word for the day was "hustle." We found that Varsity's size, attitude, and flexibility were valuable and learned to market this to the right people.

Within a month or two, we were grossing many thousands of dollars and had contracts for the Bell System in the Boise area and other parts of southern Idaho, and Utah. We rented a shop in Pocatello, bought some more used trucks, painted and lettered them, and were going full steam by spring.

This doesn't mean that everything just fell into place, and clients and customers just sprang up at the right time to fulfill all of our needs. This was far from the truth. Every time we began a new area or looked for more work in an area that we had gotten a start in, we were just like a group of Yellowstone Park bears, pawing and sniffing through the garbage cans in the parking area, looking for a morsel of food.

Our established competitors seemed to always be just a step ahead of us as they tried to convince the businesses in the area to ignore the "small-time Idaho janitor operation from out of town." But we were more like those bears than anyone knew, for once we started after a bit of business we didn't give up—we scrounged, snarled, and hung in there until we hit the first solid scrap of opportunity. Sometimes a $3,000 month start grew to $12,000 within a few months, and sometimes it was much slower. But once we committed we held, no matter what the cost or the consequences, even through unfortunate bids and meager profits.

Again now, I tried to expand the company's territory by moving Mark Browning to manage our Idaho Falls operation. We had some struggles, but gained valuable contacts and a good reputation in Idaho Falls and the Jackson Hole/Teton area.

Expanding a business, on paper or in your mind, is so simple and fun you can hardly stand it. Just pick a place, hire some people, order a telephone, print up some business cards, and presto, instant operation and new profit dollars rolling in. None of our new areas came that way. Every one was a "gut it out" experience of negative cash flow, 300 percent turnover, slow-paying accounts, and for that matter, lack of accounts. In short, we earned all we got.

Some of our best markets for extra work during this time were churches. Many times we would load up the crew in our van and pick-ups and drive 200 miles to a church or other large building and strip and refinish the floors. We would send the drapes out for dry cleaning, clean the acoustical tile ceiling, repair or replace tiles, de-lime and clean the restrooms, sand and refinish wooden floors and kitchen cabinets, and even paint the exterior of the building. We would start at eight o'clock in the morning; women from the church would often feed us lunch (we paid them for it), then we would continue working until six, eat again, and work until eleven or midnight, crawl into our sleeping bags on the church floor, and be up again early the next morning.

These were choice experiences in our lives. We loved our work—the excitement, the competition, and the striving to be the best in all that we did.

Varsity's growth was demanding not just physically and financially, but mentally and emotionally. Calls were coming in from all over, as our reputation for hard work and efficiency spread. Traveling had always appealed to me and was exciting at first, but it got old fast. Idaho and Utah were sparsely populated, and bidding and setting jobs up all over meant traveling huge numbers of miles. The little Volkswagen beetle I bought in 1965 had 125,000 miles on it when it retired in 1968, and my other cars' mileage almost equaled that.

During my first traveling year, I drove more than 65,000 miles, many times in blizzards or on icy roads and late at night. On one building inspection trip, Arlo and I drove 1,200 miles without stopping except for gas. Often I'd leave home in the morning, drive to Salt Lake City, inspect some jobs there, load supplies, and drive to Boise, Idaho, and then home again for a total of 790 miles and then clean one of our buildings the same night. On one trip Arlo and I hit a slick spot and rolled the car end over end. Neither of us was hurt, but the building we had driven 97 miles to check grossed us only $43 a month.

At this time we were cleaning a lot of those big old Venetian blinds, and one day we got a call from the county courthouse, the largest building in Pocatello—three stories high and a block long. What did they want? A dream come true—all of the blinds cleaned. There were more windows on that place than on a Chicago train, and I bid the job and got it. These were not small blinds—some were ten feet wide and over eight feet tall. We took them all down, keeping careful track of which window they came off of, took them to our shop, and cleaned them. Then I sent a couple of the crew to hang them back up. It was Saturday and this took most of the day.

THE COURTHOUSE IN POCATELLO: A BONANZA FOR A VENETIAN BLINDS CLEANER!

Sunday morning, on the way to church, I swung by the courthouse to admire our primo job and—gasp!—under each blind there was a foot of space. They were 12 inches short of the windowsill. "Oh, those dumb drama majors who hung them must have got the wrong blinds on the wrong windows," I decided, until I drove around the other side of the building and saw that all three floors of blinds were a foot short. Gadfreys—did we get the wrong blinds? After I scratched my head for a few minutes, I realized that the ribbons on commercial building blinds were cloth, not plastic like most of the home blinds we'd cleaned, and they must have shrunk! That was a long Sunday afternoon and night, as we had to take all of the blinds down, re-wet them, and re-hang them with weights, just enough weight to pull them down to the sill. I'll never forget those hundreds of clothes hangers with whatever we could find to add weight dangling from them.

The blind leading the blinds

I was always looking for a way to do a job faster, better, and cheaper. Since we were now cleaning blinds by hand, laying them out on a padded surface and washing them with a soft brush, and blinds were a high-profit item, I figured if I could invent a machine to clean them, I'd be rich, famous, and home more. So I designed an oversized vat that looked like a giant paint roller pan which could be filled with soapy water, and then a big cylinder of screening (8 feet long and 3 feet in diameter) which rotated in the pan like one of those big riverboat paddlewheels. I mounted an electric motor on the outside of the vat and attached it by pulleys to the cylinder. It was one big project and after it came together, I had it galvanized to prevent rust. It cost a lot and it weighed… well, you don't really want to know. But it was beautiful, and I got newspaper coverage as far away as Salt Lake City for inventing it. The only trouble was, it didn't work.

When the big day of tryout finally came, we hauled a load of blinds from some office and I strapped one to the clever hooks on the cylinder and switched that baby on. Two things were shredded instantly—the blind and my dreams. The drum moved so fast through the water that the blind was ripped to pieces in about 15 seconds, so I didn't have to face the bigger question of how to heat up 300 gallons of water and keep it hot. (I think I finally determined that it would cost $46 a blind to heat that massive pool to the right temperature.) Then, too, I hadn't crimped the sheet metal of the vat and after it was filled it buckled. All that time, expense, and anticipation and it crashed. The owner of a local café did give me $20 to use the cylinder for a revolving sign until people complained about how ugly it was. And a farmer bought the tank for watering cattle. Both were local—I should have sold these things somewhere far away so I didn't have to see them daily! It's a laugh now, but was a real blow back then when I had to face up to all of this lost time and money.

Most Varsity men became professional painters as well as cleaners, and pro painters warned us that painters often ended up winos. I'd made it through 35 years without imbibing any type of alcohol, so I didn't see much chance of ending up in the gutter by this route… until I learned there were other ways to get intoxicated.

We always thought we were happy at the end of an enamel paint job because the job was over. But not so—it was the paint fumes that elated our tired bodies. One day Arlo, who had never imbibed anything stronger than a Fresca, locked himself in a tiny bathroom with a gallon of high quality enamel. He had been careful to close every vent, window, and door to prevent airborne dust and debris from defiling his paint job. He went in irritable and anxious to be done and emerged two hours later somewhat less than coherent. His eyes were glistening, he stuttered and drooled as he spoke, and even laughed agreeably when we told him his wife had called and said their septic tank had overflowed. He was rummy.

We once contracted to paint a large church building in a rural area. The women's auxiliary offered to feed us at the church to save us from trying to find local diners, which were hard to come by then in the town of Teton, Idaho. Our ten-man crew had sprayed and rolled 30 gallons of enamel onto the halls and classrooms by noon. The ladies were delighted with our sparkling, happy manner as we wolfed down our food. They informed us that the supper meal was going to be even better. (We would still be there, since we still had another 50 gallons to spray and roll onto the big auditorium/cultural hall and exterior of the building.) They came through with another fine meal that evening, and it was consumed by some rather silly young men. They eyed us suspiciously now, our trustworthiness in question as they spied pantyhose around our necks and protruding from our back pockets. Unfortunately, they didn't understand about paint fumes, or that pantyhose are unequalled for straining paint to keep a painter sprayer from plugging up. The resulting gossip and a similar job in Jackson Hole, Wyoming, led us to wearing masks and paying a little more attention to ventilation.

In Jackson, we spray-painted a big old cathedral being made over into a restaurant. We noticed many flies when we started work but never saw any more during the job. The next morning we walked into a marvelous surprise. There was no red carpet anywhere, but a deep carpet of dead flies, and walking across them made a crunching noise. The fumes must have killed them.

Another time, the American Falls bowling lanes had just been refinished by some traveling pro, and the owner called us to come in that evening and help shampoo the carpet and clean the kitchen. Arlo and I and a couple of other Varsity guys and the woman who owned the lanes all went to work. The refinisher had told the owner to close the windows to keep dust out, so it was stuffy in there, and the smell of that high-power lane-coating lacquer almost knocked us over. Our eyes started to sting the minute we entered the building.

After an hour, we were all having a good time and joking—even the normally quiet and serious owner was giggling. I just figured the job was going so well we were all in a good mood, until I tried to go up a stepladder and missed the step. My legs just wouldn't go where I wanted them to, so I stepped again and missed. Gads, I've got polio, I thought, or the dumb ladder is dodging me. I didn't seem very coordinated, nor was anyone else there at this point. The ones closest to the lanes were singing like lovesick wolves, and then someone finally announced that we all needed fresh air. Driving home was almost an impossibility, and even in the cool Idaho mountain air, it took a while for reality to return.

Only a week later, the lanes in the bowling alley at Ketchum were refinished. The owner came in the next morning and flicked on the light and the tiny spark from the light switch ignited the fumes that had built up over night. The roof was blown off in the explosion that followed and in minutes the building burned to the ground. The owner was blown clear of the fire, and he lived! Assuring proper ventilation on all jobs became company policy after this.

There were other dangers for the unaware in painting. My brother Larry and I had contracted to clean and paint the ceiling of the recreation hall of a large church in Rexburg, Idaho, and to reach that 25-foot height, planned to use a portable scaffolding base mounted on large rubber caster wheels. When we started a job we would simply stand four 4-by-4 inch pillars up on the base, nail them on, and quickly construct the rest of the scaffolding with 2-by-4s and plywood.

They were holding an evening meeting in the chapel of the church and Larry and I were on the other side of the curtain constructing the scaffolding. Until we were sure we had it the right height, we only tacked each plank on with a nail or two and at some point decided to get up on the scaffold and see if we could reach the ceiling. Not thinking about our poor nailing job, both of us climbed up on the platform at the top and discovered the height was just right. To celebrate, I did a little jig, which caused our combined 350 pounds to just be too much for the nails, and the entire scaffold collapsed. I mean it disintegrated—those 20-foot 4-by-4s all fell out and the platform and all of the cross members went down. The noise in the room was like a bomb exploding when it all (plus Larry and I) came down. The people in the church meeting thought the spirits were coming and Larry and I thought our spirits were going, but neither happened. By some fortunate circumstance of the way we rode the platform down, neither of us was seriously hurt. We shortened the church meetings and lengthened the nails in the scaffolding after that.

Another time, I asked one of our workers if he could handle the large roof of the country club at a golf course. It had to be spray-painted red. He assured me he could cover every inch of it, that no job was too big or too small for him. He got the roof painted all right, as well as all of the cars parked around it (Saturday golfers). It cost an average of $400 each to clean and buff the cars. The red paint came off the roof in a year, but we could hardly get it off the cars!

The great payroll chase

Meeting payroll was still difficult. The telephone company paid right on time and never missed a check, but insurance company processing left a lot to be desired. Once, when payroll time arrived, I forgot a couple of big checks I'd written and found myself $3,200 overdrawn, with no money available, and a payroll of several thousand dollars due in three days. These were tough times, as any of you who have labored to meet a payroll know. Many times, I was in despair, trying to get enough money from accounts receivable to pay the men. I begged the people who owed us money. They were nice to me, but "the manager in Florida has to sign the check," or "the insured is in Europe and we can't issue funds until he signs the check," and so on. I begged the bankers, sold my own possessions, scrounged up any personal money I had, and was still short. I had never missed a payroll in my company's history, and so I passed out checks when payday came, determined to collect enough money by the next day to cover them. I needed only $3,500 more, exactly what a company in Casper, Wyoming, owed me for a job we did in Jackson Hole.

I called them and politely asked for my money. "Oh, without a release signed, etc., we can't issue the check. We'll mail it to you." "No!" I said. "I'll be there by eight o'clock tomorrow morning." Barbara made me a sandwich and I jumped in the car after church and headed across the Wyoming desert. I drove all night, and by eight the next morning was sitting on their doorstep. "Oh, we can't release this without the other contractor who worked on the job," they said. "It's my money, ninety days past due, I need it, and I am going to get it or else!" was my determined reply. Finally, by phone the other contractor, seeing how anxious I was to get the money, okayed my picking up the check if I could drop by Jackson Hole to get his signed release. I did so with a grin of victory, dropped off the other contractor's share of the money on the way home, and covered the payroll in time. I never included myself in that particular payroll nor in many others before and after. As business owners often do, we went without furniture, clothes, cars, and sometimes food so that our employees wouldn't have to—all part of the package of building a business.

One summer, we had a large government job in Moose, Wyoming, under the towering Grand Tetons just north of Jackson Hole. The work consisted of preparing and painting all of the houses in a small employee village, the national park headquarters, and visitor center there. This was the first job we ever did for the government, and we discovered that government jobs were truly amazing. It took three days just to read through the forms to find out what the job was, and to check to see if you could comply with all of the restrictions and specifications. It took an attorney to translate the bid specifications. If you decided you were interested, you had to sign an affidavit saying that you had looked over the job, that a government person had accompanied you, and that you did indeed understand all of the fine print. We bid the job and had to provide a staggering bond, guaranteeing our performance or we would forfeit it.

Because of the enormous size of the job, we had to fight through all of the preliminaries and spend a small fortune just to bid it, but we succeeded and got the contract. Board and room costs were unbelievable in that tourist area, so given our low profit margin, we bought a big tent and camped in the forest, cooked on a camp stove, and slept on the ground. Every day and night beneath those spectacular mountains by the Snake River (which some might view as work, and roughing it) were pure pleasure—one of our greatest outdoor experiences.

Far from a dull life

Every profession has its high points, but few equal the life of a janitor. There is rarely a situation that you can't learn a great lesson from and have a barrel of fun doing it. Not a week went by that wasn't loaded with memorable experiences.

Even a little floor buffing job at a local discount center seemed routine, for example, but wasn't. Arlo arrived there one evening at eleven o'clock (after closing time), unlocked the front door, and felt his way into the back office where the controls for the lights were located. As he concentrated on finding the electric box, he thought he heard someone breathing close by. The hair on the back of his neck stood up as he scanned the darkness. Sure enough, there was someone standing right next to him—a young burglar with a revolver in his hand! Arlo, who was armed only with a putty knife for scraping gum off the floor, hollered in a big gruff voice, "What are you doing in here?" The undoubtedly inexperienced burglar, overcome by the authority of Arlo's demand, dropped the gun and ran out the door. Arlo ran after him, captured him, and called the police. Soon an officer was leading the shaking and unsuccessful thief to a squad car. But as the officer put him in the back seat of the car and walked around to the driver's door, the burglar jumped out and took off at a dead run. The officer was no match and was soon left behind. The burglar got away and the building received its usual sweeping and buffing. Arlo's work report read: "Normal evening. P.S. Caught a burglar."

Only a few weeks after this, I was cleaning an area in the traffic department of the telephone company. I was doing the work myself to make sure nothing went wrong, because some poor relationships had developed here over a recent slip and fall. I was using a huge 120-pound floor machine to buff the floor in the women's locker and lounge area. A buffer of this size has unbelievable torque and can be hard to control, but if you know what you are doing it can be operated with two fingers. There is a big drive block under the machine faced with an inch-thick rubber pad to hold the nylon buffing pad. To make things easier I had

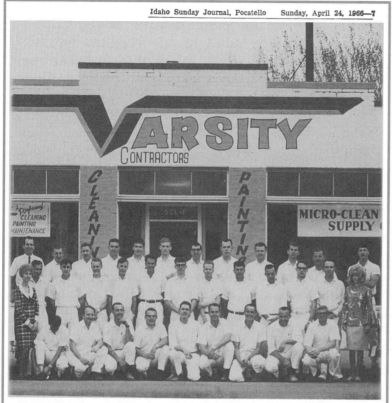

Idaho Sunday Journal, Pocatello   Sunday, April 24, 1966—7

FROM AN IDEA — Several years ago when a student at Idaho State University, was casting about for a way to finance his schooling, he organized a small group that featured home cleaning. The idea caught on and now the firm, numbering about 50 and including many university students, has expanded with offices in two states. A single contract includes servicing of 14 buildings.

Idea to Finance Schooling Pays Off for Ex-ISU Man

An idea that began with a need to finance schooling at Idaho State University has grown into a company employing 50 persons in southern Idaho and Northern Utah.

Now known as Varsity contractors, the home office is at 334 South Main Street.

Don Aslett originated the firm about 1958, featuring maintenance, painting and cleaning. Among firms with which he has contracts is Mountain States Telegraph Co., on 14 buildings in Idaho and Utah.

Richard Aslett is Pocatello office manager. Grant Barnes, a graduate of Idaho State is area supervisor at Salt Lake City. Mark Browning, former ISU student, is manager at Idaho Falls. An office is planned for Boise in November.

A conference on maintanance and an instruction school were held recently in the Pocatello office and Telephone building, including a lecture on policy on MST&T maintenance by Don Brod, plant manager. Brod conducted a plant tour.

Other instruction was given by Arlo Luke, and Don Aslett, and a cleaning demonstration by Dennis Jibson, owner of Super Clean Janitorial Service.

OCCASIONAL NEWSPAPER ARTICLES ON OUR LITTLE COMPANY, SUCH AS THIS ONE IN THE *IDAHO SUNDAY JOURNAL*, GAVE A FURTHER BOOST TO OUR GROWING BUSINESS.

the automatic switch on that would keep the buffer going without having to squeeze the trigger—sort of the "cruise control" of buffer operation. I was right in the middle of the ladies' lounge when the cord unplugged and the buffer stopped. I left it right where it died, and skipped to the end of the cord, brought it to a closer outlet, and plugged it in. But I made one little mistake. The automatic switch was still engaged and as fate would have it, one of the oldest of the hundred operators there came stiffly hobbling by just then. I was around the corner when I plugged it back in, and that woman was only three feet from the buffer when it engaged.

Without someone to control it, the big machine started with a leap. Right at the woman it came, and knocked her down. The nylon pad came out from under the machine, leaving 19 inches of rubber grabbing at the linoleum. This gave the buffer incredible traction. As the woman scrambled to her feet and started to run, screaming, the machine kept moving in her direction. Two more big leaps, and it caught up with her and beat her to the floor. I was around the corner by now and saw what had happened. Her shoe was literally ripped from her foot and torn almost in half. She lay cringing in the corner by the time the machine finally pulled its plug out.

I wasn't even going to bother finishing the job—I knew Varsity had had it! The woman got up, looked at the buffer and me and said, "My word!" Then with her broken shoe in hand, she hobbled to the lounge to recover. The most unbelievable part of the incident is that she never said one word to anyone about it, nothing! The chief operator had a big tally book and if anything was out of line, it was carefully reported. This never was. Perhaps the woman thought if she talked, we'd send a bigger buffer after her. Anyway, my salute to her. What a woman—she wouldn't even let us replace the shoe!

Most of the Varsity people were full of enthusiasm and color—they had to be to survive the constant pressure of competition. I always took jobs and customers seriously and didn't have to lighten up much because I always had some quick-witted, bold guys on the crew who took care of that. One woman, for instance, who had a very nice home, also had a pure white longhaired cat, rhinestone collar and all. She was very impressed with the job Mark Browning did painting the inside of her cupboards. Browning, with a pretty convincing straight face, explained that he'd dipped the cat in a roller pan of paint, then tossed it in each cupboard, closed the door, and then beat on the cabinet. The frightened cat distributed the paint perfectly, he claimed.

One February morning a call came from Mr. Dell Bills, of Mountain Bell in Cedar City, southern Utah. "Are you interested in ten Bell buildings down here?" he asked.

"Sure!"

The next morning I drove 550 miles to Cedar City. I looked at the main office, and then Mr. Bills and I toured his district, evaluating and bidding the phone buildings. It took an entire day of steady driving just to get around to them. The routes went over the beautiful Cedar Breaks to famous Bryce Canyon, through small famous Western towns and equally famous (and beautiful) Zion National Park into Kanab, Utah, where many Western movies have been made. We moved on to the palm-tree warm climate of St. George, and back along the cliffs to Enterprise. It began to snow, and by the time we arrived home 14 hours later, the snow was clinging to the phone lines. Some of them were weighed down to only 6 feet from the ground.

Mr. Bills called a week later and gave us the job. I came back in two weeks to open the area. I stayed there doing the work, setting up the account, and hiring and training people for 15 days, the longest time I had ever been away from home.

Lesson on the homefront

As I often tell my audiences now, do you know what the biggest, ugliest housework problem is? It's that the majority of housework is caused by men and children—yet most home chores are done by women. Like most men, I once viewed, with a certain critical eye, my wife and other women struggling feverishly to get the housework done. I ached to jump in and show those "disorganized gals" how an expert could square things away.

Soon the opportunity, along with a great lesson, came to me. I worked hard washing walls late at night to buy my wife a surprise plane ticket to Alaska. She was delighted to have her first flight ever and a chance to see her mother again. I bade her goodbye and told her to stay as many weeks as she wished, that I would care well for our six small children. (She wasted no time leaving, I assure you). But my true thoughts were, "Now that I have her out of town, I'm going to shape up this disorganized house and make it as efficient as my business!"

I woke up at four o'clock the first morning and confidently mapped out the campaign of great household efficiency about to be enacted in our home. By six-thirty the kids were up, and they saluted before they went to the bathroom! By seven-thirty, the beds were made, the dishes were done, and I was rolling to victory. We were putting some finishing touches on our new home, and my project for the day was constructing a vanity cabinet in the master bathroom—an easy half-day's work. I had just started to glue the first board when "*Waaa!*" One of the kids had biffed another. I ran out and made peace, passed out storybooks, and again picked up the hammer and board. "*Waaa!*"—someone cut a finger. Three bandages and ten minutes of comforting and mercurochrome-dabbing later, I again picked up the hammer (after scraping off the now-dry glue) and had one nail started when "*Waaa!*"—a diaper to change (a cry that was repeated all day; I'd have sworn we had four in diapers at the same time).

BARBARA ON OUR RANCH
IN THE LATE SIXTIES.

Again I returned to work, and had started the second nail, when *ding-dong* (the milkman; I slammed the cottage cheese into the fridge), then *ding-dong* (the mailman; I ran down and signed for the package), then *ring-a-ling* (the school telephoning—Laura forgot her lunch money). Then *knock-knock*—"Can I borrow...." Then *buzz*—time for lunch... *ding-dong*... time for bottles. "*Waaa!*"—diapers again, etc., etc., etc. You wouldn't believe how my morning went. (Or would you?) My building proj-ect looked like a chimpanzee special—dried glue and badly cut boards all over, and no real work accomplished. I discovered that dressing a kid once is just a warm-up—one of those kids went through four outfits by eleven-fifteen. Noon came and another surprise—those little dudes don't appreciate what you do for them, all that work cook-ing and they threw food, got it all over them, and not one of them thanked me.

Naptime came, and would you believe little kids don't all go to sleep at the same time? I've bedded down 600 head of cattle easier and faster than those six kids. When I finally got them all down, no way was I going to hammer, play the stereo, or even turn a page loudly and risk waking one of them! Fortunately, the day ended just before I did. I had two boards up on the cabinet by the time the last baby was read to sleep at midnight. The most famous housecleaner and best organizer in the West… had accomplished nothing! I was so tired and discouraged. The day before I'd bought five trucks, four people had asked me to lunch, and I'd expanded my company into a new area—but that day, nothing finished!

The next morning, I again woke at four o'clock and again decided I was going to run things like my business. I'd change all the diapers ahead for the whole day! But it didn't work. Leaving out all the gory details of the next few days, my half-day cabinet job, only half-complete, bit the dust.

A week later, my wife called to check on things. I pinched all the kids to get them howling in the background so I wouldn't have to beg her to come and save me. She did return at once, and I suddenly got efficient again.

WOMEN WHO RUN A HOME AND FAMILY ARE ABOUT TWICE AS GOOD AT "MANAGEMENT" AS THE AVERAGE BUSINESSPERSON. I FIRST TOOK NOTE OF THIS WHEN BARBARA, ON AN ERRAND RUN, COULD ACCOMPLISH IN TWO HOURS WHAT WOULD TAKE ME FOUR OR FIVE HOURS AND MUCH COMPLAINING.

Signing on… and off

I always had a secret love for art and advertising, and even took a correspondence course from an art instruction school when I was 29. My brother Larry, who had worked for me in college and was now in construction work, was a good artist and painter, so I asked him to join me in starting a little sign company. Lettering buildings and vehicles and making custom signs always seemed fascinating to me—creating things everyone looked at and that often altered life in some way.

We called the business Totem Signs, and quickly found out that our view of this business was more romanticism than reality. There weren't as many signs needing to be made as we had imagined, and there were many more good, experienced sign companies out there than we had been aware of. Roadside billboards had a meager, long-term (like 20 years from now) return. We did do a couple of high-altitude signs, including one on the front of an airport hangar, where we deserved to die on the jury-rig scaffolding we arranged on those 1890s decaying brick parapets. People liked Larry's work but paid little and late, so we did other Varsity painting work to supplement the sign income.

OUR ENERGETIC BROOD WITH THEIR KISLING COUSINS, STANDING STILL LONG ENOUGH FOR A PHOTO IN 1966.

My big debut (and only moment of glory) came when I suggested to the grocer of our little hometown of McCammon that he should cover the south side of the store's cinderblock wall with an attractive sign which I would do in exchange for $43 worth of groceries. (You see why we were never profitable.)

He said okay, and I drew up a tempting thumbnail sketch of a sack of groceries, with celery and all kinds of other things sticking out of the top, and a large "Howell's Market" lettered on the other side. I was a good letterer. But the sack of groceries ended up a waste of good paint. Looking at art on billboards is sure easier than producing it. My celery looked like sagebrush, my can of beans like a mini leaning tower of Pisa, the loaf of bread like a bald head with wrinkles, and the bag itself looked thoroughly recycled. I took the $43 worth of groceries but never parked on that end of the lot again. Fortunately, someone ran into the wall and knocked a big hole in my infamous painted bag, and when the wall was fixed, it was painted over. After this, I was demoted to the office end of the operation.

Other, more interesting and profitable businesses came along, and this business, like most of our signs, gradually faded away (although a few, many years later, are still up!), and the company was absorbed into Varsity.

Some dark days and discouragement

You don't have to look for discouragement—it will usually crop up all by itself. And if you are a venturer, doer, risk taker, or idealist you may get more than your share.

At this point my colleagues and I felt we were pretty special because we actually owned a statewide business. We had initiated creative cleaning programs with the giant Bell System, and had branched into many other types of service for them. We had around 30 telephone buildings in southern Idaho and northern Utah under contract and were looking for more.

One of the extra jobs we did for phone companies was spray painting old metal office desks and making Formica tops for them. This instantly converted a tired, utilitarian-looking desk into almost an "executive" desk. We invented the method and had done several buildings full of them. I was pretty proficient in laying Formica and using a router to shape the edges to a flawless, factory-finished looking desktop. We got a call to do the desks in the Twin Falls, Idaho phone building, and right at the same time, one of the Boise Bell managers told us the big main phone building in Boise was going to contract cleaning. (To us, this would be like getting the Empire State Building to clean!) If we'd give up our contract on a few of the small buildings we had in the area (so he could transfer some in-house cleaners rather than fire them), he'd give us the big building. Of course, we gladly gave up our few hard-earned small buildings for the one big plum, and were waiting for the go-ahead.

Everything seemed to be going our way as we started the desk job. We bought sheets of woodgrain-design Formica for the desks and took it with us. We always picked up the three-quarter-inch plywood we used under the Formica right in the town where we did the job. This time the local lumber store only had five-eighth-inch plywood. It looked almost the same and it seemed to make no difference. So we cut all of that expensive Formica to fit, mounted it on the plywood, breathed contact cement fumes for a couple of days, and left a room full of gorgeous converted desks.

On Monday morning, we were informed that all of the desktops had "potato chip" bends in them—they had warped and could be rocked back and forth easily. We went up to look and it was a mess. The five-eighth-inch wood just wasn't as rigid as the three-quarter-inch and every desktop was ruined. We tried injecting some of the tops with lacquer thinner in hypodermic needles in an attempt to salvage them, but no go. It was a nightmare and a big financial loss.

We were right in the middle of this when we learned that the telephone manager in Boise had given the contract on that big new building to his son-in-law, who had just started in the business. We were out of all the buildings we'd worked five years to get and now the big one as well. We were crushed—all of that wasted money and time, and dashed dreams and expectations.

That seemed a dark day, but we survived both the emotions and the economics. We redid the desks and made the phone company happy, got more jobs from them (and charged more for them, you can bet!). And later, the telephone manager in Boise was fired and we did get the big building after all, along with many others.

Yet more work came our way about now. Six years of intense service in the city and area of Pocatello left us rather dominant in the field of cleaning. In fact, so well known was the name Varsity that sometimes we benefited from other people's accomplishments.

The president of a big savings and loan in Pocatello was a friend of mine. He sent me and my family an invitation to watch the big Fourth of July parade from his air-conditioned second-floor office, where a 12-foot-wide window directly overlooked the parade route (probably better than the governor's view of it). I was pretty puffed up about this prestigious seating, far above the other lowly spectators crowded together out on the hot street. It was glorious to sit in a big plush corporate chair with a cool lemonade and watch the passing exhibits. (In Idaho parades then, everyone rode a horse, even the twirlers.)

My feeling that I had arrived evaporated as the parade neared the end. I could hear loud cheering and clapping, and knew something great was coming. I had a competitor, Jon Bell, a 20-year-old whose new cleaning company dared to intrude on my territory, in the town where I figured I was the cleaning king. I assumed he wasn't in my league and had ignored him until now. But there at the very end of the parade he was, with several of his employees in bright yellow jumpsuits emblazoned "Bannock Cleaning—We Clean Everything" and armed with wheelbarrows, shovels, and brooms. They were cleaning up all of the horse manure from the parade, singing as they scooped and swept. The last person would spray the soiled place with disinfectant. It was a brilliant idea, an unmatchable marketing ploy.

And there I sat, formerly fat and content, turning pale now. I'd learned a big lesson about staying in and on the job. I kicked myself for weeks for sitting on my rump, relaxed, while I was being out-created by a new young competitor! I always admired old Jon for this maneuver, but such is the redeeming value of being well known that soon afterward Varsity got a letter from the mayor, thanking us for cleaning up the manure and promising us some upcoming city work! I found out later that Jon Bell was a cousin and we became lifelong friends.

When I was first in business, expanding to another town was a real heart thumper. Moving into another state was monumental. In the early 1960s, we lettered our trucks "Idaho-Wyoming-Utah." My little college business was operating in three states, and four would be even better. We were cleaning a telephone building in Kanab, Utah, a town near the border of Arizona. Less than ten miles away in Arizona was a little town called Freedonia, and it had one single Bell phone booth. In order to add Arizona to the fledgling list on our panel trucks, I managed to negotiate cleaning it for $1.50 per time. It easily cost us $25 in expenses to drive down there and clean it, but it did qualify us to add Arizona to the states we had conquered. Vanity! And vexation. Since it was the only booth in town, and this was a pretty rugged area, it often doubled as an emergency outhouse. So we paid dearly for the right to clean it!

New heights with Bell

Early one morning some of my crew and I were shaping up our shop, when there was an anxious honking at the door. We opened it and in drove Les Hodge, in a telephone ladder truck. He informed us he had just driven this new truck off of a railroad car. (It didn't even have a license plate yet or a Bell logo.) He had a project in mind and needed the truck a few hours to pull it off, and then he would take the truck to the company garage.

The project, called "cable coating," proved to be an adventure. Long before the modern wireless transmission, the phone company ran cable that carried all phone messages. This cable was sturdy stuff, but as it aged (and was rubbed by tree branches, assailed by the weather, chewed by squirrels, hit by the shotguns of hunters, etc.), some of the insulation wore off. This left parts of the wire bare, and when it rained, you would sometimes lose your connection or get static on the line. Telephone companies dreaded loss of service or complaints and paid dearly to prevent them.

Most of Les' area was rural, and every rainstorm or blizzard resulted in more cases of trouble than he wanted, so he did some research and found a plastic-like coating called Insulite that when applied to the cable would seal up little holes and blemishes. He had ordered a 55-gallon drum of it, and since the cable was up in the air, had commandeered the not-yet-delivered ladder and bucket truck, and you don't have to guess who he selected for its maiden voyage.

I was quick to suggest that we use a big padded cotton painter's mitt, dip it in a bucket of the coating, and rub it on the line as we drove along under the phone and power lines. That was good enough for Les, and within an hour we were parked under the start of the three miles of cable with the history of the most trouble. None of us had a clue as to how to run the hydraulic ladder on the truck, but we put Arlo in the bucket, strapped him in, pushed the buttons, and up, up, up he went. As soon as he reached the line, he dipped the mitt in the bucket of Insulite and slid the mitt along the cable. Les crept along under the cable with the truck, with me coaching from the back and trying to operate controls I knew little about, and Arlo flinging the syrupy substance around. We pinned him against the cross arms of telephone poles a couple of times, but by the end of the stretch no one was dead or injured, and Arlo and the truck were covered with the plastic coating (ghastly smelling stuff). Then we all went home and tried to clean off the coating. I never did

THE VARSITY VEHICLE BANNER IN 1967:
A FOUR-STATE COMPANY NOW!

learn what the construction crew had to say when they got their new truck back with what looked like splotches of varnish all over it. We waited for the next big rainstorm in that area. It came and… zero cases of trouble. It worked!

Now Les was really enthused and offered us miles and miles of line coating, and we invented a brilliant line-coating machine made of spray heads, lambswool pads, and pulleys attached to an aluminum frame, which we mounted on a 25-foot long pole. We set the contraption on the line, fed the Insulite up under pressure, and walked along under the cable coating it. Les furnished the Insulite and paid us $100 a mile.

Applying this stuff was the meanest, toughest job you can imagine. The telephone lines ran everywhere, and we had to follow them. The cable ran over thickets of willow, thorn bush, and mesquite, and we would have to hack, saw, and muscle our way beneath the line, applying the Insulite as we went. We traveled over the tops of trees and boulders, through gullies, and where the lines went 70 feet into the air, over houses and through back yards in town, across main highways and bridges, over creeks, rivers, and lakes, through farm fields, past mean dogs and other animals. Plus it was desert hot on the site and the coating stuck to your skin, clothes, and hair and made your eyes burn.

The worst was when word got out to the other Bell System operations. Because we had just expanded our cleaning operations into Arizona, I agreed to do an 8-mile stretch of cable though some godforsaken desert north of Phoenix. It was in the rugged hills near Prescott, Cottonwood, and the historic old mining town of Jerome. Two brothers who had just gone into business with us were anxious to come on the job and help (poor souls). I drove from Idaho to Arizona armed with equipment and supplies, picked them up, and we drove to the area.

It was supposed to be a three- or four-day job, but it lasted almost two weeks. It rained and rained, and when it didn't rain, it was blisteringly hot (Idaho deserts are nothing compared to Arizona). I don't know how they ever strung cable over some of that terrain. Worst of all, my two partners were both office types and neither had ever been away from their wives for long, and after four days they were moping around and threatening mutiny. One finally did leave. One night after coating cable all day I couldn't get my pants off because there were so many cactus thorns stuck through them into my flesh. Everything else was hurting so bad, I hadn't even noticed that.

We finally reached the last day, and it was a toughie. We had to go through thickets that water couldn't even run through—the brush was brutal. But I was as driven as they were to get done. I'd been here too long, losing money most of the time. When we reached the end of the cable, the last span arched over a 200-foot-wide pond. My partner said, "There is no way!" I said, "We have to find a way, or we can't complete the contract." A rowboat was one solution, but that meant a 3-hour trip to town.

The pond was full of weeds and slimy algae, and I had a whimpering, homesick helper. But the drive to get home—home, sweet home—overcame good sense. I strapped the pressure tank on my back, hoisted the now 30-foot extension pole with the coating unit onto the line, and waded out into the pond. It turned out to be only chest deep, but it was far from the ol' swimming hole. I kept the unit on the cable and eventually emerged on the other side, covered with moss, bugs, snails, mud, and pondweed. My partner took one look at me and said, "I can't do this!" That was his last day.

The job was only a break-even promotion project to convince the telephone company in Arizona that we wanted their business. The only thing we convinced them of was that we were crazy.

I wouldn't do a job like this now for $5,000 a mile, but hopefully it helped develop character. To keep the memory of this great experience alive, I kept the cable coating equipment; it has a place of honor in my cleaning museum.

A CLOSE UP OF OUR ONE-OF-A-KIND CABLE COATING CONTRAPTION.

When you sum up ten years of growth on a progress report, it sure sounds easy. The fine print of contracts is what accomplishes it, plus years of work and investment. We loved the Bell System and had for ten years broken our butts for them, taking any crumbs of work others didn't want and always begging for more. We built a mutual trust that was soon to pay off big time. We had been gaining telephone buildings one at a time in surrounding cities, then little packages of four or five rural buildings, then the big main building downtown and the storerooms and warehouses and hundreds of telephone booths. We took anything offered.

As our business got bigger, it was next to impossible to do all of the work personally anymore. We had crews and trucks running all over and were gaining experience.

Arlo was cautious and conservative, and tended carefully to every last detail. I was creative, imaginative, sloppy, and daring. As a team we began to build a separate, specialized organization offering customized service to Bell Telephone and other telephone companies. We shared ownership of a company called Varsity Telco, and Mark Browning began running the original Varsity organization, which I owned 100 percent. Mark was our "Dr. Spock," more thorough even than Arlo, and he really stabilized and improved the operation.

For the first time ever, it seemed that things were stable—the business was running well, and I was finally beginning to get a salary that my family could actually live on. We had developed a manual of operational policy for our company and were offering not only quality but economical service to our customers. It was the proverbial calm before the storm.

If there was ever an opportunity that pushed us to a new height of growth, it was the one that came next.

LINE COATING FOR THE BELL SYSTEM:
ONE OF THE MOST CHALLENGING JOBS EVER!

Chapter 9

THE SUN VALLEY YEARS

Living the famous song,
"It Happened in Sun Valley…"

<small>SUN VALLEY, WHERE WE SPENT FIVE RICH AND EXTRAORDINARY YEARS.</small>

One of the most influential periods of my life was 1968-73, the Sun Valley years, when my fledgling (but not yet fully fledged) company took on maintenance and much more at this world-famous resort. I worked in just about every trade here, met rich and famous as well as poor people, and enjoyed powerfully contrasting seasons of fierce winter, celestial spring, mountain summer, and unforgettable fall. My company tested its mettle and grew here, and my family and I grew together and built ourselves an enormous house. I was also the leader of a growing church congregation. These five years, for both Barbara and me, seemed like an entire lifespan. Results from these years come back to us in some way almost every day of our lives.

"It Happened in Sun Valley" was a 1941 hit song about a love affair that took place in one of the ski capitals of the world, Sun Valley, Idaho. For Varsity Contractors it did indeed "happen in Sun Valley."

Sun Valley, without question, is one of the most unique resorts in the world, the place that introduced skiing to the United States. It was built in 1937 by the Union Pacific Railroad after one of Austria's best skiers tabbed the area as a mountainscape unequalled in the U.S. An Alpine-type village was built and so was the first chairlift in the country. Sun Valley's immediate popularity drew celebrities like Gary Cooper, Clark Gable, Ingrid Bergman, Ernest Hemingway, and many others. Located at 6,000 feet elevation in the Salmon River country, Sun Valley's romantic atmosphere, coupled with one of the finest ski schools anywhere, drew a wealthy and loyal group of customers. The railroad, however, unable to find the financing to continue operation, sold it to a former Olympic skier and financial tycoon, Bill Janss, of California.

I knew quite a bit about Sun Valley before Varsity's first contact with it, as both of the ranches I grew up on were only 60 or so miles south of it. Right before I left for my mission in Hawaii, I had worked here as an inter-company mail carrier and theater usher. It was these fond memories of Sun Valley that caused me to drop a business card there in late 1967 when I was cleaning telephone booths nearby. My first sales approach was given the usual "Come back later and we'll think about it." Later our Twin Falls manager, Dave Sanders, dropped off his business card and Varsity got an appointment.

While sitting out in the hall waiting for that appointment, I could hear the Sun Valley manager talking. From the conversation, it was apparent that finding good help at the resort was a major problem. This was the height of the "hippie" era and most of the help here seemed to come to work only for the free skiing privileges. When spring came and skiing conditions were less than ideal, even though Sun Valley would stay open for another month, the help would pack up and leave "like rats leaving a sinking ship," were the manager's exact words. The few employees that did stay, stayed only because they couldn't find a job anywhere else. Many of them were poorly groomed and involved in drugs; some refused to wear shoes, etc.

Finally a voice I later came to know and respect said, "All right, if you have to close down the bars because the help is so rotten, then close them down, but I want good service for the guests first!" This was E. G. "Bud" Siemons talking, operations manager of Sun Valley, and five minutes later Dave and I were seated across from him, giving our sales pitch. We really laid it on about our champion company, our quality and willingness to work, last of all adding that our employees were so clean-cut they wouldn't even use profanity. One of the Sun Valley managers sitting there said, "People like that don't exist any more!" "They do, and I can get them for you!" I quickly answered. "Good, then give us a bid," Siemons said. " I'll have things available for you when you are ready."

Siemons was good as his word—they were anxious to tell and show us all we needed to know to prepare a bid. This was no little task—it was by far the largest and most significant contract we had ever gone after. The multiple services involved included providing maid service, housemen and service janitors, cleaning hotels and condominiums, lodges, lobbies, recreation rooms, rental shops and ski rental rooms, restaurants, cafeterias, kitchens, employees' quarters, and garages. We would also provide grounds maintenance, landscaping, fencing, linen supply, convention setup, furniture moving, painting, pest control, demolition, warehouse maintenance, maintenance of ice skating rinks and bowling alleys, construction of volleyball and tennis courts, snow removal, installing and maintaining sprinkler and irrigation systems, cleaning stables (yes, horse stables), and more.

It was hard to determine a fair and accurate price for doing all this. Our best bidding and presentation minds were taxed to the limit trying to evaluate the situation and prepare the bid. Our final bid (delivered on time!) was $12,000 a month.

Harry Holmes, the dynamic general manager of Sun Valley, got involved as the size of the contract was considerable. He was quiet and unassuming, but dead accurate in his knowledge of what was going on. He seemed to like and trust me, and I felt the same about him. Mr. Holmes and Bud were convinced that we were the answer to Sun Valley's problems. Two days later, Bud announced by telephone: "Well, it's yours. Roll up your sleeves and get to work!"

The talking was over. We had just landed our biggest contract ever, one that would quickly grow to five times the original starting figure. We decided to approach a young missile engineer to be the overall manager of the operation. Rex Turner was working for Boeing Aircraft and had a fine, high-paying job with status and security. He had been working for us part-time at one of our telephone buildings near his home as a way to teach his young son (who was working there) the work ethic.

We knew he had what it would take, so we drove to Ogden, Utah, and offered him one of the biggest headaches and challenges in the history of janitoring with a resounding $700 a month starting salary—much less than he was presently receiving, plus some future stock options. Rex had one weakness (or strength, from our point of view). He had an unquenchable desire to do more than average. He could also see the future possibilities here if he could deliver, and thus accepted the job.

When our contract started there were new people all over the place, trying to find their way around in halls (some of them over a quarter-mile long), performing services of 30 different types for two different managers 24 hours a day. We started with 12 people taking the place of the 32 that had previously been required to do the same work. There were double shifts for many weeks for both crew and management until things settled down. We had some tests of patience and endurance, and finally Arlo and I decided that one of us would have to go and help on the contract for a while. I was the most qualified for the types of work involved here and familiar with the area, thus I traveled there and assisted Rex.

I traveled the 200 miles home on the weekends for a couple of weeks, but I felt that no business should require a family to be apart. When I saw a full summer in Sun Valley coming, Barbara and the kids came up and we rented a log house and spent the summer in the midst of some of the most beautiful mountains and streams in the world. While the family took advantage of the classes and pool and other things offered by Sun Valley in the summer program, my crews and I continued our super-busy schedules. We were willing to work hard to earn our money and establish a foundation with the Sun Valley company—it was a great summer for experience and progress.

More contracts were given to us early in the fall. I could see a bright future for us in Sun Valley and loved the countryside. Although I never had even thought of moving from our 60-acre paradise and newly finished big home in McCammon, two events changed my thinking. I was asked to serve as bishop (minister) of the Mormon Church in the area, and almost simultaneously, got a call from Mr. John Felthusen, a retired farmer six miles north of Sun Valley. I had tried to buy some property from him earlier, but he told me twice that he had none for sale. I learned later that John was in a barbershop getting his hair cut while some of the local lackeys that Varsity had replaced were holding a gripe session, and the subject was me. They were criticizing me as unfair for taking over the Sun Valley operation. John was an industrious farmer who, although wealthy now, never lost his strong work ethic. He was so impressed with Varsity's operation and progress that after hearing the conversation, he called to say, "For you, I think I do have some property for sale. Let's go out and look it over and you pick out what you want."

I picked ten acres of land that sloped up a mountain covered with pines and quaking aspens, and had a beautiful creek lined with cottonwoods and full of trout. "How does $2,000 an acre sound?" he asked. It was a good price, and I suspected that in a few years the property would be going for far more. (The same property later sold for four million!) "I'll take it!" "Good. You can give me $5,000 or so as a down payment after the first of the year, and we'll work the rest out later."

What a break! That afternoon I called Barbara, who had returned to McCammon to get the kids in school. After talking a few minutes we agreed that we should move to Sun Valley. "Go and find a trailer house, that's the solution for housing right now, and I'll get things ready here," I said. I scheduled the power people to wire the property, ordered a well drilled, and drew up plans for a new house we would build later.

Within a week or so, Barbara called and said she had bought a trailer. We boarded up our new home in McCammon, drained the pipes, and left it, not knowing it would be almost five years before we returned.

Moving from 4,500 square feet of living space to 600 was an adjustment, but we had made them before. We settled in, and it was a move we would never regret.

My official title in the company at this point was president of the Varsity Corporation and my duties were to stabilize and promote our entire operation in Idaho, Utah, Arizona, and Wyoming. Our Sun Valley organization was up to full strength by this time, and we were drawing employees from all over the country. Without a doubt one of the most unusual of these was Bill Zickgraf of South Carolina, who was six-foot-four and 35 years old. A former All-American swimmer, state senator, and college educated, he sparkled with Southern charm. He had brought his family of seven children to a log cabin in the mountains of Sun Valley for an experience in living in the wilds. He declined acceptance to law school to remain in the area for a while, and came to me seeking employment. The job he took would have tested anyone.

Our company had a contract to clean and service all of the toilets in the skiing areas of Sun Valley. When the mountain was filled with as many as 5,000 skiers and there were 20 restrooms open in strategic places all over, there was plenty of action for a toilet cleaner. Only four of the restrooms had water; the remaining 16 were chemical toilets that required charging every 3 to 5 hours with 5 gallons of chemical solution, hand-carried up the mountain. It wasn't difficult to train someone to do the technical parts of the job, and so much of the servicing was skiing time that you might think it was an enviable position. However, there was the matter of social status. Who wanted to be a toilet cleaner in fashionable Sun Valley?

I would interview applicants and describe, outline, and promise until their eyes glowed with eagerness to tackle the chore. But in a few days, they would begin to sneak around, trying not to be seen or recognized as the Varsity toilet cleaner. I raised the pay a dollar an hour above any other in our organization and still had difficulty keeping the position filled for long. I included a free lunch in the job and still the image of "toilet cleaner" outweighed the attraction of the slopes and the other benefits. I was about at the end of my rope when big Bill Zickgraf appeared.

"I need some work, Don." "What kind?" "I'll do anything." My pulse pounded, realizing I had a live one on the line. "I've got just the job for you, Bill. You and your family can learn to ski and you'll have a free meal." "Great, I'll take it, what is it?" I told him, and he accepted with enthusiasm. "That sounds good and I really want to learn to ski. I'll be ready to start in the morning."

The story that follows is now a legend in Sun Valley. Bill rode up the chair lift and walked through all of the locations, charting his course of action. Then he strolled into a ski shop and purchased a set of skis that looked like they'd been made from giant redwoods, and a pair of boots to match. Now he got back on the ski lift, a basket of cleaning supplies under each arm. He had never skied before and was headed to the top of the mountain to learn.

At the end of the first lift, he had to go down a hill to the next chair lift. Bill froze in fear as the slick skis headed down the slope to the lift hut. A small rail fence served to guide the skiers down the hill, but when our gallant arrived, 215 pounds of muscle, skis, and toilet supplies hit it hard, causing a spectacular derailment. Toilet articles flew everywhere, and the skiers lined up there roared with laughter. It was a moment that would have washed out any other employee, but not Zickgraf. He waved and laughed back at his audience, retrieved his goodies, put his skis back on, and continued on.

Within three weeks, there was a miracle on the mountain. Complaints about the condition of the restrooms stopped. Bill not only did a good job of cleaning, he used his spare time to develop into a fantastic skier. He was no longer the "laugh of the mountain," but a widely recognized and colorful hero of the hillsides. He hadn't let the lowly image of the janitor get him down. In melodramatic fashion, he would seize a couple of mops, one in each hand like ski poles. Then he would push off from the highest peak and gracefully glide through the skiers. The ski school students, paying $20 an hour to learn, would all stop and heads would turn as Bill, a radiant smile on his handsome face, zipped by.

There were many well-known and influential people in the ski schools. One man from the show *What's My Line?* got so excited that he offered Bill an appearance on the show. "No one would guess the skiing toilet cleaner of Sun Valley, Idaho!" he said.

BILL ZICKGRAF'S PROUD UNIFORM FOR A SKIING TOILET CLEANER.

The first aid and safety patrol officers, rugged and good looking, usually occupied the top rung of recognition, but this toilet cleaner was stealing their thunder. The safety patrol wore bright orange coats with a big white cross on them, which identified them as the ski patrol. Bill had a picture of an old-time outhouse, moon on the door and all, silk-screened onto an attractive sweatshirt. The next day, down the hill he came, with BOWL PATROL blazoned in big letters across the back and front.

Zickgraf set a precedent for service that winter, and could have written a book on his experiences. But most importantly, he totally reversed the status of the job. By August of the next year, over a dozen people were asking for it, many of them willing to do it for nothing!

Even though we were now the second biggest employer at one of the world's most famous ski resorts and I had a free lift pass, I almost never used it. Back when I was in the seventh grade, we three oldest kids all got skis for Christmas. They were long and heavy and had the old death-lock bindings. I spent hours and hours on the hills near the house, trying to stay balanced on those torture boards, tumbling and falling until I was soaking wet, my cow corral overshoes tied so tightly to the skis I almost needed a torch to cut them off. We must have strong bones in the family, because I never broke anything, but I never learned to ski, either.

Years later with some of the best gear, teachers, and slopes then available, I spent a week being lacerated and laughed at on "Baldy Mountain" trying to ski. I never could unlearn my old bad habits, so I gave up. All of my kids (who also had free passes) became expert skiers.

I did benefit, however, from my ski involvement. I got great brownie points lending my "all day, every day" free executive ski pass to my banker, lawyer, accountant, and visitors, and made lots of headlines with the inception of the "Bowl Patrol."

In our Sun Valley days we accepted our first Indian Placement child, a 12-year-old Sioux girl from North Dakota, Janet Wounded Horse Blacksmith. This was exposure to a new culture for all of us, and it required some adjusting, especially since we had six kids, ages six to fourteen years old, and two adults already in a 55-by-12-foot trailer house. Indian Placement was a church-sponsored foster care program to help often parentless Native American kids get an education in a good, solid home environment. We assumed all expenses and responsibility.

Other people frequently stayed with us at Sun Valley, too, such as 25 young people from a touring orchestra, touring actors and sports team members from schools and universities, missionaries, and cleaning crew employees away from home. There were many Sunday dinner guests and company dinners, too. Some great relationships were built here with outstanding people from all over the country. Those were among the choicest moments we ever lived.

A double feature: Teacher, preacher

Being a bishop in the Mormon Church is a non-paid position that is about the same as a pastor or minister in other churches, and in my case, this meant responsibility for a congregation of about 400 people. My church was the Sun Valley ward of the Church of Jesus Christ of Latter-day Saints. Other Mormon congregations nearby had bishops that were tractor dealers, surgeons, and even one that owned a cheese factory. And of course, I was a janitor. We were all called to this position to serve five years or so.

Being a bishop meant the entire operation was mine to staff and administer and to take care of problems: spiritual, financial, domestic, and social ones. This included looking after widows and orphans, doing marriage and drug counseling, handling welfare programs for the needy (the local city had no such program), managing Scout camps, keeping all records, and being in charge of all finances and physical facilities. Other members of the congregation serving in different capacities did most of the actual work, but I had the final responsibility.

"Ministry" was an interesting addition to running a large business, raising a large family, coaching Little League, and other community involvements. My church spiritual and temporal duties meant I was on call 24/7. It was not uncommon to get called at two or three in the morning to rush to the hospital after a car accident, or to rescue a starving family. My Sundays would start at six o'clock in a bishop's meeting and many times I wouldn't get home until ten or eleven that evening. On many weekdays and evenings there was some spiritual need to tend to or event to organize or attend. I interviewed members and assigned them to positions, conducted meetings and Sunday worship, gave sermons, performed marriages, visited the sick, and conducted funerals.

All of this church service was satisfying and educational, but demanding. Fortunately, my wife and family were equally involved in much of this and thus it was a choice medium for family togetherness. We all loved it! I had served in many other church leadership capacities earlier, and would in many more after this.

Many experiences here were scary the first time around. The one I remember best was the first wedding I ever performed. I was nervous enough myself during the ceremony, but when I glanced up at the groom, he was white as a ghost and quivering, perspiration streaming down his forehead. One look at him and I began to do a duet with him on the shakes. I finally had to hold the marriage book against my chest so I could read it. We were both immensely relieved when the ceremony was over; this was probably the first time in history that the groom and the minister embraced before the bride and groom.

That one really broke me in—after that, I performed weddings on bridges and golf courses, in classrooms, anyplace requested. I married young, old, and even hippies who threw brown rice. I remember marrying a Ray Kay and Kay Jones and at the conclusion heard some snickering in the crowd when I said, "Now I pronounce you, Ray Kay and you, Kay Kay, man and wife."

OUR SUN VALLEY HOUSE, 2,600 SQ. FT.,
WHICH WE BUILT OURSELVES FROM TOP TO BOTTOM.

Our Sun Valley house

As a family, we had been in the Sun Valley area for two years and now laid the cornerstone for another big home on the beautiful piece of property we purchased on our arrival. Wanting our house to fit the unique needs of our family and lifestyle, we designed and built it ourselves. Barbara and I learned early that trying to divide your life into separate compartments of work, play, social activities, etc., was a short-changed way to live. Our life was just one operation, consisting of our home and family, our church activities, and Varsity, and we built the house to fit this.

The house had a unique design and alpine flavor. It was built of masonry, the inside walls paneled with cedar. The exterior was sided with rough-sawn, stained pine and had exposed beams in the front from the ground to the very top floor.

OUR FAMILY AND JANET POSED IN FRONT OF THE PINE SIDING OF OUR SUN VALLEY HOME.

We made sure there was plenty of room, because as mentioned earlier, it was not uncommon to have five or ten young people besides our own children at home for activities or dinner.

There was no freestanding furniture in the living room—only built-ins. Forty people could sit in our living room, which had an enormous conversation pit backed by a huge stone fireplace. The fireplace was built by our 13-year-old son Grant and me, after Barbara and I traveled to a quarry in Oakley, Idaho, and brought back a truckload of handsome facing stone. The kitchen was 18-by-32 feet and had 44 feet of upper and lower cupboards and a 16-foot dining bar.

The house took a little over 16 months of mostly after-hours time and long Saturdays to build. We did all of the work ourselves—design, foundation, plumbing, wiring, rockwork, carpeting, and even the installation of the heating system and the glass.

The first summer we were in Sun Valley, we basically left our home in McCammon and its contents as they were. On one trip to Salt Lake, I stopped off at the house to drop off some skis and winter clothes and pick up our stereo and a tape deck. On the next trip down, I found that someone else had decided to pick up a few things—our house had been robbed! They must have used a truck. They took bikes, pumps, lawn mowers, guitars, pictures off the wall, even my Scout uniform!

At first we were devastated. Our whole house invaded! But interestingly enough, when I filed the insurance claim, the total value of what I thought we could honestly claim was just $750, and that is what we collected. Most everything we had was used and that is the value of owning things—to use them. Our total jewelry assets were $300 (Barbara's wedding rings) and she always wore them. You don't need a home full of things to lead a happy life.

There comes a time, a maturing, when you are ready to surrender some lesser things for the good of the greater, and the future. I had relished a rich upbringing full of fun and games, excitement on the ball field and court, fine hours on fishing streams and in pursuit of big game. However, with maturity and increasing responsibility to others, not just family but now thousands of customers and employees, some of the things I had long considered sacred were beginning to seem like outgrown time-takers.

I HAD ALWAYS ENJOYED FISHING AND HUNTING, BASEBALL AND OTHER SPORTS, BUT REALIZED NOW THAT I COULD GET PLENTY OF EXERCISE AND ENJOYMENT JUST TENDING TO MY FAMILY, HOME, AND BUSINESS.

This came home to me one evening when a big regional softball game was scheduled. I was 33, and hurried home from a demanding day at work with only minutes to grab my gear and get to the playing field. As I picked up my well-seasoned mitt a strange feeling gripped me, and a question popped into my mind: "What are you doing, Don? There are plenty of eager young players out there now—you've got more important things to do with your evening than play." I did. Our company was growing rapidly, we had many new employees to be trained, and 30 different projects at the resort were rolling forward at a racing pace. I had six children plus a foster Indian child, ten acres of property to develop, was building a new house, and was the bishop of a growing congregation, including a youth program that was a seven-day-a-week responsibility. I put my cleats and mitt back on the shelf, knowing I could get plenty of exercise and enjoyment just tending to my family, home, and business.

We had a struggle deciding on uniforms for the company at Sun Valley. Once we all wore "whites." Over time, linen companies talked us into using grays, browns, yellows, and finally blues. I never did like the blues because I was often mistaken for the Pepsi man, the gasman, the mail carrier, etc. The last straw came one evening when I was mistaken for a bus driver. Our company owned a big four-wheel drive Suburban with three rows of seats, and with its oversized tires it could go almost anywhere. I drove it over to the elite Sun Valley Lodge one day and parked it in the "Reserved " spot in front (a janitor's privilege). I leaped out, and as I came through the front door was met by a group of conventioneers who were more than slightly inebriated. "What time does the bus leave, Mac?" one asked me. "I'm not a bus driver," I said. "Heck you're not! That's the bus, isn't it?" he said, gesturing to the Varsity vehicle. "No Sir, that's a janitor crew truck."

"Come on, man, we need a bus!"

Drunks can be obnoxious, but they were guests. I finally got free of them and proceeded to complete my errand. When I returned, the truck was gone. I figured someone on our crew needed it (we always left the keys inside), but when I walked to the shop, it wasn't there either. I called everyone I could think of and searched all the parking lots, but there was no sign of it.

Finally, I called the Sun Valley security officer. We were cruising around in his patrol car looking for the truck when an emergency call came over the radio reporting a "tank" driving around on the sidewalks and footpaths in the condominium complex. We rushed over and there was the truck, abandoned, straddling a footbridge, not one of the four wheels touching the ground. Lined up neatly on the hood were six empty cocktail glasses. We changed our uniform color as soon as we could after that!

It was before the snow season, but ground-freezing time in Sun Valley, and we were doing some last construction work on the skiing mountain. Skiers went up by the lifts, but there were some makeshift mountain roads snaking around to the top of the 9,000-foot peak. If the road was good and dry, an ordinary pickup with plenty of weight in it might make it to the top, but four-wheel drive was generally necessary. Varsity's tool truck, an older three-quarter-ton Ford, was needed up there, but it was only two-wheel drive. So I was towing it to the top chained to a 4x4, and up the mountain some crew and I went, hitting slippery spots but managing to handle them for the most part.

On the steepest part of the trail, as we swung around a corner going up, coming down the one-lane road were some hunters in a jeep. I hit the brakes and we both stopped our vehicles. As they backed up to find an alternative branch road, suddenly I felt my vehicle easing backward. Even with the brakes on both trucks, their weight on one steep, slick north-facing spot was too much. Backward down the steep, winding mountain road, edged by sheer cliffs, we rolled, gaining speed as we went. The thought raced through my mind, "We can jump out, but… oh, these poor trucks!" I could see them in my mind careening off the edge and rolling down the hill through the rocks and pines. The choices were to jump out or run the trucks backward into the mountain. An easy decision! As soon as I hit a dry enough place in the road, I turned the wheels and jammed the back of the truck into the upper side bank. The chain yanked hard, but both trucks stopped after a few feet, raking them along the bank. I had bent vehicles but no damage to life or limb. We waited until the sun cleaned the worst of the frost from the road and then crept the rest of the way up the mountain to work.

These were the kinds of things that mothers and wives never learned about until years later.

A memorable "Varsity marathon" occurred midsummer in 1972. I was up at six o'clock and had my corporate duties done by ten. I quickly changed clothes and headed out to Bill Janss' (the owner of Sun Valley) mansion to complete a volleyball court I was building there. He had picked an old creek bed for the purpose, and there was only one cup of dirt here for every truckload of boulders. I was on a deadline and picked rocks and leveled with my tractor until eight that evening. I took a moment to watch a 7-pound rainbow trout jump in Bill's private lake, then rushed back to the office for a managers' meeting. There Mark Browning reminded me that we had promised to paint the kitchen of the Hawkes' cabin that evening as a favor to a retired rancher and his wife.

We loaded the paint and equipment and drove through the pines to the old cabin, built in the 1800s. Two hours later we had the job done and received an apple pie baked in a wood-burning stove as payment. It was midnight, and I ached for the old king bed. But I'd volunteered to show a crew in Twin Falls how to seal concrete in a large wholesale grocery outlet building, and promised I'd be there tomorrow with the seal. The only available seal of this type was in Salt Lake City, 325 miles away. A delivery had failed to come through, and I also needed to pick up some material for a ball field backstop we were building. So at one in the morning, I left for Salt Lake City in a company utility truck.

Somehow I managed to make it there, and it took two hours to measure, buy, and load the galvanized metal pipe for the backstop. To save room I hurriedly shoved the small pipes inside the larger ones, and lashed the large pipes securely to the truck rack. Then I hurried to the chemical plant and bought the seal. At eleven forty-five, I was finished and had to be in Twin Falls by four o'clock to start the floor-sealing job. I was getting sleepy by now as I started down a sloping street in the center of Salt Lake City. It was the noon rush hour, and the stoplight ahead turned red faster than I expected. Platoons of people started crossing the intersection as I hit the brakes. Like a row of rockets, the unsecured smaller pipes inside the large pipes launched out into the intersection. It was awful—the noise of those pipes banging off the truck and hitting the street at all angles, and shooting into the crowds. People were running, jumping, and dodging my barrage. Some pipes that had made it through the crowds were rolling free down the street, and some were still hanging off the truck, which looked like an octopus with rigor mortis. Anyone who hadn't run for his life was glaring daggers at me, as I (unshaven, and covered with kitchen paint) jumped out to restore my load.

Fortunately, no one was hurt, and no police arrived by the time I reloaded, so I escaped from the scene of the crime and four hours later pulled up in front of the grocery warehouse in Twin Falls, where two truckloads of crew and equipment were waiting.

Ten of us started prepping the concrete, and by eleven-thirty that night, the floor was cleaned, etched, and dry, ready for the seal. The floors were finished by three o'clock and the two-hour drive home to Sun Valley was all that was left. I stopped by the office and checked for mail and problems before heading home to catch a few winks after my 50-hour marathon. I didn't finish up until noon and didn't get to bed until nine that night, after I dealt with some church and Scout responsibilities.

Sometimes there was just no escape from schedules like this. The work had to be done and on schedule, or else! It was tough but satisfying when you succeeded. The physical work never bothered me much. It was phone calls like the one two days later from the grocery store that zoned me. "Mr. Aslett, all of our bread and cereal smells and tastes like seal!" It seems the fumes, for some reason, were readily absorbed by grain products, right through the packaging, and nothing could be done but dispose of them all.

Our grocery store inflictions didn't end with wiping out the carbohydrate inventory. A few months later, we were cleaning in one of the big chain stores (Albertsons), and our crew was using a strong ammoniated chemical to strip the floor, the fumes of which wilted every exposed vegetable in the produce department.

Winter wonderland in Varsity land

In winter mops, brooms, and patio squeegees were replaced by snow blowers, snow shovels, ice prods, and plenty of warm clothes. Although it might appear a tough, cold job, there was color and excitement for those who braved the howling wind and subzero weather.

After five years of handling snow removal for the telephone company, for example, I figured I knew all about it. Then came Sun Valley. Amazing what a few thousand feet in elevation can do for snow depth! I have a picture of us shoveling 8 feet of snow here. We were supposed to keep the paths in the condo complex plowed, and that was a no-win situation. It could snow 15 to 18 new inches overnight. We had efficient Toros that could blow away light snow in minutes, but the machines were noisy and irritated late-sleeping guests. They paid $200 per night for a room, and screamed if we showed up before eight or nine, so we had to wait until early risers had tromped 18 inches of easy snow into 3 inches of ice cement before we dared turn on the blowers.

As the winter progressed, more snow accumulated—5, 6, 7 feet of it on the roofs, and it settled into a heavy, compact sheet about 4 feet deep. It was heavy enough to finally put pressure on the doors inside the buildings. Guests got anxious when the bathroom door stuck, and the hospital people panicked when they couldn't open the operating room door. We tried everything to remove roof snow—from sawing the base of it with a wire, to heisting a blower up on the roof. We finally resorted to a special hand snow shoveling. We cut the 4-foot layer of snow into 2-foot-by-2-foot squares and slid it off. We charged $150 a roof. A good man could shovel a roof in a day.

It was a great job—up in the crisp, pure air amidst some of the most beautiful mountains in the world. The sky a blue no artist could recreate, and a perfect sun! The excuse to

CLYDE STOKER CLEARING A PATH FOR THE GUESTS (1970).

be there, besides good exercise? Profit, plus a further inducement—competition. We had great roof races. Winning required iron discipline—small, careful consistent bits and blocks and no breaks. The greedy and reckless who seemed to be winning at first paid dearly in the end.

> I WAS CALLED ONCE TO TAKE THE SNOWMAKING UNIT INTO A COURTYARD WITH AN OLD FORD TRACTOR TO PROVIDE A BLANKET OF WHITE FOR A BING CROSBY AND ANN-MARGRET SPECIAL. (ANN-MARGRET MELTED IT!)

Once the snow quit, the call of the wild wasn't over—there were the icicles. Sunny days (which caused roof snow to melt), followed by cold evenings, produced icicles you wouldn't believe on the two- and three-story condos and lodges. Many icicles were 18 inches in diameter and 10 to 15 feet long. One was 3 feet thick! We knew nothing about removing them except that if past contractors did it, we could find a way to do it better!

Another thing we knew nothing about is why those contractors carried big sheets of plywood on their trucks. That mystery was solved at the end of the first day when it was just getting dark. I was picking at the base of an enormous icicle when it came loose and at great speed struck the slanted "snow rock" (the hard mountain of snow we had shoveled off the roof during the winter). It glanced off at even greater speed, breaking right through a huge Thermopane window, sliding across the carpet, and stopping near the fireplace where a family was relaxing in front of the fire. An impressive and expensive way to discover that windows needed to be protected with plywood when you were de-icicling.

"What are you going to do about it, Don?"

Harry Holmes, general manager of Sun Valley Resort, had a reputation of being a bit cold and aloof and unsympathetic to little daily problems, but he was the undisputed power figure of the Janss Corporation. We had a nice contract on the entire resort—it worked well and saved them tons of money, and we made some, too. However the problem of coming up with cash for payroll to cover the gap until we were paid for the jobs we did followed us here, and only worsened as the size of our contracts grew. A short-term loan of any size was hard to get without a solid cosigner. I talked Holmes into it a couple of times, and then as we assumed more contracts, payrolls just kept growing.

Once I just had no solution. I had payroll and payables due, and no cash, although (as usual) plenty of sure, safe, upcoming receivables. So I took my predicament to the top, Harry's office, where even high-level managers hated to venture. I poured my heart out, explaining our growth and dire straits and my struggle to finance it all (fully expecting Harry to melt and say, "Sure, Don, how much do you need?"). Instead, he waited until I was all through and said, "Well, what are you going to do about it, Don?"

I finally got the message, the bottom line of business: My problems weren't his, or anyone else's. I stood up and said, "I'll figure something out," and walked out. I don't remember what I did, but I took care of it. (I think I even raised the price on Harry's contract in the process.) He did me a great favor with that question.

> I'D LEARNED MANY HARD LESSONS
> IN FINANCE BY NOW. MAINLY,
> THERE AIN'T NO SANTA CLAUS.
> NO ONE OUT THERE IS GOING
> TO BAIL YOU OUT OR TAKE CARE
> OF YOU. YOU EITHER DO IT ON
> YOUR OWN SOME WAY, OR SINK.

When the Sun Valley operation was at its peak, not only were we doing most of the janitorial maintenance and cleaning for the resort, we were also doing the majority of the grounds maintenance, including painting. A single contract for painting a large condominium ran as high as $25,000—quite a contrast to the $300–$600 house painting jobs on which we worked our way through college. The crew that handled these jobs was called "Outside Varsity" and was headed by Mark Browning. Mark never took second place to anyone in the quality and creativity of his work, thus "outside" income soon exceeded our cleaning gross.

During this year, it was common for five or six major outside jobs to be going at once. One month we were building a barbed wire fence four miles long for a rich rancher from New York. On that job we cleared timber, moved rocks, removed old buildings, erected large gates, and surveyed fence lines. There were some memorable moments. While dragging some cottonwood tree stumps out of the way, for instance, an unnoticed beehive was ripped apart and the angry bees decided to avenge their disturbance. They circled into attack formation and then proceeded to pursue the Varsity workers. I yelled for everyone to freeze, but men scattered in every direction. The man driving the tractor leaped off and headed out also, leaving the tractor in gear. It went down the row of newly planted expensive posts, knocking them all down like a row of dominoes. Looking back and seeing the tractor in its wake of destruction, he ran back into the bees and mounted the tractor to bring it to a stop. To this day, the tractor carries the scars of the great bee attack.

Sun Valley odd jobs? Let Varsity do it!

By this time, our presence in Sun Valley went beyond being the kings of clean. We were the demons of dirt, the cure for manure, Santa's helpers, and the deans of demolition. Every Sun Valley department from food and beverage to grounds knew Varsity was hungry and competent as odd job jockeys. We got a reputation with our big accounts (Sun Valley and the Bell System) that we would try anything, do anything, especially if told no one else could do it.

Over the years, Sun Valley provided us with every kind of job imaginable, from removing gophers in the horse corrals and recovering golf balls out of lakes, to laying fireplace fires, painting towering ski lifts, and making snow for TV specials.

One of the rules of the farm was self-reliance. If you broke it, you fixed it; if you got it stuck, you dug it out; if your fence failed **you** rounded up the runaway stock; if the tire went flat you changed it. If you needed something and it wasn't available, you made it yourself... somehow. You didn't run to the house, part in hand, whining. Ingenuity was never an option, it was a necessity.

At the time, this attitude seemed cruel. (Today it would probably be considered parental abuse.) But after you grew up, it really came in handy. Man, were we resourceful and creative. We had a shop with an anvil, forge, grinders, and other tools, and we could rivet a broken harness, ream out a bearing, or make a replacement arm for a mower support. All of this proved beneficial in my now thriving cleaning and maintenance business.

When the horse trail got too dusty, I located an old sprinkler tank on a trailer, pumped water out of the creek, and wet down the road. We built boat docks, an archery range, tennis and volleyball courts, ice rink benches, and a children's day care center playground. We silk-screened signs, made custom wooden signs, and took on dozens of other odd jobs.

When the Sun Valley Company contemplated installing automatic sprinkler systems on lodge and inn grounds and landscaping, we jumped on it. We learned how, laid in $60,000 worth of Rainbird parts, bought a sod remover, and designed and installed the whole system. Picking up trash or pick and shovel work, we did it and loved it. Anything we didn't have or couldn't buy, or that hadn't been invented, we rigged, and there was always a silent victory dance when it worked!

THE KIDS TOOK FULL ADVANTAGE OF THE ENDLESS OPPORTUNITIES FOR WINTER FUN AT SUN VALLEY.

Operation Christmas trees

Our motto at Sun Valley was "We can clean anything and will solve any of your maintenance problems." Sun Valley Company gave us the opportunity to fulfill our brag by asking us to contract "Operation Christmas Trees." On December 25 every year, hundreds of guests were snuggled comfortably into the lodge to ski and enjoy a few winter days in the West. In such a short stay, a Christmas tree was hard to come by. When a guest would call for one, a highly paid union carpenter or other maintenance employee he assigned, would round up a tree, decorate, and deliver it. This was very expensive, and the company was reluctant to pass the whole cost on to the guests. Thus in 1969, the tree project generated a $5,000 loss for the Sun Valley Company. This was a problem, and when the company approached us to handle the project, we tackled it.

Bill Zickgraf (now area manager) thought over the need, talked to the registration desk, and got a list of all the guests scheduled during Christmas. He then printed up some postcards offering 4- and 8-foot trees, decorated or "U decorate." The cards were mailed in October and in November, Bill ordered a truckload of trees and bought rooms full of decorations wholesale. He then enticed a crew of decorators and deliverers. "Enticed?" you ask. Yes, enticed. These people were paid modestly (or did it as a church fundraiser), but they might get to deliver trees to big stars of the day like Robert Redford, James Arness (Matt Dillon of *Gunsmoke*), Doris Day, June Allyson, or Art Linkletter.

As soon as a guest arrived, starting Dec. 18, Varsity's tree crew or local church fundraisers would decorate and deliver a tree, and what a great time they had! Our secretary, Carolyn, had to make an emergency delivery and guess who lifted her up by the waist to put the star on top? Steve McQueen! My wife and daughter delivered a tree to Gregory Peck and he came out in his bathrobe and in his very polite way said, "Hello, young ladies." It took two weeks to get my wife down out of the air.

When Christmas was over, crews would retrieve the trees and strip off, pack, and store the decorations for next year. It was a great project, and guests could now celebrate the holiday without putting Sun Valley in the red! By the second year, we made it profitable.

Santa's bodyguard?

Well, why not? They have Santa's helpers, don't they? Santa couldn't make it without helpers, and every once in a while he needs bodyguards, too.

Santa made an annual visit to Sun Valley. The resort furnished Santa a real sleigh and some genuine reindeer to pull him. The crowds lined up around the courtyard and railings of the Swiss-style village to greet the jolly man and his sleigh full of presents. Sun Valley furnished free hot wine and rum to everyone at this Christmas Eve event, and by the time Santa arrived on the scene, many of the children's parents had had a snort or two of the free liquor.

Soon, with a *jingle-jingle-jingle*, in all his splendor, into the courtyard Santa came. The children were squealing happily and the locally trained reindeer doing just what they had rehearsed. All was perfect until the shoving from the back of the line pushed the people in front through the barricades, causing the line to break and scores of overexcited kids (prompted by overzealous parents) massed toward Santa. The reindeer became alarmed and wheeled and stampeded right over the top of the sled. Then those famous prancing and pawing little hooves pulverized the presents and did several unpleasant, injurious, smelly things to Santa! This shortened Santa's visit considerably, due to the need for a quick trip to the hospital.

For next year's visit, Varsity was asked to provide a corps of body-guards or find a way to get Santa into the courtyard unhurt. Varsity came up with a great plan. It was spectacular, foolproof, and the would-be Santa would do it for a $200 flat fee! One of my seasonal employees was a pre-med student and a skydiver! "Give me a Santa suit and bag of toys and I'll jump and land right in the circle—guaranteed!"

The resort people were impressed, but eyeing the pinnacle on a steeple next to the courtyard, felt the risk of a Santa shish kebab was too great (especially after last year's stampede). So Varsity's crew and managers ending up guarding the line on foot so that Santa was able to meet the kids, give out candy, and retain his life and dignity.

Who says it can't be done?

One morning Bud Siemons called me into his office and spread out on his desk were plans for, I kid you not, a mountain! It was an authentic practice climbing mountain, with all the ledges, chimneys, sheer scaling cliffs, outcrops, crevices and footholds, etc., you would run into on a regular climb, only these were miniaturized. "Can you build this thing, Aslett?" Well, he was asking the right man, because it was all cinder block and concrete facing, the king of all building materials as far as I was concerned. I would have done it free just for the fun of it. (I bid the job about that low, too.)

So we built it, first laying up all the blocks and filling the cores with concrete. Once the masonry structure was up, we wrapped it in rebar (tough steel reinforcing rods) and had a swimming pool contractor come by and shoot Gunite (liquid cement) coating on it. It covered the whole thing so well our "mountain" still looks real. Some of the crew worked on it free for the adventure I convinced them it was, so we came out okay profit wise, too.

Another time Bud mentioned that they needed a boat dock on the manmade lake in the middle of a new condo development. "Let us build it." "Can you?" "Sure!"

I'd spent my boyhood in the desert so I'd never seen a boat dock close up. But I drew up and submitted a successful bid and in two days, out of a pile of logs, with the aid of a sharp chainsaw and a few clamps and bolts, there sat a boat dock. Thirty-five years later now, that dock is still there.

Then there was the time we moved the boathouse. It was a wooden shed, like a small house, up in the stable area and the "grounds" people wanted it moved to the lake beach, about a quarter of a mile away. The bids to move it from real movers with loud diesel trucks went as high as $1,600, so Mr. Siemons called us in. The building was about 10 by 15 feet, heavy, and in an awkward place for vehicles to reach. I thought about rolling it on logs with my tractor pulling, but there would be no brakes for downhill and I could just picture it floating on the lake instead of standing beside it. Then I remembered that last year, a large dome for a Playboy house had to be transported from the rail yard, and it was done by the chief playboy Hugh Hefner himself,

BUILDING A FULL-SIZE PRACTICE ROCK CLIMBING MOUNTAIN WAS ONE OF THE MORE UNUSUAL ODD JOBS WE TOOK ON FOR THE SUN VALLEY MANAGEMENT.

buying many cases of beer and rounding up a bevy of sturdy boys to carry it up where it had to go.

I put out a memo for all crew to be at the stable at 5:30 P.M., in full white uniform (for pictures, of course). I bought a case of root beer, and gave a pep talk. We surrounded the shack, picked it up pallbearer style from its slab foundation, and like a giant white-legged centipede, we propelled that thing through the pasture, down the hill, down the road, and set it on the beach. It was so much fun beating out the pros and engineers, etc., that we never billed them a penny for it. (Pure pride, I guess, but I thought it was class.)

One job the former Sun Valley hotel workforce had problems with was setting up fireplace fires. The high-class Sun Valley rental condos all had a fireplace. And what is more romantic than touching a match to a neatly prepared stack of firewood and kindling in the fireplace? What is more irritating and disappointing than the fire not burning? It would take union workers an average of an hour a fireplace to "lay a fire," and about half of those fires would never catch properly (due to wet logs, etc.). We took the contract and improved the time a bit, but about a third of our fires wouldn't burn either, and even though we were doing the job better and more cheaply than it had ever been done before, we still got "burned" with complaints.

I had seen in a sports store once a little sawdust-like pellet called a fire-starter. You set it under a log, and once lit, it would burn for 5 or

RELL AND GRANT, AND ALL OF US, WERE STRENGTHENED AND ENRICHED BY OUR TIME IN SUN VALLEY.

6 minutes, igniting the rest of the fuel. I had a couple of old sheets of a fibrous sheathing material used in house construction, and I cut them up into little cigar-sized pieces on my table saw, dipped them in melted wax, and gave them to our fire crew. Within a week, we were laying six fires an hour and one hundred percent of them burned. These little things, which we called fire sticks, would ignite the biggest, wettest log.

I went to Sun Valley management and asked if a surefire fire every time was worth five cents. "Oh yes, Mr. Aslett." We charged them five cents each for the sticks and it was a profitable home business for our kids, not to mention what it did for Varsity's ability to make fast and quality fires. There were lots of fireplaces at Sun Valley, so we set up a manufacturing center in our garage at home. We put the wax in a big turkey roaster, and heated it until it melted. Then we made a wire basket that fit into the roaster, filled it with pieces of sheathing, and it was exactly like dipping French fries into hot fat. We made thousands and thousands of fire sticks. Each of our kids had a job in the operation, and it was a great way for them to earn extra money.

I guess this is the time and place to make a small confession. I was a Scoutmaster, and the zero-degree winter campout every year was fun. Setting up camp and getting a fire going in 6 feet of snow was a bit taxing. But the boys had to learn, and as they were all on their knees, blowing and coaxing their piles of tinder and damp branches that were struggling (and failing) to be a fire, my fire was blazing almost instantly. The boys were awed. "Boy, Mr. Aslett, how do you do that?" "You'll learn, boys, just keep trying." (Those fire sticks looked just like a piece of wood.) I figured it was fair—I learned the hard way in my day, and in my old age (the ripe old age of 42), I deserved a shortcut.

The biggest decision I ever made

I had been in my own business for about 14 years now. I had the whole Sun Valley resort under many contracts besides cleaning—we were doing about every other kind of work available in a resort town. My accountant and I had bought and now ran a motel called the Red Top, and our company was expanding into other states. My dreams of building a big, successful company looked to outsiders as if they were coming to reality, but all this meant no vacations, little personal time, and worst of all very little money, as most of it went to providing capital for payroll and expansion.

At this time, the late 1960s, condos were the new and "in" thing and Sun Valley had its share. Nice Alpine-styled buildings were going up everywhere, and even novices in real estate were making lots of money selling them. I remember a local colorful character, Barry

Barsford (pure Irishman), in his heavy brogue saying about his newfound career, "Ha ha, me laddie, 'tis a license to steal!" He had moved from a little local cleaning business to being a wealthy real estate salesperson. Then a young woman who had spent most of her time hanging out with the ski bums got her real estate license and in her first year made $64,000. In those days, that was a fortune. I was taking home about $4,000 a year at best working double her hours, and hearing all of this unfocussed me enough that I said to myself, "Huh, who would be a better realtor than me?" Adding that to my entrepreneurial portfolio seemed an irresistible idea.

Most people don't have half the direction or confidence you do, but if you start looking at and listening to their success stories (we never learn all the facts between the lines), you will start wondering why your life is lacking. Many people (even basically honest ones) will fib about their kids' grades, their sex lives, gas mileage, their weight, and how much money they make. If you have doubts in any of these areas and listen to others long enough, self-doubt will ripple in.

So in the midst of my busy life, letting comparison overcome my good sense, I bought some books and started the process of obtaining my real estate sales license, hoping that all the condos wouldn't be gone by the time I was able to hang out my shingle.

It was a Friday midnight, and I was just finishing up in my office right behind the Challenger Inn. I opened the cabinet to file something and there, staring me in the face, was my neatly stacked realtor library, along with partly filled out forms and applications. An overwhelming question came to me: "Don, why not be the world's best of what you are already; why do something different?"

I sat back down in my chair and reflected on this. I already knew the cleaning and maintenance business better than anyone I could name, and I loved it. If I went into real estate it would take me years to reach the level of expertise and professionalism many people in the business reached long ago. So why change courses now? Why not start today and be not just good, but the best, in the entire building service industry?

I stood up, tossed the pile of books and binders about real estate into the trash, and went home. The next morning, I set to work with renewed determination—not just to survive or become more efficient at my profession—but to be the best in the world and make my company and myself unique.

Chapter 10

SPREADING THROUGH THE WEST

It was a big country and we had big ideas!

As the years passed, we moved Varsity's operations into a number of new states, as well as strengthened our presence in the places where we already had a foothold.

Bluffing our way to Boise

When you read about the growth of a company, it sounds good all condensed into a few pages. But there may be agony between the lines, as well as ingenuity. While I was still in Sun Valley, although we only had a few accounts in Boise, Idaho (an IBM office and a couple of phone buildings), it was not enough to justify a full-time manager. Without benefit of demographic planning, I decided we would expand to Boise from Sun Valley and move our present Sun Valley manager, Rex Turner, there to build it into a thriving operation. So one cold mountain morning (21 below zero at 5 A.M. when we left) Rex and I headed there in a van with no heater.

When we stopped in Shoshone for breakfast I was tempted to put my hands in between the hotcakes to thaw them out.

Once we got to Boise, we figured we'd do it the old way: We put on our best suits, and each of us took a street and started knocking on doors. This was not the 1950s, however. We got nothing in three long, tiring days of "cold turkey" solicitation but cold wind, café food, and "I'm sorry, maybe some other time" answers. The most common turndown was, "I'm sorry, but we already have a janitor and he is doing fine." How can you rebut that? I saw a *Mad* magazine lying in one lobby and talked the receptionist out of it to provide some clip art for an idea. I made up a little brochure, and the next day when someone hit me with, "Sorry, but I have a janitor and he/she is doing great," I gave them a copy of it. "You are lucky to have good and faithful janitors, " I said, "and when they go on vacation or are sick, we're available to come in and take their place for a day, or week, or more and will charge you exactly what they are getting. So," (and I headed for the door), "call us when they can't be there."

It worked! No one was offended, plus they knew the price was right and we were no threat to anyone. Missing janitors are common; we were in some buildings almost immediately. Once we were in a building, we knew the time it took to clean it, and usually knew how to do some things better, plus some little extras that the average janitor didn't know how or think to do. We also got to know not just the building and its needs, but all of the bosses and their assistants. An ugly brochure done in a motel room with rub-on lettering and magazine cartoons saved the day!

Two weeks after our Boise canvassing, a telephone foreman who knew us needed a cable rack dusted and vacuumed. We bid the job for $75 and got it. Cable racks were found in telephone equipment rooms. On top of 12-foot high equipment there was a steel rack two feet wide resembling a horizontal ladder, and on this lay hundreds of phone cables. The rack when full was usually only about 18 inches or less from the ceiling. Even though telephone offices were kept nearly dust free, over time dust did accumulate here. This was one of the most brutal of all maintenance jobs; the entire room full of racks had to be dusted and vacuumed from a horizontal position—either on your back or crawling along on your stomach. Every 18 inches there was a 6-foot vertical steel prong to hold the cable in place.

At three-thirty that afternoon Rex and I crawled out of the frame peak, clothes ripped, covered with dust, cuts, and bruises, but happy.

We had fulfilled the first real Varsity assignment on our newest expansion, and the area was open!

Our Boise startup was a tough one, however, and it took some real doing to build it into a profitable and smooth-running operation that would be recognized elsewhere.

Tupperware, for example, was building an enormous factory in central Idaho (Jerome) about 120 miles from Boise. We were unable to obtain a contract to service it, but were offered an opportunity to bid on the initial cleanup prior to its opening. Desperate for work, Rex bid the job as low as he could to keep the men busy. Varsity was awarded the bid and he moved the crew in. This immense building was like many football fields of concrete under one roof—acres and acres of floors. There appeared to be no end to the job, but Rex, more determined than ever, vowed to not just finish but to make money. I would send crews down from Sun Valley, 80 miles away, to help out, and they would return so beat that they couldn't even talk. Stories of unbelievable toil began to reach me, and the stories finally got so incredible that I stopped in person to check them out.

The factory was dead quiet, not a man in sight; however, there were worn-out floor pads and piles of equipment all over. The automatic scrubbers were covered with dirt and grime, their scrubbing brushes literally worn down to the block. That alone told the story—it looked like the aftermath of a battle. A maintenance man informed me that the crew had just finished a 36-hour shift, breaking only to eat two meals, and had gone to bed at a local motel. I found the motel and their room. Because it was hot the door was ajar, and lying there like a line of bodies in a morgue, was Rex and his janitor army. Their feet were sticking out of the covers, with huge blisters on the bottoms from working on concrete. The job was finished at last, and if Rex's wages weren't counted, we just broke even.

Then more news arrived. Some of the stripping and etching solution used on the concrete had flowed under the door of a room in the building and ruined more than $1,200 worth of Tupperware. This amount, which the company deducted from our check, left us with a gaping loss on the job. Tupperware parties were never the same for us after that.

Boise did eventually take hold, and with four Varsity offices it is one of our central locations today.

Arizona! A deal in the desert

One night my Sun Valley phone rang and a voice said, "Mr. Aslett, this is Bob Pothier in Phoenix, Arizona, and I wondered if I might ask you some questions about your cleaning company?"

"Sure."

"We have a small company here and need some professional advice."

I was always happy to help, even a competitor (plus we had rented his mother's house in our early Sun Valley days), and spent the next hour answering some questions about the janitorial business. He thanked me graciously. Three weeks later, he called again and asked if he and his brother drove up, would I meet with them and help them some more? I was glad to do it and arranged for my supervisors to meet with them when they arrived as well. After this we arranged for them to get some equipment wholesale, and they returned to sunny Arizona very motivated.

At this time, I met a handsome young attorney named John Preston Creer. He had been the youngest county commissioner in Salt Lake County, Utah, at the age of 29. We struck up an immediate friendship, and he did a few legal assignments for me. I mentioned the calls and visits from the Arizonans to him and he suggested offering them a merger, something they really needed and that would strengthen our presence in that state. An offer was presented and after some negotiations, an agreement made. Varsity of Arizona was in motion now in a significant way.

Setting up this corporation was the beginning of a new era in transportation for the company—flying. Driving anywhere from Sun Valley meant 160 miles before you reached any serious civilization and then hundreds of miles more to any of our other business centers. As we expanded, I was required to travel more extensively. Most trips were 400 to 800 miles, so for the first time in my life I began to fly on commercial and private airplanes to save time. When I didn't fly commercially, Rex Turner would drop by Sun Valley in his Cherokee 180 and pick me up. We'd fly to Pocatello, get in a day of meetings, and then fly home. We flew in some uncomfortable weather once in a while, but it sure beat driving.

Our strength in Arizona was our credibility with the phone company—within a month, we had added 11 new phone buildings there to our customer list.

California here we come!

Our expansions at this point all reached out from Sun Valley, as this was where the Varsity home office was presently located. No one contemplating expansion of self or business could overlook the gold coast of the West, California! Our unique foothold with the Bell System gave Arlo and I enough courage to hop in our Volkswagen bug and make some bold sales calls to the big boys at the San Francisco telephone installation. Although these were cold calls from a couple of Idaho amateurs, Varsity got a "foot in the door" and California, after a considerable number of trips there and some heavy bidding against the big competitors, joined our cleaning collection of states.

On to Denver

The next expansion in our company was the one I feel weaned us from a "farm boy company" and put us up with the big boys.

It began with an invitation from our attorney. "Hey, Don, if you're in no hurry to get back to Sun Valley stop by the house—there is someone I want you to meet." Not being much of a social mover, I declined and told him I was going to take off for home, 320 miles away on slick roads. "This guy is from Denver, Don. When I told him about your business he said his wife worked in a large building in Denver and the owners were unhappy with the janitors and looking for a good company."

"Denver is too big and far away," I told him.

"No, be at my place in an hour."

He was persuasive, and soon I was visiting with a sharp young man named Ernest Bare. He was the all-American salesperson and worked for a large housing development in Denver. I was impressed enough to investigate the building he had mentioned, especially since Denver was the headquarters of Mountain Bell, and a lot of telephone executives we knew from our work in Utah were now in Denver.

A few days later, I flew to the Mile-High City of Denver. Cities of this size overwhelmed me, especially when compared to the towns where I was raised and now called home. Ernest met me at the airport and together we called on the owner and manager of the big office building. He was encouraging, so I did a study and bid the building. Two weeks afterward I heard from him that our bid was right in there, but because we weren't established in Denver, he decided to give the job to someone else. It was a sizable bid and though the loss of it disappointed me, visions of Denver still fired me up. I had caught a glimpse of the huge telephone building downtown and my blood boiled with ambition.

We had approximately 130 telephone buildings and installations under contract at this time in other states, and I could see no reason why it should end there. Ernest was deeply involved in his own business and working with me was only a side interest, but the time was right to have him acquaint me with the Denver area. And he did.

Several of the men who knew us from the beginning days of Varsity had now been promoted to top positions with the telephone company. This made it much easier to get appointments. I got to spend an afternoon with a man we had worked with before in another Bell building, he introduced me to others, and I had a chance to really give the Varsity sales pitch to the phone people in Denver.

It was 1973, our fifth year in Sun Valley. The phone rang, and it was Ralph Walters. We'd broken our butts for him ten years before in little dinky offices in Utah and now that he was a fourth level executive—real "ruler" rank in the phone company—he remembered.

He got right to the point. "I'm over eighty buildings in the Denver area, including the million-square-foot main building downtown. Are you interested in cleaning it?" Well that is like asking a veteran cleaner if he wants to go to janitor heaven. I put down the phone, went outside did three back flips, and then picked up the phone again and calmly said, "Yes!" He asked for a per square foot price right then. I called Arlo and Rex, and we decided to boldly ask for three-and-a-half cents a square foot. I called Walters back with our price (something that never happened before or after without formal bidding), he said, "You got it! When can you start?"

This was the greatest stride we had ever made with the Bell System, and we were ecstatic and deeply appreciative—we would now be cleaning the Mountain States telephone headquarters! It was our biggest and best contract to date, over $35,000 a month. A million square feet in a single high-rise building was more space than in all of our other buildings put together!

We three flew to Denver and negotiated the final details and then met to decide who would head the operation. I had moved once (to Sun Valley), so this time it fell to Arlo and his wife and children. Pulling up roots and a family of six children is not easy; Arlo at the time was deeply involved in community affairs, a bishop in the LDS church, he played the violin and sang in the city symphony, and was loved and well thought of in the community. But he listed his beautiful new home, packed up, flew to Denver, and bought a house there—Varsity was now in Colorado!

ARLO LUKE MOVED TO DENVER IN 1973, AND THE AREA BEGAN SHOWING SUBSTANTIAL GROWTH.

Arlo jumped right in, took over contracts and situations, and produced amazing results for Varsity and for the telephone company. He had some tough going when he first arrived, however. To get quality people, he interviewed literally hundreds over two weeks. We needed 35 people, and he spent the time and money to check all 35 carefully.

Even so, 12 of the 35 never showed up for the first night of work, and never called. The second night ten more didn't show! I had sent our Sun Valley in-house operations manager and bookkeeper to Denver to set up the books, and Arlo had him working 12-hour shifts cleaning 17 floors of restrooms. When I got my office man back, he was showing the strain of his Denver visit. For a month or two turnover was high, but eventually Varsity found the quality people we needed.

Before long, things were going smoothly and profitably, and Denver began showing substantial growth. The telephone company people there were wonderful to work with and taught us much about quality control and customer service. Two of our Sun Valley managers, Duane Hunt and Dennis Parker, were transferred there.

Back to McCammon

The Denver expansion required me to leave Sun Valley and go back to Pocatello, because Varsity's original home base there was now without management leadership. In Pocatello, I would be closer to the heart of the Varsity operation as things continued to pick up. Once back in our old headquarters office, I made many changes in personnel and systems and designed some new forms and reports. Working with our CPA, we designed an accounting system for the entire company to use. I made a change in the management of Utah and within a few months, things really began to happen. Utah even began to show a slight profit for our years of investment and previous losses.

One important and permanent change in Varsity's structure had happened in Sun Valley. I was the founder of Varsity, with 100 percent sole ownership at first. After we graduated, Arlo and I split the telephone company part of our service into a second company called Varsity Telco, of which I owned 55 percent and Arlo, 45 percent. I also had a supply company called Micro-Clean Supply. Late in our Sun Valley days, at the advice of our accountant, we merged all of these entities into Varsity Contractors, Inc. I held the controlling stock, 55 percent, Arlo 30 percent, and Rex Turner, Mark Browning, and Dave Collings the remaining 15 percent. We had a board of directors and were now an official part of the corporate world.

Shortly after moving back to the ranch in McCammon from Sun Valley, we had eight teenagers living with us at one time. We accepted two more Indian placement students, Karla Dragswolf and Marty Goodbear, cousins who were both outgoing and talented. They were from the Dakota Hadasa and Mandan tribes and both had handsome Indian features. Marty kept in touch with us later, as he became a professional dancer for his culture and toured the world.

The last American Indian we had for a school year was a 16-year-old girl named Dorian Aho, also a Mandan. She was athletic, attractive, and a top student. Her mother had been beaten to death and her father was alive somewhere but out of touch. Her stay was an eventful one, with our four daughters about the same age in the house.

I was intrigued by Native American culture—what a gifted and sensitive people they are. I kept a journal during our time together and wrote a powerful book from it, which I will publish someday. What an injustice was done to these people—our visits to the reservation were an education all Americans need.

Fulfillment of another old dream

Ever since the newspaper in our little high school first published one of my poems, I felt drawn to writing. Few who knew me ever realized how much writing I did. I had notebooks full of article ideas that I planned to develop over the next few years. With the stack of letters, bids, and follow-ups I left for my secretary each day, there was always a page or two of essays, poems, and observations for future use. My poetry was like most people's poetry—no one appreciates it much except the author, but occasionally I managed to write a humorous verse or two about happenings at work, which did delight a few others, including clients. I had also noticed that people would always comment on even a business letter that was well written, and bids and proposals written with some flair and personality were accepted more often than those merely stating amounts and numbers. Even invoices sent with a nice comment or clever remark got paid faster.

I kept writing and filing what I wrote, and in 1974 finally tried to sell something.

During 16 years of working with them, I had collected, from both written and oral sources, a vast amount of information about janitorial work and other maintenance related specifically to the Bell System. I decided to tap this collection and write an article pointing out the uniqueness of a telephone maintenance operation as compared to the usual maintenance situation. The telephone industry magazine *Telephony* bought it, along with a picture and a chart. The $25 check I received for the article barely covered my secretary's time proofing and submitting it. However, that article was about as important as that first telephone call from Western Electric, for it resulted in opening one of the biggest doors thus far in my pursuit of becoming "the National Janitor."

One morning I arrived at the office and found among the eight or ten calls recorded that "Jack Poe from Northwestern Bell" had called. Anytime a telephone person I didn't know called from a Bell company we weren't working for, I always made sure I made quick contact. I had no callback number this time but fortunately, he called back.

"Mr. Aslett, this is Jack Poe from Northwestern Bell, at our headquarters building in Sioux Falls, South Dakota." AT&T headquarters in New York had recently assigned him to rewrite and update the Bell System Practice Manual on house service janitorial work. He said he knew very little about the subject of his new assignment but had read an article about it that impressed him—my article. He wanted permission to quote some of it. I told him that the article contained only a tiny taste of the information I had in that field. At first I don't think he believed me, but after two and a half hours on the phone I finally convinced him.

Those two and a half hours were the beginning of an unbelievable two and a half years to follow. We began talking on the phone regularly, and I started to send him material, including four new practices I thought the system needed. He got into the spirit of his new assignment and dug into it far beyond the call of duty. He told the home office in New York that he had found a tremendous source of information in a guy in Idaho and they should take advantage of it. They heeded Poe's message and arranged to meet with me and two of his staff.

Three weeks later, I was standing in Poe's office in Sioux Falls with two high-powered AT&T executives from the East, Wayne Gartzke and Jerry Miles, Mr. Poe, and some other local Bell people. Mr. Gartzke was a sharp, experienced telephone man who had come up through the ranks. He was seldom in a meeting more than a few minutes because of the vastness of his responsibilities. Our meeting lasted for eight hours straight, and there was an instant kinship. Gartzke knew his business, and it was refreshing to see a man so high up who so completely comprehended the field of janitorial maintenance. Gartzke recognized that I knew the business too, as it related to the Bell System, as well as anyone in the country.

After 16 years cleaning and maintaining telephone buildings and installations as a private contractor, an outsider working in the inner world of a massive, well-established, and very traditional and conservative corporation, Varsity had a proven record of cutting costs while increasing quality in the servicing of their facilities. We had streamlined and standardized operations and taken every advantage of economy of scale. We were able to find better cleaning products, equipment, and innovations that were often slow in getting through their ponderous in-house approval procedures. His bottom line after the meeting was, "There has to be some way to get your information and methods to our company—it could save us millions of dollars."

I left there convinced that in time some opportunity would come.

OUR FIRST OFFICIAL VARSITY MANAGEMENT MEETING (COMPLETE WITH MATCHING BURNT-ORANGE BLAZERS), HELD IN SALT LAKE CITY. MARK BROWNING, REX TURNER, DUANE HANSEN, ME, RICK DEBENE, DENNIS PARKER, AND ARLO LUKE.

A six-state company

In the spring of 1974 Varsity Contractors, the little one-bucket, one-ladder operation from Idaho State University, was now functioning in six Western states. This was the start, I felt, of many states to follow. We were wiping away the idea that a janitor was an end-of-the-line job, and began pulling top people nationally into our leadership.

The article I'd written for *Telephony* (and the series of articles I would write later—see p. 211) eventually played an important role in some of the biggest moves we ever made with the phone company. When a Wyoming telephone executive visiting Phoenix read the article, he returned to Wyoming and asked his man in charge to "check out this Varsity outfit." One early spring morning the plant manager of Mountain Bell in Wyoming asked, "Are you interested in looking at some work here in Wyoming?" "Yes, Sir! Where?" "Well, the whole state if you think you can offer a quality job and money-saving deal."

Elated, I told Mr. May we would be in touch later and arrange a time. I waited a week as things were busy and I had business in Arizona. The phone rang again. "Well," his gruff voice said, "what is the delay?"

"We'll be there Monday," I told him, "and travel the entire state and look at every building!" "Good, I'll contact all of the personnel involved and they will be waiting for you. Goodbye." (He was all business.)

We had learned many things about expansion by this time. The old way of sending a partly qualified man to an area and letting him "gut it out" wasn't wise. That method was a risk we didn't want to repeat.

Wyoming was large and sparsely populated, and it had extremes of weather. These two facts spelled a tough situation for making a go of it with the more than 60 phone buildings spread over the state. We had the man for those challenges, if we happened to land the contract. The man was Mark Browning. He had worked with us for eight years now and was knowledgeable and efficient in all phases of our operation—his experience at Sun Valley had taken care of that. I talked to Mark about the call from Mountain Bell and approached him about this possible new assignment. He indicated that he was interested and so that following Monday Mark, Arlo, and I headed out on a 3,000-mile bidding tour. (Arlo and I also brought our nine-year-old sons.)

We started in the Jackson Hole area in western Wyoming, swung up through Yellowstone Park and into the small town of Powell near the Montana border, and then turned south and headed through the beautiful Jim Bridger country. We drove through deserts, mountains, oil fields, and every kind of weather God ever created. At each stop we inspected and analyzed each Mountain Bell building and the phone booths and other facilities that needed janitorial service. Telephone people then were a real select group of people—they all seemed to be concerned, helpful, and polite, and it was a great experience to meet so many. Mr. May had told us the tour would take at least two weeks. We didn't have a second week right now, so when arriving in our last area for the day, we would try to get the phone people to come down to their office to see us at eight or nine in the evening. If there was a small CDO office in the area, we would run out and look at it at ten or even midnight. We were up early the next day and on our way through that huge state, where even jackrabbits needed to carry water bags to survive.

Our sons enjoyed the trip and at each stop (they weren't allowed in the buildings for security reasons), they jumped out of the car and played catch. In the evening, they made sure we selected a motel with a swimming pool. It was beautiful spring in Wyoming and the hills (full of antelope and other wild game) were solid green. We visited every town that had a telephone office or installation.

IN GRAND TETON, WYOMING, WITH MY VARSITY VW.

After the tour, we spent a week analyzing the situation and figuring prices. Far from the largest in gross income, this Wyoming prospect spanned the largest geographical area and contained more buildings in one package (more than 60, plus hundreds of booths) than we had ever bid on at once before. We prepared and presented our bid, and then waited. With a few minor adjustments, the bid was accepted. From that moment on it was Mark Browning's baby. He owned a beautiful home that he had built himself in Sun Valley, nestled in the cottonwoods near Eagle Creek. He sold it the day he listed it and was on his way. Another Varsity state was now operating.

This was cowboy country, at the height of an oil boom. If you walked into a café full of huge roughneck oil riggers and sneezed wrong, you probably wouldn't get out alive, and the doors of many of the phone booths were ripped off the hinges. Travel time here was triple anything ever before, and we earned every penny we made.

Growing pains

The process of setting up a state for a janitorial operation might sound quick and easy, but that is far from the reality. Equipment and vehicle procurement, office moving and setup expenses ran into thousands and thousands of dollars. Some small buildings that turned only $25-$75 a month profit required a $120 vacuum, a $500 floor machine, and over $400 worth of carts, chemicals, mopping gear, trash barrels, and so on. It takes a long time to get the returns on this large an investment.

It seemed that every time Barbara and I would get some money saved or be about to get the new couch or table and chairs we had waited years to buy, something big would come up in the business. It was still hard to borrow from the bank, so this meant we had to invest personal funds. Wyoming took a lot of money and was timed perfectly to take advantage of the $12,000 check I received from the sale of a piece of property. Varsity needed it worse than we did personally and so into the company $10,000 of it went. This was an old story and we had learned to expect it and live with it.

When we expanded to Denver, I had approached the bank for a loan to help foot the bill. The banker referred my request to a committee of experts in the home office and the committee said they didn't think we should expand at this time, but develop the areas we had already and save our money. That was typical advice from a group of people who didn't understand or feel the pulse and passion of our business. They were wrong, because the move to Denver contributed to business in other areas, and our company doubled in size and strength within the next 16 months.

Chapter 11

SALES CALL ON A GRAND SCALE: MY PHONE COMPANY SEMINARS

Teaching those who taught me…

The year wait

Being prepared for a "big chance" is imperative if you intend to capitalize on it. Exactly one year had passed since my initial meeting with AT&T engineers in Sioux Falls. I had heard little from Mr. Gartzke, and was impatient for action but didn't just wait by the phone. I transformed all of my notes about phone building maintenance into usable and presentable material. I wrote more practices for Bell, which I didn't give them, and researched and wrote maintenance management procedures. I visited filming studios, read up on 16 mm filming, and then wrote a script for a 20-minute "introduction to telephone building maintenance" film. I also continued to write articles for telephone magazines, hustled work for Varsity, further refined our management system, and prepared my corporate structure to run without me.

The year before I had anticipated Varsity's growth pretty accurately and had com-

LOADED UP TO TRAVEL TO ONE OF THE SEMINARS I DID FOR THE BELL SYSTEM IN THE LATE 1970S. BOTH THE NUMBER AND SIZE OF THE PROPS GOT BIGGER WITH TIME.

menced the project of replacing most of my management responsibility with a new general manager. Mark Browning was selected for this and we projected ten months ahead—September 1, 1976—as the date by which the changeover would officially be complete.

All the while, I was faced with the same old problem—all of this cost money, and Varsity was growing rapidly and constantly reorganizing. With an unwavering faith in my future with Bell, I drained every savings account and all of my own personal Varsity paychecks and poured them into the dream. There were no new cars, furniture, vacations, or fancy clothes for us. One year after the Sioux Falls meeting, I had more than $16,000 in writing and scripting expenses, and at least $25,000 in time and travel, building the idea for Bell that I knew what they needed, and could provide it. This was entirely on speculation—the assumption and faith that my chance would come. Varsity couldn't help me financially as our recent expansions had taken all of our resources.

New York calling!

Just when I began to wonder how much time was going to elapse before my investment would pay off, the telephone rang and my secretary announced that a Mr. Wayne Gartzke from New York was calling. His message was one I had been waiting to hear. "We have a country-wide engineering conference centered on operating our buildings efficiently and I feel it would be a good time for you to introduce some of your ideas and concepts to our head building managers. Are you interested?" I was not only interested, but panting like a starving wolf for such an opportunity. He accepted my enthusiastic "Yes," and informed me the conference would be broken down into three separate sessions held in Reno, Pittsburgh, and Nashville.

Three weeks later, Gartzke called me and arranged a meeting with him and two other telephone people in Denver. At this meeting we discussed and outlined the areas they wanted me to cover at the conferences. I was fascinated to learn some of the politics and priorities operating in Bell buildings and left Denver much more informed than when I arrived. Once home, I put the information together in preparation for a review to be held in Bell headquarters in the East within a few weeks. The purpose of this of course was to evaluate my material and how I presented it, to see that it would fit within their system. I intended to really knock them over, as I boiled down 17 years of experience and information into an 80-minute presentation. Then with the aid of a daughter home for the weekend from Brigham Young University, I made a visual aid—a miniature telephone building. By eleven o'clock the night before I had to leave for New York, everything was ready.

Going to New York City for the first time was a monumental experience for a person raised in a town of 160 people with a graduating class of 14. I had heard of "195 Broadway" (which was AT&T's headquarters building in downtown Manhattan) for years and to a telephone person this was Mt. Olympus. During the past year a new $2.8 million headquarters had been built in Basking Ridge, New Jersey, and this was where I was scheduled to be reviewed. It was like a dream fulfilled.

At eight-thirty the next morning I was standing in front of seven telephone company executives in a plush conference room, waiting for an eighth person to finish a long distance call and join us. He was Jerry Miles, Gartzke's boss and one of the head people over the 28,000 telephone buildings in the U.S. Miles was a youthful, well-educated man, tall and lean and analytical, and true to his Bell upbringing, conservative. The others in attendance included Gartzke, AT&T staff managers, and representatives from New Hampshire and New Jersey Bell.

Having such an important audience didn't scare me, but it unfortunately inspired me to try to lay the whole program on them in one sitting. To make it worse I constantly deviated from the main subject into philosophies and opinions. My presentation lasted two and a half hours, and I'm sure by the end, they were overwhelmed. I was dismissed for a while, and to keep me entertained was given a tour of the building. I then returned to the room and received the first real criticism I'd ever had as an adult in business.

They tore my presentation apart, adding suggestions and ideas, and commenting on everything from the spelling on my visual aids to the fact that I talked too fast and only finished about half of my thoughts and sentences. Miles was a complete gentleman, tactful and kind, but could he ever analyze. "Don, you're a great motivator and salesman with a great message. We could hear the steak cooking, we could smell it, but we never saw or tasted any meat. Give us less philosophies, more tangible things. How do you bid, how do you evaluate? Show us, tell us," etc.

To make matters worse, after my presentation I had submitted them an $85,000 proposal to redo some house service specs and writing for their whole system. It was a good, workable, factual proposal, but typed up and bound at the last minute, thus not proofread. When I listed the reasons I was the best in the world to do this, the first one was, "Because I am a professional writer." The last two words were misspelled, and that didn't seem to impress Miles much either.

By the time the critique was finished I was on my second notebook. I had been eaten alive instead of covered with glory. I was often thought of as a dominating person and as a result, most of my ideas and approaches usually got a "yes man" reaction. This particular experience, however, was a humbling one and it might even have slightly shaken my confidence. But as they finished up Mr. Miles stood up, put his hand on my shoulder, and said, "Nonetheless, we liked it. You know your stuff and we are looking forward to seeing you do your thing at the conferences."

I licked my wounds all the way home and was so busy redoing the material that I didn't look out the window of the plane all the way back to Idaho.

Four weeks later I was in Reno with a revised presentation in one hand and a fresh-off-the-camera new video in the other. From the past two days of Varsity work and travel, my nerves were ragged. Arlo from Denver, and one of our other managers, Dennis Parker, showed up to hear my report and meet Miles and Gartzke. The hotel was full so both stayed in my room on rollaway beds, and both wanted to talk, and we did so until one-thirty that morning. I was tired when I got up the next morning, too—the long-awaited day of the first conference.

The meeting included engineers and building management officials for eight telephone companies in the West and Midwest. To say the least it was inspiring to see all of those telephone executives gathered, when previously it took months, and sometimes years, just to get in touch with even one of such importance. In the next three weeks, I'd meet several hundred of the most significant (as far as buildings were concerned) people in the Bell System. Though I was well paid, it would have been worth paying them just for the exposure, which eventually proved to be even more rewarding than I had ever imagined.

This first conference, however, was not pleasant at all. The 75 Bell conferees sat at a huge U-shaped table. I was scheduled for one hour of prime time at 10 o'clock but the schedule ran late and my turn didn't come until 1:30 in the afternoon. Worrying about how I'd get a one-hour talk squeezed into the time left, I got off to a bad start, then delivered three hours worth of information in 18 minutes, followed by my 35-minute video. It was, to say the least, a disaster. I not only talked about three times too fast, but also was way over the audience's head in subject matter. The video training tape was good, but it came out poorly because of a defective VCR. Arlo was desperately signaling to me, whispering that I was blowing the whole thing. When I sat down everyone was stunned, thinking that either I was crazy or they were somehow too dumb to appreciate such brilliance.

Miles, undoubtedly embarrassed, jumped up and in a desperate attempt to recover, called me back up for a question and answer session. I talked more intelligently this time but as Arlo pointed out later, I didn't answer one question directly. I was discouraged and disappointed with myself.

At breakfast the next morning, my lower lip was almost in my plate from disgust over the previous day. Gartzke leaned over the table and said, "The first time I heard you, Don, I was impressed, informed, and inspired like I've never been, but the last two times, you just didn't have it. I've finally realized something. You're an in-charge person, and the first time, when you were running the show, you were unequalled. The last two times you were trying to sublimate and subordinate yourself to others, and you had no power. When you're in command you're great, but yesterday you were too careful." Gartzke hit the nail on the head—I knew he was right.

I left Reno convinced that eliminating the video and approaching them in my usual dominating "I know everything about this field" way would be what they wanted.

I flew home that morning, went from the airport to the office, and stayed there until my totally revised presentation was complete. Two days later, I checked into the downtown Pittsburgh Hilton at five-thirty in the evening and tuned myself up for my second presentation. From the first word this time, I captured my audience of Eastern phone executives and held them the whole time with a slower, humorously developed presentation and visual aids. I received loud applause afterwards and a mob of managers wanting my business card, more literature, more information, and some bids. Miles walked up to me and said, "Right on target, Don!" I met 60 executives altogether and received several invitations to "come speak to us."

Remembering the lesson I learned in Reno, I excused myself from all of the evening social gatherings and went to my room. There I analyzed the Pittsburgh results and questions, and further revised my presentation for the next and final conference in Nashville, Tennessee, the next week. As I was riding from the airport to downtown Nashville in a shared taxi, the stranger in the back seat with me, noticing my notebook, said, "You wouldn't happen to be that janitor from Idaho, would you?" "Yes!" "My boss wanted me to come to this conference just to hear you." This of course charged me up considerably, and Nashville went even better than Pittsburgh. This one I really enjoyed! I was confident, prepared, and experienced.

My proudest accomplishment here? At ten o'clock a coffee break was due but at ten-thirty the coffee still hadn't shown up. Gartzke called the deprived Bell men back to their seats, apologized, told them the show must go on, and that during the next session (mine!) they could go to the back of the room and grab a cup. In the 90 minutes of my presentation, not one person moved to the steaming coffee urn just 20 feet away. I loved it!

An ever-increasing audience

After I returned to my seat following my Nashville presentation, a handsome young engineer from Southern Bell, Jim Stafford, leaned over to me and whispered, "Could you put that in a clinic or seminar and bring it to Miami for my first and second level managers?" I nodded yes, and 30 minutes later had an outline for a two-day seminar including the subjects I'd covered that day plus eight more key maintenance and management issues. I slipped it to Stafford, who read it and gave me the "right on" signal. That rough outline was almost the exact material I used later to teach hundreds of local and national telephone companies the principles and secrets of precision house service management. I left Nashville encouraged—22 company heads had given me their business cards and asked me to call on them sometime.

Often I look back at the huge and beneficial effect our work with telephone companies had on our lives, both financially and otherwise, and could possibly credit it to three things: that first Western Electric job for $75 a week; to our initiative in developing and adding "services" for phone companies; or the single article I wrote for *Telephony* magazine. All of these contributed, but it was the call I got from someone reading the article that probably meant the most. Eventually, from that call, I got to be a featured speaker for the annual AT&T building engineers' meetings, held in Reno, Pittsburgh, and Nashville. This led to calls from Bell companies all over the U.S., which resulted in me putting together a two-day "house service" presentation for first, second, and third level building managers.

I did more than 70 of these seminars over the next several years, meeting most of the Bell maintenance managers in the country. This was like a sales call on a grand scale for Varsity and myself, resulting in the acquisition of more contracts and design consulting jobs on some of their major new buildings.

The seminars taught attendees how to bid and run their buildings like we, the contractors did. First I showed them how to assess where their maintenance costs and quality were right now, including all of the areas that were functioning below par and causing problems. Next I showed them how to fix all of this professionally—labor, supplies, motivation, etc. I had them bid and set up a maintenance program for my model telephone building. After this exercise they knew exactly how much a building should cost to clean and how to judge its maintenance quality level. Once they knew where they were and what they could do about it (all new and proven information not available within their company), they could return to their operations and make the needed changes. And it worked... unbelievably well!

When I was giving one of these seminars in Bridgeport, Connecticut, a manager named Boatright called me late one evening in my motel room. "Aslett, are you sure the figures you taught us today are right? I went to the office tonight and ran your rates and estimates for my building, and it came out that I should be paying $6,700 a month for cleaning and maintenance, including supplies. I have a good cleaning company and I'm paying them $18,000 a month." I asked him for the square footage of his building and other details. After 20 minutes I said, "Mr. Boatright, you get an 'A' for today—your calculations are perfect." Then I went to bed.

The next morning, as I opened the second day of the seminar, Boatright jumped to his feet. He explained how he did the Varsity arithmetic on his building last night, called me at the hotel for confirmation, then called his contractor down to the building in the middle of the night and told him the fair, correct price on his building for service was $6,700. Red-faced, the contractor lowered his price to $6,700, a nice little $11,300 instant savings per month! Talk about reinforcement! Things like this happened all over the U.S. after my presentations—it was a rather crude dog and pony show by today's standards, but it changed the industry.

My helpful (and photogenic) daughter Elizabeth and I were featured on the cover and inside the industry magazine, *Telephony,* and soon GTE, United, and Continental telephone companies began to call with new jobs for me and Varsity. While doing a seminar in Houston, Texas, an executive-looking man sitting in the front row introduced himself as Warren Brown, head of General Telephone for the Texas/Southern Florida area. My ideas were all new to him, and after returning home and applying them, he called and said they saved over three million dollars in one area the first year—a terrific return on the $135 it cost him to attend the seminar! That was a good pat on the back for me, and later we contracted to clean hundreds of GTE buildings in the Texas area for this man and his managers.

I soon became a seasoned traveling seminar teacher, at $2,000 a two-day session. Seven and a half hours straight each day of intense, top-of-lungs presentation left me exhausted at the end. By the end of the fifth seminar held near Newark, New Jersey, I was anxious to go home to the family after three weeks away and catch up on some of the scores of other projects I had in the works. I had asked Mark to attend the last two seminars to show him the mechanics of the operation, and as I was flying home with him he said casually, "By the way, the editor of *Telephony* magazine called and accepted your proposal to run the

My daughter Elizabeth and I with the model phone building used in my Bell seminars.

series of articles you approached him about." "You're kidding!" "No, here's the letter." I'd had good news before, but this was some of the best. When I'd asked the editor if he'd be interested in a 19-article series on building maintenance management, he'd written back to say, "Yes, but I don't think you can find that many subjects. Send me a one-paragraph outline of each and convince me."

I spent an afternoon summing up all of the subjects I thought might interest his readers, wrote up three of the articles, and mailed them to him before I left town to do the seminars. The letter Mark handed me was dated three weeks ago and said, "I'm convinced. Let's get six articles in and start." I didn't like the idea of owing him a bunch of articles after the glory of the start, so I was determined to write all of the rest of them right away and mail them off before I started the next round of seminars. After two weeks of early-morning starts and some help on the typewriter from Barbara, our daughter Laura, and two secretaries, the articles and accompanying illustrations were all finished and mailed. This whole experience played a part in starting me thinking about writing a book on the cleaning business.

Then I left again for three weeks of seminars, and this time Barbara accompanied me. I thought if she saw how hard I worked on these trips, she'd cry great tears of appreciation and understanding. However, the fun of seeing New York City for the first time, and telephone people taking us to dinner every night, plus lounging around the hotel or motel while I was doing my presentations, convinced her to the contrary: that I had a fat job (compared to keeping track of eight teenagers). To bring her down to earth I decided to send her in a New York cab to LaGuardia airport in Sunday traffic, but even that she found exciting.

We both enjoyed the trip so much I vowed to take her along as often as possible.

My approach to things has always been open and uninhibited. The rest of my management staff was more conservative and always worried about me giving away too much information. I would pretty well bare my soul and all of my professional secrets in teaching sessions and our people would sweat, figuring I was going to tell things Bell might turn around and use against us, or that I might build our image to heights we weren't capable of reaching. Browning decided the ultimate cure might be to get me a dog-training type collar which would give me little electrical shocks whenever I spoke out of turn.

Give me a break!

I was putting on one of my first Bell seminars, for 30 telephone executives assembled in a swanky meeting room. I started at 8 A.M. promptly, and true to my raving lunatic style of presenting, ripped into the subject with visuals and facts that created audible gasps and applause. I usually teach with an intensity that doesn't lose audiences, but at about nine-thirty I noticed nervous glances at wristwatches, squirming, eye rolling, leg crossing, and other strange movements in the group. So I cranked my speed up another notch and laid it on thicker and faster. By ten o'clock the whole room seemed in twitching turmoil, and finally a big burly guy in the back leaped to his feet and yelled, "Let us go!" "Go where?" I asked. "To the bathroom," came a chorus back.

I said, "Well, okay," and dismissed them for ten minutes, and no stampede of alarmed cattle could have equaled the surge through that door to the restrooms. I'd never seen anything like this before. Back home on the farm we used the restroom about once a day.

In the middle of the afternoon session, from one o'clock to five o'clock, I sensed another uprising brewing and asked, "Do you people have to go again?" They erupted like the Mormon Tabernacle Choir on the last hallelujah verse.

At the end of the day, the head guys called me aside and explained the birds and bees of breaks in their company. I'd never heard of a "break," and not being a coffee drinker or one who stayed up half the night drinking, I didn't have a clue that people often needed to use the bathroom several times a day!

Back on the farm, a working day had three main events: starting time, noon, and quitting time. Starting time depended on how big or far away the job was, and whether you had to wait for the dew to dry first. At noon we often ate in the field, not even turning the tractor motor off (too hard to restart). Quitting time was when the job was done or the sun went down, not when our strength gave out. Adjusting this lifetime of habit to fit seminar instruction took some doing.

I taught these seminars for three basic reasons: to establish myself, to market Varsity, and to make money. By seminar number 48, I had taught over 1,000 Bell System managers, which was the majority of them in the building or real estate group. After I'd taught the same seminar 63 times it began to get tough to keep up the drive and enthusiasm. When I had a big group it was easy, but when there were six or eight attendees it was a killer. But I needed the money to sustain myself and all of my other activities and so had no choice but to keep up the schedule. I was doing these seminars under the name System 1, a new company I started and owned, while Varsity was functioning as usual.

Here are a few comments on my seminars from attendees, including managers for New Jersey Bell, Bell of Pennsylvania, Southern Bell, South Central Bell, Wisconsin Bell, Western Electric, AT&T headquarters and AT&T Long Lines:

"Consulting and teaching telephone management seminars all over the United States, Don Aslett is one of the most unique in his field and has provided organization and direction that has saved large companies over 100 million dollars."

"I've attended hundreds of seminars since I've been with the Bell System and this was without a doubt the BEST."

"This was probably the most surprising seminar I ever attended. I fully expected to spend two dry, dreary days but to the contrary they were the most interesting days I have ever experienced."

"I enjoyed this presentation more than any other I have ever attended in my fourteen years with the company."

"Great job! If I had this kind of guidance fifteen years ago I could have done a better job."

"Most interesting and stimulating two days in many years."

"Excellent! Don holds your interest throughout. His house service manual is well written and informative. He has a dynamic personality and is a tremendous speaker. Don is witty, humorous, and able to get his points across with impact."

Varsity accounts had gradually shifted from small, one-time cleaning, painting or building jobs, construction cleanup and seasonal work, to more consistent contract cleaning: doing the same buildings, the same way every night. This more established routine was easier to track, train people for, and manage. I could now do as much or more good visiting a job site as being on the crew.

We also had enough policy and procedure in place by now that Varsity's cleaning contracts were well managed during any of my absences. Almost every manager got a turn to travel with me, for one-on-one training and meeting new contacts, be it New York, Los Angeles, Texas, or South Dakota. By 1976 the transfer of Mark Browning to general manager of Varsity was complete. I had spent two months orienting Browning to all of the operational details that I had stored up for the past 18 years. Browning knew the mechanics of the business—accounting, legal issues, and the like much better than I, but my background in contracts, politics, and personnel

IN 1976 I MADE MARK BROWNING GENERAL MANAGER OF VARSITY. HE REALLY STABILIZED AND IMPROVED OUR OPERATIONS.

was deep and detailed. Some of my sloppy "get by" practices developed through years of close friendship and association with my management and their families were now definitely a detriment to the business and in contrast to Browning's way of doing things. I hated to pinpoint deadlines or budgets; Browning demanded budgets and deadlines on everything. I hated to see employees suffer cash flow problems and often bailed them out, even with my own personal money. Browning's philosophy was if you can't carry yourself and make a profit, you're taking money you haven't earned.

Browning was a true business head, 100 percent dependable and much more suited than I to fill this job. This change freed me from many of the day-to-day responsibilities of administering a growing company.

Designing cleaning out

When I initiated my seminars for Bell in 1975, I included my primitive concept of maintenance-freeing design in them. Some of the engineers from AT&T/Bell saw merit in the concept of saving time, money, and stress on the environment through design, and hired me as a consultant to help design cleaning costs out of their largest building, a more than two-million-square-foot structure planned for Atlanta. They were impressed by my comment that one could design cleaning out of a building through wise construction, and furniture and flooring choices.

I reviewed their huge set of plans and offered ideas, did some little studies, and submitted amateur drawings of some of my

PROVIDING MAINTENANCE-FREEING IDEAS FOR BUILDING DESIGN BECAME ONE OF MY FAVORITE ASSIGNMENTS. THE BELL HEADQUARTERS IN ATLANTA WAS ONE SUCH CONSULTING JOB.

concepts to their architects. They had estimated 120 people to service the building; I told them on my first visit that if some design ideas were implemented, they could clean it with 64. We eventually did it with 63!

This job led to others like it, and during the 1980s, consultant jobs on building design became my favorite. I consulted on maintenance-reducing design for clients that included the Cincinnati school district, Alaska schools, Hawaii's Wilcox Hospital, the Wyoming Custodial Association, and American Express buildings in New York City and Florida. I also consulted on the new Bell headquarters building in Birmingham, Alabama and did a number of seminars on this subject. Later, in 1986, with my daughter Laura Simons, I published a book on it, too: *Make Your House Do the Housework*.

I was now spending time in the New York area writing house service and related practices as well as bid and contract packets for all of the telephone companies, getting to work with their lawyers, safety directors, and office managers. It was a great experience. They paid me well, and since I didn't need nightlife or entertainment, I put in good, long days for them, and was a cheap boarder. They were always

THE 85 FEET OF DOCUMENTS CREATED BY ONE OF MY SESSIONS WRITING CONTRACT SPECS FOR AT&T IN NEW YORK.

amazed when I turned in my expenses for "food and entertainment." My work was my entertainment, not being a drinker, party guy, or fan of fancy restaurants. I'd run down to the local grocery store and buy a few loaves of whole wheat bread, some jugs of apple and grape juice, a couple of bunches of bananas, some cauliflower, and Fig Newtons, and eat in my room. One ten-day billing for food was $37.86 and it was healthy eating, too.

Telephone tales

Varsity worked for the Bell System for almost 25 years, and the adventures involved in teaching and cleaning for this premium company across the country could fill a book—there were no dull or dead-end jobs here. Despite all of their carefully devised procedures and ways of going about things, there was always something new and different going on—every day was a new experience.

Curiosity killed the contract

It took us five years, for example, to finally get a shot at making a bid on the prestigious Bell Systems tower in downtown Los Angeles. My California manager and I were led into the CEO's office, just as he got a call to the next room. He politely seated us in his swank office, assuring us he would return momentarily.

In the middle of a conference desk in the room was a fancy phone system with lots of buttons. We couldn't help especially noticing one bright red button. The longer we sat, the more it intrigued us. We knew phones and phone buildings (having had contracts with over 400 such offices in several states), but we'd never seen anything quite like this. Curiosity finally overcame my manager and he pushed the red button.

Sirens! It happened to be the main fire alarm for that huge building. The whole building emptied immediately, as people scurried from their offices down stairways and into the streets. The CEO charged into his office ranting. Our appointed meeting time was replaced by the need to restore order to several thousand people. We never did get that contract, and I wasn't curious as to why.

The importance of orientation

In my work with AT&T, I had a chance to see how the greatest and most needed program in the world can be valueless, or even detrimental without proper orientation. AT&T in the New York area had joined forces with an environmental organization in a recycling program and had some classy paper holders made in which different types of recyclable paper could be placed, instead of being thrown in the wastebasket with the other trash. The janitors were all instructed carefully in the details of this new waste paper handling system.

One Monday morning the sharp white holders appeared on every one of the hundreds of desks in the building. The occupants of the desks, not oriented or introduced to the program yet, quickly found the perfect use for the important-looking new container—a place to put and organize their "urgent" documents and papers. By the next morning, pounds and pounds of important and valuable documents, notes, plans, and other papers had been picked up and shredded.

The Bell orphans

Proving innocence was never easy or clear cut when janitors were suspected of thievery, but occasionally there was some satisfaction in seeing all suspicion dropped after an accusation. The management of a large Western Electric distribution center we cleaned complained continually about "our janitors" eating Bell System food. The evidence would be found strung throughout the building the next morning. Pieces of sandwiches would be found in halls or lounges, chicken bones right in the middle of the general manager's rug or half a wiener by the computer bank. Bell management would gather up the evidence and then chastise us stiffly for pilfering food and then discarding partly eaten morsels all over. Our people pleaded innocent of disturbing even a crumb of food. The phone company insisted it was our cleaning people and continued to complain whenever food fragments appeared.

It appeared that the verdict of guilty or innocent would never be officially rendered... until a Birmingham, Alabama operation many hundreds of miles away solved the problem and cleared Varsity's good name. They received an expensive piece of communications equipment from our building and upon opening the box, they discovered, nestled snugly in the packing material, six baby kittens. These little Bell orphans indicated at least two adult cats roaming freely in our building at night and hiding out in the daytime. It was their snacks that left the chicken bones and crusts distributed throughout the building. The humane society was called, and Varsity no longer had to take the rap.

The flood of '76

In June 1976 the earthen Teton Dam, pinched between two rugged Idaho canyon walls and poised above the flat Snake River plain, sprang an early morning leak. Bulldozers tried to push fill material into the fast-dissolving structure, until a dozer was swept into the widening gap. Fortunately, warnings to the cities below helped move the people out of the path of danger, but not the little towns. Right after lunch one whole

SOME MEMORABLE SCENES FROM THE FLOOD CLEANUP THAT
FOLLOWED THE TETON DAM FAILURE IN JUNE 1976.
A BAD SCENE FOR PAPERS AND DELICATE ELECTRONICS!

side of the dam gave way, and an ocean of stored water headed for lower ground, passing through a feed yard of 10,000 cattle and a lumber mill, then carrying the drowning cattle and many logs and boards on a wild ride to the towns and cities further down the valley.

We were doing all of the cleaning, painting, and light construction for the Bell System in the area, and hours after the flood passed the entire valley still lacked lights and phone service. They called in all our crews (the Bell System was unequalled when it came to restoring service—they often had the phones working again before the sidewalks were dry). Our Varsity trucks were admitted through the roadblock guarded by the state police, and we were the first ones in. We were suddenly a valuable cog in a team of engineers and repair people. The water was gone but not the marks it left. Rooms packed with electrical and electronic equipment had been filled with five feet of water—rooms so sensitive to moisture we were never allowed to even sweat in there. Tiny delicate sensors, fuses, and dialing mechanics on the main frame were covered with mud, grasshoppers, bark, leaves, and snakes. Trained to never touch the communications gear in these buildings, now we had to manage to clean it. We removed six inches of mud and silt with scoop shovels and an old-fashioned bucket brigade.

While outsiders and reporters all wondered what was going on in the flood zone, we cleaners were there! We saw a rattlesnake wrapped around a clothesline, a TV and catcher's mitt on top of an upside-down car, automobiles from miles upstream scattered and upended over lawns, and a woman screaming because she had found a water-bloated cow in her bathroom.

What an experience, and what elation when in 30 hours the whole telephone office and its service were back on line!

The Bell breakup

Then came a big happening in communications that I believe really hurt us all: the breakup of the Bell System. Though it had served well for decades as a legally sanctioned monopoly for the sake of efficiency, suddenly it was decided that it must be split up. What a mistake! Bell provided inexpensive service, furnished all of the equipment needed with it, and installed phones within three days of a service call. The Bell labs were leaders in technology that saved lives and advanced computer knowledge. I never since have worked for a company with their quality of personnel in terms of fairness and efficiency, and they had a company loyalty that was phenomenal.

But in January 1984 the breakup was done. Years of confusion followed and we all still get 20 calls a week from competing phone companies in the aftermath. Phone irritants have increased, as have expenses, at home and in business. Phone building maintenance went that way, too. By comparison, everything afterward was disorganized as many different operations and companies struggled to run their own installations and networks. We still cleaned phone buildings but some of the spark was gone. Layers of new rules and complicated new contracts appeared, doubling the pages of specs and Occupational Safety and Health

Administration (OSHA), minority, and safety requirements. You name it—it was now harder to do.

Finally, in the mid-'90s, as the new phone companies began to settle in, the telephone company in our area, US West/Qwest, decided to stop fighting their building problems and outsource everything. They had more than 7,000 buildings spread from Seattle to North Dakota, Minneapolis to New Mexico—13 states in all. They called us into a meeting and told us they were in the business not of cleaning but of communication, information, and entertainment. And they were accordingly going to turn the maintenance of all of their buildings over to a contractor. They checked out more than a thousand contractors in the U.S., whittled that quickly down to 60, went through some strict size and reputation screening, and reduced the list to 13 prime candidates. We were still in the running. All 13 contractors submitted brief proposals, and US West cut the contenders to six. We were still in, and we traveled to Denver and made formal presentations as to why we were the best. They ended up deciding the 7,000 buildings should be divided between us and one of the other big contractors, Allied Ogden. We got most of the rural and remote buildings, which was what we were best at anyway. Later we acquired big-city buildings and installations and were back in the full-service phone business again, with 3,000 telephone buildings in the 14 Western states.

Chapter 12

THE HEART OF IT ALL: FAMILY AND COMMUNITY

A house-full means a life-full!

MY OLDEST GRANDDAUGHTER MINDY AND I IN SKAGWAY, ALASKA, IN 1983. THIS IS ONE OF MY ALL-TIME FAVORITE PHOTOS.

In all of this, an outsider looking at my business operations and personal schedule might think I had no home life. The opposite was true. My life was centered around my family—my business and travel were all appendages to it. Our concept of the home and family probably differed somewhat from the average, but our results with our family were excellent, so I like to think we did it right.

We had our six children within a seven-year span, no twins.

Nine months and three days after our marriage, we had our first child, a little blonde we named Laura, and a year later, dark-haired Karla. A year after that our first son, Grant, was born. In the next four years, we had our last three children—Elizabeth, while we were still in college and living in our first house. The 60-acre farm we moved to in 1963 was home for our last daughter, Cindy, and another son, Rell.

Each of our kids, all raised the same way by the same parents, had totally different personalities. Laura, the first and oldest, was game for anything—always open to adventure. Karla was quiet, soft, and sensitive. Elizabeth was adult, wise, and mature at the age of 10; Grant bold, independent, and self-assured. Cindy was laid back and happy-go-lucky. Rell, the youngest, was a born enterpriser—full of ideas and eager to develop them, and he could fix or build anything. They all kept and just refined these traits from childhood to maturity.

Children were welcome and a joy, and there were always plenty of them around besides our own. Our home was always open to guests and visitors, especially young people. Cousins, nieces and nephews, and our children's friends came to visit and stay, and while I was a Scoutmaster, many of my Scouts hung around for all the projects that were always underway. There were always excited comings and goings, for drill teams, sports of all kinds, FFA and Future Homemakers of America (FHA), Junior Miss pageants, trips, and lessons. Kids would stop by on their way to and from college. Some nights we would have a half-dozen young people in sleeping bags all over the house, followed by a big pancake breakfast the next morning. We often had guests from other states or countries, and once a troop of 30 Hawaiians stayed with us!

The size and openness of our house made it attractive for large gatherings. Our kids would bring guests over and there would be parties ranging from five to seventy-five kids. Teens loved the house because it had room for pool, other games, and dancing, and was big enough that they could go to the other end and play loud music without disturbing the parents. Many a community project, school party, sleigh and toboggan ride, sleepover, and reunion took place at our home. We also held Halloween parties here—one year we had a phenomenal spook alley. Girls' and boys' camps were held on our property, too, and company picnics. Besides the old log cabin on the place, we also had a ball field and a volleyball court.

When we weren't there we thought nothing of letting people live or camp out at our place, often for weeks or more at a time—relatives, employees, Scouts and their leaders, and other youth groups.

223

Other teenagers shared our home right with us. A sweet 15-year-old friend of our daughter came to live with us for two years. Right at the end of her stay, our bedroom door was flung open one morning and there stood Rell, our youngest son, accompanied by a wide-eyed, skinny kid of 16. "Dad, Mom, this is Mike, one of my classmates. He has no home and has been sleeping in his car. He's a good kid—can he live with us?" We were both sitting up in bed, stunned, but said, "Sure, put him in the back bedroom." Mike was "ours" for a year, until he graduated high school.

We treated all of these kids like our own—we gave them jobs, took them on trips, and gave them presents at Christmas. And for sure, we benefited more than they did from their stay.

The children made every hour interesting. Every time you began thinking that you, the adults, were the center of this process of living, the kids would come up with some humorous surprise or creative, off-the-wall pursuit that would remind you that besides a husband and wife there were six other major entities around intensely involved in this business of living.

We had enough resources, places, properties, and people around to always have a lot of things going on at the same time. Our family style was not a series of separate events, it was more like continually connected simultaneous projects. Everything—work, school, church activities, the business, sports, home and health maintenance, etc., was all a no-boundary blend. Fortunately, there was also very little sibling rivalry—I guess the kids were usually too busy to fight!

OUR LITTLE FAMILY IN 1964, BEFORE RELL WAS BORN IN 1965.

We had an open policy around our house from the beginning. We didn't need or use strict rules—the kids seemed to sense the boundaries and honor them, an environment I believe was created by Barbara, whose nature was more permissive than rigid. Thus our children had a wider margin of freedom than most, and their active, lively, youthful minds were an ever-present source of adventure. They were all uninhibited—as one teacher told Barbara, "If you don't believe anything Cindy (our youngest girl) tells you about me, I won't believe anything she tells me about you." All of the kids would drag home friends who were big-eyed and timid when confronted with our open style of living.

Once any of the kids was given a chore or assignment and turned loose, you could always count on a rich return. If anything had to be pulled off, with or without an instruction book, our kids could and would get it done. All our kids needed was permission (and occasionally they even skipped that), and they knew how to use the resources of a large house, lots of land and space, and nearby grandpas and grandmas.

Often they were basically on their own, with Barbara the soft but ever present backstop and mediator.

Growing up like this, our children all developed plenty of self-reliance.

I remember one evening in the Sawtooth Forest when I was involved in a

BARBARA AND I PILED ON THE TOBOGGAN WITH SIX KIDS.

big work project on a church camp. As Barbara and I were driving out on the winding mountain road we saw our second daughter, Karla, and a friend come running up the hill to meet us, screaming with delight and bearing a healthy string of brook trout they'd caught in the cold creek. The light and joy in Karla's face was unforgettable, and I don't remember any of us ever teaching her to fish.

When Grant entered his 4-H project pig in the county fair, he didn't transport it in a trailer, but loaded the monster into the back of our Suburban. With the terrified hog loose in the back of the vehicle, he managed to pick up several friends on the way, and sitting in the seat behind Grant, they were equally terrified to have a big pig snorting and oinking right behind them all the way.

My youngest son Rell came to me one day in his senior year of high school and said, "Dad, remember when you said that someday you were going to do two things, grow a beard and buy a Porsche?" (I was known for my conservatism and would never do either.) "Well, Dad, we won't hold you to the beard but there is a Porsche in the paper and it's a good deal." I interrupted, "No way, Rell!"

Well I hadn't promised, but I did make the statement, so I tried to figure a way out of this. Then it came, the perfect out! A deadbeat who owed me money and would never pay in two millennia. I handed the bill to Rell and said, "Here, collect this and you can use it to help buy the car." No chance!

Barbara and I left for Hawaii the next morning. Thirty minutes after we arrived there (twenty-four hours later), the phone rang. It was my CFO, who asked, "How do you want to insure this Porsche?" Never underestimate kids' ability when they want something!

I was of course shocked but also intrigued by the question of how he had accomplished this seemingly impossible feat of collection. "I went to see his mother," he said.

Likewise, leave it to a kid to figure out a creative way to take possession of Dad's possessions. To reduce the number of missing tools I would write or engrave "Don Aslett" on my wrenches, saws, and tapes, only to find "to Rell from" etched above my name. One Christmas, when the kids ranged from age 6 to 15, in an attempt to teach them to keep and take care of tools, I bought and marked expensive Wiss scissors for my four daughters and the best Stanley hammers for the boys and swore that if they still had these tools when they were 18, I would give them $1,000. The boys (like their dad) lost the hammers within a few months, and never collected. And the girls, like their mom, took good care of their tools and all collected the promised $1,000 at college time.

> MY LOVE OF WORK DID NOT GO UNNOTICED BY THE KIDS. RELL SAID TO ME ONE DAY, "DAD, THE LORD ALLOWED SO MUCH PLAYING TIME PER PERSON ON EARTH. INASMUCH AS YOU DON'T USE YOURS, SOMEONE IN THE FAMILY, LIKE ME, NEEDS TO USE IT UP SO IT WON'T GO TO WASTE."

Another time, getting home once from a late flight at three in the morning, my car lights caught some freshly dug ground in the meadow just below the house. I went to sleep pleased to see that the boys had shown some initiative with the farm work. I was awakened at seven-thirty by loud buzzing and cheering. I looked out the window to see that my tractor, scraper, and plow had been used to create a well-designed and creatively constructed motocross course, with ramps, gully-jumping pit, and the works. Most of the community's "dirt bikers" were there, riding at great reckless speeds and impressing rows of cheering high school girls. Every young daredevil who could jump a bike 20 feet off the ground was doing so, making as much noise as an airport and testing my homeowner's liability policy.

Not only are they dangerous and hard on the environment, I also hate the noise of dirt bikes. I dressed fast and stalked out to clear this wild bunch from my acres. Suddenly two of the finest mothers in McCammon came running up to me, each grabbing an arm. "Oh, Mr. Aslett," they said, "This is wonderful, what you are doing for the youth. Nobody would be as kind and caring as you. Thank you, thank you—the kids are having a wonderful time." They really laid it on and casting out those accursed bikes didn't seem like such a good idea after all. So I mumbled, "Glad to do it," and went back to the house. We trained and raised the kids to take the initiative, so what could I say?

We all take family for granted at times and shove it into second place behind the outside world's demands for our attention, but family is the root of it all, the ultimate bottom line. Family is so obvious, seems so strong and enduring, that we often leave it to survive on its own, and precious and cementing moments slide by, unappreciated at the time.

A PHOTO I SNAPPED OF BARBARA AND THE KIDS— CAMPING WITH 6 KIDS, WAS SHE A GOOD SPORT!

Like most parents, I was guilty of some of this too.

I rarely looked at report cards, as grades didn't mean much to me. A child's behavior told me what had to be known. Fortunately, our kids had a mother who took a more productive and saner view of school progress and prowess.

Barbara was also the master of the patience factor around home. I would persist on something, unyielding to a point, and then often be willing to say the heck with it. She would step in and rekindle any still-worthy fire I abandoned.

Only 5 percent of Scouts reach the highest rank of Eagle Scout. I scouted with my two sons to the max for years—going with them to troop camp, district camps, and national jamborees. The three of us even built and ran a day camp for Scouts one summer. But the age limit of 18 often arrives before even dedicated Scouts get their Eagle, and Grant and Rell were no exception. I begged, threatened, and shamed them for years to get them to finish the requirements, to no avail. Enough was finally enough, and with an "Okay, you two, be slacker Scouts," I abandoned the cause. Barbara quickly picked up the "project" and yes, you guessed it, both sons got Eagle Scout rank. It was that old magic called motherhood. No man grows beyond mothering, and young men at 17 are especially vulnerable. She helped them instead of hollering.

GRANT AND RELL AND I HAD MANY
ADVENTURES IN SCOUTING.

Barbara and I had our share of philosophical disagreements, which created some conflict at times. I thought sacrifice was necessary for development; she thought it foolish for anyone, especially kids, to suffer (be cold, hungry, or tired) when it wasn't necessary. I believed in preparing the kid for the path and she, the path for the kid.

I often treated outsiders such as guests or foster children equal to our own; she believed our own family came first, then others.

One common thread that kept the family united was that we were 100 percent together on church attendance and activities. We always took, never sent, our children to church. As a result they all became excellent public speakers and good teachers, and they have clean habits. Timely input from strong, talented friends and associates at church and in our business was a huge asset in raising a family as well.

Self-employed businesspeople, farmers to janitors, have another advantage, a tremendously family-friendly one. We have something much better than a family trip or two to the zoo, or annual family vacation.

Since we own our own businesses, we get to choose when, where, and how we work, as well as with whom. This gives us the liberty of doing things right with our families. This is an extension of family life that adds excitement, gives exposure and education, and builds not just relationships but character and skills. When you are the boss, you don't need to get permission to take or send your children where you or they wish to be—such as traveling along with you on jobs, trips, and projects, to company meetings and parties. Things that the normal employee would do alone, Barbara and I could do with the family. We had the option and privilege to include family and friends or the children's grandparents when and wherever we wanted. So we worked, traveled, laughed, ate, and slept side by side, be it readying the Grand Canyon for opening day, decorating Christmas trees in Sun Valley, painting together in Florida, or cleaning telephone booths in Wyoming. Bonds are built best by *doing* things together, not just being together.

LAURA'S WEDDING RECEPTION AT OUR McCAMMON HOME, JUNE 14, 1980; BACK TO FRONT: LAURA, GRANT, RELL, KARLA, LIZ, AND CINDY.

Our kids all learned independence, leadership, and hustle, and any of them, then and now, could have led the pioneers across the plains. All of them at different times worked in the business, traveled with us to help give seminars, helped me with my articles and books, and attended company meetings. They are all are super presenters, good travelers, and good parents. Karla and her husband Duff and our first grandchild moved to Skagway, Alaska in 1980 and are still there, operating the five businesses they eventually started. Both of my sons have their own businesses now, and all of my children at one time or another have run their own businesses. All are proven producers, and three so far have graduated from college.

Helping others was another big part of our family life. I gave our children some of the "whys" for doing this over the years. But Barbara gave them the "how." When Karla's father-in-law fell ill at 57 and died suddenly, for instance, I was quick to offer the widow and the rest of the family the usual "if there is anything I can do, be sure to call me."

They never did. Barbara said nothing but appraised their needs, went home, prepared our motor home with food and clean sheets, then drove it over and parked it in their yard to ease the pressure on their small home of relatives visiting for the funeral. Our children learned their mother's methods, and they all, from the time they were in grade school to now, have put them in practice—their homes are always open to lost souls. After she became a mother, Laura's home was the afterschool homesite for several latchkey kids whose parents were still at work. She'd buy extra gallons of milk and bake cookies to keep near-strangers safe and occupied. One virtue our children all possess is that they all look after other people.

Trying to sum up or describe "family" in an autobiography is like trying to crowd the history of Rome into a paragraph. A carefully recorded single week of all of the activities, emotions, and interactions involved could fill a book. Even that, of course, would never capture all of the drama and comedy of development.

Affection wasn't often paraded openly in our family, but it was there. A note like this was rare, but appreciated as a reminder of the real reasons for existence and effort:

LIZ (ELIZABETH) AT HER HIGH SCHOOL GRADUATION.

Dear Dad,
    I hope all is well with you. I want you to know how much I love you and appreciate all you do and all you've done. I know I don't express that enough, but I am grateful. I see so many things— experiences in my past that have helped me become who I am today. I'm glad I learned to work, have a good attitude, and get along with others. I only hope that I can teach my kids those things and more.
    Thank you again for the many sacrifices on our behalf.
    We love you.
                    Love, Liz

I WAS AWARE OF THE NEEDY AND OFFERED THE "CALL ME IF I CAN DO ANYTHING FOR YOU" APPROACH. BARBARA SAID NOTHING BUT SHOWED UP WITH WHAT WAS NEEDED, BE IT OUR MOTOR HOME LEFT IN THEIR YARD FOR FAMILY OVERFLOW AT A FUNERAL, OR HER PRESENCE DAY AND NIGHT AT THE BEDSIDE OF A NEIGHBOR DYING OF CANCER.

Love in a log cabin

In 1978 Barbara's mother and stepfather (Barbara lost her father when she was seven), Vera and Jerry Reed, who had been living in Alaska, were retiring and moving back to the lower 48, and we wanted them close—nothing like having grandparents around.

When we moved onto our McCammon ranch, I had arranged for a bulldozer to knock down the old log cabin on it. But when the machine arrived, I felt a strong urge to save the building, and did. I was glad I had, for as a family project, we decided to restore it now. We dug and poured a foundation around it without moving the building, then we gave it a new roof and built a new house inside it, just right for the grandparents to use free for the rest of their lives.

VERA AND JERRY REED, OUR BELOVED GRANDPARENTS-IN-RESIDENCE.

Barbara and I gave ourselves a little credit for doing this, and even for paying all of the utilities for her parents now. But our contribution was nothing when measured against what they did for our family. Having good grandparents there was a blessing beyond description. They nourished and uplifted both our kids and us, physically and emotionally, and shared our lives every day for many years. What a boost to life quality that was for all of us.

Barbara's mother was the ultimate peacemaker, and their home on our place became a refuge at times for us all. You knew you were always welcome when you walked in the door, and here was relief from rush and pressure, a place to relax, recover, and rebound. Vera and Jerry supplied any dimension for our kids that we parents missed—they were a reserve team that gave us far more than the piddly piece of real estate we gave them. They shared breakfasts, lunches, and dinners, photos, trips, and wisdom. Above all, they had *time* to spend with all of us—they were available any time of the day or night. This was a living treasure, opening avenues of education and endearment that could be obtained no other way. That little cabin wasn't the retirement center we anticipated, but a re-souling center for all of us, a role reversal where the elderly actually took care of us. It's easy to spot the strands of strength they wove into our children.

Don a politician? (not quite)

When I was in my late thirties, I received a call from the state capitol in Boise. A member of the state House of Representatives had been called away for a time during his term; he approached me to take his place in the House till he returned, kind of "rent a substitute legislator." This seemed to offer some new ground to plow, so I accepted.

MY BRIEF SPELL OF SERVICE IN THE IDAHO LEGISLATURE WAS EYE-OPENING AND EDUCATIONAL INDEED.

I didn't really know if I was a Republican or Democrat, but I found out the day I got there that I was the former. (As one cynic there put it, "a Democrat is someone who's never had to make payroll.") It was pretty darn impressive to sit in that big capitol building at my own desk surrounded by all sorts of lawmakers. I went in there with a lot of idealism about government I'd learned in school and listening to campaign promises, but there was none of that apparent here. There was a system, and although I was as smart and confident in general as many of the old pros around me, I had no clue as to how that system worked.

The first day I voted "yes" for a Democratic bill, and a bunch of Republicans jumped me and said, "Aslett, we don't do that!" "But," I said, "it was a super bill." "That's irrelevant, Don, we caucused to not support it." I told them that was stupid, and they agreed, but said that was the way it was done.

After the lynch committee left, the gentleman sitting next to me bent over and whispered, "I don't like to vote this way, but my bill is being supported by another guy so I have to go along with his." (I began to see the light.) After a few days, I got the nerve to stand up and debate a bill that concerned my field of expertise. A few minutes after I sat down, I was slipped a little note (which was a big thing there) and it said, "Nice job, Don. Love, Patricia." This really infuriated my Republican brethren because Patty was the smartest and most intimidating woman lawyer in the West, and a Democrat!

Another real revelation I received there was about lobbyists. I was taught in grade school, at Boys' State, and political science class in college that lobbyists were the scum of the earth—crooks, bribers, cheats, and sneaks. Once there, I found out that these folks, the ones keenly for or against something, were the only ones in the place who really knew much about the bills and the facts. They were the educators. You could hear all sides of an issue from the different sets of lobbyists and then you had real information (the good, the bad, and the ugly) to decide on.

I learned more about politics in my few weeks here than in my whole life previous. I learned that, in the world of politics, the talent of persuasion is superior to morality or intelligence and that all sides come to the middle in the end. I learned that the finest legal minds may not be the wisest ones, and that a small select committee can be as dumb as the whole group. And last but not least, it may not be safe to put your life in the hands of politicians, even in a good, free country.

This little stint satisfied any and all desire I might ever have to be a politician. In my fifties, I was approached by several people about running for governor, but the brief flash of ego that followed was instantly smothered by the memory of the impossibility of pleasing everyone, one battle I would never be tactful enough to fight. I was convinced by now that I could accomplish far more for town, county, state, and country as a businessperson than I ever could as a politician, and keep control of my own time and money.

Don run for governor?
If I ran for office and told people what I'd do to fix unions, foreign aid, media abuses, welfare, education, athletics, the highways, the insurance and medical industries, and the drug problem, 99 percent

of the public would be offended. The only votes I'd get would be from my wife and mother, and if I told them what I'd do about junk and clutter once I got in power, I'd lose their votes, too!

Our Alaskan adventure

Most of us have made plenty of trips, but only once or twice in our lives comes a combination of time, place, and people that really clicks. My three-week stay in Alaska in 1983 was one of these for me. Barbara's folks (Vera and Jerry Reed) had lived in Fairbanks for 15 years and

JERRY REED OUTSIDE THE CAMPER ON THE GREAT ALASKA ROAD TRIP.

they loved Alaska. Jerry had a 16mm camera and had photographed quite a bit of it. One evening as we were watching one of Jerry's films for about the fifth time in their log cabin retirement home, I made an off-the-cuff statement that my wife considered a promise: "One of these days I'll take a month off and we'll drive through Alaska and you can show us all of this in person."

From that hour on, Jerry and Vera thought of nothing but preparing for Alaska. I was, as usual, so busy that even one day off was hard to come by. I was doing my seminars across the country for the Bell System then, expanding Varsity, and fighting cash flow problems—for the past 25 years I hadn't known a single day of not being in charge of something or someone. Under senior citizen pressure, however, I finally committed to a road trip to Alaska "this next August." They marked the calendar, upgraded the camper on an old stiff-springed, three-quarter-ton '79 Ford pickup, stocked up on food and maps, and called all of their Alaskan friends and told them we were coming. I tried to get a little ahead at work and got my affairs in order, and we arranged for one of the kids to watch the house. I packed up my writing materials (I was working on my third book, *Clutter's Last Stand*), and the four of us loaded into the front seat of that pickup at five in the morning and off we went on a 6,000 mile road trip.

Jerry loved to drive, so for three weeks I didn't have to worry about anything, just enjoy togetherness with my wife and her folks and the unequalled natural beauty of Alaska. We saw glaciers, all kinds of wild animals and birds, historical sites and buildings, spectacular parks, and the Alaska Pipeline going up. We feasted on fresh salmon and halibut and wild berry jam. One day on the Denali Highway, we traveled 120 miles and never passed a single car going either way! We saw grizzlies, moose, and fresh water of every color imaginable. We panned for gold and sat in Robert Service's cabin and had his poems read to us. Every stop was a peek at paradise and add to this two ex-Alaskans who were 150 percent enthused about showing and sharing the state.

On the way home we visited Skagway, where our second daughter and oldest granddaughter, Mindy, lived. We made a sign for their ice cream store, picked blueberries, boated in the bay, and pulled in their shrimp boxes. Then we boarded a big ferry (with our camper in the hull) and went on a nice cruise up the coast with stops in Sitka, Ketchikan, and finally Prince Rupert Island. I could have written a book on each day—it was a freedom, an education, an association that would only happen once, and I was so grateful that Barbara's folks had made me do it. When I got home and went to work the next morning, I was overdrawn $51,000 at the bank—a little lag between receivables and payroll I had to quickly resolve. That was serious but it seemed (and proved) insignificant compared to the value of the trip.

Painting the town

Everyone in our community knew that a pro cleaner, painter, and construction man had equipment around. A bonanza for borrowers! After years of using my stuff, it was discovered that things worked even better if I accompanied it, so they borrowed me too. Thus I enjoyed a lifetime of donating. Two episodes I remember well both had to do with the county fair.

It seems that several of the fairgrounds buildings in Downey, Idaho, had looked shabby for years. Ernie Garrett was an energetic community advocate and a friend of mine. (And that year he was heading the fair board.) So naturally he thought, why fight to organize the whole community to deal with this when I have Don Aslett and his equipment?

He called. "Don, I have a little job down here and ten cans of paint."

"Sure, Ern, I have a half day Tuesday. I'll bring my airless sprayer."

When I got there the "cans" of paint were 5-gallon drums, and there were four livestock barns to paint, each the size of small stadiums. I gasped, and Ernie the optimist said, "We have to get it done because the fair opens in two days!"

"You mix, stir, strain, and keep the tank of the airless filled with paint, and I'll go for it," I replied.

The buildings were big but all low, with open fronts, and needed no trimming or drop cloths, just a few light fixtures shielded. An airless paint sprayer doesn't use air—it puts the paint under pressure with a hydraulic pump. This "gun," run by electricity, puts out a 3-foot blast of paint, and when the going is unobstructed, it can drain a 5-gallon drum of paint faster than a kid can slurp down a McDonald's milkshake. Since there was little preparation needed, no wind to drift the spray around, and three appreciative members of the fair board were watching in awe, Ern and I painted all four of those buildings white in five hours—a feat never repeated, not even by a whole crew. He, a 380-pound giant, was panting and the hydraulics were hot when I finished, but we did it.

The rodeo board in my hometown of McCammon heard of this tour de force to the south, and the head of the town committee, Tom (also a friend) called. "Don, we need badly to have the rodeo bleachers painted and I have the paint." "Sure," was the only choice I really had. He also promised a crew of boys (cowboys, to be exact) to help push the machine around and feed it paint. Barbara, eight months pregnant with our youngest son, came with me and my pickup load of equipment.

Tom was a nice guy, but a bargain hunter, and the paint he had was 1942 Army surplus battleship deck paint. It seemed to consist of one-third sand, one-third solvent, and one-third toxic fumes, plus eye-blinding yellow pigment. It had set up like chocolate pudding from sitting around in storage so long. All I could think of was the fact that the tip on my sprayer cost $200 (like $500 today). The miracle of converting that paint to a liquid again was comparable to raising the dead, and guess who performed it? When it came to real work, those "cowboys" were about worthless, and to entice them into the spirit of volunteerism Tom had bought a few cases of beer. They drank as Barbara and I worked. When that bright yellow paint began to cover those old, beat-up seats, cheers and rejoicing and more drinking ensued. Soon we had a bleacher full of drunks barely able to keep out of the way of the paint, and there, lugging buckets and pushing the machine around the arena, was Barbara. Not one community cowboy came to the rescue. The job was a topic at local bars for years among the cowboys, who still think they did it.

Adventures in Scouting

I was a Scoutmaster intermittently for more than ten years, and this led me into all kinds of nerve-stretching activities. Anything my Scouts did, I had to do, so I got to climb (with lineman's boots) up telephone poles, rappel off cliffs, go into claustrophobia-inspiring caves, and so on.

One troop voted to snowmobile back into a wilderness camp where you could freeze your fanny off and eat ice-cold fried eggs. Any Idaho man who can't run a snowmobile is considered a wimp, but I had al-

MY EXPLORER BOY SCOUT TROOP IN 1969, BY THE PIONEER TRAIL MARKER
WE MADE. TWO OF THESE 12-YEAR-OLDS, 10 YEARS LATER, BECAME
MY SONS-IN-LAW, DUFF RAY, AND ROBYN SIMONS.

ways considered them noisy and exercise-diminishing. A couple of local
enthusiasts loaned theirs to the troop and ten others brought their own.
I let one of the older Scouts drive mine (he was delighted) for the trip
into the mountains.

Some of the older Scouts did some fancy turns and other white-
knuckle knocking around on their machines on a foothill near camp.
Then they challenged me (as I was forever challenging them) to take a
turn. I mounted the super-powered, unfamiliar-feeling machine, opened
the throttle, and assaulted the hill. It felt easy, so I gunned it, and made
a James Bond turn just before the cliffs. But in the middle of the turn,
there was some slippage… then more… and suddenly it was either ride
the machine over the cliff or leap for my life. Being alive (even humili-
ated) seemed preferable and so I jumped. I managed to dig out of the
30-foot snowbank I landed in, but as for the snowmobile only 3 inches
of the rear tread was showing. That big fall broke one of its skis, and it
broke me forever of the urge to master those machines.

Another time, I had scheduled a Scout hike for a Friday afternoon at
4 P.M. I planned to gather everyone at our ranch and hike down to the
Indian writing rocks with them, about a mile away, and camp there for

the night. I was out of town in the East that week and scheduled to fly back early Friday morning. But my plane was delayed so I arrived home late at 4:15. All of my hike-hungry Scouts were there, in full packs, ready for an evening of pure Scouting. I'd been gone for two weeks, and the kiss from my wife when I arrived was soft and inviting. And I was so weary I would have given anything just to stay home. But the Scouts were beating on their canteens and following me around, so I grabbed my already packed gear and we were off down the valley.

Soon camp was set up and the Scouts were having the time of their lives roasting wieners over the fire. I joined in and refereed all the games and activities afterward. At dark, we all rolled our sleeping bags out on a big slab of lava rock. As the Scouts were looking up at the millions of stars in the sky, I was looking up the valley at my home on the hill and the light in the bedroom window a mile away. Just then, one of the Scouts said, "Boy, Mr. Aslett, can you think of anyplace you'd rather be than right here?" Knowing the joy and enthusiasm these kids had showed, and the memories of this they might carry all their lives, I could answer truthfully, "No, Swim, I can't think of anyplace I'd rather be than right here."

For another outing, in the dead of the coldest Idaho winter imaginable, we'd planned a toboggan run on the slopes of the Lowry farm. Two days before, I caught the flu, and by the appointed evening there wasn't a bone, muscle, or nerve in my body that didn't hurt. I had a well-established reputation, however, for never accepting excuses for missing Scout activities. So we loaded up the huge toboggans and drove to the bottom of the biggest hill on the place. Then we carried the sled and what seemed like 40 tons of other gear up the hill. I led the way, breaking a trail through hip-deep snow.

I wondered if I would make it to the top, but I did, in complete darkness. We loaded five of us onto that 8-foot toboggan, with me in front, the biggest chicken Scout behind me, and the mouthiest, mustached daredevil on the tail, and down we went.

It was ten below zero now and we were going so fast the snow flying up from the bow of the sled sprayed onto my face and stuck there, almost suffocating me. The kid behind me (who was wetting his pants with terror) grabbed me around the neck with a death grip. I was terrified we were going to hit a fence, ravine, or cliff at full speed, when a clear, joyful voice that only a fearless 13-year-old can have (the daredevil on the end) yelled out, "Wow, Mr. Aslett, ain't this fun!"

I would do it again even if I died on the hill. But at the moment, barely able to see or breathe, I felt otherwise!

Another experience no one ought to miss is leading Scouts in a winter survival hike in the Idaho mountains. The trick is picking the coldest, dreariest day, when the snow is the deepest. Then finding the most remote canyon and taking a troop of boys there to help them survive a campout. This means digging snow caves for sleeping and cooking, and a snow battle thrown in once camp is set up. I froze on every one of these expeditions, even after buying a "30 below guaranteed" sleeping bag. Meanwhile, all of my Scouts would roll their tiny sparrow-down bags out on the snow and sleep soundly with a warm smile.

My Scouts and I made more ambitious trips, too. In the mountains of New Mexico there is a 300,000-acre ranch formerly owned by the founders of Phillips Petroleum, where boys can have a tremendous wilderness experience. One summer I volunteered to take ten boys (one of my sons, Rell, included) there for 15 days. The 11 of us loaded enough equipment to field an army into a stretch van, and then we left on our thousand-mile trip.

Our first day at Philmont, we stayed at a large old hacienda that serves as the base camp. The next morning we lined up and spread out all the gear we were going to be carrying on our hike through the mountains. When the young ranger inspecting it saw my writing gear and wood rasps and saws, he said, "Sir, those cannot go—your pack must be under thirty-five pounds." He tossed them out of my pile, but as soon as he was gone, I sneaked them back.

Then we were bussed to the foot of the huge mountains, dumped out on a trail, given a map and our assigned camps, and told never to bushwhack (get off the marked trails). Hiking along at an elevation of over 10,000 feet gave me a flood of appreciation for the ranger's advice— my 55-pound pack seemed to weigh 155 by sundown.

Each day we would advance along the trail and end up at a camp where expert teachers gave us an unforgettable experience. One was a mining camp where we panned for gold and then went way back into a small, narrow mineshaft. Next was a climbing camp where we had to rappel off cliffs, then on to an archaeology camp where we looked for arrowheads and bones. A lumbering camp followed, where we climbed poles and rolled logs. There was a ten-to-fifteen-mile hike between each of these camps, and we carried all of our food and bedding on our backs. We hung even our toothpaste high in a tree every night to keep the bears away.

In the climbing camp, to show the Scouts the value of safety ropes, the trainers would hoist a kid 40 feet up a big pine tree, then trip the rope so the kid would free fall for 30 feet, but the rope would catch him before he hit the ground (sort of a pre-bungee cord experience). When my son got to the top of that tree the trip mechanism failed and he was stuck up there. In came a sudden thunderstorm—that tree and my son a perfect lightning rod. At the jamboree in Pennsylvania just a couple of years earlier a boy was killed by lightning right next to our camp, so I was in a panic, yelling at the trainers to get him down quick. They finally did, but my nerves were not the same for a while.

Our trip had other notable moments, too. One evening as we made dinner, one of the Scouts threw his cooking gear on the ground in disgust and said, "This sucks—all we do, is cook, cook, cook!" Then all of the other whiners joined in. I gathered them all together and said, "Well, guys, think of this. Each of you only has to cook once every three days. Your mothers have done this for you three times a day for your whole lives." A silence came over the group—one of those great teaching moments had just happened for them—recognition of just how much a mother does.

One night I began to make a snake stick (a wooden walking stick with a realistic-looking snake coiled around it). That's why I'd brought the rasps, saws, and sandpaper. As it took shape, the boys were enthused and wanted me to make them one. "Make your own," I said. And so every night in camp we worked on snake sticks instead of goofing around, having some great in-depth talks while doing it.

CARVING WALKING STICKS WITH A LIFELIKE SNAKE COILED AROUND THEM WAS A POPULAR PASTIME FOR MY SCOUTS.

By the time we had been out on the trail for ten days we were getting good at directions. Reading the map, we could see where a shortcut through an uncharted valley could save us a good three miles. We voted to overrule the "no bushwhacking" rule and launch out into the forest. This was a mistake, a BIG mistake. Soon we were in thickets so dense that our feet were not contacting the ground, and on all sides were no end of forests and boulders that all looked alike. One kid wet his pants, another started crying for his mother. I felt really dumb. I knew we were in trouble but pretended calm and after much thorn beating and skin raking we emerged on the trail again, saving three miles but losing three hours. Lesson learned!

The last night we camped it was Saturday night, and the next morning was a special Sunday in our faith called Fast Sunday where we go without two meals and give an amount equivalent to the cost of those meals to the poor. Because I honored the fast, so did all of the boys. We went to bed early, broke camp at three in the morning, and in the moonlit darkness walked the trail out to the big jutting ledge called the Tooth of Time. Here at sunrise we held a testimony meeting of how we felt about the trip, our parents, our lives, and our Creator. By ten o'clock on that beautiful Sunday morning, we were hiking out to go home.

We hadn't had a bath or change of clothes for 12 days, were scratched and torn, and the food in our saggy packs was long gone. All of the food we had been issued was dry, powdery stuff to which you added water. This was useful for the purpose but nothing anyone would want to eat for long. I was so hungry for a piece of real food I was tempted to chase down a deer.

We ran into a group of hikers who were leaders being trained back at the base camp, and one of them had an orange that he was tossing up and down. I told him jokingly that I would sell my birthright for that orange, and he threw it to me and said, "It's yours."

It was still Fast Sunday and in any case I wouldn't dream of eating it in front of all those hungry boys. So for the rest of our time on the trail, I would stick my fingernail into the peel and sniff the orange, and never, ever before did anything smell that good. When we got to camp, I remember still so well taking that first-in-13-days shower, and the taste of the ice-cold milk and other foods.

When the Scouts got to the phone you should have heard the moaning and groaning and exaggerations—of bears, storms, and so on. Yet when I called my wife I did the same thing. No semester at any university could have given us what we got from those 15 days.

Bedrock beliefs

One day I sat down and attempted to trace the origin of the beliefs and behavior that rewarded me the most in my life. Aside from the Scriptures and my parents, it kept boiling down to that first Boy Scout manual. The most rewarding principles were Scout-based, not school-based. Universities and the rest of the world taught the intangibles of try and effort; Scouting taught, "A Scout **IS!**"

Scouts taught me:	Universities and society taught me:
To be trustworthy	To be accepted
To be loyal	To be legal
To be helpful	To be political
To be friendly	To be hirable
To be courteous	To position myself
To be kind	To make things look and sound good
To be obedient	To be calloused
To be cheerful	To test limits
To be thrifty	To be cautious
To be brave	To be suspicious
To be clean	To trust science
To be reverent.	To consume to my income limit

I still believe the Scout manual and program is the best "how to" guide for life ever conceived.

As a totally non-buoyant skinny farm kid, I couldn't swim 50 feet without sinking, so never could pass this requirement for being an Eagle Scout. After 60 more years of involvement with Scouting I finally received the Silver Beaver award, and later both Arlo and I were inducted into the Scouting Hall of Fame.

FAMILY PHOTO 1966: BARBARA HOLDING RELL, GRANT, LIZ, ME WITH CINDY, LAURA AND KARLA STANDING BEHIND.

Chapter 13

FROM DOWN HOME TO DOWNTOWN

Plunging into diversity...

THOUGH VARSITY STARTED OUT CLEANING HOMES, BY THE 1970S WE WERE CLEANING MOSTLY BUSINESSES AND COMMERCIAL BUILDINGS OF ALL KINDS.

The client switch in our operation came much like a child's growth—one day he or she is a little boy or girl and then one morning you blink and see a man or woman. There was no conscious policy change involved here—originally we were mainly a domestic house-cleaning operation, and gradually we seemed to be cleaning mostly commercial buildings. It started with a few homeowners who happened to also own or run a business. They saw us cleaning efficiently in their home, so why not their office or store?

A number of other things contributed to this shift of service, especially the fact that the jobs in commercial work were larger—it often took 20 residential jobs to equal the return from one commercial. Commercial accounts were usually less complicated, too, because you generally had one boss and one billing. For the same amount of income in private homes, you had 20 different people to deal with, and people were often ten times as particular about their homes as the manager would be about a factory or airport. Our crews were also more comfortable cleaning an empty commercial building after 5 P.M. than being under the eye of an exacting homeowner (plus often neighbors, relatives, or friends) the whole time. Also, we were students for the first six years of our company's life, so we went to school for most of the daytime hours, and we could clean a grocery store after our studies from nine to midnight, or get up early and service the place from five to eight o'clock before morning class. I attended more than one early morning class still in uniform with wax still drying on my shoe tips.

> WHAT WAS ONCE VARSITY
> HOUSECLEANERS WAS NOW VARSITY
> CONTRACTORS, REFLECTING OUR
> BROADER BASE OF CLEANING OPERATIONS.

The '70s

Six years after Varsity became a full-time company, it was becoming well known in the western states. Our Boise operation was growing now and doing well, Arizona was moving along, and Utah was exploding. We were becoming very professional in our systems, management, and training. We did above-average work and kept good records and felt that brighter days were ahead.

We worked harder than ever, and willingly grabbed any challenge our customers offered, always looking for ways to reduce the cost and raise the quality of our work.

With this growth came new and vast responsibilities I had never before faced. This was the most frustrating decade of my life. I had a net worth of at least a million dollars in assets, yet had severely limited—or no—cash reserves. Everything we earned had to be reinvested to sustain a growing business, inventory, and payroll. This meant that our own family's cars and appliances were old, TVs going or gone.

Physical discomforts were never a real problem for me; I grew up sleeping in a bunkhouse where it got so cold at night a pitcher of water in the room would freeze solid. Some business experiences, however, were a real emotional drain; such as when trusted and outstanding managers or supervisors would succumb to greed and dishonesty and help themselves to company funds. Appropriate legal action had to be taken and in these cases, we lost not just prestige and money but good friends. Varsity always operated on self-discipline, thus opportunities for stealing and cheating were always there. We didn't have a lot of dishonesty, but we had our share. One of our top men, for example, accepted checks in behalf of the company and at the same time was running another cleaning company he had formed on his own on the side, using our equipment and funds, and servicing some of our clients. After coming out on the short end of the ledger a few times, we learned that allowing dishonesty to go unpunished was unfair to all concerned. Thereafter, dishonesty was dealt with by tighter discipline.

Then there was Vegas...

In 1970, Arlo and our southern Utah supervisor had once driven the 125 miles to Las Vegas to look over some expansion possibilities. They spent a day contacting a few businesses and trying to determine the likelihood of getting some accounts. One bank chain there expressed interest and Varsity presented them with a bid. Our bid fell within a few dollars of another local bidder and inasmuch as we weren't established there, they thanked us and went with the other bidder. We filed a copy of the bid and forgot about Nevada until late in 1974.

Arlo and I were on a plane trip to Phoenix that included a stop in Las Vegas. "Just for kicks, Don, let's check out that bank again," Arlo suggested as a way of using our layover time. I agreed, so we rented a car and I saw Las Vegas, the gambling capital of the country, for the first time. My exposure to nightlife and high rolling up to that point was almost zero.

Arriving in Las Vegas with this background, I was overwhelmed by the "action" of the place—the number of and glamour of the facilities there was unbelievable. The first view of Vegas at night outdoes any expectations—their electric bills must be unimaginable. I also saw here the largest assembly of lost-looking people I'd ever seen, including 80-year-old grandmas hanging onto slot machine handles to hold themselves up, in hopes of turning a widow's mite into a million.

We contacted the bank and found out that a new man, a senior vice president, was in charge now. We made an appointment with him and he encouraged us to pursue another bid for his bank. They liked our brochures, our clean-cut, no-smoking, no-drinking, cussing, or chasing-women appeal, and said they would like to consider us.

We did, many plane tickets later, bid and propose our way into a Las Vegas account. It wasn't the bank we'd spent thousands of dollars courting, but a large medical center operated by a builder/management development company. Getting this contract was the result of true "Varsity effort." A national Building Service Contractors Association International (BSCAI) convention was being held in Vegas at about that time. We asked two of our managers to check it out, and one of them was the man who was now managing Denver, Dennis Parker. His interest in nightlife was akin to mine and in his off hours at the convention, didn't involve himself with the usual drinking, gambling, and shows there. Instead he grabbed a handful of business cards and hit the street to hustle up business. And he got it! I was sound asleep, dreaming of mop buckets, when a call came from Vegas.

"Don, this is Dennis!"

"Parker, you horselip, it's almost 1 A.M.!"

"Oh, we are an hour behind here so it isn't as late as you think! Anyway great news!

"We found a big medical center that is unhappy with its present service." (This was the all-glass Marilyn Parkway Medical Building, nicknamed the flash cube).

I was awake after that, and for an hour we discussed making the bid. The contract was much less gross income than we could afford to move there for, but it was a good building owned by a prestigious company. When the bid was approved, we decided to take the plunge—we said yes and again Varsity shuffled its rapidly growing organization to start up and administer a new area.

We selected Dennis—our youngest manager, only 23—for the job of president and general manager of Varsity of Nevada. We'd hired him when he was 16 and his experience and abilities had been phenomenal for Varsity. We'd moved him four times in two years—Sun Valley, Boise, Denver, and now Nevada.

Dennis and his wife Susie were no strangers to work, sacrifice, and bad timing on moves. On the move to Denver, Susie was expecting her first baby exactly on moving day. She barely made it to Denver before delivering two baby janitors, Brad and Brandon. On the move to Vegas, she was again expecting almost exactly on the moving date. Dennis and I tried to have the details of a home there worked out, but the house wasn't ready yet and so they had to stay in a motel. When they finally moved into a house about a week later they breathed a sigh of relief, anticipating a little well-deserved rest before setting up an office and preparing for the opening day of business 28 days hence.

When the newly-installed phone rang, Dennis' jaw dropped, and he said, "Yes, we'll do it." "Do what?" Susie asked as he staggered to the couch and sat down. "That was Mike at the development company—the cleaning contractor just quit and walked out. They want us to start that six-story building tonight!" "Tonight?" echoed Susie. "Tonight!" Dennis said. "I told them they could depend on us to come through." Rather than a month to prepare for Varsity's debut at the building, he now had less than five hours. He hadn't contacted any prospective employees, had no supplies, and knew very little about the building. When Dennis called me and broke the news, I was packed for a flight to Salt Lake City for management meetings. I postponed the meetings and changed my ticket to Vegas.

The three of us (Susie, about eight and seven-eighths months pregnant, showed up too) worked from six that evening until five the next morning. Dennis assigned me the restrooms, and I scrubbed toilet bowls, sinks, and urinals for 11 hours straight.

The night had its highlights, because part of the clinic was open all night. Only the wildest imagination could anticipate the 3 A.M. patrons of a medical center just off the Vegas strip, including showgirls in their working costumes (what there was of them).

The building had been neglected, so we were all dragging by the time the building was clean, and the maze of locks, codes, and burglar alarms figured out. Again the next night the three of us cleaned the building, finishing in the wee hours of the morning. Meanwhile, we arranged to transfer some Varsity employees from elsewhere to help until Dennis was able to hire himself a crew.

SUSIE AND DENNIS PARKER.

I was so tired after that two-day siege that as I flew home I felt a surge of fresh appreciation for the men and women who labored nightly for our company, the employees who did the actual work.

Las Vegas, like other new areas, meant thousands of dollars for signs, trucks, office supplies, desks, scaffolding, and hundreds of other things. Every time a new account brought $80 profit a month, $1,500 worth of equipment and supplies had to be invested. Rapid growth really strained the already limited cash flow.

Happy with our work, the owner of the medical building provided other contracts, including the 16-building Valley Bank Plaza. Parker worked unbelievable hours as other new contracts began to come in, and like many Varsity managers, learned about cash flow, receivables, and payables. He soon received confirmation on a bid for a 17-story skyscraper, and Varsity was on its way in Nevada!

Varsity made its own little contributions to the color and adventure of Vegas over the years. Our office was broken into three times, the door beaten down with a crowbar, our company checks and some cash stolen. Right after the second break-in, our manager ran to the bank and told the teller not to honor any yellow Varsity checks. "Like this one?" she chirped, holding up a check she'd just cashed. "Where'd you get that?" our manager questioned. The teller leaned over and whispered, "From the guy right behind you writing another one!" The thief with our whole pad of checks under his arm was indeed 5 feet away—a silent call for the cops and he was jailed.

I got a hushed call another day telling me most of my good accounts were from the Mafia, great news! Do a poor job and end up with a complementary cement mop bucket.

Remember, janitors work at night, and Vegas is alive at night. When my employees weren't stopping robberies, being flashed, solicited by prostitutes or unions, getting beat up or their trucks vandalized, they cleaned buildings.

None of us ever forget the "first time" of anything, and we had one here. One of the vice presidents of a big prospective client company was reviewing our final bid price. Without raising his head from the document, he looked over the top of his glasses and said, "This looks pretty good, but are you sure you have everything in here?" We nodded our heads in the affirmative, and then he said it several times more and then, "Are you sure you didn't forget any of the extras?" "Like what?" we asked. "Oh…" he drawled, "like…" then he reached his hand under the table and rubbed his thumb and forefinger together briskly. We looked down at this "gimme-gimme" motion searching for a clue to what we'd forgotten. Finally, he explained a new expense unfamiliar to our ledgers—grease money, payola, bribes, or whatever. We told him we were above such skullduggery and he said, "Suit yourself, but a few bucks on the side and a trip to the Bahamas for the management do a lot to keep complaints down, competitors out, and contracts solid." Obviously politics and the movies weren't the only places this sort of thing happened!

Varsity's ledger remained free of those extras in Vegas, but he was right, it was often part of things there.

I wondered at times if we were just plain incompatible with Vegas—it seemed that even our best accounts here would end up in trouble. We had a contract to clean the Sultan Spa (name changed to protect the undressed), for instance, an exclusive women's health club. Once inside the spa, clothes were replaced by skimpy, clingy leotards, micro-bikinis, or nothing. Because everyone seems to think janitors are blind or sexless, no one made any effort to conceal herself and just flaunted at will. It didn't seem to bother the ladies to zip and bounce around half or wholly nude, but it sure cut cleaning production down. Needless to say, for our young men this became a much sought-after place to work, especially the carpeted area near the lockers and pool, which was getting worn from over-vacuuming. Then, too, new potential accounts always like to see some of your present accounts, and knowing we had the Sultan, you can guess where they all wanted to go. The Sultan and its clientele didn't appreciate periodic parades of goggle-eyed building managers.

One of our prestigious accounts in Las Vegas in the '70s was a bank chain consisting of a large downtown sky-riser and several branch banks scattered throughout the city. In one of these, coffee spills were a constant problem. Coffee with cream and sugar in it is difficult to remove, especially if not cleaned up immediately. So our custodian there did an enterprising bit of work. Unable to please the branch manager with his ability to remove coffee spots, he came up with the ingenious idea of saving all of the leftover coffee from breaks and the lunchroom for a couple of weeks. Then one night instead of shampooing the carpet with the specified coconut oil, high-foaming shampoo, he filled the tank of the machine with coffee and cleaned the whole carpet with it, staining it all the same color as the spills. The place smelled like the grand opening of a new Starbucks for a few weeks, but the carpet looked great. Ingenuity? Varsity had it.

Vegas did a lot to educate us, if nothing else. On one of our early visits there Arlo, Rex Turner, and I, like millions of tourists a year do, went out to gawk at the bright lights and crazy gamblers and have dinner. We stopped at an outdoor stage show to watch a magician. These outside shows charged no admission in the effort to entice people in to eat, drink, gamble, and watch the bigger shows inside. The magician was good, and funny—our first Vegas show! The minute he ended his act and eased off the stage six gorgeous showgirls suddenly appeared, beautiful and minimally dressed.

I think the unavailable and the untouchable fascinates us all to some degree. I didn't manage to banish this incident from my mind entirely until the afternoon I went with Dennis to bid a big hotel for a cleaning contract. The marquee as we drove up featured "the bare touch of Vegas." It was dark, quiet, and gloomy as the manager led us across the stage, then up to the dusty backstage area. There, hanging on hooks, were some of the scanty dancing costumes we'd seen—worn, frayed, smelly, stretched, and sweat-stained. I was shocked! Surely anything caressing those curves couldn't be that common—gadfreys, this was nowhere as nice as the closets and dressers at home, and not as legal, either. A great shot of perspective!

A peek at the competition

My company joined a national building contractor's organization shortly after the establishment of Varsity in Denver. Arlo and others attended meetings on various subjects which were beneficial to us. A couple of years later I was invited to a taxation and investment conference designed for top executives of maintenance companies, and soon I was checked into the Hyatt Regency in downtown Chicago.

I knew no one, so at the President's Reception spent my time observing and sizing up all of the operations and their executives. A janitor's convention is in many ways exactly like any other—in fact, if someone took down the signs, you wouldn't know the difference. Professional cleaners employ many of the same lecturers, attorneys, and economists that GM, Hilton, and bankers use. They hold their conferences in the same kinds of overpriced hotels, and managed to spread one day of instruction and information over four days of meetings. The men backslap and talk louder and louder as they drink more and more of the free alcohol. Their overdressed wives follow them around trying to get into the spirit of enthusiasm of the floor mopping conversations. The attendees leave piles of crumpled napkins and half-eaten hors d'oeuvres lying everywhere in spite of their professional cleaning know-how and training. The "big operators" tell big money and success stories that draw awestruck expressions from the younger members, who lean closer and closer trying to overhear everything without spilling their drinks.

Most of the problems you hear being discussed are basically the same ones discussed in the last three conventions, the only value of the discussion being an assurance to all that their competitors are suffering the same problems they are. The participants poke fun at the executives and owners of the businesses they contract with, with statements like, "J.P. of Acme Limited is getting better. It only takes him two weeks now to create a problem somewhere." Or "IBM doesn't know much about building maintenance, but we have them under control now."

The conference was not without advantages, however. It made me realize that although many of the companies involved were bigger and more profitable than mine at the time, none had the unique and close-knit culture Varsity did, and few of their leaders had invested as wisely in personnel and leadership. Aside from themselves, they had no one who could operate their business totally and profitably if they weren't around. When I mentioned that I had several men ready, any one of whom could take my place tomorrow as head of the entire company, they were amazed. Toward the end of the convention a constant flow of messages began to appear from their operations back home. Contractors crowded and lined the rows of telephones in the hall, some checking out early to go home and save the business.

I left my first convention inspired by not only the things I learned about the technical end of the business, but by the knowledge that our company was actually ahead of many of the rest in some important ways.

Operation Pigeon Potty

On a nice April morning, the phone rang at Varsity headquarters in Pocatello. "Don, this is Tro," the voice said. "Meet me at 138 Main at nine tomorrow morning to bid a big job." So four contractors (including me) and the owner of the building involved met the next morning. The owner got a flashlight and hammer and said, "Follow me!" We went up two flights of stairs into a room of the old hotel next door and then crawled out through a window onto the roof above the owner's store. There was a big piece of plywood over the door to a large attic over the owner's store, which he ripped off with gusto.

Then we stepped into an almost unbelievable abode. As we stood astounded, the owner quickly leaped in front of the door so we couldn't get out while the getting was good. He told us the sad tale. "Boys, this was home sweet home for thousands of pigeons for at least twenty years, and as you can see they left their mark. The smell from up here on a hot day discourages our customers, and feathers come drifting down too, so this place has got to be cleaned!" The contractor I was standing next to began to stutter, and another was in silent shock, but to be polite we all crunched through the dried pigeon refuse, then retreated back through the window and down the stairs.

I wrote up a bid and sent it in, figuring it was high enough that it would never be accepted.

Four months later, I said to our Pocatello manager, "I'll be around for a few days, so if any jobs come up, count me in." You guessed it—the pigeon job came through. Now I had two fine young men who worked with me all summer, my 13-year-old son Grant and a 14-year-old redhead named Davy Treasure. "How would you like to make a five-dollar bonus, boys?" Their eyes glistened with eagerness as they said, "YES!" "Okay, round up two snow shovels, two scoop shovels, a hoe, fifteen gunny sacks, a vacuum, and three brooms. When they had done so I presented them with a couple of respirators. "What are these for?" Davy asked. "You'll see," I said, and led the two innocent lambs up the stairs, through the window, and onto the roof of the old hotel. Then I led them into the pigeon pit—"Have all of this out in eight hours and five dollars extra is yours!"

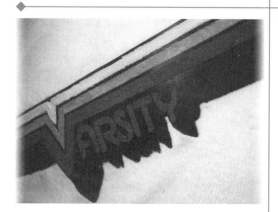

THE VARSITY LOGO IN BOLD RED, ORANGE, YELLOW, AND BLACK CARPETING GRACED ONE ENTIRE WALL OF OUR CORPORATE OFFICE IN POCATELLO.

Now pigeon dust poured forth and feathers flew. When 15 sacks were filled with pigeon poo, a sturdy rope was fastened to them and they were lowered, one at a time, two stories down into my El Camino. Where the pigeons had roosted, the droppings were 12 inches deep, level with the rafters. The two boys dauntlessly pursued their bonus. Lying exhausted on the roof after nine hours of grueling work, they were still many sacks short of victory. The job continued into the next day. No one would park by the El Camino. In the restaurant where the boys ate at noon, chicken was never considered.

Finally it was cleaned—walls and ceiling scraped, inches of bird droppings sanded off the sills, and all floors not just emptied but vacuumed and hosed. Then a giant spray gun was hoisted up and the entire interior of the room was sprayed with a latex sealant, to eliminate any remaining odor. Any holes, crevices, or openings were then well sealed to discourage any further feathered inhabitants.

The final statistics of the job:

- 4,138 pounds of dried pigeon waste removed.
- 1 truckload of other debris (including some long-dead pigeons) hauled away.
- Davy (a Scout with 30 merit badges) vowed to surrender his pigeon-raising badge.
- Grant is now cooing instead of talking.
- The sky full of pigeons hated Varsity now and performed several dive bomb attacks.

253

I put a story in our company newsletter about this epic job, with the following note:

> "The boys didn't make their five-dollar bonus. However, if we can get 50 of you readers to drop us a note expressing your empathy for them, we will give them a twenty-five dollar bonus. Grant and Davy are perched on the rafters, depending on you!"

(The boys got their well-earned bonus!)

When you are operating at a breakneck pace every day, you don't have time to sit back and admire your progress and accomplishments. At the end of 1977, a day's activities seemed much the same as 1967, and for that matter 1957. In spite of the similarities, however, there was quite a change from yesterday's Varsity to today's operation.

Instead of calls coming in from eight-thirty to four-thirty, the business phone in my home began to ring at 6 A.M. It was 8 A.M. in New York or Miami, and my morning began with calls from the East. Only a few years ago the calls were from Blackfoot, Twin Falls, Boise, and Sun Valley (all Idaho cities), plus an occasional long-distance call from Salt Lake City, 180 miles away. My call list one morning now read Miami, Raleigh, LA, Las Vegas, New York, Bridgeport, Phoenix, and Atlanta.

This ain't work!

I grew up in an environment where no one ever complained about work or "the boss"—on the farm, we were always our own bosses. The word "job" just indicated what we were doing today, not some onerous assignment. Work was kind of exciting, and finishing a job or chore something to look back on and savor.

In the cleaning business, too, most jobs were full of adventure, education, and new friends and acquaintances. Some of these were truly hard work but we couldn't wait to tackle them.

In the late '70s, we signed a rather unique contract with the Utah Parks Service, the agency that operated three big national parks in southern Utah—Bryce Canyon, Zion National Park, and the North Rim of the Grand Canyon.

These contain some of the most magnificent rock formations in the world, and sunrises and sunsets here awe onlookers. All of these areas had such heavy snows that they were only open for the summer season. As soon as the weather allowed entrance, a few weeks before the parks opened, our well organized and experienced cleaning and maintenance team would arrive (generally with the help of a snow plow), with truckloads of equipment. Then we would open up the lodges, shops, cabins, restaurants, dining rooms, and other rooms and clean them. We dusted the towering 40-foot rafters, rock walls, fireplaces, and everything else inside, stripped and waxed floors, shampooed carpet, sanitized restrooms, washed walls, sanded and re-varnished hardwood floors, and cleaned windows and counters and display cases, removing the cobwebs of winter as well as all traces of last summer's tourist wear and tear. We also raked the grounds and paths and cleaned them of debris.

We did this before the concessionaires and park staff arrived. We stayed in the cabins in the park while we were there, and the park department sent a cook who fed us like kings!

We worked long, hard days, but it was pure heaven. We had the parks to ourselves—there was no one but us amidst those massive wonders of nature. It was quiet beyond quiet, and birds, deer, and squirrels were all over, unafraid. There was no litter, no cars, no phones, no commerce—the peace and majesty of it all was unmatched. There were no TVs in the cabins either in those days, and the romance of the old log structures that my grandparents had first seen from a Model T Ford 70 years earlier gave me goosebumps. Everything was fresh and unspoiled and we worked in the middle of it for three weeks, moving from one park to the other.

The North Rim of the Grand Canyon was the last to be finished, because of the deep snow. Bryce Canyon was breathtaking, but I loved the Grand Canyon. The ghost of greatness lingered in the old buildings and there was real power in the canyon's massive size and depth. On one trip to the Grand Canyon my wife, son, and two eldest daughters came along and worked side by side with the crew, and soon everything was gleaming for opening day.

Varsity can claim a record matched by no other window cleaners in the world: we cleaned the exterior windows of the lodge overlooking the main section of the Grand Canyon where it is one mile deep, and that's high window washing! Mark Browning, a fearless mountain climber, hung on a rope outside the lodge to do it.

After work and supper, we'd walk out on the tourist trails in the dark to the canyon rim, looming a full mile above the canyon floor. It was like owning the whole canyon yourself, while feeling the spirits of all those who saw the same over the years and remained somehow to share your awe. Then at times I thought it was a bit of a sacrifice to do all this; now I realize that people sacrifice and plan for years just to visit these places during a crowded tourist time. We had it all to ourselves and got paid for it, too!

When I bid a job, I wanted to get it so I pursued every angle I could to get the job done well, yet fast enough to make a profit in the end. No matter how good you get at this, however, you still miss a few (under or overbids). When you realize you have miscalculated or left something important out of the initial quote, you take it on the chin, unless there is some better and faster way to do a good job than the way you originally planned.

Doing some deep cleaning once in the main lodge at the North Rim of the Grand Canyon, I bid to vacuum the dust, dead bugs, and cobwebs off the 20-foot-high, 60-foot-long rock wall at the end of the main dining hall. I figured that one of us could get up on a tall ladder with a backpack vacuum strapped to our back and cover the whole wall in five or six hours. When we arrived to do the job, I realized it was going to be much more difficult than I'd imagined to reach in and get decades' worth of dirt and debris out (there was still mortar dust here from its construction in 1924), and we didn't have a ladder or scaffolding capable of reaching the top safely. I feared it would actually take about two days to do the quality job I had bid. Then my eye fell on a heavy-duty kitchen hose, not just a wimpy garden hose, but a real professional model almost two inches in diameter, with water pressure to spare.

We were the only ones there, since the park hadn't yet opened for the year, and surely, I rationalized, power-hosing down the wall would do a much better job than vacuuming it, anyway. I had fishing boots in the truck, so I put them on, and we moved all of the tables and chairs out of the dining room. Then I reeled out the hose and got started.

Man, when that water, strong as the stream from a fire hose, hit the wall, dirt, dust, grit, and the carcass of every form of bug life in the canyon was flushed out and came cascading down. Bonanza! The wall looked like it had been resurrected! As soon as the water hit the floor, I had two guys with floor squeegees push the runoff through the big double doors, over the cliff, and down into the canyon.

When we were about three-quarters through, it looked as if every plumbing pipe in the complex had broken. I turned around and there stood the head man of Utah Parks. He and his fellow manager were stunned at the scene. I was terrified, but I waded over to them enthusiastically in my hip boots through 3 inches of water and shouted, "Can you believe how good that wall looks, Lamar? Looks better than new, doesn't it?" He gave a feeble affirmative nod. "Vacuuming just didn't do it, so we are biting the bullet and giving you a deluxe, expensive wash job for the same price." ("For the same price," always pleases people, even if they don't know what the original price was.) "We are getting the floor clean, too, in the process. Just look at the grime coming out of those rocks—we are doing a cleaning job that's been overdue for forty years."

By now, the two of them were nodding admiringly at the results and the savings, and walked on, satisfied, through the complex. And it did look super, three times better than if it had been vacuumed, and it only took one hour—we made a nice profit in the end. I'm just glad the floor was the old linoleum and not wood or carpet! They even hired us again the next year!

The case of the vanishing toilet paper

One of clients' most common complaints was running out of toilet paper. Even when you tried to make a scientific study of people's habits in a given place (how often they used the restroom, and which stalls), and installed double rolls in the most frequently used stalls, you never could absolutely prevent this. One time when we were cleaning at the Grand Canyon during tourist season we were really hopping to it, hoping to make a good impression on the Parks and Recreation people. In the restroom, which had enough stalls to resemble the starting gate at Santa Anita racetrack, at 7 A.M. we had every toilet paper holder newly loaded, enough to last three for four days, we thought. At 9 A.M. that same day came the famous call, "No toilet paper in the restroom!" Impossible!

Nope, sure enough a quick inspection confirmed that every single roller was bare. An old park veteran solved the mystery right away, saving us a desperate call to Scotland Yard. It was a little element of thievery. The hikers, headed to the bottom of the canyon and anticipating a pit stop in the bushes on the way down, would raid the restrooms before they left, unrolling a generous handful of it or if a roll was smaller, taking the whole thing. So back to the drawing board—what a bummer!

Driving was nonproductive, "no pay" time, so I did it in off hours, before or after our regular work, often on snowy or icy roads. I seldom knew what it was like to drive fresh. I look back and wonder how I managed not to kill myself or anyone else. Fortunately, in all of those miles, I had no accidents except a few fender benders in parking lots. We'd finish or leave a job, then drive all night to another job or (when we were still in college) an early morning class. This meant a long day's work followed by a 300- to 500-mile trip home. The ones I remember best were the trips home from our Grand Canyon jobs—there were not many interstate highways then and it took forever to get home (and Utah and Idaho were full of deer on the road).

I never used coffee, soda pop, or drugs to keep awake, and was the king of "wake-up" creativity when I got drowsy. Sticking your head out of the window or slapping your face was for amateurs. I got a bucket of snow and put it down my back, whinnied like a horse, banged my head on the steering wheel, pretended I was a tour guide, and sang all of Hank Williams' songs from "Your Cheating Heart" to "Jambalaya." One night I was so tired, some road signs came alive and ran across the road on their white post legs!

Some nights I became so exhausted I pulled off the road to sleep. As I huddled in my sleeping bag, a state patrol officer would often tap on the window to see if I was a murder victim. After a couple of hours of rest I was on my way home again, arriving in time for breakfast or church.

After one such trip, I came directly to a big job at the Blackfoot Telephone Company to help the crew. I was so tired I could hardly move, but to keep face, worked with the men at a fast clip all morning stripping floors. I was unshaven, and my clothes were wrinkled from sleeping in the car. At noon we all went to the city park to eat our lunches, then stretched out to take a ten-minute break after lunch. When the men got up to go, I couldn't move and told them I was going to rest ten more minutes. I dozed off only to be awakened by the city police, who were kicking me soundly on the bottom of my feet. "All right, you bum, get up and move along—there's no loitering in this park." My account of this thoroughly elated the men, and caused me to be more selective in both grooming and resting places.

One evening after a long day at the Grand Canyon I took off for home at 9 P.M. Four hundred miles later, I was just 25 miles from home but couldn't go any farther. So I pulled off onto a little turnoff road and backed into it, with the front of my car facing the highway. Then I fell over in the front seat to sleep a bit so I could make it home. I'd just dozed off when the sound of a diesel truck woke me. I thought I'd fallen asleep driving, and now I saw a brightly lighted tanker truck appearing to come right at me. I was on the passenger side of the front seat, so when I grabbed for the steering wheel to dodge the truck, it wasn't there. In total fear I closed my eyes to die—and *zoom!*—the truck went right by my parked car. I was fully awake now and had enough adrenalin to drive to Denver.

So stimulated was I by the event that my romantic instinct was activated, and after being gone a week was anxious to see Barbara, only a few miles away. I crawled into bed, kissed her on the back of the neck, and asked her why she hadn't waited for her lover the janitor's return. Barbara, a warm, enthusiastic, passionate lover, a few hours earlier had helped a neighbor woman whose car was out of gas. In the course of this, Barbara had for the first time in her life tried to siphon gasoline. Nothing until this (including cold showers) had ever been capable of dampening my husbandly intentions, but when she rolled over and whispered back, "Hi, Honey" in 88-octane breath, I decided that for this night the trucks and cars had won, and slept.

That's no rain cloud!

It was one of those days that could tempt a man to give in or give up. I needed money for payroll again—$2,000 by the end of the week—and it just wasn't in the bank or in any immediately collectible receivable. The only hope was to pull together and do a pile of pending "route" jobs for the telephone company, which would process my billing overnight if asked.

The route spanned more than 500 miles of south central Utah. No one really enjoyed these "must earn it" marathons. But I packed my tools, paint, ladders, and sleeping bag in the El Camino, and told Barbara that I'd be home when the job sheets were complete. I took off at daylight on Monday. Going from small town to small town, which the Utah desert country has more than its share of, I knocked out a roof repair job, a couple of weed-killing assignments, and painted some markers.

I was profitably ahead of schedule when I got to Nephi, Utah. I drove up a snaking, dusty road to a relay hut up on the side of a mountain and shuddered when I saw the height of the exhaust pipe from the diesel generator inside. I hated heights, but hated the thought of not being able to make payroll worse. So armed with a gallon of expensive 1,500-degree resistant aluminum coating, I got up on the roof and then climbed the ladder on the stack and was soon doing my favorite thing, painting. In record time, the stack was finished and gleaming wet. I was still up at the top, ready to descend, when I saw a small dark cloud moving toward me. Being a farmer, I knew it wasn't a rain cloud, plus I could hear it hum.

Within seconds I was engulfed by a mass of flying gnats—it was like a horror movie. They didn't bite, just nearly suffocated me as they filled my eyes, ears, nose, and mouth. Then suddenly, it was over. The cloud of bugs was gone except for the 90 million or so of them that were stuck to the newly painted stack. My shining aluminum stack was now a black cylinder of tiny twitching wings. My first impulse was to sit down on the roof and bawl, second was to go into the hut, start up the giant diesel engine, and burn those babies off. The third option was more rational and intelligent. The paint was good (very protective), and no one would ever see the stack up close, tall as it was and way up in the mountains as well. Starting up the motor and heating up the stack right now would probably be a big-time fire hazard anyway. So I just left it and drove off to the next job. Almost 40 years later now, I still have a strong urge to go see how many gnats are left.

I came home in four days—dirty, paint-covered, and unshaven—but having earned the $2,000. Les Hodge ran the billing through the next day!

The case of the carousing crows

Sometimes, no matter how good your cleaning service was, you just couldn't win. Our big Hewlett-Packard contract in Corvallis, Oregon, seemed like a sweet one. It was a nice building, the owners paid to keep it immaculate, and we had the programs and staff to do it. But still, in every group there is a nitpicker. There were a couple of beautiful flowering trees in the courtyard landscaping, which in the fall produced a small crabapple-like fruit. The crows in the area found these irresistible and cleaned up all of the fallen fruits for us. However, after the fruit fell it fermented quickly, and the crows always seemed to have one too many. They would fly up to the roof, and too drunk to realize that the large strips of rubber caulking up there were not big worms, they would grab and yank out sections of caulk, ruining the roof. Then they would stagger around on the roof trying to balance themselves with only half a brain, slide down the roof, and fall several stories to the ground. The engineers in the building screamed at us for letting their caulk get ripped out, and all of the bird lovers in the building screamed at us to do something about the poor crows that were falling off the roof. I don't remember what we did to remedy the situation. I think we hid!

The man who loved concrete

Probably my most torrid love affair, after the pencil and pen, was with masonry. I loved concrete—it was so permanent. Helping build a new church next door to our house and the Varsity shop, I learned how to form, pour, and finish concrete, and how to lay brick and blocks. After that I volunteered for concrete jobs whenever I could. I built many a fence and wall of masonry, and could make a concrete floor as smooth as silk. I eventually built a total of three homes and three shops out of masonry. Sometimes my birthday present would be a pallet of cinder blocks!

One day I met a man who made cinderblocks and concrete road tile in his backyard and that really intrigued me. He made his blocks and then built storage buildings out of them all over the county and rented the buildings to potato chip companies. Being a subscriber by now to a couple of concrete magazines, I noticed there was a block factory selling out in Nampa, Idaho, just 300 miles away. I'd had my eye on a piece of property about a mile and a half from our ranch, right off the interstate where a nice motel and country store could go, right on the main truck line from the East. I bought the property, 12 acres, and then bought the block plant. I hired a couple of semis to haul the dismantled plant to the property, and began to set up my own factory, a short distance from not only our home but one of the best sources of pumice (ideal for making blocks) in the U.S. at Malad, Idaho.

Everything was much simpler on paper than in the realities of construction. The cost of the parts needed for the operation's electrical system was as expensive as getting sued, and the cost of installing them was like getting sued a second time. It turned out that one didn't make blocks in the open; they had to be kiln dried to have the proper compression strength. Soon those innocent little blocks I could buy for eighty cents each had seduced me into a $50,000 investment.

I projected a good return for all this, but my timing was terrible. My newly formed System 1 consulting company started to boom with the Bell System, contracting me for seminars across the country, great money and great spin-offs for my cleaning business. So my sons and I worked late at night on the plant with lights on the tractor, when we could. Thanks to a good and dedicated son-in-law, we did get the thing set up, but he was a college student and there just wasn't time, between the two of us, to develop and run it properly. We did make blocks, but my plans to build an adjacent store and motel fell by the wayside due to the demands of my existing contracting and consulting businesses.

Shortly after this, convenience stores much like the one I had in mind popped up all over the country. One of the big chains was Flying J Truck Stops. Mark Browning and I were doing some consulting for them, writing a maintenance manual for their company, and one day I talked with their powers that be and suggested they buy my property and the little gas station that two local brothers built right next to it. They did indeed buy both places, and I gained five times my original investment. So financially, I did okay, but it hurt to not complete the project. On the other hand, a handsome Flying J installation stands there now, everything I imagined and planned, and I can enjoy it at no cost or stress.

After closing my block plant down, I sold some of the equipment to men who lived down the road, and who had the same dream

THE LOGO OF MY EXCITING, SHORT-LIVED VENTURE INTO CONCRETE BLOCK MANUFACTURE.

I did. And someone came in and stole my huge 100-foot-long conveyor, belt and all. They needed a train to haul it off—I sure would like to have seen how they did it.

ONE OF MY DREAMS WAS DASHED HERE, BUT THE WHOLE EXPERIENCE GAVE ME AN EDUCATION IN MANUFACTURE, MATERIALS TRANSPORT, REAL ESTATE, EASEMENTS, AND MORE THAT REALLY PAID OFF LATER.

Into the Sunshine State

When we were expanding Varsity to the South, a local economic advisor told me, "There are three forms of gambling in South Florida: the dog track, the racetrack, and the janitorial business." Despite the high failure rate in it, my money was on the janitor business because I knew it was choice, not chance that produced success.

The Florida operation added a new dimension to my life. Nothing was dull or uneventful. I would leave for Florida with a fresh notebook and several new pens, and return home with filled pages and used-up pens.

On one trip, there were a couple of firsts—one was a trip through the Keys to bid 24 Bell System buildings there, and the other was inspection tours through some Bell buildings with a "black light."

It seems that our quality of service in the restrooms had dropped in recent months and the Bell management, frustrated with trying to prove our deficiencies, resorted to buying a suitcase full of crime detection material, including a "black light." They then sprayed invisible "clue spray" on various parts of the floor, restroom fixtures, walls, etc. Once all the lights were out, you just switched the black light on (it was actually more like purple—ultraviolet), and any missed spots such as urine drips would gleam like a diamond. It was a real janitor killer.

When I arrived and the preliminary chitchat was over, I could see that the department chief and contract administrator were bursting at the seams to take a little tour with their new technology. On the tour, I was the main billing. We would walk into a restroom, turn out the light, turn a black light on, and in beautiful green glowing fluorescent my name D-O-N (printed as neatly as a phone man with a spray can could manage) appeared on the sides of restroom stall walls and the underside of toilet seats. I never thought I'd hate to see a three-letter word worse than a four-letter one in a restroom, but it happened.

There was no way around it—the evidence blinked out at us like a Las Vegas billboard.

One day five of us big wheels were inspecting a women's restroom after our crew cleaned it. We all went inside and turned off all the lights, but when we tried to turn on the black light it wasn't working. Suddenly a woman came into the now totally dark restroom and flipped on the light switch, and there all five of us were, huddled in a circle. "My word," she said, and whirled and ran. I never dared ask what the gossip was around the office that day and didn't want to know.

Another time several building managers got to swapping stories about how fast their custodians could carry trash from the building and dump it in the outside bins. The LA man told a story about a thug with a knife prowling around outside, so his custodian moved fast and carried a gun when he dumped the trash. A northern manager bragged on how cold it was where he came from (40 below), so his man dumped it fast, or froze. Another manager told how his janitor dumped it from the top of the building—everyone trying to top the last story.

Finally, the old Southern Bell manager, gesturing toward the chain-link fence marking the boundary between his building and the Florida swamps behind it, said, "Tell you what, men. See that little hole under that fence there?" We all looked and saw a hole and worn place under the fence. "Well about trash time, an alligator comes out and under that fence, and you ought to see my janitor dump the trash!"

Events like this continued—Florida kept you on your toes!

Carry on if it kills you?

Most of us have some little quirks even we will admit are clearly stupid, but we are hooked and hang onto them. I've had a lifetime plague of "never turning back." The Bible story of Lot's wife being turned into a pillar of salt for looking back at Sodom must have really impressed me, because once started down the road of anything there was no going back, even if it was the wrong road. Even when it was clearly time and financially wise to retrace my steps, I'd have to be forced to go back. If I got down the road a mile or two and realized I forgot something, even something major like a whole suitcase for a trip, I would rather go buy new or go without than go back.

This "no retreat" behavior came back to bite me many times. We'd make a bad bid on a contract and discover we were losing money, and needed either to drop it or go back for more money. I'd do everything possible to live with it, to manage to make a loser win. I got lots of justifiable criticism for this, but maybe this "stay on the road once committed" approach had a few blessings to compensate for the beatings it gave me.

Once this attitude almost crippled me. In the thick of a floor-stripping job a crew of ours was doing in Florida, Arlo and I stopped to see how the job was going. The answer was "not well," so we both jumped in with the crew. I'd flown in from Idaho and had only dress pants and shoes. So I took off my shoes, rolled up my pant legs, and worked in the stripper in my stocking feet. No stripper I had used before ever bothered me, but apparently this was a new super-charged formulation. The crew leader, a good friend, kept saying, "Them white feet gonna be mighty sore, Don, if you don't get out." "Nonsense—I've been stripping floors for years," I said. Even though my feet were burning by now, as were my knees, since I had to kneel to do baseboards, I kept going, and toughed it out.

Finally I had to go into the janitor closet and take off my socks. The skin and some of the flesh was gone from the top of my toes and my knees, and the exposed flesh was burned black. This stripper was about as caustic as the old oven cleaners and boy, did I suffer for the next month, wearing no shoes or oversized ones during our busiest season. It took years to heal completely, and years more for the toenails to come back. Thus I moved into the new era of rubber gloves and boots, and of reading those safety stickers I'd always glossed over.

An afternoon in the attic

To be reminded of how much water has gone under the bridge of a growing company, try reviewing 20 years of records. I did that for Varsity. We threw no records away—payroll, employee files, correspondence, job sheets, contracts, bids, etc. In 1979, it took four truckloads to move them to our new building. Mark Browning finally said of all those more than six years old, "Let's dump these!" I shivered in sentimentality and agreed, but first wanted to quickly look all of this over.

Two weeks later, I finished the project, amazed at how much effort is required to make even a tiny profit. Every one of those hundreds of files was loaded with letters, proposals, and meeting and phone call records. Often I had signed at least two-dozen letters a day—in 20 years that's a lot of letters!

I wanted to just do seminars, write, and farm, but from those old files, it was clear how influential I had been in our organization.

Even though my other managers had many impressive talents, my attic-sorting experience convinced me not to drop the reins of leadership.

The cat caper

In 1985, while meeting with the New York Port Authority's James Gresimer, who was manager at the time over the two towering 115-story World Trade Center buildings, we were discussing "unique building maintenance problems." Their most recent was cats—huge wild cats inside this swanky office complex. How could it be? Seems that as the structure was being erected, many of the city's stray cats discovered that if they hung around the construction site, the hundreds of workers would share scraps from their lunches with the cats. So for two or three years, as the building came together, not only did a cat colony grow comfortable here, but also fat and healthy. Until the last few weeks of completion the building remained open, so cats were able to move inside as the finish work progressed.

Result? When the building was complete, many experienced, untamed "Phantom of the Opera" cats were sealed inside. They hid in false ceilings, hollow wall spaces, crawlspaces, and the like, roaming and eating where they could. In one big executive meeting in the new and now fully occupied building, a fiber ceiling tile suddenly collapsed and a huge cat came flailing down and landed on the conference table, going berserk before the surprised attendees. Containing the dust-covered cat proved a bigger problem than was at hand on the business agenda, because the feline was big, wild, and terrified!

Cleaning the world's largest office building was quite an undertaking, as this quote from the *Wall Street Journal* reveals:

Tidying Up Trade Center Is a Towering Task

"... *Promptly at 5 P.M., as desk drawers are being locked and office lights flicked out, the cleaning troops report to the basement to begin setting right the wreckage of the workday just ended. Fanning out two or three to a floor, they will empty 50,000 over-flowing wastebaskets, dust as many desks, and vacuum 220 acres of carpet before the night is done. Porters tackle the building's 600 bathrooms, where they swab out 3,600 toilets and replace 14,400 rolls of toilet paper and 600,000 paper towels.*

Mundane jobs assume breathtaking proportions in a building this size. Taking down the trash—all 60 tons of it—keeps a team of 10 riding elevators up and down all night. Sweeping the stairs takes four men more than a day. (As soon as their brooms touch the ground floor, an elevator whisks them back to the top floors, where they again begin their descent.) A crew of 75 works from 1 A.M. until dawn polishing floors and shampooing 10 miles of hallway carpeting."

THINGS LEARNED AS A JANITOR—NEVER
OPEN THE WINDOWS ON BOTH SIDES OF A
15-STORY SKYSCRAPER UNLESS YOU WANT
TO SEE ALL OF THE PAPERS ON THE DESKS
SUCKED OUT ON THE DOWNWIND SIDE.

A roomful of respect

Morton-Thiokol, who made components for our space shuttles (including the infamous faulty O ring that allegedly resulted in the Challenger disaster in 1986) called me to do a training and consulting job at a remote site in northwestern Utah. It seems that the janitors there, though paid well, were on the verge of rebellion. I saw when I visited that no one could blame them. The scattered buildings were surrounded by a landscape of foot-deep mud, and there were no doormats to help cut down tracked-in dust and dirt. The janitor closet was about the size of a medicine cabinet, everything had to be transported from building to building to clean, and the office workers (mostly engineers) only multiplied the mess. It was a discouraging situation, which they figured I could fix with a rah-rah Aslett motivational rally. The objective they gave me was, "Make them feel better about themselves and their jobs, Don."

The main executive office building was nice, new, and easy to clean. I toured it with the powers that be, and was finally led to the basement cafeteria where I was to hold my workshop. The place was cold, noisy, and unattractive, and there were people constantly walking in and out (a terrible situation in which to attempt to teach). But it was the usual sort of spot to stick the janitors. "You guys are trying to tell your janitors they are important," I said, "then you give them a corner of a basement cafeteria to hold the first and only seminar for them in ten years. What about the briefing room on the main floor?"

The color drained from their faces. The room was a luxurious, presidential-size conference room. It had every amenity—padded seats, thick carpeting, fine wooden tables, recessed lights, automated screens, and a state of the art projector and sound system.

"Oh, that's for our scientists and executives. Do you realize we have $200,000 worth of tables, chairs, and visual equipment in there?" they said.

I continued to sell the upgrade. "You want to make your janitors feel important, give us that room. We are worthy to go in there and clean, entrusted with the keys and access, yet we can't sit in there and hold a seminar?"

You would have thought I asked for the plans for a secret weapon rather than the use of a vacant room. But finally, I convinced them that the very use of that forbidden room would convey the intended message better than anything I could say. A light came on in the manager's face, and he said, "Man, you're right. They would actually take better care of the room than the scientists and executives, anyway."

So use it we did, and the custodians got the message loud and clear: YOU ARE WORTHWHILE!

When I was done, the security people gathered up my props, visual aids, and handouts, carried them to the door, and bid me goodbye. Back in my office, I was going through the seminar material. There on the bottom of the pile was a strange-looking brown envelope labeled "Confidential—Failure of the O Ring." In my hands, I, a janitor in Idaho, had the secret in-house report on one of the most controversial subjects of the day. I bet I could have sold that little packet to a media source for a bundle. However, I put it in another brown envelope and sent it back to security with a note that their people had accidentally sent it home with me.

Training, of our own people or of others' employees, was a constant process now, as we had hundreds of jobs going on at once in locations all over the majority of the Western states.

OUR MANAGEMENT TEAM IN 1986. BACK: LOWELL ALLEN, TED SHARP, STEPHEN GIBSON, BOB BROWN, DAVE COLLINGS, LARRY KIRBY, MITCH DICKERSON; FRONT: JAMIE WARNOCK, ARLO LUKE, ME, MARK BROWNING, AND JIM DOLES.

Chapter 14

DOWNERS AND DELIGHTS OF JANITORDOM

A few decades in the business gave you a clear view of both sides of the broom...

My enthusiasm for our up-and-coming company blinded me at first to just where the janitor or cleanup person stood in our society's social strata. It didn't bother me then or now in the least if people couldn't tell the difference between the best profession in the world and all the others; but until it was less-than-subtly pointed out to me one day, I hadn't realized that being a janitor wasn't exactly something for which people were standing in line.

When I started the business while going to college, I received newspaper write-ups and a lot of other publicity and recognition. Everyone admired my creative cleaning activities—as long as they were leading to something bigger and better. When I finished my schooling and still remained a cleaner, my social prestige diminished greatly. Incidents such as the following brought this to my attention.

HOW MANY VARSITY FAMILY MEMBERS CAN BE STUFFED INTO YE OLDE VARSITY OUTHOUSE? COMPETITIONS ARE PART OF THE FUN AND TRADITION AT VARSITY'S ANNUAL MEETINGS, AS THE PHOTOS AT THE END OF THIS CHAPTER TESTIFY.

Journal 1962

Today had to be the epitome of how society views cleaning. I was working in the lobby of the First Security Bank's big, fancy downtown

office, polishing the floor with a brand-new buffer. It was a high moment in my life—I was almost out of college, had a nice family, a great and growing little company, was a leader in school, church, and the community. I thought I was riding the tide of social prestige along with the rest of upstanding society. In the door came a late depositor, her deposit in one hand and a spoiled, whiney kid in the other. She dragged him through the doors past me, yanking his reluctant little arm, and finally shook him in disgust and said in a stage whisper, "Behave, you little brat," and then pointing at me continued, "or you'll end up just like him!"

One of my janitors, right after he was listed in *Who's Who in Technology Today in the U.S.A*, was at the hospital registering his wife, who was about to have a baby. When the clerk asked him his occupation, he answered confidently, "Janitor." She looked up at him and said shyly, "Oh, come on, now. You don't really want me to put that down, do you?"

When we went places together, my friends would introduce me as a businessman and brag that I had many men working for me, fleets of trucks, etc. When these new acquaintances asked what kind of business, a silence would follow my answer, and after a couple of desperate glances, they would swallow and say "a *janitor*?"

I worked to keep the men's enthusiasm for the business high, battling the familiar janitor image. Arlo's wife, Jackie, struggled with the image in the beginning, as her husband, a pharmacy major, had worked his way through six years of demanding college courses while humming "rub-a-dub-dub." His real adjustment came, however, while he was working as a degreed pharmacist and still cleaning on the side.

We had a one-hour job to do at a freight terminal office, and since it was just a small job (and a day when few people would be there), we didn't bother to don uniforms or shave, and all of our good equipment was out on other jobs. We rummaged through some old supplies and managed to come up with the scroungiest mop imaginable, a couple of stiff paintbrushes, etc., and loaded them into the oldest truck we had. We were usually a classy operation, with polished trucks and clean uniforms, but that morning the two of us looked as if the Salvation Army had outfitted us. We reported to the job to dust some equipment, paint the floor, and sand some sheetrock. Paint-speckled, dirty, dusty, and dragging that wretched mop, we cut through the main terminal's plush lobby after we finished, and ran into one of the customers from the elite pharmacy where Arlo worked. This particular sharp, impeccably-dressed woman thought of Arlo as the most dignified pharmacist in town. He filled all of her prescriptions and even mixed her super-secret underarm deodorant salve. She screeched to a halt, not believing her eyes. "Arlo, is that YOU?" Like the bottom hog at the trough he gulped and said weakly, "Hi, Mrs. Burnett."

IN THE FOYER OF OUR HEADQUARTERS IN POCATELLO.

"What are you doing?" she gasped.

"Well," he cleared his throat, "I have this little business on the side."

"But Arlo—a *janitor*?"

She then looked at me critically, wheeled, and retreated. Arlo mumbled on the way home, "I looked like a troll, she was our best customer… wonder if she'll ever come in again." But by the next day, he was a true janitor, unfazed by any value judgment of his profession, ever after.

> THE JANITOR BUSINESS IS ONE OF THE TOUGHEST THERE IS; NO GLORY, LOW PAY, ODD HOURS, HARD PHYSICAL WORK, POOR TREATMENT, AND BLAME FOR ANYTHING OTHERS CAN'T BE BLAMED FOR, REGARDLESS OF WHO IS AT FAULT.

In my rural upbringing, everything was honest and real, and men and women were measured by merit, not status or appearances. So it was easier for me to accept the "janitor" image than most of the people I worked with. What we did for a living was certainly honorable, and in fact, a lot more essential than many of the jobs people usually thought highly of. When someone would proudly say, "I don't do windows,"

I always took issue and asked, "Well, who does, then? Do you make other people answer for your messes?"

I remember well our crew setting up a big convention hall once at Sun Valley. We had performed like champs on short notice. By the time the convention opened and the enthusiastic attendees poured in, we had the place perfect. I then ran to the office and changed out of my cleaning uniform into a suit and went back to oversee a few last-minute details. I was standing beside one of my uniformed crewmembers, when a portly fellow who had obviously imbibed a few too many cocktails dropped a plate stacked with hors d'oeuvres as he walked by us. Now there was taco and cocktail sauce all over the freshly cleaned rug. He turned arrogantly to my associate, and pointing at the spill, commanded, "Clean that up, boy!"

I whipped out my brand-new hanky and fell on hands and knees in my Sunday suit and quickly cleaned it up. My crewmember was incensed. "Why, I wouldn't do that for that fat slob in a million years!" he said later. I reminded him of two important facts about our profession: 1. Cleaning up after people is our job, and 2. Whether the mess-maker is obnoxious or not is irrelevant.

The majority of people do treat cleaners badly. One of our employees, a sharp little lady with a master's degree, was cleaning a men's room (the urinals, to be exact) once and had a sign up saying, "Sorry, restroom is being cleaned." In walked a well-educated, important businessman, and used the urinal right next to our cleaner, silently saying, "You don't exist."

While she was at college, my daughter Laura skied at the nearby resorts whenever she and her friends got the chance. Since she had the car that could haul the most skis and students, it was generally used as a taxi. After everyone was loaded in and they were off to the mountain, someone would always comment, "This sure is a nice car. What does your dad do for a living?" Laura always answered cheerfully, "He's a janitor." The interior of the car would go silent for a while, until someone in a politely patronizing voice would finally say, "That's nice."

How those aristocrats who made careful distinction between white- and blue-collar workers treated us was irrelevant to me. I'd cleaned up behind too many people, including the rich and famous and celebrities, to be impressed with or limited by prestige or position.

There are no dead-end jobs, only dead-end people.

Some people see a janitor's job as the end of the line. To me, it's the **beginning**. What's more important than creating a safe, healthy, happy environment? What's more important than helping people dejunk their lives and improve their environment?

Janitors, the ultimate scapegoat

If there is one thing you need to be a janitor, it is the ability to take criticism and listen to complaints. We are in a business where people take the positive for granted and report only the negative. We can empty and clean the same wastebasket perfectly 300 times and never hear a word of thanks or acknowledgment. The one night we accidentally leave it on the right side of the desk instead of the left, you'd think we had burned down the building! No matter how well or consistently you clean, your customers will gradually just expect it and say nothing. But when an occasional problem arises, they'll come to life—screaming, threatening, and even bullying you.

It didn't take long for me to discover this complaint business. At first, I figured that if I washed a woman's greasy kitchen down, she would send roses to thank me the following day. It just didn't happen that way.

Once you got out of the house they vaulted to the attic, got their expired husband's old magnifying glass, and went over every inch of wall and woodwork I had just cleaned. Most believed that no one (especially a man) could possibly clean fast and well. Things like this often followed:

I was home one day catching up on my studying when the phone rang. It was Mrs. Greasewall. "Mr. Aslett, there's a streak on my ceiling." I groaned but realized my reputation needed to be as spotless as my work. So I dressed, jumped into the old Varsity truck, and drove across town to her home (it had been a $9 job). "See, see, see!" she said, grabbing me by the arm and pulling me down to her five-foot-two eye level, "That big black streak!" I could indeed discern a mark there and went out to the truck and got all of my gear, cranked up the wall machine, and re-cleaned the spot. But the mark wouldn't budge. I was sure I'd done a good job the first time, but now, no matter how hard I cleaned this ceiling I couldn't get the streak out. By now she was whimpering and claiming, "It wasn't there before you came. I paid good money to get a good job." I had some great answers for her, but kept them confined to thoughts.

I worked and worked on it, and would probably have been there all night (as she wore a hole in the floor pacing and raving louder with each round). Suddenly, in one of her wild gestures, she hit the pole lamp and the black streak on the ceiling darted in perfect rhythm with the swing of the lamp. It was a shadow! She was more obnoxious apologizing than she was complaining, and I went home, passing another test of public relations, by no means my last. We always worked our hearts out and yielded graciously to unhappy customers.

We once cleaned a house so filthy you couldn't find the floor. The rug must have been 40 years old (so old and frayed it was uncleanable, so we didn't clean it—we just washed the walls around it). We got a summons for a lawsuit that our wall machine had cut holes in their carpet. (The wall machine weighed 21 pounds and was on big rubber casters.) To be sued in our beginning days was traumatic. We got a lawyer—our first—and went to court, and they (the whole "Beverly Hillbillies" family) came with their lawyer and wrangled over a carpet that even new would have cost $80 at the most. Finally the judge did the smart thing (neither lawyer was bright enough to think of this). He asked to see the wall machine, and when he looked at it, he just laughed. "This couldn't cut a carpet," he said. This was the first time the family themselves had seen the machine, and they were dismayed and disappointed. No case, trial over. Both sides stood up and looked at one another blankly, wondering, "What did we get out of this?" The two lawyers jumped over the bar railing, shook hands, and went off arm in arm to lunch.

The complaints never ceased, no matter how perfectly you trained the janitor or even if he was a local professor working part-time. You wouldn't believe the complaints you get when you're in charge of the cleaning. One building occupant broke his leg while flushing the toilet. Another complaint I had to work out on a busy day was one from a department store owner who said my painters working in the street display window had left the mannequins (on purpose, he claimed) in all sorts of erotic positions when they moved them, and a crowd was forming on the street. How about this accusation: "Aslett, your floors in here are too shiny. The reflection allows people to see up the ladies' dresses."

Once we were accused of stealing belts off some of the clothes racks in a department store we cleaned. All of the workers pleaded innocent. The culprit was finally caught. On our 36-inch wide space vacuum there were six belts wrapped around the giant brush roll. When the vacuum was pushed back under a slack or trouser rack, any belt end touching or near the floor was sucked off the garment. The buckle probably clicked a bit as it went in, but the janitor, lost in a world of earphone music, didn't hear it.

On one building we cleaned we were told "the account is unhappy—too many complaints." So we went all-out to please them, and no more complaints. Then they called us in and said, "There aren't enough complaints, so we must be paying you too much."

Then there is always the "comparer" who walks past the city bank whose floors are polished terrazzo and inlaid floors that resemble a sheet of glass. He comes into his old store with 1920s worn and deteriorated asphalt tile floors and demands of the janitors, "Why can't our floors look like that?" "Sir, we used the same wax and method on both." "Well, you're just not doing it right! I want this floor looking as good as the bank's! Understand?" Floor quality and use differs vastly. The bank floors take half the skill, cost, and time to make look twice as good, simply because of the fine quality of flooring they are. But try and tell that to a building owner convinced otherwise.

Complaints occasionally had their compensations. A new young, cocksure manager just given authority over a number of small rural telephone offices we cleaned took great delight in needling us over any slight misdeed, telling us each time, "I'm paid to be a hardass!" One day he told us that there was a disaster at the Lewisville community dial office and to follow him out there. We pulled in behind his car and followed. He seemed to be taking a new and longer route there, and finally Arlo nudged me and said, "Don, he can't find one of his own buildings!" And sure enough, he couldn't. He drove up and down and down and around and over hills and rural roads, hunting desperately for it. Arlo and I stayed right behind him. The longer he hunted the more stubborn he became.

After wasting half the morning and half a tank of gas he pulled over and the arrogant manner was gone. With a sheepish grin he said, "Okay, boys, where's my building?" We were the best of friends after that, and the "disaster" at the building was that the inside floor mat was left outside!

Some complaints had class. One morning our supervisor was making rounds in one of our Miami buildings and walking into an area that he generally perceived to be cleaned and shined, he noticed a little something in the middle of the floor. It was a tiny tent of folded paper, and when he reached down to pick it up, he saw the following written on the side: "Here lies Carl Cockroach, who died on this spot four days ago." And sure enough, under the little funeral tent were the rigor mortised remains of a roach. The telephone manager, instead of complaining, had found a better way to get the message across.

Planting: "Hide and seek"

Many building managers we worked for had a hard time telling if a place was really cleaned or not, and so resorted to setting "traps" around—in other words hiding little objects under, over, and behind things. They would find great glee in putting matches, pins, paperclips, coins, and notes on ledges and other places to test the cleaning person's thoroughness. Then the next morning, after everything had been cleaned, they'd rush in to see if any of their "plants" were still there. If they were, this was perfect proof that the janitor didn't do his job. The janitor of course had no defense, even though most of the time the items were planted in a place that didn't call for daily cleaning.

You can't clean every square inch of a building every night—it would cost the client a fortune. There is an acceptable middle ground in all things, including cleaning; however, many paranoid building managers never learned this. They would call us in the next morning, gloating, open their hands and reveal one marked toothpick, a leaf, nickel, or an aspirin. It was instant trial and conviction.

One telephone manager would plant marked coins in corners, behind desks, and under chair legs to see if the janitors were doing a thorough job. In this game, there were actually two tests: 1. if you found the coin, and 2. whether or not you returned it. Big hassles often developed out of these trapping practices. At times it was almost a battle of wits for the client or his employee to plant or hide an article in an obscure place and for the janitors to find it.

An example of this occurred once in a large state building Varsity cleaned. The man in charge was a real amateur in distributing his "plants," and it took our sharp supervisor only three days to decode the system and find them all. An initialed pop bottle top was always used in the lunchroom. A cigarette butt was always stuck under the bottom lid of a toilet seat. A wooden match with the head shaved to a point (for identification) was placed in an elevator door track or in back of a plant, or even on a plant leaf. And the old standby, a paper clip, so it could be distinguished from the hundreds of other clips, would be dotted with a felt tip pen and was generally tucked carefully behind the leg of a desk. Our supervisor would walk around first and pick up all of the planted items and then proceed with the regular cleaning. It was a standing joke with all of the janitors that if they just policed up all of the plants and went home, the building manager would be satisfied that his building had been thoroughly cleaned.

A classic of complaints

Of the volumes of complaints over the years, one stands out as a classic. The first call came from a building in a town 120 miles from our home office. "This is the engineering department, Don."

"How are you doing?"

"Great. Listen, Don, we don't like to complain but for the second morning now, there are big bare foot prints all over the top of two of our desks."

"Bare foot prints?"

"Yeah."

"Ah, there couldn't be. Why would anyone walk on top of an executive desk?"

On the first two identical calls like this, I talked them into believing something must be wrong with them if they were seeing bare foot prints on desks. We had a big laugh over it and figured the engineers must have been drinking the fluid out of their transits.

The third time they called, I began the same old line and the caller said, "Dammit, Don, I tell you there were bare foot prints on three desks again this morning. Now we aren't crazy—they are there! Come see for yourself"

Intrigued by the situation and aware that it was perhaps time to do something about it, I told him Arlo and I were on our way to investigate. When we arrived, they led us to the second floor and over to the desks and sure enough, there were good-size bare foot prints all over them. We thought, reasoned, and questioned, but couldn't come up with the answer. We decided that the only thing to do was to turn out all the lights and hide in the engineering room all night to catch the culprit red-footed. I left Arlo in the dark and went off to do some other business with the telephone supervisor, and soon a call came from Arlo. "The mystery is solved," he said. "Just get over here."

I was there in three minutes and entered the dark room where Arlo gestured me over to the windows. The three-story building we were in was just a few feet away from a big apartment building, so close you could shake hands from building to building. Directly across from the three desks in question were apartments serving as dorms for college girls. As all of us witnessed, the coeds dressed rather informally in their off hours, bouncing around playfully in their skivvies and some without. The Varsity men who maintained the building were also students and red-blooded young men. When they finished with their work, they must be turning off the lights and standing on the desks to get a better view. Anxious not to scratch their "bleachers," they were taking off their shoes. The tiny bit of wax powder they picked up from the freshly spray-buffed floor was enough, combined with the sweat from bare feet, to leave unmistakable tracks.

The two students showed up about then, hustling around to get their cleaning done so they could enjoy their usual late-night show. Arlo pointed out the tracks and asked them how they got there. One muttered, "A ghost?" the other, "beats me." Arlo then gave them a long lecture on trustworthiness and moral cleanliness and sent a note over to the girls' apartment suggesting the immediate installation of drapes or window shades.

We found out later that the whole engineering department was mad at us for solving the mystery!

Bank boo-boos

The lush, upscale, secure-feeling surroundings of banks did nothing to protect us from problems there.

We contracted to clean a prominent bank in Reno, Nevada in the '70s. The manager was a high-strung fellow, but he was fair. Our work there was a struggle. Reno was booming, and even dishwashers and maids and janitors were getting $9.50 an hour. We had bid the building for minimum wage ($2.15 at the time), so needless to say his building was about as shabby as our personnel's performance.

At first he was nice and suggested we be a little more thorough and not miss a third of the wastebaskets. Next, he wrote notes that it would be much better if we locked the front door of the bank after we cleaned the entrance. He gradually moved to threats and demands while we were hard-put to even find a warm body to stick a cleaner's uniform on and send there. It was a nice bank and we needed the account to stay in Reno, so our manager would work there for three days and tune it up, but after he left it would slide back to deplorable.

Finally the bank manager threatened cancellation. We begged and apologized and he yielded again (and then we backslid again). Driven to despair, he served us an official notice of cancellation of the contract. We couldn't blame him, but you wouldn't believe the sales job we did now and he, against his better judgment, pardoned us yet again. We promised him that never again would anything go wrong.

The very next night we doubled the crew and spit-polished the building. However, on the second floor when the janitor collected the trash from the wastebaskets in one of those giant plastic bags, it was a long way down to the dumpster. Why go through all of those doors and halls and all the way down the stairs, when he could just walk out on the second floor balcony and bingo, "bags away!" to the dumpster right in the alley below? This night his aim was bad and the bulging bags of confidential bank trash hit the edge of the unit and split apart. "Oh rats, " said the janitor, "I'll have to go down and pick that all up." Well, he forgot. That night a sudden squall of wind and rain came funneling up through the alley and at seven-thirty the next morning when our favorite bank manager showed up, all of the front windows of the bank were plastered with dirty, rain-soaked overdraft notices and receipts and other private papers.

Even a misaligned paper punch could throw this manager into over-drive, and I'll never forget his phone call. He was so mad he couldn't even talk—he just sputtered and snorted, trying to catch his breath and say something bad enough for the occasion. At the end of his mad murmurings, however, we did hear plainly, "You're fired!" Many years later now, I still feel that once we got our act together we should have cleaned his bank free for a few months.

At the banks we cleaned not all goofs were ours. In one branch bank, the manager was carrying a full day's transactions downstairs for processing in a big Rubbermaid trash tub he'd borrowed from our janitor closet. He stopped by the restroom on the way, set the tub on a drinking fountain while he was inside, and then forgot about it. Our janitor, walking by, saw the trash tub, picked it up, and fed the contents into a very efficient shredder. By the time they figured it out there was only one alternative: hire a small army of college students to tape and glue all of those shreds back together.

Cleaning a bank one was always conscious of the presence of money, and this proved beneficial one day when our cleaning woman was emptying the tellers' trash (which was generally just adding machine tape). She noticed some extra weight and instead of dumping the trash in the dumpster, she pawed through it and there was a huge bag of greenbacks in excess of $10,000. Someone's plan to slip out to the dumpster at midnight and get their stash was interrupted. I think we got a $25 reward for that one. Often we don't even get thanked!

A profession of honesty

Another common injustice to the janitor is the accusation of thievery. When anything comes up missing in a building, the janitor is the first one questioned.

There was never a hearing or trial on anything missing or broken. It was always the janitor! Never an apology when the owners finally found the missing object in one of their own drawers or pockets, and the rap of "thief" could stick to you just for having been a suspect. I'm sure there are cases where janitors actually have been guilty, but as a rule, they are an honest lot. Very few steal, simply because they know they will be the first suspects if anything is ever missing. We also do all we can to select trustworthy people to begin with.

My whole regional management staff was called into the office of a major company once and confronted with the fact that our employees were stealing. Their manager led us into a corner office and introduced us to the occupant of the desk. "What is missing?" he asked him. Pouting, the man pointed to a large bowl of hard candy on the corner of his desk. "There!" he said. "They took a piece of my candy." Looking at the 200 remaining pieces, my manager was thinking, "How could you possibly know one piece is gone?" So he asked about this and the victim said, "It wasn't the hard candy, it was the cinnamon bears. They ate one of my cinnamon bears." Again the manager asked him how he knew. "Because," answered the accuser, now getting emotional, "Cinnamon bears are my favorite and I counted them. There were twelve lined up around the edge—my apostles—when I went home and only eleven when I returned."

What could you say? Our janitor, in a moment of temptation, probably did snatch up and devour one of the bears. Can you believe it?—this engineer with nothing more to do than line up cinnamon bears wanted to fire a humble, hardworking janitor. We had to make a 300-mile drive on icy roads to hear this.

Janitor justice

Most managers of the companies we worked for were top people, considerate and fair. However, we've all known and maybe even worked for a few bullies and intimidators, and the impulse to someday get even with them can burn like a pilot light in back of your mind for quite a while.

In one large building we cleaned, two of the department heads, one a man and the other a woman, surely had gotten A's in "How to Make Janitors Miserable 101." The other departments loved us, but these two, for years, ragged us constantly. Our rating in that building was the highest in the whole Bell System, yet still these folks kept trying to hang us. They griped and complained, left insulting notes, bragged that they were "hard to please," talked sharply to our people, and in general bullied us.

One Friday evening there was a basketball game and we janitors all went and so didn't clean the building at our usual time slot of 6 to 9 P.M. After the game, we went out to dinner, and then after midnight, when the building was dark and abandoned, we went down to clean. Flinging open the doors of the ladies' lounge in the basement, we interrupted an intimate couch scene, starring none other than those two disagreeable department heads (who were both married... to other people). We backed out with a quick, "Excuse me"—we knew we didn't need to clean that room right then.

Talk about a miracle! You cannot believe how clean the building suddenly got. Neither ever complained again and we always had to suppress a smile when sweeping by them.

Another time, we had a contract to apply a strong and long-lasting weedkiller (called "sterilant") to a communications equipment site. We'd bought six sacks of it for this job, and were waiting to work it into our schedule (until we were going to be in the area). Meanwhile, the "know it all" and very impatient manager of the building called us every day. "When are you going to do this job?" We were going to do it soon, but no hurry, since it wasn't an emergency. He wouldn't let up, and since applying the material to ground was simple—just spread it like fertilizer or lawn seed, he figured—he proceeded to do the job himself one afternoon. He read the instructions and sprinkled the white granular stuff (over-generously) on the site. He should have read ALL of the instructions. Step 2 is to wet down the weedkiller with water so it dissolves and penetrates the soil. He didn't. There was a gully-washing rain that night and all of those undissolved granules flowed down to the adjoining property of a fantastic green thumb, a doctor whose hobby was rare and ornate trees, plants, and shrubs. The amount of weedkiller the manager applied to the tower site was enough to kill concrete, so you can imagine what it did to Dr. Green's landscape. Once it dissolved in the next rain, it killed everything.

The manager's company had to come in with backhoes, loaders, and dump trucks and remove all of the contaminated soil and replace it. Even after that, growing anything there was difficult. On our next visit to the manager's building, we never mentioned it, but we noticed he wasn't too quick to take over any of our projects after that.

LIVING WITH THE LAWS

While the public's antics often kept us laughing, at times the sheer frustration of dealing with government bureaucracy had me fuming.

I always had sympathy and even some support for the revolutionaries in history, almost all of them. Whether I shared their political and social views or not, I think I was a secret revolutionary myself. The only thing that kept me from marching, burning, picketing, and overthrowing things was the realization that how good we had it in this country overall outweighed the many improvements still needed in the system. Some things were just not fair and I accepted that as "life." Especially in business, I was a willing, if sometimes whining taxpayer.

I never really minded paying taxes—I liked having public highways and education and police protection. But I did struggle with the inefficiency and often arrogance of bureaucracy. My tax money bought city, state, and federal officials new vehicles and equipment (the best), while I, the producer, had to get by with old, worn, and repaired things. They had all of the power and people like me, the source of their money through the taxation of both businesses and private individuals, had little. The cost of fighting the system could never be justified, so I just paid and smiled.

The IRS people are a calloused bunch, and I always marveled how when I owed them $32.12, they could strong-arm me through twenty channels of penalty, fines, seizures, and other intimidations and collect it. Yet when I overpaid, getting my $525 back was lost in a world of who and what and why and when and, "We are checking it out, sir."

I had one big audit later in life where they really sieved me—every penny had to be accounted for. The amount of money I listed for charitable donations (15 percent of my income for church tithing), and travel (I was doing seminars all over), were IRS red flags. But I came out clean, got $2,500 back. Does that mean I won? No—the audit cost me weeks and over $10,000 in accounting fees.

The very next year they drew my name again and apologized, saying, "This never happens, Mr. Aslett." But again, my huge travel, printing, and church donation expenses were a red flag. They didn't realize how much of my living I made traveling to be on TV and writing books. They worked me over again and found one incident of a questionable appearance I did for a church, and disallowed a $200 deduction. I had to pay $900, and the audit cost me many times that.

That did it. I hired the best accounting firm in town and from then on did all taxes and records in "anticipating audit" style, and now I'm just waiting for an audit—it could be done in less than an hour.

I had numerous experiences with courts and lawyers, enough to find out that there may not be justice in the law. Legality is only a guideline; morality is the real line. At first I figured I could sue people who did me wrong just as others had sued me. But even if you are entirely right you have to pay plenty to prove it, so it is sometimes cheaper in time, money, and emotion to just try and forget it.

I rented some uniforms for my crew once, for instance, and they were delivered nice, clean, and new, with an invoice for $250. "Why the invoice?" I asked. "Oh, this is for the final cleaning when the contract

is over and you turn in the uniforms dirty—you are paying for it ahead."
"Okay," I said.

A year later when I turned in the uniforms for good, I got another invoice for cleaning. I wrote on it that I had already paid and sent them a copy of my receipt with the note. They kept on billing me, and I refused to pay and explained why. They never acknowledged the explanation and sued me for the $250. They were so wrong and I had clear documented evidence, so I went to my lawyer and explained the situation.

He looked it all over and agreed that I was right; they were gouging me. Even so, he added, they had legal maneuvers they could use to prevail and make me pay. There was always a risk when you go after a big company, and it would cost $300 to file, $500 for his initial fee, and lots more if it went further. (This was the old days.)

Then he gave me some free advice, the best I've ever had from a lawyer. "I know this is bugging you, Don, and they are taking advantage of you. But let me make a suggestion. Take the $300 you were going to use to file and go buy your wife a new dress. You will get more out of that than from this lawsuit, even if we win. Pay them the $250, wrong as it may be."

"No, Mr. Lawyer, this is a matter of principle, not money. Go for it!" We did, I lost, and it ended up costing me $2,000 plus lots of irritation and my wife didn't even get a cheap new dress.

I made a number of court visits over the years as an expert witness for disputes over other companies' janitorial franchises. The franchisees were usually suing the franchiser for improper or inaccurate bidding of sold contracts. I would go to the area, look over the buildings, and then go to court to testify as to what was a proper bid for the properties in question. It was fairly cut and dried, but never easy. The lawyers did everything possible to discredit me. Gadfreys, I hated that court chair, even when getting paid an expert witness fee.

Breaking in of a dust bunny

It took me till I was 22 to learn that the crooks in the world were not all on TV and in the movies. I had never really heard of anyone not paying what they owed. Bill collectors were just not part of my young life experience. The rule of the West, at least where and how I was raised, was that when you promise, you pay—period.

When I first started my business, after a job was done, I held out my hand and was paid and that was that. Then one day someone said, "Bill me," and a whole new realm of finance was revealed to me. "Send an invoice," they said, so I ended up going home and Barbara and I printed up some simple invoices and I was in big business now. I billed the guy—it was a carpet shop—$12 for stripping and waxing his showroom floor. But the invoice didn't seem to work; nothing came back, for three months. Believe it or not, a married college student really needed that $12, so I became a bill collector. I went to his shop, and was greeted by cobwebs on a locked front door. I hated this first ever realization that I was not going to get hard-earned money. Wherever he was now, and for whatever reason he did this, he had cheated me.

Accepting the idea that deadbeats would be a part of business wasn't very appetizing, but my view of humanity stayed on the positive side. When next one of my college professors (whose rug we shampooed) never paid up, I was appalled. When I faced him down he explained that his wife had divorced him and taken all their money so he couldn't pay— that was a new one. I left feeling sorrier for the guy than for my loss of money, even though he gave me a C in his psychology class that year.

Another time, a motel in Jackson Hole owed me $192. They had no complaints about the work, they just wouldn't pay. I decided to lawyer up and sue them. When the court date finally came I was number 15,450 in the line of people with claims hoping to get some satisfaction. It wasn't worth the time and life.

The first big "white collar" rip-off came from a fire loss insurance job while I was still in college. We worked three weeks painting in a residence and I billed the insurance company for a much-needed $781. Almost two months passed as the "proofs of loss" and all of the other forms were signed and approved.

Headed home late one night after a cleaning job, we saw a car straddled sideways on the centerline of the road, with a hard-drinking group of half a dozen merrymakers in and around it. The car looked familiar— it was same purple Pontiac that had been in the driveway at our recent painting job.

The driver of the car was the policyholder, and the insurance check meant to pay us had been made out to him, and he'd cashed it and blown the entire amount on a big drunken bender with a bunch of his buddies. There was nothing we could do to retrieve our money—we couldn't sue as he had no job or money. It took months of going without to recover from that loss. From then on, we required our name to be on future insurance payments along with the insured's name and never lost another bit of insurance money.

That was just the beginning, however. The deadbeats increased with the growth of my business. Not long ago, I asked my CFO how much bad debt (unpaid bills) we had written off that year—over $2 million! And many more millions in the lifetime of my little college business.

The more prestigious the business or profession, the harder dead-beats were to deal with.

We had some deadbeats within the company, too. A good boss always worries about his workers' welfare, and does his best to avoid seeing them go without. Over the years, I had many requests from my employees for advances on pay. I questioned this, fought it, and finally yielded some here.

I reached the point of disgust and anger, however, upon being advised by the payroll department that more than $30,000 worth of advanced money had never been recovered! I wrote a carefully composed announcement expressing my displeasure and making it clear that from now on, only the truly needy would get advances (87 employees were getting advances now). The pay period after my brilliant proclamation, 111 applied for advances on salary—it backfired! So I finally decided to get tough—"There will be no advances anymore for any reason!" Advances ceased, and I never heard a peep out of anyone and no one quit.

Though a slow learner and often too lenient as a businessperson, once I gained some ground, I usually kept it.

As my business grew, our human resource departments and the number of lawyers and lawsuits grew—people were suing for stress on the job, unfair drinking fountains, inconvenient parking, harassment, carpal tunnel syndrome, racial discrimination, unfair dismissal and so on. Now I had to take on a mass of government bureaucracy that used my tax money to sue me, and established codes, boundaries, covenants, and rules so complex and plentiful we couldn't even spell "handshake" anymore.

This was a minor injustice compared to what came later, after OSHA and 40 other policing organizations and departments were established. They would walk into a building and test the air or look in the janitor closet and say, "That will be $1,500 for a violation." The Immigration and Naturalization Service (INS) folks were the real barnburners. They would raid buildings (yes, make an unannounced attack) and seize any "illegal aliens" and take them away. We would show we had Social Security cards and proper documentation for them, and they would say, "They are forged" and make us go to forgery school to learn to spot altered hairlines and all the rest. We had some employees for more than ten years, sending in thousands of dollars to Social Security for them, only to have an irregularity found (it took the government that long to find it), so that we had to fire a wonderful employee or send him or her away.

Discovering the glitches and inconsistencies within some of our government departments was disheartening, and working closely with these people and trying to keep within the laws while still being good to good people was a real test. When "toe the mark," "bend over backwards to be fair" legislation and regulation proliferated, it was hard to hire, fire, or inspire anyone because of possible liability. Even when I hired others to worry about these things directly, I still had to see the host of protective measures necessary to protect us from situations and suits, and what it did to P & L's. This made life miserable for an entrepreneur.

Taking out the mental trash

Over the years I kept notes on customers and employees who, in the course of the years, had one way or another cheated me or stolen from my operation. Some put personal tires on company credit cards while buying tires for the company fleet, some did secret jobs of their own with my equipment and supplies, some came in after hours and used the company copier and reams of paper for personal projects. Still others neglected or abused things "borrowed" from the company, or took company vehicles on personal trips. These were little things that people think no one notices in a company, but almost always, one way or another, get back to the boss. I recorded these things and filed them in a private drawer at home. Most of the smaller rip-offs I let wash, but being aware of them enabled me to redirect lots of freeloading.

For the larger issues, my private "evidence" drawer preserved hope of recovery or even retaliation someday—"My day will come, you just wait!" It never seemed to, however, and finally an event occurred that caused me to ditch my entire cache of injustices. We'd done a series of construction cleanup jobs for a mall developer and billed him $1,500. He never paid us, nor did he pay ten other small contractors. We learned later that this developer was known for beating new, innocent, eager workers out of money. We were too naïve to put a lien on him and so, along with the others, we lost our money. I filed the unpaid invoice in my evidence drawer, writing across the bottom, "Get him someday."

The next year at Christmastime we decorated and furnished a Santa Claus (a tough job, by the way) for a local mall, not realizing this same deadbeat developer owned it. We billed them in January, and they claimed that they had sold the mall—we should have gotten our bill in before the end of the year, etc. They didn't pay up… three grand, and it was not collectible. When we found out it was the same guy, I added this invoice to the other in my drawer, again writing, "Get him."

Two years later, my crew in Salt Lake City, unaware of our history with this high-roller developer, did a $5,000 job for him and yes—you guessed it—along with some others we never got paid. I didn't like this guy a lot by now as what he owed Varsity approached $10,000. One afternoon a person who recognized me as a fellow contractor who'd been victimized by our mall welsher informed me that "a group of past unpaid people" had the intention of "wasting" the guy. And would I like to chip in? My first thought was that I didn't want to buy any bullets, but would be glad to pay for the gas to drop him off in the Nevada desert! But I quickly came to my senses and declined. Later that day I reflected on the fact that I (who had quit hunting, and wouldn't kill a cockroach) actually had a good feeling flash over me when it was proposed to take a man out—scary! He was such a rotten fellow, and I had harbored the irritation for so long it had poisoned my thinking. No amount of money or desire for justice was worth that.

That evening I went home and emptied the file drawer containing all my records and notes of bad debts, gyps, and other "get-them-some-day" evidence into a cardboard box and burned it in a barrel behind the house. A great feeling of relief arose with the smoke, and I was blessed thereafter with a full understanding of the doctrine and power of forgiveness.

The janitor university of lifelong learning

> Cleaning is a great way to eavesdrop on the world. Who suspects the little man or woman who sweeps the floor? Any shift can easily beat the best soap opera.

Learning to deal with bureaucracy and deleting the deadbeats out of the mental record freed up space for the more enjoyable aspects of any business.

Humor, color, and good times were a constant reward to compensate for some of the struggle and putdowns of providing cleaning services to the public. Because our accounts ranged from a quiet little house in the village to a millionaire's mansion, from schools to theaters and stadiums, offices, factories, and hundreds of other operations, our exposure to life was more than fascinating.

Since most people seem to think of us janitors as dumb or sexless, nothing is hidden from us, and there are no secrets we are not privy to. People don't hush conversation when we're around, and they're rather uninhibited about what they do and say in front of us. We also have the keys to get into anything, so they can't lock us out. We are exposed to every aspect of society, cleaning up before and after people in every type of situation, building, and profession. We clean up around people awake or asleep, working or on vacation, eating, gambling, playing, and _____ (that, too). I've cleaned after the rich (even the Kennedys), the poor, and the government. We see it all, from the parking lot to the potty.

We've all heard people who have inside knowledge of things whisper, "Man, if you saw how they make that you'd never eat it," or "you'd never fly in it," or "you'd never buy it." I quit drinking pop after working in a soda pop factory; made my meat diet more selective after cleaning a slaughterhouse; lost my interest in French fries after two years of cleaning one of the world's largest French-fry producing plants, and wouldn't drive a small car after cleaning body shops. Cleaning hospitals made me more careful not to do things to injure myself or make me ill; cleaning some offices gave me plenty of negative examples for a book on productivity.

After you've cleaned the kitchen in any restaurant, you read menus more carefully (and won't order the surprise special). And you will definitely wash the produce after you've cleaned grocery stores for a few years. Clean a few beauty salons and you'll be more careful where you clip or spray your hair, and the urge to travel is somewhat reduced after you've cleaned truck stops, rest areas, trains, or busses. The king of ugly is coffee cleanup—stains and spills.

Stadiums seem exciting when filled with thousands of excited fans. Clean them up after a game and those stands aren't so grand: cleaning gum and sticky soda pop spills off concrete, retrieving half-eaten hot dogs, picking old popcorn and peanut shells out of corners and crevices, hauling off smelly, dripping beer cans, and removing soggy programs from under seats. The only thrill I get from stadiums now is when someone underbids us for the job!

Cleaning up after people also tells you a lot about personality and character. One interesting thing we learned, for example, is that night people mess up a building more than day people. In one building, for instance, 15 people working on the night shift did more damage and vandalism, used more supplies, left things out more, and caused more cleanup than 80 to 100 people using the same building the same length of time during the day. I don't know if it is the setting of darkness (anonymity and camouflage?) or the attitude of people who come to work then. But when cleaning, the difference is really apparent.

We see enough of people's trash to chart their personality. People can be identified, analyzed, and categorized by their dirt, litter, clutter, and trash—and we see and handle it in day after day, week after week, and year after year.

Seen and cleaned

The places I got to see as a professional cleaner could also be fantastic—ones that couldn't be scheduled with the best travel agent in the world. Bidding a job at a sugar beet processing plant, I got to stand 50 feet high on a ladder inside a giant silo full of glistening fresh white sugar, enough sugar to bury a train car! Assessing another job, I explored a granite cave inside a mountain, where thousands of rare genealogical records were stored. Beyond another door deeper in the bowels of the mountain, I saw a 100-foot glass rod suspended by a thin nylon string, to measure earth tremors.

I've seen the inner workings of amusement parks, resorts, high rises, radio and television operations, casinos, and hospitals. I've been behind the scenes in Army bases, universities, churches, and factories all over the country, seeing things no one else gets to see. (Janitors get to go everyplace.) I've toured the limited access areas of trade centers, including the World Trade Center, and even the locked room in a Midwest university housing the apparatus in which the atom was split for the first time.

I worked for three weeks at the base of the Grand Tetons, helped clean up avalanches, lectured on a luxury ocean liner, and worked in 60 below zero weather in Alaska and 120-degree heat in Arizona. I cleaned or consulted in factories, plants, and buildings where everything from Harrier jets to computer chips were made. I saw the prototypes and initial plans for products that years later were nationally known brands. I've cleaned conference rooms with $120,000 tables, $4,000 chairs, and $400 ashtrays.

I've been in underground telephone communications centers almost no one even knows about, been able to stay in some of the world's most beautiful national parks when the few in my cleaning crew were the only other people there. I've felt the energy of an old Alaskan gold mining town while painting signs on the street, sealed floors in huge airport hangers, and been on emergency cleaning crews to get stores open again after a fire. We were some of the first people into Rexburg, Idaho, after the massive Teton Dam collapse (see p. 219). You see it on the news; we clean it up and get the whole story, meet the real people.

The edge called imagination

I've often been asked by the media as to where Varsity's "fun and spirited" dedication to a low-image profession came from, when did it start? I would probably call it a combination of the male thrill of competition and the creative idea of a clever woman.

All of us managers in the company were paid by the job, not the hour, so speed and efficiency really mattered. We often made a game of work, racing to see which of us could clean, paint, wax, or buff the best and fastest. You might see four of us on a long painter's plank set beneath four big church windows (full of little 8-by-10-inch panes), all of us with brushes in one hand and a pail of white paint in the other. We would each take one of those giant windows and race our way though painting the sashes, top to bottom, cutting a perfect knife-clean edge between paint and glass—no masking tape or rags allowed! The finish was usually so close we were within one or two panes of each other, just minutes apart. Mark Browning, often the winner, was ambidextrous (as proficient with his left hand as his right). So he just changed arms when the rest of us had to shift position. It was a blast!

My entry into Varsity's Vac Zoo contest (see p. 291) was this Vacasaurus Rex.

Cleaning and other jobs were so much fun we often forgot they were work. New employees thought we were crazy at first, but caught on fast.

As for that second ingredient in the Varsity recipe I mentioned, one evening after a job, the crew was assembled at our house for a get-together. Barbara had not only whipped up a good dinner, but made a cake. Not just an ordinary cake—one that was three "stories" like a building that we cleaned. She made little men out of pipe cleaners and placed them all over the cake in various poses doing all sorts of cleaning and repair. This not only delighted us, but was another step toward Varsity's reputation for not being just an ordinary maintenance organization. As time went on, we not only made building-shaped cakes, but toilet-shaped cookies and other theme treats. We even found a mold for a chocolate outhouse and served lemonade in a brand-new toilet punchbowl.

I ALWAYS ENCOURAGED CLEANERS TO LIVE THEIR PROFESSION—TO WEAR CLEANING-RELATED THINGS, DECORATE WITH THEM, TALK CLEANING, AND TEACH CLEANING EVERYWHERE THEY WENT.

Every time we Varsity people got together—for jobs, meetings, or training—we found a way to work some fun into the occasion, be it a gunfight with spray bottles or a swordfight with loaded paintbrushes. The adventure was always worth any mess that had to be cleaned up afterward.

When Varsity operations expanded to several states we needed to hold an annual company meeting to train and motivate our people, let them meet each other, and review safety procedures and other policies. We included spouses and some other family members, and our meetings were held in special places like Sun Valley, Park City, Utah, Snowbird, Jackson Hole, Yellowstone, and yes, every so often, in Pocatello, our world headquarters. But unlike normal companies who did the same old thing for convention entertainment like golf, dances, parties, or tours, we included a profession-related project and event and of course, a competition of some kind.

We began with the world's first janitor rodeo, simply making janitorial versions of the usual dramatic rodeo events. We had mop bucket chariot races, bucking floor buffers, fast draws with spray bottles, vacuum assembly races, buffer brush pogo races, mop bucket lassoing, and many other events.

It was rough and tough, and ABC even filmed it for the nationally televised program *Games People Play*. In later years we had Janitor Fashion Shows, a Janitor Carnival, Janitor Opera, Janitor Olympics, talent shows, and parades. We often modeled our events after popular headliners. For example when Evel Knievel jumped the Snake River Canyon on a motorcycle (or tried to), Arlo, our CEO, rolled down a ramp in a mop bucket and leaped over 100 rolls of toilet paper. At one annual meeting with a musical theme, we all had to make an instrument that could really be played out of cleaning gear, and perform with it! I made a guitar out of a buffer, and Arlo made a vacuum into a viola (on which he played Bach). A former professional drummer made a wonderful drum set out of metal garbage cans and a wet/dry vacuum. We had keyboards on toilet lids and speakers in wax cans. So successful was this event that the Building Service Contractors Asso-

THE TV SHOW "GAMES PEOPLE PLAY" CAME TO PARK CITY, UTAH, TO FILM THE FIRST JANITOR RODEO, NARRATED BY LAUGH-IN'S ARTE JOHNSON.

ciation later had us bring our "band" and play at the MGM Grand Hotel in Vegas. We made art out of mops one year, clocks and mailboxes out of cleaning equipment in others. Golf clubs another year, chairs another. Competition was creative and keen and soon coming from more than 20 districts and divisions of our company across the country.

Then came the famous vacuum cleaner drag race, where you took an ordinary vacuum of any kind and made a hot rod out of it. We built a track outdoors for these and raced them for a city audience. At Jackson Hole, we had a soapbox derby, where 25 districts built single-seater cars out of cleaning gear and we raced them down a hill by gravity power! At other meetings, we built obstacle courses, life-size Monopoly boards, vacuum zoos, janitor jewelry, and more, all related to our profession. Onlookers were amused if not stunned by it all. Many of these items are on display in our cleaning museum.

MAKING A V-SHIRT (FOR VARSITY) WAS THE 2006 THEME. MINE WAS MADE OUT OF A SOLID METAL WRINGER MOP BUCKET.

VARSITY CAN TURN THE DULLEST ACTIVITY INTO A HUMOROUS, HEART-WARMING EVENT.

The service projects at our company training meetings are even more impressive. Our initial one was—with a crew of 48 managers—to clean a house in ten minutes—everything: walls, floors, rugs, windows, fixtures, even the yard outside. The next year we painted a huge red barn in 60 minutes (to match TV's famous *Sixty Minutes*). At Park City, Utah, we cleaned and painted the inside of a historic Catholic Church in one afternoon. In Heber, Utah, like a swarm of ants, we crawled over and cleaned a big old steam locomotive, the Heber Creeper (see p. 492). We built rail fences at camps, refinished school floors,

PLAYING MY BUFFER BRUSH GUITAR IN
VARSITY'S MUSICAL INSTRUMENTS CONTEST.

and overhauled national park lodges, almost anything imaginable by way of maintenance. As a team of 200 managers, we even cleaned all the seats in the city stadium. While doing these things, we always wore t-shirts silk-screened with a design of the event, and of course everything (all of our labor and supplies) was provided free for the cleanee! See Chapter 24 for photographs of some of these undertakings.

Since the year 2000 we have gone from a single big project to 20 or 30 small but significant volunteer service projects across the continent, reported in displays or PowerPoint at the main meeting.

After numerous inquiries from others wishing to emulate some of these events, I wrote a book called *How to Upgrade and Motivate Your Cleaning Crews*, published by Marsh Creek Press (see p. ii). It has been a bestseller in the industry, and helps others, even people outside of our industry, put some excitement into their lives at work.

> AS A COMPANY, WE HAVE SOMETHING
> UNEQUALLED, UNIQUE. WE HAVE A
> CULTURE THAT DISTINGUISHES US FROM
> OTHER COMPANIES THAT CLEAN FOR A
> LIVING. WE MADE CLEANING NOT JUST A
> WAY TO MAKE A LIVING BUT A LIFESTYLE.

Varsity's first newsletter—"Scrubber's Scribe"

Believing that janitors needed rah-rah bulletins as much as anyone, early on I initiated a company newsletter. Thus in 1960 *The Scrubber's Scribe* was born, a monthly mimeographed report to employees and their families, and clients, on the unmitigated excitement of sweeping floors, dumping trash, and cleaning restrooms. It became a colorful little journal that many looked forward to reading, especially the adventures that only we "servants of society" are privy to.

We used clip art from anywhere, and there was no uniform, carefully thought out design or layout, to be sure, but the content often made up for the lack of presentation polish. As we moved into the world of computers and copy machines, we began to put photos into the publication, and eventually color.

I was the original careless editor, sometimes running things without giving them deep thought. My spontaneity cost me at times. If something was exciting, fresh, or struck me funny, I would (without forethought, malice, and sometimes good sense) go for it.

I've always disliked pigeons, for instance, because the wild ones in towns or cities pooped on everything and we had to clean it up. During one job where the pigeons had been around in numbers and done a fair amount of damage (see Operation Pigeon Potty), one of the crew found a dead one, still fresh and intact. On his break, he made a miniature noose and strung the pigeon up. It looked like an old-time Western lynching, and expressed our sentiments at the time. Someone snapped a picture of this, and I put it on the front page of our company newsletter, with a caption along the lines of "This is what we do to dirty birds who poop on windows."

Once that issue of our little public relations publication was out, we found that some of our biggest and best clients raised and raced pigeons. Even when I explained that the bird was dead already before we hung it, it didn't save my staff-writing job on my own newsletter.

Our Varsity newsletter, now a sleek and sophisticated thing called *Varsity Vision*, has won first place in the industry for the best publication. Of course, it now has money, talent, and machines of all kinds lavished on it. In the old "Don" days, it was hand to mouth and manual everything!

TOP TO BOTTOM: MOP CREATION, SOAPBOX DERBY ENTRIES, PINEWOOD DERBY, JANITORIAL MUSICAL INSTRUMENT, AND THE SCRUBBER'S SCRIBE.

Chapter 15

INC. TO INK: MY LIFE AS A WRITER

The pen is mightier than the mop...

HOLDING A COPY OF MY FIRST SELF-PUBLISHED BOOK AGAINST A GIANT QUILTED VERSION OF THE COVER ARTFULLY PRODUCED BY ONE OF MY SEMINAR AUDIENCES.

I make my living as a businessperson, have been called a gifted motivator, coaxed into being an entertainer, and am always dreaming of being a farmer, but in all of my spare time, I pick up a pen and write. My real passion is writing. Encouraged by the success of my books, I plan only to increase my ink and toner consumption.

We all have a message for the world, and I've felt driven to deliver mine. And I've always been willing to pay the price for this privilege—the time, the money, the risk, and the loss of privacy.

After a lifetime of writing, my conclusion is that success here is more of a "go for it" than a gift. Anyone can write, but it takes real determination to actually do it and then follow up on it. This is what I tell the would-be writers who ask me for "the secrets."

I saw and felt so much in both everyday life and business that I couldn't contain it in my mind, I had to record it in writing. Writing became a great emotional release for me—articles, letters, columns, essays, poems, and then books. My many books in print to date are only a small part of what I've written and plan to write. Writing is my favorite recreation, and any money I make from it is just an added bonus.

Sometimes being a novice is not so bad: My first book, 1978-79

After more than two decades of pro cleaning, I'd also gained a lot of knowledge, skill, and credibility in my chosen field. On occasion over the years people had called on me to give speeches, workshops, and seminars not only in cleaning, but for youth and church groups on ethics, motivation, job seeking, leadership, and the like.

My wife was the president of our church's women's auxiliary and one morning she informed me that they were planning a lesson on home care and cleaning. Since I was the local expert and she'd done me 20 recent favors for my Scouts and cleaning crews, it would be my privilege to do the presentation. I agreed, and knowing how well prepared that group's regular teacher always was, I put together a powerful, concise speech on "How to do housework faster and easier the professional way." I even built a little wooden house as a visual aid—the front would drop down to reveal a window, a wall, a floor, and other housecleaning surfaces.

The women loved the workshop, and after I finished, I felt like Elvis Presley; they rushed me, almost ripped off my shirt buttons, and begged for more material. When you've been a grubby cleaner for 25 years, you say to yourself, "Man, this is living!"

Word spread quickly that there was a man who could teach you how to clean faster and better, and he was funny. So in the next few months I did the same type of presentation for other churches, women's groups, and even a couple of home economics classes.

Everywhere I went, I showed my audiences some professional approaches they could easily apply to their own homes. I improved my visual aids and gradually strengthened the presentation and lengthened it to three hours. The more I spoke, the better exposure I received and soon health departments, government agencies, and county extension agents were calling me for lectures.

My audiences grew from 50 to 100, to 500 and even 900. I had a waiting list of people who wanted me to give seminars from Seattle to Hartford to Miami. At every one, my audiences were delighted because someone was showing them how to cut the most dreaded and unrewarding word, HOUSEWORK, from their vocabulary.

With all of these classes came a lot of questions from audiences: How this and why that and when should and what do you use? One thing was as clear as a newly cleaned window—people wanted to know more. I decided that instead of remaining afterward for hours trying to answer questions, I would write up some information and hand it out after the presentation. One day before one of my Bell seminars in San Francisco, I found myself with six free hours in a quiet hotel room. I took advantage of it to write and illustrate a little booklet I called "The Adventures of Betty Betterhouse." It looked pretty amateurish but the information was good, and new to almost everyone—how to clean toilets, walls, floors, windows, etc., fast like the professionals do. When I got home I printed up a thousand of these at a local copy shop and did my own binding with three staples.

> I SOON DISCOVERED THAT "DO IT LIKE THE PROS" WAS THE BEST NICHE TO MARKET. PEOPLE LOVE PROFESSIONAL ANYTHING; THEY KNOW IT'S SUPERIOR TO ORDINARY OLD THINGS.

I had a seminar scheduled one day in a high school auditorium in the town of Shelley, Idaho. Six hundred women came, eager to cut cleaning down to size. As I finished I pointed to the pile of Betty Betterhouse booklets and said, "If you want more information, just toss down a dollar and grab one of these." The audience jumped to their feet and mobbed the pile. When the dust cleared where the booklets had been there was a pile of dollar bills and checks.

People obviously wanted to know how to clean faster and better, so I scooped up my loot and said, "I'm going to write a book!" I saw a chance to do something no one else had ever done with a dull and often avoided subject. I spent hours thinking up new and different approaches.

At airports on layovers I always headed for the women's magazine racks, thumbing through all of the housecleaning articles I could find. There wasn't much real information here, no concrete take-a-stand material that would really help someone with housework. Much of the cleaning advice available to the consumer was just "hints and tips" and old wives' tales, many of which were not only outdated and ineffective but sometimes dangerous.

The more housecleaning articles and books I scanned, the more confident I became that good quality, motivational material to help homemakers clean and organize didn't exist. When I saw this gap, I realized I had been groomed for 25 years to fill it.

From first to final draft

Keenly motivated after seeing the demand for information, and further encouraged by my old professor Clark Carlile, I didn't waste any time getting started. Since I'd been collecting cleaning information for some time, in a couple of months of part-time work I had the book drafted on my old Olympia typewriter and a yellow pad.

I had a great gag in the book, Chapter Four, "What to Expect Out of Husbands and Children." It was nothing but four blank pages with some dirty smudges on them. It was funny, and in fact the whole book, factual as it was, was funny.

There is something about having your first book finished (at least I thought it was finished) that makes you feel powerful and arrogant,

so I let my best friend, Mark Browning, one of my managers with a brilliant mind, read it. He was too honest to be nice and was pretty critical about the attitude he saw in there; the tone of the book seemed to say, "This is the only right way to do it and if you don't clean like this, you're dumb!"

I was taken aback that there could possibly be anything wrong with my book, but I respected his wisdom and knew inside that he was right. So I revised the manuscript, eliminating some things, and adding others, and polishing it up a bit.

My creativity failed when titling time came—all of my titles were dull. Then as usual, all the way through the success of my books, a woman came through. Gladys Allen, whom I'd met and become friends with during a Scouting activity, quickly came up with a dozen titles. All of them were good but one was a grabber: *Is There Life After Housework?*

GLADYS ALLEN

"Women don't clean in dresses"

Fortunately, the artist I found to illustrate my first real book was better than good—Judi Clarke was a pro, one of Disney's cartoonists. A year before, while doing a seminar in Thousand Oaks, California, and handing out my crude Betty Betterhouse booklet, she was standing near the door as I was exiting. She caught my arm and said bluntly, "Mr. Aslett, your material is good but your artwork stinks!" "What?" I replied, really surprised to be hit on the head after my brilliant toilet cleaning performance. "Your art is awful," she repeated, and proceeded to point out at least a dozen flaws in it, such as the fact that women don't clean on ladders in dresses. In a roundabout way I asked her if she could do any better, and with a female Clint-Eastwood-like demeanor she said, "I'm good." So I had her redo it, and she *was* good.

When I finished *Life*, of course I called and asked if she would do the artwork.

I had some wild ideas about art and layout, not knowing any better and not being an experienced book writer. These proved to be a real asset in my books, after I managed to convince the "set in their ways" publishers to adopt many of them.

COVERS AND PROPOSED COVERS FOR
IS THERE LIFE AFTER HOUSEWORK? THROUGH THE YEARS.

Lost in the slush pile

Now I had a manuscript—what was I supposed to do with it? I asked and was told, "You can publish it yourself or have a publisher publish it." I was plenty busy with my business and "publisher" sounded so big and full of authority that I decided to go that route. I made about ten copies of the manuscript, got myself a *Writer's Market* (directory of publishers), copied out the names and addresses of some of the most impressive-sounding ones, and sent off my book. I was inexperienced and idealistic enough that I fully expected to hear back within a few days from all ten fighting to get my manuscript. But there was nothing… nothing… for two weeks, four weeks, and then finally after ten weeks I got a noncommittal reply from one saying that they "couldn't include it in their list at this time." Eventually I got all of my manuscripts, or most of them, back with the same kind of note (a rejection letter).

No one had even one sentence of encouragement.

This was when I first found out that "cleaning" is a hard sell. Who wants to clean? Who wants to talk about it? Who wants to read about it or pay for it? Not most people, for sure! No publisher would touch my book with a ten-foot broom handle.

But I had enough feedback from my cleaning seminars that I knew my book, once out, would sell. So I went to visit a prominent local publisher in a nearby big city. (I'd sent them a book previously.) The editor sat there behind his big desk and informed me that the topic of cleaning would not sell, that everyone hated it, and that my cutesy approach (that's what he called my cartoons and humor), would never work. My book, to have a chance, would have to be serious and solid, a factual how-to.

I kept the letter of analysis and appraisal he sent me afterward. The average successful book sells seven or eight or maybe ten thousand copies, and if you sell 20,000—wow! Forty thousand copies, fantastic! Fifty thousand is phenomenal in the book world. When this book I had presented to him eventually hit the national and foreign bestseller lists, the temptation was too much. He was so confident and "know-it-all" that a year and a half later when the book had sold over a half million

copies, I took the rejection letter he wrote to me, attached a copy of the bestseller list with my book on it, and sent it back to him!

Doing it yourself (in the dark)

The publisher route wasn't working, so on to Plan B—publish it myself. I didn't really have a clue as to how to do that, but Barbara and I (with help from our oldest daughter Laura), put the final text and art together.

Then came the first of many struggles for a cover, as you learn quickly that a book's cover design is almost as important as its title. We finally settled on a red and white gingham background with a broom on it and a cartoon figure of a woman sitting on the broom contemplating the title.

We took the finished book down to a printer in Salt Lake City, and the employees there shook their heads a bit at some of my ideas and illustrations and my farm-boy style, but they were helpful.

When it came to type design, layout, and paper choice, the three of us were close to clueless. We just decided as we went along. We picked a heavy, glossy paper that cost considerably more than what most publishers use.

"How many books do you want?" the printer asked. I always think big, and then I learned that 500 would be $3 a book, 5,000 $2 a book, 10,000 were about $1.65 a copy, and at 20,000 or more it fell to a mere $1.20 each—20,000 it was! (I had no idea at the time that the average self-published book only sells about 500 copies, mostly to friends and relatives and others taking pity.)

They printed; I scrambled to borrow enough money to pay for it. (If you think your banker is reluctant to lend you money, try borrowing $30,000 as a janitor to print a cleaning book.)

But I got the money and had the books delivered to our house, not the office, because we had some room in the garage. Gadfrey—have you ever seen 20,000 eight-and-a-half-by-eleven-inch books? They brought them in a tractor-trailer, and there wasn't room for our cars for a long time afterward.

Beginner's luck

I was doing lots of seminars then and the book sold like crazy. I sold it for $5 and before I knew it 5,000 were gone, then 10,000. Though I sold these books mainly at my seminars and by mail through the order blank in back of the book (no bookstores), 15,000 books were gone in less than a year—this is just as astounding, looking back at it now. Now that I'm older, wiser, and much better known, and have published more than three dozen books, I don't always do as well.

I made around $60,000 on this project, and for the first time in our lives, Barbara and I seemed to have some money of our own. I liked the feeling of independence—no crew to worry about or pay—just some pages of paper gave me earning power!

The book clearly could sell, but I would have to make it happen. Selling the books myself lost its glory fast, and big sales would call for exposure to large numbers of people. The population of all of southern Idaho barely equaled that of one suburb of Chicago or LA, and I couldn't spend all of my time in seminars selling books.

On to the Olympics of bookselling!

A short time later, at a seminar in northern Utah, a bookstore owner came up to me afterward and said, "Mr. Aslett, you ought to take your book to the ABA and get some national exposure." She spent an hour educating me on book peddling and politics. She gave me a few names to contact and told me if I wanted to meet some publishers and distributors, thousands of them, I should attend the American Booksellers Association Convention to be held in Chicago next weekend.

It sounded good. I was told 30,000 book-buyers would be there and I would need help to run the booth. My American Express card was strained to its limit by recent promotions so I only bought tickets for Barbara and me. She was buried at the time in preparations for our oldest daughter's wedding, but I painted a picture of fame and fortune, and printed up some business cards with her as vice president of our publishing company. We took 1,000 books, 20 cases, not knowing you didn't actually sell books there, only took orders. Our daughter Laura stayed up until two in the morning sewing up a giant gingham quilt, and our son Rell made a frame for it and affixed a real broom to the front, so it looked like a giant version of our book cover.

We can tolerate great suffering if the goal or reward is important enough. And great suffering is what it took to get all of those books out to our car and then into the airport. (Fortunately United didn't charge for excess baggage yet.) My eyeballs were protruding, my hands sore, my suit was mangled, and I smelled like a Wyoming feedlot when I finally sat down on a bench at the airport. Then the baggage conveyor belt refused to move! Our luggage alone had overloaded the conveyor and stopped it.

Three hours later in Chicago the books had to be taken out of the baggage area and onto the shuttle bus, out of the bus, up to our room, and then back down to the convention hall. We gave away 60 books, sold about 20, and had to take all of the rest back home.

We also knew nothing about booths at an exposition like this. We found a bargain booth at the last minute for $250. Little did we know that the bigger and better booths were $5,000 and $10,000 and that ours was around the corner, behind the pillars, across the forklift track, and next to the restrooms. So we showed up to peddle our single book, sitting at a bare table on the two chairs it cost us $50 each to rent, with our gingham quilt for a background.

Other publishers (in the miles of booths in huge McCormick Place) had hundreds of books in huge glittering displays, with flashing lights, animated exhibits, and people like Jane Fonda in tights, the Incredible Hulk, and Richard Simmons there in person to attract attention. One booth even had a live cougar! We were too stunned to be intimidated.

BUDGE WALLIS, GENERAL MANAGER OF WRITER'S DIGEST BOOKS, THE PUBLISHER THAT HELPED BRING MY FIRST BOOK TO NATIONAL ATTENTION.

In the next three days, I met scores of publishers and other authors in person, got acquainted with many of them, and had a taste of "book society." There was lots of big talk and strutting, but fortunately, a few people had to go to the bathroom and thus right by our booth. Two or three of them actually stopped. First was an editor from the *National Enquirer*, who paged through my book, chuckled, and then laid it down and said, "You have a bestseller there, son—too bad we don't do books." Then a trim, clean-cut man in a suit stopped, looked at my book, and asked if he might take two copies back to his office. He introduced himself as Budge Wallis, general manager of Writer's Digest Books, a well-known publisher of books for writers that also did a few books on other subjects. I gave him the books, and the rest of the show was a quick education in the book business.

A diamond in the rough beats "The Joy of Sex"

While I was getting my initiation into the book business, my cleaning company was gaining ground with one of our biggest clients, the Bell System. Two years before, I'd helped design (as a consultant on the cleaning and maintenance aspects) a big new 2.2-million-square-foot building for them in Atlanta. Now we'd been awarded the cleaning contract on this building and so were expanding into Georgia. I was in Atlanta one afternoon not long after the ABA convention and was paged out of a meeting for a call from Writer's Digest. It was Budge Wallis, and he said, "We like your book and would like to publish it. We will edit, redesign, reprint, and distribute it. We will put you on tour and on TV and pay you not the ordinary six percent royalty but a healthy ten percent of the cover cost (about a dollar a book) for royalties."

I had cleaning seminars set up all over, new cleaning contracts under way, and my company just kept on growing. I didn't have much time to try and push my book into the big leagues myself, and I didn't know how to do it, either. So I said, "Yes, Mr. Wallis, you can have it."

Later I learned that several of the critics and advisors there had looked my book over, chuckled over it, and tucked it into the reject pile. But the head editor, Carol Cartaino, read it thoughtfully. "This guy has some rough edges," she reported to the committee that decides the fate of submissions, "but he does know his stuff and this book may sell. It's a truly different approach to cleaning."

CAROL CARTAINO AT HOME ON HER OHIO FARM (SEE P. 313), BREAKING IN A NEW HELPER.

So a small but great and fast-growing publishing company in Cincinnati, Writer's Digest Books, went on to publish it. Carol really worked over the book I thought was perfect, and the trim size of the finished book was 7 by 9 inches, which was thereafter called "the Aslett size" at Writer's Digest. They put it out in the bookstores and put me on the road into a brand-new profession called publicity. Although the yellow cover they put on the book was even uglier than my original cover, in my opinion, and I was green as grass at all this, the book sold, and sold, and sold.

The book went on the bestseller list, and for ten lovely days it was even ahead of *The Joy of Sex* and *30 Days to a Beautiful Bottom*. After the book took off, Cartaino in her wisdom (here is another important job of an editor) called and said, "Can you write us another book?" "Two books on cleaning?" I whined. Since then I've done more than a dozen on cleaning; even the mundane job of cleaning has many angles.

She suggested a question and answer book, and that was all I needed. People asked me cleaning questions constantly, and I'd collected thousands and thousands of "comment cards" from my seminar audiences that often contained questions. So before long we'd assembled 100 questions

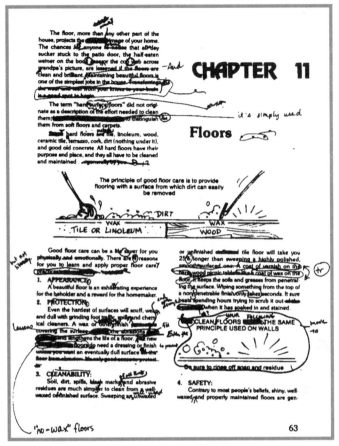

about cleaning, and I gave them short, punchy answers.

Carol toned down any over-opinionated ones, like:

"Mr. Aslett, what about those no-wax floors?"

"Lady, a no-wax floor is like a no-wash dish."

"What do you think of those hand carpet sweepers?"

"A carpet sweeper is like a girdle. It improves the surface some but doesn't do anything for what's underneath."

"My pet peed on the carpet. What can I do about it?"

"Toss that critter outside where it belongs!"

The resulting book, *Do I Dust or Vacuum First?*, coat-tailed on *Is There Life After Housework?*, and went on to sell more than half a million copies and be published in a mass-market edition, too. I'd found a great publisher and creative editor.

A rolling stone gathers no clutter

With two good books out, I was doing tons of publicity: morning talk shows and TV and radio interviews for every type of station across the country from CNN to Christian networks. Now there was something else new in my life, fan mail. It often contained good ideas and stories. Many of the "Thanks, Don, you changed my life!" letters talked a lot about one subject, Chapter Three of *Is There Life After Housework?*, which dealt with junk and clutter. It told them what they already knew—that about 40 percent of cleaning time and 60 percent of personal problems came from having too much stuff. (After all, you can't clean the floor until you can find it.)

Carol said this would make a terrific book. So I tore into the why, what, when, and how of getting rid of all the junk around the house. My research had already been done in my many years of cleaning up behind people. In those thousands of homes, businesses, and home emergencies, we cleaners saw and heard everything. The feed of additional ideas from Carol, my wife and mother-in-law, and my fans (all clutter experts), triggered lots more good material. Right in the middle of writing the book, Barbara and I took 20 days off and went on a 6,000-mile trip to Alaska (see p. 234), and I wrote as we toured and visited. Every conversation and stop at a souvenir shop or tourist trap was grist for my mill. Once in Skagway, where our daughter lived, under the pines and glaciers, watching thousands of tourists buying "stuff," I kept on writing. Carol called, and we bounced ideas off each other, I wrote my drafts in handwriting on yellow pads, and my assistant Nancy typed it all up in Pocatello. Some of the best material in the book came while on that trip.

Humbled by success

Have you ever been working on something for years and suddenly it grows into not quite a monster, but something almost as terrifying?

It was the busy spring of 1983, following some 600 radio and TV show appearances I'd made, and tons of press releases and newspaper articles. I was speaking at graduations, meeting with millionaire promoters, writing articles for major magazines, manufacturers seeking TV endorsements were calling, and "I love you—you changed my life" fan mail was pouring in. I was aware and appreciative of all this, but kind of taking it in stride. I left for New York City for a convention of professional cleaners at which I was the featured speaker. Afterward there were requests for seminars and other speaking appearances. I got back to my room and Australia was calling again. (I'd done 13 phone interviews there over the past three weeks for the British edition of *Is There*

Life After Housework?, which was selling well there.) Some important reports had arrived from the office, along with a bid decision that had to be made.

As I sat on the edge of the bed, quivering with the excitement of all this, for the first time the thought occurred to me: What am I actually doing? This is not a game or just a matter of making a buck, impressing others, or counting the shows I've been on. This was a serious reality affecting the lives of others. I was in a position now to be dangerous, and no longer had the option of just dinging around or "doing my own thing." I owed those who had built and were building me, and especially owed them a good example. I had thought of this in a fleeting way before, but suddenly the responsibility of it all really hit me. I felt humble and aware of the fact that it wasn't just me—it was us—me and you—and that "you," the public, deserved only what was good and right, the best of what I could give.

I couldn't shake this knot in my stomach as I flew to Cincinnati to edit my new book on "junk." Carol picked me up at the airport and for six days we edited and structured the book, met with publicity, production, and marketing people and in general really expanded, improved, and advanced the manuscript I had conceived a year earlier. Carol was the most masterful, intelligent person I had been around in the business, and I was overwhelmed by her wisdom and skill at extracting from me what more was needed to make the book something witty and sometimes profound that people would want to read. As she did this, each day I saw more clearly what this writing business was all about, and what the possibilities might be when I got better at it.

I left Cincinnati so stimulated by the week that I felt like running through the streets shouting, or retreating to a cabin in the woods to meditate. I flew home early on Friday morning and the national TV show *Real People* was there to film me for an upcoming show. After that came two hours of filmed interviews at my hotel. Then I traveled to a high school in Logan, Utah where I had a "Life After Housework" seminar scheduled, which was going to be filmed. Nine hundred people showed up and it was the ultimate test of nerves, as the camera operators were up on stage with me, dragging equipment around and shining lights in the audience's eyes as I was trying to give the crowd a good show (all of this effort for a show that never aired).

When all this was over, I went out and leaned against my motor home and tried to compose myself. It took three days to gather my wits and gird my loins and decide that I was in this for good, and there was no way out, unless I quit. And that's a word that never been part of my life or vocabulary.

Clutter's Last Stand was destined to impact the lives of millions of people, and as it slowly came together all of us had a sense of mission about its bottom line that "excess" erodes our spirit, wealth, health, and relationships. The book grew and came so naturally together that it almost felt inspired.

After the book was drafted, we knew it needed art, friendly cartoon art with a serious message. It was a huge project and Judi Clarke, who now had a houseful of teenagers, was busy. However, just then President Reagan laid off many FAA air controllers, including Judi's husband, so she consented to do it.

By now Writer's Digest was booming—my two books really helped put them in the "home and household" market big time and they needed Carol, as editor-in-chief, to do more on other books, and less on mine. But she was in love with our new clutter book, and so as to not disobey her boss, she took a month of accumulated vacation time and flew to California where Judi lived. She stayed in a motel and finished the book—doing the final editing by day and working with Judi by night to come up with art ideas that added greatly to the impact and readability of the book. The art in this book cost $15,000, and was worth every penny. Judi caught the feeling of the text perfectly.

Last came the usual struggle for a title. Writer's Digest finally ran a contest at the office and a young woman in the production department came through with the clever "Clutter's Last Stand."

ART BY JUDI CLARKE FROM THE TITLE PAGE OF THE FIRST EDITION OF *CLUTTER'S LAST STAND*—ME IN A STANDOFF WITH THE "JUNK MONSTER" CHARACTER THAT APPEARS THROUGHOUT THE BOOK.

I love this book—it's my favorite of the more than 40 books I've done to date. When I speak at their conferences, librarians tell me it's one of the most checked-out books ever! I've had calls and letters from thousands of people who decided not to commit suicide or give up because of it, from ministers who quote from it in sermons, and college professors who use it as a text in behavioral science classes. It's sold more than half a million copies now.

All three of my first books were bestsellers, and my royalties from June 1983 to June 1984 were around $160,000, all free and clear money—more than my total profits from the first 12 years of Varsity. Once while I was visiting Writer's Digest's home office the owner of the company, Dick Rosenthal, took me to dinner and handed me the monthly sales report, showing that they'd sold 22,000 of one of my books that month and 8,000 of another. I was naïve enough to think that was just the way the book business went. Today, to sell even 30,000 books a year I'd do back flips. We just had a hot new subject and incredibly good timing.

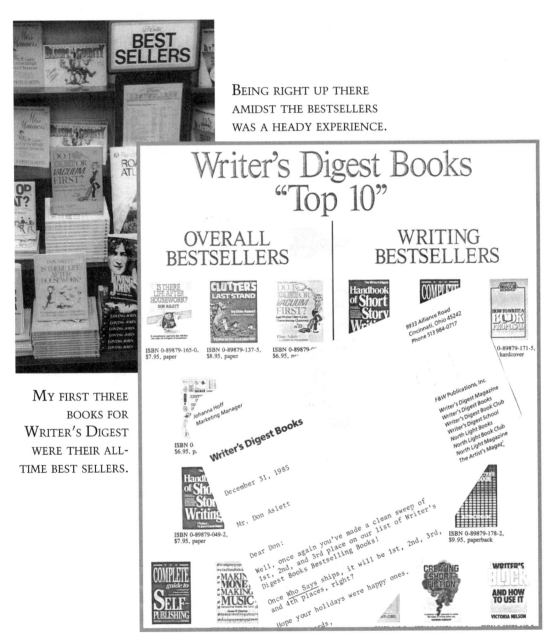

BEING RIGHT UP THERE AMIDST THE BESTSELLERS WAS A HEADY EXPERIENCE.

MY FIRST THREE BOOKS FOR WRITER'S DIGEST WERE THEIR ALL-TIME BEST SELLERS.

Writer's Digest Books "Top 10"

OVERALL BESTSELLERS

IS THERE LIFE AFTER HOUSEWORK? DON ASLETT
ISBN 0-89879-165-0, $7.95, paper

CLUTTER'S LAST STAND by Don Aslett
ISBN 0-89879-137-5, $8.95, paper

DO I DUST OR VACUUM FIRST? Don Aslett
ISBN 0-89879-, $6.95, p.

Johanna Hoff
Marketing Manager

ISBN 0-
$6.95, p.

Handbook of Short Story Writing
ISBN 0-89879-049-2, $7.95, paper

THE COMPLETE guide to SELF-PUBLISHING

MAKING MONEY MAKING MUSIC

WRITING BESTSELLERS

Handbook of Short Story Writing

COMPLETE
9933 Alliance Road
Cincinnati, Ohio 45242
Phone 513 984-0717

HOW TO WRITE A BOOK PROPOSAL
0-89879-171-5, hardcover

F&W Publications, Inc.
Writer's Digest Magazine
Writer's Digest Books
Writer's Digest Book Club
Writer's Digest School
North Light Books
North Light Book Club
North Light Magazine
The Artist's Magazine

ISBN 0-89879-178-2, $9.95, paperback

CREATING SHORT FICTION

WRITER'S BLOCK AND HOW TO USE IT
VICTORIA NELSON

Writer's Digest Books

December 31, 1985

Mr. Don Aslett

Dear Don:

Well, once again you've made a clean sweep of 1st, 2nd, and 3rd place on our list of Writer's Digest Books Bestselling Books!

Once Who Says ships, it will be 1st, 2nd, 3rd, and 4th places, right?

Hope your holidays were happy ones.

Who says a book is going to sell?

Now with three winners in a row, I thought I could do no wrong with any writing topic. My publisher and I were excited about my latest book idea, getting men to help clean. Women would swoon when the subject was mentioned. I went for it with both barrels, having progressed from audiences that were 100 percent women to at least 25 percent men and gaining. I felt I was in a good position to speak out on this, because my first cleaning crews were 100 percent men and I knew well that men could and should clean. The subject seemed perfect for the times, when women were struggling to do it all at home while often working an outside job, too. I did a nice book on this, convincing men that their help was needed and where, what, and how to clean. Artist Craig LaGory did some of the best art ever, and we put the book in kind of a Garfield oblong size and called it *Who Says It's a Woman's Job to Clean?*

The advance sale (books sold to bookstores before the book is actually published) was a staggering 72,000 copies. Writer's Digest and I could see a sure million-seller here. The media was calling and begging for interviews on the subject, and Budge and Carol and I even went to the printer and watched those babies roll off that big press.

The first weekend after the book was out I had a book signing scheduled at a bookstore in a major mall in Salt Lake City where my other books had sold well, and they shipped in stacks of this revolutionary new cleaning book. We were set up in a heavy traffic area of the mall, and when fans spotted me, they shrieked in delight. They'd run up to the table and hug me. "Love your books! Love your books! I bought the first three and they changed my life!"

"Thank you. I have had brand new one here, just for the men, only $5.95, too."

Then I'd point to or wave the shiny new book with its bright orange and green cover. We expected to sell two or three hundred books that day; we only sold two.

A month later the manager of a busy B. Dalton bookstore said to me, "Don, we've had your new book at eye level on our best aisle for thirty days and have only sold three."

I called Writer's in a panic and told them of the poor response. "Something's wrong! People aren't buying the book!"

"No! That's just a fluke. Books are flying out of here. In fact, we just printed 70,000 more." (Conservative like most book publishers, they rarely printed more than 10,000 of any book at a time.)

But all wasn't well, as the next six months would prove. This book got the most attention from the media of any book I'd ever done, but

ART BY CRAIG LaGORY FROM THE TITLE PAGE OF *WHO SAYS IT'S A WOMAN'S JOB TO CLEAN?*

actual sales were disappointing. (We're still speculating as to the reasons for this—maybe book-buyers, who are predominantly women, felt the title sounded *too* revolutionary.) I learned another new book word now called "returns," and we had them by the thousands. *Who Says* eventually sold around 100,000 copies, which is impressive by the standards of ordinary book sales, but compared to our expectations, it was a failure. Since Writer's Digest had done that second printing, there were 50,000 books left over, "remainders" as those unsold books are called when they get back to the publisher. I ended up buying them at a bargain basement price of 27 cents a book and we are still selling them slowly.

This book is still one that is sorely needed. A new (and re-titled) edition will be ready soon, so be sure to buy one for all the young men you know when you see it!

While publicizing *Who Says It's a Woman's Job to Clean?*, I made up some props that masculinized some common housework tools, like mounting a scrub brush beneath a duck decoy, putting a golf club handle on a lambswool duster, a Porsche gearshift on a pancake spatula, a tennis racket handle on a dustpan, and a saw handle atop an iron. The media loved it.

Doing housework with a hammer

The next book I completed was a combination of two of my passions. I loved not just to keep things clean, but also to design and build homes. Over the years, I'd gotten many comments from women at my seminars and in the media. "You know, Don, men are stupid—they build things that are difficult if not impossible to clean." At first this offended me; after all I was one of those construction guys with a leather carpenter's belt.

But then I started to listen to their facts and details. They were smart, and they were right. I had a lot of information on low-maintenance building in my files from my consulting jobs on commercial buildings, my own experience building homes, and the many fire and flood repairs and other diverse cleaning jobs on which my company had worked. At this time, my oldest daughter Laura was designing kitchens to help work her way through college. So we proposed a book to Writer's Digest on how you could make a new or present home low maintenance through design. *Woman's Day* magazine had interviewed me on this subject and I knew from firsthand experience that people were interested in it.

Writer's Digest gave us an unprecedented (for them) advance of $100,000 to write the book. It was a good father/daughter collaboration, and after Carol's

THE AUTHORS' PHOTO FROM *MAKE YOUR HOUSE DO THE HOUSEWORK*, WHICH I WROTE WITH MY DAUGHTER LAURA SIMONS.

edit, we had a winner. I wanted to call it "Do Your Housework with a Hammer," but yielded to Writer's Digest's choice of *Make Your House Do the Housework*. To enhance the book's credibility, Barbara and I decided to build a model low-maintenance home. It would be a great marketing move, kind of like a giant visual aid.

The book and the house were started at about the same time, but the house took ten times as long and ten times the money to finish (see p. 460). The book did better than we expected—counting book club and foreign sales, it sold more than 250,000 copies.

What makes Don Aslett's books successful?

"Don has an amazing number of new ideas, can bring any subject to life, and is a dynamic self-marketer. His love of visuals and dramatic design, his unusual approach to almost every subject, and his ability to touch and strum the chords of interest in every one of us, all add up to books that interest even people who never read books."   —Carol Cartaino, editor

ARTWORK BY BERT BETTY
FROM *PET CLEANUP MADE EASY.*

Our first special-market book

Now I was ready for a book that would help readers deal with some hard questions. There were 200 million pets (dogs and cats alone) in the U.S. in 1986 and their messes were a constant concern. Why not solve this with a new book? So we did one, called *Pet Cleanup Made Easy.*

This was the first book I didn't just sit down and write. I knew how to clean up animal poop and pee and pet hair but all of my own pets were outside of the house. Letting a cat or dog inside the house was like inviting a horse or cow in, to my farm-raised way of thinking. So we filled 24 drawers with research on everything from parakeet fallout to ferret fumes. Carol even came out to our office in Idaho for three months. Putting that book together, between Writer's Digest and our own staff, we spent more than $50,000, a huge investment. It pre-sold 26,000 copies, much to our delight.

However, since this was our first special market book, we had a surprise or two coming. We'd counted on pet stores being our big seller, but they weren't. Most of them didn't want to stock it even though they agreed it was a book all pet owners should have. People buy pets for romantic reasons—they see a little furry ball of love and companionship, and when they are just making a decision to purchase, the store didn't want to offer them a book which said in effect, "By the way, folks, you can look forward to this little cutie growing up and pooping and peeing all over." Veterinarians liked the book, too, but had little interest in selling it.

SIX BOOKS... DOZENS MORE TO GO!

The book did sell a respectable 60,000 in the end and was eventually issued by another publisher in a revised, updated edition, but I began to comprehend that the book business wasn't a pushover. However, *Pet Cleanup* did make it into a book club, as did my first three books, and I was now being quoted and interviewed regularly in major publications like *Reader's Digest, USA Today, Parents* magazine, *Woman's Day,* and *Family Circle.*

On to Manhattan!

I had a half-dozen books under my belt now, a pretty darn good sales record, and any number of new volumes in my head.

After six successful books with Writer's Digest and a long and great relationship, they began to focus more on their specialized art and writing books, while I wanted to do books that didn't fit their subject menu or format. Plus their editor-in-chief, Carol Cartaino, following a lifelong dream of living in the country, left them to buy a small farm in southwest Ohio. This would be the headquarters of a freelance editing business, and I would be her main client in her new independent life.

Mark Browning, my longtime partner in many ventures, also joined me now to help fill in the sometimes-large gap between my creative, far-reaching ideas and the mundane but important detail that makes good books. Mark and I put out a book for professional cleaners called *Cleaning Up for a Living,* and then activated and accelerated some of the other books in my idea file.

In 1987, we figured that given my past success, we were hot enough to go to the big boys in New York now, the heart of the book publishing industry. Carol, who had worked with Prentice-Hall and other well-known houses earlier in her career, agreed. We put together several good book outlines and sent them on ahead, and when eight major publishers showed strong interest, we headed for the big city. Most authors go begging; we went with the theme, "Here are several good books; if you are lucky, you might get some, and if you offer us a real attractive package, you might get them all."

We met all of the publishers who had thrown their hats in the ring, and Carol, whom I'd known for years as a soft spoken, humble intellectual, turned into a shark once she was back among her old colleagues in the book business, wheeling and dealing and interrogating. It was pretty gratifying to see a dozen of the biggest and best publishers all vying to get my books, when ten years earlier they wouldn't even open the manuscript envelope.

ART BY BERT BETTY FROM THE "ABOUT THE AUTHOR"
OF *HOW DO I CLEAN THE MOOSEHEAD?*,
MY FIRST BOOK FOR NEW AMERICAN LIBRARY.

A full-blown auction followed when we returned, as they all bid on the books with ever-better deals and advances. Advances are meant to give authors money to live on while they write the book, and also to lock in commitment between publisher and author. I never liked advances because in my rural upbringing, being paid for a job before it was done was unheard of, and putting money in the bank only to perhaps find out you weren't entitled to it seemed like folly. Any decent farmer should have his own seed money for planting. But I was assured that in the book business this was the way it was done.

Carol orchestrated the auction from her little farm in Ohio with the help of her partner, the literary agent Oscar Collier. We ended up selling four books in one shot, to two of the major players in the industry, New American Library and Dell, and getting a total advance of $210,000. (I'd come a long way from the typical beginner's advance of $5,000.)

We figured we'd hit the big time, and some good books came of it—*Not for Packrats Only* (a sequel to *Clutter's Last Stand*), *How Do I Clean the Moosehead?* (another 100 cleaning questions answered), and by special request of the editor who won the auction, *The Stainbuster's Bible.* The fourth was a giant undertaking called Don Aslett's *Cleaning Encyclopedia*, concocted as the ultimate Aslett cleaning book by Carol and the head editor of Dell. Later I did another book for Simon and Schuster, *500 Terrific Ideas for Cleaning Everything.*

Mark was the technical genius on the stain removal book and the encyclopedia while I did my creative thing on *Packrat* and *Moose.* We did seminars for income, but it was hard to get people out now for a cleaning lecture. VCRs were everywhere and people were staying home to watch them. My cleaning company had also grown into many more areas and locations and we needed Mark Browning back in it. So he left our book partnership to take over Varsity's northwest region operation, his sixth major move with the company.

As for publishers, in the end, bigger did not turn out to be better, as my books were lost amidst the thousands of other books produced by these publishers. The books were well published and received, I learned a few new things about publicity and promotion, and the books eventually earned out their big advances, but I did not feel at home. It was not the same as being a big fish in a small and eventually medium pond as I was at Writer's Digest. At the ABA now for instance, my new publisher New American Library, after telling me how important my three books were to them, passed me over at a publicity meeting to have Sylvester Stallone's mother as a guest instead. Another time, I visited the booth of the company that had not long ago spent a fortune in advances for my books, and promised all kinds of new sales records, and no one at the booth had any idea who I even was, and you could hardly find my books in their huge catalog.

The more I learned about the bigger publishing companies I worked with now, the less I liked it. The books had less attractive layout and design, it took longer to do them, and I had little meaningful contact with anyone in those giant offices. I also made less money for all of my writing and promotional efforts.

Shifting the spotlight

Book companies have one goal and that is to sell books, as quickly and as many as possible. One of the big ways to help accomplish this is publicity—any spotlight they can get on the author and the subject at hand. The more famous, funny, entertaining, or provocative the author is, the easier it is to get media attention. The publisher lines up and schedules interviews and shows for books with strong promotion potential, and also pays any expenses involved. The author only has to donate his time, and accept some wear and tear.

When I was on a book tour, an escort (driver) who knew the city and its media would generally meet me at the airport or hotel and take me to each location for interviews and appearances.

I did around five thousand different media segments—live, taped, and "phoners" (phone-in shows), on my first ten books. Then we decided to arrange all the publicity ourselves. My publicist, Tobi Haynes (now Alexander), would set up all media appearances directly, using press kits and forms that we created ourselves. I didn't like having my life and schedule in others' hands, and we were now able to do the job ourselves more efficiently and cost-effectively. We kept careful records on all of my appearances, so we could track results and select the best opportunities.

Going on up the creek with my own paddle

By this time, book writing was a habit. I had more than 30 new ideas for books in me now, and I decided that I could do better by starting and owning my own publishing company; I could write on any subject I wanted, produce my the books just the way I liked them, and own them completely.

I greatly appreciated what some good publishing companies did for me, and I'm sure they respected the effort I made for them and the money I put in their coffers. But for a farmer, there comes a time when rented ground needs to be replaced by ground you own. I had the facilities, the computers, the people, the skill, and thousands of media segments under my belt. We could produce an even better quality book for about a dollar and sell it for ten dollars, eliminating many of the middlemen. This left a great margin for my book sales at speaking engagements—I could give nice discounts and still have a good markup. Being my own publisher, I could also work on 40 new Aslett books at a time, which would terrify an ordinary publisher.

The frosting on the cake was having Carol Cartaino now available to work on all of my books. In my opinion and that of even those elite New York publishers, she's one of the best in the business—a super editor, contract negotiator, and book consultant.

My home office in McCammon, Idaho, where I do much of my writing, overlooks a beautiful green valley with rugged 8,000-foot mountains all around it. In that valley is a meandering stream called Marsh

THE COVER OF THE FIRST CATALOG OF MY PUBLISHING COMPANY MARSH CREEK PRESS.

Creek. The word "press" sounds pretty clearly like publishing, and one day Tobi combined the two in a memo and we both said, "The perfect name!" Hence Marsh Creek Press.

Thus I completed the circle from self-publisher, to an author for publishers, to larger publishers, then back to self-publishing. I liked to own and control my own things, and now I had much, much

A CARICATURE OF THE MARSH CREEK PRESS STAFF AND FREELANCERS: BERT BETTY, CRAIG LAGORY, DON, CAROL, TOBI, KERRY OTTESON, VIRGINIA AAGARD.

less bureaucracy to wade through. I went back to a smaller town mentality and enjoyed publishing again!

From cluttered file cabinets to braless cows

Some of my best books came after the first ten or twelve big sellers. Good ideas, obvious new needs, and my seminars and speaking appearances were the catalysts for many of them. The book market changed considerably (not necessarily for the better) after chain bookstores became the norm, and morning TV talk shows were less popular than they once were. On the other hand, computers made book production and printing much easier.

I was voted Idaho Business Leader of the Year in 1993. When I got to thinking about where I had learned most of my management and business skills, it always came back to being with my father on the farm and in the feedlots, barns, corrals, and pastures with the animals. So I began jotting down all of the lessons and logic that the cows, chickens, pigs, horses, sheep, and barn cats had taught me. In five days, I had the book drafted. I took it home, Carol gave it a quick edit incorporating a little more rural wisdom, and before you know it Tobi had it in type and handed it to our artist. Thus my quickest book, *Everything I*

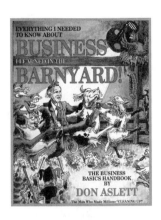

Needed to Know About Business I Learned in the Barnyard, was done. My enthusiasm for the cover was not shared by everyone (me dancing arm in arm with farm animals, cartoon style). It was probably the braless cow that offended people. A revised and expanded edition of this book—with a new cover and maybe title too—is in the works as this is written.

The same year I wrote *Barnyard,* I put together another new book called *How to Be #1 With Your Boss.* For years I had spoken at graduations and "How to Get a Good Job" weeks at schools, and to employees and managers of businesses. I had piles of notes and ideas from the real world of work on that bottom-line issue of what the boss really expects of his or her employees, and these made for the perfect book to accompany my presentations.

Since I was making some of my income as a public speaker, it also made sense to do a book (at the request of my British publisher) on that subject. They called it *Is There a Speech Inside You?* I didn't like that title and when I reissued it in the U. S., I used my own original title: *Speak Up: A Step-by-Step Guide to Presenting Powerful Public Speeches.* This was my second book designed so it could also be used as a high school or college textbook. (In 1984 I had done a textbook-type manual called *Clean It and Mean It* with Jeena Nilson, who was the State Extension Specialist of Utah State at the time.)

I also turned out a couple of small books, *Painting Without Fainting,* and *Clean in a Minute* (a short, streamlined version of *Is There Life After Housework?,* which has sold more than 130,000 copies, many of them to the military). In 1993 I helped my son Grant do *The Guide to Easy Wood Floor Care and Maintenance,* a much-needed book on a subject about which people were always asking.

Clutter was still a hot topic. I had two good decluttering books out, and one day realized that paper clutter had risen to first place among the clutter plagues at home and at the office. And my company was cleaning at least 300 million square feet of office space ev-

ART BY JOHN CALDWELL FOR
THE OFFICE CLUTTER CURE.

ery day across the country. Who better to write on the subject than me? Thus *The Office Clutter Cure* came to be. There was good stuff in that book, but almost better than the words was the art. We hired John Caldwell of *Mad* magazine fame to illustrate the book, which was worth buying just for the art.

For those still struggling with cluttered homes (packrats seem to need a periodic shot of fresh inspiration) I did two more good decluttering guides, *Lose 200 Lbs. This Weekend: It's Time to Declutter Your Life*, and *Clutter Free! Finally and Forever.* The latter included the best "confessions" and solutions from the thousands of reformed junkers who'd written and called me over the years.

After being asked hundreds if not thousands of times over the years "How do you get so much done, Don?" in 1996 I put together another of my favorite books, *How to Have a 48-Hour Day*. This was a fresh and opinionated look at a popular topic—how to get more done. The title backfired on us a little, as we found many people don't think like I do. They want a six-hour day, not a 48-hour day! But many readers claim this is the best book out there on the subject. It was later reissued by Adams Media as *DONE: How to Get Twice as Much Done in Half the Time, at Home and at the Office!*

DONE! ART BY JIM HUNT.

The next book, aimed at all the overburdened homemakers today, was called *How to Handle 1,000 Things at Once*, designed to help read-

ers get it all together in the hectic round of modern life and keep it all moving toward the results they have in mind. It incorporated wisdom from all of the "superwomen" I know and has been a steady seller.

For the year 2000, I did a large, handsomely illustrated book for the very different home cleaners of the new millennium—*No Time to Clean!*, which explained not only how to clean every part of the home faster and better, but how to cut the job of home cleaning and maintenance down to size, in a world all too full of other agendas.

In 2002, I wrote a book to encourage and help other would-be writers do their own book—a volume called *How to Write and Sell Your First Book*.

All of the above I published and produced under my own publishing company, Marsh Creek Press, although many of these books were distributed to bookstores by my old original publisher, Writer's Digest Books.

I still did some books for other publishers, too. At the request of Storey Publishing, I wrote a book with my editor Carol, called *Keeping Work Simple*. Published in 1997, it is not one of my favorites, because they had the power to "neuter" it (make it more conventional) and they did, too much so to suit me. Plus they put a cup of coffee on the cover (coffee, the biggest slower-downer of work on the planet!). But it has sold more than 35,000 copies and been translated into a half-dozen other languages.

At the request of Writer's Digest, who claimed they did a big study that revealed the need for it, Carol and I coauthored another book published in 2001 (this one hardcover) called *Get Organized, Get Published! 225 ways to make room for success.* It was and still is a super book, but after convincing us to write it, the publisher never did much to market it, perhaps because they were scaling down their writing book program by the time it came out.

All of these and many more still in the works were for the general public. For the more specialized market of my own profession, facility care and maintenance, I did four books: *The Professional Cleaner's Personal Handbook, How to Upgrade and Motivate Your Cleaning Crews,* and *Construction Cleanup,* in addition to the book I wrote earlier with Mark Browning, *Cleaning Up for a Living.* These have built and reinforced Varsity's credibility in the industry.

Another major writing partner, Sandra Phillips emerged in the late 1990s. One of my favorite book ideas, a manuscript called "Crossing the I Will Line," had such strong moral overtones that it did not fit easily with the broad-interest books I had mainly written up to now. Sandra Phillips and her husband, Dr. Reed Phillips, agreed to take the book and work on it. Dr. Phillips was in a responsible administrative position (president of Southern California University of Health Sciences) and Sandra for

An audio CD of dejunking seminar excerpts and songs produced with Sid and Alison Herron.

30 years had edited his written materials. A year and a half later, I got a call from Sandra and her husband, offering to meet me in Las Vegas and turn the book back to me.

It had been totally overhauled and re-titled *How Successful People Keep Their Lives Out of the Toilet.* I was impressed and offered to pay for the editing, but Sandra refused, saying, "just mention me in the acknowledgements." I suggested a different compromise—coauthoring the book, which we did. To date we have sold more than 6,000 copies. We've done several books together since, including *Don Aslett's Professional Cleaning System* (a nifty little instruction booklet to go with our cleaning equipment cart, see p. 456), and *Clean Break: Designs and Methods That Bring Order to Your Home.* Sandra has also made important contributions to others of my book and business projects.

Some of my older books are "born again"

In 2004, I was approached by a publisher in the Boston area (Adams Media, which had recently been acquired by my original publisher Writer's Digest). They wanted to update, redesign, and reissue some of my bestsellers, and retrofit them for the mass market (turn them into the smaller size books often sold in display racks). This could take my books to a whole new level of recognition and sales, they said. A top executive of the company flew to Pocatello and gave us the whole siren song, "We can get the Don Aslett books in the 'marts' and other places, and have a super, proven marketer on staff to do it!" Then I flew to their headquarters in Massachusetts and met with their management, editors, and designers, all of whom assured me the redone books would sell millions.

I said okay, and we agreed on seven books to be handled this way. I would also write one new one (my forty-second book)—*HELP! Around the House: A Mother's Guide to Getting the Family to Pitch in and Clean Up.* Having always disliked advances (although I took them when others such as Mark Browning and my daughter Laura were involved), I refused one for these, and took my staff off other projects to begin the revision process. A year and a half and more than $120,000 later (just for my staff and expenses, not counting my own time or the time and money Adams spent on this), we finished the eight books, all now 100 percent up to date. A handsome matching set in a new size, five and a half by eight inches, they also had new art, new layout, and new covers. Some were also re-titled.

Then we waited for the flood of sales. It was a long wait and finally from the first three released—my books with the best past sales records—a royalty check for $19,000 came, followed by a long silence

from the publisher. Many calls and emails later, we finally got a list of excuses, the leading one being "the bottom dropped out of the mass market exactly when your books came out." The returns are not all in on this experiment yet, but perhaps with some creative marketing on our part we can help to make this a worthwhile venture. So if you see a small paperback edition of one of my books somewhere, please buy one!

Once upon a flyleaf

Why autographings are such a popular part of book publicity remained a mystery throughout my writing career. I autographed thousands of books, but few of them at official "autographings." The imagined massive line at a bookstore to get an author's personal signature is a largely an illusion.

I was crushed when at my first five autograph parties, only about half a dozen people showed up to thumb through one of the 600 books stacked up around me. The majority of authors find themselves in the humiliating position at such events of waiting for a few people (if anyone) to show up. Too many of those who do appear hang around forever babbling and praising, but never buy a book. Even when I gave a free book with every book bought, or just for coming to the signing, few came. (Most of even those who *have* heard of you wouldn't miss their favorite TV program or fight traffic for a book.)

One memorable time, after $80 in cab fares, I arrived at an exclusive department store in a large mall outside of Washington, DC. I did a dynamic squeegee-waving demonstration for two hours and sold two books, one to the hardware salesperson next to me and the other to a perfume clerk across from me.

I was sent on autograph sessions from Maryland to California on another tour, and sold a grand total of 132 books. I spent over 300 hours getting to all of these places and being there for the appointed hours. My direct costs in this amounted to $250 per book sold. My publisher had about $30 in expenses for each book sold at autograph sessions of any

THE ASLETT CLASSICS, ADAMS EDITION.

kind. One well-known department store in Seattle ran a big ad in the paper for an autographing and we sold eleven books at $6.95, or a total profit of $22. They were overjoyed by the success of it. It only cost them $900 for the ad and other arrangements.

I did a quadruple header autographing session once in New Orleans (starring the great salesman Og Mandino, a sex therapist, a well-known politician, and me). All of us were popular writers and even had books on the bestseller list. The sponsor had spent $1,000 on ads for this event. I sold one book, Og sold two, and the politician one. The therapist never even got any book-buying foreplay.

I thought I must be a failure at this until I talked to other authors about it. They moaned and groaned and told me they'd never done a successful autographing, even for a bestseller. "We never sell many books at them—it's a dumb thing!" Salespeople for Prentice-Hall, Inc., told me that they set up an autographing once in Canada for Wayne Gretzky (the world famous hockey star) and not one single person showed up!

"Why do you keep doing autograph sessions, then?" I asked. "My publisher schedules them because they think other authors are making a go of them." It seemed we were all perpetuating a pointless pastime. Really now, why should anyone come to a boring autograph party to see an author sitting behind a shaky card table writing their name in a book where it has already been neatly printed at least ten times?

Getting rich from authorship

A comment I heard a lot over the years once my name and books started to really get out there: "Boy, you sure must be making money!"

One day when I heard this I said, "Yes, tomorrow I'm getting a royalty check for $40,000 for the last six months, and according to my calculations I've spent $38,500 of it already on new book ideas and their development, plus supporting the expansion that those $40,000 worth of book sales generated."

It can take a lot of fuel to run the big engine of imagination and accomplishment. While the money seemed to be rolling in, I was getting up early and thinking, planning, and writing, then into the office or onto the job for a long day's work, then an hour more of thinking and planning before I went to bed. During the day money flowed out like water for building rent and utilities, phones, new office machines, and other overhead. Almost every day memos, notes, artwork, printing, and shipping were being done, much of it never producing any income until years later, but necessary now. There were lots of people on the job, too—filing and typing, editing, researching, and helping me with my creations in other ways—and they all had to be tended, taught, and paid. Every day I had an office manager who worked furiously, as well. I had to make trips to stores, factories, and shops for new props and prop repair and modification, and trips to recording and TV studios and advertising agencies. I had to sit and listen to salespeople and promoters of all kinds with new ideas. Plus there was a constant need for correction, updating, and alteration, even on the second, third, and fourth printings of many of my publications, not to mention liability insurance in case you made a slip of the pen somewhere.

The cash flow of authorship is often "cash go."

My book pursuits had value beyond the royalties they earned and media attention they received. Because my books were based on our profession of cleaning and maintenance, I was selling "clean" to the country. Any attention they received stimulated inquiries about how building owners—and homeowners—could clean and care for their places faster, better, and cheaper. Varsity and I had the answers!

The cover of the Thai edition of *Who Says It's a Woman's Job to Clean?*

On the bookshelf in Bangkok!

Having my books published overseas was often in about the same league as cleaning a single phone booth across the border. My first publisher, Writer's Digest, sold *Is There Life After Housework?* to Exley publishers in England, and it sold big time there. Then they bought the rights to *Do I Dust or Vacuum First?* and *Clutter's Last Stand* as well. All of this made us money. I toured Great Britain doing media five times, and Australia once. They ended up selling at least 200,000 copies of my books, which for the U.K. at the time was phenomenal. These were also Writer's Digest's first foreign sales.

It was downhill after that from an economic standpoint. All kinds of other foreign editions of my books, with new covers and often new titles, too, began to appear. The Germans didn't like the title of "*Life,*" for instance, and changed it to *Polish with Your Brains,* and *Do*

I Dust or Vacuum First! became *How to Win at Housework* when it crossed the Atlantic. Eventually there were books with my byline in at least ten other countries. These foreign editions always impressed people, and you got a couple of free copies and a little prestige. But royalties rarely surpassed the cost of the stamps to find out how the books were doing there. We got a royalty check from India once for ten cents!

My own publishing company responded to foreign inquiries, even knowing it wouldn't mean much financially. We did it for the fun and adventure of it, and to see what the book would look like in another language. Foreign editions always made good displays for an office tour. It was also exciting to get international letters with their exotic stamps and cancellations. The letters often had a formality and politeness rarely seen here, using words like "humbly" never seen in U.S. business correspondence. Excessively polite requests are hard to turn down. A thousand-dollar advance, which is typical, converts into much less in foreign currency (if the bank ever does actually credit anything to your account after all the special filings and delays, discount rates, charges, and fees for foreign exchange).

Readers also write!

One of the big surprises I had, anticipating more free time when I got older and more established, was the growing necessity of response to calls and letters and now emails. When people take the time to write or call about my books or appearances, they deserve an answer. But this began to multiply into almost a full-time job. There is not a real fast way to respond to a personal, heartfelt

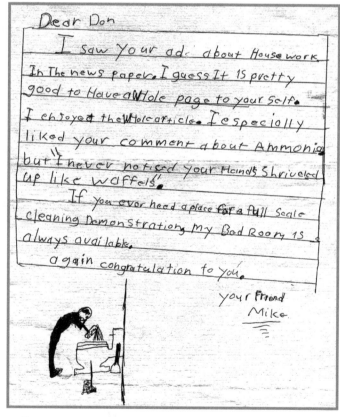

> Dear Don
>
> I saw Your ad about Housework In The news paper. I guess It is pretty good to Have a Whole page to your self. I enjoyed the Whole article. I especially liked your comment about Ammonia but "I never noticed your Hands Shriveled up like waffels".
>
> If you ever heed a place for a full Scale cleaning Demonstration, My Bed Room is always available.
>
> again congratulation to you.
>
> your Friend
> Mike

FAN MAIL WAS A CONSTANT SOURCE OF MOTIVATION. LETTERS LIKE THIS ONE TOUCHED THE HEART AND UPPED MY ENERGY LEVEL.

letter someone wrote. It needs to be read and answered. And then after I wrote a response someone else in the office had to type up my rough and mail it. And then the bad news—often when I could manage to write to someone personally, and send them a free book or whatever, I would get a longer return letter of thanks and more questions and comments. This almost made me despair.

In the late 1990s, I was averaging 20 books a week as gifts, plus personal letters written late at night or early in the morning. Because of Varsity work, I seldom took the time to do it during the day.

Typewriters don't crash

I used a manual typewriter for 20 years after electric typewriters and word processors arrived. I seldom looked up once I hunched over my 1969 Olympia typewriter. The pecking sound of this echoing through the office drove all of the computer converts insane, not so much the sound but the "stupidity" of someone (the big boss, no less) who would not switch to the latest form of automation.

BOOK NUMBER 21 IN PROGRESS, WORKING MY WAY FROM ROUGH NOTES TO MY OLD OLYMPIA MANUAL TYPEWRITER. SPREADING THINGS OUT ON THE FLOOR ALWAYS SEEMED TO SPEED UP ORGANIZATION AND INSPIRATION.

I had the same rationale as James Michener, who said he got up early and typed all of his books on a manual typewriter, and didn't worry about spelling or other fine points, just banged out his drafts.

For years, not realizing the positive side I guess, I listened to the moaning and groaning of office people losing things on their computers, suffering over corruption of some document, or trying deal with some software glitch. It drove me crazy as I pumped out pages and pages of crude but good work. My justification was that for me something didn't exist if it wasn't on a sheet of paper.

I finally laid the old aside when ribbons for manual typewriters became a special order item. Just hours before leaving my corporate office for an 18-month church mission in Boston, I let the office staff get me a laptop. I had two hours to learn to use it, and every colleague in the office crowded around showing me how to do shortcuts on this marvelous $3,000 machine. Later, I couldn't even remember how to turn it on. Fortunately, two of the young Mormon Elders in our mission area were computer geniuses so I learned not just to type but to type fast on a computer, although Bill Gates had to redesign spellcheck after I challenged it.

When I returned home, there was a top-of-the-line computer set up in my office, ready to go, my old manual having been moved to our museum—see p. 452. Today, in my prime of production, writing several books a year and overseeing five businesses as well as personal, church, and community projects, I don't personally use the Internet or do email (my staff runs it off for me). My computer still does one job only—it types.

An author's evolution

Ninety percent of my visibility was from cleaning—that was my profession, my best-known skill and the cornerstone of my credibility. But my real passion was teaching (in person or via the written word) and entertaining—I loved motivating people to change their lives for the better. Cleaning was one path into people's lives, but not the only one. The crop that brought my best harvest was books about cleaning, which all of my first ones were. The extension of cleaning was decluttering, and one aspect of that was time management. Time management was part of personal organization, which was part of personal behavior—including ways to live a more satisfying life. This gradual evolution of my subject matter not only broadened my insight and background for speaking and writing, but also led to opportunities to collect yet more information and experience.

I'm at the point now where only about 60 percent of my writing output is directly connected to cleaning. Offshoots of cleaning have moved me further into design of the homes we are cleaning, and inventions that go inside of those homes. I am also doing books on recapturing the joy of life, on writing, business, and all kinds of management. If you can succeed in one of the most competitive businesses in the world, cleaning, you might have something to offer in other fields.

> FOR THOSE IMPRESSED WITH MY
> WRITING OUTPUT, DON'T BE.
> I'M NOT THAT SMART, JUST MORE
> FAITHFUL ABOUT TAKING AND
> ASSIMILATING NOTES THAN THE
> NEXT PERSON, AND I HAVE
> A STRONG STAFF THAT
> PLUGS THE GAPS AND
> BACKSTOPS MY CARELESSNESS.

Right now I have more books in rough draft on my "writing to do" shelf than I have on the "done and published" shelf. If I live long enough, I intend to produce another two dozen or more books, to add to the 3 million copies of my titles sold so far.

Some often-quoted parts of my books:

> *You are entitled to a life of love, fulfillment, and accomplishment, but these rewards are almost impossible to obtain if you spend your life thrashing in a muddle of housework. Time—the time to love, to be, and to grow— is the most precious commodity on earth. No one's time should be wasted cleaning needlessly or inefficiently.*
>
> *A house is to live in, not for.*
>
> *The only things in life that really count are loving and being loved. Don't love what can't love you back.*
>
> *Life truly begins when you discover how flexible and free you are without clutter.*

The real reward of authorship

What kept me going and focused with my pen and paper were comments, clips, and letters like these:

"...Aslett turned a dull, dirty subject into delightful reading."
—Alyse Lounsberry, Ocala Star-Banner

"If he ever decided to get out of his lucrative housecleaning profession, he probably would manage very nicely on his writing style— smooth prose intermingled with lively humor."
—Harmon Bellamy

"No matter what else I look at, I am always reading a magnificent book about how to win freedom from clutter. It is written by an American called Don Aslett who should win a Pulitzer, a Booker, and a Nobel Prize, as well as being canonized in his own lifetime. The Secret of How to Win Freedom from Clutter *is the most challenging thing I have ever read. This man should run the world."*
—Maeve Binchy, London Daily Mail

"The book has big print, cornball headlines, imbecilic Mad *magazine-quality illustrations; but I finally started reading it. Hostilely, begrudgingly, and then I ended up hooked, and cheering."*
—Anne Lamont, reviewing Not for Packrats Only
  for Mademoiselle

"The pages of Aslett's book hold a well-balanced blend of humor, anecdotes, and 'how-to,' but one pure, simple message shines through: Time saved on housework can be used for more meaningful and enjoyable pursuits!"
—Idaho State Journal

*"Don Aslett, I love you!
(My husband knows!)"*

"Dear Don, Your two books, How to Handle 1,000 Things at
Once, *and* How to Have a 48-Hour Day, *have helped me to
triple the amount of things I can accomplish in a day!"*

"You have changed my life, Don Aslett!"

*"Dear Don, My friends and I really appreciate your anti-clutter
'Bible.' It would be our choice of book to take to a desert island
if we were castaways—along with Shakespeare and the Bible!"*

*"How could you possibly have written this book—
it's MY life story!"*

*"I was a clutterbug in the highest, most cluttered, most
catastrophic sense. I kept everything out of fear. And then
I read your book—your warm humor, your love—and I
was sold—on life—a new life of happy uncluttered
clean homemaking. I feel so free!*

*"I'm sure you hear this all the time. You saved my life,
or at least my sanity, and possibly my marriage."*

*"I cannot begin to tell you the difference
your books have made in my life."*

"I just finished reading your delightful Clutter's Last Stand, *which should be called* Swami Aslett's Guide to Enlightenment. *Your Mark Twain folksiness and Will Rogers delivery thinly disguise the wisdom of a prophet."*

"I hope your book made you a million dollars. It made me wealthy. My wealth being freedom—freedom from stuff!"

"Don Aslett, Author of Clutter's Last Stand: *YOUR BOOK IS FANTASTIC! I love it! I'm still laughing!"*

"I confess, I'm addicted. Don't stop the presses. Please continue to author. This Aslett-addict will need a fix down the road."

BESIDE THE BOOK AND VIDEO SECTION IN ONE OF MY CLEANING CENTER STORES.

Chapter 16

CLEANING AS ENTERTAINMENT

My "Life After Housework" seminars and other live appearances

My three-hour "Life After Housework" seminars were an athletic undertaking from beginning to end. Here I am demonstrating the superiority of the "ladder, plank, and box" system for reaching high places to clean.

I explained earlier how my "Life After Housework" seminars developed from a presentation I did for a church group in 1977 at Barbara's request. For about 15 years these high-energy, humor-filled, live "cleaning concerts" were a strong staple of my public appearances. They showed us the market for books, sold books and products, helped me to gain a national presence, allowed me to refine my humorous "cleaning routines," and gave valuable feedback on people's cleaning questions and needs. At the height of my seminar era, I was doing three or four of these a week.

Starting with a bang

No matter what their homes were like, people never wanted a famous professional cleaner to come inside. This made a great opener for my seminars. Several hundred women and a few men would show up to learn how to clean house faster and better, and I'd walk out on stage and shout, "Well, how did your house look when you left?" This always got a big response and a lot of laughs. I had their full attention.

When I did a seminar in the small town of Hooper, Utah, instead of the host walking on stage and reading the usual brief introduction, four women dressed in exaggerated housework attire bounced onto the stage. A piano rolled out with the familiar melody "Mr. Sandman," and—wow!—could those four sing, in perfect harmony, as good as the original Andrews Sisters recording.

This went over so well with the audience that we suggested to other seminar sponsors that they use music to introduce the event, and in the next several years, dozens of different groups thought up clever musical introductions for my appearances. Many of these were done so well that they upstaged me. Here's just a sample from my file:

"MR. ASLETT, TEACH ME TO CLEAN
BRING DOWN THE COBWEBS
MAKE MY WINDOWS GLEAM.
TEACH ME YOUR TRICKS
SO I'LL ENJOY IT.
BUT CAN I LIKE TO CLEAN A DIRTY TOILET?
ASLETT, I'M A MESS.
IT'S BOUND TO RUIN MY HAPPINESS.
SO PLEASE COME ON AND DO YOUR THING.
MR. ASLETT, TEACH ME TO CLEAN!"
—ORIGINAL LYRICS ADAPTED BY CAMILLE MEYERS

"I've Been Doing All the Housework" to the tune of "I've Been Working on the Railroad." In Alberta, Canada, they did "I'd Like to Teach the World to Clean." Then there was the "Queen of the House" version of "King of the Road." I even heard Gene Autry's old "Back in the Saddle Again" turned into "Back in the Restroom Again."

To make cleaning attractive to any audience or media (even my fellow professionals), I learned to use humor—not just make a joke or two, but non-stop, visual and hilarious humor. The most frequent comment I got following a presentation was, "Man, Don, you should be a standup comedian!" I never used other people's jokes or routines. I just pulled the funny realities and incongruities out of our day-to-day lives and cleaning activities.

Don Aslett, popular lecturer on housework, demonstrates use of extension handle for outdoor window cleaning.

Photo by Libby Frech

Move over, Mr. Clean — here comes successor

BY LIBBY FRECH   Church News correspondent

CINCINNATI, OHIO

Move over, Mr. Clean! Look out white tornado! A former bishop is sweeping the nation with the philosophy that there is life after housework.

"Home is the power lever to the world," says Don Aslett of the McCammon Ward, Arimo Idaho Stake, to radio and television audiences as he travels the nation conducting three-hour housecleaning seminars. He recently conducted one in Cincinnati.

Aslett, energetic entrepreneur of a large building maintenance firm, is also a public speaker, consultant, writer, book author, and "janitor." Admitting to the last occupation, he believes, is his key to success in motivating homemakers.

"There's only one other word besides janitor that will make people stop in silence when they ask about your career, and that's housewife. People seem to have a low image of housecleaning and housewives, but I believe that image can be changed," he said.

Several years ago his wife, Barbara, the ward Relief Society president, asked him to prepare a mini-course on housecleaning. His rapid fire delivery of professional housecleaning tips mixed with humor was so successful that he has since presented more than 100 free seminars.

As his popularity increased requests came in for his written word. He obliged by publishing a book, "Is There Life After Housework?" which was given its name by Gladys Allen, West Jordan, Utah. Writer's Digest re-published the book recently under the same title and it is available throughout the country. It will soon be published in Great Britain and Australia.

NICELY ILLUSTRATED ARTICLES, LIKE THIS ONE BY LIBBY FRECH, LENT SOME MOMENTUM TO MY SEMINARS' POPULARITY.

"YOU PUT ERMA BOMBECK TO SHAME."

"FANTASTIC! I LAUGHED ALL MY MAKEUP OFF!"

"'I was giving one of my housecleaning seminars in Caesar's Palace,' said Don Aslett, the millionaire janitor from Pocatello, Idaho. 'There was a elephant riding a bicycle on one side of me and a nude dancer on the other, and they liked me best.'

If you've seen Don Aslett in action, you'll have no trouble believing that."

—Clarence Petersen, Chicago Tribune

"His seminars, like his books, are laced with humor and he keeps his audiences entertained as he scrubs and squeegees his way through common chores in his three-piece suit."

—Los Alamos Monitor

"Seeing Don Aslett in action on TV or at one of his 'Life After Housework' seminars can have you laughing hysterically one minute and nodding your head in agreement the next, all the while envying his never-ending energy as he jumps from spot to spot, scrubbing miniature walls and windows."

—Lincoln County Journal

One of my early seminars was filmed, and for the first time in my life, I was on TV. When I saw myself on television the only thing I could say was, "Gadfrey, they must have the TV on fast forward!" My kids said, "No, Dad, that's just the way you move around up there." I looked like a speeded-up jackrabbit.

One day after one of my early seminars, I ran down to the supermarket to pick up a dustpan so I could show my audiences how to pick up water with it instead of using a mop. There was a long line at the checkout and one man, seeing only the dustpan in my hand, said, "Why don't you go ahead of me, Sir?" I accepted gratefully and to speed my way through the line, I counted out the exact amount due for the pan in nickels, dimes, and pennies and placed it in the pan. Then with great showmanship I poured the money into the cashier's hand, much to the delight of the rest of the line. Someone near the back recognized me, pointed, and in a loud voice said, "Hey, you're Don Aslett, aren't you?" Several other people in the line nodded and smiled.

My first official public recognition! I clutched the dustpan as I imagined Elvis would have his guitar, and quickly admitted, "Yes, I am." I quickly pointed out that the inexpensive dustpan I had just purchased was capable of saving three mop buckets of water and several mops, and would save hours of time when stripping and waxing floors. They all applauded, and the only thing that could have made things better was being asked to autograph a box of cereal or can of tuna fish.

THIS NEWSPAPER SNIPPET SHOWS AN ENTHUSIASTIC
VOLUNTEER FROM THE AUDIENCE
HELPING OUT DURING A SEMINAR.

Hustle! Hustle!

Guess I learned it playing ball. To make up for lack of size, coordination, or skill, I ran harder, moved faster, and even began to talk faster. As my mind raced ahead of what I was saying, I was also notorious for half-sentences, jumping from one subject to another, leaving out words, etc. My rapid-fire approach to seminar presentations could sometimes be as frustrating to the audience as trying to condense 25 years of janitorial experience into three hours was for me.

One woman wrote me a letter explaining that after two and a half hours of trying to listen to my high-speed delivery, she got a headache, got totally frustrated, and decided to go back home to her ten kids. It beat listening to me. She suggested that seeing a speech therapist might help me to slow down. Another time in Omaha, a woman walked out of the hall and said, "Have I been sleeping in there? He is on one subject and suddenly on another. I think I must have been dozing." She hadn't.

One woman, in tears, was comforted by another who had attended an earlier seminar and recorded it. "Don't worry," she said, "I took the recording home and played it on worn-out batteries and it came out just right!" Southerners seemed to have the most trouble, since they usually talk slooooow. It often took awhile for them to get a question asked. "Mr. Azslett... what do you do with all the flaws?" "The what?" "The flaws," the woman would slowly drawl out. "Flaws in what?" I'd ask back. "The flaws—you know, the flaws you walk on." "Oh, you mean the floors!" Another would ask, "Mr. Azslett, how do y'all stop 'raid mood?'" "Is that a roach killer?" I'd ask. "Noooo—'raid mood.'" With the help of an interpreter, I found out she meant "red mud."

The height of confusion came when I did a seminar in Twin Falls, Idaho. In the audience were two young deaf women and their sign language translator. Her hands were almost a blur trying to keep up with me, and when my words and sound effects were things like "geepee-geepee-geepee," "twinky," "el gunko," or "scrubbee-scrub-scrub," she would glance at me in desperation. Meanwhile the two women she was translating for laughed and their eyes sparkled, so I figured they must have been gaining something from it all. The weary translator trudged up to me afterward and awarded me and my subject matter the honor of being the most difficult ever to sign.

A real turning point came when we had a seminar scheduled at Randolph, Utah, a small town bordering Wyoming. I had the usual show gear packed in the car and a case or two of my self-published book, *Is There Life After Housework?* Barbara and my son Grant had both previously suggested that I should listen to the audience and start selling some of the pro supplies that I featured in my presentation and recommended in my book. I said that I wouldn't be caught dead being a supply peddler—that I was an author, not a pitchman.

Ignoring my protests, they loaded dozens of professional brass squeegees and a few other items into the van and set them up on a table in back of the room a few feet from my book sales table. When my cleaning show was over, I rushed back to my book table to help with the mob of bookbuyers. None came. They were all crowding and milling around the squeegee table, waving money at Grant and Barbara. I ended up selling $160 worth of books at this show, but they sold $2,000 worth of professional equipment. From then on, we always took supplies too and sure enough, they sold like crazy. There was not enough room in our truck or car anymore, especially since I'd built an 8-by-12-foot portable fold-up house that I used in my cleaning demos. So we bought a mid-sized motor home and removed the kitchen and toilet from it, leaving the foldout couch so we could take turns resting during all-night drives.

> Someone commented today that they thought the long line in the mall parking lot must be for an X-rated movie. It was just Barbara selling cleaning supplies out of the back of our motor home.

I was now in the league of the touring entertainers, the stars who go from city to city in their own bus doing gigs. We did hundreds of seminars, mostly in California, Utah, and other Western states—at schools, churches, community centers, and hotels. I did them mostly free—we made our money selling books and supplies. We had a precision family system in the summers when school was out. Once we had three or four seminars scheduled, we would plot our route and load the motor home with all of the books and cleaning gear it would hold. (We even took suitcases if there was room.) Barbara and I and two or more of our kids would leave at five in the morning to get to California by five-thirty that evening (for a seven o'clock Friday show). We'd drive into the lot of the location and I'd unload my props and set them up on stage. Barbara and the kids would set up two or three tables in the back and lay out our wares.

AT THE END OF EVERY SEMINAR THERE WAS BOOK-BUYING, AUTOGRAPHING... AND MORE QUESTIONS ABOUT CLEANING.

I'd end the three-hour seminar with a humorous account of my adventures carrying a toilet suitcase (see p. 381). Afterward there would be a rush to the tables in the back. Within 45 minutes, the place was empty, and there were empty boxes all over. We would sell $2,000-$3,500 worth of products a night (one night we sold $7,200 worth). I paid the kids $30 each for selling, and helping mothers in the audience soothe their crying babies. Then we'd load up the props and leftovers and drive all night to the next city or state, and set up for the Saturday morning show (the one with the biggest crowds), and then another one that evening. And so on, until it was time to drive the 600-plus miles home. It was exhausting but fun. Barbara and the kids were magic behind a table selling—they had it down to a science. My four daughters didn't always appreciate it, though, when I made them wear gingham dresses to match the cover of my first edition of *Is There Life After Housework*! (They were willing, however, to forget their fashion objections for a little cold cash.)

We passed out "comment cards" at the seminars, collecting home cleaning data, and eventually had more than 150,000, filled with fresh facts and insights from the home front. Before you know it, our motor home had 200,000 miles on it.

IN THE MORE THAN 100,000 "COMMENT CARDS" WE COLLECTED FROM SEMINAR AUDIENCES, THERE WERE SOME GREAT COMMENTS. SOME PEOPLE ARE REALLY DETERMINED (OR DESPERATE) TO CLEAN THINGS UP!

My unwillingness to stop perfectly good progress to eat was often exaggerated by others. I just could never see breaking stride when you were on a roll, just to eat. On one of our marathon motor-home trips where bathroom and meal breaks were pegged to the odometer, we stopped after 500 miles. As we studied the menus, someone at the table quipped, "Before I order, I want to know. How many meals are we eating for?"

Even a cleaner from Idaho could grab some share of respect from adults. Children, good for them, don't take fame or celebrity at face value, and are not impressed by wealth or big names. Proof of this occurred in Willard, Missouri.

When I showed up to do a seminar here three women met me and said there was no hotel or motel in town, so the whole church got together and drew straws. The short straw got me. A red-haired mother of six, Mrs. Harris, drew it. She was terrified to have "America's #1 Cleaning Expert" staying at her home. When I got there, there wasn't a live germ anywhere. They'd even cleaned inside the faucets!

The seminar was at a school, there was a big crowd, and my hostess (assigned to this before the great straw-drawing) Mrs. Harris now had the job of introducing me. Halfway through her introduction she stumbled a bit, trying to tell about me, and a few titters and guffaws issued from the audience. Near tears now, in a loud voice she burst out, "Well, if you think it's so funny you ought to have him staying at your house!" The crowd roared and I was on.

That evening at her home (she had made several calls to my secretary to find out my favorite everything), she served a terrific dinner including a raspberry dessert I would have sold my birthright for! She pointed out a spacious bedroom afterward and said goodnight. I sighed and got ready to crawl into that big, lovely bed. But no matter how I tried, I couldn't get into it and couldn't figure out why. I was 48 years old, and had heard about "short-sheeted" beds, but the real thing was intriguing to the point of frustration. Finally I had to dismantle "the perfect bed."

A SEMINAR UNDER THE BIG TOP—THE HOME AND FARM PROGRESS SHOW.

Next morning (Saturday), I came down for breakfast and all the kids were in suits and ties and dresses for me. Mrs. Harris, still a little nervous, was surely counting the minutes till my exit. She politely asked me how I'd slept. "Fine, " I said. Then the little four-year-old piped up, "Was it hard to get into bed?" Sister Harris' face turned red—she knew immediately what they had done. I left cheerfully, but I'll bet those kids got a long, long lesson in bed making.

"That ain't him!"

When it came to opportunities to teach cleaning, the bigger the group, the better. We had a call one day from an agricultural group in Indiana who put on a "Home and Farm Progress Show" with up to 150,000 attending over a six-day period. This would be a paid performance, and the prospects of selling books and cleaning products were also promising. It was 1,700 miles away—not bad with three driving.

This was not the same old show. When we arrived it wasn't downtown, or at a convention center or even a fairgrounds. It was 15 miles out in the farm fields, not even close to any major or small town. The show people had rented someone's entire farm, 200 to 300 acres, and set up tents, booths, and farm equipment displays all over the place. This included corrals, new cars and tractors, and of course portable eating places. It was like a huge dusty beehive. They directed our vehicles (small van and motor home) to a large yellow and white tent, and this was where I performed—capacity 600 people at a time. There were birds and bees all around and plenty of noise. On one side of me was a John Deere tractor drag race, on the other a rip-snorting "hog downs." Yes, a pig racing track—they were using Oreos to tempt the pigs to outrun each other. Fifty feet behind me was Rex Allen yodeling cowboy songs. Add some wind whipping the tent canvas, the hubbub of the passing crowd, and booth barkers selling everything from vegetable cutters to post drivers. It was a great experience with big crowds of appreciative people. A high point of the event came when I was taken back to the hotel at sunset. President Bush (George H. W.) was scheduled for a visit there. In the back seat of a limo with my shirtsleeves rolled up, I was briefly mistaken for the President. I had instant respect, until someone finally yelled out, "That ain't him!"

One foot in the toilet bowl

"How many of you have a ring in your toilet?" was a question that always got a lot of raised hands from my eager cleaning audiences. "Well don't worry, folks, there is nothing wrong with you—this is caused by the water in the bowl evaporating and the remaining minerals sticking to the side of the bowl." They would nod understandingly. This was now my big moment—I'd show them the professional secret for the sturdy old-style porcelain bowls, the wonderful, feather light, safe, and effective pumice stone.

I held it up like a Babe Ruth candy bar as I sang its praises and then did a demo with it, using it to remove a toilet ring. I did this for about a year, and one night in Hawaii, a little Japanese woman raised her hand. "Mr. Aslett, can you use these on your feet?" Believe this or not, though I was a farm boy and probably had plenty of corns and calluses I had never seen or heard of pumice used to remove them. So when she asked this question I assumed maybe she was a little finicky about putting her hand in the toilet and wanted to somehow use the pumice with her foot. So I tried to explain how she might do this with one foot in the toilet, with the pumice fastened to her foot. I thought I was giving a serious answer to a question, but she thought I was making fun of her, and the audience thought the whole thing was hilarious.

Several in the audience finally shouted out, "No, Mr. Aslett, she wants to use the pumice *on* her foot!" "I know," I said, and continued to explain that sticking your foot in the toilet was no better or easier than sticking your hand in the toilet. By now the place was in an uproar and people were showing me their feet and gesturing wildly—I told them that a pumice bar would probably fit any foot. Someone yelled out, "Corns and calluses!" and I said that I doubted the pumice would be on there long enough to cause them. Anyway, it was like a ten-minute game of ring around the conversation, and I felt like I ought to crawl into the toilet myself when I finally realized what was up. I did recover slightly by darting down into the audience and giving the woman a pumice bar—for both her feet and under the toilet seat!

> Consistent, energetic performances were not the only necessity on the seminar circuit. Driving all night in Western weather and landscape to make it home or to the next performance site could be as taxing as the show itself. Even rested, and in daylight, I was not the world's best driver. But Barbara was rarely intimidated by time, distance, weather, or road conditions. When I collapsed in a worthless heap after stepping off the stage, she piloted our loaded motor home smoothly to the next destination, without incident.

We were on a seminar trip and I'd done one the night before in Blanding, Utah. It was Valentine's Day and we were getting ourselves ready for a long motor home trip to another show the next night. There was a knock on the door, and when my wife and son opened it, in streamed 16 bubbling, enthusiastic women with trays of valentine cookies, thanking me for the show. We could hardly get them to leave! My wife turned to me and quipped, "Well, every man's dream—seventeen women in your motel room and it's legal!"

My own video!

Chris Harding from Bonneville International came to one of my "Life After Housework" seminars one day, and intrigued by my style of teaching a serious subject with a heavy dose of humor, later proposed filming the three-hour "spectacle."

Bonneville was a high-end media operation that produced a quality product, so I agreed to what proved to be a good offer. They built a super set for the production, helped me assemble and engineer my props, and then we invited a couple of hundred fans for the audience, and filmed for two days in Salt Lake City. I did the same presentation both days, giving them plenty of footage to edit. I was told by the director and camera crew that I was extra-difficult to film—I talked too fast, moved too fast, held visuals up too briefly, etc. We ended up with four cameras and my son, who knew all my seminar moves in the control room, telling them when I was about to leap, jump, or dash into the audience.

Bonneville had my own theme music written for me, and the editing and packaging of the tape was reported to cost about $85,000. The presentation, boiled down from three hours to 95 minutes, turned out well—kids and even some adults would watch it over and over. I later purchased the tape from Bonneville and folded it into our book-marketing program. It is still popular today (though I looked a little different at 49 than I do at 70).

The first two or three years on the seminar circuit my books were new, seminars were sponsored by well-organized church or community groups, and the crowds were 300 to 700 deep—everywhere! I got used to enthusiastic attendance and lots of buying of books and prod-

Don Aslett

Live

in

ST. LOUIS
at Maryville College

Don't miss his hilarious

Is There Life After Housework? Seminar

Thursday, Oct. 25, 1990
7:00 p.m.
Maryville College
Library Auditorium
13550 Conway Rd.
St. Louis, MO
Tickets $5
contact: Tom Young
1-800-727-1685
314-432-4600

Learn how:
- To prevent Housework
- Professional methods cut 75% of your housework time
- To clean your bathroom in 3 1/2 minutes!
- To get help from your family

See you at the show!

ucts. Then in the early 1990s the bubble burst. My performance had only improved with time, and I had more and better books and more national and local publicity than ever, but the crowds were smaller. This was happening to other live performers, too, but I was sure at first that it was because their performances weren't up to the standards of my "clean humor" act. I was wrong. We did more advertising than ever before, and still got fewer attendees. Was it people's ever-busier lives, or all those VCRs and home movies hitting the market? More choices in entertainment? People just staying home more?

In any case, it was an agony now, traveling hundreds or thousands of miles, renting huge auditoriums, spending plenty on publicity and then waiting at the door as the starting time drew near and seeing people come slowly in ones and twos. This didn't let up and neither did I. The worse attendance was, the more determined I got. We'd travel to every type of town and gathering, but places that used to turn out 250 to 300 excited people suddenly had no one! At one seminar in Bountiful, Utah, where previously more than 700 attended, I had a crew of six setting up props and tables, and two people showed up, a mother and daughter who never cracked a smile!

Nothing is more work, more intense than performing for a crowd. Even if you love it and make beaucoup bucks doing it, it ravishes your strength and energy and *bleeds* you. When you build yourself up for a big crowd and draw a low attendance, it still takes the same toll. It was hard to go on stage like a raving lunatic for three hours for 15 or 20 people. I did this for three years before admitting that few people wanted to spend time and money this particular way any more. About the seventy-fifth time no crowd showed up, I finally got the message. I hated to give in then; now I can't believe I didn't face up to it sooner.

I not only did seminars "live," but also many workshops and speeches. My workshop presentations alone, many of these for conventions and conferences, numbered into the hundreds. At some events, I'd do three to five sessions per day. After the first several, it can be hard to remember what you said or did in the earlier sessions, so repeating or retelling the same story was a common and embarrassing event.

Professional speaking came about so gradually I never realized I actually was a pro speaker until one day I saw it listed in a newspaper article. From high school on, I presented talks of all kinds for churches, Scouting events, community gatherings, and training seminars and sales meetings in my companies, all of this being part of life and of running a business. Most of my first speeches and seminars were free, and I sold books afterward for income. Then one group offered to pay my travel, food, and lodging expenses to come and address and inspire their workers, and others began to ask what I charged to come and speak. So I found myself speaking for $100, $500, then $1,000, then $2,000 and more. Although I had never really planned to do it, speaking became one of my favorite pastimes. Its very personal and independent nature made speeches pleasant to prepare and present, and the long-distance traveling often involved was the only negative. Humor (even more so than information) seemed to be my draw. I've been complimented more often in the course of my life for being a "wise guy" than a wise man.

The compensation I received for speaking was not always an agreed-upon fee—there were more creative compensations often representative of the group I addressed. For my many donated speeches, especially, I often received things like coats, hats, shirts, gloves, pens, pocketknives, shovels, cookbooks, aprons, quilts, trees, plaques and certificates (hundreds!), paintings, and sculptures. There have been plenty of foodstuffs, too, from a gallon of Vermont cider to apple butter and maple syrup, raspberries, and sacks of apples and potatoes, to a loaf of homemade 100 percent whole wheat bread. I've received kisses and hugs, antique washers and 1930 ironing machines, a pallet of Portland cement, a deed for a few inches of Montana property, and for speaking at a Nike convention in Philadelphia, 30 pairs of running shoes!

During this whole time I was still the controlling owner of, and active in the growing Varsity Contractors operation—books and seminars were kind of a fun side activity for me and the family, full of adventure and travel, which the kids loved. I think because of the togetherness Barbara really enjoyed them, too. We had some memorable experiences!

One day I received a request from a Bureau of Indian Affairs (BIA) agent who decided my ability to teach and inspire housework skill would benefit the Native Americans living on the Fort Hall Indian Reservation not far from Pocatello. I accepted, and showed up with my squeegees, sponges, mini-house prop.

Teaching Native Americans for the first time was a surprising experience—not until years later, working with them and having some live in our home as foster children, did I understand their temperament and culture, humor and spiritual insight. That day in a crowded conference room (the white administrators had rounded up all of the available Shoshone and Blackfoot from teepee and tract home), most of them had no idea what this paleface powwow was about or why they had been herded into this room.

At the very front, eight feet from my model demo house on the stage, sat a row of the most perfect pureblood Native American grandmothers I'd ever seen. Their dark, wrinkled faces mapped 75 to 90 years of dignity. They were handsome and noble-looking women, but remained entirely expressionless during my entire rip-roaring clean-ing snake oil show. There was not a movement or reaction from one of them the whole time. I could feel their eyes on me, but what they were thinking was impossible to tell. My best and funniest stories and examples, which normally sent crowds into hysterics, got zero reac-tion. I was sure they spoke or understood no English. During my long and unrewarding delivery of the gospel of cleaning, only once or twice did I catch a flicker of a smile from one of the younger and more mod-ern-looking women. A husky Native American attendee came up to me politely afterward and said, "You are good, white man, but you try too damn hard."

Top the American Mothers!

Being paid to speak is a strange experience. At first, you speak for nothing and usually have to, in your early years. Then suddenly people are willing to furnish you a plane ticket across the continent, and pay you a thousand or more dollars to speak for an hour.

My secretary Nancy was tough on fees. I hated to even charge, so we compromised and our fee schedule ran from zero to $8,500 (for a home show). Who do you donate to? Many organizations have some charitable aspect, and many business appearances have some spin-off value. A hard and fast policy didn't seem to cut it, so we did it by feel. What would you do if a nervous, squeaky-voiced president of the senior class called asking you to speak at their graduation—a total of eight students, and a six-hour drive on your only day off of the month? "Yes, of course," I told him. Being a giver, not a taker, had built an empire, so why change a policy that worked?

American Mothers, Inc., a little-known organization that produces our "Mothers of the Year," called one day for me to speak at their fifti-eth convention, to be held in the Waldorf-Astoria Hotel in New York. I was in a cash flow bind right then and needed paying work, not praise or motherly patting on the back, but how could anyone turn down the American Mothers? Phyllis Marriott (of the famous hotel family) as-sured us I was lucky for the privilege of addressing their elite group, rep-resenting all states of the U.S.

And so I did it on a Saturday evening following a busy week of nine other presentations and a "Life After Housework" seminar the night before. I got up at four-thirty in the morning, my son Grant drove me to the airport in Salt Lake City, and by three o'clock that afternoon, I was setting up my gear in the Waldorf-Astoria. Norman Vincent Peale was one of the other speakers and I wanted to outshine him. Three hun-dred of the most impressive women in the U.S. were there, seated at fancy table settings for the most elegant $48-per-plate dinner I had ever seen. The previous speeches had all been on serious themes, but when I got up, along with my humorous information and inspiration, they got squirted by my tiny toilet; I even jumped up on the embroidered tablecloth and sat my toilet suitcase down on it so I could read the *Wall Street Journal* there. Afterward, when a crowd of glowing mothers led me to the main lobby of the Waldorf to pose with me and my toilet suitcase, the Friars Club roasting Milton Berle in the next room took second to our excitement.

This trip to New York was an unforgettable experience, and over 40 profitable new opportunities came from that single speech.

My time in prison

A temporary receptionist we had for a week once, poked her head in the office and asked if I would be interested in speaking at a women's prison. She quickly assured me that I would enjoy it and the women there would really appreciate it. My usual eagerness for new experience prompted a "yes" out of me, and a week later I found myself being checked through prison security and ushered into a room of about 70 prisoners who qualified for this education session. All were in orange jumpsuits, and clapped enthusiastically when I was introduced and then leaned forward to listen.

I had one hour to speak, and it proved to be the best hour I'd spent in years. I expected a somber, negative, low-response crowd, but this was one of the sharpest groups of people I'd ever taught. Their sense of humor was astounding, so I got funnier yet in my organization and cleaning demos and soon many were in tears of laughter. I awarded toilet earrings, toilet erasers, and some books for good answers to the questions I posed and were they motivated! I felt a flood of love and respect for them—they were intelligent, attractive, and most of all appreciative. When the bell for dismissal rang, they all shouted, "No, no! Let us stay!" I think it was the first time the prison ever had an educational lecture that the prisoners weren't glad was over.

The administrators and guards had a brief conference and because it was only 8:30 in the evening they let me go on for another hour, and it only got better. Boy did it feel good to make a difference in how those women felt. They clapped and walked up and thanked me graciously. I replayed that experience in my mind many times in the next six months, at which time Idaho State University asked me to develop and teach a professional cleaning training course that would be televised into all of the state's prisons.

"Your stories and terrific sense of humor brought the gift of laughter to a whole room full of women who needed it desperately. A good laugh is worth way more than money in here."
—Dana J. Kobe, after I spoke at an Idaho prison

The identity advantage

No matter how well educated or well known we might be, we cleaners are usually the last and least on budgets, banquet lists, and banners. When I spoke at conventions, for instance, I got $1,500 a talk while the name brand public figure talking before or after me often got $15,000. This annoyed me, until the day I discovered my lowly profession had its up side. I was one of five people doing workshops on self-esteem, motivation, and success—all that "rah, rah, you can do it" stuff. The speakers included an astronaut, a famous entertainer, a senator, a well-known doctor, and me, the janitor. After the keynote speech the 500 attendees at this conference headed out to the sessions. My first class was slow to fill; I only had 50 or so. The second hour I had 150, and the third hour 250. The last hour I had most of them and the other presenters had only a handful.

Was I that good? Nope, it was an identity thing. Deep down inside few of the attendees really believed they could be a doctor, senator, entertainer, or astronaut. I was more believable and convincing because all knew they could be a janitor and here was one telling them they could do that and also write 40 books, make millions, be on Oprah, etc. "Gee, if that guy can do it, then so can I!"

ALTHOUGH I WAS A JANITOR, WITH THE LEAST PRESTIGE OF ALL THE SPEAKERS AT THE START OF CONVENTIONS AND WORKSHOPS, THE RESPONSE BY THE END WAS USUALLY LIKE THIS COMMENT FROM THE ASSOCIATED HOSPITALITY MANAGERS OF WASHINGTON. HUMOR AND HIGH ENERGY CAN GIVE YOU AN EDGE.

Don - earned the highest rating of all speakers -

They called me . . . the Toilet Man

"The Alaskan school system calling for you, Don." I hit the line four button and the superintendent of schools of the Delta District was indeed on the other end of the phone. "We'd like to retain you as a consultant to come here and give us some direction on our cleaning program." After a ten-minute discussion, we had a deal. Just before I hung up I asked, "Hey, can I do a couple of assemblies for the kids while I'm there?" A big silence followed. "What kind of assembly?" was his surprised reply. "A cleaning assembly," I said exuberantly—another silence. "Janitor's honor," I said, "it'll be super." Finally, "Okay." (I knew by now that when it comes to cleaning problems in schools, everyone blames the janitors, but we seldom attempt to correct the real cause—the building users' attitude.)

Grade school blood flowed again in my veins. Assemblies were the highlight of school for me—singers, jugglers, hypnotists, magicians, animal acts, firefighters, police officers—I loved them all. And now I was going to be on that stage! I hadn't the slightest idea yet what I would do when I got up there, but I knew once I committed, ideas would come.

It was Alaska's below-zero time, mid-January, when I showed up to do the job. First I spoke to the board and the school administration, then they led me to an elementary school. Into the auditorium poured 400 kids from kindergarten to sixth grade, just teeming for some tidbits from the toilet cleaner. The teachers leaned against the wall with grim looks and folded arms, wondering what a "cleaning assembly" was and why it was taking up good school time. I put on my neck mike and raced out on stage and introduced myself as being from Idaho.

"What's Idaho famous for?" I yelled. One meek little hand went up, "Potatoes." "Right!" I leaped off the stage and gave that boy an Idaho potato pin. "Now another prize for anyone who knows what I do for a living." All was quiet, and then a little girl (who must have heard a parent or teacher talking) said, "Clean toilets!" Four hundred classmates burst into laughter. "Right," I yelled, and awarded her a genuine miniature toilet key chain, complete with opening and closing lid.

The kids were solidly on board now. I removed spots and stains, dejunked desks, played germ hide and seek, and squirted a couple of kids on the front rows with water from my miniature toilet to keep them interested.

Before the assembly I had spread some litter around—wads of paper on the floor, on empty chairs, on top of the piano, etc. Now I held up a matching wad.

"Who picked these up?" Three students who had been taught at home to be neat raised their hands timidly. I rushed into the audience, praising them and giving them either a potato pin or a little toilet. "These are the real champions of the school!" I announced.

I'd also put some black poster paint "stains" and "handprints" in different places on walls and furniture earlier.

"Can you see anything else out of place?" I shouted, watching as interest and enthusiasm heightened. Several hands went up, and one at a time, I beckoned their owners up, handed them a spray bottle of all-purpose cleaner and a towel, and showed them how to "spot clean" the marks off. A buzz of "I get it now" hummed through the audience.

Next, I seized a bright red plastic clothes hanger, held it high over my head, and sang out, "What is this?"

A big chorus came back, "A hanger."

"What does it do?" I demanded.

In perfect unison the answer came, "Hangs up clothes."

I held the hanger out in front of me and froze, just looking at it for five seconds, ten, fifteen. Dead silence in the room. I turned to the students accusingly and said, "It isn't working. You told me it hangs up clothes but it isn't hanging any up." There was a stir of uncertainty in the crowd. Finally, one brave fourth-grader blurted out, "You have to put them on the hanger!" A groan of agreement rippled through the group, after which I gave a short "hang up your own clothes" demo and pep talk.

I called another volunteer up now, a little girl this time, handed her an open carton of chocolate milk, and asked her to spill it on a large piece of carpet I had on the stage. The spill caused an audible grasp and I shouted, "Uh oh, who do you call?"

An instant chorus echoed, "Ghostbusters!"

"No," I retorted, "Ghostbusters don't exist."

(One little kid piped, "The cat!")

Another kid yelled out, "Call my mom."

"No, she didn't do it. Why call her?"

I pointed to my somewhat bewildered little volunteer... "She did it." Then I showed her how to clean it up like a pro. I had her blot up the spill, and afterward do a dance on a clean towel laid on the carpet to pull the rest of the liquid out. The kids were awed.

I had the janitor sitting nearby, and now I pulled him onto the stage, shouting, "Who is this?"

A loud chorus came back, "Mr. Crenshaw, the janitor."

"Right, what does he do?"

Another coordinated chant, "Cleans the school."

"Wrong! Wrong! Wrong!" I yelled back. The kids couldn't believe they missed this one.

"Did Mr. Crenshaw mess up the school?" I asked. That stumped them.

"No."

"Then why should he have to clean it up?" No answer. "His job is to maintain the school and service it. If he has to spend all of his time cleaning behind us, he won't have time to do that. So you students do the cleaning, pick up and put away things, keep your stuff neat." All of the students nodded in approval, and the teachers were smiling now, too.

Now I walked into the audience and picked two likely candidates—boys—and asked them if they would be willing to be a live demo. They agreed, so I got their names, Harry and David, and stood them up on stage. I told the kids that this was a chance for them to vote. First, I took a spray bottle of water and slicked down Harry's hair, shined up his shoes, spiffed him up, and then pinned a carnation on him.

Then I turned to David and ransacked him—mussed up his hair, took off one shoe, pulled his shirttail out, wrinkled his trousers, and stuffed a dirty rag in his pocket. I put a stuffed animal skunk under one arm and a piece of fake rubber dog poop in his other hand.

Then I turned to the kids for the vote. "The President is coming to the school today—who shall we send to greet him, Harry or David?" A hearty reply came back, "Harry!" "One of these boys has to cook and prepare your lunch—who do you pick, Harry or David?" "HARRY!" "You have to pick one of these fellows for your friend—who do you pick?" "HARRY!" I went through this routine long enough to make the point that being sloppy and dirty is not the way to be a winner.

EVEN YEARS AFTER MY ASSEMBLIES, KIDS ARE MAKING THEIR BEDS... MOMS LOVE IT!

Time was running out, so I ended the assembly with a toilet seat race, in which I raced the biggest, fastest kid in the audience (Butch) to clean specks of black poster paint off of a toilet seat. I gave him the pro equipment, of course, so Butch polished up his seat perfectly while I was still on the top lid of mine, scouring powder flying in all directions. The kids loved it! I grabbed up Butch's seat and held it in front of his face (like a toilet picture frame). I had previously arranged for a photographer from the local paper to cover the event and told him this moment would make a prime picture. "The winner," I yelled, my other hand making a V for victory.

I quieted the now teeming kids, gave Butch a toilet key chain, and asked, "How many of you would like one of these?" Hands rocketed up and the roar of "gimmes" swelled.

"Okay, okay, your teachers have a little pledge form for each of you, that you can take home. It will ask you to do only three things for one month:

1. "Hang up your clothes. How many of you can do that?"
   (All hands shot up.)
2. "Make your bed. How many can do that?"
   (Another unanimous response.)
3. "Clean the toilet like we just did."
   (100 percent affirmation.)

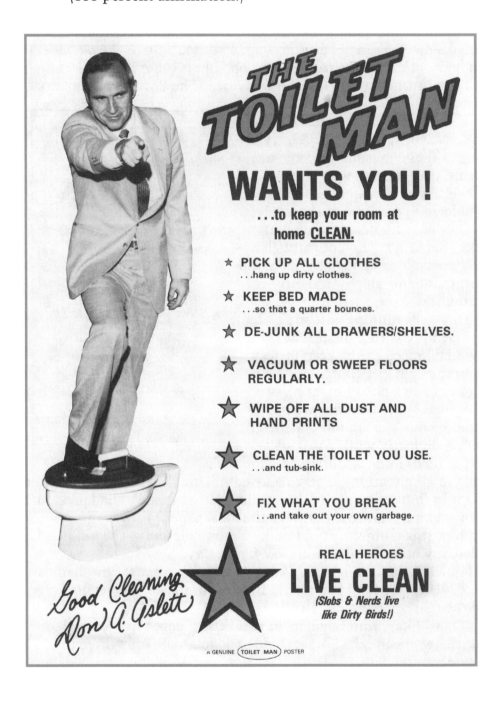

"You bring this back to your teacher in one month, signed by your parents, and I'll send you a little toilet pencil eraser—your choice of pink, white, or blue."

As the excited kids filed out, the teachers were beaming.

(The principal did get a call the next day inquiring about yesterday's curriculum, from a mother who said, "My little daughter came home, ran to the fridge, got a quart of milk and said, 'Mommy guess what we learned today?' And started to pour it out on the living room rug!")

Four and a half weeks later, not only did I have to send out 400 little toilets, but I began getting love letters from mothers asking, "Who are you, anyway? You've made such a difference in my son/daughter."

As for my new nickname, it evolved the last day of my visit to Alaska. I was finishing my consulting job at a supermarket next to the junior high, when a couple of students from the school spotted me and one yelled, "It's the Toilet Man!" In all of the classrooms facing the store, the kids surged to the windows chanting, "Toilet Man, Toilet Man!" I had to admit it had a nice ring, so I made up an Uncle-Sam style poster with that title, telling kids that the Toilet Man wanted them to clean their rooms.

Next summer at the annual convention of Alaskan school administrators, I was heralded as the best public relations program they had ever presented. This was the beginning of many more assemblies across the continent.

The best compliment I ever had from an audience was when I was giving a cleaning assembly in a grade school. The 3:15 end-of-day bell rang and not a single student moved!

Places I've taught or performed

One night, flying home from Atlanta too weary to do any serious work, I started writing down the different places I'd performed, spoken, taught, or filmed. By the time I was finished I was wide awake! These settings included:

Warehouses	Parks
Barns	Armories
Visitor centers	Bathtubs
Convention centers	Funerals
County fairs	Scaffolding
Ball fields	Elementary schools

Junior highs	Private homes
High schools	Department stores
Colleges and universities	Bookstores
Racetracks	Libraries
Theme parks	Malls
Resorts	Churches
Sports arenas	Synagogues
Rodeo grounds	Concert halls
Prisons	Lunchrooms
Mountains	Gymnasiums
Snowbanks	Restaurants
The desert	On the road
The Grand Canyon	Hospitals
Trains	Ocean liners/ships
Buses	New York penthouse
Seminaries	Stairways
Army posts	Tents
Motels/Hotels	Locker rooms
Restaurants	Disaster scenes
Television and movie sets/studios	Emergency rooms

I was not only performing in some unique places, I was putting cleaning in a new light for many people and getting off-the-wall recognition for it.

"'Who is this man who's romancing the mop? He turns everyday housework into high adventure.' Don Aslett, the most colorful custodian you're ever likely to meet, is this unique 'janitor' who is devoted to changing the way people think about cleaning out their homes—and their lives."

—*Dean and Nancy Hoch, in* This People *magazine*

"I just had to take a few minutes to thank you for the wonderful time I had listening to you speak. We came from about an hour away and some of the kids wondered if it would be worth the time to get dressed up and drive over. They ALL raved about it afterward. You have to know it went well when even all the men who had to get off tractors or quit working the cows to come commented on what a hoot it was to listen to you."

"It's disgusting—you make us want to do housework!"
—La Leche League

"Thank God I spoke before him."
—President of a university

"One of the best three hours I've ever spent."

"Your workshop on cleaning continues to rank at the very top of all the workshops presented. Our attendees applauded your enthusiasm and ability to inject energy into your... subject matter."
—Marianne B. Drew, President,
Professional Housing
Management Association

"You are the greatest thing for saving women time since the contraceptive pill!"
—Leona Jona

Chapter 17

BOOK TOURING AND PROMOTION: THE "GLAMOUR" OF AUTHORSHIP

There's no magic in marketing, just moxie!

Is There Life After Housework? proved to be a great book title; however, now I could write another book called "Is There Life After Publicity?" In 1981, Jo Hoff, publicity director for Writer's Digest Books, had asked me if I would go around the U.S. telling about "Life After Housework." This was called a media or publicity tour, and it sounded like it could have great end results, so I said, "Yes! I'll set aside the last of August, and September and October." "Fine," she said, "we'll get some good places." She did.

I received a thick envelope of plane tickets, hotel reservations, and lists of TV, radio, and newspaper appointments across the U.S.—29 cities. In four weeks I would be leaving, and even a well-traveled janitor like me felt a tingle of excitement.

There was much to do now and not enough days to do it. I had volunteered a year ago to take 40 Boy Scouts on a three-week trip to the national jamboree in West Virginia. When I returned from this and cleaned off 27 wood ticks, I had one week to soup up my visual aids and approaches for the tour. I also had a number of speaking assignments, seminars, and radio and TV

BOOK PROMOTION CHIC: AN ARTFULLY STAINED SHIRT SHOT CREATED TO HELP PROMOTE MY *STAINBUSTER'S BIBLE.*

tapings to do, in addition to all of my Varsity business. Somehow, by the night of August 22, the coast was clear.

Air service out of Pocatello was limited to a few "prop" planes at odd hours, plus the air controller strike was on, so on the big day of departure Barbara drove me to the Salt Lake airport, two hours away. Armed with my new miniature house visual aid, a big leather suitcase, and my toilet suitcase (see p. 381), I said good-bye and was off to San Francisco, scheduled the next morning to do the famous KGO *AM San Francisco* live TV show, followed by others through the day. I was really psyched to do my tour, and sure I had no equal for subject matter.

I was in my best suit by seven the next morning, determined to be early. I wanted to put a notebook in with my props and so heaved the leather bag onto the bed and unzipped it. My first thought was, what's this old girdle doing in my suitcase? Then I pawed like a frantic gopher, but there were no props. I grabbed the tag and it read "Harriet Reynolds, Anchorage, Alaska." This couldn't happen to me—only numbskulls take the wrong bag! I could see the end of my great TV career flashing before my eyes. I was sunk. The San Francisco airport was 40 minutes away, and it was rush hour.

I dove for the phone, got two slow talkers at the airport and then the freight department. Then a silence followed a promise to see if my bag was there. I spelled out my predicament, explaining that I was a famous TV star, scheduled to go on KGO in 45 minutes. The man said a delivery boy was just leaving, but thought he could catch him. He did. I had a cab waiting in front of the hotel and sat there with the erroneously claimed Anchorage bag. It was 7:45, 7:46, 7:47… I had to be at KGO at eight o'clock sharp because live TV shows don't wait. 7:48, 7:49, 7:50. He came! I gladly paid him $25 and switched cases. Then I told the cabbie I was James Bond and there was a bomb in my suitcase due to explode at 8:01 if I wasn't out of his cab. (Not a joke one would dare to make today!) As a result, I can say I've been down the hills and streets of San Francisco at more than 60 miles an hour—I left fingernail gouges in his door handle. At 8:00 A.M. I walked through the door of KGO, calm and collected, at least on the outside. My first-ever show went well—a real pro named Cheryl interviewed me, and much to the audience's delight graciously dodged my waving bowl brush. Best of all, they wanted me back! I packed my gear and caught a cab to an interview with the "Home" writer for the *San Francisco Examiner*. She was fascinated by my toilet tales and the *Examiner* ran an article with a full-page picture of me the next day, saying the Porcelain Preacher had come to town!

I had agreed to assist in any publicity needed to help make *Life* a bestseller. Writer's Digest took me at my word. An excerpt from my 1982 journals:

1981 BOOK TOUR.

Journal 1982

As I write this, seven months after the initial national tour, I've just finished the last of ten such tours. In this time, I have done 170 radio and TV appearances, 46 three-hour seminars, and been in just about every major and some of the not-so-major cities in the U.S. and Canada. Some months I traveled more than 30,000 miles—that's more than some commercial jet pilots log.

I've done every type of TV, including morning, afternoon, and evening talk shows, noon news, consumer programs, and segments from one and a half to 45 minutes—taped, live, cabled, and syndicated. I've done ABC, CBS, NBC, CNN, and three *PM Magazines*. On radio, it's been phone interviews from ten minutes to three hours, and many Q & A shows. I've taught live audiences adding up to 80,000 people, and sold cases and cases of books—in malls, on stage, and in department stores. I've been interviewed by many major newspapers and been the subject of at least 15 full-page stories, all on cleaning, mind you.

"He just doesn't die. After three radio shows, a noon TV interview, and then his 3-hour 'Life After Housework' seminar, Don still sat down to answer questions from fans in the lobby, dashed off four notes of thanks to his hosts for that day, and wrote a chapter for one of the books running through his mind—while waiting for his motel room to be ready."

—Jo Hoff, Publicity Director, Writer's Digest Books

On tour, accomplishment was measured by the number of miles traveled, times on TV, and books sold. The "tour" (which sounded romantic and exciting) was challenging, educational, and terrifying. The best shows and the late afternoon newspaper appointments were usually over by 5 or 6 P.M., and then I took a cab ride through evening traffic to catch a plane for the next city. I've spent up to $150 a day on cab fares, and since I really believe in visuals, through all of this I was carrying my miniature house prop, my toilet suitcase, three days' worth of clothes, my notebook, and often mops and extension handles. Flying means checking in well ahead, and it was usually 11 P.M. before I got to my hotel, where the restaurants most often closed at ten-thirty. (Love those granola bars.)

Barbara met me on a tour in Cleveland. I had been running a ragged schedule for more than two weeks and her companionship and help was a warm, welcome lift. Besides doing a raft of TV and radio shows and some newspaper interviews, we also did four seminars.

We had an early morning appointment the next day, then three church meetings and a fast tour of Kirtland, Ohio. We rode in a station wagon full of props and luggage, barely making it to the airport.

My nerves were frayed and Barbara and I only wanted one evening without anyone tending us, and this was going to be it. Our plane was to arrive in Detroit at three o'clock Sunday afternoon and by three-thirty we would be alone in a fancy new hotel. We planned a nice dinner and a romantic evening, topped by a late John Wayne movie. No such luck! After we arrived at the Detroit airport, they informed us that part of our luggage was lost. I accepted this, having learned by now that it did no good to threaten to kill, maim, or report anyone, and that the bellhops would eventually show up with it at about 2 A.M. (They always wake you up long enough to count out a tip for the good service of delivering the thing the minute it came in.)

We hailed a taxi at the airport and were soon headed for the city at 70 mph. I had just reassured Barbara, "It's not so bad—at least we'll get there in time for a meal." Then "thump, thump, thump," and the cab driver pulled off on the road shoulder. "Tire gone," he said apologetically. "Sounds like you lost a recap," I said, and a look at the left front tire confirmed it. The driver was standing there looking at the bedraggled piece of rubber and the still inflated bald tire it came off. I think he was intending to call for help, which would mean another hour lost because of the heavy traffic. "We can have that changed in five minutes," I assured him. I threw the luggage out of the trunk, handed him the lug wrench, grabbed the jack, and in minutes had the tire up in the air. My new suit wasn't the best for the experience, but I didn't care. I grabbed the spare and dribbled it to the front as he removed the deceased tire. While he fastened the lug nuts I threw the old tire into the trunk and piled the luggage back in—total time elapsed, ten minutes. The driver's eyes were bulging. "Man, that's the fastest I've ever seen a tire changed," he said. Again we were going down the road at 70 mph. I was a nervous wreck, and Barbara patted me affectionately—nothing more could happen. Then *boom!*—an explosion in the back of the car, and dust filled the cab. A missile, a mortar, or the Mafia must have hit us! Then a strong rubber smell: the old tire had expanded and exploded in the trunk.

That did it—even John Wayne couldn't soothe me now.

The price of performance cleaning

In March 1986, I did 14 presentations in two weeks, ranging from mountain resorts three hours from Portland to San Diego's finest hotels, to auditoriums in Williamsburg, Virginia. Preparing dynamic new material was enjoyable, doing the actual presentation and dealing with requests and questions afterward a bit of a strain but rewarding. It was the wear of travel that eventually got to me.

BARBARA'S COMPANIONSHIP AND HELP ON SOME OF MY BOOK TOURS WAS A WARM, WELCOME LIFT.

On a typical media day I left our ranch at four in the morning and drove to Pocatello, beating the opening of the sunrise pancake houses by hours. I made a quick stop at the office to sign things and leave instructions to keep all of my new books and Varsity projects progressing while I was gone. Then I drove to the airport, either Pocatello or 130 miles to Salt Lake City International, lugging oversized trunks and props across the long-term parking lot. It was always a relief to hand off my luggage at baggage check-in (with a silent prayer that it would somehow survive three plane changes and arrive when I did). Now there was a 45-minute, smoker-dodging wait for gate call, with a delay of at least 15 minutes and frequently an hour. Then you sat in a plane twentieth in line for takeoff, arrived in a strange town, found your luggage, and lugged it to a rental car. Next came trying to find where you were going from a map overlaid with Avis felt-tip marker arrows. After at least an hour's drive through fog or rain, I either arrived in time to check the setup for my presentation and then spoke, or fell into bed at eleven or midnight.

Up again at five-thirty, then speeding through heavy traffic to get to all of the shows and interviews scheduled that day. Now, a rush-hour trip to the airport, checking in and flying to the next city, finding my bags and a cab to the hotel. By ten to 11 P.M. I was reviewing my props and calling home. Then to bed at midnight or one, and up again at five-thirty, for 30 days in a row. Bottom line: books don't sell themselves.

SUCCESS WAS EASY ONCE YOU LEARNED HOW TO PASS OUT STANDING UP AND KEEP GOING.

It didn't let up—the rewards or the demands. The pressure to perform well was really intense. There were five to eight media appearances some days, and coupled with the hair-raising taxi rides in between, this took a lot of energy. I met so many producers, managers, actors, and other people that I had to start writing talk show host's names on the palm of my hand to make sure I got them right.

Taking a humorous approach really helped—I had return requests from many of the major stations and did regular appearances for four of them (Detroit, Cleveland, Cincinnati, and Indianapolis).

While on tour for my *Stainbuster's Bible*, one US Air flight attendant, taking my ticket with a flirtatious sniff, said, "Oh Sir, I love what you are wearing!" I leaned close to her and whispered, "Paint thinner. I've just been removing tar from a TV prop."

I had seven straight shows with little time between them, so I just tossed all my solvents, bleaches, acids, etc., into my travel bag along with a spotting cloth. If one of the drug dogs had sniffed my luggage it would have toppled over on its side and died.

The stain book tour took me up a notch in status. I was now approached like a doctor: "Doc, I have a stain here that...."

I was constantly reminded what a hard sell "cleaning" is. No matter how much fun I made it, how many visuals I used, or how many funny cleaning stories I told, it was still a hard sell.

After one TV show when I was on tour for *How Do I Clean the Moosehead?*, it occurred to me that if instead of showing the audience how to clean a moosehead, I showed them how to cook a moosehead, how to race moose, how to get elected to the Moose lodge, or how to give a moose mating call, my ratings would have been higher. People *have* to clean but they are a lot more interested in other things like sports, food, cars, and sex.

The things I heard most often while on tour:
1. "What kind of vitamin do you take, man?"
2. "Do you still work on the job?"
3. "Coffee, Sir?"
4. "We could sure use you in this place." [To clean it.]

Ladies on the tour

The majority of those I did business with at publishers, public relations firms, and TV stations, were women.

One thing exposure to all of the ladies of the media did teach me is that I'm definitely not a showgirl man. I really dislike candy-wrapper women parading around in glittering clothes or lack of same. Good mothers, on the other hand, I find attractive anywhere and anytime. Accomplishment was always more impressive than perfume or a perfect figure. Early in my teens, I came across this little verse: "Beauties in vain their pretty eyes may roll, Charm strikes the sight, but merit wins the soul," and that said it for me!

SOME HUMOR WAS EASY TO COME BY. SUCH AS THIS ENTRY SUBMITTED TO A JUNK CONTEST I HELD TO PROMOTE ONE OF MY DECLUTTERING BOOKS— A HEADLESS MALLARD!

When I arrived in St. Louis on a book tour once, the pretty 45-year-old escort Penguin had hired picked me up in her sun-roofed BMW, blushing, excited, almost panting, but not for me. She had driven Kirk Douglas around for two days and had just dropped him off. She carried on the whole day about his robust condition for a 74-year-old, and his dimpled chin. I thought I was rather dynamic, too, after all, I'd cleaned 10,000 toilets and Douglas only made 65 movies. I didn't see how I could fail to impress a beautiful woman, after all, I rescued old ladies from stains, held doors open for women, oohed over the city's arch, and gave her a fancy dust cloth. But she kept giving me that "Well, after Kirk…" look.

Just wait, honey, till I'm 74. I'll have cleaned 100,000 toilets!

Sometimes life as a cleaner did have a touch of macho justice, however. I boarded a plane from Salt Lake to Denver once, and a tall, attractive flight attendant, unaware passengers were boarding, backed into me, spilling her coffee. She apologized profusely, stopped, cocked her head, and stared at me. I took my seat and seated nearby were cowboy-suited "studs" with $200 hats, trim, well-tailored young business executives, and lots of macho skiers and other athletes. And then there was me, 59 years old, in five-year-old shoes and an old suit, with a worn briefcase and piles of paper all around me. Cabin service started, and when they got to my seat the tall attendant said, "I've seen you somewhere."
"Well, I am on TV a lot," I replied.

A PUBLICITY PHOTO DONE FOR THE PROMOTION OF *HOW DO I CLEAN THE MOOSEHEAD?*

Before I finished, she piped out, "It's him, it's him!" She beckoned the other two flight attendants over. "We watched you on TV in our hotel this morning. You were so funny and...."

They stopped pouring soft drinks and started pouring out questions. When they finished serving, all three came back and sat near me, laughing, and chatting, and offering me little gifts from the airlines. So I gave them each an autographed book. It was thrilling to see all those other attractive and fashionable men totally ignored, all for an old janitor!

Beauty and the Beast in Beverly Hills

Your Mind and Body, a nationally syndicated Time Warner TV show, had my name referred to them as "the best clutter expert to do a piece relating house clutter to mental and physical health." Tobi brought their proposal to me with excitement beyond her usual enthusiastic response to potential publicity.

"A big TV show called," she said, then clutching our media form to her chest blurted out, "and guess who the host is—Kim Alexis!"

"Who's she?"

"Who is she?" Tobi said, now turning red, "Why she just happens to be the biggest supermodel around today!"

"But it's LA," I whined, "the six-lane parking lot."

"But it's national," Tobi countered.

"But it's my only two free days this month...." (She knew I was weakening.)

"She'll love you, and the subject is straight from *Clutter's Last Stand.*" (Tobi knew this was my favorite book.)

Within five minutes of their call, Tobi had nailed down a plane ticket.

When I finally flew out, I was taxied to the Beverly Wilshire, the nicest hotel in LA. The health company had reserved me a suite so they could film there, too, and that made for the most expensive lodgings in my history of travel, $950 before tax. "Opulent" wouldn't do the room justice. I counted 32 lights, but couldn't manage to get enough light out of them (designer lamps with five-watt bulbs) to read the room service menu. There was enough drapery in there to serve as drop cloths for the Astrodome and it was hard to tell the bath towel from the bedspread. The phones were so fancy I couldn't figure them out, ditto the showerhead and toilet paper dispenser.

STAIN REMOVAL WAS A POPULAR SUBJECT WITH SHOW HOSTS, WHICH GAVE A BOOST TO THE PROMOTION OF MY *STAINBUSTER'S BIBLE.*

When the fatal hour of taping finally arrived, a crew of 14 geared up for an all-day session to get four minutes of film. Between them, they had clearly filmed everywhere and everyone in the business, and spent most of their time catching up with each other. Then, after they unpacked and before they set up, food arrived—bagels, cream cheese, coffee, etc.—enough to drive me crazy wondering why these $200–$600 a day technicians couldn't get up, bathe, eat, and come in ready to work.

Soon I discovered why we needed this giant suite—a wardrobe technician got set up (one bed was entirely covered with dresses), and the makeup woman had more stuff than a hiker readying for six days on the trail. I was given a script and asked to okay the cue cards while they set up lights, etc., for two hours. At last, we were ready and waiting, waiting... until finally the other talent, the host, Kim Alexis, showed up. She was beautiful, and brainy, too. Forty-five minutes more for makeup and we were ready to film. As we waited, Kim and I found common values in our children, church, and work ethic, after which she looked even prettier.

Keeping focused is essential for smooth taping, which means managing to ignore all of the distractions and interruptions, from dying batteries to retakes. This shooting had an extra distraction. The mike mounted under Kim's collar was scraping her, so they decided to mount it on her bra, and to my astonishment, they did so by pulling her sweater up right in front of everyone! A few more adjustments and we were rolling again.

Kim was quick and fresh, with a good sense of humor. It made a long day far better than tolerable, as we decluttered our way from room to room. After six hours straight I was so washed out I could barely touch the luscious lunch the hotel catered, while Kim was whisked off by impatient staff to another four hours

PROMOTING *NOT FOR PACKRATS ONLY* FOR NEW AMERICAN LIBRARY, I HAD AN UNUSUAL TOURING PARTNER—A JUNK MONSTER CREATED FROM THAT ALL-TOO-FAMILIAR CLUTTER THAT FILLS OUR CLOSETS, DRAWERS, AND GARAGES.

of voice-overs across LA somewhere. Gads, I'm glad I'm just an author and janitor.

Keeping one hand on the rudder

Blending book promotion and speaking with a growing cleaning company was not as complicated as it might appear, because they were all activities with the same goal. We had experienced managers running each of Varsity's individual areas and contracts, and I was marketing Varsity through traveling and publishing.

After more than 20 years in business, it was clear to me that nothing runs by itself. And since my life's investment and expertise was in the cleaning field, the preservation and development of Varsity was a constant concern. Leadership is a process that never ends, especially when you are the controlling stockholder. You are in on every major—and many minor—decisions. Fortunately phones, mail, and visits can sustain an operation once good management is in place. During my book promotion and speaking days I worked-in all of my Varsity duties (meetings, strategy sessions, phone calls, and written communications) just as a family fits first one child, then two, three or more into everything else that is going on. You just do it, and I did.

Book promotion in England

Back when I was attempting to teach the language to teenagers, I assumed all English was English. But during my book promotion tours in England, I soon discovered that many of our American expressions were completely unknown, or caused some consternation there. After my first couple of appearances, they attempted to clue me in nicely.

"Mr. Aslett, you do use some words, Americanisms, we might say, that aren't known here." At first they just told me. The next trip I was immediately given a neat set of typed pages: toilets are loos, diapers are nappies, a wastepaper basket is a dustbin, condo is flat, etc. One prompter told me, "Don, you use one word—janitor—a lot and it just isn't used here."

That I remembered and plugged into my interview memory. The very next morning I was on a television program watched by 8 million people. The Duke of Devonshire was one of their guests and me, the toilet cleaner. In a lovely English accent the host introduced me and asked, "Just what do you do in America, Mr. Aslett?" Determined to avoid the word "janitor," I said, "Oh, I'm just an old scrubber from Idaho." The other guests gasped in horror and the host flinched and quickly covered the microphone. I found out later that in England a scrubber is a hooker!

Two days later, I told an eager audience that what they really needed was a Doodlebug, (3M's long-handled floor cleaning tool). Again, everyone drew back in horror—later I discovered that "doodlebug" was what the British called the whistling bombs the Germans pelted them with during World War II.

> "DON ASLETT, 46, IS ONE OF THOSE
> SUPER-DYNAMIC TYPES THEY SEEM
> TO BUILD ONLY IN AMERICA."
> —LONDON **DAILY MAIL**, JUNE 19, 1982

Answering questions at a rapid rate, I would describe something as "rinky dink," or "klutzy," and then throw in a few "scruds" (a Utah swear word). In a Scottish interview I was telling a woman how to clean her tub and told her to "really scrub that dude down," only to be asked, in sweet Scottish brogue, "Mister Aslett, vots a dewed?" I told one elegant female host of a dejunking segment I'd like to look in her drawers, and the studio came unglued, and she turned red. Apparently we were each thinking of very different things.

The week of September 10, 1983 was one of life's extremes, a trip from pure contentment to terror. After leaving a newspaper interview (the first of 24 scheduled for me that week) in Bristol, England, my tour guide and I motored to Cardiff, Liverpool, and Stratford-on-Avon. Our objective was simple: fulfill all the radio, newspaper, and other publicity stops scheduled by Exley, the publisher of the British edition of my second book, *Do I Dust or Vacuum First?* The feat of crowding six to eight appearances and several hundred miles into one day was accomplished by careful planning and precision navigation through 1,500-year-old, five-foot-wide streets. What could have been a grueling impossibility was instead an inspirational experience because of my guide, Wendy Sacks, furnished by Exley—one of the smartest and most service-oriented women I ever met. She had a thorough knowledge of English roads, a fine talent for detail, and a South African accent that was a joy to hear.

Those first four days were as smooth and inspirational as any tour thus far. Our successes were one after another, and the hotels and scenery were out of the land of make-believe. I decided to write 400 more volumes, if this was what book touring could be like.

Ah, but what goes up must come down. Now I had to go to Scotland, alone. Wendy, a tactful breaker of bad news, said, "Because of schedule, I cawn't accompany you to the north. It shall be most convenient for you to catch the train and make your Friday appearances alone." After those first 1,000 percent convenient days, nothing could convince me that going alone would be anything short of being poked with a sharp stick. I begged, pleaded, and threatened to get her to call the office and change the plan… she wouldn't yield. I couldn't dent her loyalty to her orders, so not wanting to whimper publicly I stuck out my chin and said, "Okay, I will do it."

Wendy quickly locked me into my commitment by saying she was proud of me and knew I could do it regardless of the obstacles. Among the obstacles would be the waiting rental car, in which I had to make four tightly scheduled appointments, alone. (I was the kiss of death in an auto on a 40-foot wide American road, when anyone would venture to let me drive.) But Wendy had every train, hotel, and car rental precisely worked out and waved an executive goodbye as I bolted through the strange English rail gate, ticket in hand.

I said "Edinborough," to the uniformed attendant and he pointed to a train whose doors were already closing. I caught it on the run, elated that I was 15 minutes ahead of schedule (would Wendy be proud!). Little did I know that there were two trains to Edinburgh, the fast train, and the five-thirty, stop-at-every-other-house train, which I was now on. So my scheduled nine o'clock arrival at that fine Scottish city turned out to be noon. I checked into the hotel after much difficulty understanding the bellman's accent. Before I went to sleep, I reviewed the schedule. I had two radio shows, at nine and at nine-thirty, and there would be a rental car waiting afterward. Then I had 90 minutes to get to Dundee, about 90 miles away, for a big call-in show. Driving on those tiny roads terrified me without team navigation.

The two shows went so well that the second of them kept me past nine-thirty. I finished, sprinted out of the studio, and you guessed it, no rental car. At 9:45 I called Dundee, figuring if they knew it was impossible for me to get there they'd cancel and I'd get out of it and save face. But no, it was a big live show to millions, and they'd been pushing the book all week, priming those dirty-housed Scots for me. At 9:50 the rental people (who had gone off for tea) showed. I was on the phone again with Dundee, and they said an escort car would be waiting on the outside of town to take me to the studio when I got there. The rental folks dropped the keys to a tiny Ford Fiesta into my hands. Its top speed downhill seemed to be 55 mph, and it would have fit in the trunk of my Chrysler New Yorker at home. All of my driving reflexes (which weren't much to begin with) were all on the wrong side of the road. Ungentlemanly gestures and obscene verbiage were soon hurled at me and I was lost, instantly.

At 10:05 I pulled off the road and quivered. An old Scots gentleman came by and I said, "Hey, man, I'm desperate. I've got to get to Dundee in 55 minutes!" He smiled confidently and said, "Oh, yer go after dale goeener tharig stop aftar farty oohp—tarn efter updow oner lef... got at, laddie?" I said, "Huh?" I didn't understand a word he said (except "laddie"), but he did point, so I headed out, scaring a few more drivers who were driving on my side of the road. By pure accident, I hit a road that led to the motorway. I floorboarded that tiny car, and when I neared the outskirts of Dundee, there was the escort car (a sports car, no less!). I slowed up and he pulled in front of me and yelled, "Follow me!" Like a James Bond movie, I did the whole show of tire squealing and sidewalk-running, finally rushing into the studio with only one 30-second commercial between me and air time. It was a call-in show and in strange headphones, I tried to interpret Scots householders' questions from "darty tub" to "kiddie piddie."

Then I was off to Glasgow, only an hour and a half away. Three road construction projects and three hours later I pulled into the outskirts of that city. The map of downtown looked like the inside of a computer, so I wheeled the car to a stop, flagged a cab, and was on time. At this last interview, I discovered that calling Scotland "Northern England," which I had done several times today, was about equivalent to calling Canada the Northern U.S.

When the show was over, I caught a cab back to my car and headed back to Edinburgh. Once safely back in my hotel, I said to myself, "I wouldn't do this again for $100,000; I'm lucky to be alive." But the agony of those memories evaporated when the phone rang. It was Wendy, saying in that beautiful accent, "I knew you could do it!"

"While in England, Don was able to give some constructive advice to the Royal family. A caller asked if he might have some special professional cleaning advice for the imminent homecoming of Princess Di's new baby.

Don let them know that probably the dirtiest place in the palace was the doorknobs! They loved it!"

—*Scrubber's Scribe*

Daily Mail, Saturday, June 19, 1982

DON ASLETT, in London yesterday and putting to good effect his specially-made suitcase modelled on what he calls 'the symbol of my trade.' I carry it to dispel any doubt as to how I feel about my profession,' he says. 'I'm proud of it.'

Chapter 18

LIGHTS, CAMERA, ACTION: MY EXPERIENCES WITH THE MEDIA

Living for three words: "It's a wrap."

Once my book promotion got the ball rolling, I was launched into an intense and action-packed relationship with the media that continues to this day. My take on the process, after more than 26 years of it, might change your mind about wanting to be in movies. But there were some exotic experiences here for a desert-raised Idaho farm boy.

Want a hard-to-call decision on investment? Try placing a value on publicity. It became a common occurrence to get a call from afar (and almost everyplace is far from Idaho), offering to fly me there to do a segment for a "fantastic" TV program. When they described their show it always sounded like a real winner, surely superior to *Good Morning America*.

"We love Don."

"He fits our show perfectly."

"Everyone in the world will be watching!"

"We'll make him famous."

Don Aslett

AMERICA'S #1 CLEANING EXPERT

aka: King of the Toilet Ring   Don Juan of the John
      Sultan of Shine   The Toilet Man
      Urinal Colonel   Dean of Clean

Don Aslett
P.O. Box 700
311 South Fifth
Pocatello, ID 83204
208-232-6212

Home of Don Aslett's Cleaning Museum

A CELEBRITY MUST-HAVE:
THE 8x10 GLOSSY TO AUTOGRAPH FOR FANS.

"We'll pay all expenses—it will cost you nothing."

These are the five steps of publicity seduction. You know in your heart that the outfit calling is just like the last 40 that called and ended up taking two days of your time for a grand total of two minutes on the air. But maybe, just maybe, this will be "the one" that makes you a household word. You know better, but you do have the days they want open, or can squeeze the appearance in between three Varsity meetings and four speaking engagements.

"Super, stupendous, great, Mr. Aslett, we'll call you with the final date, time, and details." "We'll" is the main truth of that statement. That giant organization then proceeds to demonstrate just how many people it has on staff. A different one calls every time with different information—after eight years of this I learned to let them ramble on among themselves for weeks as they are deciding how my body and talents will be applied to their "great" show. Many of those you talk to haven't taken the time to look at any of your books or your segment proposal, or even review the preceding planning of his or her own people. To keep my courage and commitment up during this time of a thousand changes, they constantly tell me what terrific hosts they have and how much I will love them.

They may have three weeks lead time before the show, but always wait until three days before the actual flight so they can FedEx the tickets and impress you that they are willing to spend $20 or $30 on you instead of the few cents it would have cost if they'd sent them on time. Then they call you a dozen times to see if you got the tickets. Up to this hour, they have changed segment ideas at least ten times. I've sent them lists, scripts, and videotapes, and talked (sometimes in calls of more than an hour) about possible segment subjects and formats. Finally, they all agree that I should do the presentation on windows *for sure*... or maybe floors. "What do you think, Mr. Aslett?" (They haven't read a thing I sent or listened to a word I've said for the past two months.)

We now have over 25 calls and at least that many man and woman hours invested in this two-minute appearance. Just hours before I leave, they call with last-minute changes in the segment. I know this will happen so I've left my trunks open and ready for the change in props. Then I lug two 70-pound trunks to the airport—cab drivers silently curse me, and when hosts meet me at the airport, they have a tiny foreign car with a shoebox-sized trunk and no back seat. "Oh, you brought your props, Mr. Aslett?"

When I get there, the producer clasps her hands to her head, points, and yells, "Oh my gosh, it's our favorite guest! Uh, uh... (whispering quickly to the floor director 'What's his name?') Don... Don Haslett!" Then she runs up to me like she didn't know I was coming. "It's been sooo long!" and gives me either an air kiss or a halfhearted hug. "Did you bring any props, sweetie?" They never seem to have read the information sheet I provided, or to notice I am carrying a 700-pound trunk followed by a forklift with *Who Says It's a Woman's Job to Clean?* stickers all over it.

I'VE BEEN IN THE GREEN ROOM WITH BOB HOPE, JANE FONDA, MINNIE PEARL, RICHARD SIMMONS, STELLA STEVENS, RONNIE MILSAP, JERRY FALWELL, MARIE OSMOND AND MANY OTHERS!

The camera crew is seldom on time, and then the final word on it all, the executive producer, has decided what the segment will really be, and of course it doesn't resemble any of the 12 previous ideas for which I came equipped and prepared. I, of course, knew the executive producer would wait until the most inconvenient time to speak and knew there was only one subject they hadn't prepared me for, so I threw in some props for it, too—just what they want now. We finally get started shooting, and people get hungry or thirsty. By midnight, we finish and they have me on film. My name and welfare are forgotten. I end up in the alley fending for myself to get back to the hotel and home (a full day of travel tomorrow).

Most of the hosts and guests have a prerecorded communication consisting of two comments, "absolutely" and "you are very kind."

I ask a question: "Absolutely!"
"It's good to see you again."
"Absolutely."
"Where are you from?"
"You are very kind."
"How was your morning?"
"Absolutely!"
"Where is the men's room?" "You are very kind."
"How many segments are we doing?"
"Absolutely, Mr. Aslett, absolutely."

A 20-year-old intern holding a script asks, "Have you done any media before, Mr. Aslett?" "Yes, thousands of appearances." "Well," he says, "this is a camera and this is a microphone and we'll strap it on you, okay? Will that bother you?"

They never heard anything you said.

Coming in second to a dead horse

The media are usually thoroughly professional, but pretty fickle. If they have nothing else to broadcast, they bow and scrape and "sir" you to death. But let an event more appealing pop up and they don't even know you're around. I once made a special trip to *CBS Morning News* in New York. Yitzhak Rabin had been assassinated that very morning and when I got there they said, "Don who?" (Translated this means "we have something better.") This is called "preempting." Jerry Falwell once snatched my segment time; Jane Fonda munched a few of my minutes once, and a pair of polished French sex therapists shaved off some seconds. These I could accept with only a little tooth grinding, but the real insult came the morning the famous Kentucky Derby winner Swale died of a heart attack. Imagine coming in second to a dead horse!

For real news, toilet cleaning can surely wait, but it offends me on principle to be the first to go. I knew I was finally progressing when I was doing a national show live for ABC in New York, and President Reagan's speech to some visiting Russian students stretched out and went into my hour, finally eating up three segments worth. They preempted the gourmet cook who had a steaming dinner ready that had taken three hours to prepare, and Patty Duke, but not me! One of cleaning's first victories.

I soon learned that you don't schedule opportunities with the media, you contact and propose and wait, until they make the first call. Then it might be an emergency "Now!" or an often forgotten "Sometime." They use you when it fits their format and purposes, unless what you have is a real sensation, something genuinely newsworthy, and then they'll shove even a scheduled interview aside and take you.

Ninety percent of the time, the airtime they actually give you is shorter than promised. An hour show on radio often means 25 minutes of actual airtime after preliminary chitchat and advertising, etc. News, the weather, and commercials are why the station is in business and they come first.

Props: preparing, providing, and packing them

Once a TV segment was confirmed, it was always exciting. You had to hustle your own props to the set, because you wouldn't dare count on the producer to have the right stuff. For my segments, I often needed things like cat hair, fake dirt and dog poop, old engine oil, sawdust, mildew, and hard water deposits, so my staff and I would gather the visuals. If the segment happened to be on removing stains we would prepare a carpet sample to challenge the host with mustard, tar, chewing gum, or cigarette burns. After the show I'd bring all of these props home and store them, knowing there would be a next time. I always wondered if I had a wreck or was searched on the way to the airport, what the police would think, trying to figure out what all of this could possibly be. For my clutter presentations (which I did hundreds of times on stage) I had a drawer full of all kinds of junk to snatch up and show the audience—ugly, tacky, broken, worn out, but familiar stuff.

On a trip to England, going through customs at Heathrow Airport in London, a stern-faced officer asked me, "What's in the trunk?" "Junk, sir," I answered. "What do you mean, junk?" he questioned. I could see two other inspectors listening and some of the crowd in line behind me, so I knew there was an audience gathering. "Okay, there's an empty paint can, broken sunglasses, padlock with no keys, broken fly swatter, defunct wristwatch, old bowling trophy, ten-year-old *National Geographic*, an ugly old shirt, and other stuff." That set him back—all he could say was, "Anything else in there?" "As a matter of fact, yes, sir, a toilet suitcase." His humorless lips tightened, "Open 'er up, Chap."

By now everyone in viewing distance was looking and listening, and my wife, knowing what was coming, nudged me to just be serious. I had done more than 40 media appearances during that trip in England and Scotland, and this was a sensational ending, someone demanding a show! I opened my big blue travel trunk and removed a toilet eraser, toilet pencil sharpener, and a "Bowl Patrol" coat. The crowd, now more intrigued than impatient about the delay, loved it. Then the inspectors started through my junk drawer, pulling out an old distributor cap, warped trivet, empty Cool Whip container, cracked baby potty seat, etc.—even a goat brassiere. The customs officers (now two of them digging through my props) held up some of the

THE GOAT BRASSIERE THAT WON ONE OF MY CLUTTER CONTESTS—THE PROUD POSSESSION OF A COUPLE WHO HAD NEVER OWNED A GOAT....

stuff and said in a loud voice, "Why this is just junk!" I smiled triumphantly as they okayed me to repack and get back to the U.S.

Microphone machinations

I've been "miked up" (had a microphone attached to me) thousands of times. The first time they ran a mike cord not just down my shirt but my pants leg, so it wouldn't pull out, they asked if they could tape it to my sock. Since the hostess of the program was looking on, I he-manned it and said, "Naw, just tape it to my leg." The mike man murmured something about "gaffer tape" really sticking, but I glibly remarked back, "Hey, man, I've had my ankles taped to play ball plenty of times!" So he taped and I performed. I had enough pain later that day to testify that the tape TV people use for this is nothing like athletic tape! When they removed it, I thought maybe a ligament came with it. I didn't mind losing some hair, but losing skin too was more than I bargained for.

I've had microphones in my ear, three taped to me at a time, and microphones on mats I was demonstrating. I've used both "hard line" (plugged into something) and remote mikes. Wearing a remote, you soon learn not to talk about anyone anytime, because you're always "on the air." Once when I was offstage, I heard an unscheduled broadcast of my own voice saying, "Get off the stage, you old bag!" The place went dead quiet, and the celebrity involved hasn't spoken to me since.

Makeup

To someone who never even wore aftershave, stage makeup was a new experience, and one I never got used to.

If you've envied the complexion of your favorite TV personality (handsome host or comely commentator), you're wasting lots of coveting time. Only lying in a casket will you see a face with more stuff put on it than what goes on before you step before a TV camera. "It's to avoid reflections from those strong TV lights," they insist as they drag you into "makeup." The makeup appliers will trowel on an amount equal to the time available and number of guests on the show. If the show is loaded with talent, a toilet cleaner is last and if I'm lucky, forgotten.

"Lean back and relax," they say as they sponge that pink foundation paste on… and on. I evaded makeup whenever I could—my record was 18 straight major TV shows. Kathie Lee Gifford (of Regis and Kathie Lee) sometimes invited me in to talk while they washed her hair and applied makeup. She always looked fresher and more attractive without it, in a farm boy's opinion.

After a show on KGO in San Francisco where about two pounds of filler was used to make me look 14 again, I was in a hurry, so I left immediately for the airport, forgetting I was still in my studio makeup (and my collar, unbeknownst to me, looked like a Picasso drop cloth). As I stood in a crowded ticket line at the airport a delicate little man edged over to me and chirped out, "Hi guy—where are you heading?" The women all chuckled and looked at me. I finally figured out the source of my attraction and ran to the restroom to degrease! When I got back, the limousine driver, who had said very little as he escorted me around all day, leaned over and said, "Aah… Sir, this is not the best town to wear makeup around."

> I CAME OUT OF MAKEUP AT A TV STUDIO ONCE AND THE DIRECTOR LOOKED AT ME AND SAID, "IS THAT THE BEST THEY COULD DO?"

Best-dressed stress

In trying to elevate my appearance and image to "best dressed" status, I was a real failure. I guess I never overcame my sporty, aggressive willingness to dive wholeheartedly into the cause at hand. I could put on a $500 suit and 15 minutes later look as if I'd changed a car tire without a jack. (Which, in fact, I may have just done!) I often traveled with luggage that was oversize and overweight, and carrying it around always snagged clothes and stripped off buttons. Even after checking my luggage, I usually still toted a big clothes bag, my notebook, a briefcase with three or four manuscripts in it, a bulging pocket of miniature toilet key chains, and a five-foot squeegee extension handle. And when the time came to play a quick game of basketball or let grandkids ride on me, I always figured the experience was more valuable than the apparel. Of course, the paint speckles on my watch, fingernails, and ears seldom matched what I was wearing.

My colleagues made fun of me, and my daughter gave me a copy of *Dress for Success* for Christmas. My wife bought me an overcoat in an attempt to cover my stains and disharmonious colors. My parents bought me a fine sport coat and I lost it the first evening I wore it. (It was the first and only sport coat I'd ever owned.)

Occasionally, after being around some sharp dressers, I would vow to refurbish my threads and enter the competition for "Best Dressed U.S. Male," but would never even get near the semifinals. For Christmas in 1982, AM Northwest TV (which had an audience of over two million in Oregon, Washington, Montana, and Canada) asked me to do a 30-minute three-segment appearance on "Carpet Care at Christmas." I had done two extremely successful shows with them previously, my books were on the bestseller list, and the Bon Marché, a fine department store in the West, wanted me to appear, perform, and autograph at their stores. Figuring this called for a little more dress couth than I usually exhibited (since my newest suit was more than five years old), I whipped down to the Bon in Pocatello to reupholster myself for the Seattle invasion. I tried on a few $200 to $300 suits, and then spotted a real beauty on the rack. It was, the salesman assured me, their finest, a Hickey Freeman. I hadn't heard that term since I was a teenager, when a friend of mine kissed his girlfriend too hard on the neck. It was 100 percent wool and $525 with no vest, and only one pair of very snaggable-looking trousers—terrible—but considering my pending mob of admirers in the Northwest and all of the nagging I was getting about dressing better, I figured it was worth it. That suit, plus my message and good looks, would surely put me ahead of Garfield on the charts. But it didn't.

As it turned out, all I needed on that trip was Moe and Larry to have the Three Stooges back in action again. A buyer for the Bon hosted me, or tried to. I bumped my head getting into the car, dropped my clean overcoat in the gutter, and didn't have change for a tip. When I did get my coat on, the safety pin holding the lining in gleamed in the fancy hotel lights. When I tried to coolly button the only button left on it, it popped off and rolled across the hotel lobby. Making a quick turn, I knocked over a big Christmas display (with a loud crash). Getting in the elevator, I poked a woman with my window-cleaning pole. When I got my schedule out of my briefcase, I didn't latch it, and when I picked it up to leave, the contents pitched out. Showing someone how to gracefully carry a rug-cleaning machine, I struck the top of the door, and the handle snapped down and hit me on the lip, so then I had a fat, numb, bleeding lip to impress my fans.

It didn't stop when I yanked out my hotel key, and a vitamin C tablet I was carrying rolled across the floor. That $500 suit just wasn't me anyway, so I went back to my old $120 pinstripe and just got the job done.

> IN MY BRIEF TV TRAINING THE COACH STRUGGLED TO TELL ME NICELY THAT EVEN THOUGH SOMEWHAT SIMILAR, ONE DARK BLUE AND ONE BLACK SOCK DID NOT REALLY MATCH ON CAMERA.

Camera coaching

When companies hired me as a media spokesperson, their public re-

Fast talker cleans up on cleanliness

By HERB WHITNEY
The Arizona Republic

Don Aslett, "the dean of clean," shows off the rollers of an antique carpet sweeper.   Mike Smith/The Arizona Rep

lations firm would often run me through a TV training course. Many of the trainers had never been in front of a camera, yet they had all kinds of dos and don'ts for me (who had made thousands of successful appearances). Always open to doing better, however, I would follow their advice for the most part. One thing I heard again from them all was "Slow down! You talk too fast!"

"Don Aslett calls himself the 'Porcelain Preacher,' the 'Urinal Colonel,' and the 'Toilet King,' talking so fast the earhardlyhasachancetolisten. If he worked as fast as he talks, he'd have your house clean, top to bottom, in 20 minutes."
—*Tom Boone*, Dallas Times Herald

"With his conversational delivery 'tape' on double speed, he leaps from subject to subject like a gecko stalking a bug. In a world where new ideas are few and far between, he's as fresh and invigorating as a whiff of Glade in a stale bathroom."
—*Sue Dixon-Stong*, The Weekend Kauai

My energy and humor on TV were generally okay—it was some of the side references, or flippant little things I said that brought many a horrified look to hosts, and occasionally some irate mail. Just before I went on a publicity tour across the country for *Pet Cleanup Made Easy*, my editor, Carol Cartaino, handed me a little coaching slip. It is much funnier today than it was back then when I saw nothing wrong with saying "stupid dog."

Pet Lover's Phraseology Training Sheet
- Say "vet visits," not "pet repairs."
- Say "breed" rather than "make" of dog.
- "Dumb dog" is okay—"stupid dog" sounds too convincing.
- Forsake the expression, "Squirrelly pet owners."
- Skip the metaphor, "You don't just bite off and swallow a pet into your life."
- It also establishes a nice intimate tone if you say "our pets" and "your pet" instead of just "pets" or "the pet."
- "I'd never have a sandbox if I had animals!" (You aren't supposed to reveal that you don't have animals, even if you don't have any right now.)
- Try to take it easy with the expression, "Dead dog."
- No catching bats loose in the house with tennis racquets.
- Or knocking down swallow's nests.

Aslettisms

Be it overconfidence, laziness, or the simple inability to come up with the vocabulary I needed in a conversation, piece of writing, or performance, if the right word didn't come to mind I would just invent one. I did this so often these things were called "Aslettisms." At a national Scout jamboree, I served as a public health officer for the Western Region group. On staff also were three doctors and one dentist, and the doctors became so enthralled by my unique vocabulary that they put a big sign outside of our tent announcing that for 25 cents people could come in and hear me speak "Aslanian."

What were these words? Some were my replacements for swear words. When disgusted, for example, I often said, "scrud" or "for scrud sakes." When I was surprised or impressed, I often said, "Gadfrey." My overall advice to anyone seeking progress was to "show some hustle," and if anyone was not putting out full effort, I referred to this as "twinking" or "dinging." If I or anyone else was busy, making lots of dust but accomplishing little, to me that was "thrashing." To indicate great enthusiasm I always said "Snort!" My final appraisal of a non-producer is "a waste of white shirts and shower water." If I encountered people who seemed to have little personality or enthusiasm, I would ask if they "had a pulse."

Likewise, when it came to facts and statistics, if none were readily available, I would do a quick calculation from my own experience and resources and come up with something. As time went on I became convinced that my estimates were as good as "a university study shows…" or "the latest survey…." After cleaning thousands of homes and hauling off all kinds of junk (and cleaning around it), for instance, I came to the conclusion that 40 percent of all cleaning time was simply dealing with junk and clutter, not mopping and scrubbing. I used this on my media tour for my first decluttering book, *Clutter's Last Stand*, and soon all of the experts and copycats were using it as a fact and so it remains a well-established "fact" today.

Some lasting labels

In my early housecleaning days, I was referred to as "that cleaning guy;" I soon moved up to being called "the Varsity man." Then thanks to the schoolkids in Alaska, I became "The Toilet Man."

Super Janitor Don Aslett points out mistakes made by amateurs; more importantly, he stresses new professionalism in the cleaning field.

King of Custodians Shares Techniques

It was really the media who began tacking clever titles on me to give my appearances on TV, radio, and in print some extra clout. "Porcelain Preacher," was the first; others included "the King of the Toilet Ring," "Duke of the Dustpan," or the "Dean of Clean"… it never ended.

Finally one source suggested that I was unquestionably America's #1 Cleaning Expert. The title seemed to stick so I adopted it and have used it ever since. I'm sure there are some out there more technically knowledgeable about the chemistry and physics of cleaning, but there is probably no one who has embraced cleaning more wholeheartedly as not just a science and profession, but a lifestyle and almost a religion.

I've often been asked for the full list of my media nicknames:

The Porcelain Preacher	Baron of the Biffy
Billy Graham of the Pine-Sol Set	Dean of Clean
Ajax Evangelist	Minstrel of the Mop
King of the Toilet Ring	Urinal Colonel
The Pied Piper of Purification	Guru of the Loo
The Fastest Bowl Brush in the West	Jet Set Janitor
Duke of the Dustpan	Flush Gordon

Housecleaner Extraordinaire
Titan of the Toilet Bowl
The Cleaning Man
The Toilet Man
Don Juan of the John
Sultan of Shine
Czar of Cleanliness
Crusader for Clean
Squire of the Squeegee
Dean of the Dustbusters

Janitor Summa Cum Laude
Hercules of Housecleaning
The Clown Prince of Clean
The Wizard of Ooze
The Phyllis Diller of Toilets
Monsieur of Messes
Lee Iacleaner of the
   Corporate Toilet Bowl
Will Rogers of the Restroom
America's #1 Cleaning Expert

"He's more than a self-made mess-cleaning mogul. Don Aslett is a preacher, a kind of Ajax evangelist."
        —Ann L. Trebbe, The Washington Post

"Clean is the most liberating word in the English language, " said Aslett, who traded teaching high school English for a sort of Pine-Sol evangelism.

With the fervor of a carnival barker, he urges people to get rid of those knee-deep piles of pants that don't fit, baby bathtubs when the baby is 28 years old, empty margarine tubs, outdated gift calendars, petrified corsages and five pairs of white tennis shoes in various shades of gunky gray."
        —The Associated Press

"Don Aslett is known by many names, but has only one mission—to make housework as quick, easy, and painless as possible."
        —Richmond Times-Dispatch *10/27/94*

The case of the toilet suitcase

When I decided that I was going to be a janitor, I said, "Man, if I'm going to be a janitor, I'm going to be the best darn janitor this country's ever known." I'm not only a janitor at work, I'm a janitor at home, at play, in church, and every part of life, as the following bears witness.

Several years of travel revealed to me that many of my fellow travelers had luggage that identified their profession. The cowboy had boot silhouettes on his clothes bag, the engineer, a transit case, the musician, his violin case, baseball players had athletic bags, and look how much attention all the pilots get trailing their compact little flight bags through the concourses. Being #1 in the #2 business, I figured I should call some attention to my profession in my travels, and in conversation often said I would be carrying a toilet suitcase someday.

Earl Parrish, one of Varsity's Florida managers, and an expert in fiberglass molding, heard my comment and during my next trip there, I was presented with a perfect fiberglass toilet suitcase (my Stoolsonite, as I liked to call it).

As soon as I had it, I made up a business card that read:

EARL PARRISH PRESENTING ME WITH A ONE-OF-A-KIND PIECE OF LUGGAGE THAT VARSITY OF THE SOUTH WORKED HARD TO CREATE.

HI...I'M DON ASLETT!
I'm from Pocatello, Idaho

Hello . . . My name is Don Aslett. You are probably wondering about my strange luggage. It is not a porta-potty or toilet as it appears — it's my suitcase. Why do I carry it? Well, doctors carry their little black bags; lawyers and business executives carry their attache cases. I carry a toilet suitcase because I am a professional cleaner. The toilet which I (along with 8,000,000 janitors and 50,000,000 homemakers) clean regularly, is a symbol of my trade. I carry it to dispel any doubt as to how I feel about my profession — I'm proud of it.

I've been nicknamed by the media "The Porcelain Preacher," "The Billy Graham of the Pine-Sol Set," "King of the Toilet Ring," "The Urinal Colonel," "Pied Piper of Purification," "Barron of the Biffy," "Fastest Bowl Brush in the West," and others . . .

Some say I'm a janitor because a twelfth-century relative of mine was Duke of the Royal Chamber Pot. Not so, It wasn't blood lines, it was red-blooded American enterprise.

My toilet suitcase became my trademark as I traveled all over with it. It was a real attention-getter, and the media loved it. I would always close my cleaning seminars or convention speeches on the subject of the image or status of the cleaner and do a whole standup (or sitting down in this case—right on my toilet suitcase) comedy routine about getting respect for the business I was in.

I had a lot of fun with my toilet suitcase over the years. The curious would ask, "What's in there?" I'd answer confidently, "My toilet articles."

I took it into a hotel once and the desk attendant assured me that this was a first-class hotel and there was no need to bring my own.

One intrigued bystander shouted across an airline terminal once, "You sure come prepared, don't you!" Another yelled out, "Bet carrying that around really poops you out!"

Cross-legged kids approached me sometimes, asking, "Hey, does that really work?"

I used to love going through upscale hotels with my toilet suitcase. I'd enter the elevator full of men in $500 suits, diamond stickpins in their ties, fine leather briefcases, and *Wall Street Journals* under their arms. Not one would turn his head as I stood there with a life-size toilet in hand. But unbelieving eyeballs would shift slowly down to it, then dart rapidly ahead, pretending that they didn't see it, or didn't know what it was.

If you walk into the lobby of a hotel like the Waldorf-Astoria carrying a realistic-looking toilet, you will find that their speedy check-in policy is closer to instant—you are out of there and into a room *fast!*

The crowd gathered around any airport luggage carousel would suddenly come alive when the conveyor belt spit out my "suitcase." Often a kid would yell, "Look, Mom—a toilet!" and then all kinds of remarks would ripple through the crowd. "Can you imagine that?" "Must be a plumber." "Someone must really have to go a lot," etc. Then always, "I wonder whose that is?" I let it circle a few times for maximum effect, and even some of those who had already retrieved their bags would wait to see who was going to claim it.

PHOTOGRAPHERS LOVED MY TOILET SUIT-CASE, AND THIS IS ONE OF MANY SHOTS TAKING FULL ADVANTAGE OF IT.

Best of all, when my toilet suitcase came sailing through, I could safely ignore the sign that says, "Examine your luggage carefully: many bags look the same." When I did pick it up, it was always in perfect condition, because it had a sign on top that said, "If you break this, it will spill on you."

The only place my unique luggage went unnoticed was Alaska. At a luggage carousel in Fairbanks or Juneau, there are one or two ordinary, conventional suitcases (tied shut with rope), and the rest of the luggage is rolled-up bear hides, giant scuffed coolers labeled "FISH," rifle cases, surveyor's tools, wheels, propellers, and other airplane parts, and every type of tool box ever invented. Here, no one ever took a second look when my toilet suitcase came rotating by.

> "HE'S SCRUBBED THOUSANDS OF TOILETS, TAKEN 'POT SHOTS' AT PEOPLE WITH A SQUIRTING TOY TOILET, AND CARRIES A TOILET-SHAPED BRIEFCASE 'SO EVERYONE WILL HOLD THEIR BREATH WHEN I WALK BY,' HE QUIPPED."
> —BARBARA WYMAN

Tokens from the toilet man

My collection of cleaning novelties was pretty impressive, from tie tacks to talking toilet banks. The top three of my 20 or so giveaway trinkets were toilet earrings and key chains, squeegee tie tacks, and Idaho potato pins.

The earrings were authentic-looking little buggers, lids and all. I gave them to TV hosts, politicians, book editors, and other notable or famous people, and used them as prizes for right answers from audience members. After the initial shock wore off, the recipients were usually delighted by their uniqueness. Many wore them proudly. The earrings never failed to get a laugh, and best of all, made people remember my visits.

The little gold-colored squeegee tie pins I would often take off my own tie and give to special people, especially kids, in exchange for a promise that they would clean their rooms. The one-inch plastic potato pins were always popular, too—who doesn't love Idaho potatoes?

These little novelties were developed and collected initially for customer service in my Varsity operation, which was growing apace with my authorship and appearances.

Image reversal!

I didn't mind capitalizing on peoples' reaction to my lowly profession of custodian. It was okay to do janitor or maid work to get through school, but to continue in this line of work once you graduated was incomprehensible to most upscale folks who went on to teaching, engineering, medicine, manufacturing, sales and the like. There never was a way to answer "What do you do?" without people looking down afterward, avoiding eye contact with me, or saying, after a noticeable silence, "Oh, that's nice." So I finally decided to take a more aggressive stance. When someone complimented my facilities, books, or speaking and then asked me the big question, I would respond enthusiastically "I'm a janitor!" and then watch them squirm. It was a way of getting even with people caught up in status. If I wanted to heighten the effect for the snobbier, I'd say, "I clean toilets."

> AT CLASS REUNIONS OR ANYWHERE PEOPLE WERE TRYING TO IMPRESS EACH OTHER WITH THE LONGEST, MOST OFFICIAL-SOUNDING DESCRIPTION THEY COULD COME UP WITH FOR THEIR JOBS, WHEN I SAID, "I'M A JANITOR," IT WAS ALWAYS GOOD FOR A FEW GASPS.

This worked wonderfully, and then I found another little touch that was excellent for smoking out hidden prejudices. When reaching out to shake hands with someone I'd just been introduced to, I quipped, "Well, I just cleaned a toilet with this hand." This got an instant response—generally the person would jerk their hand back or at least hesitate as they calculated the possibilities of contamination.

The best response I ever got to this was on ABC's *LIVE—Regis & Kathie Lee* TV show in New York. The segment opened as I walked onstage to be greeted by the hosts. I got a quick hug from Kathie Lee and then Regis thrust his hand out to me. As I reached for it, I gave my famous line, "Hey Reg, I just cleaned a toilet with this hand." Without missing a beat he grabbed my hand and said, "That's okay, I just picked my nose with this one." They were great to work with.

I FIRST WORKED WITH REGIS ON HIS RADIO SHOW, SO HE BROUGHT ME BACK AS A REGULAR ON LIVE—REGIS & KATHIE LEE—THOSE TWO ARE PROS! KATHIE LEE STILL HUGS ME WHEN I SEE HER AT QVC!

Filming stress

Film can be wonderful when you experience it completed. But

the filming itself is seldom fun. I filmed all over, including Hollywood, Denver, Philadelphia, New York, Great Britain, Canada, and Australia. The more I did it, the more respect I had for the actors who made dozens of movies—they must have been superpeople indeed.

TV gave name recognition and sold books and products, so I did it, but it always intimidated me, even though people often praised me as being "a natural." No matter what the subject was, how well prepared I was, or how much experience I gained, filming was always a grind, and I dreaded rehearsals and retakes. Eventually I got relaxed enough to enjoy doing some segments, but for the most part doing taping was like a sentence to be served.

Onlookers who know nothing and don't need to be there wander around, get in the way, and offer all kinds of often-irrelevant opinions. This confuses and slows down those in charge and those who know a little. Things that could or should have been prepared ahead are always done in a last-minute panic. Everyone has to delay and tinker with their job, right in the middle of a take, to get attention or show others they are needed. The makeup people touch up the "talents," when only the feet are being filmed. Everyone eats or sips coffee during the filming and at the worst times. The light techs go through an experimental shift of lights for 40 minutes and end up exactly where they started (and knew was right). No matter how well or smoothly the shooting is going, the sponsor feels obliged to question or nitpick something he didn't even see. Eight people too chicken to get in front of the camera themselves are behind it gesturing and coaching. All of the crew suddenly gets faster as the budget runs out.

FILMING ON LOCATION WAS A FAMILIAR JOB, BUT NEVER AN EASY ONE.

There are always takes and retakes and then more. We always need better scripts, better starts, better endings, and even when the film is otherwise a keeper, there is often some little thing wrong. I filmed 253 "Clean in a Minute" spots once. Although they were only 51 seconds each when completed, on even the best day we would only shoot ten and many days only five. It went on for months—gathering props, writing storyboards, then worrying about lighting and sound, and doing the segment over and over and over until the timing was just right and no wrong moves were made or words slurred.

I never did get real smooth working with crews of camera operators and technicians—my movements were like lightning while the camera often moved like a snake on a cold day. They found following my moves and leaps onstage difficult—I could get off camera faster than a kangaroo.

Relief at the end of the day never came because you knew you had to do the same the next day, and the next, and the next.

You felt a real surge of relief when you heard:

- "That's a wrap!"
- "Keeper."
- "Good take."
- "That will work."
- Or clapping from the crew.

Nerves tightened when you heard:

- "One more now, just in case."
- "Uh-oh, we have an equipment problem...."
- "There's a hot spot."
- "Just one more little change."
- "Mmmmm...."
- The sound of a phone, doorbell, airplane, or garbage truck in the background somewhere.
- "Was that a short in the cord...?"
- Any silence.

I have a mental block about memorizing lines. In grade school I could memorize anything, and I can still recite long poems I learned then, yet now when it comes to memorizing a few lines for filming, forget it. When I ad-libbed I generally was smooth as silk, but if something required eight words in exact order I was worthless.

In one New York filming for Procter & Gamble, I had to open a cupboard door and say a one-liner I just couldn't get straight. Finally, after ten takes they wrote the line inside the cupboard for me to read. I became good at hiding "cheater" notes and clues, until I figured out I could just post my dialogue directly on the camera tripod.

I had this problem with live appearances, too. When I spoke at a Kiwanis convention, I might call them Rotarians, and vice versa. One time in Lake Tahoe, I had Barbara stand in the back and hold up a sign that said "ROTARY." No matter how I concentrated, this problem would crop up. I did six big-time conventions of well drillers. They hate to be called well diggers, but in my youth we called them that. So I would slip and say, "It's great to be with you well diggers today!" Big sneers confirmed my fears that I had goofed.

Likewise, somehow I locked onto "Bounty" as the word for paper towel and one year the James River Corporation, maker of Brawny paper towels, had a big "spring green" (environmental consciousness) campaign and gave me the job of spokesperson. It was awful when "Bounty," the name of one of their main competitors, would pop out when "Brawny" was in the script. A year after the tour I had to ask my publicist Tobi, "Who was it I toured for, Bounty or Brawny?"

Making cleaning more fun than sex

Although I took my responsibility to the media seriously, I found most of them would resort to almost anything to get attention. As they often told me, when there is no news—no tragedy, floods, crashes, murder, or sensational adultery to report for breaking news several times a day, they have to make news. I've since always marveled at how the local or national media can take nothing much and make it into the news of the day—now that is talent and enterprise!

I did a noted TV talk show in San Diego once with three guests. I had the third and last segment. The host led off by interviewing two homosexual men who hugged and caressed for the whole segment. Next was a sex therapist who told the host he'd had sexual relations with 269 women, professionally of course, to investigate and help them adjust to their partners. Both of these were pretty sizzling interviews. Afterward the host (whom I'd worked with before) wiped his brow off camera and apologized. "Gee, Don, I'm sorry you have to follow that kind of subject—this is going to be tough." Boastfully I replied, "Listen, Frank, the day I can't make cleaning more fun than sex, I'm going to quit." Bad brag! When the commercial was over, he greeted viewers with, "Welcome back, folks. Now we have my friend Don Aslett, who will show us how to make cleaning more fun than sex."

I can't remember what I even did for that segment, but whatever it was, it worked. Two hours later I was paged for the first time ever in an airport, with "Mr. Don Aslett, please pick up the white courtesy phone." It was Jo Hoff, publicity director for my publisher Writer's Digest. "What did you do, Don? We're being flooded with calls for your new book, *How to Make Cleaning More Fun Than Sex!*" When I told my wife about it later that evening, she said, "Well, there's a title for a book that would really sell!" I decided to drop that approach and quit while I was ahead.

At home with the home shows

I appeared often on television series related to the home, and there were so many of these it could get confusing. There was *HOME* done in Los Angeles by ABC, *Home Matters* in Philadelphia (the Discovery Channel with Susan Powell), *Our Home* in New York (Lifetime Television), and *Smart Solutions* on Home & Garden Television, plus a couple more that came and went. This kind of show was usually interested in

Former Miss America and **Home Matters** series host Susan Powell -- with contributors Mark Koebrich and Robin Young, and their guest experts -- make it easy and fun to explore gardening, crafts, cooking and collecting. **Home Matters** airs on Discovery Channel every day, from 10-11AM (ET) and Monday through Friday, from 1-2PM (ET). **Pictured:** Susan Powell. **Credit:** Photo Bureau, Inc.

EVERYONE ENDS UP WITH A FAVORITE AMONG THOSE THEY WORK WITH IN TELEVISION LAND. MINE WAS SUSAN POWELL, THE FORMER MISS AMERICA WHO HOSTED HOME MATTERS ON THE DISCOVERY CHANNEL. WE PRODUCED SOME GREAT SEGMENTS TOGETHER OVER A 7-YEAR SPAN.

short, 6- to 9-minute "how-to" segments done in the studio. These all involved lots of travel and preparation time for a few minutes of glory, and hopefully enough exposure to sell a few books.

"DON ASLETT CAN CLEAN MY HOUSE ANYTIME—HE'S THE GREATEST!"
—REGIS PHILBIN

AM CHICAGO

MY OFFICE STAFF WENT CRAZY WHEN I DID A SERIES ON CHRISTOPHER LOWELL'S SHOW.

CBS NEWS SUNDAY MORNING SENT A REPORTER AND CAMERA CREW TO SHOOT A SEGMENT IN MY OFFICE IN IDAHO. THEY TITLED IT "CLEAN SWEEP."

PAGE 4-SECTION C-IDAHO STATE JOURNAL POCATELLO-CHUBBUCK, IDAHO, THURSDAY, FEBRUARY 25, 1988

Resident Joins with Cast Of Network Home Show

Pocatello Businessman Don Aslett is joining Don Weller and Sandi Hill, former host of "Good Morning, America," on the new ABC "Home" show.

Aslett, chairman of the board of Varsity Contractors, Inc., and an acknowledged expert in the world of cleaning, will be appearing as a regular on the show.

Today on the 9:30 a.m. show, Aslett's entertaining segment on "Dejunking " was the highlight. He will also be appearing on future segments teaching professional time-saving, money-saving techniques which allow everyone greater freedom to pursue what they enjoy doing.

Aslett, an alumnus of Idaho State University, has the home office of his Varsity Contractors office here. His ABI Publishing and Housework, his retail and mail-order store, is at the same location. He is the author of 10 books on self-improvement and personal production in the cleaning field (as well as in life), which have sold more than a million copies worldwide. He has gained media attention in over 4,000 appearances in the U.S., Canada, Europe and Australia.

At left, Pocatello Businessman Don Aslett, center, with Don Weller and Sandi Hill on new ABC 'Home' show.

ABC's "Home" show was a good national show in the beginning, and Don and Sandi were super hosts, but bureaucracy or politics or whatever always seems to creep in over time. Before too long they were gone, I was gone, and the show was gone.

Aslett Keeps Hectic Pace to Help People Clear Up Clutter

By Dianna Troyer, *Idaho State Journal*, April 28, 1995

Don Aslett wasn't nervous about being on Oprah Winfrey's hour-long talk show about spring cleaning last week. After all, the McCammon resident has been Oprah's guest twice before. The first time was nine years ago, when he was on for half an hour promoting his book *Clutter's Last Stand.*

"You have to fight for the mike on talk shows," he said during a phone interview after the show. He was on seven to ten minutes.

"Time is really tight," he said about television. "The audience wants a quick visual payoff."

He should know. Since becoming the King of Clean decades ago, he's been on numerous national talk shows giving cleaning tips that his fans say have changed their lives. He's filmed more than 6,000 segments for television shows in the U.S., Canada, Europe, and Britain.

"In the last 90 days, I've done more than 132 stage presentations of about an hour, 60 media interviews, traveled 100,000 miles, and stayed in 70 hotels," Aslett said.

LAUNCHING INTO MY SPIEL FOR ONE OF MY APPEARANCES ON OPRAH!

When Oprah's off camera

Continued from article by Dianna Troyer

What's Oprah Winfrey like?

She's one of Don Aslett's favorite talk show hosts.

"Off camera, she's as funny as on camera," said Aslett, a recent guest on her show about spring cleaning. She's personable and fun. Her staff loves her. She spends a lot of time with guests off camera.

She works hard and is proof that persistence pays off. "She's like an Idahoan in that way," Aslett said.

Most people don't realize that Aslett's ten-minute appearance on Oprah required 9 hours of work. A two-minute segment of helping a family rid their house of clutter took five hours of filming.

All media appearances were gratis, unless it was a national show like Oprah or Regis and Kathie Lee, for which you would get paid a $500 guest fee. However, you had to belong to a union, the Television Actors Guild. Thus someone signed me up and I became a card-carrying "actor." The fees and dues to belong to such a prestigious organization usually ended up consuming all of the money that came in from any acting I did. A report would show a $500 payment from some show and then a deduction of $497 for dues—what a waste of good printing ink!

The "bite" style

When I wrote a book, I planned, shaped, built, and developed it for months or years, and it usually ended up hundreds of pages. For the media, you had to condense your whole message into ten seconds to ten minutes, max.

An editor at *USA Today* once counseled me on an article I was doing for them. "Remember, Don, a few short sentences should say it all. You're writing for a public that has a bite-size attention span, and often bite-size time to read."

After that, with every article, TV segment, and radio broadcast, I concentrated more on short and quick messages, no drawing things out or embroidering them. This made for better media material, except that I began to live that way, too. Before long, my meetings, projects, conversations, trips, and even relationships all began to be affected by the "bite" style.

It drove me crazy whenever I heard a speech or sermon where some-one was rambling on for 30 minutes about something that could have been said well in three. When a grandkid tried to tell me a story that was more than three sentences, I became impatient. I became totally intolerant of lines and people unable to decide quickly. People's war stories about their family, vacation, or health drove me crazy. Even re-peating choruses in music began to annoy me. I was thinking in bite size, writing that way, and treating people that way: brief, summed up, boiled-down interactions. All of this had some merit for efficiency, but as time passed, I wondered if "condensation" stripped life of some of its savor. This question triggered yet another book in the works, "How to Get the Goosebumps Back Again."

Call-ins

Radio especially loved call-ins because they involved the consumer in the broadcast, in fact they brought him or her right into it. Many people dread getting unknown calls and questions, so stations would al-ways ask, "Will you take calls?"

When I answered, "I love calls!" they booked me immediately. There were a few awkward moments, such as the woman (on a call to a major TV station in San Francisco) who explained more than anyone wanted to know about her marriage before asking how to get 30-year-old sweat stains off the armpits of a 50-year-old leather jacket. Or the man who called in a panic, wanting to know how to get ants out of his steam iron. But in 20 years of call-ins, thousands of calls, I don't think I ever had a really negative one. (Except possibly in Scotland, where my Idaho accent was hard for the natives to follow.)

```
DON ASLETT                          MONDAY, OCTOBER 9, 1989
   CLEANING EXPERT                     TOM
----------------------------------------------------------------
OUR NEXT GUEST IS KNOWN AS THE WORLD'S NUMBER ONE CLEANING EXPERT.  AS A
MATTER OF FACT HE IS THE HEAD OF ONE OF THE WORLD'S LARGEST CLEANING
COMPANIES AND HAS WRITTEN OVER 10 BOOK ON THE SUBJECT.  HIS LATEST IS
"HOW DO I CLEAN THE MOOSEHEAD?"...PLEASE WELCOME DON ASLETT.
----------------------------------------------------------------
DEMO:   DON WILL DEOMONSTRATE 4 CLEANING EXAMPLES ON THE DEMO TABLE.
----------------------------------------------------------------
1.   HOW TO GET OIL OFF THE GARAGE FLOOR.

2.   HOW TO GET A RING (LEFT OVER FROM CLEANING) OUT OF THE CARPET.

3.   HOW TO CLEAN A CHANDELIER

4.   DOG PEE
```

THE NITTY-GRITTY OF A TV APPEARANCE.

Ironically, the first national show I ever did was a call-in show and the host was a rather sharp-edged person who, as the calls and answers were going wonderfully, kept almost begging, "Now if any of you out there disagree with Mr. Aslett, feel free to call." I found that being opinionated was fine and if I stayed confident and kept it humorous the callers never wanted a fight.

The host and I always managed to make even the most timid man or woman laugh on call-in shows and always gave solid professional information. After being in the business for 40 years, as I had by this point, I had experienced (ruined, lost, fixed, or cleaned) just about everything and anything. We had people call in from cars, camps, and sick beds, and once someone called from a tractor while cultivating.

One of the most impressive linkups I remember was when I was in Hawaii, doing a call-in show on cleaning for a station in Florida, and we had a caller from Saudi Arabia. Astounding to be talking about cleaning up cat pee with the three of us 10,000 miles apart.

Spring cleaning has sprung!

Every spring, like clockwork, you could depend on calls from the major magazines for interviews on "spring cleaning." The *National Enquirer* would be first and most aggressive (I could always imagine myself clutching a mop next to Elizabeth Taylor or the Incredible Hulk, or in some Martian's kitchen). *Family Circle, Woman's Day, Glamour, Brides, Working Mother*, and dozens of others would follow.

Timing was almost more important than content in these articles—the editors and writers were mainly interested in having some expert on the subject associated with their publication, and my many books on cleaning and decluttering gave me credibility. They usually had some new spin or twist they wanted to use to lead into this time-honored subject, and even though I don't actually believe in spring cleaning, (fall cleaning is far more effective and long-lasting—see *Do I Dust or Vacuum First?*), I seldom left them disappointed.

Anything off the wall or controversial was welcome.

The battle of hint and tip

As I learned more and more about cleaning professionally, I also learned that there existed another approach called hint and tip solutions, the "home remedy" ways of cleaning things. The band aid fix, the "use the household staples" school of cleaning, such as using peanut butter or toothpaste for black marks on the wall, WD-40 for stains, vinegar and old newspapers for cleaning windows, and baking soda for just about anything. Newspaper columns and magazine articles were full of these little miracle solutions, which often needed one more ingredient to really work—a healthy serving of imagination. Vinegar was really prominent here, yet in reality it is a mild acid. Since most soils are acid based, they can't be effectively removed by vinegar. They need a cleaner from the opposite end of the pH scale—an alkaline cleaner. Thus vinegar is almost worthless as a cleaner. (Maybe it's psychological, since it squeaks.)

For 50 years I fought to keep those two words—hint and tip—from being used in any of my material. I hated to be classed with the many hint and tippers out there in the media world. I would warn writers, editors, and TV hosts that the words "hint and tip" weren't to appear in anything associated with me. I made it clear that I taught professional principles and procedures, I didn't give hints and tips. I would tell the host, for example, "But Diane, these things don't work!" And she would counter, "Yes, Don, but people have these things around the house."

One of the most notable skirmishes in the battle of hint and tip versus solid pro advice came in 2001, when I received a call from *USA Today*. The editor knew of my "professional" point of view from previous interviews, and was doing an article about a much-publicized new hint and tipper—Linda Cobb, the "Queen of Clean"—who used Tang (a powdered breakfast drink mix) to clean the toilet. "What do you think, Don?" she said. I told her that drinking Tang would probably do you more good than cleaning with it. She then asked me how my professionals clean toilets.

Three days later, the first page of the main section of *USA Today* had our pictures, side by side, in color, the Queen spooning Tang into the toilet and me kneeling to apply professional bowl cleaner. The thrust of the article was "Titans of the Toilet Clash!"

The next day calls poured in from the media. CBS, for example, offered to pay all expenses for me to come East and have a news-hour showdown with my competitor. Even the sleazy shows called, hoping to fan the flame. Knowing that there would be no way to come out ahead (even if I won) going up against up a middle-aged woman on national TV, I stayed home and stuck to my guns… or bowl cleaner.

A man in a woman's business

The question "Why is a man doing women's work?" was asked of me over and over, and it assumes, of course, that cleaning is a woman's job. The next question of "How does a man know anything about housecleaning?" was a direct challenge to my credibility.

Once the females found out that someone who cleaned for a living could provide some new and professional ways to cut cleaning time, I became their champion, the only man in recent history who had ventured publicly into (or out of) the traditional cleaning closet. Whenever I had the chance, I picked on the "non-cleaning" men unmercifully.

Even the most hardened feminist supported me, because my philosophy and seminars followed the spirit of the book I wrote for men titled *Who Says It's a Woman's Job to Clean?* I would often open my seminars by pointing out the pathetic tools most women had to use around the house: an antique vacuum that sprayed dirt all over the place, a warped pair of scissors you had to hold just right so they would cut, an old foot-treadle sewing machine, appliances with knobs and handles long gone—things they use every day. Meanwhile, the man has a $220 torque wrench set (probably never used), and a turbo-charged deluxe diesel snow blower (used once a year). This was a performance I did with many antics. Women loved it, and the men sunk sheepishly down into their seats. One night at a seminar in California, when I was at the height of my tirade, one woman yelled "Yes!" and whacked her husband on the side of his head with her purse, and the women around her cheered!

One of the highlights of my campaign to reclassify "women's work" came when I was retained to speak at a convention of Ohio election precinct officials. There were 600 attending, mostly women. An ambitious local politician, Senator Robert Taft (directly related to President Taft) was the emcee of the event. He made all the right moves until he introduced me and said, "You women are going to like Don Aslett because he will be talking about cleaning." A groan of disapproval issued forth from the audience, and Senator Taft was suddenly Senator Chauvinist. As I stepped onto the stage and passed him slinking off, I grabbed him by the arm, and asked loud enough for every last woman in the place to hear, "Senator, do you know what 'housewife's revenge' is?" Puzzled, he said, "No."

"Well, Senator, men miss the toilet all the time, and no woman should ever have to clean a toilet, let alone the misses all over the side of the toilet and tub and the floor. So when your wife is on her hands and knees cleaning men's miss messes, she really hates you, so she reaches up on the vanity counter and gets a toothbrush! (The women began to laugh.) And guess whose toothbrush it is?" The women roared in delight, and the Senator's face went white. "When she finishes scrubbing off that pee with your toothbrush, then guess what she does next, Senator?" (No answer, he's standing there like a shorn sheep.) "She rinses it out in the toilet and then puts it back. So if you occasionally have toilet breath, Senator, now you know the reason."

We've got a long way to go yet, but slowly society is grasping the idea that anyone of any gender can and should clean.

"We can't solve our environmental problems because we have this mentality that janitors and mothers are always around to clean up behind us. As I look at cleaning, we're not talking about a house, we're talking about a full-life concept. I think cleaning is the last bastion of responsibility."

—Don as quoted in *Home and Garden Quarterly*

It might appear that in this "media mania" era of my life all of my time and effort went here, and that family, church activities, Varsity, and my other businesses were "off camera." Far from it! All of this travel and media exposure not only blended in with home and business life and enhanced it, but all of it (except for full-fledged tours) took only three or four days a week, and I spent the rest of the week home and at the office with my corporate responsibilities. Interestingly, while traveling, performing, and speaking I had much more personal time to think and write than while home or at the office. Once all of the preparations for it were done, on a three-day trip east for speaking or filming only hours were spent at work, and the rest was hotel, travel, or waiting time—which turned out to be very productive for both personal and company purposes.

Interviews

Fast, fact-filled, fresh, and funny were the four ingredients the media were always after—TV, radio, or print.

By the time my interviews inched into the thousands, I had done them in hotel rooms, restaurants, lobbies, private homes, backyards, parks, airports, military bases, on buses, on paddleboats, at Scout jamborees, conventions, in church, and on paint jobs—anywhere the media could get a notepad, microphone, or TV camera. For telephone interviews, you always tried to pick or plan a place with no noise. But the best laid plans....

Desperate to do an interview with a Hollywood radio station while in Seattle once, I borrowed a security guard's phone and sat on the toilet in a tiny restroom, door closed to the extent the phone cord allowed. Unable to find any privacy in an airport another time, I did

DESPERATION CREATES A HOMEMADE "SOUNDPROOF INTERVIEW BOOTH" ON A WESTERN ROADSIDE.

a one-hour phoner with a Boston station from a bank of open phones. The airline shuttle carts ("Peep, peep…") kept passing by, and the host, concerned, asked if a garbage truck was going to back over me. I did one presentation on the loading dock of a warehouse and others in cafeterias in use.

An interview with *Prime Time America*, on one of the largest Christian networks, was scheduled for four o'clock at a Best Western in Price, Utah, where I would be speaking later. I had a 45-minute cushion of extra time just in case, and the "in case" happened, of course. As my son Grant and I started over a mountain pass on our way to the motel, the state highway department was paving and flagmen signaled a two-mile line of cars to a stop. Calling from the motel was history, and there were no cell phones then; innovation was the only solution. We turned off the road to a filling station near the top of the pass that had a single outside phone booth, occupied by the local gossip, it appeared. I circled the booth, paced, gestured, signaled to her, and sighed for ten minutes trying to get possession of that phone. At two minutes to four, she finally emerged and I leaped onto the phone. I got the host Jim Warren, but the sound of all of the passing trucks shifting at the top of the grade drowned out callers' questions. It was 96 degrees, but my son threw quilts, tablecloths, and tarps out of the motor home and draped them over the booth for a sound barrier. It was blacker and hotter than the inside of a cow, but I was then able to finish the interview without a hitch.

"I really, really enjoyed your guest on today's program. He had me in stitches talking about junk and 'stuff.' He was so funny and fun I called several friends and told them to turn on their radios. I will try to find his books tomorrow just for the entertainment value. A great laugh for an entire hour is well worth giving up some stuff for. Thank you for finding him and bringing him to us."
—Email sent to Dan Nims, KUGN, Eugene, Oregon,
about a radio interview I did from Hawaii.

The majority of interviews—radio, TV, or print—are much the same. The reporter or host asks questions, and I strive to give intelligent, informative answers with as much life and color as possible. Radio interviews range from short five-minute rah-rah sessions to two full hours of questions and call-ins. Most TV segments are 5 to 7 minutes. Yours always feel like about a minute and a half and the other guests' seem like 15 minutes, but they are usually all the same. The *National Enquirer* (which I don't buy or read, but do feed cleaning stories to occasionally) would call, tell me they had a tape recorder, and ask my permission to use it. They would call back by appointment and read the story as it was to appear and again, record my okay or corrections. All five of my stories for the *Enquirer* were done by phone, as were articles in *Brides*, *Glamour*, *Woman's Day*, *Popular Mechanics*, and many others.

When I was on tours I would meet

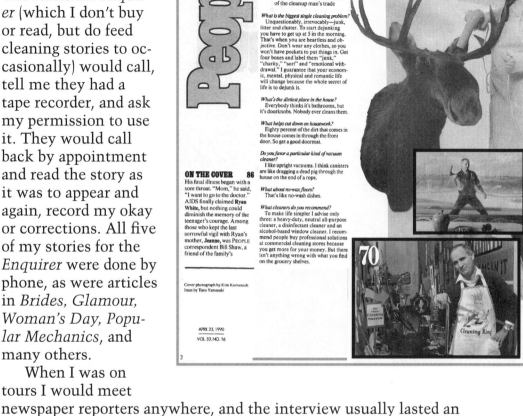

newspaper reporters anywhere, and the interview usually lasted an hour, then they took a picture or two (or thirty). The phoners across the waters—from Ireland, New Zealand, and Australia, between poor phone signals and the accents on either side, were often a strain.

People magazine was one of the biggies. An article on me appeared in the April 23, 1990 edition, which had the largest readership ever up to that point—30 million. They called us four months ahead, and it took three months to find a clear day we both could do it. Their reporter flew out from New York and we spent two days together. She came out to our ranch, drank water out of our cold well, and sat at the kitchen table for hours and just looked at the mountains, valley, cattle, and streams. She was fascinated by all the pictures of our family, kids and grandkids, and commented on "the wonder of having all this." Her enthusiasm for our lifestyle meant more to me than the article. Don't we all often take our blessings for granted, as we reload for the rat race?

"Aslett is a fast-talking, likeable, funny man who… can turn a telephone interview into a stand-up comedian's routine on housecleaning."
—*Karen Palmer,* Mansfield News Journal

"You're an inspiration, Don. I've interviewed thousands. That's literally true. Yours was the most exciting visit I've had."
—*Jerold Panas, Panas, Linzy, & Partners*

"No offense to the ladies of the night, but Don Aslett believes that cleaning is the world's oldest profession. Aslett knows [cleaning] so well that he claims he can hear mildew growing on a bathroom wall."
—*Toby Kahn writing in* People *magazine, 4/23/90*

Front page?… well, once

I clicked well with the media and was featured in many full-page spreads in major newspapers and magazines, and did finally make a front page. The last night of a ten-day tour in Great Britain, a photographer from the *Weekly World News* showed up at the publisher's home to take some pictures of America's #1 Cleaning Expert, "just to have some on file," he said. I struck every pose imaginable to complement my cleaning message. Then he said, "Just for fun, give me a funny pose." I declined to be silly, but he assured me that the Brits loved cut-ups and that a picture of me with an apron and duster would be "a riot." Reluctantly I agreed to just one shot. I put my foot on my toilet suitcase, and held the duster like a spear across my shoulder. "Now look arrogant, confident, triumphant," he said, as his Nikon clicked away.

Then I shed that silly apron and went home. About a year later, I received a phone call from an anxious daughter in Alaska. "Dad, you aren't going to believe this, but you are on the front page of a supermarket rag." "You're kidding—which one?" I asked. "That one that is about four grades below the *National Enquirer*," she said.

One of my staff rushed to the nearest supermarket to retrieve my latest publicity. Sure enough, right at the top of the front page, big as life, there was the picture—apron tied around me, chin in air, and foot on toilet, beneath a big, black headline that said, "Meet the Man Women Hate—he can clean a house in 15 minutes!" (The write-up inside was even less flattering, including a headline quoting me as saying, "If it takes more than 15 minutes to tidy up your home you are a flop as a housewife.") Fifteen years later, the picture was used again,

this time with the headline, "How to turn any man into a slave—it's just like training a dog." The accompanying article, among other things, advised women to withhold sex to get their men to do the cleaning. This was dismaying, but believe it or not, when we sought the source of the article, we couldn't pin it down. (We wrote and called and left messages, but never got an answer.) The moral being, don't pose for or say anything you wouldn't want printed.

CLEANING IS EASIER THAN TALKING ABOUT CLEANING, BUT NOT AS FAR-REACHING. A WHOLE NEW UNIVERSE OF FRIENDS, INFORMATION, BUSINESS CONTACTS, AND IDEAS FLOODED IN FROM MY TRAVEL AND APPEARANCES.

The perils of photography

I can guarantee you the glamour of being a photographed "model" is about 400 percent oversold. I was taken aback during early photo sessions at a newspaper when 15 or 20 shots were taken in two or three

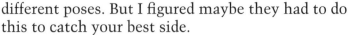

different poses. But I figured maybe they had to do this to catch your best side.

Later a small regional magazine shipped me to a studio in Salt Lake City and a photographer with shades, lights, and one assistant took 70 shots, in more positions and poses than a three-year-old could come up with.

Now a big magazine (*Family Circle*) did a story on me. Their photographer flew in and spent a full day shooting more than 350 photos in a dozen different settings and positions. They used *one* picture in the article.

Then came *People* magazine. For their story, two pro photographers (just back from Beirut) came to Pocatello with a load of lights and cameras that filled a full-size rented Lincoln. They spent two whole days shooting pictures in my office, cleaning museum, cleaning products store, home, ranch, and out at the airport, in front of a jet—1,200 pictures in all. They still didn't get everything they wanted, so two weeks later they flew me to New York for more.

I was directed to a back street in the city that made me thankful my life insurance was paid up. I rode up a rattling elevator to the studio of one of *People*'s top photographers, an ultra-businesslike young woman. She told my escort to get lost for an hour—she wanted me alone. "Loosen your tie," she snapped. I did. "I don't want drunk, just loosen it," she said. I quickly tightened it up a little. "Okay, a smile," she ordered now, and I flashed a fine one. "Don't give me that 'key to the city' look," she commanded through the camera. "I want a smile." She was definitely in charge, and she was good.

Three hundred pictures of me with a moosehead later (I was promoting *How Do I Clean the Moosehead?*), we were done. *People* used three of the 1,500-plus photos they took in all.

I still hadn't seen the full flash of fame photography. When the Eureka Company asked me to be "Mr. Vacuum" for their marketing program, at last, here was a spokesmanship offer compatible with my cleaning goals and values. They sent pages of ad layouts for my approval, and scheduled me for a "shoot" in St. Louis at Maritz Studio. (Even the cab driver raised his eyebrows and whistled when I said the name.) I was told to bring many changes of clothes, and Eureka brought representatives from two different ad agencies, their marketing people and publicist, and a graphics person. We pulled into that prestigious photography place (not a building, but a whole campus with 350 employees, they said). They'd spent the entire day setting up for this one shooting and had taken dozens of pictures already with a stand-in from all angles.

The set was freshly painted and decorated, and the photo crew had to slip on special shoes to approach me to avoid leaving any marks on the floor. Then we started in, with eight experts looking through the lens and their best photographer pulling the trigger. We just plain took pictures—the details would drive you dingy. After my initial makeup was troweled on, a makeup pro nicknamed "Bunny" hopped around all day giving me touchups. The coat and pants of my suit were "clothespinned" back to remove the slightest bag or bulge, the flaps on my pockets were taped shut, and my tie was repositioned. If I turned for an angle shot, I kid you not, the fly on my trousers had to be shifted to always appear straight. They had a ten-smile series: from slight smile and small smile to some-teeth smile and lots of teeth smile.

I posed with each of what seemed like 200 models of vacuum, and in each of these pictures, everything had to be perfect. When my suit coat didn't complement a vacuum, I raced to the dressing room and changed. You couldn't move your thumb even an eighth of an inch without permission, and the angle of everything had to be just right. I felt as if they had me on a joystick bobbing around.

The only compensation was the pictures. They were developed immediately and came out great. The last picture was of me bullwhipping three vacuums. Try making a 20-foot whip pose!

Chapter 19

AND NOW A WORD FROM OUR SPONSOR...

Selling my opinions without selling my soul...

SERVING AS A SPOKESPERSON OR MEDIA REPRESENTATIVE FOR PRODUCTS YOU RESPECT IS ANOTHER SOURCE OF INCOME AND EXPOSURE FOR A PERSON IN THE PUBLIC EYE. A PUBLICITY POSE WITH AN OLD AND NEW VACUUM FOR EUREKA.

There is another income source for the "celebrity" called spokesmanship. When a product needs publicity, the manufacturer often looks for someone to front for it, to represent it to the media. Once a public relations firm was retained by a client to publicize a cleaning-related product, they would often contact me to serve as the expert or spokesperson. If they liked me and I liked the product, we would spar around to develop a mutually beneficial arrangement. Then a tour was scheduled for which they set up the media (radio, print, and TV) and I was paid by the day (around $1,200) to cleverly introduce and display their product along with other cleaning ideas.

As a spokesman I would appear on TV and radio talk shows, news, and how-to and home shows, teaching people to clean and talking about my profession, and mention the product or sponsor somewhere in an offhand way (free advertising). I was on many major shows representing products and companies like Eureka, AstroTurf, Scotchgard, Wisk, the New Pig dust cloth, Rubbermaid, and others. The trick was to get the product and its use clearly represented without actually pitching it. The TV prop people would usually tape over any brand names on your visuals, and hosts warned you not to mention product names unnecessarily. Many liked me well enough that they would fudge on the rule about naming product brands, much to the delight of my sponsors.

My favorite experience here was when I traveled introducing a new Eureka no-cord (battery powered) vacuum. I showed up in New York to do the *LIVE—Regis and Kathie Lee* show on ABC with not only the new vacuum model, but a little plastic toy vacuum for Kathie's new baby Cody. The stage people taped every possible place on the real vacuum that could give a clue this was a Eureka product. As the segment started, Regis was trying out the sponsor's vacuum, and Kathie enthusiastically held up the toy vacuum I'd given her and yelled with great joy, "Eureka!" (which was written in two-inch letters on the toy). I got a few brownie points for that one.

Sponsorship often meant a five- to ten-city tour—the exposure (for both my books and my cleaning company) was great. An offer to be Mr. Clean in Canada for Mr. Clean's birthday, however, wasn't worth shaving my head for.

Spokesmanship, not paid endorsement

There were products I liked and used and let people know it, often resulting (because of my visibility in the industry) in a real boost in sales for the product. I did PR and ads like the one on the next page for Eureka without taking any fee or royalty for using my name and loyalty to their products. I was glad to do this for free, as long as they helped place me in speaking engagements and home shows where I did earn money. For Eureka I was featured in full-color advertising in national magazines and appeared on point-of-sale posters, banners, and other items. In the long run, ads like this helped sell my books and speaking and I'm sure gained some accounts for my cleaning company, too.

One big money opportunity that came my way was an offer to be the man in all media for the "blue water in the toilet" people, 2000 Flushes. They wanted my image and humor to enhance their product's visibility and sales. They offered and bargained, sent a delegation of PR people to Idaho, and finally flew me to their headquarters in New York to try and convince me of the enormous rewards of signing this contract for endorsement and spokesmanship.

They were nice people, and it was a good company with a popular product, but I couldn't in good faith support their claims that their product actually *cleaned* toilets the way I recommended they be cleaned (even if it doubled the sales of my books). I said no, and never regretted it. I think the final convincer was when one of their lawyers said to me in course of the negotiations, "Come on, Mr. Aslett, you know and I know that getting to the big time you have to prostitute yourself sometime."

Another time driving home from a funeral I spoke at one day, I said to my wife, "Boy, it would be nice to go to something just once where I wasn't running it or speaking at it. I'd like to just go and sit or stand somewhere sometime as a spectator, no demands or pressure to 'deliver.'" The wand waved, and I got my wish.

A publicist for The Eureka Company called and asked if I would be their "booth celebrity" at the National Housewares Show in Chicago. I'd wanted to see one of these shows for years and now would be getting paid $1,500 a day to do it, with all expenses paid in the most luxurious hotel in town. I was supposed to go and just stand there, nod, smile, absorb the goings-on and relax and just be a visual aid for a change.

When I got to Chicago, all three buildings of the enormous McCormick Center were full of buyers and sellers from all over the world. The miles of booths and displays were awesome, and the Eureka booth was not the usual 8-by-10 but 50 feet long, and it had a platform stage with a miniature living room on it at one end. The stage was my first clue that being an animated wooden Indian wasn't my destiny for these four days. One section of the "living room" had a 3-by-3-foot Plexiglas floor with a slanted mirror under it, so the audience could see under the rug (a clever idea, to demonstrate the vacuum's vigor and virtues). We would lift up the rug, sprinkle "dirt" (we used cornstarch for this) on the Plexiglas, and lay the carpet back over it. Then as we vacuumed the carpet, the cornstarch was sucked up through the rug, much to the delight of onlookers. The stage also had a new home carpet extractor and Eureka's new full-size cordless, battery powered vacuum. Red, sleek, and low, it was as sexy as any Corvette.

My job (it turned out I did have one) was to pull in potential buyers, especially from big places like Sears or Penney's. Eureka had hired a female model (who certainly overshadowed any machine) to assist me. She ran my microphone and a big TV showing me doing Eureka commercials. While I beat the carpet, she batted her eyes, sprinkled the cornstarch, and pointed at the demonstration with perfect fingernails.

I started each day at eight-thirty in the morning and ended at five or six o'clock, never leaving the booth even to eat or go the bathroom, because you never knew when that all-important client or buyer might stop by. Right across from the Eureka booth was a blender demonstration where four lovelies and a TV chef ground up ice, cabbage, and apples, and made pizzas. I'm here to testify that the average buyer, Neiman Marcus or Kmart, likes food more than a vacuum pitch.

By now my illusions of an easy job were gone. It was gut-hard work, especially demonstrating a prototype machine when parts and clamps fell off or flew into the air, or the battery fell out when six prospective buyers were watching. As one customer was bending over to study the pressure valve connection on the extractor more closely (I'd never seen or used the machine before that day), I yanked too hard and the faucet fitting blew, drenching the fellow's fine suit. By the end of the first day, I felt like a carnival huckster.

At 6 P.M., the Eureka executives were raring to go out on the town, and of course they wanted me (the "movie star") to go along. Eating for three hours in a loud, smoke-filled environment was of zero interest to me. I assured them I had collected 50 business cards from their potential customers and needed to excuse myself and go write up my notes.

I dragged myself into my room at seven o'clock, ordered a tuna fish sandwich, and started sorting contacts. Carol called me and gave me an hour's worth of little assignments that had to be completed quickly, and then I counted vacuums all night in my sleep.

I was up again at six in the morning and back on the sales floor. Later that day, I was demonstrating for our biggest audience so far, a platoon of Japanese businessmen with cameras and note pads in hand. Beauty spread the cornstarch and helped the beast inform them that I would indeed suck the deep down "dirt" from the rug. Polite nods followed, and the sound of clicking Nikons. I started up the vacuum and went into my routine when a look of horror came to the face of my lovely assistant. She was looking at the mirror under the floor, and began mouthing a silent SOS. I finally decoded her dramatics enough to realize that the cornstarch (fake dirt) was not moving. I smiled, bent down, adjusted the vacuum a notch closer to the rug, and continued. When that didn't work, I raised the suction another notch, but the cornstarch stayed put. In desperation, I dropped the vacuum all the way to the face of the carpet, giving that innocent little rug full power. The vacuum picked the rug right up off the floor and was doing its best to digest it. There was immediate loud applause from the enthusiastic Asians, impressed with a vacuum so strong it ripped the carpet off the floor. They cheered and walked into the sales area to make a deal.

After they left, I pulled the rug aside to vacuum up the powder, but it didn't budge—it stuck like glue to the glass—a little scientific phenomenon that no one expected. We couldn't remove the static electricity from it, so for the balance of the show we invented more unique new vacuum demos than you can imagine.

That was one of the longest days of my life, and I couldn't wait to collapse in that king bed. One of the advertisers from Eureka called me aside and said, "Don, Gil Dorsey (the president of Eureka) loves hockey and wants you to go with him and six others to the Blackhawks game tonight." I didn't have much choice but to say yes. So I went and there was a fine menu of fights to watch—on the ice, in the stands, or in the parking lots, plus 15,000 groaning fans, pucks flying around at 100 miles an hour, and beer spraying down your neck from the rabid fans sitting behind you. After three hours, I could hardly wait for it to end. Then in the last 30 seconds Edmonton tied and the game went into overtime. When it ended at midnight, I fired my fairy godmother.

There is a lot of pressure in doing spokesmanship media. It is actually an advertisement made to look like pure information that is selling nothing. The client usually wanted firm and consistent "mentions"; the TV people, on the other hand, wanted information without even a twinge of commercialism. It was a fine line to tread, and never easy. And there were always hours of travel, preparation, and waiting, waiting, waiting (yellow-pad time) for every five-minute segment shoot. The flood of relief after it was over, or the high after a full day that went well, was short-lived because tomorrow was the same thing with a different host in a different city.

How to Spring Green

EXPERT ADVICE FOR EARTH-FRIENDLY CLEANING

We spend **five years** of our lives cleaning. In the process, we tend to make our mark on the environment by creating excess litter as well as household waste, and by using extra energy. This year, why not use this time and effort to make a difference? While you get the house ready for spring, don't just clean, Spring Green. This brochure explains the basics for Spring Greening your home--simple things you can do to save time, money and natural resources.

Don Aslett
Cleaning expert and author of
Is There Life After Housework?

A PUBLICITY SHOT FROM A "SPRING GREEN" SPOKESMANSHIP TOUR I DID FOR THE JAMES RIVER CORPORATION.

Sweating it out for P & G

It was thunder and long underwear that most tested my commitment to hold on to the heavyweight crown of cleaning. Even the commode champ has to stay in the public eye, so I'd pledged a day to a publicity firm in New York to shoot a commercial for one of the biggest soap manufacturers in the U.S.

The shooting location was a house on Long Island, not far from the flight paths of LaGuardia and Kennedy airports. After introducing me as "the talent," the trauma of shooting three minutes of soft sell for Procter & Gamble began. As instructed, I was wearing a light blue jumpsuit to keep sweat stains undetected, and some thermal underwear under that. Plus a blue t-shirt, so no suggestive masculine hair showed at the neckline. It was hot and muggy and the client and agent wanted the words exactly, not more or less as they were in the script. The yard was full of lights, reflectors, cameras, audio consoles, directors, and crew, and I was on the side of the house trying to do a 30-second section of the script… right. On the sixth take, I did it perfectly but a dog across the street barked and ruined the audio. Then for five takes, I couldn't get everything in. Four times an airplane ruined the recording. Finally, we got a keeper, except I said "cheap" instead of "economical."

Again, again, and again I did a perfect segment, except someone stopped his car on the street to see the action or a 33-cylinder garbage truck with no muffler had to stop and start in the adjoining alley. Three hours later that 30-second part was done.

Next, because of threatening weather, they decided to film the "outside" five seconds of the story. I was supposed to come bounding out the back door, look at the camera, and say, "Remember, there is life after housework. With the right tools and techniques, you'll have more time and money for the exciting things in life." They wanted me to be a cool cat, so I had purchased a bright red and white jogging suit and flashy new sneakers. Wishing to return the outfit later to save a few dollars, they taped the bottom of the sneakers to keep them clean and tucked the un-removed labels out of sight. So I did at least 20 takes, up and down the porch, in a sweatsuit over thermal underwear in 95-degree weather, with huge cardboard tags poking at me.

Finally we went inside with the product. I'd do a perfect first time rehearsal and then stumble somewhere on the next four takes, do a gem on the fifth take but the phone would ring or the refrigerator would start up and ruin the audio.

Soon I was so tired I couldn't even read the script doing voice-overs. I was telling people to "lead the label" instead of "read the label." After 12 or 14 takes of one tough "stick to the script" section, I did a high-energy, bright-eyed convincer. The noise of the rain now outside carried into the audio and ruined the footage. By now it was 6 P.M. and I had missed my plane, which meant a 2:30 A.M. arrival home. By 7 P.M., we were shooting close-ups, no voice, but now I even missed the cupboard door handle twice.

You'll never convince me that TV talents are overpaid.

Home shows

When I was in my fifties, if someone asked, "Where is Don?" the answer was likely to be, "Oh, he's doing home shows." That means the home and garden shows, held in a big expo or convention center packed with hundreds of booths showing and selling pools, hot tubs, windows and siding, water purifiers, salad makers, cabinets, phones, statues, mops, anything! Home shows are generally held once a year for about four

Don Aslett isn't just America's #1 Cleaning Expert, he's America's favorite cleaner! For more than a decade now he's been teaching homemakers across the country how to clean faster and better, keeping them smiling all the while.

A PHOTO FROM A BROCHURE WE USED TO PROMOTE MY IN-PERSON APPEARANCES AT HOME & GARDEN SHOWS.

days in a well-populated area and each merchant or vendor pays $800 to $2,000 for a space or booth, so the name of the game is drawing a crowd. If there is no crowd, everyone loses, so the owners advertise like crazy and tap the media however they can. One way is by bringing in "celebrities" that fit the home environment, people like me, Steve Thomas (*This Old House*), or famous gardeners like Jerry Baker. The promoters would hire us to come to the shows and put on 45-minute "educational performances" three or four times a day, on a stage in some corner of the giant expo center.

When the appointed time came I would leap on the stage to entertain and educate 30 to 200 people sitting on folding chairs, then run to the booth or a table nearby to answer questions, sell books, and talk to fans. An hour later I was back on stage.

The audiences at home shows came to relax and drift through the exhibits, so you really had to bleed on stage to get their attention.

Weak performers, experts though they might be, would get eaten alive here and end up with maybe three or four people remaining and listening. Unfortunately, too, it often seemed that at these functions people left their manners home, and allowed their children to run wild. Most

Red River Valley
Home & Garden Show

2001 HOME AND GARDEN SHOW

Don Aslett

2001 Show Schedule!
Friday, February 23   3pm-9pm
Saturday, February 24   9am-6pm
Sunday, February 25   11am-6pm

Location: FargoDome
             East and West Entrances

Admission: $5, Children under 14 free when
             accompanied by an
             adult.Admission Discount
             coupon in The Forum 2/18 for
             the 2/23 show only!

Parking: $2, Charged by the FargoDome

Childcare: $2/hr for one child, $1/hr for
             each additional child from same
             family. Maximum 2-hour stay.
             Open during all show hours. Must
             be between the ages of 3-7 and
             potty trained.

THE HOME SHOW CIRCUIT WAS A REWARDING BUT DEMANDING ONE.

people came to a show like this to get something free and fill the giant free bag they grabbed at the first booth by the door. People would smoke or cuss in your face and criticize your product before you had a chance to tell them what it was. They would try to take anything that wasn't glued down, even samples chained to a table.

The negative that did most to nullify the benefits of home shows was the noise. Right next to my stage at one show was an animated rubber model of George Burns that sang, "I wish I was 90 again" 50 times an hour. In Denver, I was next to a portable child amusement center with trains, merry-go-rounds, and loud circus music. In Columbus, I shared a booth with the Columbus Zoo—three nice young people and a noisy selection of critters that screamed, snarled, and hissed. One time I was next to a large Japanese garden display and thought, "Oh boy, a quiet neighbor at last!" until they turned on the "bing-bong" music. Even my audiences (who were only there for 40 minutes) said, "Man, that drives me crazy. How do you stand it?" Show after show I was next to butchers, bakers, and candlestick makers, all with microphones, which we turned up to drown each other out.

At night, wondering how I'd get through another day, I'd tell myself, "You made more than $2,000 today, met hundreds of interesting people and some new friends, promoted Varsity and your books, and are getting a chance to visit this city. Most people would pay to do this, so quit complaining!" This forced me to admit that the home shows, though challenging, were profitable and even exciting at times.

Trying to sell people on cleaning did get to be a downer sometimes at these shows. Couples would shuffle by and I'd call out like a hustler, "Great cleaning show starting in ten minutes, don't miss it, it's worth your whole trip here!" People would actually flinch away, doing everything possible to avoid eye contact. If no crowd was building up at six minutes to starting time, I'd be out in the aisles begging people to come and listen. But even if I expected 100 and got 50, the 50 were usually so grateful and enthusiastic afterward that it was worth it.

I think the ultimate test was a home show in the Toronto area. This one was so bad the only way I survived it was by thinking how good a story it was going to make for this autobiography some day! To my left was a big inflated rubber kiddie gym, with screaming kids crawling all over it. Next to that was a guy selling a vitamin mix, running moaning blenders constantly for a crowd of people pushing for free sips of pulverized radish and cauliflower. Next to him was a piano and organ display, with the keyboards of most of the models being plunked on by would-be musicians. Right behind me was a home theater with a bass speaker that vibrated my squeegee right off the table. Next to this was a bearded gent demonstrating a metal grinding machine.

Directly to my right, however, was the ultimate distraction, a goddess-like lass in a sprayed-on bodysuit demonstrating and selling a new "thighmaster" exercise tool. All of the men the women in the audience had dragged along for the cleaning show were leaning forward and falling off their chairs, hypnotized by this fitness filly, while I was up on a makeshift plywood stage ranting and raving with a couple of skinny mops and brooms. I did four shows a day for four days and never bought a piano, a grinder, or a thighmaster. I decided that the healthiest and safest venture in the neighborhood was the Vitamix—a good decision.

One day someone asked me, "How's it going?" We all get asked that at least 10,000 times in a lifetime, and somehow a "feeling sorry for ourselves" appraisal is what often spurts out first. I answered, "Well, I spent three days filming an infomercial for Monsanto—three days of my life for nine and a half seconds of finished film." But when I thought about it, it wasn't three days of my life for nine and a half seconds at all, it was an almost impressive array of rich experiences I:

1. Would be paid royalties forever for less than ten seconds of work.
2. Had a notepad along through all of that travel, airport, hotel, and "waiting on the set" time, and wrote more than 30 pages of manuscript for the new book my publisher was waiting for, some of the best work I'd ever done.
3. Also had pages of stories, prime humor, and information from people I'd met and conversed with during that time.
4. Had four stimulating and educational hours with some of the world's best marketers.
5. Had arranged a TV spot in Europe.
6. Had written three of my best poems.
7. Also had made the decision to buy two acres of land for a corporate office in Salt Lake City someday.

In other words, at least a half-dozen other things were accomplished during those three days!

REFLECTIONS ON "FAME"

"As seen on TV"

The endorsement, even sanctification that comes with "being on television," never ceases to amaze me. People can introduce me and there will be no big response until they say, "He's been on TV." Then I get oohs and aahs and I'm much more impressive. Yet look who is on TV much of the time: dumb sweaty jocks, people whose looks are their only notable attribute, wayward politicians, liars, adulterers, thieves, murderers, molesters, spouse abusers, alcoholics and other drug addicts, and life dropouts and losers. You don't have to be worthy to be a TV celebrity—television will show anything for ratings or profits. Being sane or nice doesn't yield much news or sensation. It doesn't make sense, does it?

One thing that actually flattered me, however, was when they requested me, live or taped, for "sweeps week." That is when television networks evaluate the shows to get ratings and decide what to keep for next year. My shows were used often. One time at the American Booksellers Association convention in Atlanta, they had author interviews playing on a big screen in the center of the coliseum. One of the five picked for this from the whole country was mine—another small victory for cleaning!

At one of the booths there, a fellow hustling guests for a show said, "Let me show you the perfect interview, with energy, information, and humor." And he clicked a tape on. Halfway through it he looked back and forth and said, "Hey—you're him!"

"Every time I clean my toilet, I think of you"

Fame? Recognition? National popularity? Don't fool yourself or hold your breath. The American dream has it that you get good at something—singing, dancing, acting, or scoring—and suddenly overnight everyone knows you, seeks your autograph, and showers you with potentially profitable propositions. It doesn't really happen that way.

After years with my head in the toilet, I got good at cleaning—I knew how to do it, to write about it, to teach it, and to entertain with it. When an article on me appeared in the metropolis of Pocatello (one of Idaho's largest cities, with a population then of almost 50,000), I figured the floodgates were open. I began wondering if my local bank and post office could hold all of the mail and money that was about to tidal wave over my operations. It didn't.

When I self-published my first book, *Is There Life After Housework?*, and sold 20,000, I figured half the people in the country were thinking about me when they first got up in the morning. Then when Writer's Digest, a top-notch publisher, took my book I imagined enthusiastic homemakers storming my ranch and carrying me away, my wife running behind yelling, "Please bring him back!"

But so go the dreams. Fame wasn't and isn't like that, and for the benefit of any of you rags-to-riches dreamers I'll share a few of my first ego punctures, housework humblers, or whatever we might call them.

When Writer's Digest decided to republish my first book, *Is There Life After Housework?*, they set up a national tour to call attention to the book. The tour, described earlier, covered every major city in the U.S. Quivering with delightful thoughts of edging *Love Boat* and *60 Minutes* out of the #1 spot, I packed up my props and prepared for the first flight to San Francisco. Here there would be two segments on radio station KGO, the highly rated talk show *Jim Eason*, two other radio shows, and an interview with the *San Francisco Examiner*.

I hit the Bay City, got a full page in the paper and my radio interviews, and was a whitewashed Bill Cosby on TV. But in publicity and the media, your imagination is the only thing that penetrates the whole market.

When I finished that evening, exhausted but exuberant, the cab dropped me at the Sir Francis Drake Hotel. (I kept waiting for the cabbie to recognize me.) Although I was a couple of meals behind, I was reluctant to go to a restaurant for fear of the autograph seekers and the press, so I pulled my coat collar up and headed to a Chinese food takeout stand a few blocks away. The streets were teeming with people—any minute I knew somebody would yell out, "It's him—the Toilet Man!" and I would be inundated. But no one did, so I let my collar down and still no action, so then I took my coat off and carried it so that no one could mistake that gray suit! I whistled a cleaning song and inspected some dusty pictures—still no reaction. Armed with a couple of egg rolls, I headed back to the hotel. Frankly, I was appalled at how chicken-hearted those San Franciscans were, afraid to approach a famous figure.

Six blocks later, absent any admirers, I stood at the last light across from the hotel. I felt a tug at my sleeve and faced a lovely, classy woman. Finally she spoke, "Had a tough day, didn't you?" I sucked in my stomach, deepened my voice, and replied, "Yes, those studio lights and television shootings really take it out of you." (I was basking in having my first fan club member.) "How would you like some company in your room, a back rub and other nice things?" My fame bubble popped quickly. All I attracted with my brilliant performance in San Francisco was… a prostitute!

I ate my egg rolls alone, figuring Detroit, the next stop, would have greater appreciation for an authentic cleaning artist like me. Thirty days later I was a veteran of a full-scale author tour, but no one else (including ladies of the house or evening) had sought me out. In fact, in the next three years I did 1,500 appearances in the U.S. and at least 100 elsewhere, and still never had to hide from a mob of fans.

As I did more books and my popularity with TV, radio, and other media increased, my concept of fame shrank back to normal size. There are lots of people in the world. Few of them really care about cleaning, and only a few of those (darn few, when you get down to it) watched and held their breath when my mug squeegeed its way across the screen. I remember when I had books on the bestseller list—I did the national shows *Sonya* and *Kelly & Company* in Detroit, both top programs, and they went well! Some businessmen from a local supply company took me to a fine country club for lunch just 30 minutes after the last show.

When I sat down at the table the server eyed me, handed me the menu, and when she brought the food, said with a puzzled expression, "You sure look familiar." I suggested perhaps TV, an hour ago. "Oh," she said, "you were that funny man on TV this morning." (I had been on *Kelly* and *Sonya* many times during the previous two years.) I asked her what I was selling. "A book, I think...." "What was its name?" She had no idea. The book was shown five times on the program and the title repeated ten times.

Most of your moments of glory are short-lived or have a less than silver lining. Like the time I was coming down the escalator from the gate at the Salt Lake City airport. A young mother in the 30 or so ticket lines saw me and let out a scream that caused everyone around to look around. "Don Aslett!... Oh, Don, I was thinking about you last night!" Both the onlookers and I were stunned at this romantic burst of recognition. Then as she reached me, she grabbed me by the arm and said, "...Because my kid vomited on the carpet and it left quite a stain. I knew you'd know how to get it out."

I've had people attend my three-hour cleaning concert, roll in the aisle laughing, buy all my books, read them, and one year later sit by me on a plane and when I tell them I'm from Idaho they say, "Oh, I went to a great cleaning seminar by this guy... what was his name? Anyway, he inspired me." And they rave on. At first when I heard things like this I put my best seminar face on and flashed my squeegee tie pin and outhouse notebook, but they still didn't know it was me. I now often agree the guy was dynamite, they ought to buy a dozen more of his books before the store runs out, and never introduce myself. My ego has come a long way since that San Francisco honey's tug on my sleeve.

Overestimating your importance in life needs reality checks from time to time. In 2007, one of my Varsity managers informed me that he had just returned from a carpet care certification training session. In a room full of my own employees, the head of our Varsity University training got blank looks when he mentioned my name—the founder and majority owner of the company for which they all worked. When he asked how many there had ever heard of Don Aslett, two hands went up.

I've collected pages of thoughts and observations on the big question: "What good does fame or celebrity do?" And I've bottom-lined it out to one answer, "It gives a person power to influence the behavior of others." Real fame is the ability to do right and influence others to do the same. If you don't use the leverage of influence it gives you, then fame is all superficial—good only for passing praise and pennies.

A flood of response?

Forty years in the media, contracting, and publicity has taught me that most people waiting for results suffer from delusions of grandeur. We see and hear story after story in ads and magazines, etc., about how some ordinary (but brilliant) person came up with a good idea, and released his idea, book, or invention upon society. Floods of money and fame followed. We all read things like this and wonder what it would be like to have that kind of instant success.

By the time I was 55, I was still wondering. The ads always say, "I started this home course or mail order idea and went to my mailbox, and it was stuffed." Mine is stuffed every morning—mainly bills and flyers and ads. I'm a media star, bestselling author, popular performer, and owner of a successful mail order business, and I'm here to tell you that it just doesn't happen that way.

A good response could be three letters or orders (if you were expecting none), and a flood of mail could be five inquiries (if you generally got none). "Thousands of responses," over a span of ten years, means two letters a week.

I did Oprah… "You'll be flooded with results and sell at least 30,000 books." I didn't get one letter, and saw no marked difference in book sales. "When your name and advice go out in our newsletter, you'll be exposed to the world and overrun with calls." It went out five times, with a coded box number to measure the millions of letters, and we got three. When *Family Circle* came out to Idaho and spent $10,000 doing a five-page article on me and my cleaning techniques, they said, "We have seven million readers; you'll have it made for life." The article was well done, and we got five letters. I did a big *Woman's Day* article, too, and got no letters and heard three comments about it over the next five years. After I was featured in *People* magazine, a few friends commented, five people wrote to beg for donations, and a handful of media (that I was already appearing on regularly) called. Either something was wrong with me, or someone was overly optimistic or exaggerating.

Some little stations in the boonies would yield more than the biggies. I did big national cleaning shows claiming millions of viewers, and received almost nothing by way of response. I did the same show for Channel 2 in Salt Lake City with my daughter Laura on a Sunday night and got 750 letters in the next few days. KMOX radio out of St. Louis, gave my address and offered a one-dollar stain chart for free (seeking addresses for our mailing list), and got 100 responses. I wasn't impressed until a response consultant in the East told me that even a dozen letters after a show was a great response.

I realize now that response isn't an overnight flooding; it's a drip, drip, drip.

No truer words were ever spoken than "A prophet has no honor in his own country" (Luke 4:24). That applies well to fathers, mothers, bosses, and especially authors. While I am in demand all over, for speaking and consulting, and people are buying my books and treating them like gospel, most of this goes unnoticed at home. Very few of my family or close business associates have read any of my books or watched me on TV. I can get paid $5,000 for one day for advice and expertise, and the next day offer the same for free to close friends or family, who remain unimpressed.

I guess we all get used to the good or bad around us and just accept it as the norm. I finally gave up sharing most letters of praise and PR news with those close to me and am just letting results speak for themselves. Believe the scripture!

Chapter 20

THE FOUR-MILLION MILE CLUB: MY LIFE IN TRAVEL

It always amazes me to meet people who travel for fun...

THIS WAS AN IMPORTANT STOP ON ONE OF MY BOOK PROMOTION TRIPS TO ENGLAND, NOT TO MAKE A CALL, BUT TO POSE IN THIS "CALL BOX" (PHONE BOOTH) IN LONDON. MY COMPANY AND I HAD CLEANED SO MANY OF THESE IN THE U.S., I COULDN'T RESIST LEAVING AN ASLETT CLEANING CARD IN ONE ON FOREIGN SOIL.

Our first travel, as kids and teenagers, or in our twenties, is the most exciting thing in the world. "Getting to go" somewhere is just one step from heaven. There is always something new and exciting, and then a chance to tell everyone about it afterward. Even in the early stages of my businesses, when the demands at home and in the office had no letup in sight, a trip, even just a brief business trip somewhere, was something to look forward to, a relief and a reward.

When I gathered the material for this book, I was astounded at how many references there were to travel. I'm not talking about a few dozen comments, but hundreds of pages of... what? Mostly complaining and whining, descriptions of the irritations and inconveniences of travel. Ironically, many of my "this is my last day of travel" notes written in 1978 were almost word for word what I wrote in 1998. Forgive any excessive opinion or criticism of your hometown you find here—I guess I did a little too much traveling after awhile, and I guess I never learned.

I've flown almost 3 million miles, and driven at least 1 million, not counting all those miles on a tractor working the fields. I had 2-million miler status with Delta and didn't start keep track of frequent flyer miles until I'd been flying for years.

"Does flying bother you?" I am often asked. I practically lived in airplanes for many years, convincing myself always that the statistics often quoted to us are true, that a commercial aircraft is much safer than your automobile.

I never had even a twinge of fear getting onto a plane, but I hate flying in bad weather. One night at three in the morning, for example, between Hawaii and Los Angeles (a thousand miles from either), five miles up in the air, it felt as if we had run into a mountain. The plane plummeted, people screamed, secured carts came loose, and the plane (a DC-10) lurched and tossed. It was the first time I'd felt real fear gripping me while airborne. Finally, the plane leveled out, and we all sat tensely in our seats, overreacting to every slight bump, for the rest of the trip. Then we landed and all boarded another flight to somewhere. On the ground, you recover your bravery fast.

In another storm, over Florida, lightning was everywhere. I looked out the window and the plane seemed to be on fire, lit up with a blue glow. The off-duty pilot next to me was calmly reading a book, and seeing my concern chuckled and said, "That's called St. Elmo's fire, an electrical charge in the air that gives the illusion of fire." Nonetheless, I put my shoes on so I could die with my boots on.

The crew's downplaying of rough or bad weather always intrigued me. "There will be a little turbulence…." It is always called mild turbulence, even when it feels like the wings are about to be torn off. One time when several of the passengers were leaning over their upchuck bags after an hour of circling in the fog, we heard, "Well, we are going in now, folks, expect a vigorous landing." Now that was a new one. (And the landing lived up to it!) A couple of times in flights on small commuter planes (often called the "vomit comets"), we hit winter blizzards and clouds that felt as if they were full of rocks.

Denver was the worst, weather-wise. Even a clear May afternoon could turn into a raging snowstorm in minutes.

Once in Cincinnati, we passengers were all in the plane loaded and ready to go when we heard over the PA system: "There is a tiny mechanical problem and it will be a few minutes until takeoff." I remained in my seat and continued to write the memo I was composing. Suddenly my eyes began to sting and I looked up to see the cabin filling with the blue smoke that was pouring out of our vents. It didn't look good, but amazingly, no one panicked. No lights came on, as the pre-flight instructions promise, but we just all calmly stood up. I was in seat 11C, right behind first class, where two 300-pound brothers struggled to get their oversized luggage and fancy fishing rods out of the overhead bins. Roars, jeers, and threats pelted them: "Leave it, you idiots, and get off the plane or out of the way."

After we got off, we learned that the belts on the air conditioning had overheated, causing the rubber to smoke. Scary, but nothing serious and it would be fixed in an hour. Nevertheless, anyone who didn't want to ride that plane could go down the concourse and take another to the same destination. The passengers departed like stampeding buffalo. Knowing how peaceful it would be with only a few aboard, I stuck with the repaired plane and had plenty of room to spread out my projects.

It didn't take long as a flier to become aware of the chances of bad weather, cancelled flights, and lost luggage. I soon adopted a policy called "early" (earlier than they suggested you come to the airport), and always made sure there were two more flights that day after the one I was scheduled on to where I had to go. Thus of thousands of appearance dates and appointments, I never missed one, except for the time *all* flights were cancelled for 50+ hours right after 9-11.

Flight attendants inspired me, they were so well trained in handling passengers. There were plenty of obnoxious passengers who insulted and abused them, but in 40 years of flying, I never saw one single time where the attendants lost it. Though their role was often glorified (much of what they did was actually janitor work just like mine), they worked hard.

During a three-hour flight to Salt Lake City once, I was so weary I put all my work away, took out a pad, and observed. The friendly guy sitting across the aisle started an ambitious paper project, then had four martinis in a row, and fell asleep. Another man nearby in an all-leather outfit (including hat) twiddled his thumbs and cracked his knuckles for three hours. The Asian fellow next to me had a Japanese/English dictionary and such discipline of memorization I've never seen. The guy behind me rattled his way through a *Wall Street Journal* and two other huge papers and drank endless cups of coffee. The Neanderthal two seats up tried to visit with everyone in reach and all faked sleeping to avoid the exchange. The two college coeds up one seat to the left devoured every glamour, fashion, and "impress a man" magazine available, drank a lot of pop, and ran to the restroom incessantly. The thin pixie-cut guy in front of me, in bare-armpit attire, read a $24.95 book on *The Hero of the Grateful Dead Rock Group*. The fellow in a white shirt and expensive-looking headphones across the aisle did crossword puzzles the whole time. Others drank and ate anything available plus some stuff they brought along. A kid in back of me concentrated on seat kick-

FOR MORE THAN 25 YEARS, PLANE TRAVEL WAS A BIG PART OF MY LIFE.

ing, while someone else back there was a full-time cougher and throat clearer. Another passenger fussed with his laptop until everyone around him lost interest, so he put it away. No one looked out the window until the pilot announced that there was something to look at.

Airline aggravations

(An excerpt from one of my earlier journals.)

There are not many people or tall buildings in Idaho, so when my fame as an author, cleaner, and speaker spread, I had to travel to where there were more people and skyscrapers. This meant flying.

At first, it wasn't so bad. Western was crowing about legroom and United flaunting friendliness, and you could have an occasional extra bag without a charge. And a missed departure was at least apologized for. When fares got the squeeze, so did the seats. The seats were now spaced so close one had to assume the embryo position to ride. The flight attendants' hips seemed to get wider about now too, so they would bump your writing or reading arm on their trips by. There was little room for carry-on luggage or for that matter feet, and the half-inch clearance you finally found for your knees was invaded when the seat ahead of you came back five inches. The big hulks who take up all of the armrest plus some of your territory should be distributed evenly, but I seemed to manage to get them all. I never did master getting comfortable in an airplane seat (or even two or three of them). On all-night flights, it was easier to stay awake and write something.

The only communication between you and the crew was a constant feeding process, beginning with peanuts and drinks, then a meal and a drink, then follow-up snacks and drinks. The attendants spent the entire trip rustling and rattling food and drink, cans and wrappers, up and down the aisle.

First class upgrade meant you got to sit two seats closer to the only baggage rack in the plane. The smokers you tried unsuccessfully to avoid in the gate waiting area were here. Any peace or relaxation was shattered by noisy card shuffling encouraged by cards distributed by the crew.

Waiting in an airport was like spending time in a loud pool hall.

> AIRPLANES SELDOM KILL YOU IN A CRASH—IT'S SLOW DEATH BY THE GRADUAL ACCUMULATION OF AIR TRAVEL TIME, HOURS WHEN YOU ARE HALF DEAD WHILE STILL ALIVE.

Once in a while, when I finished a seminar or speech early and everything went well getting to the airport, I found I was a few hours ahead of schedule, and so tried to catch an earlier plane to get home sooner. Sometimes, doing this, there was an embarrassing rush. When I reached Detroit once, my plane was to leave at 9:30 for Cincinnati. I arrived at the airport at 4:50, glanced at the monitor, and would you believe there was a plane going to Cincinnati at 5:05? You normally need to check in at least 30 minutes before a flight to dispose of your luggage and get a boarding pass, but I spent the 15 minutes I had on the run. I was carrying my big "Latrine Queen" box and other props I used in my seminars, which I dragged across the airport at a trot. There was a line of others ahead of me at the gate, and at 4:57, the attendant finally asked, "Can I help you?" "Can I catch this flight?" I inquired. "Yes, I think so," he replied, and began to process my ticket.

He weighed my box and it tipped the scales at 80 pounds, so it couldn't be checked. "Can you take anything out of this to lighten it to seventy pounds?" he asked hurriedly. Surveying the contents, I decided that the two toilet seats I used for my famous toilet seat race would lighten the box enough and they did. He checked the box and said, "Now it's 5:03, but if you run you might make it." Grasping the two toilet seats tightly against my suit jacket, I made Jesse Owens look like a snail. Onlookers shook their heads in amazement that there would be such crazy people loose in an airport. They were actually rather nice— when people think you are a loose nut, possibly dangerous, they get out of your way.

I know and respect the purpose of customs at airports and borders, but learned to dislike the petty power some of the people involved liked to wield. Going into Canada once to speak at a janitor's convention, they examined me for an hour

My toilet suitcase always got very cautious handling through the system.

with questions as to my background and purpose, finally coming up with the question, "Isn't there someone in Canada who can do this as well as you, Sir?" That challenged my prowess as America's #1 Cleaner, and I said back in a smart-alecky way, "No sir, there isn't a Canadian alive who can do it." Into a special little side room I was now ushered, and grilled further.

What a mistake that was! I finally learned to humble my way through customs.

Wide-open drive time

I was doing a TV talk show in the East and the guest before me was an expert on time management and had an impressive, well documented outline of where and how we spend the hours of our lives—like three years waiting, five years in the bathroom, four years cleaning, etc. When he said two years in traffic, I laughed to myself about those poor suckers in city traffic, places like LA and New York, slow-moving parking lots. But later I got to thinking that even though I often traveled in wide open, no-traffic areas of the West, like Idaho, Wyoming, and Montana, I spent more time in all driving than they did in their traffic jams. Those almost 300,000 miles on my car and 200,000 on my motor home in a few short years didn't come from turning the speedometer ahead. Everything in the West is "distance," and driving is often the only practical alternative. I love to drive, and do so whenever I can instead of fly. Even if it takes longer, it's private and quiet.

BARBARA AND I ON A TRIP TO SALT LAKE CITY FOR A *PM MAGAZINE* APPEARANCE.

Taxi thrills

• It was nice, every once in a while, to get a cab driver who could speak English and count.

• I spent a lot of late night and early morning hours in the hands of some wild man with a cab driver's license that qualified him to "operate." It's a wonder with all these miles traveled in surface transportation, I haven't been killed or at least injured.

• Is this fun? Another 70 mph ride to the airport. I had a cab driver in New York today who was a former Kamikaze pilot who missed.

• As I left a CBS station in downtown Chicago another time, I asked the receptionist to call me a cab. "We have one right outside," she said. I stepped the 20 feet to the street and cabs buzzarded in from all directions. Seeing my arms full of suitcases, they all figured me for an airport fare and leaped out of their cars to argue over me. The guy I chose (the meanest-looking, in case a fight got started) was a giant who couldn't read, write, or drive. Reaching the hotel became secondary to survival.

• One cab I hailed once was not honoring the waiting line. He looked back—I guess to see if there was running distance—and yelled, "Jump in." "My stuff!" I yelled back, pointing to my luggage sitting on the curb. He cursed, leaped from the cab like a demon, and threw my bags in the back seat. The long-waiting other cabbies saw this scab stealing their fare, and began to yell obscenities. Three big hairy-armed irate drivers came running to teach my cabbie a lesson. "In, in, quick!" he yelled. A second after he stepped in the door he was on the road, barely out of reach of his assailants.

• An ABC limo driver picked me up for the *Regis* show, but didn't know how to get there. I gave him the address, and we drove off and got lost. "Do you know where it is?" he asked me. "I'm from Dietrich, Idaho, buddy, a town of less than 200 people—how should I know New York?" As he kept driving up and down the streets, I told him to ask another cab driver. He did ask one, and later I asked two others. But he still couldn't find it. Finally, we reached the vicinity but he couldn't find a place to park. I told him to stop, hit the trunk release, grabbed my four bags of props, and ran down the street to ABC (which turned out to be only a few blocks from my hotel).

• New York cab drivers are in a class by themselves. Not only is their endurance admirable, but their range of nationality and personality alone is worth any fare. Having made my way from Idaho through Salt Lake City, Cincinnati, and Newark on my way in one day, I was on the last leg of my journey in a New York cab. Never try to put your wallet back in your pocket while sitting down—mine was nowhere to be seen when I reached the desk of my hotel and tried to check in. I didn't have a dime, no credit cards, nothing. I was dead! Before I could panic, the cabbie who had found it halfway across town, was at my side with it. I was saved! I offered him $20, but he said, "No thanks, Sir, glad to do it."

• The stretch limo is a symbol of success, elegance, and extravagance. Clients and sponsors, and especially TV shows, often sent a stretch limousine to get me at hotels and airports. It cost more than $15,000 a foot to stretch those common Lincolns or Cadillacs—for what? I never figured out, as most of the time they only hauled one person. Going to Vegas, Akron, Memphis, Tampa, Eugene, and Indianapolis all in one week that just ran together—that was the real stretch.

Worse than tiredness was the growing interference with my privacy. I had taken on a rather intense role in public life, but the endless noise, crowding, and lines began to get to me. It almost seemed like revenge for all those cattle and pigs I hauled and herded around—I found myself being hauled and herded around to places and purposes not necessarily of my choosing. I guess I showed the wear once on a flight home when I was 49. Rather than mill and push with the crowd, I sat waiting for the others to clear out. The pilot came back to me and said, "Excuse me, Sir, do you need a wheelchair?"

Although willing to work lengthy days, I always hated interruptions. Once settled in to write, eat, or sleep I didn't want any shoulder tapping or phones ringing.

The one place I most disliked interruption was in a motel or hotel, because most of the time I arrived there following either a full day of hard travel or an intense day of filming or seminar teaching. Once that door closed, I didn't have any emotion left for dealing with anything or anyone else, including a blinking message light on a phone. But people could find more reasons to disturb you in a hotel than I could count.

I trained groups at a military base once for a long intense day, then staggered into a Marriott with total collapse in mind. I arrived soaked with perspiration, ready to jump in the shower. There was a knock at the door, the delivery of a complimentary bottle of wine I didn't want, so I sent it away. (The bearer wanted a tip, of course.) Then the manager called to see if the room was okay. Finally, I got into the shower, and another knock, asking if they could bring me anything else, since I'd passed up the wine. "No." They left, expecting another tip. Then another knock—they brought some fruit. Now it was the phone, the

WHEN I OPENED THE DOOR OF A HOTEL OR MOTEL ROOM AND DISCOVERED THAT THERE WERE TWO BEDS, A FEELING OF JOY ALWAYS FLOODED OVER ME. A PLACE TO LAY OUT ALL OF MY PROJECTS SO I COULD WORK ON THEM AS THE MOOD STRUCK ME! MUCH OF MY BEST WRITING WAS DONE IN HOTEL ROOMS IN THE EARLY MORNING OR BETWEEN APPEARANCES.

desk calling to ask if I got the fruit. I finally got to bed at eight-thirty, and was just asleep when there was a loud knock at the door. I got up, threw something on, and it was a maid with two free chocolates asking to turn down my bed. "What do you mean, turn down the bed? No thanks." And back to bed. One minute later, another knock, her again. "Well, Sir, would you like the chocolates anyway?" "Gadfreys, woman, give them to me and go away."

I went back to bed and tossed until ten, then finally fell into a deep sleep. There was a rapping at the door at what the clock dial showed as eleven-thirty—this late it must be an emergency. I rushed to the door and there stood a guy with a handcart loaded with canned goods. "Would you like a couple of cans of peas, Sir?" he asked. "What!!" "I'm giving out samples of our peas here at our convention." "Two cans of peas at midnight—are you kidding??" He wasn't. That was the worst night I remember for interruptions.

Of the many challenges of doing the telephone company seminars, none was more physically straining and risky to all concerned than the lugging around of my baggage en route. While I was at the airport checking in, my trail across the country could easily be followed by tracking the hernia operations on bellhops and baggage handlers. The first of the six pieces of luggage to be sent onto the unsuspecting conveyor was my super size aluminum suitcase, stuffed full of clothes plus a tape player, projector, manuals, and visual aids. It was so heavy I never saw a bellhop's eyes stay in their sockets when he tried to lift it. Next came my mini-skyscraper. This was a model phone building used as a visual aid. It was a mass of plastic, glass, electric wiring, and cords compacted into an innocent looking 20-by-40-by-12-inch plywood box. A frail airline check-in attendant, who had been trained not to let passengers handle their own luggage, was convinced the box was stuck to the floor. Many a bicep (and my popularity) at the ticket counter was strained when I showed up with "the box."

I finished a seminar in Philadelphia once and Arlo and I were traveling on to Pittsburgh for another. Our plane arrived on time, but a long wait at the luggage carousel was soon causing murmuring about "poor airline service." No luggage came rolling out for anyone, yet the carousel was going around. After 45 minutes of waiting, irate customers were close to violence, including that year's six-foot-five Pittsburgh Pirates batting champ. Threats and lawsuits were being bandied about by the storming customers when the carousel stopped and started again, and a voice on the loudspeaker said, "We are sorry for the luggage delay on Flight 387, but a large heavy box has jammed the system. Thank you."

A murmur of curses came from the crowd, and when the conveyor finally spit out the first piece of luggage, you guessed it, it was the big orange box with the telephone building in it. "There it is!" someone shouted. "Whose is it?" asked someone else. You can be sure that Arlo and I were not the first to claim our baggage. We decided a healthier use of time would be to wait until the crowd had thinned. After an hour, eyes still followed the box to see who the ratfink owner might be. Arlo and I remained behind a column and finally everyone had left with their baggage except the big disgruntled batter, who now had not only waited forever for his luggage, but had (during the wait) had a fight with his wife or girlfriend. Anxious not to be on the receiving end of his anger, we stepped

HEAVY

AN EXTRA TAG SEEN OFTEN ON MY SUITCASES!

forth and took all of our luggage except the box, which kept going around while we boarded the hotel limousine. We sent the driver after the box, which he managed to retrieve unmolested.

If there was any perverse pleasure I got from travel it was making bellhops earn their tips. I always liked to carry my own bags, practically an impossibility in or near a hotel. They'd spot my innocent-looking trunk or garment bag, reach down to snatch it up, and it would yank them off their feet (as usually I'd end up carrying my props or pro cleaning gear with me instead of shipping them ahead). My favorite was a box of brass squeegees that weighed about 18 pounds but looked like a box of chocolates. I could get five or six of these in a garment bag undetected. Even my briefcase, a metal Halliburton monster, could barely be lifted by bellhops when fully packed. Weight limits were more liberal in the old days.

Not the dean of haute cuisine

Performing and speaking while traveling required a lot of discipline. You can't stand in front of an audience half asleep, your mind on other things, or your stomach overloaded with food. Perhaps I was oversensitive about the obligation to do my best for every audience, but felt each one had no way of knowing how good I was before or might be next time, they only knew the performance they were experiencing. So I had to make it my best.

I didn't like to eat at banquets before speaking. Many, many times with my stomach growling and chops licking, I said "No thanks," because going on a little gaunt I focused better. After two weeks of travel, 30 media shows, speaking, and meeting fans, plus my regular business, there were evenings I wanted to go on a trash run, eat five pieces of strawberry pie, watch John Wayne on the late, late show, and sleep till 10 A.M. I couldn't do that and deliver the goods the next day, so I didn't.

When I was traveling heavily in the 1980s, publishers and clients considered it an obligation (and opportunity) to take the guest "out to dinner." Every visit I made on tour or speaking assignments, my host would want to impress me more than the previous stop. "Have you ever eaten at _____?" they would ask. "Nope," I would answer. Their face would brighten—"Ah, that's where we'll go." They'd usually pick upscale places like the Lobster Lagoon or the Prime Rib Palace. Soon I'd eaten in many of the best—even secret—restaurants from New York to San Francisco, from Atlanta to London.

After a long wait in a lobby or smoke-filled bar, we would usually end up in an elegant, under-lighted, over-promoted place, where platoons of prancing waiters with fake accents served overpriced, over-spiced food.

In a big Eastern city the restaurant I was treated to once was quaint, and overlooked a famous river. Waiters were dressed like tin soldiers and dolls, and each hors d'oeuvre was mounted on an individual tray. The bread was served with silver tongs. Making the salad at the table's edge was a professional performance—identifying, then cutting and spinning each leaf that went in. The dressing included every herb cultivated in the last three centuries.

After the salad, tiny cocktail glasses were thrust before us, which appeared to contain a couple of spoonfuls of crushed ice. "What is that?" I asked the waiter. "It is a sorbet," he said. "What is it for?" I asked. (I always thought it was an advantage to know what I was eating.) "It is to flush and cleanse your palate after the salad so you may savor the entrée better, Sir." When they served the entrée, one guy did the job while two backups stood there like stuffed penguins, nodding their heads and showing their new false teeth. After I cleared away the decorative garnishes and steamed vegetables, I found the small, discreet morsel of food I had ordered. Surely it was shriveled up from embarrassment at the pomp and circumstance required to present it.

The colorful desserts wheeled by later on a chromed-up janitor cart looked like a sculptor's experiments, and most of them had so much frosting and other decoration it completely obscured whatever the dessert started out to be. Throughout the meal, there were drinks and more drinks, and then an endless stretch at the end for coffee.

I would have traded the whole meal for a can of cold pork and beans and a mason jar of Mom's apricots or pears. My host tipped those bowing, scraping, soft-shoeing servers $20. My mother was ten times the cook and server, and I was ashamed to consider that I'd never tipped her a dime in a lifetime.

I went to the restroom to wash my hands after handling the shrimp (which was wallowing in melted butter). After I washed my greasy paws I groped for a paper towel—none! An electric hand dryer? None. Then, *thunk*, a big, clean warm towel appeared in my dripping hands. The source of the towel was a big fellow uniformed like a doorman. Surprised to find such a sharing individual in a restroom, after drying my hands I said, "Well thanks, buddy," handed it back to him, and retreated out the door. When I told the host about the mystery person dispersing cloth towels in the loo, he informed me that he was the restroom attendant, and you are required to tip him. Can you believe that? I'm glad I didn't need to do anything besides wash my hands....

Life was getting busier—my family and Varsity was growing, grandchildren appearing, and writing and preparing my presentations took time and emotion. Soon the fascination of leaving the hotel (after a day of hard work) and going out to eat from 6-10 P.M. faded. Often I had the urge to say to prospective sponsors and clients, "My fee is four thousand dollars, with a two-thousand-dollar discount if I don't have to go out to dinner."

I didn't drink, and disliked overeating and loud restaurants, so one day I said, "No more." What a relief it was to only have to go out to dinner several times a year instead of a hundred.

I've often wondered as I plowed through some unpleasantness to get to the goal, if the irritations along the way helped build character. Being a lover of pure air and lots of elbow room, when I was in travel crowds full of the smell of ghastly perfumes, aftershaves, and deodorants, I longed for the clean smell of a pigsty or corral. I lived with this on the road because it came with the package, and I tolerated it by writing about it. A few notes from my journal:

I'm tired of seeing parents yanking tiny children around like pet animals, profanity, litter, lazy servicepeople, overpriced airfares and gasoline. Listening to people talk non-stop about nothing. I'm tired of the smell of city exhaust and sewer fumes, of nose blowing, belching airplane passengers; 3000-decibel speaker announcements, and being bombarded with loud music on planes and in cabs, in lobbies, and TV and radio waiting rooms. Sick of being late on takeoff (the average seems to be 21 minutes), cancelled flights and weak airport pages, lost luggage and triumphant midnight deliveries, the noise and filth of public restrooms; tired of begging my way through squinting customs agents, having cancelled confirmed hotel reservations, being bumped off an airline flight with a boarding pass clutched in my hand; weary of paying more for short-term parking than long-term used to cost, and hearing 150 apologies a day for incompetence. (See my visual rendering of this on the next page.)

I might just become a hermit when my next book is done.

Not just New York!

I have been justifiably accused of picking on and exaggerating the flaws of big cities. New Yorkers (bless their traffic-numbed souls) often took the hit from me for LA, Chicago, Seattle, Toronto, Atlanta, Miami, Cleveland, Salt Lake City, Lihue, Hawaii, and many other places, where the crowding is just as bad. (Someday I'm going to make an "I survived another media trip to LA" t-shirt.)

How do people live... eat... sleep... work... enjoy themselves in this mass of traffic, bad manners, and confusion? When I found myself retaliating, pushing and shoving just like the natives, that was the end! A short stopover is all I can take now.

I've never understood how a human can survive in dense urbanization, in all of the noise, traffic, and awful used air. I know that they do, and most are happy and productive people, and that the Lord loves them as much, or more than Idahoans, but I sense that only a miracle will save the society of big cities. This is of course the biased impression of a farm boy from Idaho, where life is allocated in acres, not lots.

GOING TO BIG CITIES IS ALWAYS A GOOD REMINDER THAT I DON'T WANT TO GO TO HELL.

What do we do in Idaho?

As I did business and media across the country, people (especially the people in big cities) were intrigued that I was from Idaho—the "backwoods." I got "dummy from the country" treatment often, along with the question, "Well, what is there to do in Idaho?" (Where we surely roll up the sidewalks at night and sit on a stump in the yard and watch the Chevys rust.) Trying to explain the assets of Idaho brought even blanker looks. I finally came up with a comeback that made them wonder what there was to do in Dallas or Miami.

"Well, Don, what do you do in Idaho?"

"Are you talking about entertainment?"

"Yes...."

"We live in Idaho, not fight to exist. We have little pollution, traffic, or noise, and we don't have to go down to the corner store and pick over the produce to find something fresh to eat. We go out to the gardens and fruit trees and pick our own. While you folks drink reprocessed toilet-flushing water, we drink spring water out of 300-foot ice-cold wells. You have go to parks or museums to see trees and animals and nature; we have these things right in our backyard. You get on planes to go skiing, or see mountains and canyons; we can either walk or drive to them in no time. Same with hunting or fishing, in lake, river, or creek. It is all on our own land or close enough that we don't have to gas up to get there. You migrate like lemmings to crowded theaters to watch people making love on stage. In Idaho, we do it ourselves."

This usually put an end to the smart remarks.

Seattle wake-up call

I was on a book tour during which I'd logged about 400,000 of my eventual 3 million miles, and feeling like I was at the end of my endurance. I'd been on the road for 18 days, charging around from five in the morning to midnight every day, rushing from appointment to appointment and city to city. I got to Seattle at 2 A.M., and had to be back up at five the next morning to do a talk show. I finally flagged down a cab and did some of my best whimpering to the driver, telling him about my suffering and sacrifice, weather and transportation woes. I gave him a gruesome account of the last 36 hours of late planes, heavy luggage, no sleep, rush drives, no food, cancellations, etc. When I stopped to catch my breath for more dark tales of my travels, the driver (a young man working his way through college) turned to me and asked, "Who's making you do all this, Sir?"

I was stunned. The only answer was no one, or "me." I was my own boss, and it was me who created, chose, decided on, and pursued all this. That cut my future whining considerably.

The truth about my travels

The people in my home town asked my wife, when she appeared solo at the store or at church, "Where is Don?" and her answer was, "Oh, he's in Cleveland today," or "doing a book tour in Australia," or "filming in New York," or "deep in the heart of Texas speaking." Though the fascination of travel wore off for me, I kept hearing how lucky I was to get to go to all those places.

In a sense, my friends and neighbors were right; the rewards and results of all my country- and globe-hopping far outweighed the miles getting there and back. There was plenty of free juice, and I always enjoyed the great service on the flights, hoping that some of my thousands of employees were as good. On the east to west flight, I would leave New York at 4:40 P.M., and be in bed in Idaho by 10:30 that night. I would look down from a plane going 600 miles an hour and remember it took my ancestors months pushing handcarts and riding in covered wagons, to cover the same distance.

I did plenty of moaning and groaning about travel, but in retrospect, I think I was just looking for a little sympathy. It was always a thrill, time after time, to see how vast this earth is, that you could travel for 12 hours or more over nothing but water, or see your country, your ranch, from five miles up. I was now gliding through or over the clouds I'd stood in awe of as a kid, seeing structures, nature, cities, but no people from a plane. Then a few hours later I'd be traveling in a cab or darting along the sidewalk with 8 million New Yorkers.

Traveling taught me many great truths, helped establish many firm intelligences, like Wall Street is not Main Street, and the size of the town has nothing to do with the size of the people.

In truth, there wasn't a dull moment in any travel, not necessarily always the sightseeing, but the change it gave you from your usual routine and pastimes. Business associates, tour escorts, fellow guests on TV and radio programs, clients, cab drivers—from all of them I learned more than from any college professor I ever had. I got to *live* geography, sociology, and psychology, a real upgrade from classroom courses and lectures. Most of my writing and other creative efforts took place on the road. The virtues of patience, tolerance, and love were sharpened by travel, and better yet, most of all this was paid for by someone else. The blessings of it all far outweighed the blemishes.

All of this travel had a positive carryover for Varsity's expansion, and its developing "footprint." My book promotion and seminar tours pioneered a presence across the country that opened lots of doors by simple name recognition. Having the ability to take on cleaning contract work outside of our initial local areas proved to be one of our biggest assets. As our company increased in size, we could bid national accounts when a customer wanted to put all of their eggs in one basket, in other words, deal with just one contractor.

Chapter 21

WIDENING RIPPLES:
VARSITY GROWS UP AND
BRANCHES OUT

Blessings there is not room enough to receive...

THE IDAHO STATE JOURNAL

GATEWA

BUSINESS

VARSITY CONTRACTORS EXPANDS

FUTURE
WORLD HEADQUARTERS

VARSITY
CONTRACTORS
1995

Journal photo by Bill Schaefer

As construction continues, Don Aslett, president and chief executive officer of Varsity Contractors Inc., stands beside a sign announcing expansion of his company on South Fifth Avenue.

Cleaning company acquires entire block for its world headquarters

By Ronnie Anderson
Of The Journal

Local cleaning specialist Don Aslett has initiated the first phase of an expansion for Varsity Contractors Inc. in Pocatello.

It will include two 8,000-square-foot buildings to house the company's world headquarters and a training center.

He bought the city block occupied by Don Aslett's Cleaning Center. It sits between Fourth and Fifth avenues and Whitman and Bonneville streets.

> *The whole block will be called Varsity Square There is nothing like it in Pocatello. It's going to be gorgeous."*
>
> —Don Aslett
> Varsity president

"We've been really cramped here. We've got 40 people working here now, and we're just on top of each other," Aslett said.

Varsity's offices span slightly more than 12,000 square feet and house not only corporate offices, but also Aslett's antique and strange cleaning equipment collection.

Each of the buildings on the block will be one story with a low profile design and pastel concrete finish, matching the cleaning center.

"The whole block will be called Varsity Square. There is nothing like it in Pocatello. It's going to be gorgeous," he said.

uenty-One

Varsity's story of "from here to there" sounds impressive when compressed to a sentence or two: "A small-town bunch of struggling but enterprising students cleaned their way to national noteworthiness and the respect of their peers." The actual process of going from little to large was a long, long story of more of the same that started the company and keeps it going now.

We were willing, actually anxious to take on the strains and growing pains of expansion, and for some strange reason we measured our size by the number of states we were in. Expanding out of Idaho into Utah was a like signing the Declaration of Independence, and then Wyoming gave us a phenomenal big three. A single phone booth in Arizona inched us into the final four. I remember feeling a great surge of satisfaction when we were awarded a bid in our seventh state and again when a contract in state number 14 was signed. Sometimes I wonder if conquering states crowded out our concern for quality and profit. No doubt if we just developed and served well all of the opportunities within a 200-mile radius of Pocatello we would have been larger and more profitable (and had more time with our families) than we were with all of the 14 states we operated in at the time.

I THINK I WAS THE INSTIGATOR OF THIS LAND RUSH STYLE OF GROWTH, AS ONE OF MY VPS SAID HE HEARD AN ENTHUSIASTIC CLAIM IN ONE OF MY PRESENTATIONS NOT LONG AGO THAT WE WERE NOW IN 55 STATES!

Some, in fact a lot of stretch, inefficiency, and sacrifice come with new territory. At 4 to 5 percent competitive profit margins, we didn't have any extra managers or leaders hanging around, trained and ready to go, so we either had to move one of our people from another slot or just give the manager closest to the area more buildings to cover. Not many top managers old or young (even those just graduating from school) are standing in line for a cleaning career.

I guess it was kind of like family. The first and only child keeps the parents on the run and worried, but they manage when a second child comes along, and cope well by the time three and four or more are born.

As time passed in our company, new people and new departments were necessary. Where Barbara was once every department in our office—payroll, secretary, collector, scheduler, errand runner, etc., we later had a part-time, then full-time secretary, then a full-time bookkeeper, then a payroll head and then a payroll staff. Eventually an $800,000 payroll software program was added. It all happened in a connected stream of events. There were victories, reverses, gains, losses, setbacks, disappointments, and triumphs all in the stream. There was never a single incident, or a major break that made us big and rich.

The sequence for all successful business:
You dream it;
You start it;
You develop it;
You learn and like it;
You have the footings poured—the pattern made;
Now the commitment to stick to it or move to something else;
(Many businesses fail here!)
You stay, pray, pay, and compete;
You grow and grow and grow.
And live with and face the fact that some of the bureaucracy, insensitivity, and loss of touch you once noticed and disliked, even criticized in big government, universities, and corporations, is also present in parts of your own company now.
But it's operating, and thousands of employees now depend on it for sustenance. So it continues.

VARSITY IS NOW A TOTAL FACILITY SERVICES COMPANY, PROVIDING NOT JUST CLEANING BUT A WIDE RANGE OF OTHER MAINTENANCE SERVICES, INDOORS AND OUT, FOR THE PROPERTIES IT SERVES.

Women in our workforce

Varsity began as an all-male team to face and defeat dirt. Three roommates, Marvin, John, and Don, were the company. All new hires were men as no college co-eds lined up to join the Janitor Brigade and back in the 1950s and '60s it never crossed my mind that any would ever want to. The work we performed was primarily wall washing, painting, cleaning windows, cleaning up trash and litter, and after floods and fires. These were projects involving working off of high planks, straddling tall ladders, running heavy buffers, stripping grungy old floors, wading in muck and filth, cleaning smelly restrooms, and working long and often odd hours, usually outfitted in far from designer coveralls. Most of this was thought of as "men's work" and it remained so for years.

There was a "chaperonage" issue, too. Some of our jobs were too closely bid to afford motels, so we camped out for the course of the job, and slept in some of the churches we refurbished.

I never doubted that women were even more capable than men in many ways, and were hard workers. My mother and other female relatives, as I was growing up, worked in the farm fields and on the balers and combines with me. Though I never considered putting a woman on a power floor sander, when I came up against a job involving the cleaning of thousands of little figurines and other fragile home contents on a fire-damage job, I had our secretary round up a team composed entirely of college girls. They did great!

That led to placing some women in our evening jobs of contract cleaning (custodial positions) and our quality and production only improved afterward. The administration of these cleaning women was always done by a woman, mainly Barbara who made the calls and dispatched the crews.

I guess for years I waited for the female workforce to approach me, being too timid to ask, and most of them were waiting for me to approach them. I've wondered if the fact that our society has for so long tabbed cleaning as women's work is one of the reasons many women have avoided cleaning careers. The women in Varsity have increased over time, but not at the rate they have in other businesses, especially in management. But it is steadily increasing and will continue to.

My changing role in the company

Many people are interested in how and when I moved from scrubbing the boards on my hands and knees to chairman of the board of a national corporation. It was a simple evolution. I was originally the only one working on the job, and even after I hired others I was always on every job, as later were my managers. Being a boss or supervisor meant more responsibility and time on the job, not less. It always seemed to me that as soon as you gave a man a clipboard and a pickup (let him take being a boss too seriously), he became almost worthless, so we all spent a lot of time on the job with our crews. The greater your authority and pay, the tougher the parts of the job you were expected to take on. You gave your new people the easiest.

Yes, I did all of the bidding and sales at first but finished up early in the day and went to one of the jobs in progress. As the company grew, we all just wore the fits when and where they came. We took turns moving and managing when necessary, and generally the best person in a given area shifted to the leader position or reached the top niche of policymaker. I had learned many fine leadership and management skills from my parents, but I was a lousy chief executive officer (CEO). Arlo, Mark, and others were way better at this—they had the knack and discipline for formal systems and making people accountable. As Varsity grew, things went better when people like Arlo and Mark actually ran the company and I stuck to the realm of big picture thinking and motivation.

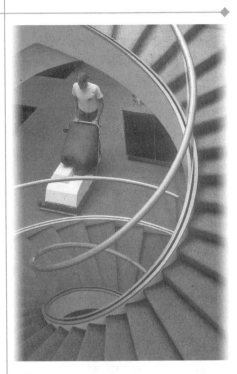

THE CLEANING COMPANY STARTED MORE THAN FIFTY YEARS AGO BY A FARM BOY NOW DOES HIGH-TECH JOBS IN THE MOST SOPHISTICATED SETTINGS.

Even though with age my commitment and efforts have only picked up, I try to stay out of the time- and energy-consuming youthful endeavors now. I still want to be out doing a paint job or buffing a supermarket floor, but the 8 to 10 hours those things require are better used now writing an article or giving a speech, which for the same amount of time has the potential for greater outcomes.

I always had a "be in the trenches" philosophy, and never liked the executive image and all that went with it. The world is too full of executives who forget how it is, forget how to produce the basic product that pays everyone's salaries and expenses. They start to value their new desk pen set or computer program over the frontline workers. Our society is executive crazy and most executives actually think they are worth what they get paid. "You are too valuable to work on the job," has been repeated to me for at least 40 years now. "You need to ride or fly around and give orders." Naturally I do want to capitalize on any wisdom and experience I've gained, but management reports just don't carry the spirit and emotion of the ranks of the regular army, the woman behind the counter, or man at the end of the shovel, or at the keyboard of a machine. My motivation and energy really blooms and grows on the front lines with the front line people—they always help me get to the root of a problem faster and more accurately than those scanning printouts and constructing giant graphs do. I always agreed with Napoleon's philosophy: "He who bivouacs with his troops needs half the army."

The contrast of then and now—always startling

When I pull the ends of time together and look at the contrast, I am stunned at what is going on in life now. I still remember well the $4.95 I paid for my first ladder for a cleaning job, and then how I stewed and connived to come up with $50 for a wall-washing machine. The big jump to our first floor machine, a giant investment of $240, made me hold my breath.

When I got my first truck for $425, I could hardly sleep at night worrying how this investment would be covered.

Fifty years later, my safety director informed me that we now owned 500 nice vehicles, some costing $30,000 or more. In one day, we bought eight new truck-mounted carpet-cleaning machines at $55,000 each, for a total of nearly half a million dollars.

Everyone was impressed that some days, while still a

In 1997, Arlo was elected president of Building Service Contractors Association International, one more sign of Varsity's growing national presence.

college student, I had 20 people working on a Saturday. Today we might have 5,000. Just a few years ago, I was astounded to know we hired 100 employees a year; this year we hired more than 10,000.

We were once thrilled to get one or two new buildings to clean, and at some point we had accumulated 140 buildings to clean in all—5 million square feet a night, an awesome achievement, we thought. Now we care for more than 300 million square feet a night. In the early days we would angle and bid to get two banks, and once in the '70s got a chain of six. In the 1990s we agreed to clean three or four hundred banks in one contract. Now we clean more than 4,000.

The more exposure we had from my books, appearances, and product sales, and Varsity's ever-expanding footprint, the greater our visibility in the industry and the more large accounts came after us. In 1997, Arlo was elected president of the Building Service Contractors of America, and Varsity today operates in all 50 states and Canada. One of our prime accounts now is shopping malls—we service more than 100 of them throughout the U.S.

ROBERT RAYL, VARSITY VICE-PRESIDENT AND LEADER OF THE "MALL GROUP," ONE OF OUR LARGEST DIVISIONS.

Other companies and affiliates have now joined our mix of maintenance contracting and consulting, publishing, and product sales, including a product manufacturing and design company (Live-Right), a computer software company (Nuvek), and a wood floor specialty division (United Varsity Contractors). Varsity is developing a new division for school maintenance (Varsity Education Services). We've planned for expansion and even bought another city block next to our Varsity corporate headquarters.

You'd think that after 50 years in the business, I'd have seen it all, but new opportunities are everywhere and contrary to the "old dog, new tricks" assumption, I am usually open and independent enough to take advantage of many of them. One day I'm involved in our new contract at the University of Texas at Austin, impressed by the three acres of carpet to care for in a facility with 50,000 students and 20,000 staff, the next day in Missouri I'm up on 30 acres of roof checking out 250 air conditioning units for which we are now responsible.

Things just get more exciting and challenging all the time.

Varsity is not just a way to make a living

So many people seem to think that business is a necessary evil, a big bad entity in life, and that we should use it to make a living and then forget it. But Varsity is not just our living—it provides much more than just financial security. It has been a powerful tool for changing lives for the better.

Everyplace we have established our operations, almost 100 percent of those working for us have had a marked life improvement. Outsiders can scarcely believe how we cater to, help, and include family whenever possible in our activities. Whenever possible, people and their needs have come first, before profit. We have been generous to a fault with requests and expectations, and always paid our employees market rate or better. Our work environment is cheerful—we provide nice facilities for staff and generous use of vehicles, phones, office machines, and the like. We've used company resources to look after the widow, the orphan, and the poor. As a company, we've donated time and money to the city and county, schools, scholarships, and churches. Community, civic, and other organizations like the Boy Scouts and Big Brothers/Big Sisters use our facilities regularly.

> I BELIEVE THAT PERSONAL GROWTH FOR THE PEOPLE I WORK WITH (AND THEIR FAMILIES) IS AS VITAL TO LIFE QUALITY AS THEIR PAYCHECKS.

We've always had something exciting going on and plenty of growth to provide new opportunities. Seldom can you find a job that provides such close and constant opportunities to better yourself, and the freedom and means to do it. We've also provided a good reputation for people to build on—our many years of hard work and investment have continually rewarded everyone involved.

I am convinced that this company has a higher purpose than cleaning, and that it will rise to be recognized even more than it is now. Our business *is* life and its end product is more spiritual than financial. We have built a tool that can help change this country for the better and help preserve decency and freedom, as well as provide good jobs in a good environment for millions of people someday. What is more worthwhile than this?

Varsity is a company of integrity, principle, and compassion. Our goal has never been just to survive or succeed, but to share. Something good like this should be continually upgraded and enhanced—not sold off or retired from. I love this business and what it has done and in my early seventies now, I'm more excited than ever by what it can do.

Varsity Contractors, Inc., mission statement:
"To reward our customers, employees, and owners a secure, exciting, and satisfying life by being 'THE' standard of excellence in the entire facility service industry."

VARSITY MANAGERS AT THE 2005 VARSITY MEETING
IN FRONT OF THE STATE CAPITOL IN BOISE, IDAHO

SOWING SEEDS FOR THE FUTURE

A bad year doesn't mean a bad idea

Part of an education in business is not letting a couple of bad years make you abandon a good crop. Just because the grasshoppers or frost ruin a yield, it wasn't the crop's fault, nor is it necessarily a reason not to replant it. And reversals often have some bright spot. Losing a game or a bid, or hitting a temporarily dead end, often left us with a new friend, or a new insight that made us smarter for the next time.

In the early 1980s we started, organized, and implemented a maid service division of Varsity—it was clearly needed and it was in our area of expertise. We called it Nation's Maid, copyrighted the name, and created some nice logos and slogans. It seemed to have all of the right elements at the right time, but like some crops some years, it just didn't yield—our management here was weak. Some competitors have thriving maid services, but ours to this day is still waiting for a replanting or a new farmer.

Likewise, it seemed like a sound and logical idea to own my own janitor supply company along with my own janitorial service. Why not buy wax, cleaners, and cleaning equipment from myself wholesale and also sell it to others? But this wasn't as easy in practice as it was on paper—things like storage, inventory, clerks, and deliveries were required, calling for capital and expertise I didn't possess at the time. The idea was good for the little company I called Micro-Clean Supply. I planted well—established product lines and purchase sources, but didn't have the laborers (or the time myself) to tend and harvest. So business died but the idea didn't.

Six years later, the climate looked better. We were a more efficient, versatile organization with some depth, so we started an entity we called Varsity Supply, figuring we could now marshal enough volume to justify direct discount purchasing of equipment and supplies. However, within a year we found ourselves in the same situation as before—it was a tagalong operation we hoped would just sort of run itself. The meager margin of supply savings involved wasn't worth the management effort; so back on the shelf it went, and back to our vendors we went.

The third planting of this idea ten years later finally found fertile ground. In my first book, *Is There Life After Housework?* I not only explained how to clean like a professional, but included a little chart of the best tools and supplies home cleaners could use, directing them to a local janitorial-supply store for the purchase. People with access to janitorial stores were happy and so were the stores.

But there are not many janitorial-supply stores even in big towns and none in small towns—so letters from people trying to locate dry sponges, pro squeegees, pumice stones, and bathroom cleaners poured in. Soon I was doing $50 worth of business a day by mail, then $100 a day ($1,500 profit a month for only a small investment in staff and space). So I printed up a primitive, one-page catalog with four products in it and included one in each book sold. This gave us $300 a day sales—a huge $4,500 a month income without going out of the office. My long-attempted supplies business was well launched without a significant startup cost.

A COVER FROM ONE OF OUR EARLY MAILORDER CATALOGS OF CLEANING SUPPLIES.

When orders and inquiries increased, we upgraded our catalog and hired a young woman named Kathy Alley (who more than 20 years later is still with us) to fill mail orders part-time in the small kitchen area of our office. Eventually she went full time and we moved her to her own building.

As the mail traffic and response grew, I hired a manager to oversee and build this part of the business. My son Grant, home from a church mission to Honduras, later modernized the operation and hired some phone answerers. Volume grew as my seminars and media appearances increased.

By this time, I had borrowed against our McCammon ranch to buy a city block in Pocatello on a main street near Idaho State University. We moved our mail order business and inventory to an old apartment on the property and put a crude "Life After Housework" sign in front, and gradually had a little retail store and some walk-in business. In 1997, we razed the block and built a large office building that fronted on the main street, including a strip mall, so it made sense to set up a full-scale store. A large, well-designed, classy cleaning-supply store with a new name soon appeared—Don Aslett's Cleaning Center. Four more stores were later added, in Boise and Idaho Falls, Idaho, Logan and Salt Lake City, Utah, with many more stores across the country on the planning board. The Cleaning Center mail-order catalog goes out to the whole country now.

This is a better "crop" than I planned, but still only one-tenth of what was just around the corner.

Doormats to dollars

My penetration into the market with some badly needed professional products for home cleaners now caught the eye of QVC, the premier TV shopping network. They were touring the country in 1997 with a telecast crew looking for new products to sell nationally. They were coming to Boise, Idaho, and invited us to offer a product. Several infomercial and home shopping network groups had called and visited my Idaho office previously with offers of "millions of dollars" to be easily made. None seemed worthy of pursuing, but a local audition with QVC seemed worth a try.

So Barbara and I took our bestselling product, Showers n' Stuff shower and tub cleaner, and did an outdoor demonstration in which I cleaned (instantly!) tough old hard-water stains and deposits off a glass shower door out of an old rental unit. We did well, according to them, and I learned a new dimension of TV. I'd been trained to provide non-commercial, educational material in my appearances, but the QVC host quietly reminded me after our test segment, "Hey, man, we're on the air to take, not teach! People are watching to buy, not be taught."

We got an award and trophy, and better yet, an invitation to go to QVC's main studio in Philadelphia and be on the show.

The QVC/Don Aslett Cleaning Center relationship after that was a heart-stopping success, going from that first $8,000 worth of products we sold in Boise to $80,000 worth on our first national TV segment, to an $800,000 session, to a $13-million gross sales year. But in between the lines of these impressive figures was a lot of effort: initial figuring and fumbling, flights from Idaho to Pennsylvania, three days of work for ten minutes on the air, finding and shipping dirty shower doors, building and shipping toilet displays, and live airings at midnight or 3 A.M.

THE GRAND OPENING OF OUR FULL-FLEDGED RETAIL CLEANING SUPPLIES STORE (LATER TO BE CALLED DON ASLETT'S CLEANING CENTER) IN THE NEW VARSITY SQUARE COMPLEX.

About this time Monsanto, manufacturers of AstroTurf doormats, did a big market research project to find out how to sell more mats. One woman in a focus group asked them why they didn't use Don Aslett. "He's been preaching mats to the world for twenty years." "Who is he?" Monsanto asked. She showed them my million-seller book pointing out the page where America's #1 Cleaner recommended a good mat outside every door.

Three of their executives were in my office the very next week wheeling and dealing. I took their mats onto QVC and away we went. They were a top seller year after year. There, in between gorgeous models selling women's clothes and jewelry, Tony Little with his power muscle machine, George Foreman and his cooking grill, inflatable beds, bug zappers, miracle laundry pellets, windmills, and birdhouses, was Don Aslett on his hands and knees, leaping through doors onto a mat, scuffing his feet, and selling doormats. I developed a demo of pouring pounds of sand and dirt into a mat, then dumping it out into a pile and asking the audience, "Do you want this in your house, ruining your nice floors, or would you like to keep it outside?" We sold out!

HERE I AM DEMONSTRATING HOW MUCH DIRT AN ASTROTURF MAT AT THE DOOR CAN KEEP OUT OF YOUR HOUSE, ON QVC.

Sometimes I would sell 5,000 mats at a whack, taking live phone calls from people raving about their merits all the while. We eventually sold more than a million mats, and the mats were a good springboard to other products. Soon I had not just ten minutes on the air but a "Don Aslett's Cleaning Secrets" hour, in which I sold hundreds of thousands of dollars worth of product, including things like shower cleaner, deodorizer, floor finish, and lots of cleaning tools. My trips to Philadelphia were now frequent. There was something humorous about entering the QVC shopping network, big on jewelry, food, and lamps, and becoming their top seller with something as mundane and ugly as a doormat.

In 2001, AstroTurf mat sales on QVC reached 250,000 annually—over $4 million worth, on which I got a commission. My percentage was small but the income was respectable and the exposure significant. Thanks to my early appearances on QVC, our cleaning products company was flooded with growth.

At this point, I sold part of the Cleaning Center to my Varsity Chief Financial Officer Dave Hermansen, a master manager who immediately made the company's marketing a science instead of continuing in my usual seat-of-the-pants style. We found a top-notch marketer, Kim Williams, who had much experience with Eddie Bauer products. She was appalled that we weren't marketing the Don Aslett name and began a transition to branding many of the products we were selling with my name and picture. We hired a professional presenter, John Holt, to represent me while while I was on my 18-month church mission (see Chapter 25). Good move. Although John didn't initially have the name or credibility in cleaning that I did, he was much better in the actual business of demonstrating and selling products. He made his points clearly and smoothly and sold like crazy. He was so good that when I returned home I didn't take back over. In fact, many QVC viewers now think he is me!

DAVE HERMANSEN AND I IN THE POCATELLO STORE.

A memorable moment in my mail-order adventures

Back when our little mail order business was doing $100 a day it was plain to see that spray bottles were a strong seller. We were ordering a few cases at a time and moving them well. My idea of getting white opaque bottles with "Life After Housework" printed on them called for a minimum 5,000-bottle order. My mail order manager gasped at this staggering figure. Then the salesman said you got a real price break on a 10,000-unit order, and that interested me. "Where is the really big price break?" I asked. "Thirty thousand," he said. At that quantity printed bottles were only 17 cents each—what a deal! And eventually we would sell them, I was sure. My staff held their breath. "He wouldn't!" they said. But I did. With my usual optimism, I went for it and ordered 30,000, and figured that having this many would push us to sell them.

But I hadn't thought through the logistics of that many bottles. I knew the order cost only about $5,000, not bad for an eternal supply of personalized bottles, but when they came (an entire tractor-trailer full) the freight bill was an unprecedented $2,300. The truck was jammed with boxes, huge ones, 3 feet high and 2 feet wide, each containing a hundred bottles. There was even a box in the empty seat beside the driver. We had to fill the shop, part of my office, the rug cleaning truck garage, and some of the sidewalk outside to get the truck unloaded. Then I drove many pickup loads home and for months our living room and garage were stacked high with boxes. Spray bottles were like locusts for three years afterward. With mail orders moving them out at a rate of 15 bottles a day, we had a five-year supply. Eventually opaque went out of style because you couldn't see the color of the cleaning solution inside. I wore holes in the boxes moving those babies around.

They led to all kinds of excitement, including a call from the principal of the high school one day. "Don, we've had a water gun episode that has affected the whole school. Your son furnished high-power spray bottles for the entire student body!" Of course, I intended to make an innocent plea and asked what made him suspect me, Mr. Clean. "Because," he said, "all of the bottles have 'Don Aslett Life After Housework' printed on them." Cornering my son Rell, I got his justification.

"Well, Dad, you taught us to be enterprising. I knew you had plenty so I loaded my car and truck full and sold them for a dollar each. They outshot the ordinary water guns unbelievably and think of the good advertisement."

I guess he might have had a point there. I eventually offered them free as giveaways. People were slow to take them, even free—they figured who had a thousand spray bottles in his living room must have a con scheme going.

Toward a cleaner world: A world-class cleaning museum

I learned early in life that the more you can do to give presence to, or add excitement to something, the more attention it will get and the more will get done on it with little or no effort. In 1977, en route to one of the four national Scout jamborees I attended as a leader, my Scouts and I stopped at the famous Ford Museum in Dearborn, Michigan. They had a well-illustrated history of everything here from pressure cookers to Presidential limousines, railroads to carpentry and mining, and suddenly I spotted a strange pump-like object labeled "1898 vacuum cleaner." My profession! I loved it, bought it, and continued along on our Scout trip.

The following summer I was in a quilt shop in Utah and spotted two old tubular "pump vacuums" mounted on the wall. That was it! There were horse museums, fire museums, farm museums, sports museums, and dozens more. Why not a museum devoted to the world's oldest and largest profession—cleaning! I decided to start one. I bought the two units for $240, and within a year, I had collected more than 50 other odd pieces of old cleaning apparatus, from sweepers to bars of soap. I displayed them in the hallway between my Cleaning Center store and the Varsity corporate office. Barbara, Grant, and I always hit the antique shops in our seminar travels after that, picking up a piece here and there. The enthusiasm caught on, and museum piece contributions began trickling in from employees, friends, and family. Visitors, employees, customers, and friends were soon able to enjoy a little tour of my collections.

One afternoon seven large boxes arrived from The Eureka Company, with a note that said they were moving to a new office and needed to get rid of some old vacuums. Inside the boxes were 11 unique pre-electric vacuums. Bonanza!—a prize beyond imagining.

The museum eventually expanded to six rooms, and included, besides old cleaning gear, facts and displays about the history of cleaning, souvenirs from my cleaning company's own history, souvenirs of notable media appearances and campaigns, championship clutter from the many clutter contests I'd held promoting my decluttering books, and some interesting photographs and old signs. Fox Network came out and did a national broadcast on the museum, and we hosted many school field trips through it. All visitors were welcome, and it was a fascinating tour through cleaning and company history.

Groundwork is in progress now to expand the museum and establish

How we used to clean and what we used to clean with is pretty astounding. These are old laundry cleaning devices. Taking a good look at, or actually trying out these antiques really shows how much better we have it today.

it as the largest and most complete of its kind in the world. It will be designed to be not just a walk-through quick display, but a spectacular, participative, educational experience for both children and adults. In 2006 I bought (for $300,000) a 220-piece antique vacuum collection from Peter Frei of Boston, including related patents, brochures, and letters dating back to 1849. So you know I'm serious and committed to this. Not long ago, in a meeting on museum planning, one of the attendees, "Mayor" McDougal said, "I wish I was excited about breathing as Don is about his museum!" The facility will be LEED certified—platinum (environmentally efficient) construction and will include a unique three-level children's cleaning world, full of exciting activities.

As the crown jewel of my campaign to clean up the world, and to promote the concept of clean as the ultimate answer to the world's needs, we are expanding my cleaning museum in Pocatello from 2,000 square feet to a five-story, 70,000-square-foot, world-class facility.

AN ARCHITECT'S RENDERING OF DON ASLETT'S MUSEUM OF CLEAN,
CONSTRUCTION OF WHICH IS UNDERWAY IN 2007.

Building blocks

In the 1990s, Varsity was still growing like crazy. Our headquarters building in Pocatello was crowded to the max, inside and out, as this was not only the company's central corporate office, but all of our regional contracting was done from here. We were renting space all over the place, and had been in and out of ten different rented offices since the beginning. I even bought an old lumberyard that got us by for a while, but the time had come to buy and build. Previous experience directed me to someone really smart about buildings and property—Glenn Marshall, the top developer in the area. He advised me to buy the whole city block that contained the old Eddy's Bakery, long since shut down now. The price was $315,000, with $60,000 down. I came up with it by once again re-mortgaging our nearly paid off home in McCammon.

We immediately made use of any livable space in existing buildings on the property, relieving some of the tight fit in our present office. I remodeled the good existing structures, tore old ruined buildings down, and sold, gave away, or razed the five houses on the block. Then we designed and built a beautiful new complex, which was on two major cross streets right in the middle of the city, just three blocks from the university where this story all began. The building and remodeling project won us the city award for most beautiful building in town two years in a row.

John Marshall (Glenn's son) was our general contractor for two attractive and deluxe buildings ("Varsity Square") that today house our corporate headquarters, a Cleaning Center retail store, my publishing company, the Live-Right offices, the temporary quarters of my Cleaning Museum, and a half-dozen commercial and retail tenants. In a few years it will be paid off (by rental income), be worth several million dollars, and generate a sizable monthly income for whoever is around after I go. Thank you, Glenn!

LEFT: ONE OF THE FIVE SMALL HOMES ON THE CITY BLOCK I PURCHASED, BEING MOVED TO A NEW LOCATION TO MAKE WAY FOR THE NEW VARSITY CORPORATE OFFICE.

RIGHT: A BACKHOE DEMOLISHING PART OF THE OLD EDDY'S BAKERY BUILDING, IN THE PROCESS OF CONSTRUCTION.

BAKERY DEMOLITION — A backhoe demolishes part of the Journal photo by Doug Lindle Eddy's Bakery building at Fifth and Bonneville last week. The old Varsity Contractors Inc., now located at 253 W. Halliday, according bakery will be remodeled to house the the corporate offices of to Lowell Allen. Plans call for houses on the block to be removed.

PUTTING THE FINISHING TOUCHES ON VARSITY SQUARE.

Just all that borders me...

I was raised with lots of land and room. Dorm rooms, apartments, and tiny town yards were a necessary temporary prison for me, so when Barbara and I bought our 60 acres in McCammon, it was a life victory.

In 1996, a 2000-acre farm next to us (I knew the place and its owner well) went up for sale. The realtor listing it drove by our well-kept, white-fenced "Aslett Acres" and dropped a sale brochure off with us. Not only was it a good buy from an investment standpoint, but it had a nice section bordering a Forest Service tract, a perfect spot for the girls' camp we had long dreamed of building. I'd seen and used numerous wonderful Boy Scout camps, but all the girls' camps I ever saw were ugly, poorly equipped, and poorly located. This 40 acres had it all—pines, cliffs, mountain views, a cold, clear creek running through it, and a nice level spot for camps and buildings. I convinced two other partners to join me and we made an offer and bought the whole 2,000 acres. The camp and a rural subdivision near it are now on the drawing board and calendar.

An old story... on new fronts

After more than 40 years, I finally had gained some success in cleaning, contracting, building, speaking, retail sales, and publishing. There remained an arena of business I always (from the age of 18) wanted to enter and that was to invent and manufacture something entirely new.

I'd invented hundreds of things in my mind and a few in my business, and some had made it to the drafting table, or even prototypes. Such as clever corrals and gates to handle cattle and hogs, floor drains for kitchens, a baseball pitching wall, forms for concrete fence posts and rails, custom workbenches and toolboxes, and even a cement alligator mascot for backyard ponds, to mention just a few. I came up with plenty of ideas over the years and dabbled in their development, but it took a kangaroo to push me into the big time.

During the preliminary groundwork on our project of building the ultimate maintenance-free house (a sequel to my initial low-maintenance—see Chapter 22), working with professors and students in Brigham Young University's Construction Management Program, my Live-Right partner, Sandra Phillips, began a strong focus on amenities inside the house. At one idea session, she stated that a home, like the commercial buildings Varsity cleans, needs a convenient way to hold, store, and transport cleaning equipment and supplies.

She brought up the idea again later, but because a door caddy for cleaning products I'd developed earlier had gone nowhere, I was pretty passive about it. Finally the combination of mobility and size (no bigger than a vacuum), plus the idea of making it like an attractive animal kids would love and want to help (a kangaroo) won me over—I could see a future.

She collected kangaroos from store shelves in Australia to Toys "R" Us, and we molded some miniature models (that looked like kangasaurus rexes). Then I spent a day in my shop and built a rough plywood prototype. When the plastics experts at the university saw it, they were ecstatic, saying it was a real winner and could be rotomolded! Sandra and I didn't have a clue what rotomold meant, but after much computer design, attendance at university plastics classes, expensive pre-prototypes, and visits to a mold factory in Los Angeles, we had a winsome 30-inch high, 12-pound plastic offspring we called the Klean-GuRoo. It took two years to fine tune and groom, to work out the details of the storage areas, wheels, axles, safety imprints, and casters. We then had to design a pouch caddy, which required an injection mold. We are now herdsmen of a troop of kangaroos, hopping around in our warehouse, and across the country in homes and schools.

As with most new products, marketing was more of a challenge than making it. When the *American Inventor* series hit national TV, Sandra's daughter-in-law Eden Phillips called and coaxed us into entering our Klean-GuRoo. We made a quick trip to California, starting at 6 A.M. we stood in line with thousands of fellow Hollywood hopefuls clutching their inventions. Our kart loaded with cleaning gear (30 items) was charming enough to catch the attention of the roving camera and interviewers not once but five times. The four-minute presentation we were allowed went off well, too, and three weeks later out of 5,000 we were in the final 50—close to the $1 million winner's circle. We returned to LA for the showdown, fully prepared and confident as we appraised the other finalists and felt we had a superior product. We were all set for a 4-0 vote, and got it, except the 4 votes were all "no's." They wanted a "sensational gadget" and our work-saver on wheels was "too practical." (Cleaning is still a hard sell!)

Wounded but wiser, and still convinced the world needed our Klean-GuRoo, we returned to other marketing approaches—stores, catalogs, mail order, home shows... and are still hopping and hoping. The Little Joey caddy that accompanies Klean-GuRoo, is an independent best seller. And we've branched into clean teeth with the novel Baby Banana Toothbrush and Teether set to hit the market in the fall of 2007.

Chapter 22

COMING FULL CIRCLE: THE SHIFTING KALEIDOSCOPE

You can go home again...

As Varsity and I grew and evolved, nothing remained static on the home front, either. There, as in business, changes are inevitable. The kaleidoscope of life keeps on turning bringing new and often unexpected designs.

No place like Idaho!

If there could be an all-encompassing word for anticipation, satisfaction, and achievement, for me it would be "home." I've lived convinced that my home state of Idaho has unequalled water, air, scenery, freedom, people, opportunities, and peace on earth. We enjoyed our home in McCammon in later years (right up to today) every bit as much now as we did when we first moved here.

Journal July 14, 1990

Today was a day of pure passion, truly a sensuous Saturday. For others it was rodeo day, parade day, fishing, boating, and water-skiing day, and all those other recreational things people crowd the roads and hills to do for fun and to enjoy and restore

BARBARA ON THE BEACH IN HAWAII, THE PARADISE TO WHICH I RETURNED THIRTY YEARS AFTER MY MISSION THERE TO BUY PROPERTY FOR OUR ENVISIONED TROPICAL RETREAT.

themselves. I stayed home and did what rewards me much better than planned play-ing—speed work!

Up early in the crisp, clean air, I went to our big garden and watered the potatoes and peas—it's marvelous to see what deep, black soil will do with a few tiny seeds. I picked a bowl of fresh currants, mashed them, Barbara boiled them into syrup, and I had them for breakfast on whole-wheat hotcakes. I grabbed a bowl of bing cherries and went outside and picked and shoveled on a new pond I was digging above the pine trees.

It was a gorgeous morning, birds singing, and sandhill cranes in swishing flight overhead. As the day went on it was hot, but even when you're soaked with sweat the cool water from the pump here comes from a hundred-foot deep well and can keep your engine running at the perfect temperature.

I ran down and built a new trail through the trees to the garden so kids wouldn't get stickers in their feet and even people in wheelchairs could go pick a tomato.

In the garage I put new plugs on two big old electrical cords. Then the family and I poured some cement around the playhouse for a mowing strip. My father-in-law invited us into his cabin to look at a new album of family pictures, reminding me of how great family is. I rushed into the house and did a one-hour radio interview on stain removal—lots of call-ins and challenges, but plenty of appreciation too.

For lunch, Barbara served fresh-baked cinnamon rolls and a large glass of guava juice. I ran back outside, and cleared some moss from the pond so that the big trout could find the shrimp. Then I put the plow on the tractor, and leveled and cultivated the new orchard planting site and anywhere else we needed soft ground for digging. I dug some fresh red new potatoes and picked some peas and Barbara made creamed peas and new potatoes for supper—absolutely exquisite! Took a breather and watched a whole tape of Tweety Bird cartoons with my granddaughter Mindy from Alaska. I was amazed at how violent they were—what a mean little bird and dumb cat!

I went back to the shop, cleaned up and fixed some things, and wrote notes for a new book. Finally at sundown I gave out. (At 55 that happens to a body.) So I show-ered and lay in bed meditating with the odors of pine and sage and cool breezes waft-ing over me. Then Barbara and I talked about our kids, church, community, and our plans for a youth camp someday. Now this was a day!

KEEPING THE WHITE FENCES ON OUR MCCAMMON RANCH SHARP
WITH THE AID OF MY SONS.

OUR HAWAII HOUSE

I mentioned earlier that we had decided to build a model low-maintenance home as a dramatic demonstration of the principles we put forth in my book *Make Your House Do the Housework*. But where should be it be built? No matter how great the house was, we figured that few people would travel to Pocatello, Idaho; Fargo, North Dakota; or Hillsboro, Ohio; to see it. The island of Kauai in Hawaii, on the other hand, had magnificent weather and scenery, and was one of the most beautiful places I'd ever been. An old Hawaiian friend from my missionary days who was now in the real estate business found us a choice 5-acre parcel of jungle—a perfect place for a model low-maintenance house. It was four miles from the ocean, and bordered a wilderness area.

Thus as I turned 51, one of the major projects and expenses of my life was underway. The potential spin-offs of this project would be phenomenal.

It had been 33 years since I had been in Kauai, and walked its red dirt roads through one of the most lush and greenest jungles on earth. Now I owned 5 acres of rain-wet jungle, complete with 110 percent humidity and tens of thousands of plants and insects. There was the sweet odor of every flower imaginable, and groves of 55-foot high bamboo! A dream come true, savoring supreme.

If you've seen *Raiders of the Lost Ark*, *Jurassic Park*, or *South Pacific*, then you've seen this place. They were all filmed here. The weather and views are so perfect, so beautiful, that it is almost boring.

The smells, gadfrey, you can *feel* the fragrance. Every worthwhile flower, vine, or fruit God made is here somewhere. And the rain—you've never seen rain until you've been here in the upper Wailua Valley, when 12 inches of rain can fall on and off within 24 hours with bright sun in between.

The intense green foliage, the red soil, the pure blue sky, and deep blue ocean trimmed with white foamy surf add up to pure delight!

The first two years we traveled to Kauai, we stayed in a hotel and went to the property daily with saws, shovels, and wicked machetes and gradually ate our way through the dense vegetation to find the best building site. The county code allowed two residential buildings on the property, a guest cottage (500 square feet maximum) and a full-size house. We built the guesthouse first, entirely of concrete with a Hawaiian lava rock exterior, and it was our Hawaiian retreat for the next 11 years as we slowly planned and worked our way toward starting in on and paying for the main house. Five hundred square feet is plenty of space for two people, plus two or three visitors, and our college-age kids managed to house up to eight there for a week or so. We let many mainland friends and locals use the house (free), and many years later now, a testimony to the durability and maintenance-freeing qualities of concrete, the guesthouse is still a great place to stay.

BARBARA AND I VISITING HAWAII IN 1971.

Our home in Hawaii was a boost to both family togetherness time and business development. I never liked my whereabouts reported as "Don's in Hawaii," as this implies vacation or loafing. We worked like dogs while in Hawaii building our low-maintenance home. Plus I did many phone interviews from there; an 8:00 a.m. morning show in the East is 3:00 a.m. in Hawaii! I also flew from Kauai to many cities in the U.S. and Europe for jobs and appearances.

After 1985 Barbara and I developed a pattern of leaving our McCammon farm in early December and living in the guesthouse until late January, at which time I often went on tour, to board meetings, or speaking engagements through February, and heavy media work in March and April. Barbara would generally stay in Kauai for the month of February, saying, "If I have to be alone in February, it's not going to be in 5 feet of snow and freezing in Idaho."

In 1994, we decided to launch into the building of the main house. On January 5, we poured the footings for this important project. Plenty of time, money, and energy went into it—dreaming about, designing, and then building it, all with the goal of a house that could provide more than just shelter and a chance to show off.

And it worked, thanks to a super contractor, Curtis Law. We met before he started, discussed the end goal, agreed on a cost-plus arrangement, shook hands, and then he built the whole thing. We never signed one single paper, not one. The land was paid for and we paid cash for the building of the house as it went along.

The house ended up a classy structure, quite different from our usual farm/ranch house style. It was made of solid concrete, over 300 cubic yards of it, and miles of steel rebar reinforcing. The floors are concrete, too, 9 inches thick (with granite tile and carpet over that), and there is not a piece of sheetrock in the place.

It has wall-hung toilets, suspended seating, few doors, and much Corian, glass, and native Koa wood. Although we didn't use an architect, we won an architectural award and an award for unique use of concrete for it. The house has also been featured on the Discovery Channel and other TV programs and in many magazine and newspaper stories.

OUR MODEL LOW-MAINTENANCE HOME,
SET IN THE MIDST OF FIVE ACRES OF LUSH TROPICAL JUNGLE.

The purpose of the house was of course family first, and it is filled many months of the year with some of our six children and many grandchildren and their friends. We are generous with it, and many parties, hula lessons, wedding receptions, and even a writing seminar have been held here.

September 13, 1996

(from letter to the kids and grandkids about our Hawaii house project)

As you may know, we have just been in Hawaii again picking and choosing things for the new house. Laura was there this week laying out the cupboards and other kitchen designs. Rell was over two weeks ago and painted the entire house on the outside. It looks like a temple. We are pouring the basketball court this week—it will be 35 feet wide and 50 feet long and have a three-point shooting line, a glass backboard, and even a fence so that when Jason misses the lay-in, the ball won't go bouncing down into the jungle. We bought three more king beds for company. The Hawaiians who came and stayed with us got together for a dinner and

ASLETT GRANDKIDS: CHRISTMAS IN HAWAII. KNEELING: MICHELLE CLARK, CAMI SIMONS, BROOKE ASLETT. MIDDLE: MAX ASLETT, GRIFFIN ASLETT, AMANDA CLARK, MICHAEL SIMONS, TODD ASLETT. BACK: ALEX ASLETT, MEGAN ASLETT, CHRISTOPHER CLARK, EMILY CLARK, CAROLYN SIMONS, AMY SIMONS, JASON CLARK.

played and sang for me, Laura, and Grandma. The food was *ono* (good).

The jungle is junglier than ever and the trees are getting big. The lime tree had buckets of limes, which I picked and made limeade. We picked two pineapples from our little patch, and one of the bamboo shoots that just came up is over six inches in diameter! Any bigger and we will make boats out of them. Two cats adopted us and we picked four stalks of bananas. All of the outside of the house is done—they are putting the glass banister on the staircase now. I finished the slanting back wall on Labor Day and don't want to see another rock for at least ten years. When you get here you can see how many thousand I laid up. All of the lighting is in, and it is like a stadium around there.

All of the jungle fruit is ripe and we are chowing down on the guava and ratberries. The wild chickens still start crowing at four in the morning. We got a new TV and ten new trees and are giving tours to lots of people who want to see the famous low-maintenance house. Your pictures will soon be up on the "brag wall." We are still planning to fly everyone over here next Thanksgiving for a week and will take a picture of the whole family on the winding stairs. We are going to have privacy trunks for everyone in the family so you can leave all of your Hawaii stuff there. The beach is saying, "Grandkids, come and play on me." The trail is finished and you can walk or even ride a bike around the whole Aslett Acres valley now (if the mosquitoes don't get you first!)

—*Grandpa Don*

One of the smartest things we ever did was design and build this house. No stock or savings account could have returned what this project has for us.

A LIFELONG DREAM COMES TO FRUITION: THE FIRST BUNCH FROM THE MORE THAN EIGHTY BANANA TREES WE NOW HAVE GROWING ON OUR HAWAIIAN PROPERTY.

We didn't do it for status or financial growth, but to increase our real "net worth" such as health, relationships, family and friends, church activities, and just plain old excitement in life. Our goals with the project have been met and are exceeding our greatest expectations. They are:

1. To provide a model and inspiration for maintenance-freeing construction.
2. To enhance enjoyment and togetherness in our marriage and our family.
3. To have something exciting and challenging to look forward to daily.
4. To further health and rest.
5. To provide a private and productive place to write and study.
6. To expand and strengthen friendships and business relationships.
7. To bring new clients and others to us for seminars, meetings, and interviews.
8. To expand and enhance our church activities.

9. To set and practice an environmental example.

This whole experience has led me to a firmer belief in inspiration and revelation. It was amazing how thought, design, and sure knowledge of our ultimate outcome here just came to me, pouring in. It appeared finished in my mind before it was even begun.

Journal November 28, 1999

At last the relief of getting back to our island! It has been a breath-holding wait all year, waiting for escape from even the pure enjoyable passion of what I do on the mainland. That big ocean, all that water, seems to do something to separate me from the complications and demands of all that is going on, layers and layers and layers of opportunities, now almost without end. This is a getaway even from too many good things.

BARBARA AND I IN 1987 BY THE SIGN (COMPLETE WITH CUSTOM-MADE CONCRETE PINEAPPLE) THAT WELCOMES VISITORS TO OUR HAWAII HOME.

This year I arrived full of plans to build, write, work, and savor more than ever. Everything we dreamed, planned, and planted seems to be climaxing, filling any vacancies, and making our yard, like our lives, lush, full, warm, and beautiful. I worked myself into almost feverish excitement in the jungle heat, thinking about all of the writing projects ahead, and everything else I have to look forward to, and of sharing it with all those special.

Wow, the Hong Kong orchid tree is literally covered with those perfect purple, white, and pink flowers. How good joy and beauty are when they are being showered from the outside and at the same time swelling from the inside.

Once we acquired and built on our house in Hawaii, our visitor list (and list of people we let stay there when we weren't there) filled several pages every year. All of this home-front hospitality and association with other people and their children was a bit of a strain on our nerves, pocketbook, and interfamily relations at times, but overall a tremendous asset to our lives. Our love for Hawaii has spread to our children, grandchildren, and many friends and relatives.

THE CIRCLE OF LIFE

MY FATHER WHEN HE WAS 26, WITH A FINE CATCH OF IDAHO TROUT.

A legacy that lives on

In 1982, my father told us all that he was having some cancer concerns, and a year later I was at his bedside when he died from the disease at the age of 74. My dad was unbeatable in management and unstoppable in accomplishment, and had the most integrity of anyone I've ever met. His presence remained just as strong after he was gone as when he was alive. His concern for others, especially family, was summed up in the last 30 seconds he lived. As he was struggling to take his final breath, he whispered to me, "Now Donny, remember on that diesel [tractor] to pull the hydrostatic gear up when you are on hills or in highway gear or it will freewheel out of control, and you could lose your life." I use his tractors, tools, methods and logic, every day—and relish it.

While Barbara and I were serving our mission in Boston (see Chapter 25), my sister Shirley called to tell me that Mother, then 87 and recovering from hip replacement surgery, had developed complications and was in critical condition, so we should come home. There was a slight possibility that she might improve, and she did, for a while. We returned and spent some great days with her in the spring of 2004. Everything seemed to indicate that she would reach 95 or 100 and make another trip or two to Hawaii when she had an aneurysm. The doctor told the family members who had been able to arrive quickly that she would only last a few hours unless by some mir-

DAD AND MOM AND THEIR GROWN CHILDREN IN 1983:
ME, DAD, MOM, SHIRLEY, DEE, LARRY, AND RICK.

acle they could stop the bleeding. They did manage to do that, and for four weeks more in the hospital, she was as alert as anyone hooked up to all kinds of medical paraphernalia can be. Just about every member of the family—all of her children, grandchildren, great-grandchildren, and numerous adopted grandchildren from Italy to Alaska—came to see her now, all of us hoping for another recovery. All of her children were at her bedside 24/7 for those four weeks, and she passed away at age 88 with both Barbara and me there.

Although I've often written and spoken of my father's influence on me, especially in the area of ethics and management, close friends and family say that my mother's influence on me was even greater. Many of the things I now find invaluable I learned from my mother. Most of the basics taught in college I already knew from "Mother classes" 24 hours a day. She was indeed the dean of the University of Motherhood. Her "ordinariness" made possible the extraordinary in all of our lives. Her wisdom and counsel, which is an inner voice in all of us now, will never stop contributing to what we are today.

- She knew how to communicate compassion and concern without saying a single word.
- She made me love cleanliness and clean life habits not by preaching, but by untiring example and perfectly chosen moments and parables.
- My mother, taught me to walk while wounded and not waffle on moral issues.
- She taught me to control sweets and eat healthy.

MOTHER IN 1995.

- My father taught me how to work, but Mother taught me to love work.
- I learned real organization watching Mother can fruit and control the kitchen while 50 other demands were at hand. She taught me the greatest management secrets of all, to be prepared and be early!
- It was Mother who showed me the pleasures of gardening, and subtly expanded my musical enthusiasms from Burl Ives to the classics of Beethoven.
- Much of my sense of humor came from Mother and her three sisters.
- It was Mother who taught me to drive a car, write poetry, and respect the elderly.
- It was she who took the time to prove the value of photographs, taking and keeping pictures.
- It was she who arranged our work so that Sundays would be clear for church.
- She was the first investor in my later corporate empire.

Mother proved that living providently was living well, and she never wasted anything.

Mother's life was so well lived that it left no need to "sell" her lifetime of accomplishments. There never was a moment of her life when she wasn't willing to put the rest of us first, and that is the ultimate measure of a human being.

Heartaches nothing can heal

As the years go by we gain some confidence in our ability to control life's outcomes, and deal with whatever comes our way. But who can be prepared for a split-second happening that removes all of that idealism forever?

As a youth leader, I was always haunted by the potential of an accident in the midst of high-adventure activities. I remember the morning when I had a van full of Scouts about to head off on a 15-day, 1,000-plus-mile trip to Philmont in the mountains of New Mexico. The boys were all excited, not a care in the world, while their mothers were unable to hide their anxiety over the possibility of some mishap. I spent the next two weeks doing everything I could to prevent such. I delivered them all home safely at the end with great relief, after exposure to bears, lightning, cliff climbing, narrow, twisting roads, rapids, and more, vowing I wouldn't put myself in that kind of position again. But I did! And was usually glad I did, after it was all over.

But then that most dreaded moment came in my own back yard, with one of the most precious young men in my life, my oldest grandson, 11-year-old Jacob.

Jacob was everything I was as a boy, only much more talented. His visits were better than those of an angel. Together we built fences, picked rocks, welded, did target practice, and made costumes for Christmas plays. When he was ten I taught him to hoe and to throw a knuckle ball, and bought him a piano. The power that child had to conjure meaning, direction, and purpose in my life was amazing. I had plans to spend the next 20 years with him, watching and helping him grow into manhood.

It was Easter weekend 1993, and the family had gathered at our ranch where for years the small merry-go-round, playhouse, and other yard entertainments had been greatly enjoyed. I'd built a sturdy cable the kids could ride down on a pulley with handlebars and was anticipating some

JACOB SIMONS IN 1992.

real excitement. I was outside with all the kids, encouraging Jacob to be the first that day to take a ride. He had the faith in me to do it, but once he got going there was more momentum than he could handle. He fell off at the end, right at my feet, and before I could catch him, he struck his head on the concrete at the base of the post. When I reached him he was unconscious, looking at me with no expression. I lost an edge for life that moment I've never recovered. Every fear and haunting thought I'd stored up about such things was suddenly a reality in my own life. The shock was so numbing I have only a blurry recollection of his father trying to revive him, then the local ambulance, then the helicopter life flight. My wife and the other grandchildren fell to their knees in prayer, while Jacob's mother Laura tried to divide her concern between her unconscious son and me.

He never did regain consciousness, and it was a week before the full responsibility for this horror settled in on me. The label "accident" didn't fit his death and never has. I built the swing, I was right with him when it happened, and all the could-haves and should-haves were on my part. Bottom line: I was careless. I know how ridiculous it is to replay things, but have replayed the prevention of this tragedy in my mind a million times since. For the first six weeks I wept the entire 20 miles to work every morning and wish I could have continued that, because once the weeping stopped, dealing with hollow places I couldn't fill was—and has been—agony. At the Scout jamboree I was committed to go to four months later, every eager face of the 30,000 boys there was Jacob's.

When someone you passionately savor, on whom you have been counting for companionship now and in the future, is suddenly taken away, there seems to be no way things can or will ever get better. You never get over it. You get used to it and learn to live with it, period. Pain like this is only eased, never entirely erased.

When a setback is something you can fix, change, or even explain to yourself, you have a good chance of overcoming it, but when something is taken away permanently, with no chance of restoration, it's a wall, period. No good news, no success can offset or soothe it.

I remember that spring, summer, and fall following the accident, hearing people comment on how beautiful things were—the fresh new green of the fields and leaves, the smell of the air, etc. There were flowers of 40 kinds on the hillsides, yet it was like having a stereo going, with the woofers and tweeters working away but no sound, just an ugly silence. I was inside a glass bubble of grief. The more beautiful the day, the worse it hurt.

Even a big new contract for my cleaning company, heavy book sales, and the birth of another new grandson were not reasons to celebrate but events I'd cheated one little boy out of. This plunged me into total despair.

And then there were all those unkept promises that came back to haunt me. "Someday, Jake, your kids will be playing on these rocks, your boys will be at this camp."

This loss is so much a part of my consciousness I often relive every moment of that horrible day in my mind in the midst of a speaking presentation, conversation, or movie. I have enough faith to not keep on asking "why," and enough responsibility to keep on living a productive life. I can even face the fact that something like this could happen again, with some other child or grandchild. But the loss of any child takes an irreplaceable part of you with them—maybe for some ultimate benefit, but I haven't identified that yet. It changes your life—crowds out unimportant things and pulls emotions out and makes you live them hourly. The loss of Jacob was the single most mind-gripping happening in my life, and despite my abiding belief in eternal life, the pain of it hasn't lessened with age—I've never healed.

> WHAT IS WORSE THAN THE LOSS OF A CHILD? ADD TO THAT A FEELING OF **RESPONSIBILITY** FOR LOSS OF A CHILD, AND YOU HAVE A HEARTACHE THAT NOTHING CAN ERASE. I LOVE LIFE, AND SEEING IT CUT SHORT IS SOMETHING WITH WHICH I NEVER HAVE BEEN ABLE TO COME TO TERMS.

My better three-fourths

People getting to know me often wonder and ask, "Man, what is your spouse like?" Most people are amazed that anyone would be able to endure me for more than a few hours. I've had many remark, "How does your wife put up with your busy schedule? She must be a good woman." That is a better description than I can come up with, except the one she writes on all her notes, cards, and letters to me, "Your ever-loving wife."

My editor presented me with a shocking appraisal when she finished reviewing my journals written over the 46-year span

A HAPPY MOMENT IN 1971.

of our marriage. "I find much written about the beginning Barbara, a medium amount on Barbara in the middle years, and very little on the later [present] Barbara. Kind of a "the honeymoon is over" observation.

PROVIDING A STRONG SHOULDER TO LEAN ON IS JUST ONE OF BARBARA'S MANY ROLES IN MY LIFE.

This probably follows the course of most human endeavors and relationships. The attained always seems somehow less worth commenting on than the process of attaining.

During the first 20 years, when we were building a family and business, Barbara and I were struggling together to survive, hence had constant interaction. At the start of our partnership, there was in our family and business just the two of us. We did all the work—me with mops, buffers, and squeegees, and her on the phone and paperwork— she was the entire "staff" otherwise.

Today, there are thousands of staff members and coworkers in our business, a vastly larger business, a huge network of friends and acquaintances, and 24 offspring (children and grandchildren). The result has been a lessening of our one-on-one time (always a concern) and a growing independence for each of us. Then, too, in the last 20 years we both have more time, money, and liberty to pursue our own interests and hobbies, much more so than in the survival years.

Barbara is still every bit as sensitive, intelligent, and affectionate as the 20-year-old I fell in love with back in 1955. She says she married me for "an exciting life," and truly, we have had very few dull moments.

The characteristic she dislikes most in me is the very thing that defines an entrepreneur: "They think they are right" (all the time!). Most people think of her as very laid back and easy-going, but Barbara is extremely strong-willed herself, and has never just gone along with all of my decisions. In many ways, we are complete opposites. She claims credit for my six successful decluttering books, for instance, because she really likes "stuff," whereas for me two pair of shoes is one too many.

A few other "Barbara bytes":

- Big business leadership usually gets more press and prestige than quiet, consistent service in the home and community. While I enjoyed the attention of print and broadcast media, Barbara served in our church as president of the Primary (managing the care of the children under twelve years old, and teaching them). Later she served as president of the Relief Society, our church's women's auxiliary that also has a sophisticated program for aiding needy families and individuals in the community.

- Barbara also has the knack for bringing important issues into full focus. While I often shotgun-spray a matter, she quickly boils it down to the bottom line, and this has often kept me out of gray areas.

- I've had "laugh sessions" with many of my friends, relatives, and business associates, as most have a good sense of humor. But none have close to Barbara's insight to humorous situations. While not the joke-telling type, she has a real talent for picking up the incongruities in things that get us both to laughing before a word is said.

- During all of my clamoring efforts and investments to change the world, Barbara is always quietly rearranging the world right around her. While my circle of friends and associates is larger, Barbara's is more loyal.

We had a scary moment early one morning in 1994 when I found Barbara gone from bed, in the kitchen on her hands and knees. I asked a dumb husband question, "Are you okay?" "Yes, I'm just grazing," she gasped, "but you better take me to the hospital." "Just not feeling well" was the only diagnosis I even considered as I drove her the 20 miles to the emergency-room. At first I couldn't comprehend the news that, "Your wife is having a heart attack." During the next week of hospitalization, tests, angioplasty, and transfer from Pocatello to Salt Lake City Hospital, we both became heart smart, realizing that age and genetics were part of our lives now. Barbara had lived a good and healthy life, but had lost her father when he was 42 from heart failure. She recovered well, but we have remained on the alert since, even opting for a bypass to promote continued heart health.

Barbara and I are reminded daily by the standard of our relationship that no success in life can compensate for failure in the home. Our fiftieth wedding anniversary is in 2007—proof that her tolerance and endurance are limitless!

"YOU ACTUALLY DID GET A 'BIG BREAK'
IN LIFE, DON—YOU MARRIED BARBARA.
IN MANY WAYS SHE HAS BEEN AN
ESSENTIAL COMPASS FOR YOUR JOURNEY
THROUGH LIFE. HOW FORTUNATE,
TO HAVE SOMEONE WHO BELIEVES
IN US NO MATTER WHAT, EVEN WHEN
WE DON'T DESERVE IT."
—MY BROTHER-IN-LAW, GENE KISLING

CHANGING PERSPECTIVES

At 16, when I was chosen as a delegate to Boys' State, it was the ultimate thrill to see my name and picture in the local paper for the first time for a reason other than sports. Having your name in print seemed then to be an important accomplishment. I devoured it, read it over and over, and made sure that parents and peers saw it.

More than 40 years later now, I realize that I don't read most of the press articles about me. Good or bad, I just toss them in a file so we can mail copies of them to people who want proof that I'm a bona fide big-time cleaner. Press is still appreciated, but after the work of the interviews themselves (the fire) is over, I have little desire to inhale the smoke. I've come full circle on others' opinions of me.

One thing you need to get used to, if you are a public figure to any extent, is being measured and evaluated constantly. At almost every seminar or workshop, for instance, there is a sheet for attendees to hand in afterward, commenting on the speaker. And even when you're sure you "knocked 'em dead" with your most brilliant presentation ever, there may well be dissenters who aren't bashful about beating on you a bit.

When I was teaching seminars for the Bell System, 72 seminars to more than 2,000 managers in all, I got 97 percent excellent ratings. After this and other favorable reviews, I figured I was hot stuff, and then came other audiences and topics not so centered in my core competency. I remember the worst of these—I was the main speaker at a press-women's convention in the Northwest. As a bestselling author, I was pretty free and bold with opinions. Half of the group raved about the humor of my talk, but the other half hated me, listing such descriptions as "arrogant," "obnoxious," and "ill-informed." Looking back, they were probably right on!

As Lincoln taught us, you can't please all of the people all of the time. Once you get over the ego shock of honest comment cards, they can be a great source of self-correction.

Any time you take a stand, you can count on others taking a stand opposite to yours. I spoke at a "Youth at Risk" conference once in Alaska to 250 of the state's adult leaders of youth. The subject turned to student alcohol abuse, and what might be done to curb its rampant presence in families in the state. I pointed out that many members of this group had recently traveled to another town in Alaska to address the problem of young people drinking, and they chose to have their meeting in a hotel rather than the new school available for the purpose. Why? Because they, the adults, couldn't be served drinks in the school. Even in our meeting that night, they had set up a bar in the back of the room. In short, without actually coming out with the word I called them hypocrites—not a great political move. I never got invited back, for sure!

Age and experience make us bolder, and these days I sometimes get much less flattering ratings than 97 percent excellent!

Another thing that comes with maturity is a deeper appreciation for life in general. You reach the point that even cutting down a growing tree makes you uncomfortable. When we moved to the farm (I was nine), my uncle made me a slingshot from a tree crotch that would shoot a marble-sized rock pretty accurately. Then I went after the starlings that pooped on our haystacks and farm machinery, though I did much more scaring away than killing.

As I got older I got to be deadly accurate with it and put a notch in it for every bird I killed. A couple of windows bit the dust, too, causing confiscation of my weapon with its 20-plus notches, and it being burned to ashes.

When I was 14, we used rifles to keep rockchucks, rabbits, and coyotes in check. Pheasant and deer hunting were big family events, and when we bagged a big buck deer, we enjoyed the venison.

But as time passed, I began to have a bad feeling about stopping a life, especially for sport. One afternoon in a gorgeous mountain setting, as I was laboring up a 9,000-foot slope, carrying a heavy rifle with a scope and ten pounds of other gear, gasping for breath while in my back pocket there was a notepad listing 60 more important things that needed doing. I stopped and asked myself: What am I doing here trying to outwit and take the life of some gentle, innocent animal? From that point on, I found killing anything distasteful, even the sneaky rat that just chewed my telephone cable. And it feels better to get our meals from the garden. Mosquitoes, centipedes, and rattlesnakes still "get it," but other varmints and insects I shoo instead of shoot.

The vocabulary of change

About the time you think you've worked out your own basic system for surviving and living a sane, even successful life, the school bell rings again. "Mold" was once something I cleaned off and out of places; today a mold is a $100,000 sculpture of aluminum used to produce new plastic cleaning tools to market. Webs were something we removed in the cleaning process; now a web is an expensive computer site developed for communication. Links were things like the coupler that held a farm implement to the tractor; now they are pathways in the information stream. I thought my vocabulary was adequate until I reached my sixties, when terms like buy/sell, succession, trusts, colonoscopy, and nonprofit foundation entered my life. Green was once mainly associated with pastures and rookies; today there is a steep fine if you overlook its environmental meaning. Harassment and political correctness were once just words in the dictionary; now you need to be aware of them every minute. "On top" once referred to reaching some high level of accomplishment; now it means all of the I's are dotted, T's are crossed, and you are liability-proof or you won't remain there.

In the 1950s, '60s, and '70s I was one of the progressive pioneers in my industry. I knew most things about most operations, had the whole of this in my knowledge base and in the scope of my own personal skills—cleaning hard floors, carpets, walls, and all of the other parts of a building, chemicals and machines, methodology, personnel, legal aspects, accounting, the trades—all of it. Everything that affected or involved my profession, I felt on top of and qualified to teach. Methods and technology are changing so fast now I couldn't keep up even by reading or attending seminars and trade shows full time. Things like safety, vehicles, payroll, health insurance, collections, and liability, which once were only one-hour, once-a-week concerns, are now incomprehensibly complicated, and I have full-time departments of five to ten people each to study and administrate them. They too fight to keep up. Even though I am older and wiser, there is too much to learn; I'm a generalist, and much of this has now passed me up.

I did all of our building startups (the first work on new contracts) personally for years, and I remember how awed and challenged we were when we had to start three buildings at once... then six. Personal involvement in every one was next to impossible when we started doing 25 at a time. Not long ago we started a new client account of 1,352 bank buildings at once, and I wasn't even invited to take part—I just got a memo about it. Years ago I was impressed that we cleaned a single lunchroom in a high rise; recently I toured one of the mall food courts we service that had 450 chairs cleaned eight times a day—that's 3,600 cleanings!

With the expansion of the areas we cleaned and services we offered, the "experience" stories I had collected over the years were dwarfed by what you'd imagine and expect when servicing 300 million square feet of floor space every day. One night a drunk drove a truck into the center of a department store we clean; the next night two of my 60-year-old female janitors pounced on and wrestled down a robber; the next day a mounted police officer's horse threw a shoe and we re-shoed the horse. Within the same week, two of my Varsity trucks crashed in an empty parking lot—into each other. We started a new contract, which a new employee sold, telling the client (a bank) how good we were. The first night he used toilet bowl cleaner on fine wooden desks. Result: red faces and $25,000 worth of damage we had to repair. Then one of our janitors (watching an X-rated tape in a big corporate training auditorium), accidentally left it in the VCR, and the next day the CEO, unaware, clicked it on in front of a room full of guests. We ran an expensive, but thorough customer safety program for the employees serving our new $500,000 a month account cleaning a large department store. The very next morning we had a "slip and fall" lawsuit from there. Elsewhere (after being carefully trained to clean up everything), a new employee did it well; he stole the telephone company manager's car right out of the building's parking lot. There is never an uneventful day in the cleaning business.

No place like home

I lived on airplanes and in cabs and limousines for at least 25 years, and had some really intense years when I knew Salt Lake City, Atlanta, LA, and Philadelphia better than home.

For the support of my many employees, and because of my commitment to publishers and clients, I kept up these kinds of schedules long past good sense. The feeling that I was having a strong influence on others was always the driver, as was the dream of where all this could go someday. But the insanity and exhaustion of nonstop travel began to dampen my relationships with family and community, and crowd the things that meant the most to me. I was fully sick of it years before I finally decided to refocus my agenda and energy. So I am concentrating more now on local and regional opportunities and projects, and things I can do by driving rather than flying. I would like to make only a couple of trips to LA and New York a year, just enough to remind me that I made the right decision as to how and where I live—in rural Idaho and Hawaii.

From my 1996 journal:

The reason I'm working on and building home and business "forts" like crazy right now (at age 62) is so that I can stay and work at home for the next 20 years, from Idaho and Hawaii. I plan on working until I'm immobile, and I want to have things set up so that people will want to come to me, rather than me having to go to them. I want to be able to work in my yard for a while and then when bones and body rebel, I can switch to the book lab. I'll also do some selected speaking. My office headquarters is being wired for TV broadcasting so that I could do CNN interviews right here from Pocatello.

My wanderlust must have been satisfied earlier, because as I get older my whole drive is not to see the world but to prove to the world that "home" is the ultimate prize. I realize that people who have been confined to one job or one place most of their lives and never got to travel much are thankful for motor homes, planes, and good maps. More power to them. I cannot comprehend, in my own life, how anyone would ever travel for pleasure. The older I get, the less willing I am to have any of my remaining time wasted, and for sure, traveling in the new millennium is more time-consuming and complicated than ever before. Newer technology and vastly increased security do nothing to enhance it.

In my sixties and seventies, my mind seemed to be focused more and more on:

Getting back home to our ranch;

Getting to Hawaii for my winter writing.

The hands of time

"His face is lined and leathery from long exposure to Idaho's sun and dry wind. At the same time, the twinkle in his eyes and his disarming smile give him a youthful, vigorous look."

'I have a personal goal to keep looking sharp,' Don says. '... Can't do that very well while traveling on airplanes and eating in restaurants, so I get out the pick and shovel on my ranch.... Helps me keep in shape.'"

—Dean and Nancy Hoch, in *This People* magazine

To do good you need to feel good

I work for exercise, and whenever possible like to find my exercise in the course of doing something useful—cleaning, decluttering, gardening, raking, building fence, shoveling dirt, sand, or snow, or playing a good rousing game with kids. I see plenty of people (too many!) who have resorted to artificial exercise in gyms or on an exer-torture apparatus at home. They spend a lot for the machine or membership and plenty of time to get there and get the exercise done. But they have nothing afterward but (hopefully) some muscles and lost calories. With physical work, you can get plenty of exercise plus some additional accomplishment and outcome—free, without having to buy and store a bunch of junk.

One blessing I never took for granted was good health and feeling good almost all the time. I can only remember a few times when I was sick with things like the flu. In 50 years on the job, I only missed a total of about six or seven days from illness or even surgery. Early in my life, I developed a passion for hard work—its results in most respects were wonderful. I felt good and gained a lot, in both friendship and material things. Plus the habit of hard work carried over into the way I approached family and community projects, and even my hobbies. I went at everything with all of my heart, mind, and might. Before long, I fell into the well-known and criticized role of workaholic. I could make even the most recreational opportunity into a real effort, and for me that's what made it recreation! In my fifties, however, it seemed that being on the go for fourteen or sixteen hours a day was getting harder, and I told my doctor that by nine o'clock it seemed that I was dead tired any more. "Nine in the morning or nine at night?" he asked. I got the message and went home and aged like everyone else, accepting late-evening tiredness as a fact of life. I vowed I'd finally learned my lesson and was going to slow down some, but that never seems to happen.

MOWING OUR YARD IN KAUAI.

Jack of all trades… master of some

I've thinned sugar beets until I couldn't straighten up and picked potatoes until my fingers were sore. I've irrigated, hauled things, and operated heavy farm equipment of all kinds. I've dug ditches and trenches, and installed sprinkler systems and dry wells, and built roads. I've planted hundreds of acres of crops and harvested the same. I can and have used almost every hand tool ever invented.

By accident and necessity in the course of my life, I learned many trades, enough that I could and did draw up plans and build a house from the ground up. In painting, I could be called a master; in cement work and masonry, I was good. Installing plastic laminate (such as Formica) a little shaky. In plumbing, I was and am slow, electrical work slower yet. Working with glass and glazing tests my nervous system. I can do sheetrock installation and taping, but if I did it for money I would make about 18 cents an hour. My welding always held, but it looked like turkey poop. At carpet laying, I was okay, until my knees turned 65.

ON MY OLD FAITHFUL MASSEY-FERGUSON AT THE RANCH.

The two worst words added to my vocabulary in later years were 1. congestion, and 2. medication. Both of these I had managed to steer clear of for years. Now the constant congestion of cities, events, and traffic was painful to the soul. And even though I live by carefully disciplined health rules, heredity began to have its day. I had high cholesterol on even the strictest diet, so I had my first regular medication at 63.

An invisible, uncorrectable condition I live with is tinnitus, or ringing in the ears. This is a constant, loud interior noise, like a million high-pitched tiny bells. I can tune this out, ignore it, or override it only when intensely occupied with an activity or project. Any additional noise added to this never ceasing, high-pitched buzzing irritates me almost to the point of wanting to jump off a cliff somewhere. No advice or input for correcting or disarming this defect has helped—sleep is the only thing that shuts the belfry down.

In the eye of the beholder

We were filming on location in a home for the Discovery Channel with a crew out of Canada, when the cameraman suddenly stopped and said, "Mr. Aslett, do you realize you look just like Sean Connery?" (The original James Bond.) Boy, did that make my morning! I "James Bonded" my way through the next several hours, figuring that even age had some merits I'd missed till now. To finish up the segment at one of my Cleaning Center stores, they filmed me with a customer. Afterward, she picked up a bottle of my new "3-in-1 Spotter" which had a picture of me in a white sport coat on the label. She held it up and exclaimed, "Wow, Mr. Aslett, look at this, you look just like an oompah loompah (the midget workmen in *Willie Wonka and the Chocolate Factory*). I looked down at it and sure, enough, I did! (a lot more than like Sean Connery). It's nice sometimes to get perspective, even if it sets you back a bit.

For some reason, the idea of aging never bothered me—I never thought about trying to replace your hair when it thinned, or understood why any man would want to color his gray hair. Who would you be fooling?

When I was out on the streets of New York a while ago buying a watch for a grandchild from a street vendor, a Chinese street artist offered me a real deal on a sidewalk portrait. We needed a new drawing for my press kit, so I sat down by her. She asked as she sketched, "You likee mo hair? You likee less wrinkle?" We earned our looks—we ought to be satisfied with them.

AT 64

AGE WILL TAKE ITS TOLL
IT HASN'T YET, BUT WILL.
I HAVEN'T ALTERED AIMS OR GOALS
SO GIVE ME ONE MORE HILL.
—DON ASLETT, DECEMBER 1999

Chapter 23

BUILDING NET WORTH: THOUGHTS ON MONEY AND CHARITY

I am my brother's sweeper...

The central purpose of most businesses is to make money. Once that goal is accomplished, however, how we spend and share it defines a person's and a business's true values.

Every year Varsity does community service projects in conjunction with our annual meeting. Here I am helping paint the sanctuary of the historic St. Mary's Catholic Church in Park City, Utah.

Payroll poor

One of the most difficult aspects of my life for many years was dealing with banks and bankers. There was always conflict as I was an idealist and they were realists.

I was taught early to earn my money, save, and spend carefully. So from the age of 13 through 23, I always had money. I paid for my own education, for my two years as a missionary in Hawaii, and for the startup of my college business. Then four new terms entered my life: payables, receivables, inventory, and cash flow. For the next 20 years, I often lived near financial despair, spending too many days and nights worrying about money. I was earning and the company was growing, but I often wasn't getting much of my cash till 90 days later, due to the red tape of big companies. Most of these jobs were profitable in the end, but labor costs on some of them amounted to $10,000, $20,000, or $30,000—a lot of money in the '50s and '60s.

The bigger we got and the more I made and gained in net worth, the larger the gap between payables and receivables grew. For years payroll was a battle of trying to minimize the overdrafts while praying for a couple of big checks to arrive on time. Especially in big growth periods, I hated paydays. Rows of gaunt-faced, hardworking fellow students lined up for their checks, with my wife, who kept the books, handing them out. We might have $50,000 owed to us, but be overdrawn $6,000. And I was out collecting, begging clients for my money so I could cover those checks. When payday came and there wasn't enough money, borrowing from a bank was my usual alternative—I didn't want to tap friends or my folks. Those bankers seemed brutal then; in retrospect I realize that their agony may have been worse than mine. Looking back at it all now, I wonder how the bankers survived me. They probably ran new loan officers through the Aslett ordeal to test them out.

Bankers are careful and conservative and have rules and guidelines that must be followed—their jobs (and the health of the national economy) depend on this. So the prospect of loaning any amount of money for any length of time to a college student, self-employed in the cleaning business, with no assets or collateral, and a family of his own to feed, would strike terror in the heart of even the best of bankers. When I did manage to extract some money from them and set an idealistic payback date, a bigger job would come in (calling for yet more money for labor and materials. The bankers always got their money in the end, but it was with a lot of begging and tense phone calls on both of our parts.

The real killer for me was missing the payback dates. I set them honestly based on what I thought were firm commitments from my customers, and when they failed to come through, so did I. Worse yet, I usually needed yet more money at this point and so I had to go with my dishonorable record to borrow another $25,000 when I hadn't yet paid back the last $25,000.

It got tougher and tougher as the business bloomed. Many times I pulled my equipment-laden truck into the bank parking lot and sat slumped over in dread for an hour or two, getting up the courage to walk one more time into that plush, polished place and beg for a chance to use their money. Even when paying hefty interest, I still felt like a beggar. I'm sure that all of the bankers within 300 miles kept abreast of my schedule and arranged their vacations for when they knew I was coming to town.

At times, much of this was caused by my own poor judgment. When the woes of the cash-flow crunch were upon me and I was hesitating at the banker's door, I could see my errors. I never charged enough or saved enough to have some working capital, I was too easy on the accounts, and went too far with employees when I should have fired them before they rang up a loss. After enough ups and downs, I began to refine things by hiring people who didn't have my deficiencies to help manage the company.

But there was one experience here that really pushed me over the edge. It was at a time when I had a proven record of accomplishment—my payback might be slow but it was always 100 percent. I had an opportunity to buy property in Sun Valley, and I traveled back to my local bank with a well thought out request (with solid collateral this time). The junior VP scanned it and said he'd show it to the big VP, who would review it and decide. I waited in the lobby for two hours past the promised time. I was sitting unnoticed behind some plants when the big VP finally came bustling in. The little VP jumped up with my carefully drafted proposal and request. The big VP was just six feet away from me when he grabbed the paper and asked, "Who is it?" "Don Aslett, the cleaner," said the little VP. "Tell him no," said the big VP, and walked away. I was asking for a $10,000 loan on a piece of land that sold later for $4 million.

From that day on, I refused to be intimidated by bankers. I went after them now as a customer making them money, not as a humble beggar. Two other bankers elsewhere scanned the same proposal and said, "Looks good to me." And one of them gave me the money. I ended up doing millions of dollars worth of business with that bank for the next 20 years.

This poverty period set a good pattern for my life. It only takes once living poor to learn to live frugally for the rest of your life. I gave up new clothes, cars, trips, and entertainment to avoid cash crunches and bank begging. Anyone who has gone without personal paychecks for months while working unbelievable hours will never waste anything, and come up with a commitment to never let yourself get there again.

As I read back in my personal journal and go through family and business records, I see that fortunately, none of this dampened our productivity, visions, hopes, or dreams. We just kept accelerating in all things. One of our toughest cash flow times was when we found the McCammon ranch and traded our city house for it—ultimately a great financial boost. (I often made the biggest and most costly moves when I was the most broke.)

One journal entry really meant a lot to me: "Mr. Glosly (the banker) thanked me today for coming in and getting a loan." I had never been treated like a valued customer before. That one "thank you" did a lot to change my perspective on banking.

Today, I haven't been inside a bank for years. The bankers politely make appointments and come to our office. Many of them are asking, competing, almost begging to get my money in their bank—a real twist of fate that I have to admit I enjoy.

> I NEVER UNDERSTOOD
> BANKERS UNTIL PEOPLE
> TRIED TO BORROW FROM ME.

On being a "moldy millionaire"

Not long ago some little kid asked if I was a "moldy [multi] millionaire"—a thought-provoking slip of the tongue, huh? One of the questionable signs of success is being thought of as a "millionaire." When I toured England, especially, I had more questions about that than anything else.

During earlier years in business when I was still putting in endless hours and struggling to survive, someone pointed out an article in the *Wall Street Journal* that said Idaho had more millionaires per capita than any other state. I didn't identify myself with that elite group then, and years later when I was included in that statistic, I still didn't comprehend it or identify with it.

Having a net worth of millions was not and is not a life-changing event for me—it is recognized by onlookers and endowment seekers to a much greater degree. There was some ego gratification in the fact that my activities had been crowned by what most people think of as the halo of success—money—but my actual lifestyle changed very little. And my emotions and perceptions, temptations and temperament were no different with an inflated bottom line.

We all hear daily the old "If I had (or made) more money I'd _____" (get rid of my troubles and be happy). Sorry, but having plenty of money only allows you the opportunity to do smart or dumb things faster.

I never was a bank account or portfolio builder. Money that made money just made money, and money doesn't mean much unless it is producing something that is enhancing life and family.

CONFUCIUS SAY,
"CAN A CLEANER EVER BE FILTHY RICH?"

The builders restructure

Most of us own some stock in some way, be it a corporate investment, retirement fund, 401K, or purely personal investment. I ended up
being a stock creator as well as a stockowner.

When we merged Varsity Housecleaners, Varsity Telco, and my little
cleaning supplies company Micro-Clean Supply into one in 1971, Varsity Contractors, we had added three new stockholders (who purchased
stock)—Mark Browning, Rex Turner, and Dave Collings. After a certain
period of time, these new stockholders were also entitled to vote on
stockholder issues. I then held 55 percent of Varsity's stock, Arlo, 30
percent, and the others the remaining 15 percent. More growth came,
and in time, the question of what to do if any of the major stockholders
died, quit, or divorced. Because controlling stock rules, and neither of
us wanted to end up with a stockholder's spouse or other family members as partners, we went to a buy/sell insurance funded agreement.
Arlo and I insured each other through Varsity with the stipulation that
upon the demise of one of the stockholders, the surviving spouse would
get a chunk of money and leave. That worked for a while, but as the
company grew and gained value, those insurance premiums moved into
hundreds of thousands of dollars. Plus neither Arlo nor I wanted the
business out of our lives, and the present arrangement was a deterrent
to Arlo and other minority stockholders, who in closely held corporations are totally at the mercy of the controlling stockholder, in this case
the Aslett family.

The more valuable the stock became, the more anxious the minority
holders were, and I was getting all sorts of advice from fellow business-
people, lawyers, and family to never surrender control. To add fuel to a
smoldering fire, in the late 1990s an Eastern investment group offered
to buy us out, and then use Varsity as a platform company to build a
huge national entity. An initial check of $6 million would come to Bar-
bara and me as part of this arrangement. But I would lose all control
of the company and its culture. And for sure, they would, within five
years, leverage and sell off our big new company—and Varsity would
not be the Varsity it is or could be.

We (the Varsity stockholders) turned down the offer, reasoning that
the business was our life—we didn't build it to sell. If they could make

it bigger, so could we. Within four years of this offer, we tripled the company's size, and still own it all.

The offer did trigger the Varsity stockholders to an awareness that it was time to consider sharing ownership further with our employees and create some stock options.

After this, I began a 5-year pursuit of a plan to ensure my own family's security as well as greater stockholder diversity and motivation. I finally decided to sell 14 percent of my stock to eight new owners, maintaining majority 41 percent but surrendering control. I didn't do it for the money. The decision was easy, as this also meant a switch from a C corporation to an S corporation, meaning that whether I was around or not at the end of the year, 41 percent of the owner distributions would go to my family. The 41 percent was secure and would be more income than the family needed after Barbara and I departed.

Sticking with simplicity

I never operated in life with a big reserve of money. I never had a "nest egg," but lived pretty providently and slowly gained substantial net worth. Operating with little cash reserve keeps you on the front lines, where you have to produce and carry your own weight and sweat things, not just hire them done. It was also incentive to take good care of my tools and vehicles. I hated waste, luxury, or extravagance in structures, food, clothing, or entertainment. It was easy to be careful about spending because I related everything to a long day of picking potatoes or thinning sugar beets. Spending $40 for a single meal bothered me even when I could afford it.

You only have to observe most of the newly rich or trust fund kids to see waste and loss of touch with the really worthwhile things in life.

Though I've made appearances and presentations all over the country and the world, I've never had more than three suits and three or four ties. I've also officiated at many marriages and funerals, and always looked good enough to get by. It takes a note in the pocket of a suit back from the dry cleaners saying, "We can't fix/clean this," before I can dispose of it.

Likewise, I wear a $12 wristwatch with my company logo on it. It tells time as well as a $400 or $4,000 watch, and I don't have to guard it when I'm traveling. I love quality but hate luxury and opulence—in dwellings, vehicles, dress, entertainment, or "toys." I see it as a waste of money, resources, and emotion—for nothing but ego. Showing off and tending overkill can use up a third of your life, or more.

Between me personally and the company, I've owned thousands of cars, trucks, and vans. Vehicles have never been a status thing for me.

I don't care how old a vehicle is or how it looks—if it is dependable, comfortable, and safe. The only car I ever had affection for was my '65 Volkswagen bug. It always started, was cheap to run and easy to park, had no room for junk, was great on snow and ice, and it always had a smiley look when you approached it.

For a company car, I drove a truck until I upgraded to a used sedan, which I drove till it reached 300,000 miles. My executives finally wrenched it away from me, saying it looked like an old Idaho irrigation vehicle, not fit for the chairman of the board of a big company. So I now drive a white Varsity van like many of my workers do; my wife and I drive a later model Buick and the '76 Ford pickup in which we went to Alaska. I still have no sentiment for vehicles—they're just transportation!

AM I MY BROTHER'S KEEPER?

(Heeding the call to service)

Being kind to animals and other people, especially children and the aged, was a doctrine my parents and grandparents lived by. You paid your way in life and did what you could for those around you who needed help or who struggled or were without.

Barbara and I followed this philosophy and raised our own children with it. Barbara and I or some other family member would occasionally leave the office to catch a school basketball game. People would spot me buying tickets or sitting in the stands and swarm up. "My daughter wants to work in Sun Valley, and if she could just get on...." "My son is having a problem with his Scout project, could you...?" "We have a graduation coming up and need an original program. Could you...?"

This never let up, and when we were home, the phone would ring with more of the same. The old "I've done my share" feeling would creep in at times but we seldom yielded to it. The rewards of service were always greater than rewards of sleep or leisure time.

ARLO LUKE AND I SERVING AS LEADERS AT THE BOY SCOUT NATIONAL JAMBOREE IN 2001.

THE DEEPEST PROMPT IN OUR
CONSCIOUSNESS IS BEING OUR BROTHER'S
KEEPER—LOOKING AFTER OTHERS, LOVING
THEM AND SHARING WITH THEM, AND
HELPING TO CREATE JOY IN THEIR LIVES.

We became only more qualified to help others as we grew older and our income increased, but as requests for help also increased we had to manage to tell the needy from the greedy (which continues to be an everyday call).

I'm not very enthusiastic about marching to save the whales or stray cats, but when a sincere and dedicated humane society worker in Hawaii asked me if I would speak at their annual fundraiser and banquet, of course I said yes, and donated $50 worth of books for the auction. A school on Kauai was having a "writing week" and asked if I would spend a day with the exceptional sixth graders, explaining how to write a book. How could you turn down those studious little people? They loved my "show" and I enjoyed doing it. Knowing I'd be in Cincinnati for a night, a church there asked me to do a "fireside" talk for youth, which I would never turn down. A rural high school in northern Idaho was holding a "lock in," where the students were locked into the school all night, for a super program of dance, food, drama, and inspirational speaker. It was worth losing a night's sleep to see 300 country students devour ethical counsel!

Then it was a grade school in the South holding a contest at a national convention where 150 kids made something original, and these things were all spread out on tables for a "famous person" to come down and judge. Also that week I read at the big local library read-a-thon, and donated my Saturday to speak at the literary club of Idaho State University. Barbara and I and the family made hundreds of "donations" like this, many at our own home.

I remember weeks of six to ten donated appearances or speeches. Most of these meant a day of time preparing for and doing them, donated books, and lots of travel. These were sometimes a strain, or even unappreciated once in a while, but they were the right thing to do. I always felt good about these donations—only once did I have a lapse in this attitude, but luckily, I was quickly cured.

I was just finishing up a terrifically busy year, and many of the appearances and presentations I had been doing were donated or "freebies" as my staff called them.

In February, I had a full schedule of home shows and trade shows. It was a profitable but brutal month and I had only one evening home, at least I thought I did. Then I realized that in a weak moment I'd agreed to do the keynote speech for an FFA banquet in Castleford, Idaho, a remote little rural community 170 miles away. I was in a "poor me" mood that afternoon as I loaded up my visual aids and headed out, and soon I was talking to myself, "Why me? I've done fifty of these! This is costing me

IN 1994 VARSITY CREWS BUILT A SPLIT-RAIL FENCE FOR THE INDIAN ROCKS SCOUT CAMP IN MCCAMMON, IDAHO.

$500 and I don't know anyone in Castleford. Somebody else ought to take their turn!" You know how you can work yourself into a frenzy of feeling sorry for yourself.

By the time I reached Castleford three and a half hours later, I had a sneer on my lip, and figured I was doing this hick town a big favor. As I walked into the old gym decorated with bright blue and gold decorations, I saw husbands and wives carrying in steaming potluck food, accompanied by FHA daughters or FFA sons. After three weeks in the East seeing very few intact families, it was good to see the affection and interaction here between parents and kids, a kind of old-fashionedness that still should be in fashion. As we ate delicious food, the emcee announced the presence of a young woman who had left Castleford after graduation and who had become an outstanding student and leader at a major university, bringing much pride and prestige to their little town. She was asked to say a few words before I started my talk. "Great," I thought, "some twinky student is going to take up some of *my* valuable speaking time."

This young lady, full of charm and confidence, stood up and thanked the group for inviting her to the banquet. She reminded everyone how good the FFA program was, and expressed appreciation for the opportunities and experiences it had given her. Then she hesitated and said, "This evening is special to me for another reason. Three years ago I hit rock bottom as a teenager. My parents had split up, and I felt like I didn't matter to anyone. I was discouraged and depressed and had decided to give up on the good life which I felt was treating me bad, and do drugs, the live-in boyfriend bit, and all that. Fold up, and coast through life. But at the depth of this critical time, we went on an FFA trip to Boise and Mr. Aslett was the speaker. He so inspired me, and filled me with will and purpose, that I returned home committed to keep life's rules, fight, endure, and excel. And I did—thanks to all of you, and to you, Mr. Aslett."

By the time she finished, I was sunk so shamefully low in my seat they thought I'd gone home. I felt like a rat for whimpering, whining, and resenting the opportunity to come and talk to a group of young people. How ungrateful could a man get? Here I had the ability and invitation to touch and change children's lives, and to think I had the nerve to pity myself for this!

That night on an exhilarating drive home, I vowed to never again "be weary in well-doing," to feel sorry about giving time or talent to others. What had been ugly on the way there was beautiful on the way home. I rolled down the window and sniffed spring thawing the fields in the crisp and now dark air. The rewards of sincere service are second to no other feeling or accomplishment in life.

The people I'm most attracted to are those who have made the transition from being a taker to being a giver, from moocher to mentor, from dragger to doer for the good of all, not just themselves.

If you want to matter, go do something that matters. Really rich people make other people's lives richer, not just their own.

Act on your first impulse to do good. Obey your own experience and instinct! Learning to follow these feelings requires some experience, some humility, and some discipline, but it's a wonderful way to set your compass. Follow that first impulse to do good—it seldom leads you astray.

MY DEFINITION OF SUCCESS?
CONDUCT THAT CREATES LASTING
JOY FOR YOURSELF AND OTHERS.

In the end what we become, not what we have or do, is the real measure of net worth. It is our progress toward achieving personal peace, not a portfolio.

As Edwin Markham said so well in his poem "Bridge Builder":

We are all blind until we see
That in the human plan
Nothing is worth the making
If it does not make the man.
Why build these cities glorious
If man unbuilded goes?
We build the world in vain
Unless the builders also grow.

VARSITY'S SERVICE PROJECT FOR 1992: CLEANUP AND RESTORATION OF THE HISTORICAL STEAM ENGINE "HEBER CREEPER" IN MIDWAY, UTAH.

Chapter 24

OUR SENIOR MISSION: ADVENTURES IN THE LAND OF NO "R'S"

Among good people with a good message.

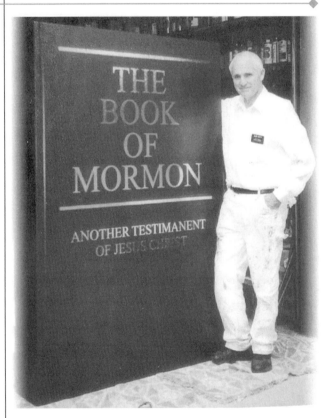

THE OVERSIZE SET OF SCRIPTURES WE MADE TO CALL ATTENTION TO OUR ROADSIDE RELIGIOUS INFORMATION BOOTH DURING BARBARA'S AND MY MISSION TO BOSTON IN 2002-2003.

The ultimate test all 45-year marriages need came in 2002, when Barbara was 65 and I was 67. Right in the middle of our busiest, most opportunity-packed prime of life, surrounded by an ever-growing number of grandkids, we decided to serve a church mission for 18 months. That's a long time to be gone at any age! Missionaries may be sent anywhere in the world, and we felt we would be sent to Hawaii, because we knew the culture and language, and had a home there. But our mission assignment was to be Massachusetts, a far cry from the rural settings we were used to. We were assigned to a small city half an hour outside of Boston—Lowell, right on the border of New Hampshire.

A senior mission in the Church of Jesus Christ of Latter-day Saints is totally volunteer. You devote all of your time to improving the spiritual and family life of the people in the designated area, and pay all of your own expenses while doing it. Your contact with the home and business you left behind, as recommended by mission guidelines, is very limited.

For the first time in many years we were *together* continuously—24/7. Alone time was the five minutes while the other was showering. Together we prayed and read scriptures, did presentations, relaxed, ate, and taught and visited others nights and mornings. All of the new friends we made in this new world were mutual friends. We drove in traffic (among the worst in the world!) together, and endured Boston's record winter and summer weather during this time.

A few excerpts from our mission journal:

Today we had to leave to enter mission orientation and training. It was three-thirty, we had to be in Utah by six, and Barbara was about as ready as I was (30 percent). We just grabbed what we'd take on a three-day trip, turned off the water and furnace, and walked outside. We took one last deep breath and scan of our ranch, the most beautiful place on earth, had a quiet prayer of commitment, said, "Let's make this count," and bolted. We didn't even lock the house or gate.

Our ten days in the mission training facility in Provo, Utah, were total severance from the past. We were just another senior couple boning up on health, public relations, proselytizing protocol, study habits, etc. There were hundreds of young 19-21 year old men and women as well as senior couples there to be trained. Of the ten couples in our orientation group one was going to Korea, one to Africa, one to Oklahoma, and one to England. Talk about people from every walk of life! Among the senior missionaries, we have ex-cops, retired military personnel, Chevron dealers, teachers, farmers, Mrs. Americas, computer executives, and a lawyer or two. We have a couple from Blackfoot, Idaho, who have done six previous missions, from Philadelphia to the Philippines!

Once we were badged, medicated, mail boxed, lunch ticketed, and read the rules, we were sent up to unpack in a little dorm room. Everything we are taking to Boston fits in the trunk and back seat of our little Buick, without blocking our view!

We were given a series of discussions to learn at our own speed, then one crisp morning they gathered our group of senior missionaries and sent us to a room where a bunch of seasoned missionary teachers and investigators evaluated our scriptural knowledge. We were like first graders taking a college entrance exam. Before we'd recovered from the spiritual humiliation of the morning's attempts, they gave us a second workover that afternoon, and some improvement was noted. They could identify us as missionaries instead of misfits. They tell us the spirit will do all the work if we just show up looking the part. The spirit is straining, but it is comforting to be with a group of others who feel as dumb as you do.

I've never seen so many dark suits, big shoes, and missionary badges in my life! It's amazing to see these hundreds of bright, well-groomed men and women singing and speaking in different languages—learning Russian, Chinese, Japanese, Korean, Spanish, and French in no time. There are dainty-looking young women heading to Africa or Ukraine. And there is never a dull moment. The leaders instruct and involve, then interrogate and evaluate you. This place is precision organized— we seniors are getting two months worth of training in eight days.

They had actors playing less-active members in real-life situations today. We knocked on doors over and over and had to impress the person who appeared with our interest in him or her with carefully chosen Scriptures. I talked half the time and Barbara the other half. In our evaluation, when asked what our approach was, Barbara said, "Don throws them into shock and then turns them over to me."

All too soon came the day of our "finals," and as our policeman so well put it, "This was more stressful than breaking up a barroom fight." We had to go into pretend malls, bus stops, grocery lines, laundromats, backyards, street scenes, etc., and make individual "contact" to get a teaching appointment.

Trained now (or at least made aware of our lacks), we packed up in the early morning of March 9. Our trip to the mission site (Provo to Boston) proved pioneer. Twenty miles up the canyon we were in a blizzard, and had icy windshields and drifts all the way east. The winds were 40 to 80 mph and coming off the Great Lakes, and as we traveled on several roads were closed right behind us.

Home away from home

We arrived at our apartment Tuesday, March 12. Our "home" is in the basement of a 600-unit complex—you get a mile jog in just taking out the garbage. The furniture is early Goodwill—love the cinderblock bookcase. This is sure different from the 6,500-square-foot, six-bedroom homes we left in Idaho and Hawaii! We unloaded everything, hung the grandkids' pictures, and were all set. Most of the other renters in the complex seem to be from India or Cambodia.

Monday morning we launched forth to find our contacts and for sure, scripture reading played a far second to map reading. Our area has six towns, and all have their own Boston Street, Boston Road, or Boston Avenue. One main road will change names several times as it passes through different towns.

People here drive at high speeds right on your back bumper so you either know your turn or you must go past it and try again. Every street looks like you've been here before. When stubborn husbands are driv-ing and frustrated wives navigating in any city, soon there is much scowling and harshness of personalities ex-posed, but mission discipline (so far) is amazing. No verbal abuse at all, just a gentle, "Gosh dear, did we miss that road again? Do you think the fourth try will work, honey?"

This is the largest Ward (congregation) in the church, around 1,500 members total, 800 of them Cambodian-Americans. The ward roster is an inch thick.

People know that we are in town, in our long black overcoats—we've had four job offers as we've passed local mortuaries!

THE NEW LOWELL WARD OF THE CHURCH OF JESUS CHRIST OF LATTER-DAY SAINTS, FOR WHICH WE SERVED OUR EIGHTEEN-MONTH MISSION.

Culture shock

Greetings from the state of Massachusetts, which I have not even come close to learning to spell. One thing is for sure... they erred in telling us this is a stateside call. Without question, this is a foreign mission, if there ever was one. What a diverse place. We have the most cosmopolitan group of people you can imagine. I analyzed the at-tendance at sacrament meeting tonight and there were hardly two of the same race, creed, or color. Sixty percent of this town seems to be Asian, Hispanic, and Indian folks. We have The Book of Mormon here in 20 different languages! When we are out meeting people, we run into many who cannot speak English—I really wonder how they get along here. We have to strain to understand the part English mixed with parts of other languages plus Boston slang. We nod our heads as if we are understanding, but are only catching a few words here and there. Sister Aslett—Barbara's title during this mission time—and I look at each other for clues.

WE HAD A PRIMARY PROGRAM TODAY WHERE SPANISH, PORTUGUESE, ITALIAN, CAMBODIAN, CHINESE, ENGLISH, AND BOSTON WERE ALL SPOKEN BY DIFFERENT KIDS AND ADULTS.

Any romanticism the quaint and historic Northeast might have is completely undone by the traffic. It is unimaginable to me how intelligent humans can creep along in a four-lane, 17-mile-long string of slowed cars night and day, month after month. And then hunt for a place to park, and pay as much for it as it costs to drive a car now. We spend two hours a day waiting at lights or for a little space to open up between cars so we can dart in.

The mere act of getting from one place to another exhausts any energy you might have had at the beginning of the day. You have to give the biggest part of your life away just to arrive somewhere!

Eighteen months of nonstop noise!

I don't think there is a quiet corner in all of Massachusetts. Apartment noise never stops: the people on all sides are on a 24-hour schedule of slamming doors, fighting, drinking and partying, playing loud music from booming entertainment centers, using washers or dryers, or vacuuming. Some people from India moved in above us and they raise elephants and train cobras in a rock-polishing machine up there. When they turn the water on and off 20 or 30 times an hour, all the pipelines in the building clank and hiss. We thought the snoring of the last guy was unbearable, but the new folks (Lord love 'em) majored in advanced, amplified snoring!

Outside is no better. The lawn people have mowers, trimmers, and blowers going constantly, the trash trucks are always crashing and dumping, and there is always a siren from a fire truck, police car, or ambulance. Nearly every day, every hour, someone is operating something that has a high-pitched motor. And dogs are barking everywhere.

We are well into the second month of our mission, after a lot of wheel spinning in the first. I see a great need for creative energy and leadership here. Many are just surviving and tending tradition day by day. They just light up and glow, even staunch old members, when you suggest some new vision and we are laying out some good paths to pursue. They've all been warned that I'm assertive, an intimidator, over-confident, arrogant, etc., so are babying Barbara and trying to ignore me for a while. But this place has need of a builder. The bottom line might be faith, but nothing moves without leadership.

At one meeting a mission leader said we needed sometimes to pull a wild card to get things accomplished. I raised my hand and asked, "What is a wild card?" The Relief Society president said, "You, Elder Aslett, are one."

One snowy evening the phone rang: the new baby (only one month old) of one of our contacts was in the hospital and the anxious mother asked for a blessing for him. It wasn't any hospital nearby, but in Concord, New Hampshire, miles of slippery killer road away. Already the interstate was jammed with accidents. Roads were treacherous and traffic just crawling along at times, but we managed to drive there and bless that tiny baby in his oxygen tent.

We did a lot to establish a traditional Pioneer Day celebration here, and the covered wagon we came up with was the hit of the show. Members brought lots of authentic pioneer gear and the church was decorated to the hilt inside and out. (These are the most decorating people we have ever met.) The evening before the holiday, we were out in the church parking lot exhausted, when a young man drove up who had been baptized two years ago. He told us his aged mother was moving tomorrow and he was on a job (he was an accountant) and couldn't leave. Could anyone in the ward help?

I know well that no moving job is little, despite his assurance that his mother had only a few boxes to move in her van. But charity subdued my intelligence and I told him I would take care of it. The next morning we were at the church at 6 A.M. setting up the Pioneer Day signs, our wagon, all of the stoves for the free pancake breakfast, and bales of hay for atmosphere (it felt good to lift and place them, even in a suit). Then I grabbed two other Elders—poor souls—and said, "We have to run over for a few minutes and help an elderly woman move," and they gullibly followed.

It was eight-thirty in the morning then, and since the woman did not in fact have a van, we had to go rent a U-Haul and that took nearly an hour. Her two other children, who were to be there at nine, were not. One was busy riding a bike and the other was getting another tattoo.

It was an old two-story house with a steep staircase just two feet wide. We hauled dressers, TVs larger than theaters, beds, cabinets, and boxes, boxes, boxes up and down those stairs and out the door—just the three of us. The humidity was at least 140 percent and inside the truck it was an oven. Before we were through we had bloody hands and ruined suits.

When it was finally all loaded up I asked her where it was going. "Oh, just around the corner, hon." It turned out to be a skyscraper apartment way across town and across the river. Her apartment was on the fourteenth floor, and the elevator was old, and about the size of our subzero refrigerator at home. Of course there was no parking in front of the building, so we unloaded it all on the grass and sidewalk, and then took it up the elevator piece by piece. Her new home was at the end of a mile-long hall, and someone sitting outside, who had stolen a shopping cart, loaned it to us for the big TV, etc.

When we got back to the house the newly tattooed daughter was there with her boyfriend, who would make Paul Bunyan look like a midget. "Think you can handle the rest of this, Butch?" I asked. Looking at we three depleted spirits, he consented, and she gave us each a bottle of water. But service pays. They did ask about the church, and why we were dumb enough to freely volunteer for such torture. I told them with a straight face that all Mormons are ordained movers

THE COVERED WAGON WE CONSTRUCTED TO ADD ATMOSPHERE TO THE PIONEER DAY CELEBRATION.

also, and they believed it. They were grateful and we were glad we did it (until the next morning when we tried to get up).

When we got back to the church, there wasn't a soul there. We had missed the whole day's events, and never tasted a pancake.

The evening was a crowning success, however—most of the wonderful program that evening came from a couple we baptized, who knew great singers and musicians in town. Everyone enjoyed the square dance so much they didn't stop till after ten. I had showed the Elders how old-time photos could be taken and printed right there with a digital setup, so people were able to leave with super pictures in their hands, which delighted many.

Best of all, we learned later that after the breakfast that morning a family of eight (the father was a top realtor in town) was taken into the chapel for a tour and the mission president helped teach them. They got the whole pioneer picture and were really impressed. One can go on a whole mission and not find and teach a family like that.

Drive-by inspiration

The locals are impressed that we "seniors" will leave home and pay our own way out here for them. They don't budge toward joining the Church, but are awed!

Finding people to teach appears to always be a struggle. Passing out tracts is a losing effort; everyone works, houses are empty. Even the smallest apartments are $800 and up and many work two and three jobs to pay the high rent. Often four and five families live in one house, and man, is it confusing to find which mailbox is which and which buzzer to press to wake up the right household!

"I've had so many doors slammed in my face," one Elder said, "that I'm beginning to look forward to it."

One contact said to the missionary who approached him, "I'll come to church, if you'll quit coming to my house and promise you won't come back."

SINCE CONSTRUCTION WORK ON THE WARD'S NEW CHURCH BUILDING WAS STILL IN THE FINISHUP STAGES, HARD HATS WERE A NECESSARY PART OF OUR MISSIONARY OUTFIT AT TIMES.

Why not have them come to us, we finally decided. Why hunt the ghettos when most of the people are out are driving around, at least 12,000 of them down Princeton Boulevard, where our beautiful new church has 450 feet of frontage space.

Our head-on approach to soliciting visitors to the new church.

You've heard of street meetings—well how about "road meetings?"

We picked up a small rug, a folding table, and a couple of folding chairs, then had three signs made and set up a mini visitor center just 15 feet off the main drag, in the newly paved driveway of the new church. On the table we put our scriptures, a framed picture of the new church, a pile of handouts, our two mono-grammed hard hats, and of course a pile of yellow pads for notes and writing. From that day on, there has been action!

Some people drive by and yell out the window, "What is this going to be, a new strip mall?" Barbara yells back, "Yeah, we'll strip you of your sins!" Then I chime in, "And the rent is only 10 percent" (tithing). We are getting some great comebacks and even a few return visitors.

MINI ROADSIDE VISITOR CENTER REPORT
(The first month's totals, carefully documented)

Cars passing our road table	31,221
Heads and eyes snapped toward the church	18,000 (6 out of every 10)
Honks	75
Halfhearted waves	1,200 (all returned)
Thumbs-up waves with smile	221
Grumpies, nasty remarks and gestures	7
Barks from interested dogs	6
People switching sides of street when they saw us	9
People walking past who couldn't understand a word we said	10
Walkers and joggers who stopped and visited	58 (100 percent)
Cars that stopped and pulled in to visit	13
Names given for contact	12
Pages of yellow pads filled with notes	112
People who took literature	45

Great plans are being made to expand this curbside converting!

Accent on angling

Thursday a young fellow about 16 came by our roadside booth with a fishing rod. Noticing his rod was broken, I asked him what happened. "A cop took it away." Why would the police take a kid's fishing pole? So I pursued it. "Is it against the law to fish down there?" (in the lake on the church property). "No," he said, "it was a big cop." And he spread his hands out to three feet. This conversation continued, with me still trying to understand why he would have had a fight with a police officer. The discussion might have gone on forever if the other kid with him hadn't remarked, "The cop he caught was only *two* feet long." It was a CARP (a fish!). They don't teach using "R's" here in Havad, gadfreys.

The apartment inspectors!

Since I was a well-known cleaner, one of our assignments was to inspect the apartments of the clean-cut young missionaries living in the area. You'd think by college age people would have some concept of cleanliness, but a visit to the dorms of these young people would quickly disabuse you of this idea. Most of them seemed to have not yet grasped the fact that Mommy or a maid wasn't part of the package of living away from home. With various creative and competition-inspiring ploys and a traveling golden outhouse trophy, Sister Aslett and I managed to get the message across in our district, and we even did a "cleaning magic

THE APARTMENT INSPECTOR.

show" for the entire Boston Mission. Once the advantages of cleanliness (and a little how-to and the right supplies) were made clear, the missionary digs showed a lot of progress. Our best propaganda motto seemed to be: "This will save your marriage someday!"

Faith in action!

It was Sister Aslett's turn to come up with a lesson for the Cruz family (one we baptized last October). I had come up with several brilliant ones previously, incorporating what I thought were some unbeatable visuals and games and old farm stories. She ignored my competitive caution that today's lesson "Better be good," and said, "Just go get in the car and drive."

"What are you going to do?" I asked.

"Just drive," she said.

"But you haven't got anything in your hands—no books, charts, games, Idaho potato pins…?" No answer, so I just drove to the Cruz's and she told them to hop in the car. "Where?" we all asked.

"Just drive." We drove to the Chelmsford Assisted Living complex with some flowers she had bought while in the supermarket. She handed them to the Cruz's smallest boy, Christopher, age five, and we went to see Sister Karl, a sharp wheelchair-bound woman in her late seventies. It was a delightful evening—when it was over the woman was close to tears and the little boy and his parents beaming over her happiness for the visit and the flowers. The Cruzes just plain know how to lift and laugh people into a higher state and did so in this rest home. What a lesson in quiet action, Sister Aslett's specialty.

Patience pays off

Endurance is a virtue Barbara and I have both always had, and it sure helps in this kind of work. When we arrived, we were assigned the Snodgrass family to help them become active in the church. The husband we only met once, and then he left for military service. For months we visited, invited the family places, and dropped off things—books, videos, tickets to dances, games—in snow, sleet, heat, and heavy traffic. We stopped by, prayed for and with them, and nothing came of it. We were treated well (on the porch) and felt the pleading in their Utah grandmother's eyes for us to continue. Which we did.

On our one-year anniversary day here, we decided to visit all 22 of our contacts (nonmembers) and in the process, drove by the Snodgrass house. We looked at each other and said, "Nope, we've done enough! We have broken our bottoms for these folks and nothing," so we drove on past. The next Sunday as I was greeting at church, through the door came the family we had given up on, and we were tickled (and ashamed). They have become my favorite family. The mother is a superwoman in the Relief Society, the girls active in the program, and the young man of the family, unable to be baptized by his father who is off in the service, wanted "that man who treated him nice" to baptize and confirm him, which I did. Another "never give up" story.

As I sat down and read my missionary journal, I noticed that many nights I was so tired I was barely able to fall into bed. I think now I lived tired. I spent too much good missionary time coddling confused people with problems who wanted sympathy more than direction, solutions, or help from a Heavenly Father. Too much time on logistics and not enough time teaching people the spirit. I was really busy, worked 12-16 hour days, but can see now that much was unproductive. Barbara was by my side the whole time—never figured out where all of her energy came from.

January 2003:
"How is the missionary work going?"

Well… we are nurturing and teaching around two dozen people from the contacts we gathered at our highway booth. We are going for the long haul here, a quality relationship, so aren't trying to get a commitment to baptism on the second meeting. In fact, we wait until they ask us, so who knows if time will run out before we do. The church is now encouraging the approach of "teaching by the spirit" (which we have been doing from the start). Several families both inside and outside the church are convinced we were sent here just for them—we shall see how that proves out. Maturity has allowed us to progress in some situations that would be a struggle for young missionaries.

Of course, the best part of missionary work is seeing the changes that come to those truly converted. A family we baptized last year are now leaders in the Ward, active in everything, giving the sacrament meeting prayers, taking the Scouts on outings, tops in choir, etc. It's a real pleasure to see them now.

KELLY WILLIAMS, A RECENTLY BAPTIZED NEW MEMBER, FELT AN INSTANT KINSHIP WITH SISTER ASLETT, ONE OF HER INSTRUCTORS.

Traffic update

Today Barbara gave me a great compliment on my Boston traffic driving, "Gee honey, you are doing so good, you are down to only one honk per intersection now!"

It's probably apparent by now that I am not a big fan of the East. The people I really like because God made the people, but He cannot be blamed for what has been done to the land here. The dictionary that the Harvard intellects put out a few centuries ago left out words like plan, vision, straight, space, polite, manners, temperance, etc. Our apartment parking lot is jammed, barely room for one car per apartment, but since everyone has two cars (except the poor senior missionaries), to make more parking room, they don't buy more land or tear something down, they do it by taking the already tight parking spaces and shrinking them. Now we have six inches to get out of our cars instead of the usual generous twelve inches. You can't damage the car next to you with

BARBARA AND I WITH TWO OF
OUR CONTACTS WHO ARE
ABOUT TO BE BAPTIZED.

your door because it there isn't enough space to get up the momentum to bang it.

Never have I seen people who love their cars so much. The poorest of the lot still drive $30,000 to $70,000 SUVs or those humpback new old-fashioned little things. The local service station attendant (there is an old-style station here where a human is actually present and pumps gas and thanks you) said it is common the week before payday for many in those big costly rigs to stop and buy a couple of dollars worth of gas. Try teaching eternal life principles to that bunch!

Winning in the weather

In 66 years of living, I never complained about weather or watched it on TV, and now, when I am supposed to be a noble sacrificing missionary, I end up whimpering about it. But the freeze or fry choice here just plain gets the best of these old bones. Sister Aslett would join in if she could get a whine in edgeways!

It is summer here now—spring didn't come for the second year in a row. It snows one day and the next day it is 90 degrees and humid. Then it rains four days in a row, one day of sun, then five days of rain. New Englanders think that this is normal weather.

Until now, all snow experience in our lives has been positive—Jerome, Dietrich, Shoshone, Sun Valley, and McCammon—even being snowed in for a week or two was exciting. Here, snow has a hard time getting to the ground because the mass of cars gather it on their hoods, tops, and trunks, and then it slides down to the dirty streets below.

This morning we got another foot of snow! The strict rule here in the apartment complex is that you have to move your car so they can plow the place. You will be towed if you don't! It being Saturday morning I was first up and out with my new, all steel, superman snow shovel, and freed our Buick. Then it was New Delhi New Year! Out they came, the rest of the inhabitants of our complex, about 80 percent of them Indians who had no clue of what to do with snow or how to drive on it. They began pecking away at it with toothbrush-sized tools. My Idaho blood raced to the rescue—I could clear and free a car in eight minutes flat. As I attempted to help them out, I would holler, "Cramp the wheel," and they would answer, "What you mean 'cramp'?" Or I would yell, "Don't gun it." And they would say back, "What you mean 'gun its'?"

Anyway the accolades in the end were worth the agony, as their impossible-to-get-out vehicles smoothly maneuvered out under this old farmer's direction.

Mundanities of missionary life

The most uncomfortable part of this is the total lack of personal privacy—quiet moments, time to shape feelings and information into some useful structure. There are only chances to hear, see, or feel fragments of things (revelations, ideas, gems of thought), and collect them like pieces of a broken vase—no time to glue them together. You can experience things, but never internalize anything. We become aware of other people's needs and problems but there is never enough solution time. I feel isolated from some of my strongest resources, and there is zero alone time to "be still and know."

We walk once in a while, and I run most every morning—great exercise in dodging trash and traffic! On Mother's Day, some of the natives brought Barbara flowers, and I fought off a Doberman to swipe some lilacs for her.

Missionary mementoes

These Northeasterners have made a great effort to transfer their clutter to Idaho with us as our time here draws to a close. People are showering us with "stuff"—we have received enough Christmas decorations to trim and light the whole Pocatello mall. We have sent six huge boxes home (UPS freight)... still Sister Aslett claws the windows of the car as I accelerate past highbrow garage sales with goodies spread all over. Even so we have acquired everything from a (perfectly good) chrome bumper hitch to a singing mouse stuffed toy, to a sewing machine from an old shoe factory that has a needle the size of a nail.

Mission cuisine

Nothing interferes with mission work like dinners and meetings. At one meeting, lunch was scheduled for noon, and when a sister walked in and announced that the meat loaf wouldn't be ready until twelve-thirty, a great groan came forth from all of the assembled Elders. Even though they were being fed a spiritual feast right then, from that moment on they couldn't keep their eyes off the clock.

We ourselves have simplified our intake. I have cooked breakfast every day of our year and a half here. It took some brilliant chemistry, but

BARBARA (TAKING A BREAK FROM THE BEARD HERE) MADE A FIRST-CLASS SANTA, BRINGING TEARS AND CHEERS TO THE HOMES OF THE NEEDY AS WE VISITED.

I developed a morning mush that smacks of health, a combo of Quaker Oats, whole wheat, and Cream of Wheat, plus a half-cup of boiled raisins. Sister Aslett grimaces at its ghastly appearance, but eats it. We have some high-pulp orange juice with this, and that is our cooking for the day.

Each morning we pray that no one will ask us or treat us to eat. People are on sure-death diets here—Dunkin' Donuts is their idea of health food. We took our name off the church food list (members consider it an honor to feed missionaries, especially senior couples). This spares us invitations to pig out and waste three hours of the evening at someone's house (some poor soul who has labored all day to come up with a killer dish to impress us). Remember we are in a foreign country here, and get fed things we can't identify, even after explanation in a language that we cannot understand. It sure is nice just to come home and have an evening of cold milk, Wheaties, and a banana.

However, the word is out that we are leaving soon, so the whole ward is hitting us up for dinner dates. We had two meals out Sunday and we both felt like cows that had feasted on third-cutting hay.

THE WARD MEMBERS ARE SUPPOSED TO INVITE THE MISSIONARIES TO DINNER, BUT NO ONE WANTS ME (THE FAMOUS CLEANER) IN THEIR HOUSE; THEY LOVE BARBARA.

Bless my soles

My loyalty for my shoes (the only pair I own) has long been undisputed. In fear I might enter the mission field with my old dilapidated McCammon farm clodhoppers, Sister Aslett found (on sale) a pair of genuine stiff black, thick-soled missionary shoes in some bargain basement in Provo. They weren't quite my size, but close enough, plus she knew I loved to suffer. Broken in during a limping first three months in the mission field, they became my favorite, worn every single day for 18 months, reduced finally to a single thin layer of insole.

On our final interview with the new mission president, he offered to give me money for a new pair of shoes—so we were shamed into securing a new pair. But we did wonder how those thick soles could have worn out when we didn't seem to walk that much. The mystery was finally solved—they were worn out in traffic, from constantly hitting the gas and brake petal or bracing feet to the floor in terror!

MY OFFICIAL MISSIONARY SHOES AFTER 18 MONTHS OF WALKING AND HARD BRAKING IN MASSACHUSETTS TRAFFIC.

Mission accomplished!

In August 2003, we completed our assignment, said a tearful good-bye to all our new friends, and drove home.

After a year and a half of absence, we found all of our family, operations, properties, and personnel prospering even better than when we left. What a testimony to the dedication and solid organization we have attained as a company—what a homecoming! Thanks to everyone, we were back with all of our operations, fresher, smarter, more sensitive, and more energetic in the cause of making great things happen.

> While we were gone our businesses had prospered tremendously, and it was shocking to see how much the grandkids had grown. And field mice had invaded our empty ranch house—another story. Once home I dove full force back into my many entities with renewed energy, while Barbara spent some long-awaited, well-deserved time with family and friends in our home in Hawaii.

Our time in the Boston area was one of much service, long hours, and impacting many lives as they impacted ours. Working around all of the intellectuals from Harvard, Yale, and Cambridge, and the many immigrants from Cambodia, Africa, Laos, and South America gave us more insight and commitment to being "our brother's keeper." We realized more than ever that "our neighbor" is not just the people on our block or in our city, and that all people have their struggles.

It was confirming and rewarding, too, to see that our past investment of time, money, and emotion in our company and my books, speaking, and seminars has been well worth it. Signs of the impact for good we've had on others' lives were everywhere. What a gospel tool all of this has been, and it's sharpened my commitment to be a much better writer, teacher, businessperson, parent, husband, and partner.

Our 18 months of missionary work as a couple was somewhat satisfactory in terms of lives changed to the better while we were there, but more so was the carryover after we returned home. Many people who didn't become part of our church became part of our lives. At least a dozen of these have bonded with us forever in love and friendship. The continual contact and exchange we have now is a real conversion to caring for each other's welfare. No better mission than that!

Many have asked, "What is the most important thing you learned out there?" and that is an easy one to answer. The church's goal of teaching the entire world will never be achieved until all of the members in every ward learn that *they* are the missionaries, not us out here hunting for people to teach. Not even all 65,000 of us out here in the field can do it. We have a little leverage as guests in a town or country to find people, but the members live daily among millions. *Home* is where you can best teach the gospel.

BY THE END OF OUR OF MISSION IT SEEMED ASTOUNDING HOW SMALL IRRITATIONS, SOME DISAGREEMENTS, EVEN OPPOSITE WAYS OF GOING ABOUT THINGS PROVE MINISCULE WHEN TWO PEOPLE ARE IN TUNE TO THE SAME GOSPEL-ORIENTED GOALS.

Chapter 25

NO MAGIC OR MIDAS TOUCH: "SECRETS" OF AN ENTREPRENEUR

*Mondays are always bright yellow,
never blue for me.*

It's interesting how other people will attribute assets or liabilities to you that you don't really have. I was always praised and respected for being a good organizer and getting a lot done—people asked me for my secrets. There aren't really any secrets—any ability I have in these areas came from watching and learning from my parents and grandparents, clients like Les Hodge, and coworkers and colleagues such as Mark Browning.

MY COMPANY CAR IS A VARSITY VAN.

Like them, I've always tried to avoid unnecessary problems. I hate to go back and fix something again, or do it over. From watching businesses and families struggle with setbacks, I realized that often the troubles people spent their time on were the result of not doing something right the first time. The "foul it up and then fix it" approach had no appeal for me—callbacks and re-dos at best left you right where you started from and that was no fun at all.

I never organized any better, or even as well, as many other people. I just spent less time on problems, so I had more time left to get other things done.

Another misconception is well illustrated by the man who came to see me once to inquire about a job—he was the "outstanding student of the year" at the local university. When Arlo asked him why he'd come, he said, "It was my wife—she said that everything Don Aslett touches turns to gold." Did I get a chuckle out of that. I sure didn't recall any "golden touches" in my life. Things never were picture perfect and almost never proceeded exactly as planned. It wasn't usually a touch that yielded any gold, but creative thinking and plenty of long, hard hours. Almost anything could be accomplished or worked out, and in some way yield something good, if you persisted long enough.

In 2006, we had a grand opening of OMNI Business Center, formerly the old federal building right across from Varsity headquarters, which I'd purchased and renovated. It had been a long process of getting to this point—it took a lot of labor and determination and at least $1 million to bring the all-but-abandoned building to the beauty it displayed that evening to over 250 Chamber of Commerce members and dignitaries attending. It was hard to miss one of the local realtors working his way through the crowd smiling with his arm in the air, saying, "It's easy to see Don Aslett's been through here waving his magic wand." Someone again reminding people that "everything Don touches turns to gold." Had he really known me and my many personal and public projects, on a scale of one to ten, in the golden touch department, I'd be lucky to come out a five.

I'm weak on technology and only average in my ability to retain things, but I have a fertile, unbounded imagination, which has dug holes in the road as often as it has transported me to exciting new destinations. Once I dream something, I have no doubt I can do it, so as you can imagine I've launched my share of losers. They may have been good ideas, good intentions, and good efforts (and often a lot of good money went into them), but often I was rudely awakened in middle of my dream. You may have noticed a few "incompletes" sprinkled throughout this autobiography. Trust me, there were more—I have a whole file in my office full of ideas and efforts I've given up on. I do have a "wand," but I think it's just a beating rod at rest!

Great achievement is often credited to a golden touch, when in fact all that was involved was a will of iron, the bend of tin, the persistence of a magnet, the endurance of brass, nerves of steel, and 14-karat calluses.

Reverses? I had plenty—the more you venture, the more you have. We entrepreneurs just don't dwell on the losers. I poured a few foundations that I never got the building up on, and there were projects like the block plant and the Red Top Motel where my plans were ahead of my pocketbook and behind the clock. Things like this do haunt me at times but have never stopped me from pouring a bunch of other foundations that I do get the buildings up on.

A businessman from a different mold

As new challenges to our company surfaced, I would often remark to Barbara, "I was never cut out to be a businessman." Running things out of the heart rather than head alone certainly had its problems and conflicts.

As Varsity continued to grow and expand, I was honored to be chosen as Idaho Business Leader of the Year in 1993. Senator Bilyeu, introducing me at the banquet that followed, called me a genius, but I don't think one person there, including family and close friends, could name a single business skill at which I excelled. I've never had many of the habits or earmarks of a good businessperson (and still don't).

- I hate budgets and never use them;
- Don't believe in resumes;
- Dislike employee reviews and detailed accountability;
- Take risks at will (live on them!);
- Exactness of communication is not my forte;
- My ability to delegate is in serious question;
- I abhor business lunches and dinners;
- I'm not a joiner;
- Wouldn't be caught dead on a golf course;
- I dodge telephones, especially cell phones;
- Don't use fancy computer programs or conventional day planners;
- Never read how-to books or articles for big corporate leaders.

Seems I'm almost anti-business, yet my life's passion and accomplishments hinge on the businesses I've developed and still own and lead.

I've got plenty of imagination, creativity, and exciting visions, which have proven pretty accurate overall. The problem is that these three attributes need a couple more virtues to balance them into workability—words like "the details," "marketing," and "cost of the project." When I decided to do something, I usually had a clear overview of why and how it would work. I had a strong why and a good where, but I was never a stickler for (or even seriously considered) the details. I suffered some real reverses from this, a few costing tons of money and some serious time losses.

Barbara tells me that my survival and success has a lot to do with getting good people to buy into my vision and cause. In Varsity, for example, the management that grew the business offset my unbusinesslike practices and took good care of detail I slopped over or neglected.

When I was 63, someone called me a multi-talented man. I refuted them, saying, "Name me just one!" After thinking a little, they finally said, "Well, Don, you have an unequalled talent for taking responsibility." I think my real talent might be motivating people to a sense of self-worth, to be better. Or as one of my partners put it, "You inspire people to achieve more, and to believe in themselves and their talents."

> Many people trying to flatter me in introductions and elsewhere have used the word "genius," because of the scope of things I've accomplished. I'm no genius, but I do have the ability to recognize genius in others and develop and showcase it.
>
> In any case, I believe that "genius" is more grunt work than gift or degrees.

Maybe it was my rural upbringing or my chosen profession, but I never felt superior to anyone, or better than him or her. Many might mistake my "overconfident plowing ahead" as arrogance or even conceit, but I always felt inferior to everyone in some way, that they had talent or ability I didn't have or would never possess. Anything I ever accomplished or did was easily explained by a big imagination, good health, no fear of risk, and just sticking it out with long hours and steady, unwavering focus. Summed up in a sentence or two, my accomplishments might seem impressive, but strung out over the 65 years of growing up, you can see it was just focus, simply enduring, and good helpers.

The only notable thing I really did in all of my book dealings or in business was develop a high profile in a low profile field—that got lots of attention.

One personality flaw I am constantly reminded of by my wife and others is that I always have to be right. A fair criticism, perhaps, but I never looked at it as always having to be right, rather that I spared no pains to *make* things right. When you are in charge, making most of the decisions around a home or business, then you are the one responsible for the ones that aren't right. I made plenty of wrong calls from bad estimates, bad timing, and bad judgments, but then I would work like heck to make a bad deal turn into something beneficial in time, and generally, it did. So instead of saying, "Gosh, that was a mistake," and then just taking the pelting and financial loss, I would say, "That wasn't the best way to do that, but if I do thus and so, it will work, just you watch!" I was often then able to reverse setbacks and poor decisions; when I did, of course I let everyone know that "it" was now profitable, or that dude I hired was now producing. This is probably what tabbed me as always thinking I was right.

> Fifteen years into our marriage, my wife said to me, "You don't ever think failure, do you? You never consider it, even." I'd never realized it, but she was right. In all that I did, I seldom if ever considered that it might fail. I never considered whether I could do something or not, only when.

Baptism into things for me was never by sprinkling, it was full immersion—all the way was the only way. I grew to hate the words "average," "moderation," "try," "probably," and "maybe." Even on paint jobs, I lived the immersion concept, as anyone who saw me right after a job would agree. Someone introducing me once remarked that I might be the only man in the world with paint on his baseball glove. Once I came home so dirty and smelly the family swears I set off the smoke alarm. How I looked on the job while putting out full production always worried others more than me. Being careful of clothes while cleaning or painting really slows you down. Just go for it and do a big cleanup at the end. Obnoxiousness or key to success?—you call it.

Thrilled by the skilled

I always liked watching real professionals work, to see just how good some people could get in their profession. It was easy to see at the ball field or concert hall or even the used car lot. An expert can walk around a car once, not even kicking the tires, and tell you everything that's wrong with it. Some can just listen to it run and rock it, and know it better than some of the computer analysis machines they hook up. Growing up on a ranch, I saw men who could guess the weight of 400-pound steers at market time and come within two or three pounds—or less.

In my business as a professional cleaner, being that good was my goal, and little by little, I entered the league of that kind of expert. After so many years, I could almost tell the condition of a building (as well as the owner's attitude toward it) just from looking in the janitor closet. I could see a cleaning supplies purchase order for a college and know what they were doing right or wrong with their floors. I could tell by counting the mop strings left behind on a floor who was bleaching their mops. Without applying standard worksheet formulas, I could appraise the time needed to clean a building and the cost of doing it in less than an hour, and be right on the money. I could tell from the trash how efficient a place was. I didn't have to discover what the problems in cleaning a place would be; I knew them before I started the job.

When you eat, drink, sleep, and live your profession, it slowly becomes second nature. It doesn't take a brilliant mind as I once thought—just sticking with it and having a passion for what you do.

Control by feel

You can get so good at something that you know by feel, or even the slightest sound, whether things are going right or wrong. I learned this running farm equipment, especially the baler. The tractor that pulls the baler is noisy enough, but the baler has noisy moving parts all over—the clanging racing of the pickup bar, the screaming of the feed auger, the whine of the power takeoff unit, and then the deafening pounding of the plunger that packs the hay into bales. You can hardly hear yourself think, and yet on the back of the baler is a quiet knotter that ties the twine around the bales. It's almost noiseless, yet amidst all of the noise, when the knotter mis-tied, I knew it. That is as amazing as a mother who has her own six children and three others playing and running all over the house, and yet if something is not right somewhere in all of that chaos, she detects it immediately and can intercede.

I got that way with business, too. I never kept the books or worked on them, but even when we were a good-size company, I could walk into the office any time and have my accounting department read me the names of the payables and receivables, and I could name the amount due or outstanding, or vice versa. The bookkeeper was astounded—though he worked with those numbers all day, he couldn't do that. It was no miracle or special skill, any one of you could do it, too, if it was your responsibility to answer for all that. It's amazing, the math skill you acquire with ownership. Often you don't have to go on a job site to find the problem. In our Vegas operation once, for example, there seemed to be excessive supply costs for the amount of floor space being cleaned. No accountant could catch it because they only look at the accuracy of invoices and dates. Field people (which all business executives should remain) can sniff it out by scanning the books—there is a problem here! And sure enough, there was. An addicted manager was buying supplies and selling them off a tailgate at a flea market to support his drug habit. I mean, how could one use 55 gallons of wax remover ($580) to strip a single floor (a $150 job)? Experiences like these proved useful in surviving now and teaching later.

A constant problem I had was that most of my planning and investment was for long-range goals. Few people think very long range, thus much of my planning received an abundance of premature criticism. I never was procedure oriented, always results oriented. If we were going to go to the Grand Canyon to work for a week, the job and its completion were 95 percent of my thrust. To the logistics of getting there, being there, or coming home, I gave little thought.

I always figured I was born 100 years too late, as all of my ambitions and dreams were of being a pioneer. I rarely followed the beaten path—blazing new ones was more my style. Maybe I was a little too visionary. I often built bridges before the infrastructure was in place, thus some feared to cross them.

Critics

The majority of my friends and associates were hesitant to correct or instruct me when I needed it, but when I encouraged them to do so, they found me lacking in plenty of ways. I was careless with detail, my directions or instructions were seldom clear, and my writing often needed translation. In general, I assumed everyone should be able to read my mind. Interesting, that after 60, the healthier, richer, happier, and more spiritual I got, the more advice about diet, money, recreation, and morality I got from others.

My best critic was Mark Browning. Although often abrupt and un-diplomatic, he had the ability to hit problems right on the nose. When I was wrong but determined to run something through by sheer force and authority, he'd never roll over and play dead. Proofreading my reports, memos, or presentations, his remarks cut to the heart of the matter. When he proofed a manual on contracts where I was instructing readers to keep things short and simple, he would circle a paragraph of rambling, convoluted sentences with a comment like, "Physician, heal thyself!" I'd be irritated at his nerve to slash my brilliant compositions, but had to admit he was right, and luckily, I always acted on it.

> ANY COMPETITIVE DOER,
> ESPECIALLY WITH A BIG
> OPINIONATED MOUTH LIKE
> MINE, GAINS PLENTY OF CRITICS!

MY TAKE ON ACCOMPLISHMENT

But if I work too hard I won't be able to smell the flowers...

Once you are suspected of being a workaholic, the famous words "take time to smell the flowers" will be presented to you more times and in more ways than you can imagine. Cards, notes, letters, calls, emails, earnest conversations, and even warnings will come your way from well-meaning associates, urging you to relax and be sure to savor life before it goes by. But have you ever noticed that the people who try the hardest to smell all the flowers are often the ones who miss the choicest blooms? Those who actively hunt for adventure have little or none, and those who are forever talking about and seeking relationships, have few.

The best way to absorb the sights, sounds, and scents of life is while covering and cultivating all the ground of production and involvement—learning, risking, building, and doing. The one who makes it all happen, who plants, grows, and weeds the flowers is the person who really savors them, not the one who merely views or sniffs them while passing by.

Many people are intimidated by "busy" people. Until they fall into the same sort of schedule themselves, they are awed by or think it impossible. But then they find out they are just as smart and capable as those remarkable supermen or superwomen. Multi-tasking is more a matter of "have to" than talent. I've always called it "wise overload:" having more to do than you ever imagined you could, and doing it well. Besides working away from home and keeping the home fires burning, there are community, church, hobbies, and educational activities, and much, much more—all part of the package. Once up to their necks in all of this, most people perform like champions.

Few Americans today understand productivity. They think that if they work, they earn, but working means nothing. If you don't produce something, if something isn't accomplished when you finish, working and trying don't count. I never had a job that paid me just for being on or at the job. I was only paid for accomplishment. Whether stacking hay, picking potatoes, shoveling snow, or cleaning toilets, no matter how many hours I labored, I only got paid for results. Putting in time was no reason to get paid, unless the job got done. It was 5¢ per bale of hay hauled and 6¢ per sack of potatoes picked, $75 to $150 per roof shoveled off, and 50¢ per toilet cleaned. Being "on" the job was no different than being in bed, unless there were results to show for it.

I ONLY KNOW HOW TO WORK AT ONE SPEED—MACH 1!

Some people make entertainment part of their schedule. I find fun in work—to me entertainment interrupts any decent day. I go to work for excitement, not to pick up money.

Mondays are always bright yellow, never blue for me.

People wonder how while buried and busy with 30 projects, you can spot and develop several new ones. Four of my best books were conceived and started during the hectic finish of six others. You just cannot put off inspiration or delay opportunity—you need to not only strike while the iron is hot, but be heating the other irons as you do. It can be done if you are really convinced that what you are doing is worth doing.

Perfection vs. production

One of the biggest obstacles to accomplishment is thinking that things have to be perfect or exact to be usable. I don't buy "do something well or not at all." If we bought that, the West would have never been settled nor any airplanes built. Most great progress was sketched out crudely first and perfected later. I'd rather get a job with an imperfect proposal than not be working.

Often accomplishing something *today* is more important than making a nice display; "right" will do as well as "just right." When purpose is more important than perfection, just do it! Seeking consensus, gathering too many opinions, can smother creativity. If you try to please everyone, you end up average. There is a time for input to stop and for output to take over—over-planning, over-preparing, and worrying too much about protocol and politics generally get in the way of progress.

Busy schedules are full of urgent demands, and great accomplishers know when to wipe their noses on their sleeves, dance in muddy boots, go hunting with any ugly gun, tell time on a dollar watch, fish with a willow branch, to eat something raw or with their fingers, or sing happy birthday out of tune. There are times to wear a wrinkled shirt, to ride without a saddle, and when whistling a tune is more desirable than assembling a 600-piece orchestra to play it.

There is a time to shoot from the hip, to quit posing for perfect form on the diving board and jump, to quit circling and land. Quit fiddling with composition and take the picture before the crisp light is lost. Quit researching and draw a conclusion!

Getting to the real work

There were two distinct divisions of work on the ranch where I was raised:

1. The chores. These were the every-day duties you could call the housework of the barnyard. The upkeep chores, including feeding, cooking, cleaning, shutting things off and turning them on, oiling machines and sharpening tools. We did all of this early in the morning or in the evening after our other work was done.

2. The "getting somewhere" processes and projects. This was the progressive or productive work—the work that created the harvests and paid the bills. We always pushed to get the chores out of the way so we could get on the real job, such as planting crops, irrigating, cultivating, or harvesting them.

In short, chores weren't counted as real work, but more like the things necessary to keep the whole afloat so we could operate.

This discipline had a great influence on my later business management, as I would find many of my colleagues and employees who interpreted preparation, philosophizing, and upkeep as producing, wasting two hours of the eight in "chore" trivia. Chores may be necessary to sustain life, but the real work is building life.

WHEN I WAKE UP IN THE MORNING, MY FIRST THOUGHT IS: HOW QUICKLY CAN I GET THE CHORES OUT OF THE WAY AND GET TO THE PRODUCTIVE, CREATIVE THINGS?

50 YEARS OF BUSINESS CARDS.

Decoration of any kind takes a lot of up-keep, which means time taken away from the productive heart of business. It took hours of combing and currying to de-burr a long mane and tail on a horse back on the ranch, and they hated every minute of it. By keeping my hairstyle short and simple, and not carrying any jewelry or cosmetic or habit baggage, I can get ready in the morning about half an hour faster than my business associates who have to fumble around with a hair dryer, aftershave, rings, necklaces, and two cups of coffee just to get them going. Bare necessity doesn't mean suffering, it means freedom to get on with what life's about!

The magic of momentum

There is magic in momentum. One of the real secrets of high production, of winning, of genuine go-getting is, once you're really going, making great headway, don't stop. When the spirit is willing, your imagination expanded, creativity pouring out—keep moving. Don't take a break, go to bed, eat, or anything, even if "it's time." Spontaneity is a source of great progress.

When you have things going, you're in the groove, and everything is rolling, don't stop and bow for applause, just go for it. When you're on the move and things are moving, don't stop to read your press or evaluate your progress or look at yourself in the mirror. When things are falling into place, you feel like you could go on forever, DO it while you can. There are times to ignore the clock, meals, nags, even tired muscles, and just keep going to the end line. Make it a marathon!

My management philosophy, which I learned watching my mother run a big household and gardens with limited resources, and watching my dad and grandparents run huge farms with many crops and hundreds of livestock, can be summed up:

- Trust people;

- Work hard;

- Never get behind;

- Keep your word;

- Be generous (more than fair) with neighbors, merchants, and helpers;

- Be in control of what you have responsibility for.

My leadership style

I have a clear-cut, simple style of leadership. I share my vision, put myself fully into the work I commit to, and give my employees a lot of rope (good pay, plenty of liberty, high expectations, and not a great deal of direction; I tell them what I want and let them go). I don't call for constant accountability, and am generous with rewards. I keep close to what is going on without always being right there.

> My people management style boils down to four simple principles: choosing my people well, expecting a lot of them, including them in what is going on, and recognizing their accomplishments.

Entrepreneurship

I grew up uninterested in any other way of making a living than working for myself. Ninety-eight percent of any money I enjoyed came in hunks after the harvest or after a year's investment in livestock. I loved independence and even though an entrepreneur usually has many more bosses than a salaried person has, I never really considered any other path. There seemed to be little excitement or future in a traditional paycheck. There were some dry (unpleasant) days, or even months, my wife reminds me, where there was no money left after paying bills and taxes. But being your own employer was how I was raised, the only choice I ever wanted.

Many people dream about self-employment, having their own company, working for themselves, and after retirement, many express regret that they never did it. I'm not the one to say if entrepreneurship is right or wrong, the best or worst choice, but I did learn from being in business myself and watching others that "fit" is a critical element of any career. Most of those raised in a 9 to 5 job environment have a different concept of responsibility and job requirements. "If I work for myself I'll never be laid off again," is true, but it doesn't mean you'll make a living. And as for working hours, I always tell starry-eyed first timers, yes, you'll have freedom with your own business—you can do anything you like after your 10- or 12-hour day. And you get to choose what job you do on Saturday. On the Sabbath, you can renew yourself and gear up for a mightier than ever Monday. As for holidays, you view them the exact opposite of normal people—as a chance to get caught up on and really roll on your work.

A side benefit of owning your own business

One of the best things about owning your own business is that you have control over your clock, calendar, and even the basic ethics of the operation. I never let my businesses support the ugly things of the world, or the ugly people, and you do run into a few.

An insurance man we were doing quite a bit of business with each year, for example, came to our office once to make a presentation. Seeing that the audience was all men, he started with two jokes, the first about seducing a 16-year-old and the second about breaking up a marriage. He knew he had blown it when no one in the room laughed. (Most of us had teenage daughters, a good marriage, and a deep belief in family values.) That was the last day he ever did business with us.

Likewise, Varsity has never supported people, causes, or groups that are down on this country or "the American way."

> IN THE CLEANING BUSINESS OR ANYWHERE, "HOW TO" ISN'T AS IMPORTANT AS "WHY DO?" WHEN THE "WHY" IS FIGURED OUT, "WHAT" AND "HOW" ARE MERE MECHANICS AND ENDURANCE.

Chapter 26

WHAT NOW? LOOKING BACK, AND FORWARD

Making it all count for something!

My all-important "portfolio" is all people. All you have to do is back up and mentally remove one or more of your key supporters during your lifetime, and where you might be is sobering. Major victories in life aren't won by a one-man army, for sure. I had many "I" ideas and plans over the years, but pulling them off was clearly a "we" process.

From ability to responsibility

An interesting thing happens as you sharpen your skills and gain a higher profile and some wealth and position. You reach a maturity that shifts your whole value system. For years in business and especially live and broadcast performances, you sweat and worry over your abilities—"Am I going to be good enough at this?" Then suddenly one day your focus switches from concern about your own abilities to the issue of responsibility. What will the result of what I do be on *others?* And believe me, this far outweighs the question of what the quality of your own individual performance might be.

In my Cleaning Center store in Boise with a heavy-duty carpet extractor.

Lifting those who lifted us

A great accomplishment may spring from a single person's idea, but rarely is it the result of a solo effort. I can't think of many things I've landed entirely on my own. There is always that support system, that network of friends, family, employees, and partners, and above all that final audience, the public, that gives structure, meaning, and impetus to our plans.

That means that what you and I achieve or have comes with a debt, needs a payback. Our employees get a paycheck, families get physical support, and friends and colleagues and the public deserve some compensation or recognition, too. As we reach our own fulfillment, glory, or profit, we need to give something back—a lift to those who lifted us.

The ever-increasing demands of my expanding businesses might give the impression at times that donors and fans have been forgotten, or that I am doing less. But that is far from the reality. I have so much more to do for so many more people and entities now, that even with all the technological aids available these days, I've had to switch to an outline rather than detail style of management. All the avenues built are still in place, and I'm still orchestrating them with enthusiasm and a greater investment of time and money than ever. I've never liked delegation but have had to consent to some form of it to keep all the bases covered anymore. But I don't plan to let my dreams or obligations or old or new helpers and fans be forgotten when I go to the great janitor closet in the sky.

Being in demand or needed is something we all secretly desire, but the thing we rarely consider is that when you've had your fill of giving and doing for others, you can't just turn it off. You've built a market for yourself, and can't just lock the door when you've achieved enough to satisfy your own needs for love, duty, or whatever. You owe… big time.

A world of wonderful women

As mentioned earlier, I was raised in a world of wonderful women. In later years, too, it was never lost on me that much, maybe most of my success resulted from women's work or influence. I had some vision, initiative, and energy, but women supplied much of what else was needed to make things work.

And they gave far more than just labor. Many of the women I worked closely with actually took on the "Aslett cause" as their own. Barbara often said that every relationship I had had to be "an affair," and she was right. I never had a casual relationship with anyone, man or woman, who worked closely with me. The many people who took on the burdens of my businesses and other undertakings as a cause, and not just for pay, I really loved, appreciated, and rewarded, and still do. I have harvested much good from their giving. I feel (and think they do too) a longtime love and loyalty. As has been proven by me and many others in years of continual association, you don't need physical contact for closeness and affection.

In many of my businesses, it was indisputably a woman's world. Men did all of the work in my cleaning company at first, because I never assumed that cleaning was women's work. As noted earlier, Barbara took all of the calls and did the bookwork for the business at first, then one, and soon two other women took over. Before long Varsity had five, ten, and twenty women in the office, and now a building full with a few men sprinkled among them.

When I began getting speaking jobs, it was always calls from women at first and my first audiences were 95 percent women. Even my later audiences were usually predominantly female, and my fan mail mostly from women. Seventy-five percent of the customers in my Cleaning Center stores are women, also.

My first writing was edited by a woman, and the artist who illustrated it was a female college student. The artist who illustrated my first two bestsellers was a woman, Judi Clarke. When my books were published by major publishers, most of the editors and publicists were women, and when they sent me on media tours, the escorts who picked me up and drove me to TV, radio, and newspaper appointments were primarily women. Most of the media hosts and writers assigned to me (probably because of my subject matter, cleaning), were also women, including Oprah, Kathie Lee, Sally Jessy Rafael, Dr. Sonya Friedman, Joan Lunden, Susan Powell of Discovery, and many others. I usually hit it off well with them, because my respect for them came through. My editor Carol Cartaino, described earlier, is a 25-plus-year partner without whom my books and my life would never have been what they are.

As my office and personal management staff grew, it was mostly women, because I found women were usually faster, smarter, and more loyal to the cause. My first office "superwoman" was Nancy Everson, a shy Wyoming farm girl. My allegiance to her was such that when she finally decided to make a trip to our guesthouse in Hawaii, my wife wondered why she didn't just walk over. Nancy worked for me for years, for college money for herself and her husband in the beginning. She didn't believe in working outside of the home when she had children, but I kept and coaxed her through three of them and gave her raises far past what her husband and most men employed locally made. But finally, when she became pregnant for the fourth time and her husband was called to be a bishop in the Mormon church, she left, despite my offer to raise her salary still higher. Later, she returned to part-time work for me more for than 26 years.

I found several talented and productive people after that, who followed Nancy's path for a shorter time, and to all of them I owe much credit for help with my books and media appearances, consulting and speaking.

I found a real keeper for me among the Varsity staff, Tobi Alexander—remarkably smart and efficient. She became operations manager for all of my personal affairs—in charge of scheduling, media, and all of my appearances and appointments everywhere. In an effort to "clone Don" for the overabundance of personal appearance opportunities that came up, she even created a booking agency for other talents at home shows on which we share the revenue. She was a talented book designer and apt at dealing with publishing personnel, and eventually became general manager and CEO of my publishing company, too. After 20 years she is still in charge. She has become a wise counselor and pulls plenty of well-earned authority when I am away. She has "processed" the last 25 books we put out and keeps an eye on 40 more always in the works.

NANCY EVERSON AND ME HARD AT WORK ON A PROJECT.

TOBI ALEXANDER

ONE THING I REALLY ENJOY AND BENEFIT FROM TODAY IS HAVING PEOPLE WITH EXPERTISE SUPERIOR TO MINE WORKING ON MY GOALS. WHAT A PRIVILEGE TO HAVE GOOD, LOYAL PEOPLE AROUND YOU!

I worked with several other women on books and seminars during the 1980s, notably Gladys Allen, a big contributor to titles and content. I did eight TV segments with Jeena Nilson for Utah State University, and a book called *Clean It and Mean It*.

Jerilynn Mecham has put together a number of artistic projects over the years including the junk man and several vac creatures. Today she is hard at work as curator of the Don Aslett Museum of Clean.

SANDRA PHILLIPS AND I AFTER A LECTURE.

Of the 25 different partnerships and businesses I've had in my life, nine of them were with women, the latest being a company called Live-Right, which provides services, information, seminars, and products designed to simplify home care and enrich family living. One of its foremost projects is researching, designing and building the ultimate maintenance-free home. This is a 50/50 LLC partnership with longtime friend Sandra Phillips, mother of eight. We met at a seminar in 1984, and she gradually became a solid contributor to my books, my companies, and my life. After reading Make Your House Do the Housework, and following the recommendations in it, she became her own general contractor to build a low-maintenance house in Southern California (getting national CBS News coverage for this).

Sandra and I are now also developing a line of long-needed and exciting new products, books, and seminars to simplify and improve home life. Sandra is a loyal, close partner, that rare person who runs and pushes right alongside of me, and even runs ahead of me on many of the same causes. An outside observer once said, "Don, you have a lot of people swinging on your gate"—Sandra is a hinge on the gate.

If I had it to do over, I would have more female partnerships and sooner, and included women in my overall management much sooner.

Today's agenda: Twenty-First Century

I'm in my seventies now and still thinking 17. Age has not erased or even dampened my feeling of destiny and commitment to leadership.

I'm still running as fast as I can, taking on more projects, making ever more friends, feeling better than ever and picking up speed, financially. I go to bed early and get up early. And I still wake up full of excitement every day.

> "BOY, GRANDPA IS OLD,
> BUT HE ACTS LIKE A KID."
> —GRANDSON MIKE SIMONS

Varsity, the little job-to-get-through-college enterprise, is now a leader in the facility care industry. We operate in all 50 states and Canada and have more than 5,000 employees and 3,000 subcontractors (smaller businesses like we used to be) working for us. Within our Varsity corporate structure, we now have a minority contracting company called System 1, a company that creates and installs computer systems, Nuvek, and a wood floor finishing company called United Varsity Contractors. I also have a speaking and consulting firm called Don Aslett, Inc., in conjunction with my publishing company, Marsh Creek Press.

LEFT: THE FRONT COVER OF MY "SPEAKING" BROCHURE—FIND OUT MORE AT WWW.ASLETT.COM

I don't think my values have changed with age, but opportunities have proliferated. I have at least 20 times more from which to select but I'm more selective now. So now comes the battle of the promising new opportunities competing with all of my existing commitments and responsibilities. Now more than ever I must consider the clock and calendar and how to wisely use the awesome two-edged sword called influence.

A 1986 GATHERING OF ALL SIX CHILDREN, DAUGHTERS AND SONS-IN-LAW, PLUS THE GRANDCHILDREN THEY HAD AT THE TIME, IN OUR MCCAMMON LIVING ROOM: DUFF & KARLA RAY, GRANT & MARGIE ASLETT, ROBYN & LAURA SIMONS, RELL & TERESA ASLETT, AND CINDY ASLETT.

What gives the most pleasure at this point is considering where I came from versus where I am today—the most astounding being the pleasure and security of family. As a young man chasing dreams of amounting to something and having someone to love, I had not even a clue then that "someone" is really plural. In my case, it means a tender, loving, super-intelligent and acutely tolerant wife, six top children, eighteen grandchildren, and now great-grandchildren. All are healthy physically, financially, and spiritually, all unselfish, and none lazy. What a pleasure that is to a patriarch!

An appreciated extra bonus has been the scriptural promise that if I followed good health habits I would "run and not be weary, walk and not faint," and surely this has been fulfilled. I've known no significant sickness or injury in more than 70 years. Another is the promise found in Malachi in the Bible that if I "paid an honest tithing," the Lord would open the windows of heaven and pour out such blessings that there would not be room to receive them. I have paid a full tithing and do indeed have so much good of everything coming my way that I cannot contain it all.

Seeds we planted years and decades ago through service or charity, or ideas we originated and thought long lost or forgotten, pop up all over the place today.

The blessing of busy

At 22, I thought I was busy and doing a lot for my family and church and the community. At 32, I'd doubled that output and figured I was in my prime of production. At 42, not only had upped my output and obligations again, but a strange thing happened—many more ideas, opportunities, and ambitions seemed to appear. At 52, I was more loaded with obligations and responsibilities than ever, and now saw more clearly the impact and outcome of all my wants and wishes if I could manage to bring them to pass.

At 62, the word "swamped" couldn't even describe my schedules and commitments. I was writing more than ever, doing more media, more speeches, and having three times the number of new people coming to me with new ideas and plans.

At 72, I feel a more intense responsibility than ever for those who are building and sustaining my visions, dreams, causes, investments, and projects. My cleaning "empire" is significant, and for maintaining Varsity's purpose and focus I am still a strong source.

THE SHOW STILL GOES ON: 2001
SHOOTING A COMMERCIAL FOR
MY CLEANING CENTERS.

My companies are not running themselves now as it might appear. Our prosperity comes from building better on what was initially built, sacrificed for, and invested in. My operations have some highly capable managers (many far better at administration than I ever was or ever will be). However, it has been adherence to well-established standards and values, and the sustaining of our unique culture, that has separated us from competitors, kept key people, and generated growth and profit.

> In my long-range planning, I felt sometime the day would come (as I became more successful) that I would feel less urgency. This never happened, or at least hasn't yet. In fact, my sense of urgency—of the importance of productivity because of the number of people and things that depend on me—has only intensified.

RETIRE... OR INSPIRE?

My work has never been work so I have nothing to retire from. You hear so many people say, "I'm going to retire soon and do what I want to do." If you aren't doing what you want to do now, in the prime of your life, something is wrong! That's like saying, "Beat me—it feels so good when you stop."

For more than 50 years now my style has been, "forge on." I would rather wear out while I'm running full speed. Being anxiously engaged in a good cause seems to be the solution for successful living—staying on the firing line, where all the action, education, and opportunities are. As long as I can stay on my feet and the old brain works, I will work. The only things I'm interested in retiring from are traffic, noise, bad entertainments, pointless meetings, interruptions, waste, excess, and clutter.

Age only brings more action

The most common advice I get these days is, "You ought to sit back and enjoy your success." My answer: "I gear up and use any success to promote good causes for myself and others." If you have the moxie to tend what you've taken in, the more you've gathered the more you need to give now, as you move into larger scale accomplishment.

Success of just about any kind means more things to sustain, and actually more risk and less control of things, as your life is spread now into many more facets and many more relationships, and you need to service all you've surrounded your-self with. There is a switch from self-preservation (which you could control to a degree) to a social obli-gation that brings with it much that is beyond your control. You find the big impressive bite you've taken of life so far now needs to be chewed and swallowed. All the seeds you've planted, even 20, 30, 40, or 50 years ago, need to be harvested. Excite-ment, suspense, challenge, and yes, even panic are more abundant in maturity. You may have learned to approach things a bit less insanely, which gives the impression you are calm and collected, but demands and expectations are higher than ever! For every thing you've over-come, three more are coming.

Maturity or success puts the viability of all of your remaining dreams and plans, everything else you have ever envisioned right on the line. Talk about suspense… it's "DO" day, man. The someday of

AGE ONLY BRINGS MORE ACTION…

all of that "gonna do someday" is here. All of your striving comes to a head now, you're really in the ring, and the bell has rung. You own all the friends and deals you made, all the ground you plowed and plant-ed—are you up to the harvest? Money, position, and fame don't immu-nize you to failure and discouragement—they make you more vulner-able to it. Can I sell my warehouse full of books (150,000!)? Can I finish the two dozen new books still in progress before my time is up? Will any of my generous loans be paid back? I've drawn the plans, have the cash, but is there time and place to build all I have in mind? Neither ventures nor the adventure that comes with them go away when you turn 50 or 60—and now in my seventies they are at an all-time high.

Don't choose to check out—you will only have more action as you age if you hang in there.

The reinforcing circle

My on-the-run, "driving" lifestyle so often commented on will hopefully not prompt the conclusion that I "fly by the seat of my pants" or act purely spontaneously in reaction to circumstances. I'm exactly the opposite.

Everything built—family, properties, church activities, careers—I thought through carefully. Most things were planned on paper, as someone going through my journals someday will discover. I planned not months and days but years or decades ahead. This may be why I'm not always overly excited by outcomes, because I've anticipated and enjoyed them in my mind already. I like to write the headlines and then live up to them.

Where our corporation and my varied other businesses are today is no accident, luck, or the result of large boardroom brainstorming sessions. It was apparent from the beginning that one entity needed to feed or complement the others. I saw and drew out a simple schematic for this.

A DIAGRAM OF
MY MASTER PLAN.

I'VE PULLED TOGETHER ENOUGH BUSINESS AND PERSONAL INTERESTS AND ENTITIES TO CREATE A MULTI-FEED REINFORCING CIRCLE, SO THAT ONE ACTIVITY OR UNDERTAKING RELATES TO, ENHANCES, AND STRENGTHENS ALL OF MY OPERATIONS.

Even better than I imagined is how well these three areas of focus integrate to sustain, strengthen, and feed each other. My first book, *Is There Life After Housework?*, for example, was intended to give information, to educate. In addition it got tons of publicity, which (with no marketing cost) got Varsity scores of cleaning contracts, and the chart of "supplies you should have" in the book gave rise to our mail order and retail cleaning products store division. That division is now selling all of my books and getting service contracts and speaking jobs that not only make money in themselves but create more contacts for service contracts, and ideas for new books. For example, where the Varsity service division might have to spend $1,500 to $2,000 or more on plane tickets, hotels, and time to make a sales call to a university in the East, Tobi could book me a speaking job at the same university for $2,500. All expenses would be paid; I'd make another $500 on book sales while there, and pass out catalogs for our stores. Best of all, the heads of the companies we would have called on, plus others, would be in my audience. This kind of interaction is, and will in the future only be more so.

> I SPEND FIVE PERCENT OF MY TIME THINKING ABOUT THE PAST, 15 PERCENT ABOUT THE PRESENT, AND 80 PERCENT THINKING ABOUT TOMORROW.
> —DON ASLETT AS QUOTED BY PETER WARD, **LOWELL SUN** 10/9/02

Crusade for clean

A big-picture perspective from someone whose profession is cleaning up after people:

The results of my lifelong crusade (books, lectures, and cleaning businesses) to clean up convinces me that a little effort by all of us to clean up the world could change the face of the planet, and the quality of our own lives beyond even the most optimistic imaginings. Imagine how good it would feel and be to always have clean air, clean water, clean food, clean clothes, clean health habits, clean homes, clean yards, clean thoughts, clean language, clean dealings in business and elsewhere, and a clean conscience. If we all made even a small effort in behalf of cleanliness, we would need half the hospitals, police force, lawyers, psychologists, janitors, and planetary resources. Stress and sickness would be drastically reduced. Clean is the perfect problem solver, the big timesaver. That miracle cure we all are on the lookout for is in our pocket already, basically unused.

Simply being clean could replace most of the self-help and motivation books and seminars. Clean is the master manager. Clean gives us space and freedom, physical and emotional. Clean saves money, cuts depreciation, promotes safety, prevents waste, saves the environment, and makes things pleasant to feel, see, and smell. Best of all clean affects how you are treated. People treat you to your level of cleanliness, and you treat yourself to the same level.

> IT'S WHAT WE ARE ALL AFTER,
> A ONE-WORD SHORTCUT TO PEACE,
> PERSONAL HAPPINESS,
> AND EVEN WEALTH, AND IT'S
> BASICALLY FREE—IT'S **CLEAN**.

Unfortunately, we have slipped to relying on others to administer our cleanliness level. For example, notice the signs across the country such as "Adopt a Highway." These are well-meaning but have a "repair" mentality and give the impression that someone else is responsible for our mess. By adopting a highway we aren't cleaning up the world, we are reinforcing bad behavior, and just keeping even at a big cost of time and money. We have slipped to believing there are departments, companies, agencies, custodians, mothers (mother nature as well our own moms) on earth to clean up after us. We toss trash all over and then someone (or a group) out there is supposed to fix this—pick it all up and dispose of it, and renew it to its original setting. The correct sign on the highway should be, "Adopt a Habit" (of picking up after yourself).

Keeping clean is not asking for great sacrifice, just a few minutes a day of consideration for our fellow man and our surroundings. Think of what would be the most valuable single thing a student could learn in school. Reading? Writing? Arithmetic? Computer tech? I say all of these are a far second to learning and leaving school with one single principle ingrained. Namely, "I am responsible for my own messes and outcomes. When I mess up, financially, health-wise, morally, in my job, etc., it's not my parents' fault, or the fault of my teachers, my peers, society, the government, the weather, or God. It's just me." If we only learned that one lesson, to be responsible for our own outcomes, we could and would have a cleaner world. Schools with eight janitors need only one to clean restrooms. The students themselves, kindergarten through college, should clean their own school, the best curriculum any educational institution could offer. Three minutes a day per student could save billions of dollars a day in school upkeep costs.

Likewise, if all of us who stayed in motels and hotels left rooms neat (which also would only take about three minutes), maids could clean 25 rooms in a day instead of 12-15 of the trashed rooms they usually encounter. If everyone in offices took three minutes a day to clean and clear their surroundings, our professional cleaning services and consumption of our planet's resources could be reduced up to 30 percent—and how many billions would that save?

Bigtime "cleanup" of the world is only more of us doing it on a smalltime, daily basis. When you live clean, eat clean, think clean, and avoid excess, what does it matter who else knows, because you know. Clean will alter your life for the good unbelievably—it will give you confidence, power, savings of time and money, control of emotions, and personal peace. Clean will change you and this country first, and a change for the good in the world is a natural carryover. Let's do it!

Interesting how when we get a grim diagnosis from the doctor, we launch into a frantic effort to get our affairs in order. We go all out to prepare to die, yet now while living now we won't put out much effort to remove or change things that are really interfering with our lives. Why not get our "house" (our world and planet) in order while it really counts, not when it's too late?

Now what?

I have my favorite "wall hanger" right by my desk: "All this mileage—make it count for something!" It's all been a "trip," with a nice share of success and security now, but I have far from arrived yet. The motors are all still humming, and there is still plenty of open road ahead. This autobiography is a mid-life accounting report—time now to take a breather, before the second half.

Is the world any better because of all of this mileage? I think so. For sure, it's a little cleaner, and janitorial work and housework have a little more presence and prestige. And for sure, there is more coming! I love my profession, and love what it can do for the world.

If I can do it, so can you!

Anyone impressed or depressed by this account of my custodial exploits to date needs to bear in mind that what is recorded here is just the highlights of a unique profession and a busy family and personal life. Between the lines, there was an abundance of stops, strains, and stumbles.

You can do better than all of this if you haven't already. Lack of talent, ability, or even opportunity is not a limitation. Any "left out" or lesser circumstances can easily be compensated for or conquered by endurance, persistence, and dedication to a cause and love of people. Many "gifts" are wasted by people who can do things so well, so easily, they put out just enough to get by. We, the common people of the world, have to struggle to survive and achieve, and in the process, we generally can and do perform equal or better than the naturally talented "best." It breaks my heart to see anyone surrender their dreams and ambitions because they feel inferior. Being in debt, being born on the wrong side of the tracks, losing a job, a game, poor test results, having crooked teeth, an out-of-date computer, being too short or too tall, or even being "the janitor" doesn't make you lesser, it just offers more chances to develop other gifts and talents.

Final counsel for success

- Keep your hand in the toilet (and your heart in your business).
- Your business needs to be your friend, not your taskmaster. It should be kind and giving, not a taker of your life. If your work doesn't please you, you need to change it or change yourself (or both). You don't work just to make money or to put yourself in the position to be free someday. ***Your work itself has to be freedom.*** If you like your life's work, you will never have to do a day's work in your life. Liking what you do and knowing it has real value is the key to self-motivation, energy, and personal satisfaction.
- Listen to successful peers, not success peddlers, for direction.
- Plan your life well and career planning will take care of itself.
- Bear in mind that one of the biggest keys to personal success is recognizing and accepting responsibility for your own outcomes, instead of depending on or blaming others.
- Spend more time making the news and less time reading or watching it.
- If something is really important to you, do it NOW—don't save the best for later.

- Be generous with your resources (time, talent, property, and money) from the beginning—don't wait until you are in a position to do it someday. Use good judgment, but do your good deeds as you go along so you can enjoy the rewards as you go along.
- Remember that you lose your audience when you lose simplicity.
- Keep anxiously engaged in good causes.

LET ME DO WHILE OTHERS LOOK
AND WRITE, NOT USE, THAT HOW-TO BOOK.
NO WAITING FOR THE END WITH DOUBT
I WANT THE STAGE... TILL TIME RUNS OUT.
                              —DA HONOLULU 1981

APPENDIX

Answering the Most Often-Asked Questions: Your Chance to Interview Don!

Biographies should answer some big questions about people—hopefully most of your questions were answered earlier in this book. Let me address just a few of the most common here.

"What got you into cleaning? How did you ever decide to become a janitor?"

This intrigues quite a few people. Why would anyone enjoy sweeping floors and gathering trash?

Aside from the fact that I enjoy it immensely and it has given me a good living, I guess it stems back to my childhood experiences.

On the farm, it didn't take long to learn that "clean" paid off. Any junk—empty sacks, pieces of wire, old boards, or broken tools—left around would eventually cause an accident. Someone would stumble over it, it would draw flies and rats, or injure or choke an animal. Untucked shirts got caught in augers or power takeoffs, unclean facilities caused fires or cave-ins, carelessly tossed twine or baling wire damaged equipment and delayed jobs. Our equipment was kept clean so

it always worked well, and our fields were kept clear of rocks and litter.

Keeping the weeds cleaned up around the house and yard kept insects and rattlesnakes away and the cockleburs out of the animals, and a clean, shiny shovel was much easier to dig with than a dirty one. It took less time to care for the animals when their barns, corrals, and lots were kept clean, and even the irrigation water ran three times faster through clean ditches. Everything that came out of the thresher or combine clean brought a higher price. Clean was clearly a bargain!

Even as a child I could see, too, how much better my parents did because they always kept their personal effects clean and neat and contained, when so many of our neighbors and relatives were always losing things, and wasting time hunting or replacing them. Early on, it was clear how good clean clothes or a clean bed felt, and how much better I fared with a clean desk in grade school than my pals who kept a crammed desk.

The advantages of clean were obvious everywhere, and I bought in to it. As the years went on, observing the efficiency of military order and cleanliness, watching the Bell Telephone system work, and seeing the greater effectiveness of edited (clean) essays in my writing, only reinforced this belief. Cleanliness made things simple, and made good sense. It was a ticket to enjoying life with less hassle. What got me into clean as a career, in short, was simply wanting to possess the most efficient tool and channel for living life to the max.

"Are you a clean freak or compulsive cleaner?"

Far from it. I neither schedule cleaning nor worship it—perfection in cleaning is an impossibility, as the minute you finish cleaning something, the soiling process is usually starting again. Although we keep it clean, we use our house hard and don't get excited if a fly dies in a window track. Getting just about anything done in life creates some dust, shavings, trimmings, or dirt. There is nothing wrong with making a mess, especially in the process of doing something useful. But you don't want to leave a mess when you're done, to get in the way or fall over, or have to clean up "later."

What means the most to me is order—being squared away with no excess or unnecessary things in the way of progress. I like things neat and sanitary, not polished.

"When you started your little business as a college student did you ever imagine it would be this enormous someday?"

As people survey the size of Varsity now, and all of my books and work with the media, I often hear this question. And I can answer it honestly with a big YES! I had big dreams and expectations of myself, and a strong imagination, and I did comprehend this business becoming a giant one someday. There were some surprises, though.

First—It took about 30 years longer than I thought it would.

Second—It was at least 50 times harder to accomplish than I anticipated. It's easy to do things in your mind or imagination or on paper, but on the real road, there is plenty of wear and tear, emotional even more than physical.

Third—Thousands more spin-off opportunities than I foresaw resulted from building a life and business. All of the exposure and experience I had opened doors daily with people and places.

Things never just fell into place as success stories so often indicate. I made fewer bad judgment calls as life went on, but the struggle to overcome the laziness inside us all, the urge to just to do enough to "get by," was always present.

I could always see the vision of what could be done and exactly how to do it, and had no fears of failing to do it, but generally, I was looking high at my objective, *over* all the obstacles and struggles. If I had looked straight through to it, I probably wouldn't ever have thought I could do it.

"What did you most want to achieve when you started out?"

Just making a living or surviving, has never been the main focus in my life. I got past that at the age of 14. So the answer to this big question is that I wanted to count for something, to make a difference, to be needed and loved, make a significant mark on others. Above all, I wanted to influence others lives for the good, and I worked at this as earnestly when I started out as I do now.

"How does 'success' feel?"

No different than the process of trying to achieve it, because success is never final. Our dreams, imaginings, and expectations of ourselves only get more ambitious with age. The field widens, even if the body or brain may be slowing down a bit.

Success doesn't have a cruise control or a parking lot; you never "reach" success. You might be succeeding, be achieving satisfaction in something, bringing in a sack of gold, but success is purely a process. There's no cutoff, and we can put many gauges on it, but never a lid. It's all relative, too, as the lives of some of the poorest, most ignorant people are rich and fulfilled, while some of wealthiest and most educated are miserable. Success is conduct that brings joy to yourself and others, nothing more. Where does that end? It doesn't!

"What is the most impressive sight you've seen or place you've been?"

Compared to some world travelers, I'm definitely a novice, but I have seen a lot for an Idaho janitor. As for things that most impressed me, I would name nine:

1. Home—there is never anywhere more beautiful, comfortable, exciting, productive, or restful than home. Being there or coming back

to it always gives me goosebumps, whether it's our ranch in Idaho or our retreat in Kauai.

2. In front of an audience, feeling the warmth and teaching some good life-changing principles.

3. Farm fields at harvest—impressive and rewarding, the payoff of all the effort.

4. Alaska—I am always stunned by it, every trip there. Spending as much time as I have in Idaho, Montana, and Wyoming, I'm used to vast, rugged places, but Alaska is beyond description. The awesomeness—sheer size and number—of everything there (waters, glaciers, forests, wildlife) never ends. Big, wild, and challenging, Alaska is a bigger glimpse of the marvel of creation, the fresh new world we are all looking for.

5. Mt. McKinley: More than 20,000 feet high, it dwarfed the Idaho mountains I had considered phenomenal.

6. The original atomic laboratory. As a janitor, I was ushered into a now restricted and abandoned room in a Midwest university, and stood by a large dark apparatus where the atom was first split, groundwork for the first atomic bomb. It gave me an eerie, sober feeling I will never forget.

7, 8, and 9. I've seen hundreds of parks, grounds, and monuments and some were "ho hum" and some "wow!" But only a few have really seized me, prodding the spirit and inner self. My first visit to Gettysburg (taking Scouts there en route to a jamboree) had an impact that has never left me. For the first time in my life, I realized the force and magnitude of the Civil War. The frailty of humanity seemed to come into focus here, and the price of social struggles. That this could happen (as precious as even one life is) in America to people all focused on freedom and life quality is incredible. I've been haunted and more appreciative of the value of "peace" since that visit.

Two other such places were Little Bighorn Battlefield National Monument, which brings home the impact of our injustices to the Native Americans, and Punchbowl, the National Memorial Cemetery of the Pacific on Oahu. I stood here and read name after name, imagining my own 18-year-old son's name among the tens of thousands of young people who went with their future to the bottom of the ocean. All as a result of man's scramble to get more.

"How do you keep going? Where do you get all of your energy?"

An AT&T executive once told me that one of the prime ingredients for success is a high energy level, and if what he said is true, mine has helped me. It's allowed me to still be going strong when others need to rest. I believe, however, that much of the energy we have is not physical strength but an emotional factor—motivation. I've been asked hundreds of times, "Don't you get tired, sick, or discouraged once in a while?" The answer is that I have and I do, but when duty calls, you can't let tiredness, sickness, or discouragement deter you—you simply do the job anyway, as there is no other choice, or no one else to do it. Rain or shine, in sickness or health, the toilets must be cleaned.

Even if I don't feel well, teaching is a sure cure for what ails me, because once I stand in front of an audience, frayed nerves, strained, tired eyes, or sore back disappear and I am living.

I also have the gift of not being able to recognize sheer drudgery. Work is never work—play is work because after play you are tired, sore, broke, and that is it. After work, you are all of the same only have a big, fat accomplishment sitting there to show for it. And during the work, you can always look forward to that exciting end.

An "unbelievably tough schedule" is not always what it appears from the outside. In fact many of the "overworked" people you see are more relaxed, healthier, and more content than the only semi-busy or non-busy folks stressing out trying to find something worthwhile to do. When work is pure enjoyment, in your control, and nicely varied, it isn't work. Plus, people who do a lot usually have proportionate rewards. More people need them, so they are more loved, admired, and appreciated, which is super motivating.

Another frequent question is, "What drives you?"

I've always had a strong sense of destiny. Ever since my consciousness clicked in, I've had a clear sense of purpose and a belief that I count, am needed, and have a responsibility to help look after others. You have to believe that you matter in this overwhelming sea of people and traffic today, and that what you do matters—to others first and then yourself.

I can foresee results before I get them, and this is another source of my drive to go after things. To me the pains of today are nothing compared to the results of tomorrow. For me looking forward to and working toward what can be is the ultimate of living. My feeling of personal destiny is so strong it often pushes me to the point of exhaustion.

"Instead of 'Aslett's Acres,' his ranch should be called 'Type A Acres.'"

"He has the kind of energy children possess. His transmission doesn't seem to have a reverse or low gear."

"Don is just about the right pace for the rest of us when he's suffering from sleep deprivation. He is already on spin cycle by the time I get up."

"I want a cup of whatever he drinks."
—Lisa Staib

"How do you get so much done?"

I never figured out how "much" is measured—by comparison? Expectation? Assignment? I've just done as much as I can, as fast as I can, as often as I can, for as many people as I can. Add to that, the experience and wisdom of age, long hours, clear goals and strong commitment to them, good health, endurance, willingness to take risks, and a love of work and service. Incredible accomplishments can easily come from being anxiously engaged in a good cause. (If you want to know more about this subject, check out my book *DONE!: How to Accomplish Twice as Much in Half the Time, at Home or at the Office.*)

"Do you ever relax?"

The biggest worry people seem to have about me is that I might be deprived of relaxation or pleasure—judging by the all of the "stop long enough to smell the roses" comments. Those who never developed a passion for work and the fun and relaxation it provides can never be given a satisfactory answer. I usually relax in harness, but when I do have some free time, I love to write (poetry, especially), and to design structures (such as corrals, houses, barns, and inventions).

RELAXING WITH MY GUITAR, WHICH I'VE ENJOYED SINCE MY TEENAGE EFFORTS TO MASTER MY FIRST TUNE ON IT.

"You are such a dejunker—just what <u>do</u> you keep?"

Being outspoken on the liabilities of excess and clutter, a subject I've written six books on so far, I've been often asked, "Just what *do* I keep?" I can sum it up in two short paragraphs.

Valueless to me are big wardrobes, unnecessary decorations, plaques and trophies, play tools, jewelry, trendy, short-lived publications, and junk foods and beverages.

Valuable I keep and cherish: useful tools and equipment, musical instruments, antiques related to my profession, meaningful photographs, good books, good cameras, and land or buildings that can or do house good causes or create some income.

I judge "stuff" (objects, property, or projects) by one qualification: Does "it" (the thing in question) enhance yours or someone else's life? If it does or will, then it's worth keeping.

"What is your home like?"

Big, and open—we seldom lock our doors and we've never worshipped a house—it's just a tool to take on life. We live fairly simply—I think over-decorated houses are a pain. We've always had houses for sharing, not show—they get lots of traffic and use, are never immaculate, but people seem to always be comfortable there. Each of our houses have been different, too, self-designed, not standard, so there is lots of room to run, build, play, entertain guests, or sleep, and it's easy to get from one place to another.

"How do people (especially your wife) stand being around you all the time, with your intensity and impatience?"

People who stand around while I am doing things, I tend to ignore; those who choose to be around me learn to ignore me, so it probably balances out. As for Barbara, people on the outside are usually more awed by entrepreneurial industry than those who live with it. In any case, as numerous people have put it, "Your wife deserves a special place in heaven." On the positive side, with intensity often comes some pretty good earnings, excitement, education, and entertainment, and most people find that offsets any obnoxiousness or insensitivity I might be guilty of.

"How do you keep your sanity?"

Many people have asked how I kept my sanity under the barrage of things always going on, where I had to function in high gear constantly even when discouraged or disappointed. I was never on the edge or even close to it because I had a wife who was not only smart and perceptive, but gentle, loving, and stable—the anchor and balance every entrepreneur needs. My children were adults at age 15, and they gave me further focus, stability, advice, and help when I needed it. Plus being my own boss and having 200 projects going at once, I can switch when something gets me down or gets to be too much for me—just change projects or production lines. This is one big helper, a productive release.

Another is keeping healthy, getting enough sleep, plenty of hard physical work, and no nerve-taxers, like coffee, tea, pop, alcohol, drugs, etc. When you feel good, it takes a lot to get you down.

Since I am a high-strung type A, another thing that helps me survive is writing about whatever is irritating or consuming me. I make a book or article of it, and thus not only get all of my feelings out, but also make a profit on it. That's pretty delightful and healing.

Another way I keep from succumbing to "too much" or "too busy" is to avoid working close to deadlines. I get things done well before they are due, so that when and if my schedule crowds up from an unexpected overload, I still have room to maneuver.

"How do you manage to make everything fun?"

That's actually easy. When you take a profession or pastime society places at the bottom (where you cannot get much lower)—any positive you can manage to connect with it is a milestone. Cleaning is a dull and dreaded subject—people don't expect much from it but drudgery, and certainly aren't prepared to get a laugh or a lift from it, so you can take them by surprise.

People made my life fun, so I lived and worked from my earliest years to make everyone's fun. If there is any secret to this it is simply:

I've learned to give anything I do a real presence.

DECKED OUT AS THE
"KING OF CLEAN" FOR MY
FUN-FILLED, SPOOFY
APPEARANCE ON THE
DEBORAH DUNCAN SHOW
IN DALLAS ON RECRUITING
THE MAN OF THE HOUSE
TO HELP CLEAN.

There are hundreds of tools out for accomplishing this, and most of them cost little or nothing. I use poems, photos, drawings, mottos, signs, and posters. I rename people, times, and places (give them funny nicknames). You can also make the undertaking a contest, competition, or race. The dullest work party or project is dripping with possibilities for humor!

Another way to make things funny is to point out the incongruities in them, or to exaggerate them—the truth turned up a little and enhanced. For instance, take ordinary vacuuming. You can take every aspect of vacuuming from choosing a vacuum, to vacuuming stairs and edges, to bag changing, and make it funny. You can exaggerate just about any of the little irritants of vacuuming from running over (and picking up) things you shouldn't, to struggling with the cord. I can do a 15-minute comedy routine about vacuuming that keeps people in stitches.

Making things fun is not a talent, it is a decision to not be ordinary or accept the ordinary. There isn't a dull subject or happening, only dull speakers or teachers. Anyone can give anything personality—and it does people good to see someone laughing and smiling, cleaning toilets!

"DON HAS A SWISS ARMY KNIFE
IMAGINATION. HE ALWAYS MANAGES
TO MAKE THINGS EXCITING."

"Do you have any fears or phobias?"

Aside from disliking confrontation and time-wasting situations, and heights, I have a fear of being caught up with everything—all finished, nothing left to do. I have nightmares of being locked up somewhere where I couldn't work, write, or teach. I fear idleness of any kind, and that the years I have left will not be enough for all that I still want to do.

"You don't still work on the job any more, do you?"

This is the question I hear most often, and the answer to this one is easy: Yes, I do, more than ever. There is a false idea around that success is reaching a point where you make others do all the work while you just rake in the money and live in leisure for the rest of your life. I'm on the other end of the spectrum—I believe that the higher you get on the success chain, the longer and harder you should work, and more responsible you should become. I work a little smarter, but just as hard as I did from the age of 16 on, and expect to continue this until age or health restrictions shut me down. For me, age and more money in the bank have just created a bigger and better selection of work to do, a nice position to be in. I am still working twelve-hour days on one job or another—the only thing missing now in my work pattern is the "grunt work," as they call it. I'd still rather be on a tractor with a disc behind me, than behind a desk, but now all the "experts" tell me I can't afford to work on a hands-on, front-line job.

The question most often asked of my wife is, "Is he that funny at home?"

When you meet her, be sure to ask her.

"Don, do you help your wife around the house?"

I like to think I "run" things around our house… including the vacuum cleaner, dishwasher, lawnmower, window squeegee, toilet plunger, carpet shampooer, paint roller, garbage compactor, waffle iron, taxi service, mop bucket, broom, sprinkler, hose, and dust cloth. I believe that men should be full partners in home cleaning, and I love to see the results of the process, so it's no problem at all.

"How do you manage to write so much?"

Two reasons. One, there is a lot to write about, and two, I write all the time. It takes very little effort or money to capture what you hear, see, and feel in the course of each day. I carry a notepad with me everywhere—while traveling, eating, dressing, sitting in church or in meetings, even in bed. I don't like a rigidly scheduled writing life, and it doesn't fit the pattern of my other responsibilities. But I make the most of every available moment. If you want to write, you don't have to wait until you're on vacation or unemployed. You can write in time fragments, "down time," waiting time, and bits and pieces. The way steady daily progress adds up is like the miracle of compound interest, or watching a tiny drip of water fill a barrel!

I travel with several book projects at all times, even on an overnight flight or a one-day jaunt. Sometimes I never touch the stuff I bring, but if the mood or opportunity is there, I can act on it. Often I can do in one hour, in a motel room or snowed in or stalled somewhere, what would take a day in an office setting.

Another thing that makes it easy is that I have well-organized places for what I write, or any notes I take, and these things are filed regularly, so I never have loose or backlogged notes. Thus when and if the time for a topic comes, I have a nice set of notes to refine and expand upon.

The only glitch in writing for me is losing pens. I look forward to the afterlife as an opportunity to reunite with all of the pens, measuring tapes, and pocketknives I've lost!

> I'M CONSTANTLY ASKED, "HOW CAN YOU WRITE SO MUCH—FIVE BOOKS ON CLUTTER," ETC.? EASY ANSWER: I CLEAN UP BEHIND PEOPLE AND I TRAVEL. THAT'S ALL YOU NEED!

"What would you do different if you could do it all over?"

First, a few of the smaller things:

• I'd take a course in small engine repair. For sure, I've owned all the hard-starting, nonworking lawnmowers, pumps, tillers, and go-kart motors ever produced. And I've spent far too many hours pulling on a rope over and over like a fool, changing sparkplugs, and kicking and beating on these things, when probably a few knowing touches and adjustments here and there would have kept them all running smoothly. Those stubborn little motors have been responsible for strained backs, marriage strains, lost contracts, and hired helpers quitting.

• I'd learn nail sizes (the proper way to identify nails, instead of having to refer to them as "big ones" or "little ones." This has caused lots of mistakes in communication, and wasted time and gas.

• I'd learn the names of Mexican and Asian dishes. I never know dim sum from moo goo gai pan or a chimichanga from a quesadilla. I have to ask again or guess, every time. So I waste time and often end up with the wrong thing.

•I would have memorized more poems when young. I could and did easily memorize many then, and can still quote them 50 years later. I have to beat my brain now to memorize one or two lines for a TV shooting. I'd also publish my own poetry sooner.

• I'd learn the number keys on the keyboard by touch. I spend a lot of time on a keyboard, and always have to break my stride and speed when a number comes up. A little thing? Add up the thousands of pages I've typed over the years and it would have been well worth learning them in typing class when I was 16.

On the more serious side, if I included all of my personal blemishes here, it would fill more pages than you would care to read: "You talk too fast," "You don't finish sentences," "You're intolerant," "You intimidate," "You dress terribly," "You always have to be right," "You're a workaholic," " You're the worst speller in Idaho (maybe the USA)," "Your jaws pop," "You come on too strong," etc.

One thing I'd surely change, I see now, is the impression I often created that "my view should be your view, on all matters." You could call this being pushy or overbearing, a mode I seem to function in all too often. Things said in jest often contain some truth, and one afternoon several of my office staff and a couple of visiting partners in a "fun poking" mood typed up the following and gave it to me:

If Don isn't hungry, no one is hungry.

If Don isn't tired, no one is tired.

If Don isn't cold, no one is cold.

If Don doesn't have to go to the bathroom, no one has to go.

(On and on it went, with a whole list of my habits and attitudes as inflicted on others.) One of the things mentioned was work—"If Don thinks all work is fun then we should all think all work is fun."

I always believed this, that work was fun—I was convinced that work had all the elements of happiness and reward while play just got in the way. In my youth I so greatly enjoyed the satisfactions of harvest time and of haying, thinning beets, picking spuds, and even cleaning that all of this fell under recreation for me.

The trouble is I don't keep this attitude to myself, often unconsciously imposing the same standard and schedule on those around me. It wasn't until my grandchildren looked at me as insane that it occurred to me that I might have a perverted view of work. I would say, "How can anyone lie on a beach, in a hot tub, golf, water ski, or watch TV when they could weed, paint, or plant or build something?" The kids would drawl back, "I don't think so, Grandpa." The old "what's fun for Don must be fun for the family," I see now, was an attitude I'd temper some if I could do it all over.

I realize now, too, that because life was always exhilarating, I just ignored some of the barbs and bumps along the way. The person at the wheel and with the vision, focused on outcome, is often less sensitive to the ruts in the road to the finish line. Most of my visions and decisions were idealistic. Even if I could logically see the lack of time, money, and resources to get the job done, or buy or build something, I still went for it, figuring a little forcing of the issue and application (more hours!) would compensate for the shortage of resources, and it generally did.

However, when it didn't, and obligations and expectations were knocking at the door, it was crying time in the janitor closet. There was a price to be paid whenever there was a bad judgment by "the boss," and at times I made more than my share of such judgments. I reflect now on the pain this must have caused some of the people around me, especially family, pain that I myself just brushed off as part of the package. I justified it all by looking at the big picture, expecting everyone else to see it too—to ignore the 10 percent bad and savor the 90 percent of accomplishment and real potential.

I never could find any other gears in the gearbox of life than high. Reflecting back, if I had it to do over, I would probably do much the same, only this time not inflict my schedules so much on others.

Another thing I regret is any time I spent on trivia. One evening, for example, I must have spent two or three hours watching old movies that I'd seen six times already. Then later, going through one of my "memory drawers," I realized that in my oldest granddaughter's lifetime (she was then 25 and I was her only living grandfather), I—a writer—had only written her four letters. And I regularly teach, write, and preach about time use and effectiveness! Unfulfilled intentions haunt me.

Fortunately, I still have the time and commitment to "un-haunt" some of these I can:

- Be kinder and more sensitive to the people close to me;
- Listen more and talk less;
- Be quicker to respond to requests;
- Play with children more;
- I'd call and write to those in need and down in spirit more. I did this some, maybe even more than most, but far less than I could and should have. I would have touched thousands of people by now. I had the time, information, and money to do it, too, but sometimes the moment slipped by.

WHAT DO I REGRET MOST? INSENSITIVITY AND UNEXPRESSED SENSITIVITY.

"What do you feel best about in your life?"

I feel good today about many things, especially the fact that I was able to earn enough that my wife never had to work outside of the home and thereby had the time she needed to do an expert, loving job of raising our six children.

It also means a great deal to me when people report that their lives were influenced to the good by my writing, speaking, or one of my businesses.

A more mundane thing I really feel good about is that from the very beginning of my business, right up to 2006, I never took more salary than I needed to live providently. Even as chairman of the board and majority owner of Varsity, and sole owner of other companies, I took less salary than my top managers, and left or put back most of my profits into the business, with total faith that someday the value and investment would be returned to me. And it has been.

INDEX

S

DON ASLETT'S
MUSEUM OF CLEAN

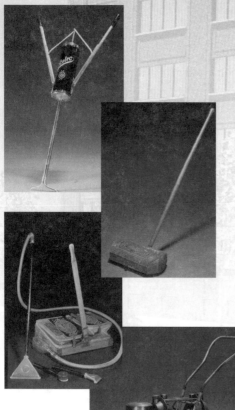

Don Aslett has the lifetime goal of selling the value of "clean" as the solution—the answer—to the world's social and personal needs. You can be a part of this unique, exciting project in Pocatello, Idaho:

1. Visit the museum with friends and family; enjoy a firsthand look at a scope of "clean" that will stimulate the imagination.

2. Be on the lookout for unique antiques—even modern information and items—that you can add to the museum.

3. Make a tax-deductible contribution to the Museum of Clean. We are a self-funded, non-profit organization.

Send your contribution to:
Don Aslett's
Museum of Clean
PO Box 700
Pocatello, ID 83204
208-232-3535

Visit us:
Don Aslett's
Museum of Clean
700 South First Avenue
Pocatello, Idaho 83201

www.donaslett.com